THE HISTORY OF AL-ṬABARĪ

AN ANNOTATED TRANSLATION

VOLUME XXXIX

Biographies of the Prophet's Companions and Their Successors

AL-ṬABARĪ'S SUPPLEMENT TO HIS *HISTORY*

The History of al-Ṭabarī

Editorial Board

Ihsan Abbas, University of Jordan, Amman

C. E. Bosworth, The University of Manchester

Franz Rosenthal, Yale University

Everett K. Rowson, The University of Pennsylvania

Ehsan Yar-Shater, Columbia University (*General Editor*)

Estelle Whelan, *Editorial Coordinator*

Center for Iranian Studies
Columbia University

SUNY

SERIES IN NEAR EASTERN STUDIES

Said Amir Arjomand, Editor

We note with profound regret the death on October 13, 1997, of Dr. Estelle Whelan, who capably coordinated and saw through the press the publication of most of the volumes in this series, including the present one.

The preparation of this volume was made possible in part by a grant from the National Endowment for the Humanities, an independent federal agency.

Bibliotheca Persica
Edited by Ehsan Yar-Shater

The History of al-Ṭabarī

(Ta'rīkh al-rusul wa'l-mulūk)

VOLUME XXXIX

Biographies of the Prophet's Companions and Their Successors

translated and annotated
by

Ella Landau-Tasseron

The Hebrew University of Jerusalem

State University of New York Press

Published by
State University of New York Press, Albany

Printed in the United States of America

For information, address State University of New York Press, State University Plaza, Albany, N.Y., 12246

Library of Congress Cataloging-in-Publication Data

Tabarī, 838?–923.
[Tārīkh al-rusul wa-al-mulūk. English. Selections]
Biographies of the Prophet's companions and their successors / translated and annotated by Ella Landau-Tasseron
p. cm.—(SUNY series in Near Eastern studies) (The history of al-Ṭabarī = Ta'rīkh al-rusul wal'l mulūk ; v. 39)
(Bibliotheca Persica)
Includes bibliographical references and index.
ISBN 0-7914-2819-2 (alk. paper).—ISBN 0-7914-2820-6
(pbk. : alk. paper)
1. Muḥammad, Prophet, d. 632—Companions—Biography—Early works to 1800. 2. Muslims—Saudi Arabia—Biography—Early works to 1800. 3. Muslim women—Saudi Arabia—Biography—Early works to 1800. I. Landau-Tasseron, Ella. II. Title. III. Title: Ṭabarī's supplement to his History. IV. Series. V. Series: Ṭabarī, 838?–923. Tārīkh al-rusul wa-al-mulūk. English ; v. 39. VI. Series: Bibliotheca Persica (Albany, N.Y.)
DS38.2.T313 1988 vol. 39
[BP75.5]
297.6'48—dc21
[B] 97-45138
CIP

10 9 8 7 6 5 4 3 2 1

Preface

The History of Prophets and Kings (*Ta'rīkh al-rusul wa'l-mulūk*) by Abū Ja'far Muḥammad b. Jarīr al-Ṭabarī (839–923), here rendered as *The History of al-Ṭabarī*, is by common consent the most important universal history produced in the world of Islam. It has been translated here in its entirety for the first time for the benefit of non-Arabists, with historical and philological notes for those interested in the particulars of the text.

In his monumental work al-Ṭabarī explores the history of the ancient nations, with special emphasis on biblical peoples and prophets, the legendary and factual history of ancient Iran, and, in great detail, the rise of Islam, the life of the Prophet Muḥammad, and the history of the Islamic world down to the year 915. The first volume of this translation contains a biography of al-Ṭabarī and a discussion of the method, scope, and value of his work. It also provides information on some of the technical considerations that have guided the work of the translators. The thirty-ninth volume is a compendium of biographies of early members of the Muslim community, compiled by al-Ṭabarī; although not strictly a part of his *History*, it complements it.

The *History* has been divided here into thirty-nine volumes, each of which covers about 200 pages of the original Arabic text in the Leiden edition. An attempt has been made to draw the dividing lines between the individual volumes in such a way that each is to some degree independent and can be read as such. The page numbers of the Leiden edition appear in the margins of the translated volumes.

Al-Ṭabarī very often quotes his sources verbatim and traces the chain of transmission (*isnād*) to an original source. The chains of transmitters are, for the sake of brevity, rendered by only a dash (—) between the individual links in the chain. Thus, "According to Ibn Ḥumayd—Salamah—Ibn Isḥāq" means that al-Ṭabarī received the report from Ibn Ḥumayd, who said that he was told by Salamah, who said that he was told by Ibn Isḥāq, and so on. The numerous subtle and important differences in the original Arabic wording have been disregarded.

The table of contents at the beginning of each volume gives a brief survey of the topics dealt with in that particular volume. It also includes the headings and subheadings as they appear in al-Ṭabarī's text, as well as those occasionally introduced by the translator.

Well-known place names, such as, for instance, Mecca, Baghdad, Jerusalem, Damascus, and the Yemen, are given in their English spellings. Less common place names, which are the vast majority, are transliterated. Biblical figures appear in the accepted English spelling. Iranian names are usually transcribed according to their Arabic forms, and the presumed Iranian forms are often discussed in the footnotes.

Technical terms have been translated wherever possible, but some, such as "dirham," and "imām," have been retained in Arabic forms. Others that cannot be translated with sufficient precision have been retained and italicized, as well as footnoted.

The annotation is aimed chiefly at clarifying difficult passages, identifying individuals and place names, and discussing textual difficulties. Much leeway has been left to the translators to include in the footnotes whatever they consider necessary and helpful.

The bibliographies list all the sources mentioned in the annotation.

The index in each volume contains all the names of persons and places referred to in the text, as well as those mentioned in the notes as far as they refer to the medieval period. It does not include the names of modern scholars. A general index, it is hoped, will appear after all the volumes have been published.

For further details concerning the series and acknowledgments, see Preface to Volume I.

Ehsan Yar-Shater

Contents

Preface / v

Abbreviations / xiii

Translator's Foreword / xv

Tables 1. Genealogy of Quraysh / xxviii
2. Genealogy of the Hāshimites / xxix

Excerpts from the Book Entitled the Supplement to the Supplemented: Biographies of Companions and Their Successors

[Women Who Died before the Emigration (*Hijrah*) / 3

[Those Who Died in the Year 8 (629/630)] / 4

[The Year 9 (630/631)] / 11

[The Year 11 (632/633)] / 12

[Those Who Died in the Year 14 (635/636)] / 19

[Those Who Were Killed in the Year 16 (637/638)] / 22

[Those Who Died or Were Killed in the Year 23 (643/644)] / 22

[Those Who Died in the Year 32 (652/653)] / 23

Those Who Died or Were Killed in the Year 33 (653/654) / 25

[Those Who Were Killed in the Year 36 (656/657)] / 27

Those Who Died or Were Killed in the Year 37 (657/658) / 28

Those Who Died or Were Killed in the Year 40 (660/661) / 36

Those Who Died in the Year 50 (670/671) / 37

Those Who Died or Were Killed in the Year 52 (672) / 40

Those Who Died or Were Killed in the Year 54 (673/674) / 40

[Those Who Died in the Year 64 (683/684)] / 51

Those Who Died in the Year 65 (684/685)] / 52

Those Who Died or Were Killed in the Year 68 (687/688) / 54

Those Who Died or Were Killed in the Year 74 (693/694)] / 57

Those Who Died in the Year 78 (697/698) / 58

Those Who Died or Were Killed in the Year 80 (699/700) / 59

The Names of Those Companions Who Outlived the Prophet and Transmitted Traditions and Knowledge / 95

The Clients (*Mawālī*) of the Banū Hāshim / 98

The Allies (*Ḥulafā'*) of the Banū Hāshim / 100

Those of the Banū al-Muṭṭalib b. ʿAbd Manāf b. Quṣayy Who Transmitted [Traditions] from the Prophet / 102

The Allies of the Banū Nawfal b. ʿAbd Manāf b. Quṣayy / 104

The Names of the Campanions Who Outlived the Prophet and from Whom Knowledge Was Transmitted, of the Banū Asad b. ʿAbd al-ʿUzzā b. Quṣayy b. Kilāb / 105

The Names of Those Who Transmitted [Traditions] from the Prophet, of the Banū ʿAbd al-Dār b. Quṣayy b. Kilāb / 106

The Names of Those Who Transmitted [Traditions] from the Prophet, of the Banū Zuhrah b. Kilāb, Brother of Quṣayy b. Kilāb / 107

Those Who Transmitted [Traditions] from the Prophet, of the Allies of the Banū Zuhrah / 110

The Names of Those Who Transmitted [Traditions] from the Prophet, of the Banū Taym b. Murrah / 111

[Those Who Transmitted Traditions], of the Banū Makhzūm b. Yaqaẓah b. Murrah b. Kaʿb / 111

The Allies of the Banū Makhzūm Who Outlived the Prophet and Transmitted [Traditions] from Him / 116

Those of the Banū ʿAdī b. Kaʿb b. Luʾayy b. Ghālib Who Outlived the Prophet and Transmitted [Traditions] from Him / 117

[Those of the Banū Jumaḥ Who Outlived the Prophet and Transmitted Traditions from Him] / 118

[The Companions] of the Banū ʿĀmir b. Luʾayy b. Ghālib [Who Outlived the Prophet and Transmitted Traditions from Him] / 118

[Those of the Kinānah Who Outlived the Prophet and Transmitted Traditions from Him] / 119

[Those of the Tamīm Who Outlived the Prophet and Transmitted Traditions from Him] / 123

Those of the Banū Ḍabbah b. Udd b. Ṭābikhah b. al-Yās b. Muḍar [Who Outlived the Prophet and Transmitted Traditions from Him] / 125

Those of the Banū Ja'dah b. Ka'b b. Rabī'ah b. 'Āmir b. Ṣa'ṣa'ah [Who Outlived the Prophet and Transmitted Traditions from Him] / 126

Those of the Banū Numayr b. 'Āmir b. Ṣa'ṣa'ah [Who Outlived the Prophet and Transmitted Traditions from Him] / 127

[Those of the Banū Taghlib Who Outlived the Prophet and Transmitted Traditions from Him] / 129

The Names of Those Who Believed in the Prophet and Followed Him during His Lifetime, Then Outlived Him and Transmitted [Traditions] from Him, of Yemenī Tribes / 130

The Names of Some of Those Belonging to Other Yemenī Tribes Who Believed in the Prophet and Followed Him during His Lifetime, Outlived Him, and Transmitted Traditions from Him / 137

The Names of the Ash'arīs Who Transmitted [Traditions] from the Prophet / 147

The Names of [the People of] Ḥaḍramawt Who Transmitted [Traditions] from the Prophet / 148

Of the Kindah / 149

Those Who Transmitted [Traditions] from the Prophet, of the Rest of the Azd / 150

Of the Hamdān / 151

The Biographies of the Women Who Embraced Islam during the Prophet's Lifetime: Those of Them Who Passed away before the Emigration / 161

Those of Them Who Died during the Prophet's Lifetime after the Emigration / 161

The Prophet's Wives Who Died during His Lifetime / 163

The [Death] Dates of the Prophet's Daughters, Paternal Aunts, and Wives Who Died after Him / 166

The Death Dates of the Prophet's Wives Who Died after Him / 169

Biographies of the Women Whose Death Dates Are Known, of the Emigrants, Anṣār, and Others Who Were the Prophet's Contemporaries, Believed in Him, and Followed Him / 191

Names of the Hāshimī Women Believers Who Outlived the Prophet, Transmitted Traditions from Him, and Had [Their] Knowledge Transmitted from Them / 195

Clients [of the Banū Hāshim] / 199

Arab Women [Married into the Quraysh] Who Outlived the Prophet and Transmitted [Traditions] from Him, Having Given Him the Oath of Allegiance and Embraced Islam during His Lifetime / 201

The Death Dates of Successors and People of the Following Generations, of [Our] Deceased Forefathers Who Had Been Scholars and Transmitters of Traditions / 206

Successors Who Died in the Year 32 (652/653) / 206

Those Who Died in the Year 81 (700/701) / 208

Those Who Died in the Year 83 (702/703) / 209

Those Who Died in the Year 105 (723/724) / 215

Those Who Died in the Year 111 (729/730) / 228

Those Who Died in the Year 112 (730/731) / 229

Those Who Died in the Year 150 (767/768) / 250

Those Who Died in the Year 161 (777/778) / 257

Qurashī [Women], [Younger] Contemporaries of Companions of the Prophet, from Whom Knowledge Was Transmitted / 278

The Following are Names and *Kunyah*s Mentioned in the *History* / 281

The Women Contemporary with the Prophet Who Gave Him the Oath of Allegiance and Are Known by Their *Kunyah*s / 286

The *Kunyah*s of People Who Outlived the Prophet and Were Known by Their Names, Not by Their *Kunyah*s / 287

Those of the Prophet's Companions Who Were Known by [the Names of] Their Patrons or Brothers or by Their [Own] Nicknames or by Their Grandfathers, Instead of Their Actual Fathers / 300

The Names of the Successors Who Were Known by Their *Kunyah*s / 303

The *Kunyah*s of the Successors Who Were Known by Their Names, Rather than by Their *Kunyah*s / 314

The *Kunyah*s of People of Subsequent Generations Who Were Known by Their Names, Rather than by Their *Kunyah*s / 332

Bibliography of Cited Works / 339

Index / 357

Abbreviations

AO: *Acta Orientalia*
AOH: *Acta Orientalia Hungarica*
BSOAS: *Bulletin of the School of Oriental and African Studies*
EI[1]: *The Encyclopaedia of Islam*, 1st edition. Leiden, 1913–42.
EI[2]: *The Encyclopaedia of Islam*, 2nd edition. Leiden, 1960–.
IC: *Islamic Culture*
IOS: Israel Oriental Studies
IQ: *Islamic Quarterly*
JAOS: *Journal of the American Oriental Society*
JASB: *Journal of the Asiatic Society of Bengal*
JESHO: *Journal of the Economic and Social History of the Orient*
JNES: *Journal of Near Eastern Studies*
JPHS: *Journal of the Pakistan Historical Society*
JRAS: *Journal of the Royal Asiatic Society*
JSAI: *Jerusalem Studies in Arabic and Islam*
JSS: *Journal of Semitic Studies*
MIDEO: *Mélanges de l'Institut Dominicain d'Études Orientales du Caire*
MW: *Muslim World*
WZKM: *Wiener Zeitschrift für die Kunde Morgenländes*
ZDMG: *Zeitschrift der Deutschen Morgenländischen Gesellschaft*

Translator's Foreword

In the introduction to his *History* al-Ṭabarī declares his intention to append to the work biographical notes on the Prophet's Companions, their Successors, and transmitters of traditions from subsequent generations. This, no doubt, is the work entitled *The Supplement to the Supplemented: Biographies of Companions and Their Sucessors* (*Dhayl al-mudhayyal min taʾrīkh al-ṣaḥābah wa-al-tābiʿīn*), contained in an incomplete form in this volume.[1]

In spite of its title, the book does not belong to the literary genre of "supplement" (*dhayl*, literally, "a tail"), which consists of histories or biographical dictionaries written by later authors as continuations of earlier works. The author of a "supplement" would usually start the book where the earlier author had left off and would tend to follow the style and patterns used by his predecessor. The result, however, was most often an independent work. For al-Ṭabarī's *History* such "supplements" were written by Muḥammad b. ʿAbd al-Malik al-Hamadhānī, Abū Aḥmad al-Farghānī, and ʿArīb b. Saʿd al-Qurṭubī.[2]

I wish to thank those who helped me in my efforts to understand de Goeje's introduction, written in Latin: Prof. Benjamin Z. Kedar, Dr. Milka Levi-Rubin, and Mr. Nils Grede. The difficulties that de Goeje's text presented even after all their assistance do not reflect upon their efforts. Thanks are also due to Prof. Yohannan Friedmann for some valuable comments and to Dr. Estelle Whelan for her kindness and patience throughout the years that it took to complete this work.

1. *Introductio*, p. xiii; Rosenthal, "Introduction," 89–90.

2. *Dhayls* were sometimes called *ṣilah* or *takmilah*, "continuation" or "completion." The works of al-Hamadhānī and al-Qurṭubī were published in combina-

Describing al-Ṭabarī's work, al-Sakhāwī says the following:

> The great *History* includes the sources of the [various] reports, [as well as] the accounts of the world history, but it is limited by the author's purpose, namely, to supply information about history, wars, and conquests. Only rarely does [al-Ṭabarī] deal with disparaging transmitters or declaring them trustworthy (*al-jarḥ wa-al-taʿdīl*), because his work on biographies suffices in this respect (*iktifāʾan bi-taʾrīkhihi fī al-rijāl*). Thus the information he gives [in the *History*] about the great religious teachers (*al-aʾimmah*) is not exhaustive, for his interest lay in conveying clear detailed accounts of wars and conquests, stories of ancient prophets and kings, past nations, and bygone generations. He adduced [all this information], together with its sources and many chains of transmission; he was erudite in all these and other matters.
>
> Al-Ṭabarī wrote a supplement to the above-mentioned *History*; moreover, he supplemented the supplement as well.[3]

The supplements mentioned by al-Sakhāwī have nothing to do with our *Supplement to the Supplemented* (*Dhayl al-mudhayyal*). De Goeje was probably right in concluding, although hesitantly, that al-Sakhāwī is alluding here to what is better known as "the two sections."[4] The original *History* apparently reached the end of the first civil war; the first section covered the Umayyad period, the second the ʿAbbāsid period, up to the year 302/914–15.[5]

Al-Sakhāwī, however, also mentions al-Ṭabarī's *Dhayl al-mudhayyal* in this paragraph, referring to it as "his (al-Ṭabarī's) work on biographies of traditionists" (*taʾrīkhihi fī al-rijāl*). He

---

tion with al-Ṭabarī's *Dhayl al-mudhayyal* by Dār al-Maʿārif in Cairo (1977) and Dār al-Fikr in Beirut (1987). See also Ibn al-Nadīm, I, 565; al-Sakhāwī, 302; Ibn Ḥajar, *Iṣābah*, I, 3; al-Kattānī, 98–99. On the genre see Farah.

3. *Wa-lahu ʿalā taʾrīkhihi al-madhkūr dhayl, bal dhayyala ʿalā al-dhayl ayḍan.* See al-Sakhāwī, 301–2. See also Rosenthal, *History*, 488, for a different translation of the passage.

4. *Introductio*," p. xv.

5. Rosenthal, "Introduction," 133; Yāqūt, *Irshād*, 2456–57; Ibn al-Nadīm, I, 565.

considers it to be of another genre than, and independent from, the *History*.

There are thus two unusual aspects of al-Ṭabarī's historical and biographical work. First, he supplemented his own *History*; his supplements did not remain independent but were integrated into the main work. Second, he entitled his biographical work "A Supplement," even though it did not belong to the *dhayl* genre. It should, of course, be noted that in al-Ṭabarī's time this genre had not yet been developed, so that he was not deviating from any convention.[6] However, it is no accident that most of the later biobibliographical sources, al-Sakhāwī included, avoid the genuine title of the book, referring to it simply as *Ta'rīkh al-rijāl* (Biographies of Traditionists).[7] On the other hand, quotations from the work appear either under the original title, sometimes in shortened form, or under al-Ṭabarī's name alone.[8]

The biographical literature, to which *Dhayl al-mudhayyal* properly belongs, is unique to Muslim culture. It has deep roots in pre-Islamic Arab interest in genealogy, but at the same time it is an outgrowth of the characteristic Muslim way of preserving knowledge. Prophetic traditions (*ḥadīths*) and other accounts were discussed and passed on among members of the Muslim community, and in the process much was falsified and invented. Becoming aware of this fact, Muslim scholars developed a source critique, the "science of traditionists" (*'ilm al-rijāl*), to help them evaluate transmitted material. Personal merits of the transmitters, as well as facts about their lives (like death dates and dwelling places), were checked. If, for example, it was found that a

---

6. Cf. a later author, Abū Shāmah of the thirteenth century, who wrote a supplement to his own work; al-Sakhāwī, 305.

7. In the context of the genre of biographies the word *rijāl*, literally, "men," serves as a technical term for "traditionists" or "transmitters." For references to al-Ṭabarī's *Ta'rīkh al-rijāl*, see *Introductio*, p. XIII; Rosenthal, "Introduction," 89–90; Gilliot, "Oeuvres," 71; al-Sakhāwī, 301; al-Dhahabī, *Siyar*, XIV, 273; idem, *Ta'rīkh*, XXIV, 283; Ismā'īl al-Baghdādī, II, 26; Ibn Khayr, I, 227; Ibn 'Asākir, XV, 165. See also Goldziher, "Literarische Thätigkeit." Of all the sources only Yāqūt (*Irshād* 2444, 2457) and Ibn Khayr call the work *Dhayl al-mudhayyal*.

8. Citing by the author's name alone was the common practice in the literature. For quotations from the *Dhayl*, see, e.g., Ibn Qudāmah, 237; al-Quhpā'ī, IV, 109; Ibn Ḥajar, *Iṣābah*, I, 559, II, 376; Ibn 'Abd al-Barr, I, 12. In al-Dāraquṭnī, V, 2564, the editor gives a list of dozens of references; some of them are not correct, and some are lacking in the extant version of the *Dhayl*.

certain person claimed to have transmitted from someone whom he could not have met, the material he transmitted was to be rejected. In the case of Companions, their Islamic records, or services to the cause of Islam (*sābiqah*), were mentioned, as well as any detail or anecdote connecting them with the Prophet. In the case of subsequent generations, the degree of the person's piety and sometimes his political or sectarian biases would be recorded. Many variations developed in the genre, however, in both the content and the arrangement of the collected biographical details. Often, the biographies contain material totally irrelevant to the purpose of the genre mentioned above, for example, physical descriptions, personal traits (e.g., generosity), and historical events in which the subjects were involved. Such is the case with *Dhayl al-mudhayyal.* On the other hand, there are works that contain only an evaluation of the person's trustworthiness. This subgenre is more properly called "the disparaging and declaring as trustworthy" (*al-jarḥ wa-al-taʿdīl*).

The earliest works in the genre date from the late second/eighth to the beginning of the third/ninth century. They were often arranged in categories of time and place, or tribes, called "layers" (*ṭabaqāt*, meaning also "generations"). Variations of this method were also followed, in part, in *Dhayl al-mudhayyal.*[9]

The present volume is merely a collection of excerpts from *Dhayl al-mudhayyal,* as indicated by the title found on the second part of the Cairo manuscript: *The Second Part of Excerpts (muntakhab) from the Book [Called] The Supplement to the Supplemented: Biographies of Companions and Their Successors, Compiled by Abū Jaʿfar Muḥammad b. Jarīr b. Yazīd al-Ṭabarī, Transmitted from Him by Abū ʿAlī Makhlad b. Jaʿfar b. Makhlad b. Sahl b. Ḥumrān al-Bāqarḥī.*[10] It is not possible to infer from this title the identity of the compiler of the excerpts. It may have

---

9. Among the earliest authors in this genre were Yaḥyā b. Maʿīn (d. 203/818), Muḥammad b. ʿUmar al-Wāqidī (d. 204/819), his pupil and scribe Muḥammad b. Saʿd (d. 230/845), Khalīfah b. Khayyāṭ (d. 240/854), Muslim b. al-Ḥajjāj (d. 261/875), and Muḥammad b. Ismāʿīl al-Bukhārī (d. 256/870). See al-Sakhāwī, 315, 336–57; al-Kattānī, 96–105, 108–10. The genre is much more complex than is possible to describe in the present context. See further Hafsi; Gibb, "Islamic Biographical Literature"; Juynboll, *Muslim Tradition,* 134–90; Auchterlonie, 2–3.

10. Loth, 581.

been the transmitter Abū 'Alī Makhlad b. Ja'far, as Loth and Rieu thought, or any other transmitter of subsequent generations, a view preferred by de Goeje and Rosenthal.[11] It is perhaps worthy of note that Makhlad b. Ja'far (d. 369/979–80) was accused of buying books, among them al-Ṭabarī's *History*, and transmitting them in a nonnormative way, that is, without having studied them with a teacher and without having acquired an authorization for transmission (*ijāzah*).[12] Such a character was perhaps more likely than others to have taken a free hand with al-Ṭabarī's work, making a rather confused and deficient abridgment from it.

According to Yāqūt,[13] the original *Dhayl* followed a genealogical order (*'alā tartīb al-aqrab fa-al-aqrab*), partly reflected in the extant collection of excerpts. Presumably some chronological order was maintained as well, reflected in the text in rudimentary fashion. However, no ordering principle governs the present text as a whole. The semichronological order followed in the beginning is abandoned at some point to make way for various disconnected rubrics. Occasionally the material bears no relation to the rubric under which it occurs, and chapters end and begin without any indication. Some entries are recorded twice, without the use of cross-refereces. When a cross-reference does appear, the reference is to a chapter omitted from the collection.[14]

Dhayl al-mudhayyal also included an introduction lacking in the present collection. Of its content we know only one statement, of an extreme nature: Al-Ṭabarī, who founded his own school of law, declares everyone who contradicts his views to be an infidel. He states that he would not accept the testimony of, or trust traditions transmitted by, people who held Qadarī, Shī'ī, or Khārijī doctrines, nor would he accept (legal) arguments based on reasoning.[15] In spite of this statement, he held Abū Ḥanīfah in great esteem[16] and included in *Dhayl al-mudhayyal* many Shī'īs

---

11. Loth, 582; *Introductio*, pp. XIII, XIV; Rosenthal, "Introduction," 89.
12. Al-Khaṭīb al-Baghdādī, *Ta'rīkh*, XIII, 176–77; Ibn Ḥajar, *Lisān*, VI, 9.
13. Yāqūt, *Irshād*, 2457.
14. Al-Ṭabarī, III, 2478; see also *Introductio*, p. XIV. For a detailed analysis of the structure of the *Dhayl*, see Landau-Tasseron, "Biographical Work."
15. Yāqūt, *Irshād*, 2463, but see a different interpretation of the passage in Rosenthal, "Introduction," 90.
16. Yāqūt, *Irshād*, 2463; see al-Ṭabarī, III, 2510 (the biography of Abū Ḥanīfah).

and also others of different persuasions. his statement, however, may signify that his pursuit of the "science of traditionists" (*'ilm al-rijāl*) arose from a broader interest than usual. Not only the transmission of the prophetic tradition but also the application of religious law was to profit from his biographical work.

While recording the biographies of eminent members of the Muslim community al-Ṭabarī mentions the great historical events in which they were involved. Wishing to be concise, he refers the reader to another place for further details, saying: "The accounts about him were already recorded in our book entitled *The Supplemented* (*al-Mudhayyal*)."[17] There is a mystery here. It appears that a book by someone as well known as al-Ṭabarī is virtually unknown. De Goeje found only two references to *al-Mudhayyal* in the literature, one in an anonymous work on astrology and chronology, the other in Ḥamzah al-Iṣfahānī's book.[18] The latter refers to *al-Mudhayyal* as a very famous work,[19] but no biobibliography, whether ancient or modern, records a book by al-Ṭabarī under this title. What was this *Mudhayyal*, then, and how did it relate to the *History* and to the present volume, *Dhayl al-mudhayyal*?

Loth defines *Dhayl al-mudhayyal* as an "'Appendix zum Supplement' seines (al-Ṭabarī's) grossen Geschichtswerks." The *Mudhayyal* was, in his opinion, the work announced by al-Ṭabarī in the introduction to the *History*; it was a preparatory work (*Vorarbeit*) in which al-Ṭabarī collected material for the *History*. The *Dhayl* was extracted from a more comprehensive work (*al-Mudhayyal*?).[20] Loth thus conceives of the three titles, *Ta'rīkh*, *al-Mudhayyal*, and *Dhayl al-mudhayyal*, as applying to three different works. He seems to be confusing the *Dhayl*, announced in the introduction to the *History*, with *al-Mudhayyal*. There is no evidence that *al-Mudhayyal* was a *Vorarbeit*. His rendering of the title *Dhayl al-mudhayyal* as "Appendix zum Supplement" is

17. Al-Ṭabarī, III, 2321, 2335, 2476, 2498. For the reference occurring on page 2358, see p. xxii, below.
18. *Introductio*, p. XIV. The anonymous work is *Dustūr al-munajjimīn*; see Blochet, 12.
19. Ḥamzah al-Iṣfahānī, 121.
20. Loth, 582.

not accurate either. *Mudhayyal*, the passive form of "to append," "to supplement," means "the supplemented," as mentioned by de Goeje.[21]

From de Goeje's careful phrasing it is difficult to infer whether he conceived of *al-Mudhayyal* as an abridgment of the *History* or as a different title for it, so that the two would in fact be one work. The difficulty lies perhaps in the *History* itself. By this title de Goeje sometimes means the extant text of the *History*, that is, the published version of *Ta'rīkh al-rusul wa-al-mulūk*, at other times a much longer version said by some sources to have existed.[22] I hope to clarify this matter in what follows.

If de Goeje meant to say that *al-Mudhayyal* was identical with the *History* as we have it today, he was probably right. There is no real evidence that a longer version actually existed. The description of *al-Mudhayyal* by Ḥamzah al-Iṣfahānī fits the *History* very well and cannot be applied to any other work by al-Ṭabarī. Unfortunately, the quotation given by al-Iṣfahānī from *al-Mudhayyal* cannot be located in the *History*, but this in itself does not prove the existence of a longer version. De Goeje adduces many other instances of quotations lacking in the Leiden edition. This phenomenon is common and is often encountered, in relation not only to the *History* but to many other texts as well. To give but one example, al-Ṭabarī quotes from Ibn Sa'd passages lacking in the Sachau edition.[23] This does not necessarily mean that the extant text, edited by Sachau, is an abridgment of Ibn Sa'd's "original" *Ṭabaqāt*.

The very title *al-Mudhayyal* proves that this work is identical with the *History*. It will be recalled that al-Ṭabarī planned to, and did, supplement the *History* with biographical notes, which makes the *History* a supplemented work, a work to which something was appended, in other words, a *mudhayyal*.

An additional proof of this identification can be found in analysis of the preposition *min*. One of al-Ṭabarī's own references to *al-Mudhayyal* runs as follows: "His story is already recorded in our book entitled *al-Mudhayyal min mukhtaṣar ta'rīkh al-rusul wa-*

21. *Introductio*, p. XIII.
22. *Introductio*, especially pp. XIV, XV–XVI. On the longer version, see below.
23. See al-Ṭabarī, III, 2359, 2378, 2387, 2505, 2516, 2517, 2519, 2520.

al-mulūk (The Supplemented Work: The Abridged History of the Prophets and Kings).[24] This title is constructed precisely as is the title of the present volume, *Dhayl al-mudhayyal min ta'rīkh al-ṣaḥābah wa-al-tābi'īn*. The first two words are a nicely put, but too general, title; *min*, literally "namely," specifies the real subject matter of the work (*min mubayyinah*). In other words, *Dhayl al-mudhayyal* is identical with *Ta'rīkh al-ṣaḥābah wa-al-tābi'īn*. In precisely the same way *al-Mudhayyal* is identical with *Mukhtaṣar ta'rīkh al-rusul wa-al-mulūk*. The latter, however, is by no means an abridgment of the *History* as we know it but the *History* itself. This is proved by the fact that one of the *History* manuscripts bears the title *The Abridged History of the Prophets and Kings*.[25] This title perhaps reflects al-Ṭabarī's modesty, as Rosenthal suggests. It may, however, also be explained by the following story: Al-Ṭabarī asked his pupils (or scribes): "Do you have enough energy for [writing down] the Qur'ān exegesis?" They asked how long it was, and he said "Thirty thousand pages," whereupon the people retorted: "We shall have died before finishing such a task." So al-Ṭabarī abridged the work in 3,000 pages. Then he asked the people: "Do you have enough energy for [writing down] the world history from Adam to our own time?" They asked how long it was, and his answer was as before, whereupon they responded as before. Al-Ṭabarī then said, "We are in God's hands! People have no ambition any more." He sat down and abridged the *History* in 3,000 pages.[26]

As noted previously, it is not certain that there ever existed a version of the *History* ten times longer than the extant text. This story may be a mere anecdote expressing wonder at al-Ṭabarī's achievement. The fact remains that the *History* as we know it is also called *The Abridged History*. We are thus left with three titles for the same work, the famous *History* edited by de Goeje and others: *The Abridged History of Prophets and Kings*, *The Supplemented Work* (*al-Mudhayyal*), and *History of the Prophets*

---

24. Al-Ṭabarī, III, 2358.
25. Rosenthal, "Introduction," 130–31.
26. *Introductio*, p. LXXXIII (the Arabic text); al-Khaṭib al-Baghdādī, II, 163; al-Dhahabī, *Siyar*, XIV, 274–75; Yāqūt, *Irshād*, 2442; Ibn al-Jawzī, *Muntaẓam*, XIII, 216.

and Kings. It is doubtful that the last refers to an original ten times (or otherwise) longer than the extant text.

In the matter of *Dhayl al-mudhayyal* de Goeje's opinion is entirely clear. He thinks that this title includes both *al-Mudhayyal*, or abridgment (of the *History*), and the biographical notes.[27] In the same vein Rosenthal holds that by the title *al-Mudhayyal*, mentioned by al-Ṭabarī in our volume, *Dhayl al-mudhayyal* was meant and that the two are in fact identical.[28] The problem with this view is that it cannot be harmonized with the technique of citation used by al-Ṭabarī. When he writes, "I already said this in my book entitled *al-Mudhayyal*," he must be referring to a work separate from the one in which he makes the reference, that is, *Dhayl al-mudhayyal*. Had the two titles referred to the same book, al-Ṭabarī ought to have used the terms set for cross-references.[29]

There are, however, other grounds for reconsidering de Goeje's opinion. He bases himself on the descriptions of *Dhayl al-mudhayyal* by al-Dhahabī and Ibn Khayr al-Ishbīlī, who mention al-Ṭabarī's "book on *ta'rīkh* known as *Dhayl al-mudhayyal*," which contained "twenty parts."[30] From these descriptions de Goeje drew his conception of *Dhayl al-mudhayyal* as a large work containing historical material (*ta'rīkh*) near in size and content to the *History* itself. But a "part" (*juz'*) is by no means identical with a "volume." It is unspecified and may be of any size. For example, each *juz'* in the manuscript of excerpts from *Dhayl al-mudhayyal* comprised no more than twelve to eighteen pages.[31] Twenty parts, then, do not necessarily correspond to the length of the *History*. As for the word *ta'rīkh*, it does not always mean "history." "The oldest works called *ta'rīkh* were collections of biographies," as Rosenthal observed in his *History of Muslim Historiography*.[32] It is also worthy of note that Ibn Khayr al-Ishbīlī acquired *Dhayl al-*

27. *Introductio*, pp. XIV–XV.
28. Rosenthal, "Introduction," 89.
29. For example, *wa-qad dhakartu fīmā maḍā min hādhā al-kitāb* or *wa-qad taqaddama*.
30. *Introductio*, pp. XIV–XV; Ibn Khayr, 227; al-Dhahabī, *Ta'rīkh*, XXIV, 283; idem, *Siyar*, XIV, 273.
31. Loth, 581.
32. See Rosenthal, *History*, 13–14.

mudhayyal through a chain of transmitters, which included Ibn ʿAbd al-Barr.[33] This author, himself a genealogist and biographer, used *Dhayl al-mudhayyal* in his own biographical dictionary, *al-Istīʿāb*.[34] Therefore *Dhayl al-mudhayyal*, as described by al-Dhahabī and Ibn Khary, was not a history combined with biographies but a purely biographical work, a *ta'rīkh fī al-rijāl*. There is no evidence that it was combined with al-Ṭabarī's *History*, in an "abridged" form or otherwise.

The sources used by al-Ṭabarī cannot be properly analyzed, as the present volume does not contain the original text of the *Dhayl*. It may, however, be mentioned that al-Wāqidī's *Ṭabaqāt* was one of the main sources.[35] Al-Ṭabarī quotes both al-Wāqidī and Ibn Saʿd, which means that he knew both al-Wāqidī's original, now lost, and its adaptation by al-Wāqidī's pupil and scribe. Other early historians, genealogists, and biographers cited in the extant *Dhayl* are Abū Maʿshar Najīḥ (d. 170/787),[36] Abū Mikhnaf (d. 157/774),[37] Abū ʿUbaydah (d. 209/824),[38] al-Madā'inī (d. 225/840),[39] Ibn Isḥāq (d. 150/767),[40] Mūsā b. ʿUqbah (d. 141/758),[41] Abū Zurʿah (d. 281/895),[42] and Ibn al-Kalbī (d. 204/819).[43] Countless other informants are mentioned, and research into this matter is a project in itself.

The deficiencies of the present form of the *Dhayl* include a total lack of uniformity and consistency. Some entries are made up of long stories, others of mere names; still others contain traditions transmitted by the persons discussed with hardly any biographical details. The information is often rudimentary, so that one can hardly distinguish among eminent Muslims, insignificant Com-

---

33. Ibn Khayr, I, 227.
34. Ibn ʿAbd al-Barr, *Istīʿāb*, I, 12.
35. On this work, see F. Segzin, I, 297 (no. 12); al-Sakhāwī, 317; Muṣṭafā, I, 164.
36. Al-Ṭabarī, 2333, 2347, 2433, 2444, 2503, 2535.
37. Ibid., 2317, 2367.
38. Ibid., 2443, 2356, 2459.
39. Ibid., 2324, 2332, 2333, 2337, 2338.
40. Ibid., 2296–97, 2303, 2312.
41. Ibid., 2306, 2324, 2328.
42. Ibid., 2401, 2473.
43. Ibid., 2300, 2306, 2317. Note that the quotations from the early historians may be at second hand, that is, copied by al-Ṭabarī not from the originals but from other sources. On this issue, see Landau-Tasseron, "Reconstruction."

panions, tribal chiefs, caliphs, and names invented for chains of transmission (*isnāds*). This situation is probably owing partly to the fact that the present form is not the original one, partly to the availability or otherwise of biographical details.

By the time Muslim scholars started to inquire about people mentioned in chains of transmission many of these people had been forgotten. Moreover, some of them never really existed, for many traditions and *isnāds* were fabricated, a fact that generated the whole field of inquiry in the first place. Additional confusion was caused by the fact that many people in Muslim society bore similar or identical names. Yet Muslim scholars did their utmost to obtain biographical information, with varying degrees of success. I therefore thought it useful to add references to other biographical works, for both completeness and comparison. The choice of sources for the purpose was difficult, given the enormous wealth of biographical works published to date and augmented daily with new publications. I finally chose Khalīfah b. Khayyāṭ (d. 240/854), Aḥmad b. Yaḥyā al-Balādhurī (d. 279/892), and Ibn Ḥibbān al-Bustī (d. 354/965), knowing that other choices could be equally valid. My decision was not arbitrary, however. Khalīfah b. Khayyāṭ wrote precisely in the same genres used by al-Ṭabarī some fifty years later: history arranged according to years (annals) and biographies arranged according to categories (*ṭabaqāt*). Al-Balādhurī, preceding al-Ṭabarī by a generation, wrote a special kind of integrated combination of history and biography. Ibn Ḥibbān, a generation later than al-Ṭabarī, divided the biographical material he collected into three different works: one dealing with famous scholars, another with trustworthy scholars, and a third with dubious transmitters. The first is arranged according to categories (time and place), the last two alphabetically.[44] Additional light may thus be shed on what material was circulating in al-Ṭabarī's lifetime and on the differences and similarities between near-contemporaneous authors in dealing with this material.

The obvious source to compare with *Dhayl al-mudhayyal* is Ibn Sa'd's *Ṭabaqāt*, but it does not serve the purpose just defined pre-

44. Only the first, *Mashāhīr*, was systematically combed for parallels; the other two works were used occasionally.

cisely because it is a reflection of al-Ṭabarī's main source, al-Wāqidī's *Ṭabaqāt.* I therefore did not comb Ibn Sa'd's work for parallels but traced back to it only al-Ṭabarī's explicit quotations and some of de Goeje's references. There is much more of Ibn Sa'd (and al-Wāqidī) in the *Dhayl* that I did not point out, and the expert reader is invited to check Ibn Sa'd with the help of its excellent indexes.

The task of systematically combing the works of Khalīfah, al-Balādhurī, and Ibn Ḥibbān, as well as tracing parallels in Ibn Sa'd, was carried out by Ṭāriq Abū Rajab. As a true book lover, he sometimes exceeded his brief and, ignoring my strict warnings about lack of space, occasionally came up with additional interesting references. I hereby express my gratitude to him for his invaluable assistance.

In addition to the aforementioned works, other sources were occasionally consulted, when the person discussed seemed important in some way. I have no space to explain all my decisions, and I admit that they were somewhat arbitrary. A person who seems important to me may be utterly insignificant in someone else's opinion. A great many sources I left untouched for lack of space. For further research one may want to obtain information about additional biographical works from Auchterlonie's guide.[45] Some recent works not included in this guide are the following: *al-Ṭabaqāt*, by Muslim b. al-Ḥajjāj; *al-Ta'rīkh*, by Yaḥyā b. Ma'īn; *Mu'jam rijāl al-ḥadīth*, by al-Khū'ī; *Mawsū'at rijāl al-kutub al-tis'ah*, by al-Bandārī and Ḥasan. Prophetic traditions quoted by al-Ṭabarī may be traced in *Tuḥfat al-ashrāf*, by al-Mizzī, and *Mawsū'at aṭrāf al-ḥadīth*, by Muḥammad Zaghlūl. Last but by no means least, the recent monumental work by Josef van Ess should be mentioned, with its rich information about early sects, scholars, and religious figures of the second and third centuries of the Muslim era.[46]

The references described are meant for experts. As this volume is aimed primarily at the nonexpert, many notes are given to make the text and context comprehensible. Lack of space compelled me to have as little recourse as possible to cross-references. Both

45. Auchterlonie.
46. For all these works, see "Bibliography of Cited Works."

names and concepts were annotated only once each, usually when first occurring in the text. The index should therefore be used when an unexplained item occurs, in order to locate the explanation in a previous (or sometimes later) note.

Another matter omitted for lack of time and space was checking the chains of transmission (*isnād*s), which include hundreds of names. I did, however, try to identify persons mentioned only by their first names or nicknames by collating *isnād*s from both the *History* and the *Dhayl*. The identification, when there is one, is recorded between brackets. The latter device also served for inserting additions into the text, for the sake of comprehensibility.

Surely the present volume leaves much to be desired. Thinking of the improvements I would like to introduce in it, I can only cite al-Ṭabarī's pupils' response to his suggestions: *hādhā mimmā tafnā al-aʿmār qabla tamāmihi.*

I nevertheless hope that this volume will be of some use to nonexperts and experts alike.

Ella Landau-Tasseron

Table 1. Genealogy of Quraysh

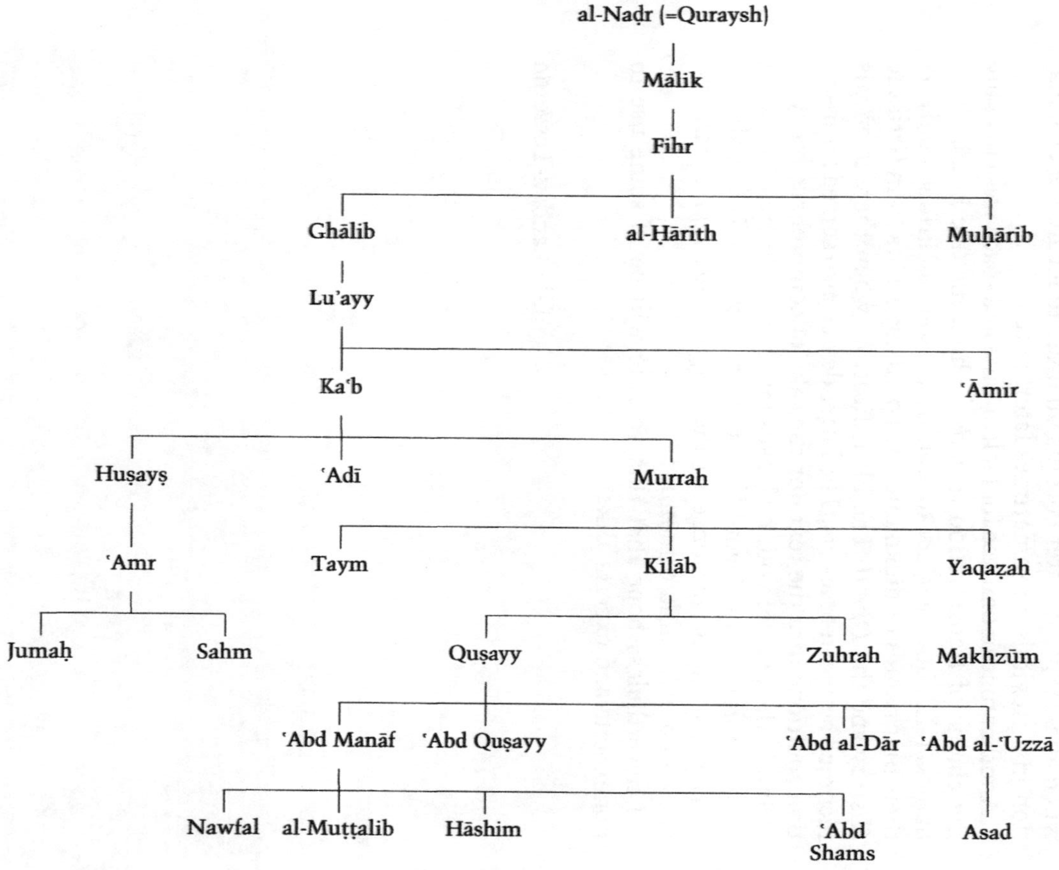

Table 2. Genealogy of the Hāshimites

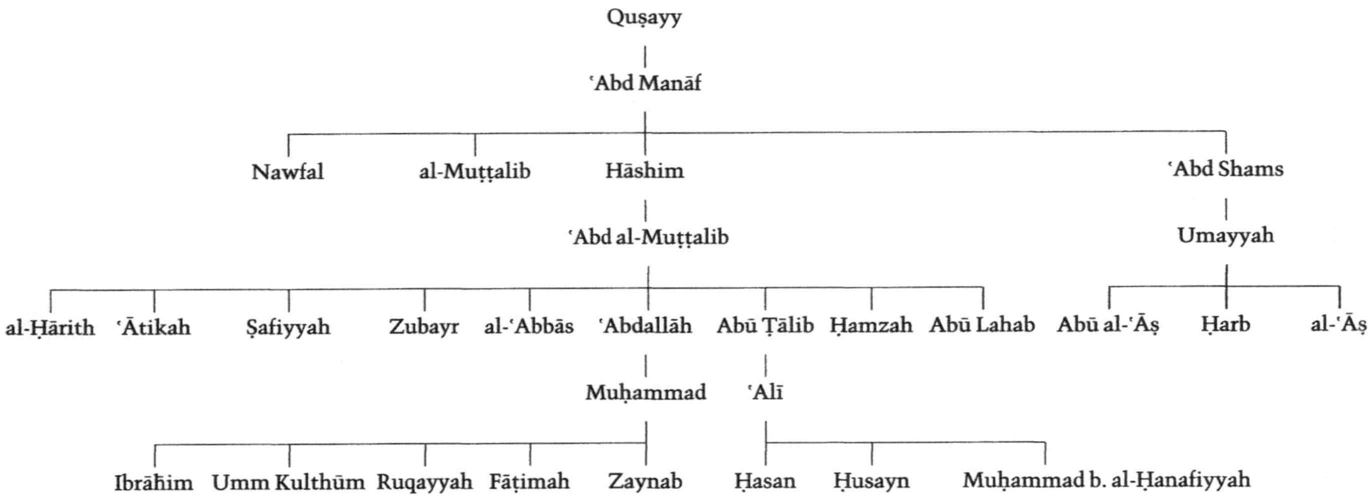

Excerpts from the Book Entitled *The Supplement to the Supplemented: Biographies of Companions and Their Successors*

In the name of Allāh, the Merciful, the Compassionate: [2296]

Abū Ja'far Muḥammad b. Jarīr b. Yazīd al-Ṭabarī wrote in his book *The Supplement to the Supplemented: Biographies of Companions and Their Successors*:

*[Women Who Died Before the Emigration (*Hijrah*)]*

Among the women who died in Mecca before the Prophet's Emigration [to Medina] was his wife, Khadījah, daughter of Khuwaylid b. Asad b. 'Abd al-'Uzzā b. Quṣayy.[1]

Khadījah's *kunyah*[2] was Umm Hind. Hind, after whom she was named, was her son from Abū Hālah b. al-Nabbāsh b. Zurārah, her husband before [she married] the Prophet.[3]

---

1. A member of the Qurashī clan Asad b. 'Abd al-'Uzzā; see Ibn Ḥazm, *Jamharat*, 117–25. On the Quraysh, the Prophet's tribe, see "Ḳuraysh," *EI*², V, 434–35 (W. M. Watt); Kister, "Mecca and Tamīm"; idem, "Some Reports Concerning Mecca." Khadījah was the Prophet's first wife and the first to believe in him when he was inspired. She also bore most of the Prophet's children. See Guillaume, 82–83, 107–13, 191; Lings, 34–36, 44–45, 96; Kister, "The Sons of Khadīja"; "Khadīdja," *EI*², IV, 898–99 (W. M. Watt); Muir, 24–25; Ibn Hishām, I, 198–203, 253–57; al-Balādhurī, *Ansāb*, I, 396–405; Ibn Ḥanbal, *Faḍā'il*, 847–56; al-Ṣāliḥī, 35–76.

2. The Arabs' polite way of addressing people is by referring to their parenthood, so that one is addressed as "father/mother of so-and-so." This specific kind of by-name is called a *kunyah*, sometimes rendered as *agnomen*.

3. On Abū Hālah and his clan, see Kister, "On Strangers and Allies," 120–26.

She died three years before the Emigration, at the age of sixty-five. This information was transmitted to me by al-Hārith [b. Muḥammad]—[Muḥammad] Ibn Sa'd—Muḥammad b. 'Umar [al-Wāqidī]—Muḥammad b. Ṣāliḥ and 'Abd al-Raḥmān b. 'Abd al-'Azīz.

Khadījah died in the month of Ramaḍān that year and was buried in al-Ḥajūn.[4]

[Those Who Died in the Year 8] (May 1, 629–April 19, 630)

Among those who died at the beginning of the year 8 was Zaynab, daughter of the Prophet.[5]

Zaynab was the Prophet's eldest daughter.

The cause of her death was as follows: When she was sent away from Mecca to the Prophet [in Medina] Habbār b. al-Aswad and another man overtook her; as it was reported, one of them pushed her, whereupon she fell on a rock, miscarried her child, and lost a lot of blood. She had this injury and ultimately died of it.

Among those who were killed was Ja'far b. Abī Ṭālib b. 'Abd al-Muṭṭalib b. Hāshim b 'Abd Manāf.[6]

Ja'far was killed as a *shahīd*[7] in [the battle of] Mu'tah.[8]

---

4. A mountain in Mecca where a cemetery was situated; see Yāqūt, *Mu'jam al-buldān*, II, 215.

5. "Zainab bint Muḥammad," *EI*[1], VII, 1200 (V. Vacca). Cf. Guillaume, 314–16; Lings, 158–59; Ibn Sa'd, VIII, 20–24; Ibn Hishām, II, 308–12; al-Balādhurī, *Ansāb*, I, 269, 357, 397–400; Khalīfah b. Khayyāṭ, *Ta'rīkh*, 56; al-Ḥalabī, II, 205–6, III, 106; Ibn al-Jawzī, *Muntaẓam*, III, 124–25; al-Dhahabī, *Siyar*, II, 247; al-Ṭabarī, *Ta'rīkh*, I, 1348–50. See also p. 13, below.

6. The Prophet's uncle. See "Dja'far b. Abī Ṭālib," *EI*[2], II, 372 (L. Veccia Vaglieri); Khalīfah b. Khayyāṭ, *Ta'rīkh*, 49–50; idem, *Ṭabaqāt*, 4–5; Ibn Ḥanbal, *Faḍā'il*, 889–91; al-Balādhurī, *Ansāb*, I, 283–84.

7. A Muslim killed in battle against infidels is promised paradise unconditionally; he is a *shahīd*, usually translated as "martyr." Although the translation is literally accurate, the connotations of the two terms are completely different. Martyrdom connotes the death of a powerless, suffering individual at the hands of an oppressor, whereas *shahādah* connotes mainly fearlessness in battle. I have therefore chosen to leave *shahīd* untranslated.

8. A town east of the Dead Sea, where a Muslim raiding force was defeated by a Byzantine force in the year 8/629. See "Mu'ta," *EI*[2], VII, 756–57 (F. Buhl); Guillaume, 531–40; Muir, 392–95; Lings 286–90; Watt, *Muḥammad at Medina*, 53–55; al-Wāqidī, 755–69; Ibn Hishām, IV, 15–30; al-Ṭabarī, *Ta'rīkh*, I, 1614–18; Ibn Abī Shaybah, *Muṣannaf*, IV, 577.

According to [Muḥammad] Ibn Ḥumayd—Salamah [b. al-Faḍl] and Abū Tumaylah—Ibn Isḥāq—Yaḥyā b. ʿAbbād—his father: My stepfather[9] belonged to the Banū Murrah b. ʿAwf,[10] and took part in that raid; that is, the raid of Mu'tah. He told me [the following]:[11] "By God, it is as if I [can even now] see Jaʿfar as he jumped [2297]
down from his roan mare, hamstrung her, and fought the enemy until he was killed."

It was reported that Jaʿfar was the first Muslim who hamstrung [his horse].[12]

According to Muḥammad b. ʿUmar [al-Wāqidī]—ʿAbdallāh b. Muḥammad b. ʿUmar b. ʿAlī—his father: A Byzantine soldier hit him, that is, Jaʿfar, and cut him in half; one half fell in a vineyard. Thirty or thirty-odd wounds were found on one half of his body.

Jaʿfar had been converted to Islam before the Prophet entered the house of al-Arqam to preach from there.[13] He then emigrated to Abyssinia in the second emigration,[14] with his wife Asmā' bt. ʿUmays, where he stayed until after the Prophet's Emigration to Medina.[15] He returned from Abyssinia to the Prophet while the latter was in Khaybar, in the year 7/628.[16]

---

9. *Abī alladhī arḍaʿanī*, meaning the husband of the child's wet nurse. Cf. Ibn Isḥāq, *Sīrah*, 218; al-Wāqidī, 13, 688.

10. An important north Arabian tribe; see "Murra," *EI²*, VII, 628–30 (E. Landau-Tasseron).

11. Cf. Guillaume, 534; Ibn Abī Shaybah, *Muṣannaf*, IV, 577; al-Ḥalabī, III, 77; Ibn al-Athīr, *Kāmil*, II, 113–14; al-Ṭabarī, *Ta'rīkh*, I, 1614.

12. Arab warriors of pre-Islamic times practiced *ʿaqr*, that is, cutting their own horses' hamstrings during battle to prevent the possibility of fleeing the enemy. Muslim scholars debated the permissibility of this act and placed restrictions upon it. The original pre-Islamic social significance of the custom was obfuscated in Islamic times by the argument that the purpose of hamstringing was to prevent a victorious enemy from obtaining Muslim horses from a Muslim defeat. See Ibn Hudhayl, I, 40, 48 (text), II, 207, 225 (translation). Mercier is incorrect in translating *ʿaqr* as having the horse killed.

13. See p. 47, below.

14. While Muḥammad was active in Mecca, some dozens of his followers emigrated to Abyssinia at his suggestion, for reasons that are not entirely clear, probably in A.D. 615–17. The followers gradually returned, though some stayed till 7/628. See Guillaume, 146–53, 167–69; Lings, 81–84; Watt, *Muḥammad at Mecca*, 109–17; Caetani, I, 262–84.

15. That is, in the year 622. See Guillaume, 221–27, 281; Lings, 118–22; "Hidjra," *EI²*, III, 366–67 (W. M. Watt).

16. Khaybar was a Jewish settlement north of Medina, conquered by Muḥammad in Muḥarram 7/May 628. See Guillaume, 510–19; Lings, 263–69; "Khaybar," *EI²*, IV, 1137–43 (L. Veccia Vaglieri); al-Ṭabarī, *Ta'rīkh*, I, 1575–84.

Ja'far was killed in Jumādā I, 8/September 629, having been one of the Prophet's commanders of the expedition sent against the Byzantines.[17]

Ja'far's *kunyah* was Abū 'Abdallāh.

Zayd al-Ḥibb ("the beloved")[18] b. Ḥārithah b. Sharāhīl b. 'Abd al-'Uzzā b. Imri' al-Qays b. 'Āmir b. al Nu'mān b. 'Āmir b. 'Abd Wadd b. 'Awf b. Kinānah b. 'Awf b. 'Udhrah b. Zayd al-Lāt b. Rufaydah b. Thawr b. Kalb b. Wabarah b. Taghlib b. Ḥalwān b. 'Imrān b. al-Ḥāf b. Quḍā'ah—whose [real name] was 'Amr—b. Mālik b. 'Amr b. Murrah b. Mālik b. Ḥimyar b. Saba' b. Yashjub b. Ya'rub b. Qaḥṭān.[19]

It was reported that in pre-Islamic times Zayd's mother, Su'dā bt. Tha'labah b. 'Abd 'Āmir b. Aflat b. Silsilah of the Banū Ma'n of Ṭayyi',[20] [once] paid a visit to her family and brought Zayd along
[2298] with her. Horsemen of the Banū al-Qayn b. Jasr[21] raided the tents of the Banū Ma'n, the clan of Zayd's mother, and seized Zayd, who was then already grown up, [a young man] of full stature. They brought him to the market at 'Ukkāẓ[22] and offered him for sale, whereupon Ḥakīm b. Ḥizām b. Khuwaylid b. 'Abd al-'Uzzā b. Quṣayy purchased him for his paternal aunt, Khadījah bt. Khuwaylid, for 400 dirhams. When the Prophet married Khadījah she gave him Zayd, and he took him.

Zayd's father, Ḥārithah b. Sharāḥīl, said after he had lost him:

---

17. That is, Mu'tah.

18. So called because the Prophet loved him. See "Zaid b. Ḥāritha," *EI*[1], VII, 1194 (V. Vacca); Ibn Sa'd, III/1, 27–32; al-Zubayr b. Bakkār, 316–22; Khalīfah b. Khayyāṭ, *Ta'rīkh*, 49–50; idem, *Ṭabaqāt*, 6; al-Balādhurī, *Ansāb*, I, 467–73, III (Maḥmūdī), 283–84; Ibn Hishām, I, 264–66.

19. The key names in this long genealogy are Qaḥṭān, the eponym of all the so-called "southern" (Yemeni) Arabs; Quḍā'ah, a large confederation with branches extending as far north as Syria already in pre-Islamic times; and Kalb, one of the most powerful tribes of the Quḍā'ah. See "Kalb b. Wabara," *EI*[2], IV, 492–94 (A. A. Dixon); "Ḳuḍā'a," *EI*[2], V, 315–18 (M. J. Kister); "Ḳaḥṭān," *EI*[2], IV, 447 (A. Fischer [A. K. Irvine]).

20. A large confederation of southern origin, owning large territories in Najd. See Ibn Ḥazm, *Jamharat* 398–404; Caskel, II, 57–61.

21. A powerful tribe of the Quḍā'ah confederation; see Ibn Ḥazm, *Jamharat* 453–54.

22. An important market held every year in the vicinity of Mecca. See "'Ukkāẓ," in Glassé, 407; Kister, "Mecca and Tamīm," 146, 156.

I weep for Zayd not knowing what became of him.
    Is he alive, is he to be expected, or has Death come over him?
By God I ask yet do not comprehend.
    Was it the plain or the mountain that brought about your end?
I wish that I knew: Will you ever return?
    In this world only for your coming back I yearn.
The sun reminds me of him when it dawns,
    evoking his memory as the dusk falls.
When the winds blow they stir up memories like dust.
    O how long my sorrow and fear for him last!
I shall hasten all my reddish-white camels all over the earth, toiling. [2299]
    Neither I nor the camels will be weary of wandering
All my life long, until I die,
    for every man is mortal, even though hopes lie.
To ʿAmr and Qays[23] do I entrust [Zayd's fate]
    and to Yazīd and then to Jabal.

He means Jabalah b. Ḥārithah, Zayd's elder brother. By Yazīd he means Zayd's half-brother, Yazīd b. Kaʿb b. Sharāḥīl.

People from [the tribe of] Kalb came to Mecca on pilgrimage and saw Zayd. They recognized one another, and Zayd said: "Convey the following verses to my family, for I know that they have grieved for me." Then he said:

Carry a message from me to my people, for I am far away,
    that close to the House[24] and the places of pilgrimage I stay.
So let go of the grief that has deeply saddened you,
    and do not hasten all your camels all over the earth.
I live with the best of families, may God be blessed;
    from father to son, of Maʿadd[25] they are the noblest.

---

23. Brothers of Ḥārithah, Zayd's father; see Ibn Ḥajar, *Iṣābah*, I, 563 (s.v. Zayd b. Ḥārithah).

24. That is, the Kaʿbah.

25. Maʿadd, together with his "son" Nizār and his "father," ʿAdnān, are considered the patriarchs, or eponyms, of the tribes believed to be of northern origin. In fact these are generic names for these tribes, and as such they are interchangeable.

The Kalbī people went away and informed Zayd's father. He exclaimed: "My son, by the Lord of the Kaʿbah!" They described Zayd's situation and the people with whom he was staying. Ḥārithah and Kaʿb, sons of Sharāḥīl, then set out to ransom Zayd. They came to Mecca and asked about the Prophet, whereupon they were told that he was in the mosque. They went in to [see]
[2300] him and said: "O son of ʿAbdallāh, O son of ʿAbd al-Muṭṭalib, O son of Hāshim,[26] O son of the chief of the clan! You are the people of God's sanctuary; you live next to it and you are protected by it.[27] By His house you set captives free and feed the prisoners.[28] We come to see you about a member of our family who is staying with you, so be benevolent and kind toward us in the matter of his ransom, for we will pay you handsomely." The Prophet asked "Who is he?" and they replied "Zayd b. Ḥārithah." The Prophet said "I would like to suggest something else," so they asked "What is it?" He said: "I shall invite him and give him the option. If he opts for [leaving with] you, you can have him without paying a ransom, but if he chooses [to stay with] me, by God, I am not the sort of person who would prefer anyone over the one who had chosen him." The two of them said: "You have been kind and more than fair toward us."

The Prophet then called Zayd and asked him "Do you recognize these people?" Zayd said "Yes." The Prophet asked "Who are they?" and Zayd replied "This is my father, and this [other person] is my paternal uncle," and the Prophet said "And I am the one whom you have known and whose companionship you have experienced, so choose between me and them." Zayd said "I am not the kind of person who would choose anyone in preference to you; to me you are like a father and a paternal uncle." The two men said to him "Woe to you, O Zayd, would you prefer slavery to freedom, your father, your paternal uncle, and to your family?" He said

---

26. See Table 2, p. xxix.

27. On the exclusive status of the Quraysh, Muḥammad's tribe, in relation to the Kaʿbah, see Kister, "Mecca and Tamīm"; his views are challenged by Crone, *Meccan Trade*. See also Rubin, "Īlāf"; Simon, *Meccan Trade*.

28. This seems a contradiction in terms. The variant *al-jāʾiʿ* "the hungry" for "the prisoners" (*al-asīr*) seems more appropriate; see al-Ṭabarī, *Taʾrīkh*, 2300 note *b*).

"Yes, for I have seen something in this man, and I am not the kind of person who would ever choose anyone in preference to him." The Prophet, having witnessed this, took Zayd out to the Ḥijr[29] and said "O all those who are present, witness that Zayd [hereby] becomes my [adopted] son, with mutual rights of inheritance." When Zayd's father and paternal uncle saw this, they were satisfied and went away.

[Zayd b. Ḥārithah] was thus called Zayd b. Muḥammad until God revealed Islam. I was told all this by al-Ḥārith [b. Muḥammad]—Ibn Sa'd—Hishām b. Muḥammad [al-Kalbī]—his father [Muḥammad al-Kalbī], Jamīl b. Marthad al-Ṭā'ī, and others.

[Hishām] related part of the story on the authority of his [2301] father—[Bādhām] Abū Ṣāliḥ—['Abdallāh] Ibn 'Abbās. Through the chain of transmission going back to Ibn 'Abbās, [Hishām] related [the following]: The Prophet gave to [Zayd] in marriage Zaynab bt. Jaḥsh b. Ri'āb al-Asadiyyah, whose mother was Umaymah bt. 'Abd al-Muṭṭalib b. Hāshim.[30] Zayd later divorced her, and the Prophet married her. The Munāfiqūn[31] made this a topic of their conversation and reviled the Prophet, saying "Muḥammad prohibits [marriage] with the [former] wives of one's own sons, but he married the [former] wife of his son Zayd." As a result of this God revealed the following verse: "Muḥammad is not the father of any of your men, nay, he is the messenger of God and the seal of the prophets . . . ," etc.[32] God also revealed the verse "Call them by their fathers' names,"[33] so from that day onward [Zayd] was called

---

29. The sacred place in front of the Ka'bah where sacrifices were made, oaths taken, etc.; see Rubin, "Ka'ba."

30. That is, a paternal aunt of the Prophet. When Jaḥsh, originally of the bedouin tribe of Asad, decided to settle in Mecca, he became an ally of the leader Umayyah b. 'Abd Shams and married Umaymah, daughter of the rival leader, 'Abd al-Muṭṭalib, grandfather of the Prophet. See Muḥammad Ibn Ḥabīb, *Munammaq*, 357; Kister, "On Strangers and Allies," 138–39.

31. Usually translated as "the Hypocrites," this term refers to Muḥammad's opponents among the Muslims in Medina. See "Munāfiḳūn," *EI*², VII, 561–62 (A. A. Brockett); Lings, 237–39; al-Balādhurī, *Ansāb*, I, 274–83.

32. Qur'ān, 33:40 On the doctrine of the Seal of the Prophets, see Y. Friedmann, "Finality."

33. Qur'ān 33:5. This may also be translated as "trace their pedigrees back to their [real] fathers," and, indeed, the verse has both meanings at once. The declara-

Zayd b. Ḥārithah, and [other] adopted sons were named after their [real] fathers. Al-Miqdād was called [ibn] 'Amr after he had been named al- Miqdād b. al-Aswad since al-Aswad b. 'Abd Yāghūth had adopted him.

Zayd was killed in Jumādā I/September that year at the age of fifty-five.

It was reported that his *kunyah* was Abū Salamah.

According to Muḥammad b. 'Umar [al-Wāqidī]—Muḥammad b. al-Ḥasan b. Usāmah b. Zayd[34]—his father: The Prophet was ten years Zayd's senior. Zayd was a short, flat-nosed man, of a very dark brown skin; his *kunyah* was Abū Usāmah.

Zayd participated in the battles of Badr and Uḥud[35] and was appointed deputy in Medina when the Prophet left for the raid of al-Muraysī'.[36] Zayd also took part in the event of the Ditch (al-Khandaq), the expedition to al-Ḥudaybiyyah, and the conquest of Khaybar.[37] He was one of the famous archers among the Prophet's Companions.

---

tion was aimed at refuting the charge of incest raised against Muḥammad. See pp. 26, 180–82, below.

34. That is, great-grandson of Zayd.

35. Badr lies southwest of Medina; it was the site of the Muslims' first victory over their major enemy, the Quraysh. The battle took place in the spring of 2/624, two years after the Prophet's Emigration. Uḥud is a mountain near Medina where Muḥammad and his followers were defeated by the Quraysh and their allies in the year 3/625. See Kennedy, 35, 37–38; Watt, *Muḥammad at Medina*, 1–16, 21–29; Guillaume, 289–314, 370–426; Wellhausen, *Muḥammad*, 37–91, 101–48; Caetani, I, 472–96, 541–65; Ḥamīdullāh, *Battlefields*, 15, 20; "Badr," *EI*², I, 867–88 (W. M. Watt); al-Wāqidī, 12–172, 199–333; Ibn Hishām, II, 257–374, III, 64–178; al-Balādhurī, *Ansāb*, I, 288–308, 311–38; al-Ṭabarī, *Ta'rīkh*, I, 1284–1359, 1383–1425.

36. In the year 5/626. See al-Wāqidī, 404–13; Wellhausen, *Muḥammad*, 175–90. It was also called the raid of Banū al-Muṣṭaliq; see Ibn Hishām, III, 302–9. Here, however, Abū Dharr, not Zayd, acted as the Prophet's deputy. See also Guillaume, 490–93; al-Ṭabarī, *Ta'rīkh*, I, 1511–17.

37. Al-Khandaq (the Ditch) is the name given in Muslim tradition to the siege by the Quraysh and their allies of Medina in the year 5/627. It is related that the Muslims dug a ditch to defend the town, and the besiegers eventually dispersed without achieving any result. See "Khandaḳ," *EI*², IV, 1020 (W. M. Watt); Watt, *Muḥammad at Medina*, 35–39; Guillaume, 456–61; Wellhausen, *Muḥammad*, 190–210; Caetani, I, 611–26; al-Ṭabarī, *Ta'rīkh*, I, 1463–85. Al-Ḥudaybiyyah is a place near Mecca where Muḥammad concluded a ten-year peace treaty with the Meccans. See "Ḥudaybiya," *EI*², III, 539 (W. M. Watt); Watt, "Expedition"; Lecker, "Ḥudaybiyya-Treaty"; Hawting, "Ḥudaybiyya"; Guillaume, 499–510; Lings, 247–56; Wellhausen, *Muḥammad*, 241–64; al-Ṭabarī, *Ta'rīkh*, I, 1528–59.

Thābit b. al-Jidhʿ of the Banū Salimah of the Anṣār, that is, Thābit b. Thaʿlabah b. Zayd b. al-Ḥārith b. Ḥarām b. Kaʿb.[38]

Al-Jidhʿ was [the nickname of] Thaʿlabah b. Kaʿb, who was so called, as was reported, because of his bravery and courage. Another version of the name is Thābit b. Thaʿlabah al-Jadhaʿ.[39] [2302]

Thābit witnessed the ʿAqabah meeting with the seventy Anṣārīs who swore allegiance to the Prophet that night.[40] He [also] participated in the battles of Badr, Uḥud, and the Ditch and the expedition to al-Ḥudaybiyyah, the conquest of Khaybar, the conquest of Mecca, the battle of Ḥunayn, and the [siege of] al-Ṭā'if,[41] where he was killed and became a *shahīd*.

[The Year 9]
(April 20, 630–April 8, 631)

In the year 9/630, in Shaʿbān/November, Umm Kulthūm, daughter of the Prophet, died.[42]

The Prophet said the ritual prayer over her bier, and it was reported that ʿAlī b. Abī Ṭālib, al-Faḍl b. al-ʿAbbās, and Usāmah b. Zayd descended into her grave.[43] She is the one to whom Umm

---

38. Khalīfah b. Khayyāṭ, *Ta'rīkh*, 55; Ibn Saʿd, III/2, 110–11; al-Balādhurī, *Ansāb*, I, 247. On the Anṣār see "Anṣār," *EI*², I, 514–15 (W. M. Watt); Hasson, "Contribution."

39. *Jidhʿ* means a palm trunk (conveying the notion of hardiness), whereas *jadhaʿ* means a strong young man.

40. See "ʿAḳaba," *EI*², I, 314 (W. M. Watt); Guillaume, 198–207; Kister, "Papyrus."

41. In the year 8/630 Mecca fell to the Muslims with hardly any resistance. It was then that most of the Quraysh, in particular the noble families, were converted to Islam. Shortly afterward the Thaqīf, the ruling tribe of the nearby town al-Ṭā'if, organized a bedouin army, which was defeated by Muḥammad at a place called Ḥunayn. Muḥammad then laid siege to al-Ṭā'if but had to withdraw without achieving any result. Shortly afterward, however, the Thaqīf joined Islam of their own volition. See Kennedy, 42–43; Guillaume, 540–61, 587–92; Watt, *Muḥammad at Medina*, 65–73; Wellhausen, *Muḥammad*, 319–73; Caetani, II, 105–79; Ḥamīdullāh, *Battlefields*, 36; Kister, "Ṭā'if"; al-Wāqidī, 780–992; Ibn Hishām, IV, 31–129, 182–88; al-Balādhurī, *Ansāb*, I, 353–68; al-Ṭabarī, *Ta'rīkh*, I, 1618–44, 1654–74.

42. Khalīfah b. Khayyāṭ, *Ta'rīkh*, 57; al-Balādhurī, *Ansāb*, I, 401.

43. Descending into the grave of the deceased was apparently a pre-Islamic custom, at least in Medina. It was sometimes, but not regularly, practiced by the Prophet in person. Historians of Medina mention five such instances. See ʿUmar b. Shabbah, I, 121–24; al-Samhūdī, III, 897–99. The practice continued in early Islam;

'Aṭiyyah referred when she said: "I washed one of the Prophet's daughters."[44]

According to Anas b. Mālik: When Umm Kulthūm was laid in her grave the Prophet said "Let no one who has become impure by approaching his wife tonight, descend into the grave"; he said: "Is there among you anyone who has not become impure by approaching his wife tonight?" Abū Ṭalḥah[45] said "I, O Messenger of God"; so the Prophet said "Descend," and Abū Ṭalḥah did so.

[The Year 11]
(March 29, 632–March 17, 633)

In the year 11/632, on 3 Ramaḍān/November 22, Fāṭimah, daughter of Muḥammad [the Prophet], passed away, at the age of twenty-nine or so.[46]

Opinions differ as to the time of Fāṭimah's death. According to Abū Ja'far Muḥammad b. 'Alī,[47] she died three months after the
[2303] Prophet, whereas, according to Yazīd b. Abī Ziyād—'Abdallāh b. al-Ḥārith, it was eight months [after the Prophet].

According to Muḥammad b. 'Umar [al-Wāqidī]—Ma'mar [b. Rāshid]—[Ibn Shihāb] al-Zuhrī—'Urwah [b. al-Zubayr]—'Ā'ishah [the Prophet's wife], and also Ibn Jurayj—al-Zuhrī—'Urwah: Fāṭimah died six months after the Prophet, and this is the sound [account], according to Ibn 'Umar [al-Wāqidī]. She died on Monday the 3rd of Ramaḍān 11/November 22, 632.[48]

---

see, e.g., Ibn Ḥajar, *Iṣābah*, IV, 380, s.v. Fāṭimah al-Zahrā'; 'Abd al-Malik Ibn Ḥabīb, *Ta'rīkh*, 96, 101. However, it is not included among Muḥammad's funerary practices as recorded by Ibn Qayyim al-Jawziyyah, I, 139–46.

44. That is, in preparation for her burial. Umm 'Aṭiyyah, an Anṣārī woman, is connected with traditions about washing the dead and otherwise; see Ibn Ḥajar, *Iṣābah*, IV, 476–77.

45. Zayd b. Sahl, an Anṣārī and a close Companion of the Prophet. See Ibn Ḥajar, *Iṣābah*, I, 566–67; Ibn Manẓūr, *Mukhtaṣar*, IX, 134–41; al-Dhahabī, *Siyar*, II, 27–34.

46. See "Fāṭima," *EI*², II, 841–50 (L. Veccia Vaglieri); al-Amīn, II, 535–639; Ibn Sa'd, III/2, 11–20; Khalīfah b. Khayyāṭ, *Ta'rīkh*, 60–61; al-Balādhurī, *Ansāb*, I, 402–5; Ibn Ḥanbal, *Faḍā'il*, 754–65; al-Suyūṭī, *Thughūr*; 'Abd al-Malik Ibn Ḥabīb, *Ta'rīkh*, 84, 98; al-Ṭabarī, *Ta'rīkh*, I, 1869.

47. That is, Muḥammad al-Bāqir; see pp. 229–30, below.

48. *Laylat al-thulathā'* is Monday because the Arabs count the days by the nights that precede them. According to Cattenoz, however, this date was a Sunday.

According to Ja'far [al-Ṣādiq] b. Muḥammad, her *kunyah* was Umm Abīhā.[49]

Abū al-'Āṣ b. al-Rabī' b. 'Abd al-'Uzzā b. 'Abd Shams b. 'Abd Manāf b. Quṣayy.[50] Abū al-'Āṣ's name was Miqsam. His mother was Hālah bt. Khuwaylid b. Asad b. 'Abd al-'Uzzā b. Quṣayy, and his maternal aunt was Khadījah bt. Khuwaylid, the Prophet's wife. The Prophet gave his daughter Zaynab to him in marriage before [the rise of] Islam, and she bore him 'Alī and Umāmah. 'Alī died in childhood, whereas Umāmah lived and was married to 'Alī b. Abī Ṭālib after the death of Fāṭimah, the Prophet's daughter.

Abū al-'Āṣ b. al-Rabī' participated in the battle of Badr on the side of the unbelievers and was taken prisoner by 'Abdallāh b. Jubayr b. al-Nu'mān al-Anṣārī.[51] When the Meccans sent [a delegation to negotiate] the ransom of their prisoners, 'Amr b. al-Rabī', brother of Abū al-'Āṣ, came to ransom his brother.

According to [Muḥammad] Ibn Ḥumayd—Salamah [b. al-Faḍl]—Muḥammad [Ibn Isḥāq]—Yaḥyā b. 'Abbād b. 'Abdallāh b. al-Zubayr—his father, 'Abbād—'Ā'ishah: When the Meccans sent [a delegation to negotiate] the ransom of their prisoners, Zaynab, the Prophet's daughter, sent valuables as a ransom for Abū al-'Āṣ. She sent a necklace that [her mother] Khadījah had given her before conducting her to Abū al-'Āṣ for the first time, to consum- [2304]
mate their marriage. When the Prophet saw it his heart softened toward her a great deal, and he said [to his followers] "If you think it appropriate to set the prisoner free on her behalf, and [also] to

49. Meaning "mother of her father," a unique *kunyah* the sense of which is by no means clear. Whenever it is mentioned it is not explained; the same applies to Faṭimah's granddaughter and to Muḥammad b. al-Ḥanafiyyah's daughter, both called Umm Abīhā; see al-Balādhurī, *Ansāb*, III, (Maḥmūdī) 271; Ibn Isḥāq, *Siyar*, 251. This appellation is found in the context of the Nuṣayrī-'Alawi religion, where it refers to belief in reincarnation. Fāṭimah is believed to be the reincarnation of Āminah, the Prophet's mother, who is in turn the reincarnation of the Virgin Mary. As proof of this argument Fāṭimah's *kunyah*, Umm Abīhā, is adduced. See al-Ṭabarānī, "Majmū' al-a'yād," 175. I owe this information to my colleague Meir Bar-Asher. Fāṭimah, however, is commonly compared by the Shī'īs to the Virgin Mary without involving the doctrine of reincarnation or this strange *kunyah*.

50. Ibn Ḥibbān, *Mashāhīr*, 56; al-Wāqidī, 553–55; Wellhausen, *Muḥammad*, 233–34; al-Ṭabarī, *Ta'rīkh*, I, 1346–49, 1350–52. See also the references in note 5. The clan's name is 'Abd Shams, of the Quraysh.

51. A prominent Anṣārī who was killed in the battle of Uḥud; see Ibn Ḥajar, *Iṣābah*, II, 287.

return to her that which belongs to her, do so." They said "Yes, O Messenger of God!" So they set Abū al-ʿĀṣ free and returned to Zaynab that which belonged to her.

Abū-al-ʿĀṣ remained married to Zaynab, even though he was still a pagan.[52] Shortly before the *fatḥ*, that is, the conquest of Mecca,[53] he went to Syria [carrying] merchandise [for sale], as well as goods that the Quraysh delivered through him. After he finished his trade and was on his way back he came across one of the Prophet's raiding parties; according to another version, it was the Prophet himself who had sent the party [to raid] the caravan Abū al-ʿĀṣ was traveling with on its way back from Syria.[54] [The party] comprised 170 mounted raiders under the command of Zayd b. Ḥārithah. This occurred in Jumādā I, 6/October 627. The party appropriated goods and took some of the caravan's passengers prisoner, but Abū al-ʿĀṣ escaped, and they could not overtake him. The party returned [to Medina] with the booty, and Abū al-ʿĀṣ came at night and entered [the dwelling of] Zaynab, the Prophet's daughter, seeking her protection. She granted him protection for as long as he was occupied with retrieving his property.[55] In the morning the Prophet came out for the morning prayer. He uttered the formula "God is great" (*Allāh akbar*), and the people did the same; according to [Muḥammad] Ibn Ḥumayd—Salamah [b. al-Faḍl]—Muḥammad Ibn Isḥāq—Yazīd b. Rūmān: Zaynab called out "O people, I have granted protection to Abū al-ʿĀṣ b. al-Rabīʿ." On finishing the prayer the Prophet came before the people and said: "O people, did you hear what I heard?" They replied "Yes," whereupon he said: "By He Who holds Muḥammad's soul in His

52. Literally, the sentence reads "Abū al-ʿĀṣ remained with her, professing paganism [or, in spite of his paganism]," but as the story continues it becomes evident that Zaynab lived in Medina, whereas Abū al-ʿĀṣ lived in Mecca. They were separated until Abū al-ʿĀṣ was converted to Islam; see note 57.

53. The term *fatḥ* usually refers to the conquest of Mecca in the year 8/630. The original meaning may have been different, although still connected with the sanctuary in Mecca; see Hawting, "Ḥudaybiyya."

54. The raid of al-ʿĪṣ; see the references in note 50, above.

55. Literally, "in the matter of demanding his property." Granting protection, *jiwār*, was common in pre-Islamic times. Protection was sometimes granted against all hazards, at other times only against certain stipulated ones. See Goldziher, *Muslim Studies*, I, 22–23; p. 116, below.

hands, I never knew about any of this until I heard of it [now], just as you did. [Know that] the lowest-ranking Muslim [is authorized] [2305] to grant [someone] protection from other Muslims."[56] The Prophet then retreated and went to see his daughter Zaynab. He said to her "O daughter, treat Abū al-ʿĀṣ well, but do not let him touch you, because you are not lawful to him."[57]

According to Ibn Isḥāq—ʿAbdallāh b. Abī Bakr: The Prophet sent [a message] to the raiding party that had looted Abū al-ʿĀṣ's property, saying: "You know this man's standing in relation to us; now you plundered property that belongs to him. If you act in a commendable way, you will return that which belongs to him, and this would be pleasing to us. However, if you refuse to do so [you will be excused], because it is booty imparted to you by God, and you are more entitled to it [than anyone else]." They said "O Messenger of God, of course we will return it to him." They returned Abū al-ʿĀṣ's property to him, to the point that someone would even come with a rope, another with a worn-out leather bag and a waterskin, yet another with a peg, until they returned to him all his property; nothing was missing. Abū al-ʿĀṣ then left for Mecca, where he handed every Qurashī proprietor, that is, those who had delivered goods through him, the property that belonged to them. Then he said "O people of Quraysh, has there remained with me any property belonging to any of you that you did not yet retrieve?" They said "No, may God reward you; indeed we found that you are faithful and noble." He said: "I testify that there is no god but Allāh and that Muḥammad is His servant and messenger. I

56. That is, the Muslim community was legally responsible for the safety of anyone granted protection by any individual Muslim, regardless of the circumstances. This saying, here attributed to the Prophet (a *ḥadīth*), may have originated during the Muslim conquests after Muḥammad's death, as a solution to the problem of the treaties with enemies. For example, objections were raised when Khālid b. al-Walīd concluded a peace treaty with leaders of Damascus, because he was not commander-in-chief. Yet the commander-in-chief, Abū ʿUbaydah, ratified the treaty, saying "the lowest ranking Muslim. . . ." See al-Balādhurī, *Futūḥ*, 122. Note that Abū ʿUbaydah does not attribute the saying to the Prophet. See the discussion, e.g., in Abū Yūsuf, 61, 63 (where the example of Zaynab is mentioned), 68–69 (where protection granted by a slave is discussed). See also Ibn Abī Shaybah, *Muṣannaf*, VII, 689–90; Ibn al-Murtaḍā, V, 452; Ben Shemesh, III, 65–66; cf. al-Wāqidī, 793.

57. The Muslims had to divorce their pagan spouses; see note 59.

was prevented from embracing Islam while I was staying with Muḥammad only by the fear that you would think I [did so] merely to embezzle your property. Now that God has returned it to you and I am free from it, I become converted to Islam." Abū al-ʿĀṣ then departed and went to the Prophet.

According to Ibn Isḥāq—Dā'ūd b. al-Ḥuṣayn—ʿIkrimah, the client[58] of [ʿAbdallāh] Ibn ʿAbbās—Ibn ʿAbbās: The Prophet returned Zaynab [to her husband Abū al-ʿĀṣ] by force of their initial marriage, without renewing it, after six years [of separation].[59]

Abū al-ʿĀṣ returned to Mecca after embracing Islam and did not participate in any military [or other] event with the Prophet.[60]
[2306] He later moved to Medina, where he died in Dhū al-Ḥijjah 12/February 634, during the caliphate of Abū Bakr. He appointed al-Zubayr b. al-ʿAwwām as the executor of his will.

According to Hishām b. Muḥammad [al-Kalbī]—Maʿrūf b. Kharrabūdha: Abū al-ʿĀṣ b. al-Rabīʿ went on a [business] trip to Syria; remembering his wife Zaynab, the Prophet's daughter, he recited the following verses:

I remembered Zaynab when passing through Iram,[61]
and I said: "Blessed be the man[62] who dwells by the holy place.

58. A client, in Arabic *mawlā*, is a person linked to another in any of a number of legal ways called *walā'*; see "Mawlā," *EI*², VI, 874–82 (P. Crone).

59. See al-Ṭabarī, *Ta'rīkh*, I, 1347. According to others, Abū al-ʿĀṣ had to pay the bride price and marry Zaynab again; e.g., al-Balādhurī, *Ansāb* I, 399. See the legal discussion in Abū Yūsuf, 100.

60. The term *mashhad* (pl. *mashāhid*), literally, "a scene," refers to battles, as well as to other events in the life of the Prophet (e.g., the treaty of al-Ḥudaybiyyah). Participation with the Prophet in these events imparted great prestige to his followers and constituted their claim to fame, as well as to material benefits after the Prophet's death. A person's record is called *sābiqah*, i.e., "priority, privilege."

61. The text is vocalized *warrakat* in the third person (as also in Ibn Saʿd, VIII, 21), in order to make it conform to the meter. This vocalization seems impossible, however, because Iram is written with an *alif* at the end (*iramā*), which means that it is the object, not the subject of the verb. See al-Amīn, XXXIII, 214, who has *adraktu*, "I arrived at," for *warraktu*; the editor remarks that he does not understand the verse. See also al-Marzubānī, 332 (*jāwaztu* "I passed through"); Ibn Manẓūr, *Mukhtaṣar*, XXIX, 44 (*waradtu* "I reached"). Iram is explained here as another name for Damascus.

62. Literally, "May God grant rain unto the man. . . ."

May God reward the virtuous daughter of the reliable one![63]
That which a husband knows he will praise.

ʿIkrimah b. Abī Jahl—Abū Jahl's name was ʿAmr—b. Hishām b. al-Mughīrah b. ʿAbdallāh b. ʿUmar b. Makhzūm.[64]

According to Muḥammad b. ʿUmar [al-Wāqidī]—Abū Bakr b. ʿAbdallāh b. Abī Sabrah—Mūsā b. ʿUqbah—Abū Ḥabībah, the client of al-Zubayr [b. al-ʿAwwām]—ʿAbdallāh b. al-Zubayr: On the day of the conquest of Mecca ʿIkrimah b. Abī Jahl ran away to the Yemen, fearing that the Prophet would kill him.[65] His wife Umm Ḥakīm bt. al-Ḥārith b. Hishām, who was a clever woman, had already become a follower of the Prophet. She went to the Prophet and said "My cousin[66] ʿIkrimah fled from you to the Yemen, fearing that you would kill him, so grant him protection." The Prophet said "I grant him the protection of God; whoever meets him must not harm him."[67] Umm Ḥakīm set out to look for ʿIkrimah and caught up with him somewhere on the coast of Tihāmah, already embarked on a boat. She started waving to him, saying: "O cousin, I come to you from the man who is the kindest [2307]
toward his kin,[68] the most just and the most virtuous of all people. Do not ruin yourself [by fleeing], for I have asked him to grant you protection, and he did." ʿIkrimah said "Did you do that?" and she replied "Yes, I spoke with him, and he granted you protection." So ʿIkrimah went back with her. As he drew near Mecca the Prophet told his Companions "ʿIkrimah b. Abī Jahl will come to you as a

63. *Al-amīn* "the reliable one" was an epithet of the Prophet.

64. Ibn Saʿd, V, 329, VII/2 126; Khalīfah b. Khayyāṭ, *Taʾrīkh*, 88, 100; idem, *Ṭabaqāt*, 20, 299; Ibn Ḥibbān, *Mashāhīr*, 59; al-Rāzī, 147–48; Ibn Abī Shaybah, *Muṣannaf*, IV, 577; al-Mizzī, *Tahdhīb*, XX, 247. The Makhzūm was a leading clan among the Quraysh; see Ibn Ḥazm, *Jamharat*, 141.

65. See a similar story told about Ṣafwān b. Umayyah; al-Ṭabarī, *Taʾrīkh*, I, 1644–46.

66. ʿIkrimah and his wife were paternal first cousins; see Ibn Ḥazm, *Jamharat*, 145.

67. Cf. al-Ḥalabī, III, 106–7; Ibn al-Athīr, *Kāmil*, II, 123–24.

68. *Awṣal al-nās*. Being kind to one's family, i.e., practicing *ṣilat al-raḥim*, was one of the highly appreciated social values in both the pre-Islamic and the Islamic periods. It is distinct from tribal group solidarity, *ʿaṣabiyyah*, which was condemned by Islam.

believer and an Emigrant;[69] do not curse his father,[70] for to curse the dead [only] harms the living and does not reach the dead." 'Ikrimah then arrived at the Prophet's door with his wife. She, however, preceded him, asked permission to see the Prophet, and went in. 'Umar informed the Prophet that 'Ikrimah had arrived, at which the Prophet rejoiced and jumped to his feet—he did not [even] have his cloak on—out of joy for 'Ikrimah's [arrival]. He said [to the woman] "Bring him in," whereupon 'Ikrimah came in and said "O Muḥammad,[71] this woman here informs me that you have granted me protection." The Prophet said "So you are protected." 'Ikrimah reported: At that point I said "I declare that there is no god but Allāh alone; He has no partner, and you are the servant of God and His messenger." I [also] said "You are the most just, truthful, and faithful of all people." I said this bowing my head because I felt ashamed before him. Then I said "O Messenger of God, forgive me all my enmity toward you and all the campaigns[72] in which I hastened [to participate] so as to support paganism." The Prophet said "O God, forgive 'Ikrimah all his enmity toward me and all the campaigns in which he hastened [to participate] in order to avert [others] from Your path." [Then] I said "O Messenger of God, instruct me with what you know is best, so that I shall know it." The Prophet replied "Declare that you testify that there is no god but Allāh and that Muḥammad is His servant and messenger, and exert yourself in the path of God." 'Ikrimah then said[73] "By God, every sum of money I spent on averting [others] from the path of God I shall doubly reciprocate,

---

69. The Emigrants, *Muhājirūn*, constituted the elite of the Muslim community, both during the Prophet's lifetime and afterward. In this class were included those who emigrated to Medina with the Prophet and afterward until the conquest of Mecca. In some instances bedouins who remained in their own territory but committed themselves to Islam were also included. The account of 'Ikrimah's conversion is an attempt to include the Quraysh, who were converted after the conquest of Mecca, in the Islamic elite. See also p. 115 and note 541, below.

70. That is, Abū Jahl, who had been a fervent opponent of the Muslims and was killed in the battle of Badr; see "Abū D̲jahl," *EI*², I, 115 (W. M. Watt).

71. Unbelievers addressed the Prop̲het by his name, whereas Muslims always said "O Messenger of God," as indeed 'Ikrimah does later in the story.

72. Or, undertakings, deeds; see *Glossarium*, s.v. *markab*.

73. The story reverts to the third person at this point.

[spending it] in the way of God." He later exerted himself in battle and was killed, becoming a *shahīd*, at the battle of Ajnādayn[74] during the caliphate of Abū Bakr.

In the year of his Pilgrimage[75] the Prophet appointed 'Ikrimah tax collector of the tribal confederation of Hawāzin.[76] 'Ikrimah was in Tabālah[77] when the Prophet died.

[Those Who Died in the Year 14] *(February 25, 635–February 13, 636)*

Among those who died in the year 14 was Nawfal b. al-Ḥārith b. 'Abd al-Muṭṭalib b. Hāshim b. 'Abd Manāf.[78] [2308]

Nawfal's *kunyah* was Abū al-Ḥārith, after his son al-Ḥārith. It was reported that Nawfal was the eldest convert to Islam among the Banū Hāshim. He was older than his paternal uncles Ḥamzah[79] and al-'Abbās, older [too] than his brothers Rabī'ah, Abū Sufyān, and 'Abd Shams,[80] sons of al-Ḥārith.

Nawfal b. al-Ḥārith was taken prisoner [by the Muslims] at Badr.

According to Ibn Sa'd[81]—'Alī b. 'Īsā al-Nawfalī—his father—his paternal uncle Isḥāq b. 'Abdallāh b. al-Ḥārith—'Abdallāh b. al-

---

74. A battle between the Muslims and a Byzantine force, usually said to have taken place between al-Ramlah and Bayt Jibrīn in Palestine in the year 13/634. Both the location and the date are, however, disputed; see Donner, *Early Islamic Conquests*, 128–30.

75. Three months before his death, in 10/632, the Prophet performed a pilgrimage to Mecca. This occasion is called "the Farewell Pilgrimage" (*ḥajjat al-wadā'*).

76. The Hawāzin was a large tribal confederation, attached to the town of al-Ṭā'if; see "Hawāzin," *EI²*, III, 285–86 (W. M. Watt). As for tax collectors sent by the Prophet, there are various lists; see p. 83, below.

77. A place on the way to the Yemen, about 150 miles south of Mecca; see Yāqūt, *Mu'jam al-buldān*, I, 816–17.

78. Of the Prophet's clan, the Banū Hāshim. See Khalīfah b. Khayyāṭ, *Ta'rīkh*, 104; idem, *Ṭabaqāt*, 6; Ibn Ḥibbān, *Mashāhīr*, 58.

79. An early convert who was killed in the battle of Uḥud; see Ibn Ḥajar, *Iṣābah*, I, 353–54.

80. The Prophet changed his name to 'Abdallāh; see note 234, below. He is counted among the Companions; see Ibn Ḥajar, *Iṣabah*, II, 292.

81. Ibn Sa'd, IV/1, 31.

Ḥārith b. Nawfal: When Nawfal b. al-Ḥārith was taken prisoner at Badr the Prophet said to him "Ransom yourself, O Nawfal." The latter replied "I have nothing to pay as ransom, O Messenger of God," whereupon the Prophet said: "Ransom yourself with your lances, which [are stored] at Juddah."[82] Nawfal said "I testify that you are the messenger of God." He then ransomed himself with those lances, which numbered 1,000.

The Prophet established the bond of brotherhood (*mu'ākhāh*) between Nawfal and al-ʿAbbās b. ʿAbd al-Muṭṭalib.[83] In pre-Islamic times the two were equal partners,[84] and they loved each other.

Nawfal took part in the conquest of Mecca, the battle of Ḥunayn, and the siege of al-Ṭā'if, on the Prophet's side. He stood firmly by the Prophet at Ḥunayn;[85] he had [also] supplied the Prophet with 3,000 lances for that battle, whereupon the Prophet said to him "O Abū al-Ḥārith, it is as if I look at your lances smashing the idolators' backbones."[86]

Nawfal b. al-Ḥārith died one year and three months after ʿUmar b. al-Khaṭṭāb's accession to the caliphate.[87] ʿUmar said the prayer over his bier and walked with [the mourners] to al-Baqīʿ,[88] where Nawfal was buried.

---

82. A town on the Red Sea shore; see "Djudda," *EI*², II, 571–72 (R. Hartmann [Phebe Ann Marr]).

83. After the Emigration to Medina Muḥammad instituted "brotherhood" (*mu'ākhāh*) between pairs of Muslims. Among other things such "brothers" inherited from one another. See Watt, *Muḥammad at Medina*, 248–49. Guillaume, 234–35; Simon, "L'institution"; Muḥammad Ibn Ḥabīb, *Muḥabbar*, 71; al-Balādhurī, *Ansāb*, I, 270.

84. That is, their partnership included all their property (*shirkat al-mufāwaḍah*), as opposed to partnership in part of the property only (*shirkat al-ʿinān*).

85. This is worthy of note because at a certain point during this battle most of the Muslims defected, and it took a second offensive to gain victory. See al-Wāqidī, 897–907; p. 25, below.

86. *Ka-annī anẓuru ilā rimāḥika*. . . . This expression denotes foreknowledge of events and is often used as a literary device to anticipate later developments in the story. Here it also points to the prophetic powers of Muḥammad.

87. In the year 13/634.

88. Al-Baqīʿ was the first Islamic cemetery in Medina, instituted during the Prophet's lifetime. Most of the Companions, the members of the Prophet's family, and many Successors (*tābiʿūn*) were buried there. See "Baḳīʿ al-Gharḳad," *EI*², I, 957–58 (A. J. Wensinck [A. S. Bazmee Ansari]); ʿUmar b. Shabbah, I, 86–133.

Abū Sufyān b. al-Ḥārith b. ʿAbd al-Muṭṭalib b. Hāshim.[89]

He was the Prophet's milk brother because Ḥalīmah[90] nursed him [too] for a few days.

Abū Sufyān had amicable [relations] with the Prophet. [However], when the Prophet was sent [on his divine mission] Abū Sufyān became his enemy and composed satirical poems against him and his Companions. He showed hatred toward the Prophet for twenty years, never remaining behind when the Quraysh set out to fight Muḥammad. When there was talk about the Prophet's going to Mecca in the Year of the Conquest (*fatḥ*), God put the belief in Islam in the heart of Abū Sufyān. He thus met the Prophet before the latter camped at al-Abwāʾ.[91] Abū Sufyān embraced Islam, together with his son Jaʿfar, and set out with the Prophet to participate in the conquest of Mecca and the battle of Ḥunayn. [2309]

Abū Sufyān related [the following]: When we met the enemy in battle at Ḥunayn I jumped off my horse, my sword unsheathed in my hand, while the Prophet was looking at me; God knows that I wished to die for him. Al-ʿAbbās then said "O Messenger of God, this is your [milk] brother and paternal cousin Abū Sufyān b. al-Ḥārith, so regard him with favor." The Prophet said: "I do. May God forgive him all his enmity toward me." The Prophet then turned to me, saying "My brother, upon my life!" and I kissed his foot in the stirrup.

Abū Sufyān b. al-Ḥārith died in Medina four months minus thirteen days after the death of his brother Nawfal b. al-Ḥārith. According to another report, he died in the year 20 (December 21, 640–December 9, 641). ʿUmar b. al-Khaṭṭāb said the prayer over his bier, and he was buried in the corner of the court of ʿAqīl b. Abī Ṭālib in al-Baqīʿ. He had dug a grave for himself three days before he died.

---

89. Al-Balādhurī, *Ansāb*, I, 361, 365, 477, 539, III (Dūrī), 296; Khalīfah b. Khayyāṭ, *Ṭabaqāt*, 6; Ibn Ḥibbān, *Mashāhīr*, 44; Ibn Saʿd, IV/1, 34–37; Ibn Qudāmah, 105–8.

90. Ḥalīmah was a bedouin woman who was hired as wet nurse for Muḥammad. See Guillaume, 70; Ibn Ḥajar, *Iṣābah*, IV, 274.

91. Cf. Ibn Saʿd, IV/1, 34. Al-Abwāʾ is a place on the road from Mecca to Medina. One of Muḥammad's first military expeditions was to this place; see "Abwāʾ," *EI*², I, 169 (W. M. Watt); al-Wāqidī, 11–12; Wellhausen, *Muḥammad*, 34. The same place served the Quraysh as a campsite on their way to fight the Prophet at Badr (2/624); see al-Wāqidī, 145; Wellhausen, 80.

[Those Who Were Killed in the Year 16] (February 2, 637–January 22, 638)

Among those who were killed in the year 16 was Sa'd b. 'Ubayd b. al-Nu'mān b. Qays b. 'Amr b. Zayd b. Umayyah b. Zayd.[92]

He was called Sa'd the Reciter.[93]

Sa'd's *kunyah* was Abū Zayd.

[2310] According to Anas b. Mālik, Sa'd was one of the six who collected the Qur'ān during the Prophet's lifetime.[94]

Sa'd took part in the battles of Badr, Uḥud, the Ditch, and all the [other] battles, on the Prophet's side. He was killed as a *shahīd* in the battle of al-Qādisiyyah[95] in the year 16/637, aged sixty-four.

That same year Māriyah, the mother of Ibrāhīm son of the Prophet, died.[96] 'Umar b. al-Khaṭṭāb said the prayer over her bier. Her grave is in al-Baqī'.

Those Who Died or Were Killed in the Year 23 (November 19, 643–November 6, 644)

Among them was 'Umar b. al-Khaṭṭāb b. Nufayl b. 'Abd al-'Uzzā b. Riyāḥ b. 'Abdallāh b. Qurṭ b. Razāḥ b. 'Adī b. Ka'b.[97]

---

92. An Anṣārī, father of 'Umayr b. Sa'd, who was one of 'Umar's governors in al-Kūfah. See Khalīfah b. Khayyāṭ, *Ta'rīkh*, 103; Ibn Ḥibbān, *Mashāhīr*, 29.

93. That is, reciter or reader of the Qur'ān. See "Ḳur'ān," *EI*², V, 426 (A. T. Welch); Ibn al-Jazarī.

94. There is a debate over the meaning of *jama'a al-qur'ān*, *jama'a* signifying both "to collect" and "to comprise, [to be in possession of] the whole of. . . ." Accordingly the phrase could mean "collected" or "memorized the whole of the Qur'ān." In the prevailing Muslim tradition it is maintained that the Qur'ān was collected by order of the third caliph, 'Uthmān, but there are also traditions that it had already been collected during the Prophet's lifetime. See Jeffery, 5–7; Burton; Wansbrough, chap. 1; Sharon, "Umayyads," 131, n. 37. In addition, there is confusion regarding the identity of Abū Zayd, who collected (or memorized) the Qur'ān. See p. 284, below; Ibn Ḥajar, *Iṣābah*, II, 31.

95. Al-Qādisiyyah, in southwestern Iraq, was the site of a decisive victory by the Muslims over the Persians, probably in the year 16/637. See "Ḳādisiyya," *EI*², IV, 384–87 (L. Veccia Vaglieri); Kennedy, 67; Donner, *Early Islamic Conquests*, 203–10 and passim; Kamāl; al-Ṭabarī, *Ta'rīkh*, I, 2213–2361.

96. A Coptic concubine of the Prophet. The son she bore him died in infancy. Like 'Ā'ishah, Muḥammad's most beloved wife, she was charged with and acquitted of adultery. See "Māriya," *EI*², VI, 575 (F. Buhl); Caetani, II, 237–38; Khalīfah b. Khayyāṭ, *Ta'rīkh*, 106; al-Balādhurī, *Ansāb*, I, 448–53.

97. The second caliph, of the Qurashī clan the Banū 'Adī. See "'Omar ibn al-

'Umar's *kunyah* was Abū Ḥafṣ.

According to Ibn Sa'd[98]—Ya'qūb b. Ibrāhīm b. Sa'd—his father—Ṣāliḥ b. Kaysān—Ibn Shihāb [al-Zuhrī]: The possessors of the Scriptures (*ahl al-kitāb*)[99] were the first to give 'Umar the name Fārūq,[100] and the Muslims transmitted it from them; no report has reached us of any mention of this name by the Prophet.[101]

According to Ibn 'Umar [al-Wāqidī][102]—Abū Bakr b. Ismā'īl b. Muḥammad b. Sa'd—his father: 'Umar was stabbed on Wednesday, the 26th of Dhū al-Ḥijjah, 23/November 3, 644, and was buried on Sunday morning, the 1st of Muḥarram, 24/November 7, 644.

[Those Who Died in the Year 32] *(August 12, 652–August 1, 653)*

Among them was al-Ṭufayl b. al-Ḥārith b. al-Muṭṭalib b. 'Abd Manāf.[103]

He was a brother of 'Ubaydah b. al-Ḥārith, who had fought a duel against 'Utbah b. Rabī'ah[104] at the battle of Badr.

Khaṭṭāb," *EI*¹, III, 982–84 (G. Levi Della Vida); Kennedy, 57–70; Ibn Sa'd, III, 190–274; Khalīfah b. Khayyāṭ, *Ta'rīkh*, 126–27; idem, *Ṭabaqāt*, 22; Ibn Ḥanbal, *Faḍā'il*, 244–448; Ibn Ḥibbān, *Mashāhīr*, 23; Ibn al-Jawzī, *Ta'rīkh*.

98. Ibn Sa'd, III/1, 193.

99. *Ahl al-kitāb*, literally "People of the Book," originally referred to Jews and Christians and later extended to include Zoroastrians. They all have a special legal status within the Muslim state and as such are termed *ahl al-dhimmah*. The latter term (and status) was sometimes applied to members of yet other religions, including non-Arab idolators. See "*Ahl al-kitāb*," *EI*², I, 264–66 (G. Vajda); "*Dhimma*," *EI*², II, 227–31 (C. Cahen); Fattal; Bat Ye'or; Friedmann, "Temple."

100. For the most recent discussion of 'Umar's surname al-Fārūq, see Bashear, "Title."

101. But see al-Ṭabarī, *Ta'rīkh*, I, 2728–29, where this same report is preceded by another, in which it is related that it was the Prophet who gave 'Umar this name.

102. Cf. al-Ṭabarī, *Ta'rīkh*, I, 3726.

103. Ibn Ḥibbān, *Mashāhīr*, 34; al-Balādhurī, *Ansāb*, I, 429; Ibn Sa'd, III/1, 35. The clan's name is the Banū al-Muṭṭalib, related to the Prophet's clan, the Banū Hāshim. See Ibn Ḥazm, *Jamharat* 72–74; al-Zubayrī, 92–97.

104. Duels were often fought in the course of battles, not necessarily deciding the final outcome. 'Utbah b. Rabī'ah, of the 'Abd Shams clan, was one of the Qurashī leaders who bitterly opposed the Prophet and, while Muḥammad was still in Mecca, attempted to find a way to end his preaching. He was eventually killed at Badr by the Muslims. See Guillaume, 118, 132–33, 191, 296–98; Ibn Ḥazm, *Jamharat*, 76.

Al-Ṭufayl b. al-Ḥārith took part in the battles of Badr, Uḥud, and all the [other] battles, on the Prophet's side.

He died in the year 32 at the age of seventy.

Al-Ḥuṣayn b. al-Ḥārith b. al-Muṭṭalib b. 'Abd Manāf.[105]

He was a brother of 'Ubaydah and al-Ṭufayl, sons of al-Ḥārith.

[2311] He died that same year, a few months after his brother al-Ṭufayl.

Al-Ḥuṣayn had participated in Badr, Uḥud, and all the [other] battles on the Prophet's side.

Al-'Abbās b. 'Abd al-Muṭṭalib b. Hāshim b. 'Abd Manāf, the paternal uncle of the Prophet.[106]

His mother was Nutaylah, daughter of Janāb b. Kulayb b. Mālik b. 'Amr b. 'Āmir b. Zayd Manāh b. 'Āmir—also named al-Ḍaḥyān—b. Sa'd b. al-Khazraj b. Taymallāh b. al-Namir b. Qāsiṭ b. Hinb b. Afṣā b. Du'miyy b. Jadīlah b. Asad b. Rabī'ah b. Nizār b. Ma'add b. 'Adnān.[107]

Al-'Abbās' *kunyah* was Abū al-Faḍl [after] al-Faḍl, his eldest son.

It was reported that al-'Abbās was three years the Prophet's senior: The latter was born in the year of the Elephant,[108] whereas al-'Abbās was born three years before that.

Al-'Abbās participated in the conquest of Mecca, the battle of Ḥunayn, the siege of al-Ṭā'if, and the expedition to Tabūk[109] on

---

105. Al-Balādhurī, *Ansāb*, I, 308; Ibn Sa'd, III/1, 36.

106. That is, the eponym of the 'Abbāsid dynasty. Al-'Abbās was a late convert, and his descendants reshaped his biography in the process of legitimizing their rule. See "'Abbās b. 'Abd al-Muṭṭalib," *EI²*, I, 8–9 (W. M. Watt); Sharon, *Black Banners*, 35, 93–99 and passim; Khalīfah b. Khayyāṭ, *Ta'rīkh*, 144; idem, *Ṭabaqāt*, 4; Ibn Ḥanbal, *Faḍā'il*, 915–49; Ibn Ḥibbān, *Mashāhīr*, 27–28; Ibn Sa'd, IV/1, 1–22; *Akhbār al-dawlah*, passim.

107. The meaningful names in this long chain are al-Namir b. Qāsiṭ, a tribe of the great Rabī'ah confederation, and 'Āmir al-Ḍaḥyān, who was a powerful chief in his time. See Caskel, II, 22–23; Ibn Ḥazm, *Jamharat*, 300–2; "Rabī'a and Muḍar," *EI²*, VIII, 352–54 (H. Kindermann).

108. The Year of the Elephant was the year in which the Yemenī ruler Abrahah the Abyssinian attacked Mecca but was repelled with God's intervention. The event is recorded in Qur'ān 105 and in Arab histories. Traditionally the event is placed in the year A.D. 570, and so is Muḥammad's birth. Actually Abrahah's campaign took place in the 550s. See Kister, "Campaign"; Conrad, "Abraha."

109. A town on the northern frontier of Arabia. Muḥammad made a great campaign there in the year 9/631 but retreated after ten days because of discontent among his followers. See "Tabūk," *EI¹*, VII, 593–94 (F. Buhl); Guillaume,

the Prophet's side. At the head of his family, he stood firmly by the Prophet in the battle of Ḥunayn, while [other] people retreated, deserting the Prophet.

According to Ibn 'Umar [al-Wāqidī][110]—Khālid b. al-Qāsim al-Bayāḍī—Shu'bah, the client of Ibn 'Abbās: Al-'Abbās' spine was straight, and he used to tell us that when 'Abd al-Muṭṭalib[111] died his spine was [even] straighter than his.

Al-'Abbās died on Friday, 14 Rajab 32/February 19, 653, during the caliphate of 'Uthmān b. 'Affān,[112] at the age of eighty-eight. He was buried in al-Baqī', in the burial ground of the Hāshim family.

It was reported that when al-'Abbās died his body was washed by 'Alī b. Abī Ṭālib, together with 'Abdallāh, 'Ubaydallāh, and Qutham, sons of al-'Abbās.[113]

According to Muḥammad b. 'Alī,[114] al-'Abbās b. 'Abd al-Muṭṭalib died in the year 34 (July 22, 654–July 10, 655). 'Uthmān [b. 'Affān] said the ritual prayer over his bier, and he was buried in al-Baqī'.

Those Who Died or Were Killed in the Year 33 (August 2, 653–July 21, 654) [2312]

Among them was al-Miqdād b. 'Amr b. Tha'labah b. Mālik b. Rabī'ah b. Thumāmah b. Maṭrūd b. 'Amr b. Sa'd b. Zuhayr—according to some, it is Sa'd b. Dahīr—b. Lu'ayy b. Tha'labah b.

602–14; Wellhausen, *Muḥammad*, 390–416; Caetani, II, 238–53; al-Wāqidī, 989–1025.

110. Ibn Sa'd, IV/1, 20.

111. That is, al-'Abbās' father and the Prophet's grandfather.

112. The third caliph, who ruled in the years 23–35/644–56.

113. The body of the dead was washed by relatives or close friends. 'Alī and al-'Abbās both belonged to the Hāshim clan, and it is feasible that there were close ties between them. However, in view of the political rivalry between the descendants of 'Alī (supported by the Shī'ah) and those al-'Abbās (the 'Abbāsid dynasty), reports of the close ties between the two eponyms may be biased. See Sharon, *Black Banners*, chap. 4; Madelung, "Hāshimiyyāt"; compare the scene in which 'Alī, al-'Abbās, the latter's two sons al-Faḍl and Qutham, and two others are depicted washing the dead body of the Prophet; Guillaume, 687–88. This story helped the Shī'ah to explain 'Alī's failure to demand the caliphate that day.

114. Perhaps Muḥammad al-Bāqir is meant here; he provided other information about the family as well. See, e.g., p. 12, above.

Mālik b. al-Sharīd b. Ahwan b. Fās b. Duraym b. al-Qayn b. Ahwad b. Bahrā' b. 'Amr b. al-Ḥāf b. Quḍā'ah.[115]

Al-Miqdād's *kunyah* was Abū Ma'bad.

In pre-Islamic times al-Miqdād became an ally[116] of al-Aswad b. 'Abd Yāghūth, of the Zuhrah clan.[117] The latter adopted him, and so he was called al-Miqdād b. al-Aswad, but when [God] revealed the Qur'ānic verse "Call them by their fathers' [names],"[118] he was [again] named al-Miqdād b. 'Amr.

According to Ibn Isḥāq and Ibn 'Umar [al-Wāqidī], al-Miqdād participated in the second emigration to Abyssinia. He [also] took part on the Prophet's side in the battles of Badr, Uḥud, the Ditch, and all the [other] battles. He was one of the famous archers among the Prophet's companions.

According to Ibn Sa'd[119]—Muḥammad b. 'Umar [al-Wāqidī]—Mūsā b. Ya'qūb—his paternal aunt—her mother, Karīmah, daughter of al-Miqdād: She described her father to them saying: He was tall, brown, big-bellied, with a lot of hair on his head. He used to dye his beard yellow; it was of medium size, neither big nor small.
[2313] He was wide-eyed, his eyebrows were knitted, and his nose was hooked.

[According to Karīmah]: Al-Miqdād died in al-Jurf, [a place] three miles away from Medina,[120] in the year 33. People carried

115. The meaningful tribal name here is Bahrā', of the great Quḍā'ah confederation. See Ibn Ḥazm, *Jamharat*, 441; "Bahrā'," *EI²*, I, 938 (C. E. Bosworth). On al-Miqdād, see "Miḳdād b. 'Amr," *EI²*, VII, 32–33 (G. H. A. Juynboll); Khalīfah b. Khayyāṭ, *Ṭabaqāt*, 16–17; idem, *Ta'rīkh*, 144; Ibn Ḥibbān, *Mashāhīr*, 46; Ibn Sa'd, III/1, 114–16; al-Balādhurī, *Ansāb*, I, 204–5; Muḥammad Ibn Ḥabīb, *Munammaq*, 363–64.

116. An alliance, *ḥilf*, was a legal act by which an individual was admitted into a clan and accorded the same rights and obligations as the members of the clan. The clan was usually represented by one of its members (in this instance al-Aswad b. 'Abd Yāghūth). See "Ḥilf," *EI²*, III, 388–89 (E. Tyan); Crone, *Roman, Provincial and Islamic Law*, 51–56. This sense of *ḥilf* should be distinguished from *ḥilf* in the sense of an alliance between two groups, concluded for the purpose of a common military enterprise.

117. An important clan of the Quraysh. See Watt, *Muḥammad at Mecca*, 5–8 and passim; Caskel, II, 2–4. Al-Aswad was the Prophet's maternal cousin, yet he opposed Islam; see Mu'arrij b. 'Amr al-Sadūsī, 61.

118. Ibn Sa'd, III/1, 114; see also p. 9, above.

119. Ibn Sa'd, III/1, 115.

120. See Yāqūt, *Mu'jam al-buldān*, II, 62. The place was apparently a base whence the Muslim armies set out for raids. See, e.g., al-Wāqidī, 1125; al-Ṭabarī, *Ta'rīkh*, I, 1796 and passim.

his body on their shoulders to be buried in Medina, and ʿUthmān b. ʿAffān said the ritual prayer over his bier. He was seventy years old or so when he died.

According to Ibn Saʿd[121]—Muḥammad b. ʿAbdallāh al-Asadī—ʿAmr b. Thābit—his father—Abū Fāʾid: Al-Miqdād drank castor oil, then died.

[Those Who Were Killed in the Year 36] (June 30, 656–June 18, 657)

Among those who were killed in the year 36 was al-Zubayr b. al-ʿAwwām b. Khuwaylid b. Asad b. ʿAbd al-ʿUzzā b. Quṣayy.[122]

Al-Zubayr was converted to Islam at an early stage; it is reported that he was the fourth or fifth convert.

According to Hishām b. ʿUrwah [b. al-Zubayr]—his father: Al-Zubayr embraced Islam when he was sixteen years old. He never failed to participate in all the campaigns undertaken by the Prophet. He was fifty-odd years when he was killed.

Al-Zubayr emigrated to Abyssinia twice.

The Prophet established the bond of brotherhood (*muʾākhāh*) between al-Zubayr and [ʿAbdallāh] b. Masʿūd.

It was reported that al-Zubayr was neither tall nor short, light-bearded, dark-toned, and hairy.

According to al-Ḥārith [b. Muḥammad][123]—ʿAbdallāh b. Maslamah b. Qaʿnab—Sufyān b. ʿUyaynah: The inheritance left by al-Zubayr amounted to 40 million [dirhams].[124]

They [also] reported[125] that on the day of the battle of the Camel,[126] that is, Thursday the 10th of Jumādā II that year/

121. Ibn Saʿd, III/1, 115.

122. One of Muḥammad's closest Companions, of the Qurashī clan Asad. See Khalīfah b. Khayyāṭ, *Taʾrīkh*, 161, 168; idem, *Ṭabaqāt*, 13; Ibn Ḥibbān, *Mashāhīr*, 25–26; Ibn Ḥanbal, *Faḍāʾil*, 733–38; ʿAbd al-Malik Ibn Ḥabīb, *Taʾrīkh*, 114–15; Ibn Saʿd, III/1, 70–73.

123. Ibn Saʿd, III/1, 71.

124. Literally, "Al-Zubayr's inheritance was divided according to forty millions" (i.e., that amount was taken as the basis for dividing the inheritance). On al-Zubayr's legendary wealth, see Ibn al-Zubayr, 203.

125. This can refer either to the just-mentioned chain of authorities or to another, unspecified one.

126. In the year 36/656 al-Zubayr, his associate Ṭalḥah b. ʿUbaydallāh (see be-

December 5, 656, after the battle had taken place, al-Zubayr rode his horse, named Dhū al-Khimār, and left for Medina. He was killed [on the way] in Wādī al-Sibā' and was buried there.[127] 'Urwah [b. al-Zubayr] said: My father was killed in [the immediate aftermath of] the battle of the Camel, aged sixty-four.

[2314] Ṭalḥah b. 'Ubaydallāh b. 'Uthmān b. 'Amr b. Ka'b b. Sa'd b. Taym b. Murrah.[128]

His *kunyah* was Abū Muḥammad. His mother was al-Ṣa'bah bt. 'Abdallāh al-Ḥaḍramī.

Ṭalḥah was killed, in [the immediate aftermath of] the battle of the Camel, by Marwān b. al-Ḥakam.

Ṭalḥah had a son named Muḥammad and surnamed al-Sajjād (the Worshipper). Ṭalḥah's *kunyah* was [Abū Muḥammad] after [this son]. He was killed with his father, Ṭalḥah, in the battle of the Camel.

Ṭalḥah was an early convert to Islam, [yet] he did not take part in the battle of Badr.

Those Who Died or Were Killed in the Year 37 (June 19, 657–June 8, 658)

Among them was 'Ammār b. Yāsir[129] b. 'Āmir b. Mālik b. Kinānah b. Qays b. al-Ḥuṣayn b. al-Wadhīm b. Tha'labah b. 'Awf b. Ḥārithah b. 'Āmir al-Akbar b. Yām b. 'Ans—that is, Zayd—b. Mālik b. Udad b. Zayd b. Yashjub b. 'Arīb b. Zayd b. Kahlān b.

---

low), and the Prophet's widow 'Ā'ishah fought against the fourth caliph, 'Alī b. Abī Ṭālib, the casus belli being their request that 'Alī punish the murderers of the third caliph, 'Uthmān b. 'Affān. According to the prevailing versions, Ṭalḥah and al-Zubayr were not killed in battle but repented their move and retreated. They were nevertheless killed by 'Alī's supporters. See Kennedy, 76; Wellhausen, *Arab Kingdom*, 51–53; "Djamal," *EI*², II, 414–16 (L. Veccia Vaglieri); Caetani, IX, 23–225; 'Armūsh; al-Ṭabarī, *Ta'rīkh*, I, 3111–3224.

127. A *wādī* on the way from southern Iraq to the Ḥijāz; see Yāqūt, *Mu'jam al-buldān*, III, 29.

128. A close Companion of the Prophet, of the Qurashī clan Taym. See "Ṭalḥa b. 'Ubaidallāh," *EI*¹, VIII, 640–41 (G. Levi Della Vida); Khalīfah b. Khayyāṭ, *Ta'rīkh*, 160, 165; idem, *Ṭabaqāt*, 18; Ibn Ḥanbal, *Faḍā'il*, 743–48; Ibn Ḥibbān, *Mashāhīr*, 25; al-Balādhurī, *Ansāb*, I, 437; Ibn Sa'd, III/1, 152–61.

129. "'Ammār b. Yāsir," *EI*², I, 448 (H. Reckendorf); Ibn Sa'd, III/1, 176–89; Khalīfah b. Khayyāṭ, *Ta'rīkh*, 173; idem, *Ṭabaqāt*, 21, 75, 189; Ibn Ḥanbal, *Faḍā'il*, 857–61; Ibn Ḥibbān, *Mashāhīr*, 74; al-Balādhurī, *Ansāb*, I, 156–75, V, 48–52.

Saba' b. Yashjub b. Ya'rub b. Qaḥṭān. [The tribe] Banū Mālik b. Udad belong to Madhḥij.[130]

It was reported that Yāsir b. 'Āmir, the father[131] of 'Ammār b. Yāsir, and his two brothers al-Ḥārith and Mālik came from the Yemen to Mecca looking for a brother of theirs. Al-Ḥārith and Mālik returned to the Yemen, whereas Yāsir stayed in Mecca and entered into an alliance (*ḥilf*) with Abū Ḥudhayfah b. al-Mughīrah b. 'Abdallāh b. 'Umar b. Makhzūm.[132] Abū Ḥudhayfah gave a slave girl named Sumayyah bt. Khabbāṭ in marriage to Yāsir, and she bore him 'Ammār, who was freed by Abū Ḥudhayfah. Yāsir and 'Ammār stayed with Abū Ḥudhayfah until he died. Then God brought Islam [into the world], and Yāsir, Sumayyah, 'Ammār, and his brother 'Abdallāh b. Yāsir adhered to it. Yāsir [also] had a son older than 'Ammār and 'Abdallāh, Ḥurayth by name, who had been [2315]
killed in pre-Islamic times by [people of the tribe of] Banū al-Dīl.[133]

After Yāsir's death Sumayyah was given in marriage to al-Azraq, a Byzantine slave of al-Ḥārith b. Kaladah al-Thaqafī.[134] Al-Azraq was one of the Ṭā'ifī slaves who went out to the Prophet during the siege of al-Ṭā'if, and the Prophet set them free; among them was [also] Abū Bakrah.[135]

---

130. *Wa-banū mālik bn udad min madhḥij.* The text here is not accurate: the Banū Mālik b. Udad were not part of the Madhḥij but identical with it (the structure of the sentence does not allow interpretation of *min* as *mubayyinah*). Madhḥij was a toponym and also the name of a large, powerful tribal group of Yemenī origin. According to the Arab genealogists, the real name (and pedigree) of this group is Mālik b. Udad. See "Madhḥidj," *EI*², V, 953–54 (G. R. Smith [C. E. Bosworth]); Ibn Ḥazm, *Jamharat*, 397, 405. See also note 406, below.

131. The text has *rabā* instead of *abā*, obviously an error. The Cairo edition, 508, has a hypercorrection (*rabbā*, "raised"), whereas the Dār al-Fikr edition, 504, has *abā*.

132. A leader of the powerful Qurashī clan the Makhzūm, who died before Islam, so that not much is known about him. See al-Zubayrī, 300.

133. There are a few tribes by that name, all belonging to the confederation of Rabī'ah. See Ibn Ḥazm, *Jamharat*, 295, 298.

134. A member of the tribe of Thaqīf, the people of the town al-Ṭā'if. He lived in pre-Islamic times, learned the craft of medicine in Persia, and was known as the Arab doctor of his time. See Hawting, "Development."

135. A son of the aforementioned al-Ḥārith b. Kaladah by a slave girl named Sumayyah (not identical with 'Ammār's mother). He was freed by the Prophet and became a well-known Companion. His offspring attained high positions in both learning and administration. See Ibn 'Abd al-Barr, *Istī'āb*, IV, 23; see Ibn Ḥajar, *Iṣābah*, IV, 334–35, for the confusion between Sumayyah the slave girl of Abū Ḥudhayfah and mother of 'Ammār and Sumayyah the slave girl of al-Ḥārith b. Kaladah and mother of Abū Bakrah and Salamah. Contrary to our text, Salamah b. al-Azraq was not the half-brother of 'Ammār).

Sumayyah bore al-Azraq [a son], Salamah b. al-Azraq, who was 'Ammār's half-brother. Salamah's offspring later claimed that al-Azraq had been the son of 'Amr b. al-Ḥārith b. Abī Shamir from Ghassān[136] and an ally (*ḥalīf*) of the Banū Umayyah.[137] [Indeed] al-Azraq and his offspring attained a high position in Mecca. They married into the Umayyad family and had children with them.

'Ammār's *kunyah* was Abū al-Yaqẓān.

According to all the biographers I have mentioned, 'Ammār emigrated to Abyssinia in the second emigration.

According to Ibn 'Umar [al-Wāqidī]—'Abdallāh b. Ja'far: The Prophet established the bond of brotherhood (*mu'ākhāh*) between 'Ammār b. Yāsir and Ḥudhayfah b. al-Yamān. 'Abdallāh b. Ja'far said: Ḥudhayfah did not take part in the battle of Badr, yet he was an early convert.[138]

[The biographers] all agree that 'Ammār b. Yāsir participated in the battles of Badr, Uḥud, and the Ditch, and all the [other] events, on the Prophet's side.

According to Ibn 'Umar [al-Wāqidī]—'Abdallāh b. Nāfi'—his father—['Abdallāh] Ibn 'Umar, who related the following: I saw 'Ammār b. Yāsir during the battle of al-Yamāmah[139] [standing] high on a rock, shouting: "O Muslims, are you running away from
[2316] Paradise? I am 'Ammār b. Yāsir; come over to me."[140] I was look-

---

136. Ghassān was an Arab kingdom in Syria dependent on Byzantium, on the southern border of which it was situated. Arab genealogists acknowledge the Ghassān as a tribal group, while admitting that its constituents were not the descendants of one and the same eponym. See "Ghassān," *EI*², II, 1020–21 (I. Shahîd); Ibn Ḥazm, *Jamharat*, 460, 472–74.

137. The family that produced the first dynasty in Islam (41–132/661–750) and had held the leading position in Mecca before and during the Prophet's lifetime. See Hawting, *First Dynasty*; Munajjid.

138. There were two Companions by that name. The one meant here was a man of bedouin origin, of the tribe of 'Abs, whose father had come to Medina in pre-Islamic times and became an ally of the Awsī clan of Banū 'Abd al-Ashhal; see Ibn Ḥajar, *Iṣābah*, I, 317–18; p. 133, below. The brotherhood was established before the battle of Badr, so Ḥudhayfah's participation in it proves that he was an early convert.

139. In the year 13/633, against the Banū Ḥanīfah and their allies in al-Yamāmah (in the eastern part of the Arabian peninsula), led by their (false) prophet Musaylimah. This was part of the so-called apostasy wars (*riddah*), in Abū Bakr's time. See Shoufani, 83–84; Caetani, II, 723–62.

140. According to an ancient custom, a warrior cries out his own name in the course of battle, evoking his own and his ancestors' past heroic deeds, thus encour-

ing at his ear, which had been cut and was dangling, while he fought vehemently.

According to Ibn 'Umar [al-Wāqidī]—'Abdallāh b. Abī 'Ubaydah—his father—Lu'lu'ah, the client of Umm al-Ḥakam bt. 'Ammār b. Yāsir: On the day 'Ammār was killed, Hāshim b. 'Utbah was carrying the flag;[141] 'Alī's companions suffered great losses, until the time for the afternoon [prayer] came. When the sun began setting 'Ammār moved behind Hāshim, advancing past him. 'Ammār was holding [a vessel with] a mixture of milk and water and was awaiting sunset in order to break his fast. When the sun had set and he had drunk the mixture he said: "I heard the Prophet say 'Your last meal in this world will be a mixture of milk and water.' " He then went forward and fought until he was killed. He was ninety-four years old.

According to Ibn 'Umar [al-Wāqidī]—'Abdallāh b. al-Ḥārith—his father—'Umārah b. Khuzaymah b. Thābit: Khuzaymah b. Thābit [b. al-Fākih al-Anṣārī] was present at the battle of the Camel but never drew his sword. He was [also] present at the battle of Ṣiffīn, where he said: "I shall never stray from the right path, [as I will wait] until 'Ammār is killed so that I can see who kills him, for I have heard the Prophet say 'The unjust party will kill ['Ammār].' " When 'Ammār was killed Khuzaymah said "The wrong way is now clear to me." Then he went forward and fought until he was killed.

'Ammār's killer was Abū Ghādiyah of the Muzaynah tribe.[142] He stabbed him with a lance, and 'Ammār fell. ['Ammār] was fighting [seated] in a litter that day; he was killed at the age of ninety-four. When he fell [as a result of Abū Ghādiyah's blow] [2317]

aging his fellow tribesmen and intimidating the enemy. 'Ammār here encourages the people also by reminding them that death in battle will earn them paradise.

141. The reference is to the battle of Ṣiffīn, in the year 37/657, between the fourth caliph, 'Alī b. Abī Ṭālib, and his opponent Mu'āwiyah b. Abī Sufyān, who later founded the Umayyad dynasty. See Kennedy, 78–79; Wellhausen, *Arab Kingdom*, 75–112; Petersen, 186–96; Hinds, "Ṣiffīn"; Hawting, *First Dynasty*, 28; Caetani, IX, 429–541; Naṣr b. Muzāḥim; al-Ṭabarī, *Ta'rīkh* I, 3256–3349 (3317–22 on 'Ammār). Cf. Ibn al-Jawzī, *Muntaẓam*, V, 118–19.

142. There were at least two persons by the name Abū Ghādiyah. According to Ibn Ḥajar, *Iṣābah*, IV, 150–52, following many other scholars, the Abū Ghādiyah who killed 'Ammār was not the one of the Muzaynah but the one of the tribe of Juhaynah. Both are counted among the Companions. Cf. Naṣr b. Muzāḥim, 339–42.

another man bent down over him and pierced his head. The two men started quarreling, each claiming "It was I who killed him," whereupon ʿAmr b. al-ʿĀṣ said "Indeed, these two are contesting [the 'right' to enter] hell."[143] Muʿāwiyah heard this, and when the two men were gone he said to ʿAmr: "I never saw anything like what you did. These people fought with devotion for our cause, and you tell them 'You are contesting [the "right" to enter] hell?' " ʿAmr said: "By God, this is so and, by God, you do know this [too]. I wish I had died twenty years before this."

According to Ibn ʿUmar [al-Wāqidī]—ʿAbdallāh b. Jaʿfar—Ibn Abī ʿAwn: ʿAmmār was killed when he was ninety-one years old; he had been born before the Prophet. [He was killed like this]: Three men approached him, namely, ʿUqbah b. ʿĀmir al-Juhanī, ʿUmar b. al-Ḥārith al-Khawlānī, and Sharīk b. Salamah al-Murādī.[144] They drew near him together while he was saying "By God, [even] if you beat us [so hard] that you make us reach the palm trees of Hajar,[145] we know that we are in the right and you in the wrong." All [three] of them pounced on him and killed him. Some people claim that ʿUqbah b. ʿĀmir killed him, whereas others hold that it was ʿUmar b. al-Ḥārith al-Khawlānī.

Abū Jaʿfar [al-Ṭabarī] says: According to Hishām b. Muḥammad [al-Kalbī]—Abū Mikhnaf: ʿAmmār did not desist from urging on Hāshim b. ʿUtbah, who was carrying the flag, until he [announced a] charge. Then ʿAmmār got up, leading his squadron, and Dhū al-Kalāʿ rose up to him, leading his own squadron.[146] They fought

143. Or, "These two will be quarreling nowhere but in hell." ʿAmr, who supported Muʿāwiyah, implies that Muʿāwiyah acted wrongfully and was bound to go to hell together with his supporters. See also Naṣr b. Muzāḥim, 333, 341.

144. ʿUqbah b. ʿĀmir was a famous Companion credited with the transmission of many prophetic traditions, a poet who mastered the art of writing, and a Qurʾān reader who had a version of the holy book different from the canonical ʿUthmānī text (see note 94, above, but he is not recorded by Jeffery). He supported Muʿawiyah against ʿAlī and was later appointed governor of Egypt. See Ibn Ḥajar, *Iṣābah*, II, 489; al-Kindī, 35–36. The two other persons mentioned here are apparently much less well known; see Ibn Manẓūr, *Mukhtaṣar*, X, 306.

145. Oases situated in the eastern part of the Arabian peninsula, also known as al-Aḥsāʾ or Ḥasā; see "Ḥasā," *EI*², III, 237–38 (F. S. Vidal).

146. Cf. Naṣr b. Muzāḥim, 333. Dhū al-Kalāʿ, of the Yemenī people of Ḥimyar, was a powerful local king in the Yemen in pre-Islamic times. He was converted to Islam as late as the time of the second caliph, ʿUmar, and became one of the most powerful leaders of the Yemenī tribes in Syria. He supported Muʿāwiyah against

and were both killed, and both their squadrons were entirely [2318] destroyed. Ḥuwayy al-Saksakī[147] and Abū Ghādiyah al-Muzanī [were the ones who] fell on ʿAmmār and killed him. [Later] Abū Ghādiyah was asked "How did you kill him?" He said "When our squadrons moved toward each other, he called out 'Is anyone prepared to fight a duel?'[148] A man of the Sakāsik came forward, they exchanged blows with their swords, and ʿAmmār killed the Saksakī. Then he called [again], 'Is anyone prepared to fight a duel?' A man of the Ḥimyar came forward, they exchanged blows with their swords, and ʿAmmār killed the Ḥimyarī, [but] the latter had weakened him. [Then] ʿAmmār called out [again]: 'Who is prepared to fight a duel?' I came forward, and we exchanged blows. His hand had already weakened, and I stooped and dealt him another blow, whereupon he fell, and I hit him with my sword until he died. People shouted 'You have killed Abū al-Yaqẓān; may God kill you.' I said 'Go away; I do not care who you were.'[149] I swear that I did not recognize him that day." Muḥammad b. al-Muntashir said to Abū Ghādiyah "O Abū al-Ghādiyah, on the day of Judgment your adversary will be *mārandar*," meaning "bulky."[150] Abū Ghādiyah laughed.

According to Ibn ʿUmar [al-Wāqidī]—ʿAbdallāh b. Abī ʿUbaydah b. Muḥammad b. ʿAmmār—his father—Luʾluʾah, the client of Umm al-Ḥakam bt. ʿAmmār, who described ʿAmmār to them saying: He was brown-toned, tall, flabby, his eyes dark blue, his shoulders broad. He was not in the habit of dyeing his white hair.

ʿAlī and was killed in the battle of Ṣiffīn. See Hasson, *Recherches*, 167–70; Crone, *Slaves*, 95; Naṣr b. Muzāḥim, passim. On Ḥimyar, see note 405, below.

147. Ḥuwayy seems famous mainly for killing ʿAmmār (but he is not mentioned by Naṣr b. Muzāḥim or by al-Ṭabarī in the story of ʿAmmār's death); see Ibn Ḥazm, *Jamharat*, 431–32; Ibn al-Kalbī, *Nasab maʿadd*, 196. His son was one of the notables of Damascus; see Ibn Manẓūr, *Mukhtaṣar*, XIX, 203. Ḥuwayy's clan, the Sakāsik, was part of the powerful Yemenī tribe of Kindah; see "Kinda," *EI²*, V, 118–20 (A. F. L. Beeston). The Kindī branches that settled in Syria after the Muslim conquest were ardent supporters of Muʿāwiyah; see Hasson, *Recherches*, 112–15.

148. See note 104, above.

149. Apparently Abū Ghādiyah is addressing ʿAmmār, who is already dead.

150. Vocalized *māzundar* in Ibn Saʿd, III/1, 187; see also al-Balādhurī, *Ansāb*, I, 173. Although glossed by Arabic *ḍakhm*, "big, bulky," the meaning of this Persian word is by no means clear. De Goeje suggests "terrible, grave"; *Glossarium*, s.v. *mārandar*.

According to Ibn ʿUmar [al-Wāqidī], it was unanimously agreed [among the scholars] that ʿAmmār was killed [while fighting on
[2319] the side of] ʿAlī b. Abī Ṭālib at Ṣiffīn, in Ṣafar, 37/July 657. He was ninety-three years old and was buried at Ṣiffīn.

ʿAbdallāh b. Budayl b. Warqāʾ b. ʿAbd al-ʿUzzā b. Rabīʿah b. Jurayy b. ʿĀmir b. Māzin b. ʿAdiyy b. ʿAmr b. Rabīʿah.[151]

ʿAbdallāh participated in the conquest of Mecca, the battle of Ḥunayn, and the expedition to Tabūk on the Prophet's side. He was killed in the battle of Ṣiffīn, [fighting] on the side of ʿAlī, the Commander of the Faithful.[152]

Khuzaymah b. Thābit b. al-Fākih b. Thaʿlabah b. Sāʿidah b. ʿĀmir b. Ghayyān b. ʿĀmir b. Khaṭmah b. Jusham b. Mālik b. al-Aws.[153]

[He was] the man of the two testimonies.[154]

Khuzaymah's *kunyah* was Abū ʿUmārah. He had two brothers, Waḥwaḥ and ʿAbdallāh.

Khuzaymah carried the banner of [his clan, the] Khaṭmah, on the day of the conquest of Mecca. He participated in the battle of Ṣiffīn on ʿAlī's side and was killed there, in the year 37.

Saʿd b. al-Ḥārith b. al-Ṣimmah b. ʿAmr b. ʿAtīk b. ʿAmr b. Mabdhūl—[whose real name was] ʿĀmir—b. Mālik b. al-Najjār.[155]

Saʿd was a Companion of the Prophet. He participated in [the

---

151. Ibn Ḥibbān, *Mashāhīr*, 135; Khalīfah b. Khayyāṭ, *Taʾrīkh*, 177; al-Ṭabarī, *Taʾrīkh*, I, 3289, 3297, 3299; Ibn Ḥajar, *Iṣābah*, I, 141. The clan's name is Banū ʿAdī b. ʿAmr, of the Muḍar; see Ibn Ḥazm, *Jamharat*, 239.

152. ʿAbdallāh was commander of the infantry; see Naṣr b. Muzāḥim, 102, 111, 205, and passim.

153. Khalīfah b. Khayyāṭ, *Ṭabaqāt*, 83; Ibn Ḥibbān, *Mashāhīr*, 77; al-Balādhurī, *Ansāb*, I, 170; Ibn Saʿd, IV/2, 90–92, IV, 33; Naṣr b. Muzāḥim, 363. Khuzaymah's clan was the Banū Khaṭmah, a part of the Aws (one of two tribes making up the Anṣār).

154. *Dhū al-shahādatayn*, so called because the Prophet highly estimated him and considered his testimony equal to that of two men; see Ibn Ḥajar, *Iṣābah*, I, 425–26.

155. The Banū al-Najjār was an important clan of the Khazraj (the other of the two tribes making up the Anṣār).

battle of] Ṣiffīn on the side of ʿAlī b. Abī Ṭālib and was killed there. He was the brother of Abū Juhaym b. al-Ḥārith b. al-Ṣimmah.[156]

Abū ʿAmrah, that is, Bashīr b. ʿAmr b. Miḥṣan b. ʿAmr b. ʿAtīk b. ʿAmr b. Mabdhūl.[157]

Abū ʿAmrah was the father of ʿAbd al-Raḥmān b. Abī ʿAmrah, who transmitted [traditions] from ʿUthmān b. ʿAffān.

Abū ʿAmrah was killed in [the battle of] Ṣiffīn [while fighting] on ʿAlī's side.

Hāshim b. ʿUtbah b. Abī Waqqāṣ b. Uhayb b. ʿAbd Manāf b. Zuhrah.[158] [2320]

Hāshim embraced Islam on the day of the conquest of Mecca. He is [the one known as] al-Mirqāl (the swift runner). He was one-eyed, as he had lost an eye at the battle of Yarmūk.[159]

Hāshim was a nephew of Saʿd b. Abī Waqqāṣ.

He fought on ʿAlī's side at Ṣiffīn, where he was in charge of the infantry. He is the one who said:

A one-eyed man [I am], who seeks a place for his kin,[160]
Who experienced life till he was wearied.
His enemies he must beat or else himself be beaten.

He was killed at Ṣiffīn.

Abū Faḍālah al-Anṣārī.[161]

---

156. A minor Companion, who was credited with the transmission of certain important traditions; see Ibn Ḥajar, *Iṣābah*, IV, 36.

157. Al-Balādhurī, *Ansāb*, III (Dūrī), 294; Khalīfah b. Khayyāṭ, *Ṭabaqāt*, 105; Naṣr b. Muzāḥim, 187, 357–59; al-Ṭabarī, *Taʾrīkh*, I, 3270–71, 3290. He was of the Banū al-Najjār, of the Khazraj (Anṣār).

158. Ibn Ḥibbān, *Mashāhīr*, 34; Khalīfah b. Khayyāṭ, *Taʾrīkh*, 176–77; Ibn Qudāmah, 389–91; Naṣr b. Muzāḥim, passim; al-Qummī, III, 156–57; al-Ṭabarī, *Taʾrīkh*, I, 3322–24. He belonged to the Qurashī clan the Banū Zuhrah and was known as a brave warrior.

159. One of the major battles of the Muslim conquest of Syria; see Donner, *Early Islamic Conquests*, 133–36, 142; al-Ṭabarī, *Taʾrīkh*, I, 2090–2121.

160. See al-Ṭabarī, *Taʾrīkh*, I, 2324; Naṣr b. Muzāḥim, 327, 355; Ibn al-Athīr, *Kāmil*, III, 314.

161. Although said to have participated in the battle of Badr, he appears to be a rather obscure Companion; see Ibn Ḥajar, *Iṣābah*, IV, 155 (full name not mentioned).

He was one of the participants in [the battle of] Badr. He was killed at Ṣiffīn, [fighting] on 'Alī's side.

Sahl b. Ḥunayf b. Wāhib b. al-'Ukaym b. Tha'labah b. 'Amr b. al-Ḥārith b. Majda'ah b. 'Amr b. Ḥanash b. 'Awf b. 'Amr b. 'Awf.[162]

His *kunyah* was Abū Sa'd or, according to another version, Abū 'Abdallāh.

Sahl's ancestor was 'Amr b. al-Ḥārith, the one called Baḥzaj (calf of a wild cow).[163]

Sahl participated in [the battles of] Badr and Uḥud. At Uḥud he stood firmly by the Prophet while others retreated from him, and he pledged himself before the Prophet to fight to the death. That
[2321] day he shot arrows defending the Prophet, whereupon the latter said "Give arrows to Sahl, for he is easy [in spending them]."[164]

Sahl also participated in the [event of the] Ditch and all the [other] battles on the Prophet's side. He fought at Ṣiffīn on the side of 'Alī b. Abī Ṭālib.

According to Ibn 'Umar [al-Wāqidī]—'Abd al-Raḥmān b. 'Abd al-'Azīz—Muḥammad b. Abī Umāmah b. Sahl—his father: Sahl b. Ḥunayf died in al-Kūfah in the year 38 (June 9, 658–May 28, 659); 'Alī b. Abī Ṭālib said the ritual prayer over his bier.

Those Who Died or Were Killed in the Year 40 (May 17, 660–May 6, 661)

Among those who were killed that year was the Commander of the Faithful 'Alī b. Abī Ṭālib—the latter's name was 'Abd Manāf—b. 'Abd al-Muṭṭalib b. Hāshim b. 'Abd Manāf b. Quṣayy.[165]

'Alī's *kunyah* was Abū al-Ḥasan.

---

162. Ibn Ḥibbān, *Mashāhīr*, 80; Khalīfah b. Khayyāṭ, *Ta'rīkh*, 181; idem, *Ṭabaqāt*, 85; Ibn Sa'd, III/2, 39–41. The clan, 'Awf b. 'Amr, belonged to the Aws (Anṣār); see Ibn Ḥazm, *Jamharat*, 336.

163. There is some confusion in the genealogy of Sahl. See Ibn al-Kalbī, *Nasab ma'add*, 372; idem, *Jamharat*, 630; Ibn Ḥazm, *Jamharat*, 336.

164. Ibn Sa'd, III/2, 40. There is a play on words here, as *sahl* means "easy." See also Ibn 'Abd al-Barr, *Istī'āb*, II, 92; al-Mizzī, *Tahdhīb*, XII, 185.

165. The Prophet's paternal cousin and son-in-law and the fourth caliph (35–40/656–661. See "'Alī b. Abī Ṭālib," *EI²*, I, 381–86; al-Amīn, III/1–3; Ibn Sa'd, III/1, 11–27; Khalīfah b. Khayyāṭ, *Ta'rīkh*, 182–83; idem, *Ṭabaqāt*, 4–5; Ibn Ḥibbān, *Mashāhīr*, 24; Ibn Ḥanbal, *Faḍā'il*, 528–728.

It was reported that 'Alī was struck on Thursday, 17th Ramaḍān/January 24, 661, and died on Saturday, the 19th of that month/January 26, 661.[166] The information about him is already recorded in our book *al-Mudhayyal.*

Isḥāq b. 'Abdallāh b. Abī Farwah asked Abū Ja'far Muḥammad [al-Bāqir] b. 'Alī "What did 'Alī look like?" He said "A man of dark-brown complexion and heavy eyes,[167] bald, big-bellied, and rather short."

Those Who Died in the Year 50 (January 29, 670–January 17, 671)

Among them was Sa'īd b. Zayd b. 'Amr b. Nufayl b. 'Abd al-'Uzzā b. Riyāḥ b. 'Abdallāh b. Qurṭ b. Razāḥ b. 'Adī b. Ka'b b. Lu'ayy.[168]

His *kunyah* was Abū al-A'war.

Sa'īd's father, Zayd b. 'Amr b. Nufayl, had abandoned the religion of his people, the Quraysh.[169] He died while the Quraysh were building the Ka'bah, five years before the Prophet was [first] inspired,[170] and it is related that the Prophet said "He will be resurrected as a community unto himself."[171]

---

166. The dates do not correspond to the weekdays mentioned here. According to Cattenoz' tables, the 17th of Ramaḍān was a Sunday and the 19th a Tuesday. *Laylat al-jum'ah* and *laylat al-aḥad* are rendered as Thursday and Saturday because the Arabs count the days by the nights that precede them.

167. *Thaqīl al-'aynayn*, perhaps bulging eyes or drooping eyelids.

168. One of the earliest converts and a close Companion of the Prophet. See "Sa'īd b. Zaid," *EI*[1], VII, 66–67 (A. J. Wensinck); Ibn Ḥibbān, *Mashāhīr*, 26; Khalīfah b. Khayyāṭ, *Ta'rīkh*, 205; idem, *Ṭabaqāt*, 22; Ibn Qudāmah, 424–26. According to 'Abd al-Malik Ibn Ḥabīb, *Ta'rīkh*, 122, he died in the year 46/666–67. The clan's name is Banū 'Adī, of the Quraysh.

169. Much has been written about the pre-Islamic Arab monotheists, the *ḥanīfs*; the most recent study is Rubin's "*Ḥanīfiyya.*"

170. The precise date of this event is not known but is usually placed in about A.D. 610. See Conrad, "Abraha," especially 233–35; on the construction history of the Ka'bah, see Rubin, "Ka'ba."

171. Ibn Sa'd, III/1, 277. Cf. al-Ṭabarī, *Jāmi'*, II, 8–10: As the role of Muḥammad's community on Judgment Day is to testify that God's messengers indeed conveyed the messages, the argument here may be that Zayd's testimony will be equivalent to that of the whole community. It is usually the archmonotheist, the patriarch Abraham, who is referred to as *ummah*, interpreted as "leader" or "teacher of what is good"; see Qur'ān 16:120; al-Ṭabarī, *Jāmi'*, XIV, 191–92.

[2322] Sa'īd b. Zayd had been converted to Islam before the Prophet entered the house of al-Arqam to preach from there.[172] He participated with the Prophet in [the battle of] Uḥud, the Ditch, and all the [other] events except [the battle of] Badr.

According to Ibn 'Umar [al-Wāqidī]—'Abd al-Malik b. Zayd, a descendant of Sa'īd b. Zayd—his father: Sa'īd b. Zayd died in al-'Aqīq,[173] and people carried him on their shoulders to Medina, where he was buried. Sa'd [b. Abī Waqqāṣ?][174] and ['Abdallāh] Ibn 'Umar descended into his grave.[175] He was seventy-odd years old when he died in the year 50 or 51/670–71 or 671–72. He had been exceptionally tall, of brown complexion, and hairy.

Al-Mughīrah b. Shu'bah b. Abī 'Āmir b. Mas'ūd b. Mu'attib b. Mālik b. Ka'b b. 'Amr b. Sa'd b. 'Awf b. Thaqīf—whose [real] name was Qasiyy—b. Munabbih b. Bakr b. Hawāzin b. 'Ikrimah b. Khaṣafah b. Qays b. 'Aylān b. Muḍar b. Nizār.[176]

Al-Mughīrah's *kunyah* was Abū 'Abdallāh, and he was called Mughīrah al-Ra'y (Mughīrah of the sound opinion), for he was very shrewd.

Al-Mughīrah went to the Prophet, embraced Islam, and stayed with him; thus al-Mughīrah took part in the minor pilgrimage (*'umrah*) of al-Ḥudaybiyyah in Dhū al-Qa'dah of the year 6/April 628.

According to Ibn 'Umar [al-Wāqidī]—'Abdallāh b. Muḥammad b. 'Umar b. 'Alī—his father—'Alī [b. Abī Ṭālib]: When al-Mughīrah b. Shu'bah threw his signet ring into the Prophet's grave I said "Let it not be said by people that you descended into the Prophet's grave, and don't you [go around] telling people that your

---

172. See p. 47, below.

173. The valley west of Medina; several eminent Qurashīs built castles there. See "'Akīk," *EI*², I, 336–37 (G. Rentz); 'Umar b. Shabbah, I, 146–52, 165–67; al-Samhūdī, III, 1039–71.

174. Note that a similar account ("died in al-'Aqīq and was carried to Medina") is given about Sa'd b. Abī Waqqāṣ; see Ibn Ḥibbān, *Mashāhīr*, 26.

175. See note 43, above.

176. First governor of al-Kūfah for Mu'āwiyah. See "al-Mughīra b. Shu'ba," *EI*², VII, 347 (H. Lammens); Hawting, *First Dynasty*, 40; Khalīfah b. Khayyāṭ, *Ṭabaqāt*, 53, 131, 183; Ibn Ḥibbān, *Mashāhīr*, 75; al-A'ẓamī, *Kuttāb*, 107–8. His tribe, the Thaqīf of the town al-Ṭā'if, played a leading role in the early Muslim state; see Donner, *Early Islamic Conquests*, 78 and passim.

signet ring is in his grave."[177] So 'Alī went down, for he had seen where the ring had fallen, picked it up, and gave it to al-Mughīrah.

According to Ibn 'Umar [al-Wāqidī]—Muḥammad b. Abī Mūsā al-Thaqafī—his father: Al-Mughīrah died in al-Kūfah in Sha'bān, 50/September 670, during the caliphate of Mu'āwiyah, at the age of seventy. He had been an extremely tall man and one-eyed; it was [also] said that he had woolly, curled, chestnut-colored hair, in which he used to make four partings. He had a big head, contracting lips, broken front teeth, thick arms, and broad shoulders. [2323]

Al-Ḥasan b. 'Alī b. Abī Ṭālib.[178]

According to Ibn 'Umar [al-Wāqidī]—'Abdallāh b. Ja'far [b. 'Abd al-Raḥmān b. al-Miswar]—Umm Bakr bt. al-Miswar [b. Makhramah]: Al-Ḥasan b. 'Alī was poisoned a few times [but] always escaped death until the last poisoning, of which he died because his liver had been destroyed [by it]. When he died the women of the Banū Hāshim wailed a [whole] month for him.[179]

According to Ibn 'Umar [al-Wāqidī]—Ḥafṣ b. 'Umar—Abū Ja'far [Muḥammad al-Bāqir?]: The people mourned seven days for al-Ḥasan, suspending [trade in] the markets.

According to Ibn 'Umar [al-Wāqidī]—'Ubaydah bt. Nābil—'Ā'ishah bt. Sa'd: The women of the Banū Hāshim put on mourning garments for a [whole] year, [lamenting] al-Ḥasan.

According to [al-Wāqidī]—Dā'ūd b. Sinān—Tha'labah b. Abī Mālik: We were in attendance of Ḥasan b. 'Alī on the day he died, and we buried him in al-Baqī'. I saw al-Baqī' [so crowded with people that], if I had thrown a needle there, it would inevitably [2324] have fallen on someone's head.

According to 'Alī b. Muḥammad [al-Madā'inī]—Maslamah b.

---

177. Ibn Sa'd, II/2, 77–78. Such sayings would have earned al-Mughīrah prestige. As he was a controversial figure, the point of the story is that such prestige was denied him.

178. 'Alī's eldest son, the second imām of the Shī'ah. See "al-Ḥasan b. 'Alī", *EI*[2], III, 240–43 (L. Veccia Vaglieri); al-Amīn, IV, 3–109; Khalīfah b. Khayyāṭ, *Ta'rīkh*, 194; idem, *Ṭabaqāt*, 5; Ibn Ḥanbal, *Faḍā'il*, 766–89; Ibn Ḥibbān, *Mashāhīr*, 24–25; al-Balādhurī, *Ansāb*, III (Maḥmūdī), 5–74; 'Abd al-Malik Ibn Ḥabīb, 119–20.

179. Cf. Abū al-Layth al-Samarqandī, fol. 72a–b. Lamenting the dead (*nawḥ, niyāḥah*) was a pre-Islamic practice, banned in many sayings attributed to the Prophet. Shedding tears for them (*bukā'*) was, however, permitted; see "Niyāḥa," *EI*[2], VIII, 64–65 (T. Fahd); Juynboll, *Muslim Tradition*, 96–108.

Muḥārib: Al-Ḥasan b. 'Alī died on the 5th of Rabī' I 50/April 2, 670. 'Alī b. Muḥammad says that, according to another version, he died in the year 51 (January 18, 671–January 7, 672) at the age of forty-six.

Those Who Died or Were Killed in the Year 52 (January 8, 672–December 26, 672)

Among them was Abū Ayyūb.[180]

His name was Khālid b. Zayd b. Kulayb b. Tha'labah b. 'Abd b. 'Awf b. Ghanm b. Mālik b. al-Najjār.[181]

All [the biographers] are unanimous that he was one of the seventy Anṣār who swore allegiance to the Prophet on the night of the 'Aqabah meeting.

The Prophet established the bond of brotherhood (*mu'ākhāh*) between Abū Ayyub and Muṣ'ab b. 'Umayr.[182]

Abū Ayyūb participated in [the battles of] Badr, Uḥud, and the Ditch and all the [other] events on the Prophet's side.

Abū Ayyūb died when Yazīd b. Mu'āwiyah raided Constantinople during the caliphate of his father, Mu'āwiyah.[183] His grave is at the foot of the fortress in Constantinople, in the Byzantine territory. It was reported that the Greeks frequent his grave, renovate it, and pray there for rain in times of drought.[184]

Those Who Died or Were Killed in the Year 54 (December 16, 673–December 5, 674)

Among them was Ḥakīm b. Ḥizām b. Khuwaylid b. Asad b. 'Abd al-'Uzzā b. Quṣayy.[185]

---

180. "Abū Ayyūb," *EI*², I, 108–9; Khalīfah b. Khayyāṭ *Ta'rīkh*, 197; idem, *Ṭabaqāt*, 89; Ibn Ḥibbān, *Mashāhīr*, 49; al-Balādhurī, *Ansāb*, I, 242, III (Dūrī), 53; al-A'ẓamī, *Kuttāb*, 33–34.

181. The clan's name is Banū al-Najjār, of the Khazraj (Anṣār).

182. An early convert, of the Qurashī clan the Banū 'Abd al-Dār, who was the Prophet's deputy in Medina before the Emigration; see Ibn Ḥajar, *Iṣābah*, III, 421–22.

183. In the year 49/669–70. See al-Ṭabarī, *Ta'rīkh*, II, 86; al-Manbijī, 69 and n. 6. On Yazīd, who reigned after his father Mu'āwiyah, see Hawting, *First Dynasty*, 40–44 and passim; "Yazīd," *EI*¹, VIII, 1162–63 (H. Lammens).

184. Ibn Sa'd, III/2, 50.

185. A nephew of Khadījah, the Prophet's wife, of the Qurashī clan the Banū

According to Ibn ʿUmar [al-Wāqidī]—al-Mundhir b. ʿAbdallāh—Mūsā b. ʿUqbah—Abū Ḥabībah, the client of al-Zubayr [b. al-ʿAwwām]—Ḥakīm b. Ḥizām: I was born thirteen years before the People of the Elephant came [to raid Mecca]; I was [already] a mature man[186] when ʿAbd al-Muṭṭalib intended to sacrifice his son ʿAbdallāh, as his vow was due to be fulfilled;[187] this was five years before the Prophet was born.[188]

Ḥakīm b. Ḥizām participated in [the war] of the Fijār together with his father, Ḥizām b. Khuwaylid, who was killed in the sec- [2325] ond Fijār war.[189]

Ḥakīm's *kunyah* was Abū Khālid. He had [four] sons: ʿAbdallāh, Khālid, Yaḥyā, and Hishām; their mother was Zaynab bt. al-ʿAwwām b. Khuwaylid b. Asad b. ʿAbd al-ʿUzzā b. Quṣayy.[190] According to another version, the mother of Hishām b. Ḥakīm was Mulaykah bt. Mālik b. Saʿd, of the Banū al-Ḥārith b. Fihr.[191] All of Ḥakīm's sons joined the Prophet on the day of the conquest [of Mecca] and were counted among his Companions.

It was reported that Ḥakīm b. Ḥizām reached the age of 120. When Muʿāwiyah made the Pilgrimage [to Mecca] he passed by him. Afterward Muʿāwiyah sent Ḥakīm a pregnant she-camel so that he might drink her milk. That was after Muʿāwiyah had asked him what food he ate, whereupon Ḥakīm replied "As for chewing, there is none of that for me," so Muʿāwiyah sent him that pregnant she-camel. He also sent him a gift, which, however, Ḥakīm refused to accept, saying "After the Prophet died I took nothing

---

Asad. See Ibn Ḥibbān, *Mashāhīr*, 31; Khalīfah b. Khayyāṭ, *Taʾrīkh*, 211; idem, *Ṭabaqāt*, 13–14; Ibn Qudāmah, 270–72.

186. Literally, "I had brains"; see also note 108, above, on the Year of the Elephant.

187. ʿAbd al-Muṭṭalib, grandfather of the Prophet, vowed that if he had ten grown-up sons he would sacrifice one of them to God. The lot fell to ʿAbdallāh, father of the Prophet, who was then ransomed with a hundred camels. See Ibn Hishām, I, 160–64; Guillaume, 66–68; al-Ṭabarī, *Taʾrīkh*, I, 1073–78.

188. See p. 24, above.

189. A series of pre-Islamic battles between the Quraysh with their allies and several other tribal groups, see E. Landau-Tasseron, "Sinful Wars."

190. That is, they were nephews of the famous Companion al-Zubayr b. al-ʿAwwām.

191. A Qurashī clan. Fihr is in fact considered as the real eponym of the tribe, Quraysh being a byname. See Caskel, II, 4; al-Zubayrī, 443–46; Ibn Ḥazm, *Jamharat*, 12, 176–78.

[from the government]. Abū Bakr and 'Umar invited me to take my lawful share, but I refused to do so."[192]

According to Ibn 'Umar [al-Wāqidī]—Ibn Abī al-Zinād—his father: Ḥakīm b. Ḥizām was asked "What does wealth consist of, O Abū Khālid?" He replied "Having few dependents."

According to Ibn 'Umar [al-Wāqidī]: Ḥakīm b. Ḥizām came to Medina, where he settled and built a house (*dār*).[193] He died in Medina in the year 54, during the caliphate of Mu'āwiyah, at the age of 120.

Makhramah b. Nawfal b. Uhayb b. 'Abd Manāf b. Zuhrah b. Kilāb.[194]

His mother was Ruqayqah bt. Abī Ṣayfiyy b. Hāshim b. 'Abd Manāf.

Makhramah had [eight] sons: the eldest, Ṣafwān, after whom he was called [Abū Ṣafwān]; al-Miswar; al-Ṣalt al-Akbar, (the mother of Ṣafwān and the other two was 'Ātikah bt. 'Awf b. 'Abd 'Awf b. 'Abd b. al-Ḥārith b. Zuhrah, the sister of 'Abd al-Raḥmān b. 'Awf. She was an Emigrant, and her mother was al-Shifā' bt. 'Awf b. 'Abd
[2326] b. al-Ḥārith b. Zuhrah, who was also an Emigrant); al-Ṣalt al-Aṣghar; Ṣafwān al-Aṣghar; al-'Aṭṭāf al-Akbar; al-'Aṭṭāf al-Aṣghar; and Muḥammad.

Makhramah b. Nawfal embraced Islam on the conquest of Mecca. He was an expert on the genealogy and traditions of the Quraysh and had knowledge about the stones utilized as demarcations of the sanctuary [in Mecca] (*anṣāb al-ḥaram*). 'Umar [b. al-Khaṭṭāb] used to send him, together with Sa'īd b. Yarbū' Abū Hūd, Ḥuwayṭib b. 'Abd al-'Uzzā, and Azhar b. 'Abd 'Awf, to renew these demarcations of the sanctuary, because these [people] had knowledge of them.[195]

---

192. Ḥakīm is referring to the pension awarded the Muslim veterans among others. On the system of the pensions instituted by 'Umar (*dīwān*), see Puin; "'Aṭā'," *EI*², I, 729–30 (Cl. Cahen); "Dīwān," ibid. II, 323–24 (A. A. Dūrī).

193. *Dār* may refer to a plot containing a courtyard and one or more buildings.

194. Of the Qurashī clan the Banū Zuhrah. See Ibn Ḥibbān, *Mashāhīr*, 58; Khalīfah b. Khayyāṭ, *Ta'rīkh*, 211; idem, *Ṭabaqāt*, 15; Ibn Qudāmah, 291–92.

195. See Ibn Ḥajar, *Iṣābah*, I, 29–30 (the biography of the Qurashī Companion Azhar b. 'Abd 'Awf), II, 51–52 (the biography of the Qurashī Companion Sa'īd b. Yarbū'). The sacred territory in Mecca was demarcated with the help of stones,

Makhramah b. Nawfal lost his eyesight [some time] during the caliphate of 'Uthmān.

Makhramah b. Nawfal participated in the battle of Ḥunayn with the Prophet, who gave him fifty camels from the spoils. However, according to Ibn 'Umar [al-Wāqidī], 'Abdallāh b. Ja'far denied that Makhramah was given any of that [booty] and said that he never heard any of his family mention this.[196]

Makhramah died in Medina in the year 54/673–74, during the caliphate of Mu'āwiyah; he was 115 years old when he died.

Ḥuwayṭib b. 'Abd al-'Uzzā b. Abī Qays b. 'Abd Wadd b. Naṣr b. Mālik b. Ḥisl b. 'Āmir b. Lu'ayy.[197]

According to Ibn 'Umar [al-Wāqidī]—Ibrāhīm b. Ja'far b. Maḥmūd b. Muḥammad b. Maslamah al-Ashhalī—his father: Ḥuwayṭib b. 'Abd al-'Uzzā al-'Āmirī lived 120 years, sixty of them in the Jāhiliyyah and sixty in Islam.[198] When Marwān b. al-Ḥakam became governor of Medina for the first time Ḥuwayṭib came to see him, together with other senior leading [members of [2327]
the community], that is, Ḥakīm b. Ḥizām and Makhramah b. Nawfal. They all had a talk; then [the people] went home. After that Ḥuwayṭib came to see Marwān one day and talked with him. Marwān asked "How old are you?" Ḥuwayṭib told him, whereupon Marwān said "O old man, you were a late convert to Islam; even youngsters preceded you."[199] Ḥuwayṭib said: "God is the One whose help is sought. I had intended to be converted more than once, [and] every time your father forbade me and hindered me from doing so, saying: 'Will you debase your honor and leave

---

believed to have been first put there by Abraham under the guidance of the angel Jibrīl; see al-Azraqī, I, 358–60.

196. The informant 'Abdallāh b. Ja'far was a descendant of Makhramah; see al-Wāqidī, I, and index.

197. Ibn Sa'd, V, 335–36; Khalīfah b. Khayyāṭ, *Ta'rīkh*, 211; idem, *Ṭabaqāt*, 27; Ibn Ḥibbān, *Mashāhīr*, 60; al-Balādhurī, *Ansāb*, I, 362; al-Mizzī, *Tahdhīb*, VII, 468–69; Ibn al-Jawzī, *Muntaẓam*, V, 273–75. The 'Āmir b. Lu'ayy are a Qurashī clan. See Caskel, II, 3–4; al-Zubayrī, 412; Ibn Ḥazm, *Jamharat*, 12, 166–68.

198. Jāhiliyyah is the name given in the Muslim tradition to the pre-Islamic period. The name signifies both "ignorance" (of God) and "the state of being unbridled or unrestrained." See Goldziher, *Muslim Studies*, I, 201–8. It can usually be translated simply as "pre-Islamic times," unless the text seems to make a point of the contradistinction Jāhiliyyah vs. Islam.

199. On the importance of precedence (*sābiqah*) see note 60, above.

the religion of your forefathers for a newly created religion, becoming a follower [of someone else]?'" Marwān, by God, held his tongue and regretted what he had said to him. Then Ḥuwayṭib said "Did not 'Uthmān [b. 'Affān] inform you of what he had endured from your father upon his conversion?" Marwān became [even] more upset, and Ḥuwayṭib said:

> Among the leading members of the Quraysh who remained faithful to the tribe's religion until the conquest of Mecca, no one was more averse than I to what he adhered to; but destiny [compelled me]. I participated in the battle of Badr on the side of the idolators, and I saw wonders;[200] I saw angels kill and take prisoners between heaven and earth, and I said [to myself] "This is a [divinely] protected man." I did not mention what I saw [to anyone]. Then we all retreated to Mecca; we stayed there, and the people of the Quraysh embraced Islam one after the other. When the event of al-Ḥudaybiyyah occurred I was there, and I witnessed the peace treaty; [moreover], I acted as a go-between until it was achieved. All this [time] I wanted to be converted to Islam, but God refused [to let anything happen] except what He willed. When we wrote the peace treaty of al-Ḥudaybiyyah I was one of the witnesses, and I said [to myself]: "The Quraysh will only be vexed by Muḥammad. I am pleased to have pushed him [away from Mecca] with the palms of my hands." When the Prophet came to Mecca for the minor pilgrimage of the consummation[201] I and Suhayl b. 'Amr[202] were among those who stayed in Mecca, in order to oust the Prophet in due time, that is, [after] three [days]. When the three [days] had elapsed I came with Suhayl b. 'Amr, and we said "Your stipu-
> [2328] lated time has elapsed, so get out of our territory." The

200. Literally, "examples" [from which a lesson should be learned], or "warnings."

201. *'Umrat al-qaḍiyyah*; in the treaty of al-Ḥudaybiyyah the Quraysh agreed that the Prophet should enter Mecca for three days during the following year (i.e., 7/ May 11, 628–April 30, 629), in order to perform a minor pilgrimage. See Ibn Hishām, IV, 12–14; Guillaume, 530–31; Lings, 280–85.

202. An eminent Qurashī leader of the 'Āmir b. Lu'ayy clan, a late convert but a faithful Muslim. See al-Zubayrī, 417–19; Ibn Ḥajar, *Iṣābah*, II, 93–94.

> Prophet called out "O Bilāl, let no Muslim of those who had come with us remain in Mecca after the sun has set."[203]

According to Ibn 'Umar [al-Wāqidī]—Ibrāhīm b. Ja'far b. Maḥmūd—his father, and Abū Bakr b. 'Abdallāh b. Abī Sabrah—Mūsā b. 'Uqbah—al-Mundhir b. Jahm—Ḥuwayṭib b. 'Abd al-'Uzzā: When the Prophet entered Mecca in the year of the conquest (*fatḥ*) I was seized by a great fear. I left my house and scattered my children to safe places; then I reached the garden of 'Awf and stayed there. Suddenly I saw Abū Dharr al-Ghifārī; he was a friend of mine, and friendship is always helpful. When I saw him I ran away, [but] he called "Abū Muḥammad!" I said "At your service." He asked "What is the matter with you?" I said "Fear." He said "You do not have to fear; [I grant] you protection in the name of God."[204] I walked back to him and greeted him, and he said "Go home." I said: "Is there a way home for me? By God, I do not think that I shall reach it alive before I am found and killed, or else my house will be broken into and I will be killed there. Besides, my children are [scattered] in various places." Abū Dharr said "Assemble your children in one place, and I shall bring you home." He brought me [home], then started calling at my door "Ḥuwayṭib has been granted protection, so he is not to be harassed." Abū Dharr then went to the Prophet and told him [all about it], whereupon the Prophet said "Didn't we grant everyone protection except those whom I ordered killed?" Then I was calmed, and I brought back my children. Abū Dharr came back to me and said: "O Abū Muḥammad, how much longer? Until when? [Others] preceded you to all the battlefields, and you missed a lot of advantages, [yet] there is still much good [to be had];[205] go to the Prophet and embrace Islam so that you will be safe.[206] [Know that] the Prophet

---

203. The point of the story seems to be that the Prophet is a man who keeps his word. First, he complies with the demand to leave the town. Second, only those Muslims who had come with him for the *'umrah* are to leave. This is in agreement with the Ḥudaybiyyah treaty that forbade new Meccan converts to emigrate to Medina, except by permission of their patrons.

204. Literally, "you are protected by God's protection." See note 56, above.

205. See note 60, above.

206. *Aslim taslam.* In this particular context safety is not relevant because Ḥuwayṭib has already been granted protection. This, however, was a slogan often

is the most kind, forbearing, and generous of all people. His honor
[2329] is your honor, and his power is your power." I said "I shall go with you to him." So I went with him to the Prophet in al-Baṭḥā'.[207] Abū Bakr and 'Umar were with him. I stood near him and asked Abū Dharr "What does one say to him by way of greeting?" He answered: ["One says]: 'Peace be with you, O Messenger of God, and God's mercy.'"[208] This I said, whereupon he replied "And peace be with you, O Ḥuwayṭib." I said "I testify that there is no god but Allāh and that you are God's messenger." The Prophet said "Praise be to God, Who led you to the right path." The Prophet was glad about my conversion. He asked for a loan from me, and I lent him 40,000 dirhams. Then I participated in [the battle of] Ḥunayn and [the siege of] al-Ṭā'if with him, and he gave me 100 camels from the spoils of Ḥunayn.

According to Abū Ja'far [al-Ṭabarī]: Ḥuwayṭib later went to Medina and settled there. He had a house at al-Balāṭ, by the Qur'ān copyists' [quarter].[209]

According to Ibn 'Umar [al-Wāqidī]—'Abd al-Raḥmān b. Abī al-Zinād—his father: Ḥuwayṭib sold his house in Mecca to Mu'āwiyah for 40,000 dinars. [People] said to him "O Abū Muḥammad, 40,000 dinars?!" He said "What are 40,000 dinars to a man who has five children?"[210] 'Abd al-Raḥmān b. Abī al-Zinād said "By God, at that time he was among the recipients of the monthly [rations] of food."[211]

Ḥuwayṭib b. 'Abd al-'Uzzā died in Medina in the year 54/673–74, during the caliphate of Mu'āwiyah, at the age of 120.

---

used by the Prophet when inviting tribal or foreign leaders to join Islam. See, e.g., Ḥamīdullāh, *Majmū'at al-wathā'iq*, 32, 35, 77, 81.

207. That is, Mecca; see Yāqūt, *Mu'jam al-buldān*, I, 662.

208. The pre-Islamic formal greetings were deliberately changed in Islam; see, e.g., al-Wāqidī, 964.

209. *'Inda aṣḥāb al-maṣāḥif*. Al-Sam'ānī, V, 308–9, equates the appellation Maṣāḥifī with *kāna yaktub al-maṣāḥif* ("he was a Qur'ān copyist") and with *ṣāḥib al-maṣāḥif*. I thank Dr. Estelle Whelan for this reference. Al-Balāṭ was the area around the Prophet's mosque in Medina, so called because it was paved with stones. See 'Umar b. Shabbah, I, 16–17 (al-Balāṭ), 252–53 (Ḥuwayṭib's house); al-Samhūdī, II, 734–47 (Ḥuwayṭib's house in 743–44, 746).

210. Al-Zubayrī, 426.

211. *Qūt*. See Ibn al-Farrā', 239; Abū 'Ubayd, 107.

Al-Arqam b. Abī al-Arqam b. Asad b. ʿAbdallāh b. ʿUmar b. Makhzūm.[212]

Abū al-Arqam's name was ʿAbd Manāf, and al-Arqam's *kunyah* was Abū ʿAbdallāh.

According to Ibn ʿUmar [al-Wāqidī]—Muḥammad b. ʿImrān b. Hind b. ʿAbdallāh b. ʿUthmān b. al-Arqam b. Abī al-Arqam al-Makhzūmī—his father—Yaḥyā b. ʿImrān b. ʿUthmān b. al-Arqam: [2330]
My grandfather ʿUthmān b. al-Arqam used to say "I am the son of the seventh [member] of the Muslim community, for my father was the seventh [person] to embrace Islam."

Al-Arqam's house was on the Ṣafā;[213] this was the house where the Prophet stayed in the beginning of Islam, calling upon the people to [believe in] Islam, and many people were converted to Islam there.[214]

Al-Arqam b. Abī al-Arqam participated in [the battles of] Badr, Uḥud, and the Ditch and all [the other] events on the Prophet's side.

According to Ibn ʿUmar [al-Wāqidī]—Muḥammad b. ʿImrān b. Hind—his father: [When] al-Arqam b. Abī al-Arqam was dying he willed it that Saʿd [b. Abī Waqqāṣ] say the ritual prayer over his bier. Marwān b. al-Ḥakam was [then] the governor of Medina for Muʿāwiyah, whereas Saʿd was staying at his castle in al-ʿAqīq. Al-Arqam died, and Saʿd demanded that [the funeral] be suspended [until his arrival]. Marwān said "Should [the burial] of a Companion of the Prophet be suspended on account of someone's absence?" Marwān thus wanted to say the ritual prayer, but ʿUbaydallāh b. al-Arqam, backed by the Banū Makhzūm, refused Marwān this, and a quarrel broke out between them.[215] Then Saʿd

---

212. An early convert of the Qurashī clan Makhzūm, whose leaders opposed the Prophet. See Ibn Ḥibbān, *Mashāhīr*, 57; Ibn Saʿd, III/1, 172–74; Ibn Qudāmah, 388–89; al-Aʿẓamī, *Kuttāb*, 44–45.

213. A hill in Mecca, opposite the Kaʿbah, see Yāqūt, *Muʿjam al-buldān*, III, 397. Certain rituals are performed between this hill and the Marwah during the pilgrimage.

214. Ibn Saʿd, III/1, 173. Our text, as well as Cairo, 519, and Dār al-Fikr, 515, have *wa-fī*, "in," instead of *wa-hiya al-dār*, "this was the house," evidently an error.

215. Performing the burial ritual was in fact the governor's task, as was the conducting of the Friday prayer. Political opposition was expressed by refusal to join the prayer under the governor's leadership, and perhaps the present incident had a similar political significance.

arrived and said the prayer over al-Arqam's bier. This was in Medina in the year 55 (December 6, 674–November 24, 675).

Al-Arqam died at the age of eighty-odd years.

Abū Maḥdhūrah.[216]

His name was Aws b. Mi'yar b. Lawdhān b. Rabī'ah b. 'Uwayj b. Sa'd b. Jumaḥ.

Abū Maḥdhūrah had a full brother by the name of Unays, who was killed as an infidel at Badr.

According to Ibn Sa'd[217]—someone who traced the pedigree of
[2331] Abū Maḥdhūrah: His name was Samurah b. 'Umayr b. Lawdhān b. Wahb b. Sa'd b. Jumaḥ, and he had a full brother by the name of Aws.

Abū Mahdḥūrah fathered 'Abd al-Malik and Ḥudayr.

He died in Mecca in the year 59 (October 23, 678–October 12, 679). He never emigrated but remained living in Mecca until his death.

Al-Ḥusayn b. 'Alī b. Abī Ṭālib.[218]

Al-Ḥusayn was born at the beginning of Sha'bān, 4/January 626; his *kunyah* was Abū 'Abdallāh.

Al-Ḥusayn fathered [several children].

(1) 'Alī al-Akbar, who was killed with his father at al-Ṭaff.[219] His mother was Āminah bt. Abī Murrah b. 'Urwah b. Mas'ūd b. Mu'attib of the Thaqīf, and her mother was the daughter of Abū

---

216. A member of the Qurashī clan the Banū Jumaḥ; see Ibn Ḥazm, *Jamharat*, 159–63. Genealogists tend to confuse him with his brother. See Ibn Ḥajar, *Iṣābah*, IV, 176; Ibn Ḥibbān, *Mashāhīr*, 56–57; Khalīfah b. Khayyāṭ, *Ṭabaqāt*, 24; Ibn Ḥanbal, *Faḍā'il*, 977; al-Balādhurī, *Ansāb*, I, 527, IVa, 183; Ibn Qudāmah, 461.

217. Ibn Sa'd, V, 332–33.

218. 'Alī's second son and the third imām of the Shī'ah. See "Ḥusayn b. 'Alī," *EI*², III, 607–15 (L. Veccia Vaglieri); al-Amīn, IV, 110–404; al-Balādhurī, *Ansāb*, III (Maḥmūdī), 142–210 and passim; Khalīfah b. Khayyāṭ, *Ta'rīkh*, 221, 224, 226; idem, *Ṭabaqāt*, 5, 230; Ibn Ḥibbān, *Mashāhīr*, 25; Ibn Ḥanbal, *Faḍā'il*, 766–88; al-Ṭabarī, *Ta'rīkh*, II, 227–390.

219. The reference is to the massacre at Karbalā' near al-Kūfah, al-Ṭaff being the designation of the district; see Yāqūt, *Mu'jam al-buldān*, III, 539. This is where al-Ḥusayn and many members of his family were killed by the Umayyad governor while trying to reach their supporters in al-Kūfah. See "Karbalā'," *EI*², IV, 637–39 (E. Honigmann); Kennedy, 89–90; see also the references in the preceding note and below.

Sufyān b. Ḥarb.[220] According to Muḥammad b. 'Umar [al-Wāqidī], Ḥassān b. Thābit[221] composed [the following verses] about Āminah:

Around us the sun of daytime does wander.
    Who has ever seen a sun wandering in the evening?
Among the Quraysh the best protector[222] is her mother's father.
    And her uncles, they are the Thaqīf, if you inquire.

According to Abū Ja'far [al-Ṭabarī], these verses are attributed to 'Umar b. Abī Rabī'ah[223] and belong to his poetry. He recites the following:

Around us an evening sun does wander.
    Who has ever seen a sun wandering in the evening?
Among the Quraysh the best protector is her mother's father,
    and, if you trace her pedigree, her uncles are the Thaqīf.

(2) 'Alī al-Aṣghar, to whom are traced all of al-Ḥusayn's descendants, whereas 'Alī al-Akbar had no progeny. The mother of 'Alī al-Aṣghar was a concubine. According to 'Alī b. Muḥammad [al-Madā'inī], her name was Sulāfah, [but] Abū Ja'far [al-Ṭabarī] says that, according to others, her name was Jaydā.

['Alī al-Aṣghar] was a virtuous man and a leader.

(3) Ja'far, who had no progeny. [2332]

(4) Fāṭimah, whose mother was Umm Isḥāq bt. Ṭalḥah b. 'Ubaydallāh.

[Umm Isḥāq] had been married to al-Ḥasan b. 'Alī. When he was about to die he enjoined [his brother] al-Ḥusayn to marry her, which he did, and she bore him Fāṭimah.

(5) 'Abdallāh, who was killed together with his father.

---

220. Abū Sufyān was one of the most important leaders of the Quraysh at the time of the Prophet and the father of Mu'āwiyah, founder of the Umayyad dynasty; see "Abū Sufyān," *EI*², I, 151 (W. M. Watt).

221. A Medinan pre-Islamic poet who embraced Islam and became the poet of the Prophet, serving the Islamic cause with his verses, see p. 72, below.

222. *Awfā qurayshin bi-dhimmatin*, i.e., among the Quraysh he is the most loyal where the granting of protection is concerned. Such a praise indicates not only his personal character but his high social status as well because effective protection could be granted only by influential people.

223. A famous love poet of the Umayyad period. See "Omar b. Abī Rabī'a," *EI*¹, III, 979 (I. Kratschkowsky); al-Ṣafadī, XXII, 492–501; Jabbūr.

(6) Sukaynah, whose mother was al-Rabāb bt. Imri' al-Qays b. 'Adī b. Aws b. Jābir b. Ka'b b. 'Ulaym b. Hubal b. Kinānah b. Bakr b. 'Awf b. 'Udhrah b. Zaydallāt b. Rufaydah b. Thawr b. Kalb. Al-Ḥusayn b. 'Alī composed [the following verses] about al-Rabāb and Sukaynah:

I swear that I love the house
where Sukaynah and al-Rabāb abide.
I love them both and shall my money spend.
My admonisher will have no words to chide.
Even if scolded I shall not comply,
never in my life, until in the earth I lie.

According to 'Alī b. Muḥammad [al-Madā'inī]—Ḥammād b. Salamah—Abū al-Muhazzam: We were at a funeral, and Abū Hurayrah was with us. When we returned al-Ḥusayn found difficulty in ascending the road. Abū Hurayrah started to shake the dust off al-Ḥusayn's feet with his garment. Al-Ḥusayn said "You, Abū Hurayrah, do that!" Abū Hurayrah replied "Let me be, for if people had known what I know about you they would have carried you on their shoulders."

According to Abū Ja'far [al-Ṭabarī]—anonymous—Khālid b. Khidāsh: When the people of Fakhkh[224] were killed Ḥammad [b. Salamah] would not participate in teaching sessions[225] for about a month, and I saw that he was sad. Later he resumed teaching, [but
[2333] he was] in a poor state and for two or three months often shed tears; I heard him say "We love the descendants of 'Alī as much as we love Islam."[226]

According to Muḥammad b. 'Umar [al-Wāqidī]—Abū Ma'shar [Najīḥ b. 'Abd al-Raḥmān]: Al-Ḥusayn was killed on the 10th of Muḥarram, [61/October 10, 680]. Al-Wāqidī says that this is the correct [version].

---

224. That is, the Shī'ī rebels led by al-Ḥusayn b. 'Alī b. al-Ḥasan b. al-Ḥasan b. al-Ḥasan b. 'Alī b. Abī Ṭālib, in the year 169/785–86. See "Fakhkh," *EI*², II, 744–45 (L. Veccia Vaglieri); van Arendonck, 62–65; al-Ṭabarī, *Ta'rīkh*, III, 551–68. An edition of *Akhbār fakhkh* by the fourth-century author Aḥmad b. Sahl al-Rāzī is currently in preparation by Māhir Jarrār.

225. *Labitha . . . lā yajlis*, literally, "would not sit," apparently in an assembly; see "Madjlis," *EI*², V, 1031–33 (ed.). Because Ḥammād was a traditionist, it is logical that the reference here is to his teaching sessions.

226. Love of the 'Alid family is a major precept of the Shī'ī creed.

According to Muḥammad b. 'Umar [al-Wāqidī]—'Aṭā' b. Muslim—'Āṣim b. Abī al-Najūd—Zirr b. Ḥubaysh: The first head ever to have been put up on a spar was that of al-Ḥusayn.

According to 'Alī b. Muḥammad [al-Madā'inī]—'Alī b. Mujāhid—Ḥanash b. al-Ḥārith—an old man from [the tribe of] al-Nakha': Al-Ḥajjāj [b. Yūsuf][227] said: "Let those who did heroic deeds stand up." Some people stood up and told [their stories]. Then Sinān b. Anas got up and said: "I am the one who killed al-Ḥusayn."[228] Al-Ḥajjāj said "A brave act [it was indeed]!" Sinān then returned to his home and lost his speech and his mind. He used to eat and excrete on the spot.

[Those Who Died in the Year 64] *(August 30, 683–August 17, 684)*

Among those who died in the year 64 was al-Miswar b. Makhramah b. Nawfal b. Uhayb b. 'Abd Manāf b. Zuhrah b. Kilāb.[229]

His *kunyah* was Abū 'Abd al-Raḥmān, and his mother was 'Ātikah bt. 'Awf b. 'Abd 'Awf b. 'Abd b. al-Ḥārith b. Zuhrah b. Kilāb, sister of 'Abd al-Raḥmān b. 'Awf. She was counted among the Emigrants who gave the oath of allegiance to the Prophet.

Al-Miswar b. Makhramah was eight years old when the Prophet died.

According to Ibn 'Umar [al-Wāqidī]—'Abdallāh b. Ja'far [b. 'Abd al-Raḥmān b. al-Miswar b. Makhramah]—Umm Bakr, daughter of al-Miswar b. Makhramah, and Abū 'Awn: Al-Miswar was hit by a ballista stone that was fired at the Ka'bah. [The stone] broke up,

---

227. The powerful governor of al-Kūfah, nominated by 'Abd al-Malik (reigned 65–86/685–705). See Hawting, *First Dynasty*, 58–71; "al-Ḥadjdjādj," *EI²*, III, 39–43 (A. Dietrich).

228. Sinān b. Anas was a member of the Nakha' tribe. For his role at Karbalā', see al-Ṭabarī, *Ta'rīkh*, II, 362, 366–67; al-Balādhurī, *Ansāb*, III (Maḥmūdī), 202–5. It is noteworthy that the most fervent supporter of al-Ḥusayn's father, 'Alī b. Abī Ṭālib, was Mālik al-Ashtar, of the same tribe of southern origin (Nakha') but a different clan. See Ibn Ḥazm, *Jamharat*, 415; Naṣr b. Muzāḥim, index s.v. Mālik b. al-Ḥārith al-Ashtar; Ibn al-Kalbī, *Nasab ma'add*, 291–92, 294. For the role of al-Nakha' in Kūfan politics, see Djaït, "Yamanites," 159–61, 166.

229. A member of the Qurashī clan the Banū Zuhrah. See Ibn Ḥibbān, *Mashāhīr*, 43; Khalīfah b. Khayyāṭ, *Ṭabaqāt*, 15; al-Zubayrī 264; 'Abd al-Malik Ibn Ḥabīb, 125; Ibn Qudāmah, 292–93. See also his father's biography, p. 42, above.

and a chip hit al-Miswar's cheek while he was standing praying. This made him ill for a few days; then he died. [His death occurred] on the day when the news of Yazīd's death was announced in Mecca.[230] Ibn al-Zubayr had not [yet] declared himself caliph at that time [but demanded] that the ruler be elected by a council (*shūrā*).[231]

According to Muḥammad [Ibn 'Umar al-Wāqidī]—'Abdallāh b.
[2334] Ja'far—Abū 'Awn and Umm Bakr, daughter of al-Miswar: Al-Miswar died on the day Yazīd b. Mu'āwiyah's death was announced [in Mecca], on the 1st of Rabī' II, [64/November 27, 683]. He was then sixty-two years old.

Abū Ja'far [al-Ṭabarī] says: Al-Miswar was born two years after the Emigration and died on the 1st of Rabī' II, 64/November 27, 683. I was informed that Yaḥyā b. Ma'īn held that al-Miswar b. Makhramah died in the year 73 (May 23, 692–May 12, 693), but this view is mistaken.[232]

Those Who Died in the Year 65 (August 18, 684–August 7, 685)

Among them was Sulaymān b. Ṣurad b. al-Jawn b. Abī al-Jawn—whose name was 'Abd al-'Uzzā—b. Munqidh b. Rabī'ah b. Aṣram b. Ḍabīs b. Ḥarām b. Ḥubshiyyah b. Ka'b b. 'Amr b. Rabī'ah b. Ḥārithah b. 'Amr Muzayqiyā b. 'Āmir Mā' al-Samā' b. Ḥārithah al-Ghiṭrīf b. Imri' al-Qays b. Tha'labah b. Māzin b. al-Azd.[233]

Sulaymān's *kunyah* was Abū Muṭarrif.

---

230. Cf. al-Ṭabarī, *Ta'rīkh*, II, 426: here al-Miswar dies fighting. The occasion is the second *fitnah* ("civil war"), which lasted from 61–73/680–92. The events described here took place in the year 64/683. See Rotter; and also the biography of 'Abdallāh b. al-Zubayr below.

231. The call for the appointment of caliphs by a council (rather than by inheritance or force) was often voiced in early Islam by those opposing the government, see Crone, "Meaning of the 'Abbāsid Call."

232. The mistake arises from the confusion between the two sieges on Mecca, in 64/683 and 73/692, see Ibn Ḥajar, *Iṣābah*, III, 420 (s.v. Miswar b. Makhramah). On Yaḥyā b. Ma'īn, a traditionist and biographer (d. 233/847), see F. Sezgin, I, 106–7; Sayf.

233. Ibn Ḥibbān, *Mashāhīr*, 81; Khalīfah b. Khayyāṭ, *Ta'rīkh*, 258; idem, *Ṭabaqāt*, 107, 137. The clan's name is Ḥarām b. Ḥubshiyyah of the Khuzā'ah confederation, traced here to the southern tribe Azd and elsewhere (e.g., Ibn Ḥazm, *Jamharat* 237–38; see also Ibn al-Kalbī, *Nasab ma'add*, 439, 456–60) to the northern confederation of Muḍar. See "Khuzā'a," *EI*[2], V, 76–80 (M. J. Kister).

Sulaymān was converted and became a Companion of the Prophet. His name had been Yasār, but the Prophet named him Sulaymān upon his conversion.[234]

[Sulaymān b. Ṣurad was a man of] noble demeanor and respected among his people. He was among the Muslims who settled in al-Kūfah.[235] He participated in [the battle of] Ṣiffīn on ʿAlī's side and was [later] one of those who wrote to al-Ḥusayn b. ʿAlī, asking him to come to al-Kūfah. When al-Ḥusayn did come, [however], Sulaymān failed to fight on his side.[236]

After al-Ḥusayn was killed regret came over Sulaymān, al-Musayyab b. Najabah al-Fazārī, and all those who had deserted al-Ḥusayn and failed to fight on his side. They said "There is no atonement for what we did unless we sacrifice ourselves while seeking to avenge al-Ḥusayn's blood." They [therefore] encamped at al-Nukhaylah[237] on the 1st of Rabīʿ II, 65/November 15, 684; appointed Sulaymān b. Ṣurad their leader; and set out for Syria [2335] seeking to avenge the blood of al-Ḥusayn. They numbered 4,000 men[238] and were called "the Repenters" (*al-tawwābūn*); we have already recorded their story in our book entitled *al-Mudhayyal.*[239]

Sulaymān b. Ṣurad was killed in this episode by Yazīd b. al-Ḥuṣayn b. Numayr,[240] who shot an arrow at him and killed him; his head was carried off to [the caliph], Marwān b. al-Ḥakam, by Adham b. Muḥriz al-Bāhilī,[241] together with the head of al-Musayyab b. Najabah.

Sulaymān was ninety-three years old when he died.

---

234. The Prophet often changed people's names if they contained references to an idol or were otherwise not pleasing. Yasār was a common name of slaves. See Kister, "Call Yourselves."

235. On the foundation of al-Kūfah during the period of the conquests, the most recent work is Djaït, *Al-Kūfa.*

236. That is, at Karbalāʾ. See al-Balādhurī, *Ansāb*, III (Maḥmūdī), 149–53 (on the role of Sulaymān).

237. A place near al-Kūfah, where ʿAlī was encamped before setting out for the battle of Ṣiffīn. See al-Ṭabarī, *Taʾrīkh*, I, 3256, 3259; Yāqūt, *Muʿjam al-buldān*, IV, 771.

238. A formulaic number; see Conrad, "Abraha."

239. See Hawting, *First Dynasty*, 51; idem, "The *Tawwābūn*"; al-Balādhurī, *Ansāb*, V, 204–13; al-Ṭabarī, *Taʾrīkh*, II, 497–513, 538–76.

240. Son of the Umayyad general al-Ḥuṣayn b. Numayr. See Hawting, *First Dynasty*, 48–49; al-Balādhurī, *Ansāb*, V, 210; Naṣr b. Muzāḥim, 128.

241. The first Muslim to be born in Ḥimṣ; he was a commander in the Umayyad army. See al-Ṭabarī, *Taʾrīkh*, I, 3305, II, 559, 564, 568; Naṣr b. Muzāḥim, 267–68; Ibn Manẓūr, *Mukhtaṣar* IV, 230–32; al-Suyūṭī, *Wasāʾil*, 100; al-Ṣafadī, VIII, 330.

Those Who Died or Were Killed in the Year 68 (July 18, 687–July 5, 688)

Among them was 'Abdallāh b. al-'Abbās b. 'Abd al-Muṭṭalib b. Hāshim b. 'Abd Manāf b. Quṣayy.[242]

His mother was Umm al-Faḍl Lubābah al-Kubrah bt. al-Ḥārith b. Ḥazn, of the Banū Hilāl b. 'Āmir.[243]

According to 'Alī b. Muḥammad [al-Madā'inī]: 'Abdallāh b. al-'Abbās fathered [several children].

(1) 'Alī, the leader among ['Abdallāh's] offspring. He was born in the year 40/660–61 or, according to another version, in the year of [the battle of] the Camel, that is, 36/656–57. He was the handsomest and comeliest of the Quraysh on earth and the most [devoted to] prayer among them, so that he was named al-Sajjād (the one who prostrates himself habitually).[244] The caliphate was in the hands of his descendants.

(2) Al-'Abbās, 'Abdallāh's eldest, after whom he was called [Abū al-'Abbās], (3) Muḥammad, (4) 'Ubaydallāh, (5) al-Faḍl, (6) Lubābah.

Their mother was Zar'ah bt. Mishraḥ b. Ma'dī-Karib b. Walī'ah; Mishraḥ was one of the four kings.[245]

Al-'Abbās, 'Ubaydallāh, al-Faḍl, and Muḥammad, sons of 'Abdallāh b. al-'Abbās, had no offspring. As for Lubābah bt. 'Abdallāh, she was married to 'Alī b. 'Abdallāh b. Ja'far b. Abī Ṭālib[246] and bore him [children], who [in their turn] had offspring.

---

242. Cousin and Companion of the Prophet, considered as the greatest authority on Qur'ān interpretation. He was the ancestor of the 'Abbāsid dynasty. See "'Abd Allāh b. 'Abbās," *EI²*, I, 40–41 (L. Veccia Vaglieri); Jeffery, 193–94; Sharon, *Black Banners*, 82–84; Ibn Ḥibbān, *Mashāhīr*, 28; Ibn Ḥanbal, *Faḍā'il*, 844–47; al-Balādhurī, *Ansāb*, III (Dūrī), 27–55; *Akhbār al-dawlah*, passim; Abū al-Naṣr.

243. That is, 'Āmir b. Ṣa'ṣa'ah, an important tribal confederation of northern origin. Some of its branches were closely related to the Quraysh in pre-Islamic times. See "'Āmir b. Ṣa'ṣa'a," *EI²*, I, 441–42 (W. Caskel); Kister, "Mecca and Tamim," 132–34, 136–39, 157; Ibn Ḥazm, *Jamharat*, 272–92.

244. The Shī'ah reserve this honorary epithet for the fourth imām, 'Alī Zayn al-'Ābidīn, see al-Amīn, V, 409.

245. Traditions mention four kings of the tribe of Kindah who came to the Prophet and embraced Islam but apostatized after his death and were killed. See Ibn Ḥazm, *Jamharat*, 428; al-Kalā'ī, 229; al-Ḥillī, 78–79; al-Ṭabarī, *Ta'rīkh*, I, 2004; Lecker, "Kinda."

246. An eminent member of the Ṭālibī family and the ancestor of the further progeny of that family. See Ibn Ḥazm, *Jamharat*, 68; Ibn Qudāmah, 118; al-Zubayrī, 82.

(7) Asmā' bt. 'Abdallāh. She was married to 'Abdallāh b. 'Ubaydallāh b. al-'Abbās, to whom she bore Ḥasan and Ḥusayn;[247] [2336] her mother was a concubine.

According to Ibn 'Umar [al-Wāqidī]: The scholars in our midst agree that Ibn 'Abbās was born shortly before the Banū Hāshim came out of the ravine where they had been besieged.[248] This was three years before the Emigration. Ibn 'Abbās was thirteen years old when the Prophet died. This is proved by what he says in a tradition transmitted by Mālik [b. Anas]—[Ibn Shihāb] al-Zuhrī—'Ubaydallāh b. 'Abdallāh [b. al-'Abbās]—'Abdallāh b. 'Abbās: I was riding a donkey during the Farewell Pilgrimage together with al-Faḍl, and I passed by the Prophet while he was praying. I was already nearing puberty at that time.

According to Dā'ūd b. 'Amr al-Ḍabbī—['Abd al-Raḥmān b. 'Abdallāh] Ibn Abī al-Zinād—his father and 'Abdallāh b. al-Faḍl b. 'Ayyāsh b. Abī Rabī'ah b. al-Ḥārith—the reliable source—Ḥassān b. Thābit: We, that is, the Anṣār, demanded [something] from 'Umar [b. al-Khaṭṭāb] or 'Uthmān [b. 'Affān]—Ibn Abī al-Zinād has doubts [about who it was]—so we brought along 'Abdallāh b. 'Abbās together with several of the Prophet's Companions. Ibn 'Abbās spoke, and they spoke, and they mentioned the Anṣār and their merits (*manāqib*), but the ruler excused himself [and refused the request];[249] it was a major request we made. [The ruler] went on addressing them until they stood up and condoned [his position], except Ibn 'Abbās, who said "Nay, by God, the Anṣār cannot be forsaken [after] the help and shelter they gave [to the Prophet]." He mentioned their excellence and said "Here is the poet of the Prophet, who defended him [with his poetry]." 'Abdallāh did not cease from addressing [the ruler] with impressive speech, refuting

---

247. *Akhbār al-dawlah*, 118. I could find hardly any detail on this 'Abdallāh, except that he transmitted traditions. See Ibn Ḥajar, *Tahdhīb*, V, 267; Ibn Qudāmah, 161; al-Zubayrī, 29.

248. As part of their struggle against the Prophet, the Quraysh are said to have proclaimed a boycott of the Prophet's relatives, i.e., the clans of the Banū Hāshim and the Banū al-Muṭṭalib. See Ibn Hishām, I, 375–80, II, 14–21; Guillaume, 159–61, 172–75.

249. The enumeration of the merits (*manāqib*) of a group or an individual was a common practice among the Muslims, inherited from pre-Islamic times; see Goldziher *Muslim Studies*, I, 45–46. There was emphasis on the merits of the Anṣār in particular, precisely because in practice they were gradually deprived of political power; see Hasson, "Contribution."

all his arguments, until he had no alternative but to comply with our demand. So we departed, our demand carried out with the help of ['Abdallāh's] words. I then passed by the mosque, by the people who had been together with [Ibn 'Abbās] but had not achieved what he had; I said so that they would hear "Indeed, he was the most worthy of you to achieve this." They said "No doubt." I said, referring to 'Abdallāh "By God, this is the vestige of prophethood and the legacy of Aḥmad,[250] and he was the most worthy of it
[2337] among you."[251] And I said, referring to 'Abdallāh:[252]

When he speaks he leaves no words for others;
his are not disjointed but carefully chosen words.
Adequate he is, fulfilling the hearts' desires,
leaving the guileful speechless, both in earnest and in jest.
The highest [merit] you attained easily;
the highest peak you gained, being neither base nor lowly.

According to Khālid b. al-Qāsim al-Bayāḍī—Shu'bah, [the client of Ibn 'Abbās]—Ibn 'Abbās: I was born three years before the Emigration, while we were in the ravine [boycotted], and I was thirteen years old when the Prophet died.

Ibn 'Abbās died in the year 68 at the age of seventy-one.

According to Ibn 'Umar [al-Wāqidī]—Muḥammad b. 'Uqbah and Muḥammad b. Rifā'ah b. Tha'labah b. Abī Mālik—Sh'ubah, the client of Ibn 'Abbās: 'Abdallāh b. 'Abbās died in al-Ṭā'if in the year 68 at the age of seventy-two.

According to Ibn 'Umar [al-Wāqidī]—Isḥāq b. Yaḥyā—Abū Salamah al-Ḥaḍramī: I saw the grave of Ibn 'Abbās, and [Muḥammad] Ibn al-Ḥanafiyyah was tending it;[253] he ordered that the top of the grave be made flat.[254]

According to 'Alī b. Muḥammad [al-Madā'inī]—Ḥafṣ b. Maymūn [b. Mihrān]—his father: 'Abdallāh b. 'Abbās died in al-Ṭā'if.

---

250. That is, the Prophet, see Qur'ān, 61:6.
251. The story alludes to the 'Abbasids' right to the caliphate.
252. Ḥassān b. Thābit, I, 331–32.
253. See note 113, above.
254. On the interdiction to elevate graves and to build over them, see Ibn Qayyim al-Jawziyyah, I, 146. A construction was, however, built over Ibn 'Abbās' grave at a much later date; see al-'Ujaymī, 66–67.

A white bird came and entered the bier.[255] When he was laid in the grave we heard a voice reciting "O confident soul, go back to your Lord pleased and pleasing."[256]

According to anonymous source(s)—'Alī b. Muḥammad [al-Madā'inī]: 'Abdallāh b. 'Abbās died at the age of seventy-four. [2338]

Those Who Died or Were Killed in the Year 74 (May 13, 693–May 1, 694)

Among them was Abū Sa'īd al-Khudrī.[257]

His name was Sa'd b. Mālik b. Sinān b. Tha'labah b. 'Ubayd b. al-Abjar—whose name was Khudrah—b. 'Awf b. al-Ḥārith b. al-Khazraj.[258]

Some [scholars] claim that Khudrah was the mother of al-Abjar.

Qatādah b. al-Nu'mān al-Ẓafarī of the People of Badr[259] was Abū Sa'īd's half-brother by his mother.

According to Ibn 'Umar [al-Wāqidī]—al-Ḍaḥḥāk b. 'Uthmān—Muḥammad b. Yaḥyā b. Ḥabbān—Ibn Muḥayrīz [al-Jumaḥī] and Abū Ṣirmah—Abū Sa'īd al-Khudrī: I joined the Prophet on the raid of Banū al-Muṣṭaliq. According to Ibn 'Umar: He was then fifteen years old. He also participated in the [siege of the] Ditch and the events (*mashāhid*) that occurred afterward.

According to Ibn 'Umar [al-Wāqidī]—Sa'īd b. Abī Zayd—Rubayḥ b. 'Abd al-Raḥmān b. Abī Sa'īd—his father—Abū Sa'īd: I was presented before the Prophet on the day of the battle of Uḥud; I was thirteen years old. My father took me by the hand and said "O Messenger of God, he is large-boned, even if short." The Prophet examined me closely from head to foot and said "Send him back"; so he sent him back.[260]

---

255. The text has *bayna al-na'sh wa-al-sarīr*, both words signifying "bier." Cf. in al-'Ujaymī, 65 (where the bird enters inside the shrouds); Ibn al-Jawzī, *Muntaẓam*, VI, 75; al-Dhahabī, *Siyar*, III, 358; al-Ṣafadī, XVII, 234.

256. Qur'ān, 89:27.

257. An eminent Anṣārī. See Ibn Ḥibbān, *Mashāhīr*, 30; Khalīfah b. Khayyāṭ, *Ta'rīkh*, 268; idem, *Ṭabaqāt*, 96.

258. The clan's name is Banū Khudrah, of the Khazraj (Anṣār); see Ibn Ḥazm, *Jamharat*, 472.

259. That is, those who had participated in the battle of Badr. See note 60, above.

260. The account revolves around a point of law, i.e., the age of legal majority in Islam. See "Bāligh," *EI*², I, 993 (ed.); Conrad, "Abraha," n. 94.

According to Ibn ʿUmar [al-Wāqidī]—ʿAbd al-ʿAzīz b. ʿUqbah—Iyās b. Salamah b. al-Akwaʿ: Abū Saʿīd al-Khudrī died in the year 74.

Those Who Died in the Year 78 (March 30, 697–March 19, 698)

[2339] Among them was Jābir b. ʿAbdallāh b. ʿAmr b. Ḥarām b. Thaʿlabah b. Ḥarām b. Kaʿb b. Ghanm b. Kaʿb b. Salimah b. Saʿd b. ʿAlī b. Asad b. Sāridah b. Tazīd b. Jusham b. al-Khazraj.[261]

His *kunyah* was Abū ʿAbdallāh.

[Jābir] was present at [the meeting in] al-ʿAqabah among the seventy Anṣār who gave the Prophet the oath of allegiance there. He was one of the youngest among them. [Later] he wanted to take part in the battle of Badr, but his father ordered him to stay behind to keep watch on his sisters, who numbered nine. His father also left him behind when he went out for [the battle of] Uḥud. [Jābir] participated in the subsequent events.

According to Ibn ʿUmar [al-Wāqidī]—Ibrāhīm b. Jaʿfar—his father: I asked Jābir b. ʿAbdallāh how many raids the Prophet had launched, and he said: "The Prophet had personally launched twenty-seven raids, and I participated in sixteen of them with him. I could not go with a raid until my father was killed at Uḥud, [because] he always left me behind to keep watch on my sisters, who numbered nine. The first raid in which I took part at [the Prophet's] side was Ḥamrāʾ al-Asad,[262] [then the rest] to the last of his raids."

According to Muḥammad b. ʿUmar [al-Wāqidī]—Khārijah b. al-Ḥārith: Jābir b. ʿAbdallāh died in the year 78 at the age of ninety-four after having lost his sight. I saw a striped cloth on his bier.

---

261. Al-Balādhurī, *Ansāb*, I, 248; Khalīfah b. Khayyāṭ, *Taʾrīkh*, 261; idem, *Ṭabaqāt*, 102; Ibn Ḥibbān, *Mashāhīr*, 30. The name of Jābir's clan is Banū Salimah of the Khazraj (Anṣār); see Ibn Ḥazm, *Jamharat*, 358.

262. On the day after the defeat at Uḥud, in Shawwāl 3/625. See al-Wāqidī, 334–40; Wellhausen, *Muḥammad*, 149–51. Cf. Ibn Hishām, III, 108, 110–11; Guillaume, 390–91.

Abān b. 'Uthmān,[263] who was the governor of Medina, said the ritual prayer over his bier.

Those Who Died or Were Killed in the Year 80 (March 9, 699–February 25, 700)

Among them was 'Abdallāh b. Ja'far b. Abī Ṭālib b. 'Abd al-Muṭṭalib.[264]

His *kunyah* was Abū Ja'far, and his mother was Asmā' bt. 'Umays.

According to Ibn 'Umar [al-Wāqidī]: 'Abdallāh b. Ja'far died in Medina in the Year of the Juḥāf (sweeping), that is, the torrent that occurred in the interior of Mecca and swept away pilgrims and camels together with their loads.[265] Abān b. 'Uthmān, who ruled as governor of Medina on behalf of 'Abd al-Malik b. Marwān, said the ritual prayer over his bier. He was ninety years old when he died.

According to 'Alī b. Muḥammad [al-Madā'inī]: 'Abdallāh b. [2340] Ja'far died in the year 84 (January 24, 703–January 13, 704) or 85 (January 14, 704–January 1, 705).[266]

'Amr b. Ḥurayth b. 'Amr b. 'Uthmān b. 'Abdallāh b. 'Amr b. Makhzūm.[267]

His *kunyah* was Abū Sa'īd.

---

263. Son of the third caliph 'Uthmān b. 'Affān, of the Umayyad family. He served as governor of Medina for 'Abd al-Malik (65–86/685–705) but was dismissed after seven years. He is considered an important authority on prophetic tradition and the Prophet's campaigns. See "Abān b. 'Uthmān," *EI*², I, 2–3 (K. V. Zetterstéen); Duri, *Rise of Historical Writing*, 24–25.

264. Of the Prophet's clan, Hāshim; see the genealogical table. See also "'Abdallāh b. Ja'far," *EI*², I, 44 (K. V. Zetterstéen); Ibn Ḥibbān, *Mashāhīr*, 27; Khalīfah b. Khayyāṭ, *Ta'rīkh*, 279; Ibn Qudāmah, 116–18. See his father's biography, pp. 4–5, above.

265. Al-Ṭabarī, *Ta'rīkh*, II, 1040.

266. The text is garbled here (*sanat arba' aw khams wa-thamānīn sanah*). Cf. Ibn Ḥajar, *Iṣābah*, II, 289. Note that from this point onward no chronological order is maintained in the *Dhayl.*

267. Of the Qurashī clan Banū Makhzūm. See Ibn Ḥibbān, *Mashāhīr*, 79; Khalīfah b. Khayyāt, *Ta'rīkh*, 276; idem, *Ṭabaqāt*, 20; Ibn Qudāmah, 388. On his political role in Umayyad times, see also al-Balādhurī, *Ansāb*, IVa, 213–15, 221–22, V, 351–52.

'Amr was twelve years old when the Prophet died. According to Abū Nu'aym al-Faḍl b. Dukayn, 'Amr b. Ḥurayth died in al-Kūfah in the year 85/704, during the caliphate of 'Abd al-Malik b. Marwān.

'Aqīl b. Abī Ṭālib b. 'Abd al-Muṭṭalib b. Hāshim.[268]
He was one of those who were taken prisoner in the battle of Badr, and, as he had no money, al-'Abbās b. 'Abd al-Muṭṭalib ransomed him.

According to Ibn Sa'd[269]—'Alī b. 'Īsā al-Nawfalī—his father—his paternal uncle Isḥāq b. 'Abdallāh—'Abdallāh b. al-Ḥārith: Al-'Abbās ransomed himself and his nephew 'Aqīl for eighty ounces of gold or, according to another version, for a thousand dinars.

According to Ibn Sa'd[270]—'Alī b. 'Īsā—Abān b. 'Uthmān—Mu'āwiyah b. 'Ammār al-Duhnī—Abū 'Abdallāh Ja'far [al-Ṣādiq] b. Muḥammad: On the day of [the battle of] Badr the Prophet said "Go and have a look who of my family, the Banū Hāshim, is here."[271] 'Alī b. Abī Ṭālib went and saw al-'Abbās [b. 'Abd al-Muṭṭalib], Nawfal [b. al-Ḥārith b. 'Abd al-Muṭṭalib], and 'Aqīl. 'Alī withdrew, and 'Aqīl called out to him "O son of Umm 'Alī, by God you have seen us." So 'Alī went to the Prophet and told him that he saw al-'Abbās, Nawfal, and 'Aqīl. The Prophet drew near until he stood very close to 'Aqīl and said "O Abū Yazīd, Abū Jahl has been killed." 'Aqīl said: "In that case, no one will contest you [for authority] in Tihāmah.[272] If your [words] take effect on the people, [fine]; if not, dominate them [by force]."

According to Abū Ja'far [al-Ṭabarī], there is a report saying that 'Aqīl returned to Mecca and stayed there. Later, at the beginning
[2341] of the year 8/629, he went to the Prophet as an Emigrant and took part in the expedition of Mu'tah. He then returned and became ill,

268. The Prophet's paternal cousin, brother of 'Alī. See "'Aḳīl b. Abī Ṭālib," *EI*², I, 337 (L. Veccia Vaglieri); Ibn Ḥibbān, *Mashāhīr*, 27; al-Balādhurī, *Ansāb*, I, 301, 365, III (Dūrī), 296; Ibn Qudāmah, 112.
269. Ibn Sa'd, IV/1, 29.
270. Cf. Ibn Sa'd, IV/1, 29; al-Dhahabī, *Siyar*, I, 218–19.
271. That is, among the prisoners.
272. The strip of land along the west and south coasts of Arabia, see "Tihāma," *EI*¹, VIII, 763–65 (A. Grohmann).

so he is not mentioned [among the participants] in the conquest of Mecca, [the siege] of al-Ṭā'if, and [the battle of] Ḥunayn.

It was reported that ʿAqīl b. Abī Ṭālib died after having lost his sight, during the caliphate of Muʿāwiyah.

Rabīʿah b. al-Ḥārith b. ʿAbd al-Muṭṭalib b. Hāshim b. ʿAbd Manāf.[273]

He is the one about whom the Prophet said, on the day of the conquest of Mecca: "I say, every [open case of] blood revenge and every privilege of the Jāhiliyyah are hereby rendered null and void.[274] The first case of blood revenge that I thus declare annulled is that of Rabīʿah b. al-Ḥārith." The Prophet said: "The first case of blood revenge that I declare annulled is that of Rabīʿah b. al-Ḥārith," even though Rabīʿah was alive only because there was a vendetta Rabīʿah was entitled to seek in pre-Islamic times.[275] [The story is as follows]: A small child of Rabīʿah was given to a wet nurse from the Banū Layth b. Bakr,[276] who were in a state of war with the Hudhayl.[277] This son of Rabīʿah b. al-Ḥārith, who was a small child, crept out in front of the tents, and the Hudhayl threw a rock at him, which hit him and crushed his head. The advent of Islam occurred before Rabīʿah b. al-Ḥārith could avenge his son's blood, and the Prophet declared annulled [the obligation] to seek vengeance for that blood and did not let Rabīʿah approach his son's assassin.[278] This is what is meant by the Prophet's annulling the revenge for his blood: It means that he invalidated Rabīʿah's right to seek vengeance for it because it was one of the pre-Islamic vendetta cases, rendered void by Islam.[279]

---

273. A cousin of the Prophet. See Ibn Ḥibbān, *Mashāhīr*, 57; Khalīfah b. Khayyāṭ, *Ta'rīkh*, 127; idem, *Ṭabaqāt*, 5–6; Ibn Ḥazm, *Jamharat*, 70; Ibn Saʿd, IV/1, 32–33; Ibn Qudāmah, 103.

274. Literally, "are under these two feet of mine."

275. Seeking blood revenge was both an obligation and a right, ending only with the seeker's death.

276. A clan of the northern tribe of Kinānah whose territories lay in the vicinity of Mecca. See "Kināna," *EI*², V, 116 (W. M. Watt); Ibn Ḥazm, *Jamharat*, 180.

277. A northern tribe, in the vicinity of Mecca and al-Ṭā'if. See "Hudhayl," *EI*², III, 540–41 (G. Rentz); Ibn Ḥazm, *Jamharat*, 196–98.

278. Or "did not enable Rabīʿah to take action against his son's assassin." See also Ibn Ḥazm, *Jamharat*, 70.

279. Islam modified the pre-Islamic law of vengeance; see Coulson, 18.

As for the slain son of Rabīʿah, there is disagreement over his name. According to Ibn ʿUmar it was Ādam b. Rabīʿah, whereas others say that it was Tammām b. Rabīʿah and yet others hold that it was Iyās b. Rabīʿah.

All [the scholars] agree that Rabīʿah b. al-Ḥārith was [several] years older than his paternal uncle al-ʿAbbās b. ʿAbd al-Muṭṭalib.

[2342] It was reported that Rabīʿah b. al-Ḥārith did not take part in [the battle of] Badr with the idolators [because] he was away [on a trip to] Syria. Later, during the period of the Ditch, he went to the Prophet as an Emigrant. He participated in [the battle of] Ḥunayn on the Prophet's side and was among those of the Prophet's family and Companions who persevered [with the fighting].[280]

Rabīʿah died after his brothers Nawfal and Abū Sufyān, during the caliphate of ʿUmar b. al-Khaṭṭāb.

ʿAbdallāh b. al-Ḥārith b. ʿAbd al-Muṭṭalib b. Hāshim b. ʿAbd Manāf.[281]

His name was previously ʿAbd Shams, and when he was converted the Prophet called him ʿAbdallāh.[282]

[ʿAbdallāh b. al-Ḥārith] left Mecca before the conquest (*fatḥ*) and went to the Prophet as an Emigrant. He accompanied the Prophet on one of his raids and died in Ṣafrāʾ.[283] The Prophet buried him in his gown, that is, the Prophet's gown, and said about him: "He is happy; [the ultimate] happiness overtook him."[284]

Jaʿfar b. Abī Sufyān b. al-Ḥārith b. ʿAbd al-Muṭṭalib b. Hāshim.[285]

He was one of those Companions who persevered [with the fighting] on the Prophet's side at the battle of Ḥunayn.

Jaʿfar and his father remained with the Prophet until the latter's death.

---

280. See p. 25, above.

281. Brother of Rabīʿah of the preceding biography, see Ibn Ḥajar, *Iṣābah*, II, 292.

282. See note 234, above.

283. A place near Badr, see Ibn Manẓūr, *Lisān*, IV, 465.

284. *Saʿādah*, "happiness," refers to the attaining of Paradise. See also note 7, above.

285. He belonged to the Prophet's clan, Hāshim, see al-Balādhurī, *Ansāb*, III (Dūrī), 296–97.

Ja'far died in the middle of the caliphate of Mu'āwiyah, may God damn him.[286]

Al-Ḥārith b. Nawfal b. al-Ḥārith b. 'Abd al-Muṭṭalib b. Hāshim.[287]

Al-Ḥārith was [already] mature in the Prophet's lifetime.

He became a Companion on the conversion of his father.[288] His son 'Abdallāh was born during the Prophet's lifetime; the baby was brought to the Prophet, who performed on him the ritual of rubbing the palate with chewed dates (*taḥnīk*) and blessed him.[289]

According to Ibn Sa'd[290]—'Alī b. 'Īsā—his father: Al-Ḥārith b. Nawfal moved to al-Baṣrah during the governorship of 'Abdallāh b. 'Āmir b. Kurayz,[291] built a house (*dār*) on a piece of land, and settled there. He died in al-Baṣrah at the end of the caliphate of 'Uthmān.

'Abd al-Muṭṭalib b. Rabī'ah b. al-Ḥārith b. 'Abd al-Muṭṭalib b. Hāshim.[292]

'Abd al-Muṭṭalib transmitted [traditions] from the Prophet; he [2343] was [already] mature in the Prophet's lifetime.

According to Ibn 'Umar [al-Wāqidī]—Ibn Sa'd—'Alī b. 'Īsā al-Nawfalī: 'Abd al-Muṭṭalib b. Rabī'ah stayed in Medina until the time of [the caliphate of] 'Umar b. al-Khaṭṭāb. He then moved to Syria, where he built a house (*dār*) and settled. He died in Damascus during the caliphate of Yazīd b. Mu'āwiyah.

---

286. The text as a rule uses terms of blessing after the names of the Prophet and the Companions, which I omit in the translation. Here the custom is reversed. On the traditional Muslim attitude toward the Umayyads, see Hawting, *First Dynasty*, 11–20.

287. Of the Prophet's clan. See Ibn Ḥibbān, *Mashāhīr*, 63; al-Balādhurī, *Ansāb*, I, 440, III (Dūrī), 297; Ibn Qudāmah, 100–1.

288. See p. 19, above.

289. See Gil'adi. Cf. al-Ṭabarī, *Ta'rīkh*, I, 1935.

290. Ibn Sa'd, IV/1, 39.

291. Maternal cousin of the third caliph, 'Uthmān, and governor of al-Baṣrah on his behalf; see "'Abdallāh b. 'Āmir," *EI²*, I, 43 (H. A. R. Gibb).

292. A member of the Prophet's clan. See Khalīfah b. Khayyāṭ, *Ta'rīkh*, 246; idem, *Ṭabaqāt*, 7; al-Balādhurī, *Ansāb*, III (Dūrī), 24–25, 295–96; Ibn Qudāmah, 103–4.

'Utbah b. Abī Lahab—whose name was 'Abd al-'Uzzā—b. 'Abd al-Muṭṭalib b. Hāshim b. 'Abd Manāf.[293]

According to Ibn Sa'd[294]—'Alī b. 'Īsā b. 'Abdallāh al-Nawfalī—Ḥamzah b. 'Utbah b. Ibrāhīm al-Lihbī—Ibrāhīm b. 'Āmir b. Abī Sufyān b. Mu'attib and other Hāshimī shaykhs of ours—Ibn 'Abbās—his father al-'Abbās b. 'Abd al-Muṭṭalib: When the Prophet arrived in Mecca on its conquest he said to me "O 'Abbās, where are your nephews 'Utbah and Mu'attib? I do not see them." I said "O Messenger of God, they withdrew to the side, together with other idolators of the Quraysh." The Prophet said "Go and bring them to me." So I rode to 'Uranah,[295] [where they were staying,] and went to them and said "The Prophet invites you." They hastened to ride with me and came to the Prophet. He called on them to embrace Islam, and they did, giving him the oath of allegiance. Then the Prophet stood up, took their hands, and, walking between them, led them to the *multazam*, that is, the area between the door of the Ka'bah and the Black Stone.[296] He prayed for a while, then left, his face reflecting joy. I said to him "O Messenger of God, may God make you joyful; I see joy reflected in your face." The Prophet said "Yes, I had asked a gift from God, these two cousins of mine, and he gave them to me."

According to Ḥamzah b. 'Utbah: Shortly after this the two ['Utbah and Mu'attib] went with the Prophet to Ḥunayn and took
[2344] part in the battle. That day they were among those of the Prophet's family and Companions who persevered with [the fighting] on the Prophet's side.[297] Mu'attib lost an eye in that battle.

None of the men of the Hāshim clan remained to live in Mecca after its conquest except 'Utbah and Mu'attib, sons of Abū Lahab.

---

293. Abū Lahab b. 'Abd al-Muṭṭalib, an uncle of the Prophet, was one of his fiercest enemies. See Rubin, "Abū Lahab." On 'Utbah, see al-Balādhurī, *Ansāb*, I, 131, 401; Ibn Qudāmah, 143.

294. Ibn Sa'd, IV/1, 41–42.

295. A valley near 'Arafāt, to the east of Mecca; see Yāqūt, *Mu'jam al-buldān*, III, 657.

296. According to the Muslim tradition, a prayer uttered in this particular place is bound to be answered. There is, however, a view placing the *multazam* at the rear of the Ka'bah, see al-Azraqī, I, 246–49.

297. See p. 25, above.

Usāmah, son of Zayd b. Ḥārithah, the Prophet's beloved.[298]
His *kunyah* was Abū Muḥammad. His mother was Umm Ayman, whose name was Barakah, the nurse and client of the Prophet.
Usāmah was born in Mecca. He grew to manhood without experiencing anything but Islam, never adhering to any other religion. He emigrated to Medina together with his father, Zayd, who was, as some people say, the first man to have been converted to Islam.[299] Usāmah never left the Prophet's side.
According to Ibn Sa'd—al-Faḍl b. Dukayn—Ḥanash [b. al-Ḥārith]—his father: The Prophet appointed Usāmah at the age of eighteen.[300]
According to Ibn 'Umar [al-Wāqidī]: The number of Usāmah's descendants, both men and women, never exceeded twenty in any given generation.
Usāmah was twenty years old when the Prophet died. He then settled in Wādī al-Qurā[301] and later in Medina. He died in al-Jurf at the end of the caliphate of Mu'āwiyah.

Abū Rāfi', client of the Prophet.[302]
His name was Aslam.

298. Ibn Ḥibbān, *Mashāhīr*, 30; Khalīfah b. Khayyāṭ, *Ta'rīkh*, 65, 216; idem, *Ṭabaqāt*, 6–7; Ibn Ḥanbal, *Faḍā'il*, 834–37; al-Balādhurī, *Ansāb*, I, 470–76.

299. The identity of the first Muslim became a point of debate among the Muslims. According to Sunnī Islam, the first to have believed in the Prophet was Abū Bakr, a merit that, among others, made him worthy of the caliphate. According to the Shī'ah, however, the first Muslim was 'Alī. A neutral view places this merit with Zayd b. Ḥārithah, whose descendants had nothing to do with the contention for power.

300. Ibn Sa'd, IV/1, 46. Shortly before his death the Prophet prepared an expedition against the Byzantines, appointing the young Usāmah as commander, to avenge the death of his father, Zayd, killed in Mu'tah. The Prophet died, and Abū Bakr dispatched the army in spite of loud protests from Muslims objecting to Usāmah because of his young age. See al-Ṭabarī, *Ta'rīkh*, I, 1796–97, 1845–48.

301. The fertile valley to the north of Medina; see "Wādī al-Ḳurā," *EI*[1], VIII, 1077–78 (A. Grohmann).

302. Ibn Ḥibbān, *Mashāhīr*, 53; Khalīfah b. Khayyāṭ, *Ta'rīkh*, 186; al-Balādhurī, *Ansāb*, I, 477–78, III (Dūrī), 21. Al-Ṣadr, 30, says that he was 'Alī's appointee over the treasury of al-Kūfah and the first Shī'ī to compile a collection of traditions and legal issues.

Abū Rāfi' had been a slave of al-'Abbās b. 'Abd al-Muṭṭalib and was given as a present to the Prophet. When the latter received the good news of al-'Abbās' conversion to Islam he set Abū Rāfi' free.

Abū Rāfi' emigrated to Medina after [the battle of] Badr and stayed with the Prophet. He participated in [the battles of] Uḥud and the Ditch, and all the [other] events. The Prophet gave his client Salmā to him in marriage, and she participated with him in [the conquest of] Khaybar.

Salmā bore Abū Rāfi' [a son], 'Ubaydallāh b. Abī Rāfi', who acted as scribe for 'Alī b. Abī Ṭālib.

Salmān al-Fārisī.[303]

His *kunyah* was Abū 'Abdallāh.

The Ditch was the first military action in which Salmān took part.

[2345] According to Ja'far b. Sulaymān—Hishām b. Ḥassān—al-Ḥasan: Salmān's pension ('aṭā') was 5,000 [dirhams a year], and he was appointed over 30,000 men. He used to collect firewood clad in a cloak, half of which he used for covering himself, whereas the other half he spread.

Each time his pension was due he did not take it and lived off his own handwoven palm leaves.[304]

According to Ibn 'Umar: Salmān al-Fārisī died during the caliphate of 'Uthmān b. 'Affān.

Al-Aswad b. Nawfal b. Khuwaylid b. Asad b. 'Abd al-'Uzzā b. Quṣayy.[305]

He was an early convert to Islam in Mecca and emigrated to Abyssinia in the second emigration. According to Mūsā b. 'Uqbah,

---

303. A famous Companion, see "Salmān al-Fārisī," *EI*[1], IV, 116–17 (G. Levi Della Vida); Ibn Ḥibbān, *Mashāhīr*, 76; Khalīfah b. Khayyāṭ, *Ta'rīkh*, 173; idem, *Ṭabaqāt*, 7. He is credited with having suggested to the Prophet the digging of the Ditch for defense against the besieging Quraysh in the year 5/627.

304. *Ya'kulu min safīf yadihi*, literally, "he ate from the plait of palm leaves of his hand." The parallel text adduced by de Goeje from Ibn al-Athīr's *Usd al-ghābah* has *wa-akala min kasb yadihi kāna yasuffu al-khūṣ*, "he ate from the earnings of his hand; he wove palm leaves." See also Ibn Sa'd, IV/1, 62.

305. A member of the Qurashī clan Asad b. 'Abd al-'Uzzā. He was a nephew of Khadījah, the Prophet's wife, and an early convert. See al-Balādhurī, *Ansāb*, I, 202; Ibn Qudāmah, 274.

it was Nawfal b. Khuwaylid [not his son al-Aswad] who embraced Islam and emigrated to Abyssinia.[306]

Muḥammad b. ʿAbd al-Raḥmān b. al-Aswad b. Nawfal b. Khuwaylid.[307]
His *kunyah* was Abū al-Aswad. He is the one known as "the orphan of ʿUrwah b. al-Zubayr."[308]

Abū al-Rūm b. ʿUmayr b. Hāshim b. ʿAbd Manāf b. ʿAbd al-Dār b. Quṣayy.[309]
His mother was Byzantine. He was a half-brother of Muṣʿab b. ʿUmayr.
According to Ibn ʿUmar [al-Wāqidī], Abū al-Rūm was an early convert in Mecca and emigrated to Abyssinia in the second emigration. He also took part in [the battle of] Uḥud.

Jahm b. Qays b. Shuraḥbīl b. Hāshim b. ʿAbd Manāf b. ʿAbd al-Dār b. Quṣayy.[310]
Jahm was an early convert to Islam and emigrated to Abyssinia in the second emigration. This is unanimously accepted [among the scholars]. His wife, Ḥuraymalah bt. ʿAbd al-Aswad b. Khuzay- [2346]
mah b. Uqaysh b. ʿĀmir b. Bayāḍah al-Khuzāʿiyyah, and the two sons she had borne him, ʿAmr and Khuzaymah, sons of Jahm, were with him. Ḥuraymalah died in Abyssinia.

Al-Walīd b. al-Walīd b. al-Mughīrah b. ʿAbdallāh b. ʿUmar b. Makhzūm.[311]
According to Ibn ʿUmar [al-Wāqidī] on the authority of Muḥammad b. ʿAbdallāh[312]—[Ibn Shihāb] al-Zuhrī—ʿUrwah [b. al-Zu-

306. Notwithstanding, Nawfal is also said to have been a fierce opponent of Islam in its early period; see Ibn Ḥajar, *Iṣābah*, I, 46.

307. Khalīfah b. Khayyāṭ, *Taʾrīkh*, 421, see also al-Aʿẓamī, *Maghāzī*, 61–62.

308. ʿUrwah was his guardian according to the will of his father, ʿAbd al-Raḥmān.

309. A member of the Qurashī clan Banū ʿAbd al-Dār (this Hāshim is not identical with the Prophet's ancestor). See Ibn Ḥazm, *Jamharat*, 125–27; al-Balādhurī, *Ansāb*, I, 203; Ibn Qudāmah, 245.

310. Al-Balādhurī, *Ansāb*, I, 203; Ibn Qudāmah, 247. The clan is the same as in the preceding biography.

311. Brother of the famous Companion and general Khālid b. al-Walīd, of the Qurashī clan Makhzūm. See Ibn Ḥajar, *Iṣabah*, III, 639–40; Ibn Qudāmah, 349–50.

312. The reference is perhaps to Ibn Abī Sabrah; see, e.g., al-Wāqidī, 1097.

bayr] and on the authority of Ibrāhīm b. Jaʿfar—his father: Salamah b. Hishām,[313] ʿAyyāsh b. Abī Rabīʿah,[314] and al-Walīd b. al-Walīd left [Mecca], emigrating to [Medina to join] the Prophet. People from the Quraysh went after them to bring them back but failed to overtake them. When the three reached the edge of the basalt area of Medina (*ḥarrah*) al-Walīd's finger was cut and bled, whereupon he said:[315]

What are you but a bleeding finger?
    It is in the path of God that you suffer.

[Later] he had a heart failure and died in Medina. Umm Salamah bt. Abī Umayyah[316] mourned him and said:

For al-Walīd b. al-Walīd b. al-Mughīrah, O my eye, let your
    tears flow.
The like of al-Walīd b. al-Walīd Abū al-Walīd protect the clan
    [against its foe].

The Prophet said "Do not say this, Umm Salamah, but say 'Death has come justly, this is what you turned away from.'"[317]

Ibn Umm Maktūm.[318]

Opinions differ as to his name. The Medinan scholars say that it was ʿAbdallāh, whereas the Iraqis and Hishām b. Muḥammad [al-Kalbī] hold that it was ʿAmr b. Qays b. Zāʾidah b. al-Aṣamm b.
[2347] Rawāḥah b. Ḥajar b. ʿAbd b. Maʿīṣ b. ʿĀmir b. Luʾayy. He was called by the name of his mother, Umm Maktūm, whose [full] name was ʿĀtikah bt. ʿAbdallāh b. ʿAnkathah b. ʿĀmir b. Makhzūm b. Yaqaẓah.

Ibn Umm Maktūm was an early convert to Islam in Mecca. He

---

313. Cousin of al-Walīd and brother of Abū Jahl. See Ibn Ḥajar, *Iṣābah*, II, 68–69; Ibn Manẓūr, *Mukhtaṣar*, X, 94–96.

314. Cousin of al-Walīd, apparently of the Meccans who were converted after the Muslim conquest of their city. See Ibn Ḥajar, *Iṣābah*, III, 47.

315. Ibn Manẓūr, *Mukhtaṣar*, X, 95. In al-Bukhārī's *Ṣaḥīḥ*, II, 202 (*jihād*, 9) the verse is attributed to the Prophet, who was wounded in a battle. I thank Prof. Yohanan Friedmann for this reference.

316. That is, the Prophet's wife. She belonged to the same clan as al-Walīd.

317. Qurʾān, 50:18. The Prophet's objection is raised by the pre-Islamic (*jāhilī*) style of the lament.

318. Of the Qurashī clan ʿĀmir b. Luʾayy; see Ibn Ḥazm, *Jamharat*, 171. He was an early convert, and the Prophet often appointed him as deputy in Medina when he left on raids. See, e.g., al-Balādhurī, *Ansāb*, I, 310–11 and passim; Ibn Qudāmah, 488–89.

was blind. He came to Medina as an Emigrant, [but] opinions differ as to the time of his arrival. According to Muḥammad b. ʿUmar [al-Wāqidī], he arrived shortly after [the battle of] Badr and lived in the house of the Qur'ān reciters, which was the house of Makhramah b. Nawfal.[319]

[Ibn Umm Maktūm] used to act as muezzin for the Prophet in Medina, together with Bilāl. Whenever the Prophet went out on a raid he appointed him to lead the public prayer in Medina.

Ibn Umm Maktūm carried the Muslim banner in the battle of al-Qādisiyyah. He later returned to Medina, where he died.

Abū Dharr Jundab b. Junādah b. Sufyān b. ʿUbayd b. Ḥarām b. Ghifār b. Mulayl b. Ḍamrah b. Bakr b. ʿAbd Manāh b. Kinānah b. Khuzaymah b. Mudrikah b. Alyās b. Muḍar b. Nizār.[320]

According to Ibn ʿUmar [al-Wāqidī]—Mūsā b. ʿUbaydah—Nuʿaym b. ʿAbdallāh al-Mujmir—his father: Abū Dharr's name was Jundab b. Junādah; this was [also] the opinion of Muḥammad b. ʿUmar [al-Wāqidī], Hishām b. Muḥammad [al-Kalbī], and other historians. Ibn ʿUmar says that, according to Najīḥ Abū Maʿshar, Abū Dharr's name was Burayr b. Jundab.

According to [Ibn ʿUmar al-Wāqidī]—Abū Bakr b. ʿAbdallāh b. Abī Sabrah—Mūsā b. ʿUqbah—ʿAṭā' b. Abī Marwān—his father: Abū Dharr said "I was the fifth [person] to embrace Islam."

According to Abū Jaʿfar [al-Ṭabarī]: Abū Dharr returned to his [2348] clan's territory after his conversion, where he stayed until after the battles of Badr, Uḥud, and the Ditch. He then joined the Prophet in Medina.[321] According to Ibn Saʿd[322]—ʿAbdallāh b. ʿAmr Abū Maʿmar al-Minqarī—ʿAbd al-Wārith b. Saʿīd—al-Ḥusayn al-Muʿallim—Abū Buraydah: When Abū Mūsā al-Ashʿarī arrived [in al-Kūfah] he met Abū Dharr and started seeking his company. Al-Ashʿarī was a short, slender man, whereas Abū Dharr was black and hairy. Al-Ashʿarī started clinging to him, and Abū Dharr would say "Go away and leave me alone," and al-

---

319. Cf. ʿUmar b. Shabbah, I, 241, 253.

320. "Abū Dharr," *EI²*, I, 114–15 (J. Robson); Cameron, *Abū Dharr*; Ibn Ḥibbān, *Mashāhīr*, 30–31; Khalīfah b. Khayyāṭ, *Ṭabaqāt*, 31–32; al-Balādhurī, *Ansāb*, V, 52–56; Ibn Saʿd, IV/1, 161–75. He was an early convert of the Ghifār clan, which belonged to the northern tribe of Kinānah; see Ibn Ḥazm, *Jamharat*, 176.

321. Cf. Landau-Tasseron, "F. McG. Donner," 501 (about Muhājirūn who returned to their clans).

322. Ibn Saʿd, IV/1, 169.

Ash'arī would say "Welcome, O brother," whereupon Abū Dharr would push him and say "I am no brother of yours; I was your brother before you were appointed governor." Later Abū Dharr met Abū Hurayrah, who sought his company and said to him "Welcome my brother," whereupon Abū Dharr replied "Go away and leave me alone; did you not act as governor on behalf of those [rulers]?" Abū Hurayrah said "Yes." Abū Dharr asked "Did you trespass by building luxurious buildings or [unlawfully] acquiring estates or flocks?" Abū Hurayrah said "No," whereupon Abū Dharr said "You are my brother."[323]

According to Ibn Sa'd[324]—al-Faḍl b. Dukayn—Ṣāliḥ b. Rustam—Abū 'Āmir—Ḥumayd b. Hilāl—al-Aḥnaf b. Qays: Abū Dharr, as I saw him, was a tall, dark-brown-toned man with white hair and a white beard.

According to Abū Ja'far [al-Ṭabarī], Abū Dharr died during the caliphate of 'Uthmān in al-Rabadhah.[325]

Buraydah b. al-Ḥuṣayb b. 'Abdallāh b. al-Ḥārith b. al-A'raj b. Sa'd b. Rizāḥ b. 'Adī b. Sahm b. Māzin b. al-Ḥārith b. Salāmān b. Aslam b. Afṣā b. Ḥārithah b. 'Amr b. 'Āmir, that is, Mā' al-Samā'.[326]

His *kunyah* was Abū 'Abdallāh.

Buraydah was converted to Islam when the Prophet passed by him during his Emigration [to Medina].

According to Ibn 'Umar [al-Wāqidī]—Hāshim b. 'Āṣim al-
[2349] Aslamī—his father: While emigrating from Mecca to Medina the Prophet arrived at al-Ghamīm.[327] Buraydah b. al-Ḥuṣayb went to him [there], and the Prophet called on him to join Islam. Buraydah

323. Abu Dharr, considered one of the first ascetics in Islam, expresses here the negative attitude toward government as such, because of the corruption often involved in it. See Goitein, "Attitudes"; Kister, "Social Concepts"; 'Athāmina, "'Ulamā'." As for Abū Hurayrah, he was accused of corruption by the caliph 'Umar, the present account notwithstanding; see al-Balādhurī, *Futūḥ*, 82.

324. Ibn Sa'd, IV/1, 169.

325. Al-Rababhah is an Islamic town about 200 kilometers southeast of Medina; see al-Rāshid, *Al-Rabadha.* Abū Dharr, who lived in Syria, was exiled to this place because the governor, Mu'āwiyah, had had complaints against him. See al-Ṭabarī, *Ta'rīkh*, I, 2858–62, 2895–97.

326. A part of the decendants of this 'Āmir, including Buraydah's clan, the Aslam, formed the large tribal confederation called Khuzā'ah, the genealogy of which is confused. On Buraydah see Ibn Ḥibbān, *Mashāhīr*, 100–1; al-A'ẓamī, *Kuttāb*, 47; Ibn Sa'd, VII/1, 3–4, VII/2, 99–100; Khalīfah b. Khayyāṭ *Ta'rīkh*, 246.

327. A place near Medina, see Yāqūt, *Mu'jam al-buldān*, III, 817–18.

was converted with those who were with him, numbering about eighty families. The Prophet said the evening prayer, and they prayed standing behind him.

According to [Ibn ʿUmar]—Hāshim b. ʿĀṣim al-Aslamī—al-Mundhir b. Jahm: That night, the Prophet taught Buraydah a part of *sūrat Maryam.* After [the battles of] Badr and Uḥud Buraydah went to the Prophet in Medina and learned the rest of it. He became a resident of Medina, stayed with the Prophet, and participated in the raids from that point onward.[328]

After the Prophet's death Buraydah remained in Medina until [the area of] al-Baṣrah was conquered and a garrison was established there.[329] He moved to al-Baṣrah, took possession of a piece of land, [and built a house (*dār*) there]. He then left for Khurāsān, to participate in raids there. He died in Merv during the rule of Yazīd b. Muʿāwiyah, and his offspring stayed there.

Diḥyah b. Khalīfah b. Farwah b. Faḍālah b. Zayd b. Imriʾ al-Qays b. al-Khazj, that is, Zayd Manāh—b. ʿĀmir b. Bakr b. ʿĀmir al-Akbar (senior) b. ʿAwf b. Bakr b. ʿAwf b. ʿUdhrah b. Zayd al-Lāt b. Rufaydah b. Thawr b. Kalb b. Wabarah b. Taghlib b. Ḥalwān b. al-Ḥāf b. Quḍāʿah.[330]

Diḥyah was an early convert [but] did not take part in [the battle of] Badr. It was said that he resembled [the angel] Jibrīl.

Diḥyah participated on the Prophet's side in the events that followed [the battle of] Badr. He lived until the time of the caliphate of Muʿāwiyah.

Aws b. Qayẓī b. ʿAmr b. Zayd b. Jusham b. Ḥārithah and his two [2350]
sons, Kabāthah and ʿAbdallāh, sons of Aws.[331]

They took part in [the battle of] Uḥud.[332]

ʿArābah b. Aws b. Qayẓī came with them on the day of Uḥud,

---

328. Buraydah was appointed to several tasks by the Prophet; see, e.g., al-Wāqidī, 404–5, 410.

329. "Baṣra," *EI*², I, 1085–86 (Ch. Pellat); al-Ṭabarī, *Taʾrīkh*, I, 2377. See also Donner, "Tribal Settlement"; al-ʿAlī, *al-Tanẓīmāt al-ijtimāʿiyyah.*

330. A member of the ʿUdhrah, a part of the great tribe Kalb. On Diḥyah, see recently S. Bashear, "Mission"; Ibn Ḥibbān, *Mashāhīr*, 94; al-Balādhurī, *Ansāb*, I, 377, 531.

331. Of the Ḥārithah clan, of the Aws (Anṣār), see Ibn Ḥajar, *Iṣābah*, I, 87.

332. They were, however, among those who ran away. See al-Balādhurī, *Ansāb*, I, 326.

but he was considered too young [to fight] and was sent back.[333] ʿArābah is the one about whom al-Shammākh b. Ḍirār[334] says:

If you carry my saddle and bring me to ʿArābah,
then choke with your aorta's blood.[335]

ʿUthmān b. Ḥunayf b. Wāhib b. ʿUkaym b. Thaʿlabah b. al-Ḥārith b. Majdaʿah b. ʿAmr b. Ḥanash b. ʿAwf b. ʿAmr b. ʿAwf.[336]

His *kunyah* was Abū ʿAbdallāh.

ʿUthmān was sent by ʿUmar b. al-Khaṭṭāb to supervise the survey of the land of Iraq [for the assessment of taxes].[337] [Later] he acted as governor of al-Baṣrah for ʿAlī [b. Abī Ṭālib], when the oath of allegiance was taken on the latter's behalf.[338]

[ʿUthmān b. Ḥunayf] died in al-Baṣrah during the caliphate of Muʿāwiyah.

Ḥassān b. Thābit b. al-Mundhir b. Ḥarām b. ʿAmr b. Zayd Manāh b. ʿAdī b. ʿAmr b. Mālik b. al-Najjār, the Prophet's poet.[339]

His *kunyah* was Abū al-Walīd.

Ḥassān was an early convert [but] did not participate in any battle with the Prophet, [owing to] his cowardice.

He died during the caliphate of Muʿāwiyah at the age of 120; sixty years of his life he had lived during the Jāhiliyyah and sixty during Islam.

Nawfal b. Muʿāwiyah b. Ṣakhr b. Yaʿmur b. Nufāthah b. ʿAdī b. al-Dīl b. Bakr b. ʿAbd Manāh b. Kinānah.[340]

---

333. See note 260, above.

334. A pre-Islamic poet of the northern Dhubyān tribe. On him see al-Hādī, *al-Shammākh b. ḍirār*, on the tribe, 52–74.

335. The poet apparently addresses his (she)-camel, meaning to say that if he reaches ʿArābah he need make no further journey. The verse is part of a poem, see p. 74, below.

336. Of the clan Banū ʿAwf b. ʿAmr, from the Aws (Anṣār). See Ibn Ḥazm, *Jamharat*, 336; Ibn Ḥibbān, *Mashāhīr*, 49; al-Balādhurī, *Ansāb*, I, 163.

337. See Dennett, 23; Morony, 37, 101–6; see also 484–85.

338. On the advent of new caliphs, it was the duty of the governors to secure the oath of allegiance from the subjects in the provinces. See al-Ṭabarī, *Taʾrīkh*, I, 3087, and 3115–21 for ʿUthmān's role during ʿAlī's time.

339. See "Ḥassān b. Thābit," *EI²*, III, 271–73 (W. Arafat); Ḥassān, I, 3–7 (introduction by W. Arafat); Ibn Ḥibbān, *Mashāhīr*, 32. The clan's name is Banū al-Najjār, from the Khazraj tribe (Ansār), see Ibn Ḥazm, *Jamharat*, 346.

340. Ibn Ḥibbān, *Mashāhīr*, 62; Khalīfah b. Khayyāṭ, *Ṭabaqāt*, 34. The clan's name is in fact Banū al-Du'il, from the Kinānah tribe; see Ibn Ḥazm, *Jamharat*, 184–85.

His family was the leading one among the Banū al-Dīl, and his father, Mu'āwiyah, was the chief of the Banū al-Dīl in the battle of al-Fijār.[341] Ta'abbaṭa Sharran[342] said about him:

No, by [the life of] her father, we did not alight at 'Āmir's [2351]
or by 'Āmir's or by Nawfal the Nufāthī.[343]

[Nawfal's] son, Salmā b. Nawfal, was the most generous among the Arabs. The Ja'farī poet said about him:

We select chiefs who are not leaders at all;
nay, the praiseworthy chief is Salmā b. Nawfal.[344]

According to Muḥammad b. 'Umar [al-Wāqidī]—Abū Bakr b. 'Abdallāh b. Abī Sabrah—Jūthah b. 'Ubayd al-Dīlī: Nawfal b. Mu'āwiyah al-Dīlī lived sixty years during the Jāhiliyyah and sixty years during Islam. He participated with the idolators of the Quraysh in [the battles of] Badr, Uḥud, and the Ditch, where he was harmful [to the Muslims], acquiring fame thereby. He later embraced Islam and took part in the conquest of Mecca, [the battle of] Ḥunayn, and [the siege of] al-Ṭā'if on the Prophet's side.

Nawfal settled in Medina with the Banū al-Dīl. He transmitted [traditions] from the Prophet.

Nawfal died in Medina during the caliphate of Yazīd b. Mu'āwiyah, may God curse them both.[345]

'Arābah b. Aws b. Qayẓī b. 'Amr b. Zayd b. Jusham b. Ḥārithah b. al-Ḥārith.[346]

His father, Aws b. Qayẓī, and his brothers 'Abdallāh and Kabāthah, sons of Aws, took part in [the battle of] Uḥud, whereas he was considered too young (*ṣaghīr*) and was sent back.[347] He was allowed [to participate] in the Ditch (Khandaq).

---

341. On these pre-Islamic battles, see Landau-Tasseron, "Sinful wars."
342. A pre-Islamic poet; see F. Sezgin, II, 137–39.
343. Cf. Abū al-Faraj al-Iṣfahānī, XVIII, 214 (Ibn Qawfal instead of Nawfal; that is, the verse does not allude to Nawfal). The two 'Āmirs mentioned are 'Āmir b. al-Ṭufayl and 'Āmir b. Mālik, both of them tribal chiefs in the confederation 'Amir b. Ṣa'ṣa'ah.
344. Cf. Abū al-Faraj al-Iṣfahānī, XII, 76; Ibn Ḥajar, *Iṣābah*, II, 70; al-Mubarrad, 75 (where the name is Salm, not Salmā). There is no clue to the identity of the poet in any of these sources.
345. See note 286, above.
346. See p. 71, above; Ibn Ḥajar, *Iṣābah*, II, 473.
347. See note 260, above.

According to Ibn ʿUmar [al-Wāqidī]—ʿUmar b. ʿUqbah—ʿĀṣim
[2352] b. ʿUmar b. Qatādah: At the time of Uḥud ʿArābah b. Aws was fourteen years and five months old, and the Prophet sent him back and refused to allow him [to participate in the battle].

According to Muḥammad, ʿArābah was the one eulogized by al-Shammākh b. Ḍirār. The latter came [once] to Medina, and ʿArābah loaded his camel with dates:

I found ʿArābah al-Awsī unequaled
in his involvement in charity.
His right hand always receives
the hoisted flag of nobility.[348]

ʿUbaydallāh b. al-ʿAbbās b. ʿAbd al-Muṭṭalib.[349]

ʿUbaydallāh fathered Muḥammad, after whom he was called [Abū Muḥammad], al-ʿAbbās, and al-ʿĀliyah, who was married to ʿAlī b. ʿAbdallāh b. al-ʿAbbās. She bore him Muḥammad b. ʿAlī, among whose descendants the ʿAbbāsid caliphate was inherited.

[ʿUbaydallāh also fathered] ʿAbd al-Raḥmān and Qutham, who were killed by Busr b. Abī Arṭāh al-ʿĀmirī in the Yemen.[350]

ʿUbaydallāh b. al-ʿAbbās was one year younger than ʿAbdallāh b. al-ʿAbbās. He heard and transmitted [traditions] from the Prophet and lived to the time of Yazīd b. Muʿāwiyah.

ʿAlī b. Abī Ṭālib appointed ʿUbaydallāh b. al-ʿAbbās governor of the Yemen. He also appointed him to lead the pilgrimage, and he did, in the year 39/660. That year the people agreed that Shaybah b. ʿUthmān b. Abī Ṭalḥah [should conduct the pilgrimage], and so he did.[351]

---

348. These verses, as well as the one on p. 72, above, are part of a poem, for which see al-Shammākh, 96–97. See also Ibn Ḥazm, *Jamharat*, 341; al-Balādhurī, *Ansāb*, I, 277; Abū al-Faraj al-Iṣfahānī, VIII, 102; al-Mubarrad, 75, 396. Here the phrase "right hand" is explained as "powerfully."

349. Cousin of the Prophet. See al-Balādhurī, *Ansāb*, III (Dūrī), 24, 55–65; Khalīfah b. Khayyāṭ, *Taʾrīkh*, 173, 182, 214.

350. This occurred in the year 40/660, during the attempt of Muʿāwiyah's general Busr to seize the Ḥijāz and the Yemen from ʿAlī's men. ʿUbaydallāh was governor of the Yemen for ʿAlī; see al-Ṭabarī *Taʾrīkh*, I, 3451–52.

351. These are in fact conflicting versions as to who conducted the pilgrimage in the year 39/660. According to one of them, it was ʿUbydallāh b. ʿAbbās. According to the other, Muʿāwiyah, contending with ʿAlī for power, sent a representative of his own to perform this task. The latter, however, was not accepted, so a compromise was reached, under which a neutral person (Shaybah b. ʿUthmān) con-

'Ubaydallāh b. al-'Abbās was a brave and generous leader. He used to slaughter a camel every day [and distribute the meat]. He was in charge of the vanguard [of the army] dispatched by al-Ḥasan b. 'Alī against Mu'āwiyah.[352]

'Ubaydallāh's full brother, Qutham b. al-'Abbās.[353]

Qutham participated in raids in Khurāsān when Sa'īd b. 'Uthmān governed it.[354] Sa'īd wanted to give him a thousand shares of the spoils, but Qutham said: "No. First allocate the fifth (*khums*) [which is due to the public treasury],[355] then give the people their lawful shares, and afterward you can give me what you want."

Qutham was a pious, virtuous man; he died in Samarkand.

Abū Ja'far [al-Ṭabarī] said: According to 'Alī b. Muḥammad [al-Madā'inī]: Qutham b. 'Abbās was a governor of Mecca on behalf of [2353]
'Alī and conducted the pilgrimage.

It was said that he resembled the Prophet.[356]

Ma'bad b. al-'Abbās and Kathīr b. al-'Abbās.[357]

According to 'Alī b. Muḥammad al-Madā'inī, the mother of Kathīr and Tammām was a Byzantine concubine whose name was Musliyah.

Kathīr died in Yanbu'[358] from an ulcer in the throat.

Tammām b. al-'Abbās.[359]

---

ducted the pilgrimage. See al-Ṭabarī, *Ta'rīkh*, I, 2448. On Shaybah b. 'Uthmān, see Ibn Sa'd, V, 331; Ibn Ḥajar, *Tahdhīb*, IV, 329–30. Cf. also note 371, below.

352. For conflicting accounts of 'Ubaydallāh's role in the relations between al-Ḥasan and Mu'āwiyah, see al-Ṭabarī, *Ta'rīkh*, II, 1–2; al-Balādhurī, *Ansāb*, III (Maḥmūdī), 33–34, 37–38.

353. He worked in the service of 'Alī b. Abī Ṭālib. See "Ḳutham b. al-'Abbās," *EI*², V, 551 (C. E. Bosworth); al-Balādhurī, *Ansāb*, III (Dūrī), 65–66.

354. Sa'īd was governor of Khurāsān. See al-Ṭabarī, *Ta'rīkh*, II, 177–80; Ibn Manẓūr, *Mukhtaṣar*, IX, 334–36; Khalīfah b. Khayyāṭ, *Ṭabaqāt*, 240; Muḥammad Ibn Ḥabīb, *Mughtālīn*, 165–68.

355. A fifth (*khums*) of all booty is said to belong to God, to be used for special purposes. See Ben Shemesh, I, 23–24, II, 51–53, III, 51–55.

356. See the list of those who resembled the Prophet in Muḥammad Ibn Ḥabīb, *Muḥabbar*, 46–47; and also Ibn Ḥazm, *Jamharat*, 60, 69, 70, 73.

357. Al-Balādhurī, *Ansāb*, III (Dūrī), 22, 66 (on Ma'bad), 60 (on Kathīr, who was a scholar).

358. An oasis near Medina; see Yāqūt, *Mu'jam al-buldān*, IV, 1038–39.

359. He worked in the service of 'Alī b. Abī Ṭālib. See Khalīfah b. Khayyāṭ, *Ta'rīkh*, 185; al-Balādhurī, *Ansāb*, III (Dūrī), 60; al-Ṭabarī, *Ta'rīkh*, I, 3107.

He was one of the most violent men of his time. He was the youngest of his father's sons.

'Abdallāh b. Zam'ah b. al-Aswad b. al-Muṭṭalib b. Asad b. 'Abd al-'Uzzā b. Quṣayy.[360]

His mother was Qarībah al-Kubrā (senior) bt. Abī Umayyah b. al-Mughīrah b. 'Abdallāh b. 'Umar b. Makhzūm; her mother was 'Ātikah bt. 'Abd al-Muṭṭalib b. Hāshim.[361]

'Āmir b. Kurayz b. Rabī'ah b. Ḥabīb b. 'Abd Shams b. 'Abd Manāf b. Quṣayy.[362]

His mother was al-Bayḍā', that is, Umm Ḥakīm bt. 'Abd al-Muṭṭalib b. Hāshim.

'Āmir b. Kurayz was converted to Islam on the day of the conquest of Mecca and lived to the [time of the] caliphate of 'Uthmān b. Affān. He went to al-Baṣrah to his son 'Abdallāh b. 'Āmir while the latter was governor there on behalf of 'Uthmān b. 'Affān.

Abū Hāshim b. 'Utbah b. Rabī'ah b. 'Abd Shams b. 'Abd Manāf.[363]

He was converted to Islam on the day of the conquest of Mecca. [Later] he left for Syria, where he settled until his death.

Qays b. Makhramah b. al-Muṭṭalib b. 'Abd Manāf.[364]

Al-Ṣalt b. Makhramah b. al-Muṭṭalib b. 'Abd Manāf b. Quṣayy.[365]

He was converted to Islam on the day of the conquest of Mecca.

---

360. Of the Qurashī clan Banū Asad b. 'Abd al-'Uzzā. See Ibn Ḥibbān, *Mashāhīr*, 63; Khalīfah b. Khayyāṭ *Ta'rīkh*, 230; idem, *Ṭabaqāt*, 14; Ibn Qudāmah, 277.

361. Aunt of the Prophet, famous for a dream in which she foresaw the battle of Badr. See Ibn Hishām, II, 258–59; Muḥammad Ibn Ḥabīb, *Munammaq*, 337–38, see also 33, 50; Ibn Ḥajar, *Iṣabah*, IV, 357–58.

362. A member of the powerful Qurashī clan the Banū 'Abd Shams and notorious for his stupidity. See al-Balādhurī, *Ansāb*, I, 82; Ibn Ḥajar, *Iṣābah*, II, 256.

363. A member of the Qurashī clan the Banū 'Abd Shams. See Khalīfah b. Khayyāṭ, *Ta'rīkh*, 172; idem, *Ṭabaqāt*, 12; Ibn Qudāmah, 217–18.

364. Ibn Ḥibbān, *Mashāhīr*, 63; Ibn Qudāmah, 235; al-Zubayrī, 92. He belonged to the Qurashī clan the Banū al-Muṭṭalib b. 'Abd Manāf; see Ibn Ḥazm, *Jamharat*, 72–74. The next five biographies are of people of the same clan.

365. Khalīfah b. Khayyāṭ, *Ta'rīkh*, 233.

Juhaym b. al-Ṣalt b. Makhramah b. al-Muṭṭalib b. 'Abd Manāf.[366]

'Abdallāh b. Qays b. Makhramah b. al-Muṭṭalib b. 'Abd Manāf.[367]
He was converted to Islam on the day of the conquest of Mecca.

Rukānah b. 'Abd Yazīd b. Hāshim b. al-Muṭṭalib b. 'Abd Manāf b. Quṣayy.[368] [2354]
He was converted to Islam on the day of the conquest [of Mecca]. He then went to Medina, where he settled until his death, at the beginning of the caliphate of Mu'āwiyah.

His full brother 'Ujayr b. 'Abd Yazīd b. Hāshim b. al-Muṭṭalib.[369]

Abū Nabiqah.[370]
His name was 'Abdallāh b. 'Alqamah b. al-Muṭṭalib b. 'Abd Manāf.

Al-Aswad b. Abī al-Bakhtarī—the latter's name was al-'Āṣ—b. Hāshim b. al-Ḥārith b. Asad b. 'Abd al-'Uzzā b. Quṣayy.[371]
Al-Aswad was converted to Islam on the day of the conquest [of Mecca], whereas his father Abū al-Bakhtarī was killed in the battle of Badr as an idolator.

Habbār b. al-Aswad b. al-Muṭṭalib b. Asad b. 'Abd al-'Uzzā b. Quṣayy.[372]

---

366. He served the Prophet as a scribe. See al-A'ẓamī, *Kuttāb*, 51–52; Ibn Qudāmah, 237.
367. He lived in Medina and fulfilled certain functions there for al-Ḥajjāj b. Yūsuf. See Ibn Ḥibbān, *Mashāhīr*, 114; Khalīfah b. Khayyāṭ, *Ta'rīkh*, 294; al-Balādhurī, *Ansāb*, V, 374.
368. Ibn Ḥibbān, *Mashāhīr*, 61; Khalīfah b. Khayyāṭ, *Ṭabaqāt*, 9; Ibn Qudāmah, 234; al-Zubayrī, 95–96.
369. Ibn Ḥajar, *Iṣābah*, II, 466; Ibn Qudāmah, 235.
370. Ibn Ḥajar, *Iṣābah*, IV, 196; Ibn Qudāmah, 237–38.
371. A member of the Qurashī clan Asad b. 'Abd al-'Uzzā. According to al-Zubayr b. Bakkār, he was accepted as neutral leader during the war between 'Alī and Mu'āwiyah; see Ibn Ḥajar, *Iṣābah*, I, 42.
372. Al-Balādhurī, *Ansāb*, I, 357–58; Ibn Qudāmah, 219. See also p. 000, above (biography of Zaynab).

It was reported that Habbār used to relate [the following story]: When the Prophet came out and preached [the belief in] Allāh I was among those who showed hatred toward him, opposed him, and harmed him.

[When] the Prophet sent someone to Mecca to fetch his daughter Zaynab some people from the Quraysh obstructed her way, and Habbār was among them. He poked her and wounded her back with a lance, and she lost the baby she was carrying; she was then brought back to the dwellings of the Banū ʿAbd Manāf. Habbār b. al-Aswad had committed a grave sin against Islam, and the Prophet allowed his blood to be shed with impunity. Whenever he sent a party on a raid he gave orders concerning Habbār, saying "If you seize him put him between two logs of firewood and burn him." He would then say: "Only the Lord of Fire is entitled to torture with fire.[373] If you seize him cut off his hands and feet, then kill him."

Abū Jaʿfar [al-Ṭabarī] said: According to Muḥammad b. ʿUmar
[2355] [al-Wāqidī]—Wāqid b. Abī Thābit—Yazīd b. Rūmān—al-Zubayr b. al-ʿAwwām: The Prophet never sent a raiding party without telling them "If you seize Habbār, cut off his hands and feet, then [execute him by] hitting his neck."[374] By God, I used to look for him and ask about him, and God knows that, had I seized him before he went to the Prophet, I would have killed him. Then he came to the Prophet while I was sitting with him and started making excuses to the Prophet, saying: "O Muḥammad, curse those who curse you and harm those who harm you. I hastened to curse and harm you [while] I was forsaken [by God], but God has helped me and led me to Islam." I looked at the Prophet, who bowed his head out of shame for Habbār's excuses. The Prophet said "I forgive you, for [conversion to] Islam nullifies whatever was [committed] before it."[375] Habbār was hated more than any-

---

373. Arabic *nār* signifies both "fire" and "hell," so the sentence means that only God, Who controls [heaven and] hell, may exact punishment by fire. As a rule, the Muslims refrained from executions by fire. Cf. al-Balādhuri, *Futūḥ*, 107.

374. Cf. al-Wāqidī, 857.

375. *Al-islām yajubbu mā kāna qablahu*, a *ḥadīth* reflecting the tolerance of Islam toward former enemies who repented. Even the false prophet Ṭulayḥah, who embraced Islam after his defeat in the apostasy wars, was forgiven and considered a good Muslim and eventually a *shahīd.* On him, see Ibn Ḥajar, *Iṣābah*, II, 234. See the *ḥadīth* in Ibn Ḥanbal, *Musnad*, IV, 199.

one; the Prophet heard about his forbearance in the face of harassment and said [to him] "O Habbār, curse those who curse you."

According to Ibn ʿUmar [al-Wāqidī]—Hishām b. ʿUmārah—Saʿīd b. Muḥammad b. Jubayr b. Muṭʿim—his father—his grandfather: I was sitting with the Prophet in his mosque, among [others of] his Companions, on his return from Jiʿrānah[376] when Habbār b. al-Aswad appeared at the Prophet's door. The people saw him and said "O Messenger of God, here is Habbār b. al-Aswad." The Prophet said "I saw him." Someone wanted to go up to him, but the Prophet motioned him to sit down. Habbār then [approached until he] stood very close to the Prophet and said: "O Messenger of God, peace be with you. I testify that there is no God but Allāh, and I testify that you are the messenger of God. I had roamed the country, fleeing from you; I had wanted to join the non-Arabs, but then I remembered you and your kindness, your [2356] virtue, your compassion, and your forbearance to those who act impetuously toward you. O Messenger of God, we have been idolators, but God has led us to the right path through you and saved us from damnation. Forgive my impetuous ways and whatever you heard about me, for I admit my wickedness and confess my sin." The Prophet said: "I forgive you, for Allāh treated you benevolently by showing you the way to Islam. [Conversion to] Islam nullifies whatever was [committed] before it."

Hind b. Abī Hālah—whose name was al-Nabbāsh—b. Zurārah b. Waqdān b. Ḥabīb b. Salāmah b. Ghuwayy b. Jirwah b. Usayyid b. ʿAmr b. Tamīm.[377]

Abū Hālah and his two brothers, ʿAwf and Unays, came to Mecca and entered into an alliance (*ḥilf*) with the Banū ʿAbd al-Dār b. Quṣayy b. Kilāb. The [brothers] remained to live with them in Mecca, and Abū Hālah married Khadījah bt. Khuwaylid. She bore him two sons, Hind and Hālah. Hālah died, whereas Hind

---

376. A place 10 miles from Mecca where the Prophet assembled the spoils from the battle of Ḥunayn for distribution in the year 8/630. See al-Wāqidī, 939–49; Wellhausen, *Muḥammad*, 373–81; Ibn Hishām, IV, 130–43; Guillaume, 592–97.

377. Khalīfah b. Khayyāṭ, *Ṭabaqāt*, 43, 199. He was of the Tamīmī clan Usayyid, which had a special status in Mecca in pre-Islamic times. See Ibn Ḥazm, *Jamharat*, 210; Kister, "On Strangers and Allies," 120–26. On the large, powerful confederation of Tamīm (of northern origin), see Kister, "Mecca and Tamīm"; "Tamīm," *EI*¹, IV, 643–46 (Levi Della Vida); Caskel, II, 7–10.

lived to see [the advent of] Islam and was converted. Al-Ḥasan b. ʿAlī [b. Abī Ṭālib] transmitted [traditions] from him; he used to say "I was told by my maternal uncle Hind b. Abī Hālah."[378]

According to [Abū ʿUbaydah] Maʿmar b. Muthannā: Hind was passing through al-Baṣrah, and died there. The market was canceled that day, and there was no loading and unloading of ships. They said "The brother of Fāṭimah, the brother of Fāṭimah, may God bless her!"[379]

Al-Muhājir b. Abī Umayyah b. al-Mughīrah b. ʿAbdallāh b. ʿUmar b. Makhzūm.[380]

[He was a] full brother of Umm Salamah bt. Abī Umayyah, the Prophet's wife.

The name of Abū Umayyah b. al-Mughīrah was Suhayl. He is [the one known as] Zād al-Rakb (provider for the passengers). Whenever he set out on a journey, he took it upon himself [to pay] the expenses of his companions and fellow travelers on that journey. He was therefore called Zād al-Rakb.[381]

According to Ibn ʿUmar [al-Wāqidī]—Abū Bakr b. ʿAbdallāh b.
[2357] Abī Sabrah—al-Muhājir b. Mismār: The Prophet was angry with al-Muhājir b. Abī Umayyah, so the latter said to Umm Salamah "Speak to the Prophet for me, for today is your day with him." So she let him enter her house, and when the Prophet came in he was taken by surprise as al-Muhājir approached him from behind and seized him by the waist. The Prophet laughed, and Umm Salamah said [to the Prophet] "Regard him with favor, may God regard you with favor." So the Prophet regarded him with favor and appointed him over Ṣanʿāʾ. Al-Muhājir left [for Ṣanʿāʾ], and when [on his way

378. Being the son of Khadījah from her first marriage, Hind was half-brother of Fāṭimah, daughter of the Prophet and mother of al-Ḥasan. See the genealogical table 2, p. xxix.

379. *Ṣalawāt allāh ʿalayhā*, a formula used specifically after mention of the Prophet's name. As a rule, other formulas are used after mention of members of the Prophet's family, such as "peace be upon him/her" or "may God be pleased with him/her." See Robson; Ibn al-ʿArabī.

380. A member of the Qurashī clan Makhzūm and one of the Prophet's tax collectors. See Khalīfah b. Khayyāṭ, *Taʾrīkh*, 62, 84; al-Balādhurī, *Ansāb*, I, 529; al-Rāzī, 145–46; Ibn Qudāmah, 372–73.

381. Muḥammad Ibn Ḥabīb, *Muḥabbar*, 137; Ibn Qudāmah, 370.

there] he arrived in Mecca he learned of the rise of al-ʿAnsī in Ṣanʿāʾ.[382] He returned to Medina, where he stayed until the Prophet's death. Abū Bakr then appointed him over Ṣanʿāʾ, and he left to take his post. [Ibn ʿUmar al-Wāqidī] said to Ibn Abī Sabrah "But, according to the version I have, the Prophet sent al-Muhājir as governor, and he was in Ṣanʿāʾ when the Prophet died." Ibn Abī Sabrah replied "That [which I told you] is what I was informed by Muhājir b. Mismār."

Ṣafwān b. Umayyah b. Khalaf b. Wahb b. Ḥudhāfah b. Jumaḥ b. ʿAmr b. Huṣayṣ.[383]

His *kunyah* was Abū Wahb.

According to Ibn ʿUmar [al-Wāqidī]—ʿAbdallāh b. Yazīd al-Hudhalī—Abū Ḥuṣayn: The Prophet asked Ṣafwān b. Umayyah for a loan of 50,000 [dirhams?] while he was in Mecca, and he lent it to him.

According to Muḥammad b. ʿUmar [al-Wāqidī]: Ṣafwān always remained a good Muslim, [but] we have no information of his taking part in any raid with the Prophet or after the latter's death. He remained to live in Mecca until his death at the beginning of Muʿāwiyah's caliphate.

ʿAbdallāh b. Saʿd b. Abī Sarḥ b. al-Ḥārith b. Ḥubayb b. Jadhīmah b. Mālik b. Ḥisl b. ʿĀmir b. Luʾayy.[384]

ʿAbdallāh was an early convert and one of the Prophet's scribes. He later apostatized and was [again] converted to Islam on the day of the conquest of Mecca. The information about him is already [2358]
[recorded] in our book entitled *The Supplemented: The Abridged History of the Messengers and Kings.*

---

382. Al-Aswad al-ʿAnsī posed as a prophet in the Yemen some time before Muḥammad's death. The Prophet succeeded in having him killed. See "Aswad al-ʿAnsī," *EI*², I, 728 (W. M. Watt); al-Kalāʿī, 213–15; Ibn Ḥubaysh, 124–25.

383. A member of the Qurashī clan Jumaḥ; see Ibn Ḥibbān, *Mashāhīr*, 56; al-Balādhurī, *Ansāb*, I, 304–5, 362–63; Khalīfah b. Khayyāṭ, *Ṭabaqāt*, 24; Ibn Qudāmah, 452–54.

384. A statesman and general of the Qurashī clan the Banū ʿĀmir b. Luʾayy. See "ʿAbdallāh b. Saʿd," *EI*², I, 51–52 (C. H. Becker); Ibn Ḥibbān, *Mashāhīr*, 90; al-Balādhurī, *Ansāb*, I, 358; Khalīfah b. Khayyāṭ, *Taʾrīkh*, 64, 13–35, 157; al-Aʿẓamī, *Kuttāb*, 83–89.

Al-Aqra' b. Ḥābis b. 'Iqāl b. Muḥammad b. Sufyān b. Mujāshi' b. Dārim b. Mālik b. Ḥanẓalah b. Mālik b. Zayd Manāh b. Tamīm.[385]

He was a member of the Tamīmī delegation that came to the Prophet, and the latter gave him 100 camels from the booty of Ḥunayn. Al-'Abbās b. Mirdās composed verses about this.[386]

Ṣa'ṣa'ah b. Nājiyah b. 'Iqāl b. Muḥammad b. Sufyān b. Mujāshi'.[387]

Ṣa'ṣa'ah went to the Prophet and embraced Islam. Among his posterity were the poet al-Farazdaq b. Ghālib b. Ṣa'ṣa'ah[388] and the preacher 'Iqāl b. Shabbah b. 'Iqāl b. Ṣa'ṣa'ah.[389]

Al-Zibriqān b. Badr b. Imri' al-Qays b. Khalaf b. Bahdalah b. 'Awf b. Ka'b b. Sa'd b. Zayd Manāh b. Tamīm.[390]

Al-Zibriqān's real name was al-Ḥuṣayn. He was a poet and [so] handsome [that] he was called "the moon of Najd." He was a member of the Tamīmī delegation that went to the Prophet and was appointed by the latter to collect the legal alms (*ṣadaqah*) from his people, the Banū Sa'd b. Zayd Manāh b. Tamīm. He was in this post when the Prophet died. [Then] the Arabs apostatized and refused to pay the legal alms, but al-Zibriqān firmly adhered to Islam, collected the alms from his people, and handed them over to Abū Bakr.[391]

---

385. "Akra' b. Ḥābis," *EI²*, I, 343 (M. J. Kister). He was a tribal chief of the Tamīmī clan Mujāshi'; see Ibn Ḥazm, *Jamharat*, 230–31.

386. Although the text so implies, there was no connection between the participation of al-Aqra' in the delegation and his receiving the gift; see Landau-Tasseron, "Processes." On the Prophet's gifts to tribal leaders after the battle of Ḥunayn and the Sulamī al-'Abbās b. Mirdās' protest against receiving only four camels, see al-Wāqidī, 946–47.

387. Of the Mujāshi'; see Ibn Ḥibbān, *Mashāhīr*, 69–70. He was famous for his objection to the pre-Islamic custom of burying alive female babies; see, e.g., Abū al-Faraj al-Iṣfahānī, XIX, 2–3.

388. A famous poet who flourished in the Umayyad period; see "al-Farazdaḳ," *EI²*, II, 788–89 (R. Blachère).

389. A companion of the Umayyad caliphs Hishām and al-Walīd II. See al-Balādhurī, *Ansāb*, VI, 228; Ibn Manẓūr, *Mukhtaṣar*, XVII, 91–93; al-Ṭabarī, *Ta'rīkh*, I, 1730, 1755–56, 1820.

390. A tribal chief of the Tamīmī clan the Bahdalah. See Ibn Ḥazm, *Jamharat*, 219, 466; al-Balādhurī, *Ansāb*, I, 530; Landau-Tasseron, "Processes," 254.

391. See Kister, "*Illā biḥaqqihi*"; Bashear, "*Zakāt*"; Shoufani, *Al-Riddah*.

Mālik b. Nuwayrah b. Jamrah b. ʿUbayd b. Thaʿlabah b. Yarbūʿ b. Ḥanẓalah b. Mālik b. Zayd Manāh b. Tamīm.[392]

According to Ibn ʿUmar [al-Wāqidī]—ʿUtbah b. Jabīrah—Ḥu- [2359] ṣayn b. ʿAbd al-Raḥmān b. ʿAmr b. Saʿd b. Muʿādh: The Prophet returned to Medina from the pilgrimage in the year 10/632. When he saw the new moon of Muḥarram of the year 11/632 he sent tax collectors to several Arab [tribes].[393] He appointed Mālik b. Nuwayrah, who had already embraced Islam, to collect the legal alms from the Banū Yarbūʿ.

Mālik was a poet, and his nickname was al-Jafūl.[394]

Labīd b. Rabīʿah b. Mālik b. Jaʿfar b. Kilāb, the poet.[395]

According to Ibn ʿUmar [al-Wāqidī]—Mūsā b. Shaybah b. ʿAmr b. ʿAbdallāh b. Kaʿb b. Mālik b. Khārijah b. ʿAbdallāh b. Kaʿb: The delegation of the Banū Kilāb went to the Prophet in the year 9/630–31. They were thirteen people, including Labīd b. Rabīʿah, and were lodged at the house of Ramlah bt. al-Ḥadath.[396] They came to the Prophet, greeted him with the Islamic greeting,[397] and embraced Islam, whereupon they returned to their tribe's territory.

According to Ibn Saʿd[398]—Naṣr b. Bāb—Dāʾūd b. Abī Hind—[ʿĀmir b. Sharāḥīl] al-Shaʿbī: ʿUmar b. al-Khaṭṭāb wrote to al-

---

392. A member of the Tamīmī clan the Yarbūʿ. See Ibn Ḥazm, *Jamharat*, 224–28; "Mālik b. Nuwayra," *EI*², VI, 267–69 (E. Landau-Tasseron).

393. Cf. al-Wāqidī, 973, where the tax collectors are said to have been sent on the emergence of the new moon in the year 9/630. Al-Wāqidī's sources here are different, and Mālik b. Nuwayrah is not included in this list. These two lists, both quoted on the authority of al-Wāqidī, can also be found in Ibn Saʿd, II/1, 115; Ibn Ḥubaysh, 23–24; al-Kalāʿī, 43, and others. For yet other lists, see Khalīfah b. Khayyāṭ, *Taʾrīkh*, 63; al-Balādhurī, *Ansāb*, I, 529–30; al-Yaʿqūbī, II, 122; Ibn Hishām, IV, 246; al-Ṭabarī, *Taʾrīkh*, I, 1750; Muḥammad Ibn Ḥabīb, *Muḥabbar*, 125–28; and also Shoufani, *Al-Riddah*, 96.

394. That is, "the one who frightens [the camels away]," referring to the story that he scattered the *ṣadaqah* camels (and gave them back to those who had paid them). *Jafūl*, however, also means "hairy."

395. A member of the Jaʿfar b. Kilāb from the ʿĀmir b. Ṣaʿṣʿah tribe. See Ibn Ḥazm, *Jamharat*, 284–87; "Labīd b. Rabīʿa," *EI*², V, 583–84 (C. Brockelmann).

396. This is al-Wāqidī's version; other scholars call her Ramlah bt. al-Ḥārith. Her house is mentioned in the *Sīrah* and elsewhere as a lodging. See Ibn Ḥajar, *Iṣābah*, IV, 305; al-Wāqidī, 192, 975, 988; Ibn Saʿd, VIII, 327; Ibn Ḥubaysh, 122.

397. See p. 000, above.

398. The parallel text in Ibn Saʿd could not be traced.

Mughīrah b. Shu'bah, his governor in al-Kūfah: "Invite the poets who live in your jurisdiction, and ask them to recite the poetry they composed both in pre-Islamic and Islamic times; then write to me about it." So al-Mughīrah invited them. He said to Labīd "Recite to me the poetry you composed both in pre-Islamic and Islamic times." Labīd replied "Allāh gave me *sūrat al-Baqarah* and *sūrat Āl 'Imrān*[399] instead of that." Al-Mughīrah then said to al-Aghlab al-'Ijlī[400] "Recite to me," and he said:

Is it *rajaz* or a poem[401] that you need?
What you ask can easily be achieved.

Al-Mughīrah wrote about this to 'Umar, and he wrote back:
[2360] "Cut al-Aghlab's pension by 500 [dirhams], and add them to Labīd's." Al-Aghlab traveled to 'Umar, [came before him], and said "Would you cut my pension for obeying you?" 'Umar then wrote to al-Mughīrah "Return to al-Aghlab the 500 you have cut, [but] leave intact the increase in Labīd b. Rabī'ah's pension."

Ḥubshī b. Junādah b. Naṣr b. Usāmah b. al-Ḥārith b. Mu'ayṭ b. 'Amr b. Jandal b. Murrah b. Ṣa'ṣa'ah b. Mu'āwiyah b. Bakr b. Hawāzin.[402]

The Banū Murrah b. Ṣa'ṣa'ah are the Banū Salūl; Salūl was a woman, the mother of the Banū Murrah, that is, Salūl bt. Dhuhl b. Shaybān b. Tha'labah; and they are known by her [name].

Ḥubshī b. Junādah was a Companion of the Prophet. He fought on the side of 'Alī [b. Abī Ṭālib] in the battles he led.

Abū Umāmah al-Bāhilī.[403]

His name was Ṣudayy b. 'Ajlān, from the Banū Sahm b. 'Amr b. Tha'labah b. Ghanm b. Qutaybah b. Ma'n b. Mālik b. A'ṣur—whose name was Munabbih—b. Sa'd b. Qays b. 'Aylān.

---

399. Chapters 2 and 3 of the Qur'ān.

400. A poet born before Islam; he died in 22/642. See "al-Aghlab," *EI*², I, 247 (C. Pellat).

401. *Rajaz* is a certain kind of meter, in which the verses are less rigidly structured than in a regular poem; see "Radjaz," *EI*², VIII, 375–78 (M. Ullmann).

402. Ibn Ḥazm, *Jamharat*, 271–72; Khalīfah b. Khayyāṭ, *Ṭabaqāt*, 55–56.

403. The male ancestor of the tribe was Mālik b. A'ṣur, but it was known as Bāhilah, after Mālik's wife. Their pedigree is confused. See Ibn Ḥazm, *Jamharat*, 245–47; Khalīfah b. Khayyāṭ, *Ta'rīkh*, 293; idem, *Ṭabaqāt*, 46, 302.

Zayd al-Khayl b. Muhalhil b. Zayd b. Munhib b. 'Abd Ruḍā b. al-Mukhtalis b. Thuwab b. Kinānah b. Mālik b. Nābil b. Aswadān—whose name was Nabhān—b. 'Amr b. al-Ghawth b. Ṭayyi' b. Udad b. Zayd b. Yashjub b. Ya'rub b. Qaḥṭān.[404]

The mother of Ṭayyi' was Dallah bt. Manjishān b. Killah b. Radmān b. Ḥimyar,[405] whose mother gave birth to her on a hill by the name of Madhḥij, so Dallah was called Madhḥij after that hill [2361] and all her descendants are called Banū Madhḥij.[406]

Ṭayyi' had been named Julhumah, and he was called Ṭayyi', according to a certain opinion, only because he was the first to have plastered the [walls of the] watering places (*ṭawā al-manāhil*), and some say that it was because he was the first to have plastered the walls of a well.

Zayd al-Khayl died in a place called Fardah,[407] while returning after [visiting] the Prophet.

According to Hishām [Ibn al-Kalbī]—his father: The clan of Zayd al-Khayl was called the Banū al-Mukhtalis. Zayd had several children:[408]

(1) Miknaf b. Zayd, after whom Zayd was called [Abū Miknaf]. He embraced Islam and ranked among the Prophet's Companions. He took part in the wars of apostasy (*riddah*) [on the Muslim side] under the command of Khālid b. al-Walīd and showed courage.

(2) Ḥurayth b. Zayd; he was a horseman. He ranked among the Prophet's Companions and took part in the wars of apostasy under the command of Khālid b. al-Walīd. He [also] was a poet.

(3) 'Urwah b. Zayd. He took part in the battles of Qādisiyyah,

---

404. The clan's name is Banū al-Mukhtalis, the larger group being the Nabhān; see Ibn Ḥazm, *Jamharat*, 403–4. Zayd was a poet and tribal chief in pre-Islamic times; see Landau-Tasseron, "Ṭayyi'," 57.

405. An ancient Arab people from southern Arabia, incorporated by Arab genealogists into the tribal scheme as a son of Saba' (ancient Sheba). See "Ḥimyar," *EI*¹, II, 310–12 (J. H. Mordtmann); Ibn Ḥazm, *Jamharat*, 432; Caskel, II, 66–73.

406. Theoretically all Arab tribes had male eponyms. When it was obvious that a tribe's name had been otherwise coined, a story was adduced by the genealogists to explain it.

407. A mountain or, according to another version, a watering place in the territory of Ṭayyi', see Yāqūt, *Mu'jam al-buldān*, III, 871.

408. On Zayd's children and their role in the apostasy wars, see Landau-Tasseron, "Ṭayyi'," 57–59.

Quss al-Nāṭif, and Mihrān[409] and showed courage. He composed verses about it.

Zayd al-Khayl was a poet.

ʿAdī b. Ḥātim al-Jawād (the generous) b. ʿAbdallāh b. Saʿd b. al-Ḥashraj b. Imriʾ al-Qays b. ʿAdī b. Akhzam b. Rabīʿah b. Jarwal b. Thuʿal b. ʿAmr b. al-Ghawth b. Ṭayyiʾ.[410]

His *kunyah* was Abū Ṭarīf.

ʿAdī b. Ḥātim took part in the battles of Qādisiyyah,[411] Mihrān, Quss al-Nāṭif, and Nukhaylah. He was the standard bearer. He fought in the battle of the Camel on the side of the Commander of the Faithful ʿAlī b. Abī Ṭālib, where he lost an eye and his son was killed. He [also] took part in the battles of Ṣiffīn and Nahrawān on ʿAlī's side.[412]

ʿAdī died during the rule of al-Mukhtār[413] in al-Kūfah, at the age of 120.

[2362] ʿAmr b. al-Musabbiḥ b. Kaʿb b. Ṭarīf b. ʿAṣar b. Ghanm b. Ḥārithah b. Thuwab b. Maʿn b. ʿAtūd b. ʿUnayn b. Salāmān b. Thuʿal b. ʿAmr b. al-Ghawth b. Ṭayyiʾ.[414]

---

409. Quss al-Nāṭif is another name for the battle of the Bridge in Iraq in the year 13/634 or 14/635. See Donner, *Early Islamic Conquests*, 191–92; al-Balādhurī, *Futūḥ*, 251–52; al-Ṭabarī, *Taʾrīkh*, I, 2174–83. Mihrān is another name for the battle of Nukhaylah in Iraq, which took place before al-Qādisiyyah, but cf. the biography of ʿAdī b. Ḥātim, below, where the two names seem to refer to two disparate events; Nukhaylah is also known as al-Buwayb. See al-Balādhurī, ibid., 253–55; Donner, ibid., 198.

410. A tribal leader who embraced Islam and was appointed tax collector by the Prophet. See Ibn Ḥibbān, *Mashāhīr*, 75; Khalīfah b. Khayyāṭ, *Taʾrīkh*, 68–69; al-Ḍabbī, 23–25. The clan's name was Banū Thuʿal. See also Landau-Tasseron, "Ṭayyiʾ," 53–56, 59–60.

411. See al-Ṭabarī, *Taʾrīkh*, I, 2221, where he is said to have been the commander of the Ṭayyiʾ.

412. A town in Iraq, the site of ʿAlī's victory over the Khawārij who rebelled against him in the year 37/658; see Wellhausen, *Arab Kingdom*, 84–86.

413. Leader of a successful pro-ʿAlid revolt. He ruled al-Kūfah in 66–67/685–87; see "al-Mukhtār," *EI*², VII, 521–24 (G. R. Hawting).

414. A member of the Banū Thuʿal, he is considered to be one of the *muʿammarūn*, those who lived more than 120 years. See Ibn Ḥajar, *Iṣābah*, III, 16, and also "Muʿammar," *EI*², VII, 258 (G. H. A. Juynboll).

He was the best archer among the Arabs, and [the poet] Imru' al-Qays[415] said about him:

How many archers of the Banū Thuʻal
draw their hands out of the hiding place?

Wabarah b. al-Jaḥdar al-Maʻnī of the Banū Daghsh said:[416]

The raven pushed—I wished that it did not—
causing me and Salmā and Umm al-Ḥawshab to part.[417]
I wished that the core of that raven's heart
by ʻAmr's perfectly made arrows was shot.

ʻAmr b. al-Musabbiḥ lived 150 years. He lived to the Prophet's time, went to see him, and embraced Islam.

Al-Ashʻath b. Qays, that is, al-Ashajj (scarface), b. Maʻdī-Karib b. Muʻāwiyah b. Jabalah b. ʻAdī b. Rabīʻah b. Muʻāwiyah al-Akramīn b. al-Ḥārith b. Muʻāwiyah b. al-Ḥārith b. Muʻāwiyah b. Thawr b. Murattiʻ b. Kindah.[418]

[Al-Ashʻath] was a Kindī; Kindah's [real] name was Thawr b. ʻUfayr b. ʻAdī b. al-Ḥārith b. Murrah b. Udad b. Zayd b. Yashjub b. ʻArīb b. Kahlān b. Saba' b. Yashjub b. Yaʻrub b. Qaḥṭān.

Al-Ashʻath's [real] name was Maʻdī-Karib, but his hair was always disheveled, so he was nicknamed al-Ashʻath (the disheveled). His *kunyah* was Abū Muḥammad.

---

415. See "Imru' al-Ḳays b. Hudjr," *EI²*, III, 1177–78 (S. Boustany); Tuetey. The verses are in al-Sandūbī, *Sharḥ dīwān Imri' al-Qays*, 86, and Ibn al-Kalbī, *Nasab maʻadd*, 239, from which apparently al-Ṭabarī quoted it; cf. Ibn Ḥajar, *Iṣābah*, III, 16 (*wa-qāla Ibn al-Kalbī thumma al-Ṭabarī . . .*)

416. Ibn al-Kalbī, *Nasab maʻadd*; Ibn Manẓūr, *Lisān*, I, 743 s.v. *l.gh.b* (both variants omitting the obscure part about Umm al-Ḥawshab). In Ibn al-Kalbī, 236, the poet is called Wabarah b. Salāmah and the family the Banū Da's of the Ṭā'ī clan Maʻn. Note Jaḥdam/Qaḥdham in Ibn al-Kalbī (apparently corresponding to our text's Jaḥdar).

417. The raven is the symbol of separation from the beloved in ancient Arabic poetry. Salmā is obviously the beloved's name. I could not find out what Umm al-Ḥawshab refers to.

418. Of the Banū Jabalah of Kindah; see Ibn al-Kalbī, *Nasab maʻadd*, 139. Al-Ashʻath was an important leader both in pre-Islamic and Islamic times. He served ʻUthmān as a governor and ʻAlī as a general and played a crucial role in Kūfan politics. See "al-Ashʻath b. Ḳays," *EI²*, I, 696–97 (H. Reckendorf); Crone, *Slaves*, 110–11; Lecker, "Kinda"; idem, "Judaism Among Kinda"; Khalīfah b. Khayyāṭ, *Ta'rīkh*, 129, 149, 175–77; Ibn Ḥibbān, *Mashāhīr*, 78.

[2363] Al-Ash'ath went to see the Prophet with seventy [other] riders from Kindah. He later took part in the wars of apostasy (*riddah*), was taken prisoner, and was sent to Abū Bakr.[419] He repented and remained to live in Medina until 'Umar b. al-Khaṭṭāb, during his caliphate, urged the people to participate in the military expeditions to Iraq.[420] Al-Ash'ath joined [a regiment] under [the command of] Sa'd b. Abī Waqqāṣ and took part in the battles of Qādisiyyah, Madā'in, Jalūlā', and Nihāwand.[421] He chose for himself a piece of land in al-Kūfah when the Muslims founded the garrison, built a house (*dār*) among [the other members of] the Kindah, and lived there until his death.

Al-Ash'ath was present at the Arbitration (*taḥkīm al-ḥakamayn*).[422] 'Alī wanted to appoint 'Abdallāh b. al-'Abbās as arbiter to confront 'Amr b. al-'Āṣ,[423] but al- Ash'ath b. Qays refused [to accept this], saying: "This case should not be judged by two Muḍarīs! One of the arbitrators must be a Yemenī."[424] So 'Alī appointed Abū Mūsā al-Ash'arī, and al-Ash'ath was one of the witnesses to the document [of arbitration].

Al-Ash'ath's brother Sayf b. Qays.[425]

---

419. On the apostasy of the Kindah after the Prophet's death and al-Ash'ath's leading role, see Ibn Ḥubaysh, 131–41; al-Kalā'ī, 222–42; Lecker, "Kinda"; Lecker, "Judaism."

420. The former apostates were not allowed to take part in the conquests until a shortage of manpower was felt, during Umar's caliphate; see Landau-Tasseron, "F. McG. Donner," 506–8. In addition, the Muslims were reluctant to raid Iraq, where they had suffered setbacks in the beginning; see al-Balādhurī, *Futūḥ* (Beirut), 252–53.

421. Al-Madā'in (Ctesiphon) in Iraq, Jalūlā' and Nihāwand in Persia were Sasānian cities and sites of battles during the Muslim conquests. See Donner, *Early Islamic Conquests*, 209–10; al-Ṭabarī, *Ta'rīkh*, I, 2431–44, 2457–74, 2596–2637; al-Balādhurī, *Futūh*, 262–65, 302–7.

422. The battle of Ṣiffīn between 'Alī and Mu'āwiyah (37/657) ended with an agreement to arbitration; see Hinds, "Ṣiffīn Agreement."

423. 'Amr, Mu'āwiyah's appointee, was known as an exceptionally shrewd person (*dāhiyah*).

424. The Muḍar (the "northern" tribes) and the Yemen (the "southern" tribes) were in fact the two rival factions that dominated the political life of the Umayyad period. It should be noted that in the tribal context the designations "southerners" and "northerners" are not geographical but genealogical terms. The names Qays and Kalb are also used to denote these factions. See Crone, *Slaves*; Landau-Tasseron, "Waning of the Umayyads."

425. Ibn al-Kalbī, *Nasab ma'add*, 141; Ibn Ḥajar, *Iṣābah*, II, 104.

He went with al-Ash'ath b. Qays to see the Prophet. The latter told him to act as the [clan's] muezzin, and so he did until his death.

Their brother Ibrāhīm b. Qays.[426]
He went to see the Prophet together with al-Ash'ath and embraced Islam.

Al-Ḥārith b. Sa'īd b. Qays b. al-Ḥārith b. Shaybān b. al-'Ātik b. Mu'āwiyah al-Akramīn.[427]
He went to see the Prophet.

Amānāh b. Qays b. al-Ḥārith b. Shaybān b. al-'Ātik b. Mu'āwiyah al-Akramīn.[428]
He went to see the Prophet and embraced Islam. He lived a long life, and the poet 'Ūḍah b. Badā said about him:[429]

I wish to live long, O Umm Khālid,
just as Amānāh b. Qays b. Shaybān did. [2364]
He lived so long "he is not a mortal" people would say;
many an old man and youth he saw pass away.
After a [long] period of time
a great calamity befell him like Naṣr b. Duhmān.[430]
As if among the living not an hour did he linger,
[now] he is placed in the grave's custody, shrouded in linen.

Amānāh's son Yazīd b. Amānāh joined [his father] in his visit [to the Prophet]. He embraced Islam and later apostatized and was killed as an apostate in the battle of Nujayr.[431] This was reported by Hishām b. Muḥammad [al-Kalbī].[432]

---

426. Ibn Ḥajar, *Iṣābah*, I, 15.
427. The clan's name is Shaybān; it was of the Kindah tribe; see Ibn al-Kalbī, *Nasab ma'add*, 159; Ibn Ḥajar, *Iṣābah*, 279.
428. Uncle of the aforementioned al-Ḥārith.
429. Ibn al-Kalbī, *Nasab ma'add*, 160; Ibn Ḥajar, *Iṣābah*, I, 62–63. The poet belonged to the Nakha'.
430. A folkloric figure connected with several stories and proverbs. According to one of them, he lived a very long time and, after having aged, was again rejuvenated. See al-Zamakhsharī, I, 254–55.
431. Al-Nujayr was a fortress of the Kindah in Ḥaḍramawt where the Kindī apostates were besieged and defeated by the Muslims. See note 419, above.
432. Ibn al-Kalbī, *Nasab ma'add*, 160.

Ma'dān b. al-Aswad b. 'Abdallāh b. al-Ḥārith al-Wallādah b. 'Amr b. Mu'āwiyah b. al-Ḥārith al-Akbar (senior).[433]

Ma'dān was nicknamed al-Jafshīsh.[434]

He came to see the Prophet together with al-Ash'ath b. Qays. He is the one who said to the Prophet "O Messenger of God, are you not one of us?" The Prophet remained silent. [This was repeated] twice, and the third time the Prophet said: "We do not trace our pedigree through the female line, and we shall not disown our male ancestors. We are the descendants of al-Naḍr b. Kinānah."[435] Al-Ash'ath said [to Ma'dān] "May God break your teeth; why did you not keep quiet?"

According to the tradition of Kindah, al-Jafshīsh was the one who said:

We obeyed the Messenger of God, for he spoke the truth,
 but, [I] wonder, what is the kingship of Abū Bakr to us?
Will he, when he dies, beqeath it to a young camel?
 this by God is a backbreaking [upheaval].[436]

[2365] This was reported by Hishām b. Muḥammad [al-Kalbī],[437] but Muḥammad b. 'Umar [al-Wāqidī] held that these two verses were composed by Ḥārithah b. Surāqah b. Ma'dī Karib al-Kindī, who

433. The clan is Banū al-Ḥārith al-Wallādah of the Kindah. 'Abdallāh's original name was Shayṭān, "devil," changed by the Prophet, see p. 53, above; Ibn al-Kalbī, *Nasab ma'add*, 172.

434. Opinions differ as to the identity of al-Jafshīsh. I could not, however, find an explanation of the nickname. See Ibn Ḥajar, *Iṣābah*, I, 240–41. My search in the direction of south Arabian yielded no results either. See also Lecker, "Kinda."

435. Several tribal groups attempted to establish their kinship with the Quraysh, the ruling tribe, either through the Prophet himself or otherwise. See E. Landau-Tasseron, "Asad," 13; idem, "Murra."

436. These verses are variously attributed to several poets. They reflect the reluctance of many Arab tribes to submit to the hegemony of Medina after the Prophet's death, in the so-called apostasy period. See p. 82, above. For these verses, see al-Ḥuṭay'ah, 329–30; al-Ṭabarī, *Ta'rīkh*, I, 1875–76; Ibn 'Asākir, *Tahdhīb*, VII, 96; Ibn Ḥubaysh, 15, 133; al-Kalā'ī, 37, 227; Yāqūt, *Mu'jam al-buldān*, II, 286–87 (s.v. "Ḥaḍramawt"); Ibn A'tham, I, 49; see also Kister, "*Illā bi-ḥaqqihi*'," 35. The second verse mockingly refers to the *kunyah* "Abū Bakr," literally, "father of the young camel"; c.f. al-Ṭabarī, *Ta'rīkh*, I, 1890. See also Muḥammad Ibn Ḥabīb, *Muḥabbar*, 185, where a Kindī woman by the name of Umm Ma'dān is listed among those who rejoiced in the Prophet's death, together with Malkah, daughter of Amānāh.

437. Ibn al-Kalbī, *Nasab ma'add*, 173. The composer of the verses, however, is here Abū Hunayy Masrūq b. Ma'dī Karib.

withheld the legal alms from [the tax collector] Ziyād b. Labīd and joined those who apostatized.[438]

Qays b. al-Makshūḥ—whose [real] name was Hubayrah—b. ʿAbd Yāghūth b. al-Ghuzayyil b. Salamah b. Bidā b. ʿĀmir b. ʿAwbathān b. Zāhir b. Murād.[439]

Qays's father, Hubayrah, was nicknamed al-Makshūḥ because he had a complaint in his flank resulting from a fire (*kushiḥa bi-al-nār*); that is, he had a burn on his flank (*kashḥ*). He had been a leader of the Murād, and [so was] his son Qays.

[Qays] was the [best] horseman of the Madhḥij tribe. It was reported that he was the one who had pierced the head of [al-Aswad] al-ʿAnsī. The [tribal confederation of] Muḍar used to call him Qays Ghudar (treacherous), to which he would reply "I am not treacherous, but I inflict death on Muḍar."[440]

According to Muḥammad b. ʿUmar [al-Wāqidī]—ʿAbdallāh b. ʿAmr b. Zuhayr—Muḥammad b. ʿUmārah b. Khuzaymah b. Thābit: When ʿAmr b. Maʿdī Karib heard about the Prophet he said to Qays b. al-Makshūḥ al-Murādī: "O Qays, you are the leader of your tribe at present. We have heard that a man of the Quraysh, by the name of Muḥammad, has arisen in the Ḥijāz, claiming to be a prophet. Let us go to him and learn the truth about him. If he is a prophet, as he claims, the matter will be clear to us when we meet him; [in that case] we should follow him. If he is not [a prophet], we will learn the truth about him. If someone else from your tribe precedes us to him, [that man] will assume leadership and rule us, and we will be his subordinates."[441] Qays refused [the suggestion]

---

438. See Ibn Ḥubaysh, 133; al-Kalāʿī, 226–28.

439. There are two people by that name, see Ibn al-Kalbī *Nasab maʿadd*, 335, 351. The one discussed here, famous for his part in killing the false Yemeni prophet al-Aswad, belonged to the Banū Zāhir of the tribe of Murād. See Ibn al-Kalbī, *Nasad maʿadd*, 335; Khalīfah b. Khayyāṭ, *Taʾrīkh*, 84, 102; Ibn Saʿd, V, 383. For the Murād, a part of Madhhij that dwelt in the Yemen east of Najrān, see Ibn Ḥazm, *Jamharat*, 406–7; "Murād," *EI²*, VII, 591–92 (G. Levi Della Vida).

440. Ibn al-Kalbī, *Nasad maʿadd*, 335. This exchange reflects the enmity between the "northern" and "southern" confederations. See note 424. Qays's reply rhymes in Arabic.

441. This statement presupposes a ruling status for the Prophet. Rise to leadership of a clan could depend on a person's connections with rulers of states outside the clan (such as al-Ḥīrah and Ghassān in pre-Islamic times, the Prophet and the caliphs in Islamic times).

and said that the idea was foolish. ʿAmr b. Maʿdī Karib rode to Medina leading ten of his fellow tribesmen, embraced Islam, and returned to his [tribe's] territory.[442]

[2366] Ṣafwān b. ʿAssāl, of the Banū al-Rabaḍ b. Zāhir b. ʿĀmir b. ʿAwbathān b. Zāhir b. Murād.[443]

As a pension recipient he counted as one of the Jamal.[444]

He embraced Islam and was a Companion of the Prophet.

ʿAmr b. al-Ḥamiq b. al-Kāhin b. Ḥabīb b. ʿAmr b. al-Qayn b. Razāḥ b. ʿAmr b. Saʿd b. ʿAmr b. Kaʿb b. ʿAmr.[445]

He gave the oath of allegiance to the Prophet during the Farewell Pilgrimage and ranked among the Companions after that.

ʿAmr was among those who took part in the assault on ʿUthmān b. ʿAffān.[446] He later participated with ʿAlī b. Abī Ṭālib in the battles led by him. He was killed in the Jazīrah by Ibn Umm al-Ḥakam.[447]

According to Ibn ʿUmar [al-Wāqidī]—ʿĪsā b. ʿAbd al-Raḥmān—[ʿĀmir b. Sharāḥīl] al-Shaʿbī: The first head to have been carried [to the ruler] in Islamic times was the head of ʿAmr b. al-Ḥamiq.[448]

Kurz b. ʿAlqamah b. Hilāl b. Juraybah b. ʿAbd-Nuhm b. Ḥulayl b. Ḥubshiyyah b. Salūl b. Kaʿb b. ʿAmr b. Ḥārithah b. ʿAmr Muzay-

---

442. See al-Ṭabarī, *Taʾrīkh*, I, 1732–34, for a similar version. The chain of authorities is different.

443. Ibn Ḥibbān, *Mashāhīr*, 80; Khalīfah b. Khayyāṭ, *Ṭabaqāt*, 74–75, 134; Ibn al-Kalbī, *Nasab maʿadd*, 335.

444. A clan of the Murād; see Ibn Ḥazm, *Jamharat*, 476–77. The tribal leaders received the pensions (*ʿaṭāʾ*) on behalf of their people and were responsible for distributing them individually. Sometimes people were listed with clans other than their own for the purpose of receiving pensions.

445. Of the Khuzāʿah confederation. See Ibn Ḥibbān, *Mashāhīr*, 94; Khalīfah b. Khayyāṭ, *Ṭabaqāt*, 107, 136; idem, *Taʾrīkh*, 176, 197; al-Balādhurī, *Ansāb*, IVa, 236–37; Muḥammad Ibn Ḥabīb, *Muḥabbar*, 292, 490; Naṣr b. Muzāḥim, passim.

446. The reference is to the murder of the third caliph, ʿUthmān, in the year 35/656, see Kennedy, 69–75.

447. He was killed in retaliation for the murder of ʿUthmān. Ibn Umm al-Ḥakam, ʿAbd al-Raḥmān b. ʿAbdallāh b. ʿUthmān al-Thaqafī, was Muʿāwiyah's governor of Mosul; see al-Ṭabarī, *Taʾrīkh*, II, 127–28.

448. Cf. Muḥammad Ibn Ḥabīb, *Muḥabbar*, 292; al-Suyūṭī, *Wasāʾil*, 81; Ibn Qutaybah, *Awāʾil*, 41.

qiyā' b. 'Āmir Mā' al-Samā' b. Ḥārithah al-Ghiṭrīf b. Imri' al-Qays b. Tha'labah b. Māzin b. al-Azd b. al-Ghawth b. Nabt b. Mālik b. Zayd b. Kahlān b. Saba' b. Yashjub b. Ya'rub b. Qaḥṭān.[449]

Kurz embraced Islam on the day of the conquest of Mecca. He lived a long life. [Once] one of the signs marking the [boundaries of] the sacred territory in Mecca (*a'lām al-ḥaram*) could not be found. Marwān b. al-Ḥakam wrote to Mu'āwiyah about it, and he wrote [back] "If Kurz b. 'Alqamah is still alive, ask him to lead you to it." [Marwān] did this, so Kurz is the one who set the boundaries of the sacred territory in Mu'āwiyah's time; they are in the same position even now.[450]

Al-Ḥaysumān b. Iyās b. 'Abdallāh b. Ḍubay'ah b. 'Amr b. Māzin b. 'Adī b. 'Amr.[451] [2367]

He had a leading position within his clan. He embraced Islam and was a good Muslim (*ḥasuna islāmuhu*).[452]

Mikhnaf b. Sulaym b. al-Ḥārith b. 'Awf b. Tha'labah b. 'Āmir b. Dhuhl b. Māzin b. Dhubyān b. Tha'labah b. al-Dūl b. Sa'd Manāh b. Ghāmid b. 'Abdallāh b. Ka'b b. al-Ḥārith b. Ka'b b. 'Abdallāh b. Mālik b. Naṣr b. al-Azd.[453]

Mikhnaf embraced Islam and ranked among the Companions. His family was the leading one among the Azd in al-Kūfah. He had three brothers: 'Abd Shams, who was killed in the battle of

---

449. The clan's name is Banū 'Abd Nuhm, it was of the Khuzā'ah confederation. See Ibn Ḥazm, *Jamharat*, 236; Ibn al-Kalbī, *Nasab ma'add*, 444. Kurz was the one who went after the Prophet when the latter emigrated but miraculously lost track of him; see Ibn Ḥajar, *Iṣābah*, III, 291.

450. Ibn Ḥazm, *Jamharat*, 236, and see p. 42, above. Marwān was Mu'āwiyah's governor in Mecca.

451. The clan was the Banū 'Adī of the Khuzā'ah confederation; see Ibn Ḥazm, *Jamharat*, 239. Al-Ḥaysumān is known as the one who brought the Quraysh the bad news of their defeat at Badr; see also al-Balādhurī, *Ansāb*, I, 294; Ibn Ḥajar, *Iṣābah*, I, 366, quoting, among others, al-Ṭabarī (*Ta'rīkh*, I, 1338); Ibn al-Kalbī, *Nasab ma'add*, 454.

452. This phrase usually denotes people whose sincerity was doubtful, e.g., people who had apostatized then embraced Islam again.

453. The clan was the Banū Tha'labah b. 'Āmir of the Azd, one of the most important southern tribal confederations in Umayyad times. Mikhnaf was one of the main leaders. He served 'Alī as governor of Iṣfahān and as a general in the battle of Ṣiffīn. See Ibn al-Kalbī, *Nasab ma'add*, 482; Ibn Ḥazm, *Jamharat*, 377; Khalīfah b. Khayyāṭ, *Ṭabaqāt*, 113; Naṣr b. Muzāḥim, 104–5, and passim; also "Azd," *EI*^{2}, I, 811–13 (G. Strenziok).

Nukhaylah; al-Ṣaqʿab, who was killed in the battle of the Camel; and ʿAbdallāh, who was [also] killed in the battle of the Camel.[454]

Among the descendants of Mikhnaf b. Sulaym was Abū Mikhnaf Lūṭ b. Yaḥyā b. Saʿīd b. Mikhnaf b. Sulaym.[455] Accounts of people's battles (*ayyām al-nās*) are transmitted from him.

Fayrūz b. al-Daylamī.[456]

His *kunyah* was Abū ʿAbdallāh. He belonged to the descendants (*abnāʾ*) of the Persians who had been sent by Khusraw to the Yemen, conquered it, and drove out the Abyssinians.[457]

According to ʿAbd al-Munʿim: They later traced their pedigree to the Banū Ḍabbah,[458] saying "We had been taken prisoner in pre-Islamic times."[459] ʿAbd al-Munʿim was mistaken in what he said, for [the story] was like this: Ḍabbah b. Udd had three sons. One of them assaulted another descendant of Ḍabbah and killed him. His father wanted to kill him [in retaliation], so he ran away and set-
[2368] tled in the Daylam mountains,[460] where he fathered several children. His descendants claim even today that they have in their possession his saddle and utensils.

Fayrūz is the one who killed al-ʿAnsī, that is, al-Aswad b. Kaʿb al-Kadhdhāb (the liar), who claimed to be a prophet in the Yemen. The Prophet said "He was killed by the virtuous man Fayrūz b. al-Daylamī."

---

454. Cf. Khalīfah b. Khayyāṭ, *Taʾrīkh*, 172.

455. "Abū Mikhnaf," *EI*², I, 140 (H. A. R. Gibb); Duri, *Rise of Historical Writing*, 43–44; Muṣṭafā, I, 178–79; U. Sezgin, *Abū Miḫnaf*.

456. Khalīfah b. Khayyāṭ, *Ṭabaqāt*, 7; idem, *Taʾrīkh*, 84; Ibn Ḥajar, *Iṣābah*, III, 210; Ibn Saʿd, V, 389.

457. The reference is to the Persian intervention in the Yemen under Khusraw Anūshirwān (531–79), see "Abnāʾ," *EI*², I, 102 (K. V. Zettersteén); al-Ṭabarī, *Taʾrīkh*, I, 901–66.

458. Ḍabbah b. Udd, of the northern Muḍar confederation. See "Ḍabba," *EI*², II, 71–72 (W. Caskel); Ibn Ḥazm, *Jamharat*, 203. Genealogists mention that "the [Persian people] Daylam are said to be descendants of Bāsil b. Ḍabbah," without further explanation. See Ibn Ḥazm, loc. cit.; al-Wazīr, 135.

459. Change (or forgery) of genealogy was common, often accomplished by manipulating the history of a female ancestor, e.g., claiming that she had remarried and brought along her son from the previous marriage, so that he (and his descendants) were erroneously traced to the stepfather; here the argument is that a male ancestor from the Ḍabbah had been captured and remained among the Abnāʾ so that his descendants were thought to belong to that group.

460. In the highlands of Gīlān; see "Daylam," *EI*², 189–90 (Minorsky).

Fayrūz went to see the Prophet and transmitted [traditions] from him. Some people transmitted [traditions] from Fayrūz, saying "I was told by al-Daylamī al-Ḥimyarī," whereas others say "On the authority of al-Daylamī," which is the same thing; it is Fayrūz al-Daylamī. He was called al-Ḥimyarī only because he lived among the Ḥimyar and was their ally.

Fayrūz died during the caliphate of 'Uthmān.

The Names of Those Companions Who Outlived the Prophet and Transmitted Traditions and Knowledge[461]

The names of those who lived after the Prophet from the Banū 'Abd al-Muṭṭalib b. Hāshim b. 'Abd Manāf.[462]

Al-'Abbās b. 'Abd al-Muṭṭalib, the paternal uncle of the Prophet, and his sons al-Faḍl, 'Abdallāh, and 'Ubaydallāh. All of them lived during the time of the Prophet and transmitted [traditions] from him, and knowledge was transmitted from them.

The oldest among al-'Abbās' children whom I have mentioned was al-Faḍl, after whom al-'Abbās was called [Abū al-Faḍl].[463] He was the first of them to die. He died before his father, in Syria, in the plague of 'Amwās.[464]

'Abdallāh [b. al-'Abbās] was the one who broadened the people's knowledge. He was given a long life and lived until the days of the war between Ibn al-Zubayr and 'Abd al-Malik b. Marwān.[465] I have already mentioned his death date and other details about him.

'Ubaydallāh was the youngest of al-'Abbās' three sons; 'Abdallāh was a year older than he. 'Ubaydallāh died before 'Abdallāh,

---

461. In fact, the next chapters (up to p. 119) deal with members, allies, and clients of Qurashī clans: the Banū Hāshim, al-Muṭṭalib, Nawfal, Asad, 'Abd al-Dār, Zuhrah, Taym b. Murrah, Makhzūm, 'Adī b. Ka'b, Jumaḥ and 'Āmir b. Lu'ayy.

462. That is, the Prophet's clan.

463. Ibn Ḥibbān, *Mashāhīr*, 28; al-Balādhurī, *Ansāb*, III (Dūrī), 23–26; Khalīfah b. Khayyāṭ, *Ta'rīkh*, 87–88; idem, *Ṭabaqāt*, 4.

464. 'Amwās, ancient Emmaus in Palestine, was the site of a Muslim military camp during the conquests. Many fell victim there to the plague of the year 18/639. See "'Amwās," *EI²*, I, 460–61 (Sourdel-Thomine); Conrad, "Plague," chap. 5.

465. That is, the second civil war, see pp. 51–52, above.

during the time of Yazīd b. Mu'āwiyah, whereas 'Abdallāh's death occurred two years later.

The mother of al-Faḍl, 'Abdallāh, 'Ubaydallāh, and Qutham was
[2369] the same [woman], that is, Umm al-Faḍl Lubābah al-Kubrā (senior) bt. al-Ḥārith b. Ḥazn, of the Banū Hilāl b. 'Āmir.

In addition to these, others among al-'Abbās' children transmitted knowledge and traditions, such as Kathīr, Tammām, and Ma'bad. None of them, however, is known really to have heard [traditions directly] from the Prophet, except those whom I mentioned.

'Alī and 'Aqīl, sons of Abū Ṭālib b. 'Abd al-Muṭṭalib; al-Ḥasan and al-Ḥusayn, sons of 'Alī b. Abī Ṭālib; and 'Abdallāh b. Ja'far b. Abī Ṭālib. All of them outlived the Prophet and transmitted knowledge and traditions. I have already mentioned their death dates and the periods of their lives.

Al-Ḥārith b. Nawfal b. al-Ḥārith b. 'Abd al-Muṭṭalib b. Hāshim b. 'Abd Manāf.

Among his offspring was 'Abdallāh b. al-Ḥārith b. Nawfal, who was accepted [as leader] by the people of al-Baṣrah during the time of [the strife between] the Zubayrī and the Marwanī factions.[466] His nickname was Babbah.

[Al-Ḥārith] lived during the Prophet's time and transmitted [traditions] from him.

Some traditions transmitted by al-Ḥārith from the Prophet: According to 'Alī b. Sahl al-Ramlī—Mu'ammil b. Ismā'īl—Sufyān—'Āṣim b. 'Ubaydallāh—'Ubaydallāh b. 'Abdallāh b. 'Utbah—'Abdallāh b. al-Ḥārith b. Nawfal—his father: Whenever the Prophet heard the muezzin call "I testify that there is no God but Allāh; I testify that Muḥammad is the Messenger of Allāh" he would say "[It is] as he says." When the muezzin called "Come to prayer" the Prophet would say "There is neither might nor power

466. The reference is to the second civil war (*fitnah*). In the confusion after the death of Yazīd b. Mu'āwiyah (64/683) people in the provinces ousted their official governors and chose others in their place. See al-Balādhurī, *Ansāb*, V, 132, 188 (read *bi-babbah* instead of *baynahu*), 190, 273; Ibn Ḥazm, *Jamharat*, 70; Ibn Ḥibbān, *Mashāhīr*, 115.

but in God." And when the muezzin reached the [line] "Come and be saved" the Prophet would say "There is neither might nor power but in God."[467]

According to Hilāl b. al-ʿAlāʾ al-Raqqī—Ḥafṣ b. ʿUmar Abū ʿUmar al-Ḥawḍī—Hammām—Layth—ʿAlqamah b. Marthad—ʿAbdallāh b. al-Ḥārith—his father: The Prophet taught us how to say the prayer over the dead: "O God, forgive our living and our dead; make peace between us and bring our hearts together. O God, this is your servant so-and-so son of so-and-so; we know nothing but good [about him], [but] You know him better. Forgive us, and forgive him." I was the youngest among the people [present], and I asked: "What if I do not know good things [about him]?" The Prophet replied: "Say only what you know." [2370]

ʿAbd al-Muṭṭalib b. Rabīʿah b. al-Ḥārith b. ʿAbd al-Muṭṭalib b. Hāshim b. ʿAbd Manāf.

According to the biographers, he was [already] a mature man in the Prophet's lifetime. He transmitted from him a few traditions, among them the following. According to Abū Kurayb [Muḥammad b. al-ʿAlāʾ]—[Muḥammad] Ibn Fuḍayl—Yazīd b. Abī Ziyād—ʿAbdallāh b. al-Ḥārith—ʿAbd al-Muṭṭalib b. Rabīʿah b. al-Ḥārith b. ʿAbd al-Muṭṭalib: I was with the Prophet when al-ʿAbbās came in to see him. Al-ʿAbbās was angry, and the Prophet asked him "What is it that made you angry?" Al-ʿAbbās said: "O Messenger of God, what is it between us and the Quraysh? When they meet one another they do so with cheerful countenance, and when they meet us it is otherwise." The Prophet flew into a rage until his face reddened and the vein between his eyes was filled with blood; whenever he became angry [this vein] would be filled with blood. When he relaxed he said "[I swear] by He who holds Muḥammad's soul in His hand, belief does not enter a man's heart until he loves you for the sake of God and His messenger." Then he said "O people, whoever harasses al-ʿAbbās, it is as if he harassed me; indeed, one's paternal uncle is like one's father."[468]

---

467. See "Adhān," *EI*², I, 187–88 (T. W. Juynboll).

468. *ʿAmm al-rajul ṣinw abīhi. Ṣinw* means "growing from one root, a brother," but the sentence conveys more than the undeniable fact that "one's uncle is the brother of one's father." The idea that one's paternal uncle is like a father to one

Rabīʿah b. al-Ḥārith b. ʿAbd al-Muṭṭalib b. Hāshim.

His *kunyah* was Abū Arwā.

[2371] Rabīʿah is the one about whom the Prophet said, on the day Mecca was conquered "I say, every [open case of] blood revenge and every privilege from pre-Islamic times are hereby rendered null and void, and the first case of blood revenge that I thus declare annulled is that of Rabīʿah b. al-Ḥārith."[469] The reason for this was that a son of Rabīʿah was killed in pre-Islamic times, and the [right and obligation] to avenge his blood was canceled by Islam. The Prophet did not enable Rabīʿah to pursue the vendetta against the assassin of his son.

Rabīʿah outlived the Prophet until ʿUmar's caliphate and transmitted [traditions] from him. It was reported that he was two years older than his paternal uncle al-ʿAbbās b. ʿAbd al-Muṭṭalib.

A tradition traced back to him: According to Muḥammad b. Ḥumayd—Jarīr [b. ʿAbd al-Ḥamīd]—ʿAṭāʾ [b. al-Sāʾib]—ʿAbdallāh b. Rabīʿah—his father—a man of the Quraysh: I saw the Prophet in pre-Islamic times standing at [the place of assembly at] ʿArafāt with the idolators; then I saw him in Islamic times standing at the same place,[470] so I knew that it was God who made him stand like this.[471]

*The Clients (*Mawālī*) of the Banū Hāshim*

Those who outlived the Prophet, transmitted [traditions] from him, and from whom knowledge was transmitted.

Salmān al-Fārisī.

His *kunyah* was Abū ʿAbdallāh.

According to al-Ḥārith b. Muḥammad—Ibn Saʿd[472]—Ismāʿīl b. ʿAbdallāh b. Zurārah al-Jarmī—Jaʿfar b. Sulaymān—Hishām b.

---

figures in other prophetic traditions as well and served the propaganda of the ʿAbbāsid dynasty against the Shīʿah; see Goldziher, *Muslim Studies*, II, 100, 102, 107. The point that the people should love al-ʿAbbās also reflects the specific struggle against the Shīʿah, for whom the love of ʿAlī and his family was a central feature of the creed.

469. See p. 61, above.

470. Or "in the same way."

471. See "ʿArafa," *EI²*, I, 604–5 (A. J. Wensinck, and H. A. R. Gibb).

472. Ibn Saʿd, IV/1, 62.

Ḥassān—al-Ḥasan: Salmān's pension was 5,000 [dirhams], and he was appointed over 30,000 people. He used to gather firewood clad in a cloak, half of which he used for covering himself; the other half he spread. Each time his pension was due he did not take it but lived off his own handwoven palm leaves.

According to Ismā'īl b. Mūsā al-Suddī—Sharīk—Abū Rabī'ah al-Iyādī—Ibn Buraydah—his father: The Prophet said "God has ordered me to love four [people]." The Prophet was asked: "Who [2372]
are they? Tell us their names." He said "'Alī is one of them"—he said that three times—" and Abū Dharr and al-Miqdād [b. al-Aswad] and Salmān. God has ordered me to love them and told me that He loves them."

Salmān died in al-Madā'in during 'Uthmān's caliphate.

Abū Rāfi', the Prophet's client.

His name was Aslam.

Abū Rāfi' had been a slave of al-'Abbās b. 'Abd al-Muṭṭalib, who gave him [as a present] to the Prophet. The latter freed him and gave him his client Salmā in marriage. She bore Abū Rāfi' his son 'Ubaydallāh b. Abī Rāfi'.

Usāmah b. Zayd al-Ḥibb (the beloved) b. Ḥārithah.

His *kunyah* was Abū Muḥammad.

His mother was Umm Ayman, the Prophet's client and nurse.

It was reported that Usāmah was twenty years old when the Prophet died. After the Prophet's death he settled in Wādī al-Qurā but returned later to Medina and died in al-Jurf at the end of Mu'āwiyah's caliphate.

Thawbān, the Prophet's client.[473]

His *kunyah* was Abū 'Abdallāh.

Thawbān was one of those whom the Prophet favored by granting them freedom. He remained with the Prophet until the latter's

473. Thawbān b. Yuḥdad, of Yemenī origin. See Khalīfah b. Khayyāṭ, *Ta'rīkh*, 211; idem, *Ṭabaqāt*, 7; Ibn Ḥibbān, *Mashāhīr*, 85; Ibn Manẓūr, *Mukhtaṣar*, V, 346–49.

death, whereupon he moved to Syria and settled in Ḥimṣ. He had a house (*dār*) there [that he gave away as] charity (*ṣadaqah*).[474]

It was reported that Thawbān belonged to the clan called Ḥakam b. Sa'd al-'Ashīrah.[475]

Ḍumayrah b. Abī Ḍumayrah.[476]

He transmitted from the Prophet the following [tradition]. According to Yūnus b. 'Abd al-A'lā—['Abdallāh] Ibn Wahb—Ibn Abī Dhi'b [al-'Āmirī]—Ḥusayn b. 'Abdallāh b. Ḍumayrah—his father—his grandfather Ḍumayrah: The Prophet passed by Umm Ḍumayrah, who was weeping. He asked her: "Why are you weeping? Are you hungry or cold?[477] She answered "O Messenger of God, I was separated from my son." The Prophet said "A child
[2373] should not be separated from its mother." The Prophet then sent to the man who owned Ḍumayrah, asking him to come [and see him], and bought Ḍumayrah from him for a young camel.

Zayd Abū Yasār, the Prophet's client.[478]

He transmitted from the Prophet the following [tradition]. According to Mūsā b. Ismā'īl—Ḥafṣ b. 'Umar al-Shannī—his father 'Umar b. Murrah—Bilāl b. Yasār b. Zayd, the Prophet's client—his father—his grandfather: The Prophet said: "Whoever says 'I ask forgiveness of God, beside Whom there is no god, the Ever-Living, the Self-Existing. To Him I come back' he will be forgiven even if he runs away from an army while it is on the move."

*The Allies (*Ḥulafā'*) of the Banū Hāshim*

Abū Marthad al-Ghanawī.[479]

---

474. *Ṣadaqah* means charity, legal alms, and also property the fruits of which are given away by the owner for charity or other good purposes. For the latter sense, the term *waqf* is more common.

475. A southern clan; see Ibn al-Kalbī, *Nasab ma'add*, 300–2; Ibn Ḥazm, *Jamharat*, 407–9.

476. Counted among the Companions, with no details. Ibn Ḥajar, *Iṣābah*, II, 214.

477. Literally, "naked."

478. Zayd b. Būlā, a black slave freed by the Prophet, see Ibn Ḥajar, *Iṣābah*, I, 561.

479. Kannāz b. al-Ḥuṣayn b. Yarbū'. See Khalīfah b. Khayyāṭ, *Ṭabaqāt*, 8, 47; Ibn

According to Muḥammad b. Bashshār—'Abd al-Raḥmān [b. Mahdī]—'Abdallāh b. al-Mubārak—'Abd al-Raḥmān b. Yazīd—Busr b. 'Ubaydallāh—Abū Idrīs—Wāthilah b. al-Aṣqa'—Abū Marthad al-Ghanawī—the Prophet: Do not sit on graves, and do not pray toward them.[480]

His son Marthad b. Abī Marthad.[481]

He was killed in the battle of al-Rajī'.[482]

According to Sulaymān b. 'Abd al-Jabbār—Ismā'īl b. Abān—Yaḥyā b. Ya'lā al-Aslamī, who was trustworthy—'Alī b. Mūsā—al-Qāsim [Abū 'Abd al-Raḥmān al-Shāmī]—Marthad b. Abī Marthad al-Ghanawī, who was one of the participants in [the battle of] Badr—the Prophet: If you want your prayer to be accepted, let the best among you act as imām and lead the prayer, for they are your deputation [which mediates] between you and your Lord.

His grandson Unays b. Marthad b. Abī Marthad al-Ghanawī.[483] [2374]

His *kunyah* was Abū Yazīd.

The age difference between him and his father was twenty-one years.

Unays participated on the Prophet's side in the conquest of Mecca and the battle of Ḥunayn. He was the Prophet's spy in the battle of Awṭās.[484]

Abū Marthad was an ally (*ḥalīf*) of Ḥamzah b. 'Abd al-Muṭṭalib.[485]

According to Zakariyā' b. Yaḥyā b. Abān al-Miṣrī—Abū Ṣāliḥ, al-Layth's scribe—al-Layth b. Sa'd—Yaḥyā b. Sa'īd—Khālid b. Abī

Ḥibbān, *Mashāhīr*, 39. The Ghanī belonged to the northern Qays confederation. See Caskel, II, 21–22; Ibn Ḥazm, *Jamharat*, 247–48; Ibn al-Kalbī, *Jamharat*, 463–70.

480. This tradition must be part of the religious debate over the veneration of the dead. See Goldziher, *Muslim Studies*, I, 209–38.

481. Khalīfah b. Khayyāṭ, *Ṭabaqāt*, 8.

482. An event in which six deputies of the Prophet, sent to teach Islam to some bedouin clans on their request, were murdered (3/625). See Ibn Ḥishām, III, 178–85; al-Wāqidī, 354–63; Guillaume, 426–29.

483. Ibn Ḥibbān, *Mashāhīr*, 37–38.

484. Part of the events of Ḥunayn in the year 8/630. See Ibn Hishām, IV, 97; al-Wāqidī, 915.

485. So was his son Marthad. See Mu'arrij, 28–29; Ibn Ḥazm, *Jamharat*, 247; al-Balādhurī, *Ansāb*, I, 270.

'Imrān—al-Ḥakam b. Mas'ūd al-Najrānī—Unays b. Abī Marthad—the Prophet: "There will be a deaf and dumb internal struggle (*fitnah*), a deaf, dumb, and blind one.[486] Those who will lie down during this war will be better than those who will sit, those who will sit better than those who will stand, those who will stand better than those who will walk, those who will walk better than those who will run. Whoever comes [demanding the people's allegiance], let [those who are present] stretch their necks [in support]."[487] So I was told by Zakariyā' b. Yaḥyā, who said: Unays b. Abī Marthad al-Anṣārī. But [in fact] it is Unays b. Marthad b. Abī Marthad al-Ghanawī, of the clan of Ghanī b. Ya'ṣur b. Sa'd b. Qays b. 'Aylān b. Muḍar.

Those of the Banū al-Muṭṭalib b. 'Abd Manāf b. Quṣayy Who Transmitted [Traditions] from the Prophet

Among them was Rukānah b. 'Abd Yazīd b. Hāshim b. al-Muṭṭalib b. 'Abd Manāf b. Quṣayy.

He was among those who embraced Islam upon the conquest [of Mecca]. He outlived the Prophet and died at the beginning of Mu'āwiyah's caliphate.

Qays b. Makhramah b. al-Muṭṭalib b. 'Abd Manāf b. Quṣayy.

[2375] Jubayr b. Muṭ'im b. 'Adī b. Nawfal b. 'Abd Manāf.[488]

His *kunyah* was Abū Muḥammad or Abū 'Alī. He embraced Islam before the conquest [of Mecca] and settled in Medina, where he died during the caliphate of Mu'āwiyah.

---

486. That is, endless, or leading to the wrong course; see Lane s.v. *bkm*.

487. Cf. al-Ṭabarī, *Ta'rīkh*, I, 3153, where a similar saying is voiced by Abū Mūsā al-Ash'arī. "Stretching the neck" is a metaphor for lending support; cf. al-Balādhurī, *Ansāb*, I, 581. This and many other traditions in the same vein reflect the great fear and aversion Islam felt toward disunity and hence toward opposition to the government. In certain circles it was held that even the worst ruler was better than none at all. See Kister, "Social Concepts"; "Fitna," *EI*², II, 930–31 (L. Gardet); Lewis, *Islam in History*, chap. 6.

488. Of the Banū Nawfal, brother clan of Hāshim and al-Muṭalib; see al-Zubayrī, 197–205; Ibn Ḥibbān, *Mashāhīr*, 32; Khalīfah b. Khayyāṭ, *Ṭabaqāt*, 9; Ibn Qudāmah, 239–40.

Jubayr's father, Muṭʿim b. ʿAdī, was one of the notables of the Quraysh. He had granted the Prophet protection from the idolators, and when the battle of Badr occurred and people from the Quraysh were taken prisoner the Prophet said "If Muṭʿim b. ʿAdī had been alive I would have freed those foul-smelling [idolators][489] on his behalf."[490] [The Prophet said this] because [Muṭʿim] had done him a favor.[491]

Ḥassān b. Thābit said about [Muṭʿim b. ʿAdī]:[492]

If glory had had the power to grant a man immortality,
 Muṭʿim's glory would have saved him [from obscurity].
You protected the Prophet from them, and they as your slaves [obeyed]
 as long as the *talbiyah* was uttered and *iḥrām* observed.[493]

Jubayr transmitted many traditions from the Prophet.

ʿUqbah b. al-Ḥārith b. ʿĀmir b. Nawfal b. ʿAbd Manāf b. Quṣayy.[494]

He transmitted [traditions] from the Prophet.

According to [Muḥammad] Ibn Bashshār—ʿAbd al-Wahhāb [b. ʿAbd al-Majīd al-Thaqafī]—Ayyūb—ʿAbdallāh b. Abī Mulaykah—ʿUqbah b. al-Ḥārith: Al-Nuʿaymān, or Ibn al-Nuʿaymān, was brought [to the Prophet] after he had been drinking [alcohol]. The Prophet ordered the people present in the house to beat him, and I was among them. We beat him with shoes and palm branches.

---

489. Idolators are referred to as dirt and foul-smelling creatures; see Ibn Manẓūr, *Lisān*, XIII, 426–27.

490. Al-Zubayrī, 200; Ibn Qudāmah, 240; Ibn Hishām, II, 20. The usual practice, both in pre-Islamic and in the Prophet's times, was to free prisoners against a ransom, unless the captor granted them their freedom as a special favor to themselves or to someone who interceded on their behalf.

491. That is, by granting him protection on his return from al-Ṭaʾif. According to another version, Muṭʿim was the one who instigated the anulling of the Qurashī boycott of the Banū Hāshim; see Ibn Hishām, II, 15–16.

492. Ḥassān, *Dīwān*, I, 198–99; Ibn Hishām, II, 19–20.

493. Meaning "always." The *talbiyah* was the formula expressing devotion to the gods in pre-Islamic times. *Iḥrām* was the state of consecration observed by those who performed the pilgrimage to Mecca. Both rituals are also performed in Islam with the necessary modifications. See "Iḥram," *EI*², III, 1052–53 (A. J. Wensinck and J. Jomier); "Talbiya," *EI*¹, IV, 640 (A. J. Wensinck); Kister, "*Labbayka.*"

494. Ibn Ḥibbān, *Mashāhīr*, 64; Khalīfah b. Khayyāṭ, *Ṭabaqāt*, 9; al-Zubayrī, 204–5.

[2376] *The Allies of the Banū Nawfal b. ʿAbd Manāf b. Quṣayy*

ʿUtbah b. Ghazwān b. Jābir b. Uhayb b. Nusayb b. Zayd b. Mālik b. al-Ḥārith b. ʿAwf b. Māzin b. Manṣūr b. ʿIkrimah b. Khaṣafah b. Qays b. ʿAylān b. Muḍar.[495]

His *kunyah* was Abū ʿAbdallāh or Abū Ghazwān.

ʿUtbah was an early convert and was among those who emigrated to Abyssinia in the second emigration. He was the one who selected the site of al-Baṣrah, founded the garrison there, and built its [first] mosque.[496]

ʿUtbah transmitted [traditions] from the Prophet, among them the following. According to Muḥammad b. Bashshār—Ṣafwān b. ʿĪsā al-Zuhrī—ʿAmr b. ʿĪsā Abū Naʿāmah al-ʿAdawī—Khālid b. ʿUmayr and Shuways Abū al-Raqqād—ʿUtbah b. Ghazwān: I saw myself [in a situation where I was] one of seven [people] standing by the Prophet; we had no food but acacia leaves, until the flesh inside our mouths became ulcerated. Once I stumbled on a mantle and split it in two to share it with Saʿd.[497]

Among their allies was Yaʿlā b. Umayyah b. Ubayy b. ʿUbaydah b. Hammām b. al-Ḥārith b. Bakr b. Zayd b. Mālik b. Ḥanẓalah b. Mālik b. Zayd Manāh b. Tamīm.[498]

His mother was Munyah bt. Jābir b. Uhayb b. Nusayb b. Zayd b. Mālik b. al-Ḥārith b. ʿAwf b. Māzin b. Manṣūr, the paternal aunt of ʿUtbah b. Ghazwān.

---

495. The clan is the Banū Māzin b. Manṣūr, of the northern Qays confederation; see Ibn Ḥazm, *Jamharat*, 260; Ibn Ḥibbān, *Mashāhīr*, 66; Khalīfah b. Khayyāṭ, *Taʾrīkh*, 95–98; idem, *Ṭabaqāt*, 10; al-Balādhurī, *Ansāb*, I, 201; Ibn Saʿd, III/1, 69, VII/1, 1–3.

496. Cf. al-Ṭabarī, *Taʾrīkh*, I, 2377–88; see also Donner, "Tribal Settlement in Basra."

497. Cf. al-Ṭabarī, *Taʾrīkh*, I, 2380. A tradition much more important than this one is ascribed to ʿUtbah by al-Ṭabarānī, i.e., the *man kadhdhaba* tradition, in which the Prophet says "Whoever tells lies about me, let him seek for himself a place in hell"; see Ibn Ḥajar. *Iṣābah*, II, 455. On this tradition, see Juynboll, *Muslim Tradition*, 96–133.

498. The clan is the Banū al-ʿAdawiyyah of the great northern tribe of Tamīm. It is called after a female ancestor and includes the descendants of Zayd b. Mālik (Yaʿlā's ancestor) and those of two of his brothers; see Ibn Ḥazm, *Jamharat*, 228–29. On Yaʿlā, who served as governor and judge under the first three caliphs, then joined ʿAlī, see Khalīfah b. Khayyāṭ, *Taʾrīkh*, 91, 158; idem, *Ṭabaqāt*, 45; Ibn Ḥibbān, *Mashāhīr*, 58.

'Utbah and Ya'lā b. Umayyah were among the allies of al-Ḥārith b. Nawfal b. 'Abd Manāf b. Quṣayy. Ya'lā b. Umayyah, his father, [2377] Umayyah b. Ubayy, his brother Salamah b. Umayyah, and his sister Nafīsah bt. Munyah were converted to Islam. Ya'lā participated on the Prophet's side in [the battle of] Ḥunayn, [the siege of] al-Ṭā'if, and [the expedition to] Tabūk. He and his brother Salamah transmitted [traditions] from the Prophet.

The Names of the Companions Who Outlived the Prophet and from Whom Knowledge Was Transmitted, of the Banū Asad b. 'Abd al-'Uzzā b. Quṣayy b. Kilāb

Among them was al-Zubayr b. al-'Awwām b. Khuwaylid b. Asad b. 'Abd al-'Uzzā b. Quṣayy.

His mother was Ṣafiyyah bt. 'Abd al-Muṭṭalib b. Hāshim b. 'Abd Manāf, the paternal aunt of the Prophet.

His *kunyah* was Abū 'Abdallāh.

It was reported that al-Zubayr was the fourth or fifth convert. He emigrated to Abyssinia twice and did not fail to participate in all the Prophet's military activities.

The Prophet established the bond of brotherhood (*mu'ākhāh*) between al-Zubayr and 'Abdallāh b. Mas'ūd.

Al-Zubayr was killed in Wādī al-Sibā' on Thursday, 10 Jumādā II 36/December 5, 656, while returning to Medina from the battle of the Camel, and was buried there. He was then sixty-four years old.

Al-Zubayr transmitted many traditions from the Prophet.

His son 'Abdallāh b. al-Zubayr.[499]

His mother was Asmā' bt. Abī Bakr.

'Abdallāh was born in Shawwāl 2/March–April 624. It was reported that his mother, Asmā', emigrated to the Prophet while

499. The first child born among the Emigrants in Medina, a Companion of the Prophet, and a close associate of his maternal aunt the Prophet's wife 'Ā'ishah, on whose side he fought against 'Alī. He established a rival caliphate in Mecca in 64–73/683–92 and was eventually killed by the Syrian army dispatched by the caliph 'Abd al-Malik (these events were part of the second civil war, or *fitnah*). See "'Abdallāh b. al-Zubayr," *EI²*, I, 54–55 (H. A. R. Gibb); Hawting, *First Dynasty*, 46–49; Rotter; al-Balādhurī, *Ansāb*, V, 188–204; al-Kharbūṭalī.

pregnant with him. His *kunyahs* were Abū Bakr and Abū Khubayb.

Ḥakīm b. Ḥizām b. Khuwaylid b. Asad b. 'Abd al-'Uzzā b. Quṣayy.

His mother was Umm Ḥakīm bt. Zuhayr b. al-Ḥārith b. Asad b. 'Abd al-'Uzzā b. Quṣayy.

[2378] According to al-Ḥārith [b. Muḥammad]—Ibn Sa'd[500]—Muḥammad b. 'Umar [al-Wāqidī]—al-Mundhir b. 'Abdallāh—Mūsā b. 'Uqbah—Abū Ḥabībah, the client of al-Zubayr—Ḥakīm b. Ḥizām: I was born thirteen years before the People of the Elephant arrived. I was [already] a mature man when 'Abd al-Muṭṭalib intended to sacrifice his son 'Abdallāh, as his vow was due to be fulfilled. This was five years before the Prophet was born.

Ḥakīm's *kunyah* was Abū Khālid. He died in Medina at the age of 120, during the caliphate of Mu'āwiyah.

He transmitted [traditions] from the Prophet.

Ḥakīm counts among the converts of the conquest [of Mecca], and so do his sons Khālid and Hishām. The two of them embraced Islam together with him on the day of the conquest of Mecca. Two brothers of theirs, 'Abdallāh and Yaḥyā, sons of Ḥakīm b. Ḥizām, were also converted to Islam on that day.

The Names of Those Who Transmitted [Traditions] from the Prophet, of the Banū 'Abd al-Dār b. Quṣayy b. Kilāb

Among them was Shaybah the Ḥājib (doorkeeper) b. 'Uthmān, that is, al-Awqaṣ (the short-necked) b. Abī Ṭalḥah—whose [real] name was 'Abdallāh—b. 'Abd al-'Uzzā b. 'Uthmān b. 'Abd al-Dār b. Quṣayy.[501]

He embraced Islam at Ḥunayn, while the Prophet was fighting the Hawāzin.[502] He transmitted [traditions] from the Prophet.

500. The parallel text in Ibn Sa'd could not be traced.

501. Of the 'Abd al-Dār, traditionally the doorkeepers of the Ka'bah. Shaybah and 'Uthmān b. Ṭalḥah received the keys of the Ka'bah from the Prophet in confirmation of their position. See al-Zubayrī, 252–53; Ibn Qudāmah, 250 (read *dafa'a* for *rafa'a*); Khalīfah b. Khayyāṭ, *Ṭabaqāt*, 14; Ibn Ḥibbān, *Mashāhīr*, 56.

502. Several Qurashīs participated in the battle of Ḥunayn (after the conquest of Mecca) without having embraced Islam first.

ʿUthmān b. Ṭalḥah b. Abī Ṭalḥah b. ʿAbd al-ʿUzzā b. ʿUthmān b. ʿAbd al-Dār b. Quṣayy b. Kilāb.[503]

He emigrated to the Prophet during the armistice of Ḥudaybiyyah, in Ṣafar 8/June 629.

Abū al-Sanābil b. Baʿkak b. al-Ḥārith b. al-Sabbāq b. ʿAbd al-Dār [2379]
b. Quṣayy b. Kilāb.[504]

He counts as one of the converts of the conquest [of Mecca].

The Names of Those Who Transmitted [Traditions] from the Prophet, of the Banū Zuhrah b. Kilāb, Brother of Quṣayy b. Kilāb.

Among them was ʿAbd al-Raḥmān b. ʿAwf b. ʿAbd ʿAwf b. ʿAbd b. al-Ḥārith b. Zuhrah b. Kilāb.[505]

Saʿd b. Abī Waqqāṣ—whose name was Mālik—b. Uhayb b. ʿAbd Manāf b. Zuhrah b. Kilāb b. Murrah.[506]

Saʿd's *kunyah* was Abū Isḥāq.

Al-Miswar b. Makhramah b. Nawfal b. Uhayb b. ʿAbd Manāf b. Zuhrah b. Kilāb.

His *kunyah* was Abū ʿAbd al-Raḥmān.

He was the son of ʿAbd al-Raḥmān b. ʿAwf's sister.

Al-Miswar was eight years old when the Prophet died. He transmitted [traditions] from the Prophet, among them the following.

---

503. Al-Zubayrī, 252–53; Ibn Qudāmah, 249–50; Khalīfah b. Khayyāṭ, *Ta'rīkh*, 190; idem, *Ṭabaqāt*, 14; Ibn Ḥibbān, *Mashāhīr*, 51; al-Balādhurī, *Ansāb*, I, 361, III (Dūrī), 16.

504. Ibn Ḥibbān, *Mashāhīr*, 43; Khalīfah b. Khayyāṭ, *Ṭabaqāt*, 14–15; Ibn Qudāmah, 252–53.

505. A wealthy and respected Qurashī, one of Muḥammad's closest Companions. He played a crucial part in the election of the third caliph, ʿUthmān. Khalīfah b. Khayyāṭ, *Ṭabaqāt*, 15; Ibn Ḥibbān, *Mashāhīr*, 26; Ibn Ḥanbal, *Faḍā'il*, 728–32; al-Balādhurī, *Ansāb*, I, 203–4.

506. An early convert who was a close and trusted Companion of the Prophet. Later he served as the chief commander of the conquering Muslim army in Iraq and the governor of al-Kūfah. He took a neutral stand in the strife between ʿAlī and Muʿāwiyah and died some time in the years 50–58/670–78. See "Saʿd b. Abī Waḳḳāṣ," *EI*[1], IV, 29–30 (K. V. Zettersteen); Khalīfah b. Khayyāṭ, *Ṭabaqāt*, 15; Ibn Ḥibbān, *Mashāhīr*, 26; Ibn Ḥanbal, *Faḍā'il*, 748–54; al-Balādhurī, *Ansāb*, V, 16–21 and passim; Ibn Qudāmah, 287–88.

According to Ma'mar [b. Rāshid] al-Baḥrānī—Abū 'Āmir—'Abdallāh b. Ja'far b. al-Miswar b. Makhramah—Umm Bakr bt. al-Miswar—al-Miswar: I was standing behind the Prophet while he was performing ablutions, when a Jew passed by. The Jew said "Lift his garment off his back." I approached to lift the Prophet's garment, and the Prophet sprinkled my face with water.

Nāfi' b. 'Utbah b. Abī Waqqāṣ b. Uhayb b. 'Abd Manāf b. Zuhrah b. Kilāb.[507]

Nāfi' counts as one of the converts of the conquest, for he embraced Islam on the day of the conquest of Mecca. He was the brother of Hāshim b. 'Utbah al-Mirqāl (the swift runner).

Nafi' b. 'Utbah transmitted [traditions] from the Prophet, [among them the following]. According to Muḥammad b. Khalaf al-'Asqalānī—Rawwād b. al-Jarrāḥ—al-Mas'ūdī—'Abd al-Malik
[2380] b. 'Umayr—Jābir b. Samurah—Nafi' b. 'Utbah—the Prophet: You will fight the [inhabitants of the] Arabian peninsula, and God will conquer them; you will fight the Byzantines, and God will conquer them; you will fight the Persians, and God will conquer them; you will fight the Deceiver,[508] and God will conquer him.[509]

'Abd al-Raḥmān b. Azhar b. 'Awf b. 'Abd 'Awf b. 'Abd b. al-Ḥārith b. Zuhrah b. Kilāb.[510]

He participated in [the battle of] Ḥunayn on the Prophet's side.

'Abd al-Raḥmān transmitted [traditions] from the Prophet, [among them the following]. According to Yūnus b. 'Abd al-A'lā al-Ṣadafī—['Abdallāh] Ibn Wahb—Usāmah b. Zayd al-Laythī—Ibn Shihāb [al-Zuhrī]—'Abd al-Raḥmān b. Azhar: It is as if I can see the Prophet even now looking for Khālid b. al-Walīd's camel among the [rest of the] camels on the day of Ḥunayn. While he was at that a man was brought before him who had been drinking [alcohol]. The Prophet told the people "Beat him." Some of them

507. Khalīfah b. Khayyāṭ, *Ṭabaqāt*, 15, 126; Ibn Ḥazm, *Jamharat*, 129.

508. Al-Dajjāl, a figure parallel to the Antichrist, is the embodiment of evil in Islamic eschatology. War against him is one of the Portents of the Hour; see "al-Dadjdjāl," *EI*², II, 76–77 (A. Abel).

509. Cf. Ibn Qudāmah, 290–91; Yūsuf b. Yaḥyā al-Sulamī, 276–77.

510. Khalīfah b. Khayyāṭ, *Ṭabaqāt*, 16; Ibn Ḥibbān, *Mashāhīr*, 52; Ibn Qudāmah, 302–3.

beat him with their shoes, other with sticks, still others with rods, that is, green palm branches. The Prophet then took some earth and threw it in the man's face.[511]

'Abdallāh b. al-Arqam b. 'Abd Yāghūth b. Wahb b. 'Abd Manāf b. Zuhrah b. Kilāb.[512]

He transmitted [traditions] from the Prophet, among them the following. According to Tamīm b. al-Muntaṣir al-Wāsiṭī—Yazīd, that is, Ibn Hārūn—Muḥammad, that is, Ibn Isḥāq—Hishām b. 'Urwah—his father—'Abdallāh b. al-Arqam b. 'Abd Yāghūth—the Prophet: If any of you feels something in his stomach when [2381] the time for prayer has come, let him go first to the lavatory.

Ṣafwān [b. Makhramah b. Nawfal] al-Zuhrī.[513]

According to [Muḥammad] Ibn Ḥumayd—al-Ḥakam b. Bashīr—Bashīr b. Salmān—al-Qāsim b. Ṣafwān al-Zuhrī—his father—the Prophet: Delay the noon prayer until the cooler time of the day, for the heat pertains to hellfire.[514]

'Abdallāh b. 'Adī b. Ḥamrā' al-Zuhrī.[515]

According to 'Abdallāh b. Yūsuf al-Jubayrī—Aḥmad b. 'Abd al-Raḥmān al-Ḥarrānī—Ḥajjāj b. Abī Manī'—'Ubaydallāh b. Abī Ziyād—[Ibn Shihāb] al-Zuhrī—Abū Salamah b. 'Abd al-Raḥmān—Abū 'Amr b. 'Adī b. Ḥamrā' al-Zuhrī: Standing at al-Ḥazawwarah[516] in the market of Mecca, the Prophet said "By God, you are the best place on earth"; or [in another version]: "[By God, you are] the place that I love the most on God's earth. If I had not been forced out of you, I would not have left you."

---

511. Cf. p. 103, above.

512. He served 'Umar and 'Uthmān as treasurer; see Khalīfah b. Khayyāṭ, *Ta'rīkh*, 130, 157; idem, *Ṭabaqāt*, 16; al-Balādhurī, *Ansāb*, V, 58–59; Ibn Qudāmah, 294.

513. Ibn Ḥajar, *Iṣābah*, II, 190.

514. Cf. Abū Zur'ah, 607–8, where the tradition is attributed to another person.

515. Ibn Ḥibbān, *Mashāhīr*, 63; Ibn Qudāmah, 304.

516. The old marketplace in Mecca, later incorporated in the area of the Holy Mosque (i.e., the Ka'bah); see Yāqūt, *Mu'jam al-buldān*, II, 262; al-Azraqī, 301, 497.

Those Who Transmitted [Traditions] from the Prophet, of the Allies of the Banū Zuhrah

ʿAbdallāh b. Masʿūd b. Ghāfil b. Ḥabīb b. Shamkh b. Fār b.
[2382] Makhzūm b. Ṣāhilah b. Kāhil b. al-Ḥārith b. Tamīm b. Saʿd b. Hudhayl b. Mudrikah b. al-Yās b. Muḍar.[517]

His *kunyah* was Abū ʿAbd al-Raḥmān.

Masʿūd b. Ghāfil, ʿAbdallāh's father, had entered an alliance with ʿAbd b. al-Ḥārith b. Zuhrah[518] in pre-Islamic times.

Al-Miqdād b. ʿAmr b. Thaʿlabah b. Mālik b. Rabīʿah.

He is called al-Miqdād b. al-Aswad.

In pre-Islamic times [al-Miqdād] concluded an alliance with al-Aswad b. ʿAbd Yāghūth b. Wahb b. ʿAbd Manāf b. Zuhrah b. Kilāb. Al-Aswad adopted him, and he was called al-Miqdād b. al-Aswad until God revealed the [following verse] in disapproval of His Prophet: "Call them by their fathers' names; this is more just in the eyes of God." Consequently he was called al-Miqdād b. ʿAmr.

Khabbāb b. al-Aratt b. Jandalah b. Saʿd b. Khuzaymah b. Kaʿb, of the Banū Saʿd b. Zayd Manāh b. Tamīm.[519]

Khabbāb had been taken prisoner and sold in Mecca. [A woman named] Umm Anmār bt. Sibāʿ of the Khuzāʿah tribe, allies of ʿAwf b. ʿAbd ʿAwf b. ʿAbd b. al-Ḥārith b. Zuhrah, bought Khabbāb and set him free. According to another version, Khabbāb's mother and the mother of Sibāʿ were the same. At any rate, Khabbāb b. al-Aratt joined the family of Sibāʿ[520] and as a consequence claimed to have entered an alliance with the Banū Zuhrah.

---

517. The tribe's name is Hudhayl; see Ibn Ḥazm, *Jamharat*, 197. ʿAbdallāh b. Masʿūd was a close Companion of the Prophet of humble bedouin origin. He held important positions in the caliphates of ʿUmar and ʿUthmān and was known as one of the greatest experts on the Qurʾān and religious law. See "Ibn Masʿūd," *EI*², III, 873–75 (J.-C. Vadet); Jeffery, 20–24; Schacht, *Origins*, 231–33; Khalīfah b. Khayyāṭ, *Ṭabaqāt*, 16; Ibn Ḥanbal, *Faḍāʾil*, 837–44; Ibn Ḥibbān, *Mashāhīr*, 29; al-Balādhurī, *Ansāb*, I, 204–5, V, 36–38.

518. An important family from the Qurashī Zuhrah clan; see al-Zubayrī, 265.

519. Of the Tamīmī clan Saʿd b. Zayd Manāh; see Ibn Ḥazm, *Jamharat*, 215. On Khabbāb, see Kister, "On Strangers and Allies," 126–27; Khalīfah b. Khayyāṭ, *Ṭabaqāt*, 17; Ibn Ḥibbān, *Mashāhīr*, 76; al-Balādhurī, *Ansāb*, I, 175–80.

520. That is, either as a family member or as a client; freedmen became allies, or clients, of their former masters. See Crone, *Roman, Provincial and Islamic Law*, 36–38.

Khabbāb transmitted many traditions from the Prophet.

Shuraḥbīl b. Ḥasanah.[521]

Ḥasanah was his mother, of the 'Adūl clan.[522] His father was 'Abdallāh b. al-Muṭā' b. 'Amr b. Kindah, an ally of the Banū Zuhrah.

The Names of Those Who Transmitted [Traditions] from the Prophet, of the Banū Taym b. Murrah[523] [2383]

Among them was Abū Bakr 'Abdallāh b. Abī Quḥāfah—whose name was 'Uthmān—b. 'Āmir b. 'Amr b. Ka' b b. Sa'd b. Taym b. Murrah.[524]

[Those Who Transmitted Traditions], of the Banū Makhzūm b. Yaqaẓah b. Murrah b. Ka'b

Khālid b. al-Walīd b. al-Mughīrah b. 'Abdallāh b. 'Umar b. Makhzūm.[525]

His *kunyah* was Abū Sulaymān.

Khālid's mother was 'Aṣmā', that is, Lubābah al-Ṣughrā (junior), bt. al-Ḥārith b. Ḥazn b. Bujayr b. al-Huzam b. Ruwaybah b. 'Abdallāh b. Hilāl b. 'Āmir b. Ṣa'ṣa'ah. She was the sister of Umm al-Faḍl bt. al-Ḥārith, also called Lubābah, the mother of al-'Abbās b. 'Abd al-Muṭṭalib's sons. Khālid b. al-Walīd was thus a maternal cousin of 'Abdallāh b. al-'Abbās and a nephew of Maymūnah bt. al-Ḥārith, the Prophet's wife.

---

521. He was one of the Prophet's scribes and a commander during the conquests. See Ibn Ḥibbān, *Mashāhīr*, 41; al-Balādhurī, *Ansāb*, I, 214; al-A'ẓamī, *Kuttāb*, 72.

522. She was a client of a member of the Jumaḥ; see Ibn Ḥazm, *Jamharat*, 162; Ibn Ḥajar, *Iṣābah*, IV, 272. I could not trace the clan 'Adūl.

523. A Qurashī clan; see Ibn Ḥazm *Jamharat*, 135–40.

524. That is, the first caliph, who was the Prophet's closest Companion and father-in-law. See "Abū Bakr," *EI*[2], I, 109–11 (W. M. Watt); Khalīfah b. Khayyāṭ, *Ta'rīkh*, 64–90; idem, *Ṭabaqāt*, 16–17; Ibn Ḥanbal, *Faḍā'il*, 65–106.

525. An important general in Muḥammad's time and later, during the apostasy wars and the beginning of the conquests. He was dismissed by the second caliph, 'Umar b. al-Khaṭṭāb. He was nicknamed "the sword of God." "Khālid b. al-Walīd," *EI*[2], IV, 928–29 (P. Crone); Khalīfah b. Khayyāṭ, *Ṭabaqāt*, 19–20; Ibn Ḥanbal, *Faḍā'il*, 813–17; Ibn Ḥibbān, *Mashāhīr*, 56; Ibn Qudāmah, 345–49; al-A'ẓamī, *Kuttāb*, 60–62; Akram.

Khālid transmitted traditions from the Prophet.

'Ayyāsh b. Abī Rabī'ah b. al-Mughīrah b. 'Abdallāh b. 'Umar b. Makhzūm.[526]

He was half-brother of Abū Jahl b. Hishām, their mother being Asmā' bt. Mukharribah b. Jandal b. Ubayr b. Nahshal b. Dārim b. Ghanm.[527]

'Ayyāsh was among the emigrants to Abyssinia together with his wife Asmā' bt. Salamah b. Mukharribah;[528] she bore him his son 'Abdallāh b. 'Ayyāsh in Abyssinia. 'Ayyāsh later returned to Mecca [where he stayed] until the Prophet died, whereupon he
[2384] moved to Syria and participated in the holy wars.[529] He then returned to Mecca, where he lived until his death.

'Ayyāsh transmitted [traditions] from the Prophet; among the traditions transmitted from him is [the following]. According to Muḥammad b. Sahl b. 'Askar al-Bukhārī—'Abd al-Razzāq [b. Hammām al-Ṣan'ānī]—Ma'mar [b. Rāshid]—Ayyūb [b. Abī Tamīmah][530]—Nāfi' [client of 'Abdallāh Ibn 'Umar]—'Ayyāsh b. Abī Rabī'ah—the Prophet: A wind will come before the Hour[531] and will take the souls of all the believers.

'Abdallāh b. Abī Umayyah b. al-Mughīrah b. 'Abdallāh b. 'Umar b. Makhzūm.[532]

His mother was 'Ātikah bt. 'Abd al-Muṭṭalib b. Hāshim b. 'Abd Manāf.[533] He was the brother of Umm Salamah, the Prophet's wife.

'Abdallāh participated on the Prophet's side in the conquest of Mecca, [the battle] of Ḥunayn, and [the siege of] al-Ṭā'if. He was hit and killed by an arrow during the siege of al-Ṭā'if. This is what

526. Ibn Ḥibbān, *Mashāhīr*, 64; al-Balādhurī, *Ansāb*, I, 208–10; Ibn Qudāmah, 375–76.

527. The clan is the Nahshal, from the Tamīm tribe; see Ibn Ḥazm, *Jamharat*, 230; Ibn Ḥajar, *Iṣābah*, IV, 232.

528. Ibn Ḥajar, *Iṣābah*, IV, 229.

529. That is, the conquests.

530. See Motzki, 3.

531. That is, the Day of Judgment.

532. Maternal cousin of the Prophet and an opponent of Islam until the year 8/630. See Ibn Qudāmah, 373–74; al-Balādhurī, *Ansāb*, I, 145–46.

533. Ibn Ḥajar, *Iṣābah*, IV, 357–58.

the biographers say, and there is no disagreement among them over this point.

'Umar b. Abī Salamah b. 'Abd al-Asad b. Hilāl b. 'Abdallāh b. 'Umar b. Makhzūm.[534]

It was reported that the Prophet fostered him from the time he was nine years old.

'Umar participated in [the battle of] the Camel on the side of 'Alī [b. Abī Ṭālib], who later appointed him governor of Fārs. He died in Medina during the caliphate of 'Abd al-Malik b. Marwān. He transmitted traditions from the Prophet.

'Umar's brother Salamah b. Abī Salamah outlived the Prophet [and died during] the caliphate of 'Abd al-Malik b. Marwān, but no transmission from the Prophet is recorded from him. He was older than his brother 'Umar b. Abī Salamah. Umm Salamah, the Prophet's wife, was the mother of both of them. Their father, Abū Salamah, died during the Prophet's lifetime. His name was 'Abdallāh b. 'Abd al-Asad.

'Amr b. Ḥurayth b. 'Amr b. 'Uthmān b. 'Abdallāh b. 'Umar b. Makhzūm.

His *kunyah* was Abū Sa'īd.

It was reported that 'Amr was twelve years old when the [2385]
Prophet died. He settled in al-Kūfah, where he died in the year 85 (January 14, 704–January 2, 705).

'Amr transmitted traditions from the Prophet, among them the following. According to Abū Kurayb [Muḥammad b. al-'Alā']—Ibn Numayr and Wakī' [b. al-Jarrāḥ]—Ismā'īl b. Abī Khālid—al-Aṣbagh, client of 'Amr b. Ḥurayth—'Amr b. Ḥurayth: I used to pray together with the Prophet. At the dawn prayer he used to recite [the following verse]: "I swear not by [the stars] that lag, that run, and that fade away."[535] It is as if I can [even now] hear his voice.

---

534. Ibn Ḥibbān, *Mashāhīr*, 50; Khalīfah b. Khayyāṭ, *Ta'rīkh*, 184, 294, 303; Ibn Qudāmah, 383.

535. Qur'ān 81:15–16, trans. Bell, II, 639.

According to Abū Kurayb [Muḥammad b. al-'Alā']—Wakī' [b. al-Jarrāḥ]: He recited [the following]: "When the sun shall be veiled."[536]

According to 'Abd al-Ḥamīd b. Bayān al-Qannād—Muḥammad b. Yazīd—Ismā'īl b. Abī Khālid—Aṣbagh, client of 'Amr b. Ḥurayth—'Amr b. Ḥurayth: I prayed with the Prophet the dawn prayer; it is as if I can [even now] hear his voice, reciting "I swear not by [the stars] that lag, that run, and that fade away." My mother then took me to him, and he prayed for my sucess in gaining a livelihood.

'Amr's brother Sa'īd b. Ḥurayth.[537]

He was older than 'Amr.

It was reported that Sa'īd participated on the Prophet's side in the conquest of Mecca, at the age of fifteen. He settled in al-Kūfah, together with his brother 'Amr, after the Prophet's death.

Sa'īd transmitted [traditions] from the Prophet, among them the following. According to [Muḥammad] Ibn Bashshār—'Abd al-Wahhāb b. 'Abd al-Majīd—Ismā'īl b. Ibrāhīm b. Muhājir—'Abd al-Malik b. 'Umayr—'Amr b. Ḥurayth—his brother Sa'īd b. Ḥurayth—the Prophet: He who sells a house and does not buy another one instead is not likely to see blessing in that money.

[2386] 'Abdallāh b. Abī Rabī'ah—whose name was 'Amr—b. Makhzūm.[538]

He was a full brother of 'Ayyāsh b. Abī Rabī'ah and the father of the poet 'Umar b. 'Abdallāh b. Abī Rabī'ah.

'Abdallāh b. Abī Rabī'ah embraced Islam on the day of the conquest of Mecca. His name had been Baḥīr, and the Prophet renamed him 'Abdallāh when he was converted.[539]

'Abdallāh transmitted from the Prophet [the following]. According to Sulaymān b. 'Abd al-Jabbār—Zakariyā' b. 'Adī—Ḥātim—Ismā'īl b. Ibrāhīm al-Makhzūmī—his father—his grandfather, the last reported that the Prophet borrowed from him [a sum of

---

536. Qur'ān 81:1, trans. Bell, II, 638.

537. Khalīfah b. Khayyāṭ, *Ṭabaqāt*, 20, 126; Ibn Qudāmah, 388.

538. He served the Prophet, 'Umar, and 'Uthmān as governor in the Yemen; see Khalīfah b. Khayyāṭ, *Ta'rīkh*, 128; idem, *Ṭabaqāt*, 21; Ibn Qudāmah, 377–78.

539. See note 234, above.

money] between 13,000 and 19,000 [dirhams?]. When the Prophet returned from [the battle of] Ḥunayn he called him and said: "Take your money, may God bless your family and your property. The reward for lending money is only full back payment and praise."[540]

ʿIkrimah b. Abī Jahl—whose name was ʿAmr—b. Hishām b. al-Mughīrah b. ʿAbdallāh b. ʿUmar b. Makhzūm.

He embraced Islam after the conquest of Mecca.

According to Aḥmad b. ʿUthmān b. Ḥakīm al-Awdī—Shurayḥ b. Salamah—Ibrāhīm b. Yūsuf—his father—Abū Isḥāq [al-Sabīʿī]—ʿĀmir b. Saʿd [b. Abī Waqqāṣ]: When ʿIkrimah b. Abī Jahl came to the Prophet the latter said to him "Welcome, O rider and passenger," or "Emigrant."[541] [ʿIkrimah] related: I said "What shall I say, O Messenger of God?" He replied "Say 'I testify that there is no God but Allāh and that you are God's messenger.'" I said this, then I continued "What shall I say, O Messenger of God?" He replied "Say, 'O Messenger of God, I ask you to bear witness that I am an Emigrant.'" I said that, whereupon the Prophet said "I will grant you today anything you ask [provided that it is something] I would have granted anyone else." I said: "I shall not ask you for money, as I am one of the richest among the Quraysh, but I ask you to forgive me for having fought against you and for having spent money in order to divert [others] from the [2387]
path of God. If I live long [enough], I shall double that amount [and spend it on the opposite purpose]."

Al-Sāʾib b. Abī al-Sāʾib, father of ʿAbdallāh b. al-Sāʾib.[542]

According to Muḥammad b. ʿUmar [al-Wāqidī], he was the Prophet's partner in pre-Islamic times; so it is according to al-Ḥārith—Ibn Saʿd—[Muḥammad b. ʿUmar]. According to Hishām b. Muḥammad b. al-Kalbī, however, the Prophet's partner in pre-

---

540. Apparently this is a tradition against usury, strictly forbidden in Islam.

541. The narrator is not sure of the correct wording and gives two alternatives. The significance of the difference is that, according to the prevailing view, the status of Emigrant was not granted to people who were converted after the conquest of Mecca (*lā hijrah baʿda al-fatḥ*). The second version contradicts this view.

542. Khalīfah b. Khayyāṭ, *Ṭabaqāt*, 20; Ibn Qudāmah, 386. ʿAbdallāh was also a Companion, known for being the Meccan expert reader; see Ibn Ḥajar, *Iṣābah*, II, 314; al-Ṣafadī, XVII, 187–88; Ibn Saʿd, V, 329; Ibn al-Jazarī, I, 419–20.

Islamic times was ʿAbdallāh b. al-Sāʾib b. Abī al-Sāʾib. At any rate, the one discussed in this biography is al-Sāʾib.

According to Abū Kurayb [Muḥammad b. al-ʿAlāʾ]—Muṣʿab b. al-Miqdām—Isrāʾīl—Ibrāhīm b. Muhājir—Mujāhid—al-Sāʾib: ʿUthmān b. ʿAffān and Zuhayr b. Umayyah brought me [to the Prophet]. They asked permission to go in to see him and [upon receiving it, went in and] praised me before him. The Prophet said "I know him better [than you do]; were you not my partner in pre-Islamic times?" I said: "Yes, may my father and my mother be ransom for you.[543] You were a very good partner; you never quarreled or competed [unfairly]." [Hearing this,] the Prophet said to me: "O Sāʾib, contemplate the virtues you had in the Jāhiliyyah, and adhere to them in Islam. Act hospitably toward your guest, be benevolent toward orphans, and respect those to whom you granted protection (*jār*)."[544]

Al-Sāʾib b. Abī al-Sāʾib and his son ʿAbdallāh embraced Islam on the day of the conquest of Mecca. ʿAbdallāh's *kunyah* was Abū ʿAbd al-Raḥmān. As for Qays b. al-Sāʾib, he was a paternal cousin of ʿAbdallāh b. al-Sāʾib. [His full name] was Qays b. al-Sāʾib b. ʿUwaymir b. ʿĀʾidh b. ʿImrān b. Makhzūm. According to al-
[2388] Wāqidī, he was Mujāhid's patron. Al-Wāqidī reported [the following] on the authority of ʿAbd al-Ḥamīd b. ʿImrān—Mūsā b. Abī Kathīr—Mujāhid: The following verse was revealed in connection with my patron Qays b. al-Sāʾib: "Those who can afford it may ransom [the duty to fast] by feeding a poor man. . . ."[545] So he broke the fast and fed one poor man against each day.

The Allies of the Banū Makhzūm Who Outlived the Prophet and Transmitted [Traditions] from Him

ʿAmmār b. Yāsir b. ʿĀmir b. Mālik b. Kinānah b. Madhḥij.

It was reported that Yāsir and his two brothers al-Ḥārith and Mālik came to Mecca from the Yemen, searching for a brother of theirs. Al-Ḥārith and Mālik returned [later] to the Yemen,

543. A formula often used when addressing the Prophet, indicating the speaker's reverence toward him.

544. *Jār* means at once a neighbor, a person who is given protection, and the one who grants protection. See also note 55, above.

545. Qurʾān 2:184.

whereas Yāsir remained in Mecca and entered an alliance with Abū Ḥudhayfah b. al-Mughīrah b. ʿAbdallāh b. ʿUmar b. Makhzūm. Abū Ḥudhayfah's name was Muhashshim, or Muhāshim, and he was one of Those Who Mocked the Prophet (*mustahzi'ūn*).[546] Abū Ḥudhayfah gave Yāsir in marriage a slave girl of his named Sumayyah bt. Khabbāṭ; she bore him ʿAmmār, who was freed by Abū Ḥudhayfah. Yāsir, Sumayyah, and ʿAmmār were converted upon the rise of Islam. ʿAmmār participated on the Prophet's side in all the events (*mashāhid*). He outlived the Prophet and transmitted [traditions] from him. He was killed in [the battle of] Ṣiffīn, [fighting] on ʿAlī's side.

Those of the Banū ʿAdī b. Kaʿb[547] b. Lu'ayy b. Ghālib Who Outlived the Prophet and Transmitted [Traditions] from Him

ʿUmar b. al-Khaṭṭāb b. Nufayl b. ʿAbd al-ʿUzzā b. Riyāḥ b. ʿAbdallāh b. Qurṭ b. Razāḥ b. ʿAdī b. Kaʿb.
His *kunyah* was Abū Ḥafṣ.

ʿUmar's son ʿAbdallāh.[548]
His *kunyah* was Abū ʿAbd al-Raḥmān.

[ʿUmar's] brother Zayd b. al-Khaṭṭāb b. Nufayl.[549]
His *kunyah* was Abū ʿAbd al-Raḥmān. [2389]
Zayd was older than his brother ʿUmar and an earlier convert. He was the standard-bearer in the battle of Yamāmah. It was reported that he did not cease to advance, carrying [the flag], and to fight with his sword until he was killed.

Saʿīd b. Zayd b. ʿAmr b. Nufayl b. ʿAbd al-ʿUzzā b. Riyāḥ b. ʿAbdallāh b. Qurṭ b. Razāḥ b. ʿAdī b. Kaʿb b. Lu'ayy.
His *kunyah* was Abū al-Aʿwar.

---

546. See Muḥammad Ibn Ḥabīb, *Muḥabbar*, 158–60; Ibn Isḥāq, *Siyar*, 273–75.
547. A Qurashī clan; see Ibn Ḥazm, *Jamharat*, 150–59.
548. He was admired for his piety, honesty, and erudition in prophetic traditions and customs. See "ʿAbdallāh b. ʿUmar," *EI*², I, 53–54 (L. Veccia Vaglieri); Schacht, *Origins*, 25; Ibn Qudāmah, 406–8.
549. Ibn Qudāmah, 419–20; Ibn Ḥibbān, *Mashāhīr*, 30; Khalīfah b. Khayyāṭ, *Ta'rīkh*, 108, 112; idem, *Ṭabaqāt*, 22.

Sa'īd was an early convert. He had embraced Islam before the Prophet entered the house of al-Arqam to preach from there. Sa'īd did not take part in [the battle of] Badr, but he did participate in Uḥud and [all] the Prophet's battles that took place afterward.

[Those of the Banū Jumaḥ Who Outlived the Prophet and Transmitted Traditions from Him]

Ṣafwān b. Umayyah b. Khalaf b. Wahb b. Ḥudhāfah b. Jumaḥ.

He outlived the Prophet and transmitted [traditions] from him. He belonged to the converts of the conquest [of Mecca].

According to Yūsuf b. Ḥammād al-Ma'nī—'Uthmān b. 'Abd al-Raḥmān al-Jumaḥī—Muḥammad b. al-Faḍl b. al-'Abbās: Ṣafwān b. Umayyah came to see us while we were having a feast. When the food was served he said "Eat the meat with your front teeth, for I heard the Prophet say 'Eat meat with your front teeth, for it is more appetizing, more wholesome and more enjoyable [in this way].'"

Abū Maḥdhūrah the muezzin.

His name was Aws b. Mi'yar b. Lawdhān b. Rabī'ah b. Sa'd b. Jumaḥ. There is another version of his name and genealogy: Samurah b. 'Umayr b. Lawdhān b. Wahb b. Sa'd b. Jumaḥ. He had a full brother named Aws.

He outlived the Prophet for some time and transmitted [traditions] from him.

[2390] According to Mūsā b. Sahl al-Ramlī—Muḥammad b. 'Amr b. 'Abd al-Raḥmān b. 'Abdallāh b. Muḥayrīz—his father 'Amr b. 'Abd al-Raḥmān—his father—his grandfather, 'Abdallāh b. Muḥayrīz: I saw Abū Maḥdhūrah, the Prophet's Companion, and he had a lot of hair [on his head]. I said "O Uncle, why don't you cut your hair?" He said "I wouldn't cut hair the Prophet had stroked and blessed."

[The Companions] of the Banū 'Āmir b. Lu'ayy b. Ghālib [Who Outlived the Prophet and Transmitted Traditions from Him]

Ibn Umm Maktūm, the Prophet's muezzin.

There are different opinions as regards his name. The Medinan genealogists hold that it was ʿAbdallāh, whereas, according to the Iraqi genealogists, it was ʿAmr. All are agreed, however, about his genealogy: He was the son of Qays b. Zā'idah b. al-Aṣamm b. Rawāḥah b. Ḥajar b. Maʿīṣ b. ʿĀmir b. Lu'ayy. Another version has Zā'idah b. al-Aṣamm b. Harim b. Rawāḥah.

Ibn Umm Maktūm outlived the Prophet and transmitted [traditions] from him.

According to [Muḥammad] Ibn Ḥumayd—Yaḥyā b. al-Ḍurays—Abū Sinān—ʿAmr b. Murrah—Abū al-Bakhtarī—Ibn Umm Maktūm—the Prophet: Had you known what I know, you would have laughed little and wept a lot.

ʿĀmir b. Masʿūd.[550]

He transmitted [traditions] from the Prophet.

According to Muḥammad b. ʿUmārah al-Asadī—ʿUbaydallāh b. Mūsā—Isrā'īl—Abū Isḥāq—an old man of the Quraysh by the name of ʿĀmir b. Masʿūd—the Prophet: Fasting in winter is like spoils easily acquired, for the nights are long and the days are short.[551]

[Those of the Kinānah Who Outlived the Prophet and Transmitted Traditions from Him][552]

Nawfal b. Muʿāwiyah b. ʿAmr b. Ṣakhr b. Yaʿmur b. Nufāthah b. ʿAdī b. al-Dīl. [2391]

He outlived the Prophet and transmitted [traditions] from him.

According to Muḥammad b. ʿAbdallāh b. ʿAbd al-Ḥakam—Ibn

550. I was not able to trace an ʿĀmirī by this name (as al-Ṭabarī's rubric necessitates). There is, however, a rather well-known Jumaḥī named ʿĀmir b. Masʿūd who was elected governor by the Kūfans at the beginning of the second civil war. See al-Balādhurī, *Ansāb*, IVa, 87, 100–1, V, 190. The description here ("an old man of the Quraysh") is not appropriate for such a figure. However, Ibn Ḥajar *Iṣābah*, II, 260, *Tahdhīb*, V, 70, ascribes to this Jumaḥī the same tradition recorded in the *Dhayl*. See also Ibn Qudāmah, 456. It is worthwhile noting that this tradition is not recorded in Zaghlūl's *Mawsūʿat aṭrāf al-ḥadīth.*

551. There is a play on words here: "spoils easily acquired" is in Arabic *ghanīmah bāridah*, and the latter word's common meaning is "cold."

552. No heading is given in the text. The biographies following Nawfal's are of people of the Layth and Ghifār clans. Both these and al-Dīl, Nawfal's clan, belonged to the Kinānah tribe.

Abī Fudayk—Ibn Abī Dhi'b [al-'Āmirī]—Ibn Shihāb [al-Zuhrī]—Abū Bakr b. 'Abd al-Raḥmān b. al-Ḥārith b. Hishām—Nawfal b. Mu'āwiyah al-Dīlī—the Prophet: Whoever misses a prayer, it is as if he were deprived of his family and property.

Sulaymān b. Ukaymah al-Laythī.[553]

He transmitted [traditions] from the Prophet.

According to Sa'īd b. 'Amr al-Sakūnī—al-Walīd b. Salamah al-Filasṭīnī—Ya'qūb b. 'Abdallāh b. Sulaymān b. Ukaymah al-Laythī—his father—his grandfather: We said to the Prophet "We hear traditions, and we cannot repeat them [exactly] as we heard them." The Prophet replied "There is no harm done as long as you do not make forbidden things lawful or lawful things forbidden and as long as you convey the correct meaning [of the tradition]."[554]

Faḍālah al-Laythī.[555]

He transmitted [traditions] from the Prophet.

According to al-Ḥasan b. Qaza'ah al-Bāhilī—Maslamah b. 'Alqamah—Dā'ūd b. Abī Hind—Abū Ḥarb—'Abdallāh b. Faḍālah—his father: I went to the Prophet and embraced Islam; he informed me about the prayer times, and I said "O Messenger of God, these are hours at short intervals, and I am a working man, so give me a general guideline." The Prophet said "Do your best not to neglect the two *'aṣrs*." I asked "What are the two *'aṣrs*, O Messenger of God?" He replied "The prayer before dawn and the one before sunset."[556]

---

553. Called Sulaym in Ibn Ḥajar, *Iṣābah*, II, 73. The tradition is recorded here with the same *isnād*.

554. The issue raised here is the permissibility of transmitting paraphrased traditions, a practice apparently common in the early days of Islam; in later times transmission verbatim was required. See Goldziher, *Muslim Studies*, II, 186–87 (*riwāyah bi-al-ma'nā* vs. *riwāyah bi-al-lafẓ*).

555. Khalīfah b. Khayyāṭ, *Ṭabaqāt*, 30; Ibn Ḥajar, *Iṣābah*, III, 208. Biographers are confused about this obscure figure.

556. *'Aṣrayn* and *'aṣrān*, both dual forms of *'aṣr*, literally meaning "the two afternoon prayers," but the Arabic allows the combination of two different things under a dual appellation, for example, al-'Umarāni, which means not "the two men named 'Umar" but "Abū Bakr and 'Umar." For the time of the prayers, see Rubin, "Morning and Evening Prayers"; "Mīḳāt," *EI*², VII, 26–27 (A. J. Wensinck).

According to Isḥāq b. Shāhīn al-Wāsiṭī—Khālid b. ʿAbdallāh— [2392]
Dā'ūd—Abū Ḥarb—ʿAbdallāh b. Faḍālah al-Laythī—his father: The Prophet taught me, among other things, [the following]: "Observe the five prayers." I said: "I have work to do at such hours, so give me a general guideline that will suffice if I observe it." The Prophet said "Observe the two *ʿaṣrs*." This meant nothing in our dialect, so I asked "What are the two *ʿaṣrs*?" He said "The prayer before dawn and the one before sunset."

Shaddād b. Usāmah b. ʿAmr, that is, al-Hādi, b. ʿAbdallāh b. Jābir b. Bishr b. ʿUtwārah b. ʿĀmir b. Layth.[557]

His wife was Salmā bt. ʿUmays, sister of Asmā' bt. ʿUmays al-Khathʿamiyyah.

Shaddād transmitted from the Prophet [the following]. According to Mūsā b. Ismāʿīl—Jarīr b. Ḥāzim—Muḥammad b. ʿAbdallāh b. Abī Yaʿqūb al-Ḍabbī—ʿAbdallāh b. Shaddād b. al-Hādi—his father: The Prophet came out to us in one of the—I think he said: two evening prayers (*ṣalātay al-ʿashiyy*)—carrying one of his daughter's children, al-Ḥasan or al-Ḥusayn. He moved forward and placed him at his right foot. The Prophet bowed for a long time during his prayer. I raised my head from among the people, and there was the Prophet bowing, the child riding his back. I resumed bowing, and when the Prophet [was finished and] was
about to leave people asked him "O Messenger of God, at this [2393]
prayer you performed the bowing in a way you [never] did before; was it a [divine] order or inspiration?" He said "Nothing of this kind; only this [grand]child of mine rode my back, and I hated to rush him before he was satisfied."

Khufāf b. Īmā' b. Raḥḍah b. Khurbah b. Khalāf b. Ḥārithah b. Ghifār.[558]

Khufāf transmitted from the Prophet [the following]. According to [Muḥammad] Ibn Bashshār—ʿAbd al-Wahhāb b. ʿAbd al-Majīd—Muḥammad b. ʿAmr—Khālid b. ʿAbdallāh b. Ḥarmalah—al-Ḥārith b. Khufāf b. Īmā' b. Raḥḍah—Khufāf b. Īmā': The Prophet prostrated himself, then raised his head and said: "May

557. Khalīfah b. Khayyāṭ, *Ṭabaqāt*, 8, 30, 127; Ibn Ḥajar, *Iṣābah*, II, 141–42.

558. A bedouin who threw in his lot with the Prophet as early as the year 2/624. See al-Ṭabarī, *Ta'rīkh*, I, 1311; Khalīfah b. Khayyāṭ, *Ṭabaqāt*, 33.

God forgive the Ghifār and be in peace with the Aslam. O God, curse Ri'l, Dhakwān, and 'Uṣayyah."[559] Khufāf said: This is why the unbelievers were cursed.

Rāfi' b. 'Amr, al-Ḥakam b. 'Amr's brother.[560]

He transmitted [traditions] from the Prophet.

According to 'Abd al-Raḥmān b. al-Walīd al-Jurjānī—Muslim b. Ibrāhīm—Sulaymān b. al-Mughīrah—Ḥumayd b. Hilāl—'Abdallāh b. al-Ṣāmit—Abū Dharr: the Prophet said "My community after me," or he said:[561] "There will be in my community people who will read the Qur'ān, but it will not pass through their throats. They will fall out of the religion as [swiftly] as an arrow bolts when shot and will not return [to believe]. They will be the worst of mankind and of [the whole] Creation." Sulaymān said "I am very much inclined to think that he said 'The trait [by which they will be known] will be their [internal] disagreement.'"[562]

[2394] 'Abdallāh b. al-Ṣāmit related: I met Rāfi' b. 'Amr al-Ghifārī, al-Ḥakam b. 'Amr's brother, and I said to him "I [transmit a tradition I] heard from Abū Dharr, where he said such-and-so," and I mentioned to him this report. He said: "Why does this surprise you? I heard it from the Prophet."

Naṣr b. 'Abīdah al-Naṣrī.[563]

He transmitted [traditions] from the Prophet.

According to Muḥammad b. 'Umārah al-Asadī—'Ubaydallāh b. Mūsā—Isrā'īl—Abū Isḥāq—'Abdah b. Ḥazn al-Naṣrī: Camel herders and shepherds held a disputation for rank in the Prophet's

---

559. The clan names Ghifār and Aslam originate in the roots *gh-f-r* and *s-l-m*, denoting forgiveness and peace respectively. Ri'l, Dhakwān, and 'Uṣayyah are clans of the Sulaym tribe. On the last three see Lecker, *Banū Sulaym*, passim. They were involved in the massacre of the Prophet's Companions at Bi'r Ma'ūnah in the year 4/626; see Kister, "Expedition of Bi'r Ma'ūna."

560. Khalīfah b. Khayyāṭ, *Ṭabaqāt*, 32; Ibn Ḥibbān, *Mashāhīr*, 68. He was of the Ghifār clan; his brother al-Ḥakam was governor of Khurāsān in the time of Mu'āwiyah. See also al-Ṭabarī, *Ta'rīkh*, II, 79.

561. That is, another version.

562. Al-Ṭabarī, *Ta'rīkh*, I, 1682; Ibn Hishām, IV, 139. This is a political tradition aimed against disunity, hence against disobedience to the rulers. See note 487, above.

563. There is a confusion regarding his name and identity; see below, where he is called 'Abdah b. Ḥazn; Ibn Ḥajar, *Iṣābah*, II, 434.

presence.[564] The camel herders said: "What are you, shepherds, do you [ever] surpass anyone for any [merit] or gain anything [worthwhile]?[565] These are merely wretched sheep you graze, then bring back in the evening." [Thus] the camel herders silenced the shepherds, whereupon the Prophet said: "Dā'ūd was sent [as a prophet], and he had been a shepherd; Mūsā was sent [as a prophet], and he had been a shepherd. And I was sent [as a prophet], and I had grazed the sheep of my family at Ajyād."[566] So the shepherds won the contest from the camel herders.

[Those of the Tamīm Who Outlived the Prophet and Transmitted Traditions from Him][567]

Al-Farazdaq's paternal uncle.

He transmitted from the Prophet [the following]. According to Yazīd b. Hārūn—Jarīr b. Ḥāzim—al-Ḥasan—Ṣa'ṣa'ah b. Mu'āwiyah, the poet al-Farazdaq's paternal uncle. This is what Yazīd said.[568] [Anyway, Ṣa'ṣa'ah] came to the Prophet, and [the latter] read to him the following verse: "Whoever has done a particle's weight of good shall see it, and whoever has done a particle's weight of evil shall see it."[569] Whereupon [Ṣa'ṣa'ah] said "This suffices me; I shall not hear another [verse]."[570]

Sulaym b. Jābir al-Hujaymī, Abū Jurayy.[571] [2395]

---

564. Competitions for superiority (*mufākharah*) were common in pre-Islamic times. They consisted of an argument held by the competitors in public or in the presence of an arbiter; see Goldziher, *Muslim Studies*, I, 57–63.

565. *Hal tajubbūna shay'an aw tuṣībūnahu.* The Cairo and Dār al-Fikr editions (both, incidentally, on p. 567!) have *taḥubbūna*, "you like," which does not make sense here, whereas the variant adduced by de Goeje is *takhubbūna.* The meaning "surpass" for *tajubbūna* is to be found in Kazimirski, s.v. *j-b-b.*

566. A place in Mecca; see Yāqūt, *Mu'jam al-buldān*, I, 138.

567. No heading is given in the text, but the next three biographies are of Tamīmīs.

568. Ibn Sa'd, VII/1, 25. Note that al-Farazdaq's pedigree is al-Farazdaq b. Ghālib b. Ṣa'ṣa'ah, so that his paternal uncle should be son of Ṣa'ṣa'ah, not son of Mu'āwiyah. There is a confusion between Ṣa'ṣa'ah b. Mu'āwiyah, uncle of the famous Tamīmī leader al-Aḥnaf b. Qays, and Ṣa'ṣa'ah b. Nājiyah, al-Farazdaq's grandfather; see Ibn Ḥajar, *Iṣabah*, II, 185–86.

569. Qur'ān 99:7–8; Bell, II, 672.

570. This expresses admiration; cf. Ibn Ḥajar, *Iṣābah*, II, 186.

571. Ibn Ḥibbān, *Mashāhīr*, 73; Khalīfah b. Khayyāṭ, *Ṭabaqāt*, 42, 179.

According to Isḥāq b. Ibrāhīm al-Ṣawwāf—Yūsuf b. Yaʿqūb al-Sadūsī—'Abd al-Wāḥid b. Wāṣil—Abū Ghifār—Abū Tamīmah—Abū Jurayy: I came across someone surrounded by people who obeyed him. They were content with whatever he told them. I said to myself "This is a man!" [I asked] who he was, and I was told that he was God's Messenger. I said "May peace be upon you O Messenger of God, may peace be upon you." The Prophet said "'May peace be upon you' is a greeting for the dead; you should say 'Peace be upon you.'"[572] So I said "Peace be upon you, O Messenger of God; are you [indeed] God's Messenger?" He said: "Yes, I am the Messenger of God, Who will hear your prayer if any harm comes to you or a drought befalls you. And, if you enter a land or [another version:] a desert and your riding beast is lost and you pray to Him, He will guide it back to you." I said "Let my father and mother be ransom for you, O Messenger of God; [please] instruct me." The Prophet said "Do not curse anyone." I never cursed after this any free man or slave or sheep or camel. [The Prophet also] said: "Do not skimp on good deeds; if you speak to your brother, do so with a cheerful face, for this is a good deed. Raise your garment (*izār*)[573] halfway up your leg, or else [leave it] down your ankles. Beware of letting loose your garment, for this is vanity, and God does not like vanity. And, if someone admonishes you for something he knows about you, do not [retaliate by] admonishing him for something you know about him, for the evil outcome of such an act will affect you."

Ḥarmalah al-'Anbarī.[574]

He transmitted [traditions] from the Prophet.

[2396] According to Ibn al-Muthannā—'Abd al-Raḥmān b. Mahdī—Qurrah b. Khālid—Dirghāmah b. 'Ulaybah b. Ḥarmalah al-'Anbarī—his father—his [grand]father: I went to the Prophet together with [other] delegates from the clan. [While we were there] he led

572. The difference is in the order of the words, which cannot be translated very well into English. The greeting for the dead is *'alayka al-salām*, whereas the usual greeting is *al-salām 'alayka.* Cf. Ibn Qayyim al-Jawziyyah, II, 26; Abū al-Layth al-Samarqandī, fol. 34a–b.

573. That is, that which covers the lower part of the body.

574. Ḥarmalah b. 'Abdallāh b. Anas, a rather insignificant Companion of the Tamīmī clan Banū al-'Anbar; see Khalīfah b. Khayyāṭ, *Ṭabaqāt*, 42. On the 'Anbarīs, see Landau-Tasseron, "Processes."

the morning prayer for us. I looked at the faces of the people and hardly knew them, that is, because of the darkness.[575]

Those of the Banū Ḍabbah b. Udd b. Ṭābikhah b. al-Yās b. Muḍar [Who Outlived the Prophet and Transmitted Traditions from Him]

Salmān b. ʿĀmir al-Ḍabbī.[576]

He transmitted traditions from the Prophet, among them the following. According to Bishr b. Diḥyah al-Baṣrī—Ḥammād b. Zayd—ʿĀṣim—Ḥafṣah bt. Sīrīn—al-Rabāb, a woman of the Banū Ḍabbah—Salmān b. ʿĀmir—the Prophet: Have dates for breakfast, and if no dates are available, have water, for water is pure.

ʿAbdallāh b. Sarjis al-Muzanī.[577]

He transmitted [traditions] from the Prophet.

According to Naṣr b. ʿAlī al-Jahḍamī—Nūḥ b. Qays—ʿAbdallāh b. ʿImrān—ʿĀṣim al-Aḥwal—ʿAbdallāh b. Sarjis al-Muzanī—the Prophet: Following the right course, being temperate, and aiming at what is right form one of twenty-four parts of prophecy.[578]

Maysarah al-Fajr, who was, as was reported, Budayl b. Maysarah's father.[579]

He transmitted [traditions] from the Prophet.

According to [Muḥammad] Ibn Bashshār—ʿAbd al-Raḥmān—Manṣūr b. Saʿd—Budayl—ʿAbdallāh b. Shaqīq—Maysarah al-Fajr: [2397]
I said "O Messenger of God, when was it ordained that you should

575. *Ghalas* means the darkness at the end of the night. This tradition is about the correct time for the morning prayer.

576. Khalīfah b. Khayyāṭ, *Ṭabaqāt*, 39, 177.

577. As he is included in the chapter on Ḍabbah, he is probably not of the well-known Muzaynah tribe but of the ʿAmr b. Udd, a brother tribe of Ḍabbah, known as Muzaynah after their female ancestor. See Ibn Ḥazm, *Jamharat*, 201. ʿAbdallāh was an ally of the Qurashī clan Makhzūm. His being the Prophet's Companion is disputed; see Ibn Ḥajar, *Iṣābah*, II, 315–16.

578. That is, such behavior is characteristic of prophets and therefore commendable. Other commendable traits or modes of behavior are characterized in the same way. See Abū Dā'ūd, *Sunan, Kitab al-Ādāb*, no. 3; Mālik, al-*Muwaṭṭa'*, *Kitāb al-shaʿar, no. 17*.

579. Said to belong to the ʿĀmirī tribe the Banū ʿUqayl but apparently known only in connection with this tradition. See Ibn Ḥajar, *Iṣābah*, III, 470; Khalīfah b. Khayyāṭ, *Ṭabaqāt*, 59; Ibn Saʿd, VII/1, 41.

be a prophet?" He replied "At the time when Ādam was in the process of being created."[580]

Those of the Banū Ja'dah b. Ka'b b. Rabī'ah b. 'Āmir b. Ṣa'ṣa'ah[581] *[Who Outlived the Prophet and Transmitted Traditions from Him]*

The poet Nābighah of the Ja'dah.[582]

His name was Qays b. 'Abdallāh b. 'Udas b. Rabī'ah b. Ja'dah. He transmitted [traditions] from the Prophet.

According to 'Umar b. Ismā'īl al-Hamdānī—Ya'lā b. al-Ashdaq al-'Uqaylī—al-Nābighah: I recited poetry to the Prophet, saying:

Our glory reached the skies, our forefathers' too,
yet it is a higher rank we aspire to.
There is no good in deliberateness (*ḥilm*) without
bursts of anger (*bawādir*) to keep its purity intact.
There is no good in impetuousity (*jahl*) without
a firm man (*ḥalīm*), who accomplishes when starting an act.[583]

The Prophet said: "You [spoke] well, Abū Laylā"—he said that three times—"may your teeth not be broken. What is the rank [you aspire to], O Abū Laylā?" I said "Paradise." He said "Paradise, if God so wills."

The poet Ḥumayd b. Thawr al-Hilālī.[584]

---

580. Literally, "when Ādam was between spirit and body."

581. A clan of the great northern confederation 'Āmir b. Ṣa'ṣa'ah; see Ibn Ḥazm, *Jamharat*, 289.

582. "Al-Nābighah al-Dja'dī," *EI*², VII, 842–43 (A. Arazī); al-Sandūbī, 371–84; Abū Zayd al-Qurashī, II, 773.

583. The verses are part of a long poem; see Abū Zayd al-Qurashī, II, 774–86 (66, 72, 73). On the concept of *ḥilm*, i.e., moral integrity, deliberation, mildness, as opposed to *jahl*, i.e., impetuousity, hastiness, passion, see Goldziher, *Muslim Studies*, I, 201–8.

584. Of the 'Āmirī tribe the Banū Hilāl; he flourished in the first/seventh century. See "Ḥumayd b. Thawr," *EI*², III, 573 (J. W. Fück); Abū al-Faraj al-Iṣfahānī, IV, 97–98.

Those of the Banū Numayr[585] *b. ʿĀmir b. Ṣaʿṣaʿah [Who Outlived the Prophet and Transmitted Traditions from Him]*

Abū Zuhayr al-Numayrī.[586]

He transmitted traditions from the Prophet, among them the following. According to Muḥammad b. ʿAwf al-Ṭāʾī—Muḥammad b. Ismāʿīl—Ḍamḍam—Shurayḥ—Abū Zuhayr al-Numayrī—the Prophet: Do not fight locusts, for they are counted among the greatest armies of God.[587]

Yazīd b. ʿĀmir al-Suwāʾī.[588]

He had fought on the idolators' side in the battle of Ḥunayn and [2398] was later converted to Islam. He transmitted [traditions] from the Prophet.

According to Muḥammad b. Yazīd al-Adamī—Maʿn, that is, b. ʿĪsā al-Qazzāz—Saʿīd b. al-Sāʾib al-Ṭāʾifī—his father—Yazīd b. ʿĀmir: When the Muslims retreated in the battle of Ḥunayn, the Prophet stretched out his hand to the ground and picked up a handful of soil. He advanced with it toward the idolators who were pursuing the Muslims, threw it in their faces, and said "Go back, may your faces be deformed." We withdrew, every one of us noticing the others' taking motes out of their eyes.

Ḥubshī b. Junādah b. Naṣr b. Usāmah b. al-Ḥārith b. Muʿayṭ b. ʿAmr b. Jandal b. Murrah b. Ṣaʿṣaʿah.

He was a Companion of the Prophet and transmitted traditions from him.

---

585. Ibn Ḥazm, *Jamharat*, 279–80; Caskel, II, 15.

586. Confused with one Abū Zuhayr al-Anmārī; see Ibn Ḥajar, *Iṣābah*, IV, 77–78 (including the locust tradition).

587. Cf. Qurʾān 7:133. The black spots on their wings are inscriptions identifying God as the Lord of the world, Creator and Commander of the locust army; see al-Kashshī, 54. There is a debate among scholars whether or not the killing of locusts is permissible. See Abū al-Layth al-Samarqandī, fol. 90a–b; Kister, "Locust's Wing." On the permissibility of killing lizards, snakes, and ants, see Muslim, *Ṣaḥīḥ*, 1752–60 (*kitāb al-salām*, 37–39).

588. Khalīfah b. Khayyāṭ, *Ṭabaqāt*, 54, 285; Ibn Ḥajar, *Iṣābah*, III, 659. On the ʿĀmirī clan Suwāʾah, see Ibn Ḥazm, *Jamharat*, 273.

According to Ismā'īl b. Mūsā al-Suddī—Sharīk—Abū Isḥāq—Ḥubshī b. Junādah al-Salūlī—the Prophet: 'Alī [b. Abī Ṭālib] belongs to my family, and I belong to his family. No one should pay my debt but me or 'Alī.[589]

According to [Muḥammad] Ibn Ḥumayd—Ḥakkām [b. Salm]—'Anbasah [b. Sa'īd]—Abū Isḥāq—Ḥubshī b. Junādah: I heard the Prophet say: "Alī belongs to my family, and I belong to his family. No one should transmit my messages except myself or 'Alī." He said it on the Farewell Pilgrimage.[590]

Abū Maryam Mālik b. Rabī'ah al-Salūlī, father of Burayd b. Abī Maryam.[591]

He transmitted traditions from the Prophet.

According to [Muḥammad] Ibn Ḥumayd—Jarīr [b. 'Abd al-Ḥamīd]—'Aṭā' [b. al-Sā'ib]—Burayd b. Abī Maryam—his father: The Prophet stood among us on a certain occasion and told us about the events that will occur until Doomsday.

[2399] Al-Hirmās b. Ziyād al-Bāhilī.[592]

He transmitted traditions from the Prophet, among them the following. According to al-'Abbās b. Abī Ṭālib—'Abdallāh b. 'Imrān al-Iṣbahānī—Yaḥyā b. Ḍurays al-Rāzī—'Ikrimah b. 'Ammār—Hirmās: I was riding behind my father,[593] and I saw the Prophet riding a camel and uttering the formula *labbayka*. He was per-

---

589. One of the merits of the first caliph, Abū Bakr, which made him qualified to rule (in the eyes of Sunnī Islam), was his participation with the Prophet in the Emigration. The Shī'ī propaganda counterbalanced this argument with the claim that 'Alī remained in Mecca and joined the Prophet in Medina later for one of two purposes (or both): to cover up, at peril of his own life, for the Prophet until he was safely far from Mecca or to pay the Prophet's debts. In addition, the very expression "'Alī belongs to my family and I to his," was used in Shī'ī propaganda to legitimize the Shī'ī claim to rule.

590. This is a tradition legitimizing the Shī'ī claim to power by making 'Alī the sole authorized transmitter of messages from the Prophet. The messages mentioned here refer to the Prophet's divine mission. Note that in his speech at the Farewell Pilgrimage the Prophet asked the audience several times "*hal ballaghtu*?" that is, "have I effectively transmitted the divine message?"

591. Khalīfah b. Khayyāṭ, *Ṭabaqāt*, 55, 183; Ibn Ḥibbān, *Mashāhīr*, 71.

592. Khalīfah b. Khayyāṭ *Ṭabaqāt*, 47, 289; Ibn Ḥibbān, *Mashāhīr*, 413.

593. That is, on the same riding beast.

forming the Ḥajj and the lesser pilgrimage (*'umrah*) together [on that occasion].[594]

[Those of the Banū Taghlib[595] Who Outlived the Prophet and Transmitted Traditions from Him]

Ḥarb b. 'Ubaydallāh's maternal grandfather.[596]

He transmitted [traditions] from the Prophet.

According to [Muḥammad] Ibn Ḥumayd—Jarīr [b. 'Abd al-Ḥamīd]—'Aṭā' [b. al-Sā'ib]—Ḥarb b. 'Ubaydallāh—his maternal grandfather, who was a man of the Banū Taghlib:[597] We embraced Islam and went to the Prophet. I said [to him] "My people have embraced Islam, so teach us." He said "Go and teach them about the prayer and the giving of legal alms." He then informed me about the legal alms due on camels, cattle, sheep, gold, and silver.[598] I turned [to go] away, having memorized everything he taught me, except the legal alms. I went back to him and said "I have memorized everything, except the legal alms." So he taught me again, but when I turned [to go] away I forgot them [again]. So I went back to him and said: "I have memorized everything but the legal alms. Shall I [simply] tax them the tenth [of their property]?" the Prophet said "No, the tenth is obligatory only on Jews and Christians, not on Muslims."[599]

---

594. There was a debate about the permissibility of performing the Ḥajj and the lesser pilgrimage (*'umrah*) together, see Rubin, "Great Pilgrimage." On the formula *labbayka*, see p. 103, above.

595. A large confederation of northern origin. They dwelt in southern Iraq before Islam and professed Christianity, continuing to adhere to it after the Muslim conquests. See Caskel, II, 27; Ibn Ḥazm, *Jamharat*, 303–7, 469.

596. The origin of such an entry would be a chain of transmission (*isnād*) running "Ḥarb b 'Ubaydallāh heard his maternal grandfather . . ." This grandfather is ignored in most of my sources; Ḥarb himself was a Kūfan of the tribe of Thaqīf. See Ibn Ḥibbān, *Thiqāt*, IV, 172; Ibn Ḥajar, *Tahdhīb*, II, 198.

597. Abū 'Ubayd, 212.

598. See Ben Shemesh, I, 94–103, III, 45–50, 54–57, for detailed sums of legal alms, as well as debates on various types of property.

599. See the discussion on the permissibility of levying the tenth (*'ushr*) in Abū 'Ubayd, 211–18; Ben Shemesh, I, 103–9, II, 78–83, III, 30. The Banū Taghlib who remained Christians refused to pay the *jizyah* (poll tax taken from non-Muslims) because it involved humiliation, whereas they were proud Arabs. A compromise was reached according to which they paid a tenth of their property. See Abū 'Ubayd, 217; Ben Shemesh, I, 54–58; cf. van Arendonck, 143, 325–26 (appendix VI).

The Names of Those Who Believed in the Prophet and Followed Him during His Lifetime, Then Outlived Him and Transmitted [Traditions] from Him, of Yemenī Tribes

Among them [were people] of the offspring of Aws b. Ḥārithah b. Tha'labah b. 'Amr b. 'Āmir b. Ḥārithah b. Imri' al-Qays b. Tha'labah b. Māzin b. al-Azd b. al-Ghawth b. Nabt b. Mālik b. Zayd b.
[2400] Kahlān b. Saba' b. Yashjub b. Ya'rub b. Qaḥṭān.[600] Qaḥṭān is the ancestor of all the Yemenī lineages.

The genealogists disagree about the pedigree of Qaḥṭān [himself].[601] Some trace him back to Ismā'īl b. Ibrāhīm, saying that his [name] was Qaḥṭān b. al-Hamaysa' b. Tayman b. Nabt b. Ismā'īl b. Ibrāhīm. Hishām b. Muḥammad [al-Kalbī] held this genealogy [as true]. He quoted his father as saying that he had been contemporaneous with [older] scholars and genealogists who traced Qaḥṭān's pedigree in this way. Other [genealogists] argue that the [name] was Qaḥṭān b. Fāligh b. 'Āḇir b. Shālakh—there is a version with *kh* and one with *ḥ*—b. Arfakhshad b. Nūḥ, may God bless him and all the other prophets.[602]

The mother of [the clans] al-Aws and al-Khazraj, sons of Ḥārithah, was al-'Anqā', that is, Qaylah bt. Kāhil b. 'Udhrah b. Sa'd, that is, Sa'd b. Hudhaym. [This Sa'd] was traced back to Hudhaym because the latter, who had been an Abyssinian slave, raised him, so Hudhaym's name became predominant in Sa'd's genealogy. In fact, Sa'd's [genealogy] was Sa'd b. Zayd b. Layth b. Sūd b. Aslum b. al-Ḥāf b. Quḍā'ah.

Sa'd b. Mu'ādh was the Aws' leader until his death on the Prophet's return from the attack on the Banū Qurayẓah.[603] I have already recorded his biography.[604]

---

600. By Aws b. Ḥārithah the Medinan tribe is meant; it belonged to the great southern confederation of the Azd.

601. See, e.g., Ibn Ḥazm, *Jamharat*, 7–8. About the permissibility of such debates, see Goldziher, *Muslim Studies*, I, 95–96.

602. *Ṣallā Allāh 'alayhi*; see note 379, above.

603. The last Jewish tribe in Medina, besieged by the Prophet in the year 5/627. The men were executed, the women and children taken into slavery. See Kister, "Massacre."

604. Not found in this fragment (*Muntakhab min dhayl al-mudhayyal*). See on him *EI*[1], IV, 30 (K. V. Zettersteén); Khalīfah b. Khayyāṭ, *Ṭabaqāt*, 77; Ibn Ḥanbal, *Faḍā'il*, 818–26.

Khuzaymah b. Thābit b. al-Fākih b. Thaʿlabah b. Sāʿidah b. ʿĀmir b. Ghayyān b. ʿĀmir b. Khaṭmah.

He transmitted traditions from the Prophet.

According to al-ʿAbbās b. Abī Ṭālib—Saʿd b. ʿAbd al-Ḥamīd b. Jaʿfar al-Anṣārī—ʿAbdallāh b. Muḥammad b. ʿImrān b. Ibrāhīm b. Muḥammad b. Ṭalḥah b. ʿUbaydallāh—Khuzaymah b. Muḥammad b. ʿUmārah b. Khuzaymah b. Thābit—his father—his grandfather—Khuzaymah b. Thābit—the Prophet: Beware of the prayer of the wronged, for it is carried by the clouds, because God says "By My Might and Glory, I shall help you, even if it will take time."[605] [2401]

Khuzaymah b. Thābit's brother.

He transmitted traditions from the Prophet, among them the following. According to ʿAbd al-Raḥmān b. ʿAbdallāh b. ʿAbd al-Ḥakam—Abū Zurʿah [al-Dimashqī]—Yūnus [b. Yazīd al-Aylī]—Ibn Shihāb [al-Zuhrī]—ʿUmārah b. Khuzaymah b. Thābit. [Now], Khuzaymah b. Thābit was the man whose testimony was considered by the Prophet as equivalent to that of two people. ʿUmārah quotes his paternal uncle [that is, Khuzaymah's brother], who was a Companion of the Prophet [as saying]: Khuzaymah b. Thābit saw himself in a dream, prostrating himself above the Prophet's forehead. Khuzaymah went to the Prophet and told him [about it], whereupon the Prophet lay down and said "Make your dream true." So Khuzaymah prostrated himself above the Prophet's forehead.

ʿAbdallāh b. Ḥanẓalah b. al-Rāhib.[606]

He transmitted [traditions] from the Prophet.

According to Muḥammad b. Ismāʿīl al-Sulamī—al-Ḥasan b. Sawwār, Abū al-ʿAlāʾ—ʿIkrimah b. ʿAmmār—Ḍamḍam b. Jaws—ʿAbdallāh b. Ḥanẓalah b. al-Rāhib: I saw the Prophet performing

---

605. "God says" means "there is a verse in the Qurʾān," but this particular sentence is not in the Qurʾān. According to De Goeje, this may be a paraphrase of Qurʾan 22:41.

606. An eminent Anṣārī killed in Medina by the caliph's army in the battle of al-Ḥarrah, one of the events of the second civil war (in the year 64/683). See "ʿAbd Allāh b. Ḥanẓala," *EI*², I, 45; Khalīfah b. Khayyāṭ, *Taʾrīkh*, 227–30; idem, *Ṭabaqāt*, 236–37.

the circumambulation of the House[607] riding a she camel, without striking or urging her, without calling "Go on! go on!"

'Uwaymir b. Ashqar, of the Banū Ḥārithah b. al-Ḥārith.[608]
He transmitted [traditions] from the Prophet.

According to al-'Abbās b. al-Walīd al-Bayrūtī—his father—al-Awzā'ī[609]—Yaḥyā b. Sa'īd al-Anṣārī—'Abbād b. Tamīm—'Uwaymir b. Ashqar al-Anṣārī al-Māzinī, [who related] that [once] he had slaughtered his sacrificial animal before the Prophet
[2402] prayed.[610] He then went to the Prophet and told him [about it], whereupon the Prophet ordered him to go back [and go on with] the offering.

According to Yūnus b. 'Abd al-A'lā al-Ṣadafī—['Abdallāh] Ibn Wahb—'Amr b. al-Ḥārith and Mālik b. Anas—Yaḥyā b. Sa'īd al-Anṣārī—'Abbād b. Tamīm—'Uwaymir b. Ashqar al-Anṣārī [who related] that [once] he had slaughtered a sacrificial animal on the Day of the Sacrifices before sunrise. He mentioned this to the Prophet, who ordered him to go back and sacrifice another animal.[611]

According to [Muḥammad] Ibn Sinān al-Qazzāz—Mūsā [b. Ismā'īl Abū Salamah]—Ḥammād [b. Salamah]—Yaḥyā b. Sa'īd—'Abbād b. Tamīm—'Uwaymir b. Ashqar, who had slaughtered before the Prophet prayed, and the Prophet ordered him to do it again.

Mujammi' b. Jāriyah, of the Banū 'Amr b. 'Awf.[612]
He transmitted traditions from the Prophet.

---

607. That is, the Ka'bah.

608. Khalīfah b. Khayyāṭ, *Ṭabaqāt*, 105.

609. An early, famous Syrian jurist; see his biography p. 255, below.

610. That is, during the festival of 'Īd al-Aḍḥā, on Dhū al-Ḥijjah 10.

611. This tradition is the exact opposite of the previous one, reflecting the jurists' debate on this point. The difference between the two depends on the reading of one letter. *Ya'ūda li-ḍaḥiyyatihi* in the first tradition means "to go back to his sacrifice," whereas *ya'ūda bi-ḍaḥiyyah ukhrā* in the second tradition means "to come back with another sacrifice." De Goeje's explanation that *li-ḍaḥiyyatihi* means *bi-ukhrā* ("with another one") is unwarranted.

612. Considered one of the Munāfiqūn ("the Hypocrites"), i.e., those Muslims who opposed the Prophet on certain occasions. See Ibn Ḥajar, *Iṣābah*, III, 366; al-Balādhurī, *Ansāb*, I, 276.

According to al-Ḥasan b. 'Arafah—Ismā'īl b. 'Ayyāsh al-Ḥimṣī—'Abd al-'Azīz b. 'Ubaydallāh—Ya'qūb b. Mujammi' b. Jāriyah—his father: The Prophet walked in the funeral of a man of the Banū 'Amr b. Awf. Upon arriving at the cemetery he said: "Peace be upon [you], grave dwellers"—he said that three times—"[upon] those among you who were believers and Muslims. You have arrived ahead of us, and we shall follow you. May God forgive us and you."

Ḥudhayfah b. al-Yamān, Abū 'Abdallāh.[613]
He originated in the [tribe of] 'Abs b. Baghīḍ and [later] became an ally of the Banū 'Abd al-Ashhal.[614] He transmitted many traditions from the Prophet.

Abū Ayyūb Khālid b. Zayd b. Kulayb b. Tha'labah b. 'Abd b. 'Awf b. Ghanm b. Mālik b. al-Najjār, that is, Taymallāh b. Tha'la- [2403]
bah b. 'Amr b. al-Khazraj.[615]
Abū Ayyūb was present at the 'Aqabah meeting with the seventy Anṣārīs. He took part on the Prophet's side in [the battles] of Badr, Uḥud, and the Ditch and all the [other] events. He transmitted many traditions from the Prophet.

Thābit b. Qays b. Shammās b. Imri' al-Qays b. Mālik al-Agharr b. Tha'labah b. Ka'b b. al-Khazraj b. al-Ḥārith b. al-Khazraj.[616]
He transmitted traditions from the Prophet.
According to Yūnus b. 'Abd al-A'lā al-Ṣadafī—['Abdallāh] Ibn Wahb—Dā'ūd b. 'Abd al-Raḥmān al-Makkī—'Amr b. Yaḥyā al-Māzinī—Yūsuf b. Muḥammad b. Thābit b. Qays b. Shammās—his father—his grandfather, who reported that he entered the Prophet's [house to see him], and the Prophet said "O Lord, re-

613. An eminent Companion who served as a general during the conquests. See Khalīfah b. Khayyāṭ, *Ta'rīkh*, 29, 120–25, 131–32, 135; idem, *Ṭabaqāt*, 48–49; Ibn Ḥibbān, *Mashāhīr*, 74–75.
614. A clan of the Aws (Anṣār).
615. The following biographies are of people of the Khazraj, the brother of the Aws.
616. The spokesman of the Anṣār and their commander in the battle of Yamāmah in the apostasy wars; see Khalīfah b. Khayyāṭ, *Ṭabaqāt*, 94; Ibn Ḥibbān, *Mashāhīr*, 34.

move the sorrow from Qays b. Shammās."[617] The Prophet then took some earth from Buṭḥān,[618] put it in a vessel containing some water, and poured it on him.

Abū al-Yasar Ka'b b. 'Amr.[619]

He transmitted [traditions] from the Prophet.

According to Ḥumayd b. Mas'adah al-Sāmī—Bishr b. al-Mufaḍḍal—'Abd al-Raḥmān b. Isḥāq—'Abd al-Raḥmān b. Mu'āwiyah—Ḥanẓalah b. Qays—Abū al-Yasar al-Badrī[620]—the Prophet: Whoever wishes that God would shade him in His shadow—and he motioned with his hand—let him sell to the poor on credit, or discount [some money] for him.

'Ubayd b. Rifā'ah al-Zuraqī.[621]

According to Ḥawtharah b. Muḥammad al-Minqarī and Sa'īd b.
[2404] al-Rabī' al-Rāzī—Sufyān—'Amr—'Urwah b. 'Āmir—'Ubayd b. Rifā'ah al-Zuraqī: Asmā' said: "O Messenger of God, the Banū Ja'far are hit by the evil eye. Shall we seek a [counter]charm for them?" He said "Yes; had anything come before predestination, it would have been the evil eye."[622]

Khallād b. Rifā'ah b. Rāfi'.[623]

He transmitted [traditions] from the Prophet.

According to 'Ubaydallāh b. Sa'd al-Zuhrī—his paternal uncle—Sharīk—'Abdallāh b. 'Awn—'Alī b. Yaḥyā—Khallād b. Rifā'ah b.

---

617. Note that it is not Thābit but his father who is blessed. This may be because the blessing is uttered in rhymed, rhythmic prose. The addition of "Thābit" would have spoiled the rhythm, whereas the omission of Shammās would have spoiled the rhyme.

618. One of the three wadis of Medina. See Yāqūt, *Mu'jam al-buldān*, I, 662; al-Samhūdī, 1071–72.

619. Khalīfah b. Khayyāṭ, *Ṭabaqāt*, 102; Ibn Ḥibbān, *Mashāhīr*, 39.

620. That is, one who participated in the battle of Badr.

621. Khalīfah b. Khayyāṭ *Ṭabaqāt*, 253; Ibn Sa'd, V, 204.

622. Practices connected with magic or sorcery had pagan origins and were therefore objectionable, but often they could not be abolished; hence the debates on them that arose among Muslims and the ascription to the Prophet of their condemnation or otherwise. See Fahd, chap. 4; cf. Guillaume, 240 n.

623. Brother of the former; see Khalīfah b. Khayyāṭ, *Ṭabaqāt*, 100.

Rāfiʿ, who was counted among the participants in [the battle of] Badr: A man came to the Prophet, who was sitting, and prayed close to him. When he had finished he approached the Prophet and greeted him. The Prophet said "Pray again, because [it is as if] you did not pray." He prayed as before, and when he had finished, approached the Prophet and greeted [him]. The Prophet said to him "Pray again, because [it is as if] you did not pray." The man said "O Prophet of God, teach me." The Prophet said: "When you turn towards the Kaʿbah utter the formula 'God is the greatest,' then recite whatever God wishes you to recite;[624] when you lower your head put your hands on your knees and stretch your back. You have to make room for lowering your head. When you raise your body straighten your spine so that your bones return to [their right places in their] joints. Make room for your prostration, and when you raise your body sit on your left thigh. Do the same in every lowering of the head and every prostration until you finish [your prayer]."

Ziyād b. Labīd b. Thaʿlabah b. Sinān, one of the Banū Bayāḍah b. ʿĀmir b. Zurayq.[625]

He transmitted [traditions] from the Prophet.

According to Ibn Wakīʿ—his father—al-Aʿmash—Salām b. Abī al-Jaʿd—Ziyād b. Labīd: The Prophet mentioned something and said: "That [will be] at the time when knowledge will have died out." We said "O Messenger of God, how will knowledge die out [2405]
while we read the Qur'ān and teach it to our children, who [in their turn] will teach it to their children until Doomsday?"[626] He said: "May your mother be bereaved of you, O Ziyād.[627] I thought that you were one of the most learned men in Medina. Do not

---

624. That is, of verses of the Qur'ān.

625. An eminent Anṣārī; he was appointed by the Prophet as tax collector in Ḥaḍramawt. See Khalīfah b. Khayyāṭ, *Ta'rīkh*, 62, 84; idem, *Ṭabaqāt*, 100–1; al-Balādhurī, *Ansāb*, I, 245, 529.

626. The issue raised here is that of religious authority and whether or not a Muslim needs an interpreter and mediator between himself and God (such as the [Umayyad] caliph, the *'ulamā'*, the Shīʿī Imam). See Crone and Hinds; Landau-Tasseron, "Cyclical Reform."

627. This is not a curse but a term of reprimand.

these Jews and Christians read their Bible and their Gospel, [yet] know nothing of what is in them?"

Abū Ibrāhīm al-Anṣārī's father.[628]

According to Muḥammad b. 'Abdallāh b. Bazī'—Bishr b. al-Mufaḍḍal—Hishām al-Dastawā'ī—Yaḥyā b. Abī Kathīr—Abū Ibrāhīm al-Anṣārī—his father, who heard the Prophet pray over the dead, saying: O God, forgive our living and our dead, our present and our absent [members], our male and our female [members], our young and our old.

According to Ibn al-Muthannā—al-Walīd b. Muslim—al-Awzā'ī—Yaḥyā—Abū Ibrāhīm, [who was] a man of the Banū 'Abd al-Ashhal—his father, who heard the Prophet pray in a funeral, saying: "O God, forgive the first and the last among us, and our living and our dead, our male and our female, our young and our old, our present and our absent. O God, do not deprive us of the reward [of this act], and do not lead us astray after this."

Yaḥyā recorded on the authority of Abū Salamah—the Prophet, a similar tradition, to which he added: Whomever You resurrect, let him be a Muslim, and whomever You take unto You, do so while he is a believer.

'Umayr al-Anṣārī.[629]

He transmitted [traditions] from the Prophet.

According to Ibn Wakī'—his father—Sa'īd b. Sa'īd al-Taghlibī or al-Tha'labī—al-Ṭabarī was not sure about it[630]—Sa'īd b. 'Umayr al-Anṣārī, who ranked among those who took part in Badr—the
[2406] Prophet: Whoever of my community prays for me sincerely and from [the depth of] his soul, God will reward him by blessing him ten times,[631] by raising him ten degrees, by writing ten good deeds to his credit, and erasing ten evils from his record.

---

628. Khalīfah b. Khayyāṭ, *Ṭabaqāt*, 124.

629. 'Umayr b. 'Uqbah b. Niyār; see Ibn Ḥajar, *Iṣābah*, III, 34; *Tahdhīb*, IV, 62.

630. Evidently this is a remark by a scribe or the student who took down the material from al-Ṭabarī by dictation, as was the custom among the Muslim scholars.

631. Literally, "God will pray for him ten times, as a reward for it." For *ṣallā* in the sense of "bless," see note 379, above.

The Names of Some of Those Belonging to Other Yemenī Tribes Who Believed in the Prophet and Followed Him during His Lifetime, Outlived Him, and Transmitted Traditions from Him

Those of the Khuzā'ah, who are the offspring of Ka'b, Mulayḥ and 'Adī, sons of Rabī'ah b. Ḥārithah b. 'Amr Muzayqiyā' b. 'Āmir Mā' al-Samā' b. Ḥārithah al-Ghiṭrīf b. Imri' al-Qays b. Tha'labah b. Māzin. [The Khuzā'ah belong to the tribe of] Azd b. al-Ghawth b. Nabt b. Mālik b. Zayd b. Kahlān b. Saba' b. Yashjub b. Ya'rub b. Qaḥṭān.

Al-Ḥuṣayn b. 'Ubayd b. Khalaf b. 'Abd Nuhm b. Juraybah b. Jahmah b. Ghāḍirah b. Ḥubshiyyah b. Ka'b b. 'Amr, the father of 'Imrān b. Ḥuṣayn.[632]

He transmitted [traditions] from the Prophet.

According to [Muḥammad] Ibn Ḥumayd—Hārūn b. al-Mughīrah—'Amr, that is, Ibn Abī Qays—Manṣūr—Rib'ī—'Imrān b. al-Ḥuṣayn—his father, [who related] that he had come to the Prophet before embracing Islam and said: "O Muḥammad, 'Abd al-Muṭṭalib was better for his people than you. He used to feed them liver and meat of camel humps, whereas you harm them."[633] Then he said "Teach me," whereupon the Prophet replied "Say 'O [2407] God, guard me against the evil of my [own] soul, and make me resolve upon the right course.'" Al-Ḥuṣayn came to the Prophet [again] after he had embraced Islam and asked "What shall I say?" The Prophet said "Say 'O God, forgive [the sins I committed] secretly and openly, by mistake and intentionally, knowingly and ignorantly.'"

Sulaymān b. Ṣurad b. al-Jawn b. Abī al-Jawn—that is, 'Abd al-'Uzzā—b. Munqidh.

Sulaymān's *kunyah* was Abū Muṭarrif. His name had been Yasār before he embraced Islam, but the Prophet gave him the name Sulaymān on the occasion of his conversion.[634]

---

632. Ibn Ḥibbān, *Thiqāt*, III, 88; Ibn Ḥajar, *Iṣābah*, I, 337–38. According to the latter source, his conversion to Islam is not certain.

633. Literally, "you hurt their throats."

634. See note 234, above.

He participated in the battles of the Camel and Ṣiffīn on the side of ʿAlī b. Abī Ṭālib. According to another version, he did not take part in the Camel, but there is no disagreement [among historians] over his participation in Ṣiffīn. He was killed by Yazīd b. al-Ḥuṣayn b. Numayr at ʿAyn al-Wardah, near Qarqīsiyā', as the Repenters' leader and commander.

Sulaymān transmitted traditions from the Prophet.

According to Naṣr b. ʿAlī al-Jahḍamī—his father—Shuʿbah—ʿAbd al-Akram, who was someone from al-Kūfah—his father—Sulaymān b. Ṣurad: The Prophet came to us and we spent several nights unable to get, or [another version] it was impossible to get, food.

Ḥubaysh b. Khālid al-Ashʿar b. Khulayf.[635]

He transmitted from the Prophet the following. According to Abū Hishām Muḥammad b. Sulaymān b. al-Ḥakam b. Ayyūb b. Sulaymān b. Thābit b. Yasār al-Kaʿbī al-Rabaʿī—his paternal uncle Ayyūb b. al-Ḥakam b. Ayyūb—Ḥizām b. Hishām—his father Hishām b. Ḥubaysh—his grandfather Ḥubaysh b. Khālid, a Companion of the Prophet: When the Prophet left Mecca emigrating to Medina he was accompanied by Abū Bakr, the latter's client ʿĀmir
[2408] b. Fuhayrah, and their guide, ʿAbdallāh b. al-Urayqiṭ of the Banū al-Layth. [On their way] they passed by the two tents of Umm Maʿbad al-Khuzāʿiyyah. She was a strong woman, free yet dignified in her discourse with men;[636] she used to sit erect[637] in the court in front of the tent and [order] drink and food to be served. They sought to buy from her meat and dates but did not obtain any

635. Brother of Umm Maʿbad, the protagonist of the following story. He was himself a Companion and was one of the few killed during the conquest of Mecca; see Ibn Ḥajar, *Iṣābah*, I, 310.

636. *Barzah*, from the root *b-r-z* meaning to appear, protrude, be seen. The term implies that also in pre-Islamic times the norm for women was to keep distance from men (for Umm Maʿbad is not yet converted), but there was a possibility of closer, yet not dishonorable, contacts. See de Goeje's *Glossarium* under b-r-z; see Abū al-Faraj al-Iṣfahānī, XIV, 159 on the conduct of Sukaynah, daughter of al-Ḥusayn. I thank my colleague, Prof. Albert Arazi for this reference.

637. *Taḥtabī. Iḥtibā'* is a peculiar manner of sitting, with the legs and back confined together in a garment, considered characteristic of the Arab and Muslim nobility; see al-Dhahabī, *Mīzān* (ed. Bijāwī), III, 272, no. 6403. I owe this reference to Prof. M. J. Kister.

of this for [at that time] the people were poor (*murmilīn*); Abū Hishām [replaces this word with] *mushtīn*, that is, suffering from want during the winter, but according to al-Ṭabarī it should be *musnitīn*, that is, going through a period of drought. [Anyway], the Prophet then saw an ewe in the corner of the tent and asked "What is this ewe, O Umm Maʿbad?" She replied "This is an ewe that was too exhausted to [join] the sheep." He asked "Does she have any milk?" to which she replied "She is too exhausted for this." He asked "Will you permit me to milk her?" She said "Yes, [I swear] by my father and mother, if you think that she has milk, do milk her." The Prophet had her brought before him, passed his hand over her udder, mentioned the name of God, and prayed for Umm Maʿbad that her ewe [be blessed]. The ewe parted her legs widely, let the milk flow abundantly, then stood ruminating. The Prophet asked for a vessel [big enough] to sustain the [whole] family and milked into it in a stream until it was covered with froth. He then gave Umm Maʿbad to drink until her thirst was quenched, and he gave his companions to drink until their thirst was quenched, and he was the last to drink, so they [all] quenched their thirst. The Prophet then milked [the ewe] into the vessel again until he filled it.[638] He left it with Umm Maʿbad, accepted the oath of allegiance from her, and left [with his companions].

Shortly afterward her husband, Abū Maʿbad, arrived, driving a few lean goats, so emaciated that they were staggering, even in the morning;[639] there was hardly any marrow in their bones. When Abū Maʿbad saw the milk he was surprised and asked: "Where did you get this, O Umm Maʿbad, the sheep pasturing far away [or else] not pregnant? There is no milking ewe in the tent, [is there]?" She replied "No, by God, but a blessed man passed by us, whose story is such-and-so." Abū Maʿbad said "Describe him to me, O Umm Maʿbad." She said "I saw a radiant man with a luminous [2409]
face and harmonious build unspoiled by thinness and not tainted by small-headedness." Such is the version of Abū Hishām, but it

638. Cf. the version about ʿAbdallāh b. Masʿūd milking an ewe for the Prophet and Abū Bakr on their way to Medina in Kister, "Land Property," 275. For a list of miracles performed by the Prophet, see Ibn Ḥazm, *Jawāmiʿ al-sīrah*, 7–14.

639. *Tasāwakna huzlan ḍuḥan*; See note a to p. 2408.

should be "unspoiled by fleshiness and not tainted by [excessive] leanness."[640] "He is comely and fine-looking, with large black eyes and thick eyelashes." Abū Hishām's version is "long [eyelashes]." "His voice is [like] neighing (ṣahl)"; the shaykh[641] says: This is a mistake, it should be *ṣaḥal* with *ḥ* [that is, a rough voice]. "His neck is long, his beard thick, his brows fine, arched, and joined. When silent he has an air of dignity, and when he speaks he is stately and lustrous. He is the most handsome and majestic person [when you observe him] from a distance and the nicest and kindest when close to [you]. His speech is sweet and clear, like strung beads shed from their string; [he speaks] neither too little nor too much. He is of middle stature, neither loathsome for tallness nor offensive to the eye for shortness. He seemed like a branch that [stands out] between two others, being the most beautiful to look at and the most harmoniously proportioned among the three.[642] He had companions surrounding him who, when he spoke, listened silently to what he said (*naṣatū li-qawlihi*)." Al-Ṭabarī remarks: It should be *anṣatū li-qawlihi.*[643] "When he commanded they hastened to fulfill his command; they rushed and served him promptly, without his being stern or reproachful [to them] (*mufannid*)." Abū Hishām says that this is a mistake; it [should be] "or aggressive" (*mu'tadin*).[644] Abū Ma'bad said: "By God, this is the man of the Quraysh we were told about in Mecca. I intended to become a companion of his, and indeed I shall if I find a way to do so." Then a loud voice was heard in Bakkah;[645] people heard it but did not know to whom it belonged. It recited the following:[646]

---

640. The version from Abū Hishām (as given by de Goeje) is *lam ya'ibhu nuḥluhu wa-lam tuzri bi-hi ṣuqlah.* The corrected version is *lam ta'ibhu thujlah wa-lam tuzri bi-hi ṣuqlah.* Cairo and Dār al-Fikr (both, incidentally, 578) have *nuḥlah* or *niḥlah* instead of *nuḥluhu.*

641. That is, al-Ṭabarī; see p. 143, below.

642. That is, the Prophet, Abū Bakr, and the latter's client.

643. That is, in the fourth form, rather than in the first. The dictionaries, however, have both forms in the same sense.

644. The number of scribal errors in this passage points to its extremely rich and difficult language.

645. Bakkah is another name for Mecca; see Yāqūt, *Mu'jam al-buldān,* I, 706.

646. See al-Ṭabarī, *Ta'rīkh,* I, 1241.

May God the Lord of the people grant the best reward [2410]
to the two companions who drank at midday at the two tents of Umm Maʿbad.
They stopped there, bringing true guidance, and she followed.
Happiness is the lot of one who becomes a companion of Muḥammad.
O come, clan of Quṣayy,[647] [see] how God removed from your midst
leadership and priceless noble deeds.
Let the Banū Kaʿb rejoice in their woman's undertaking,
as she stayed there for the believers, waiting.
Ask your sister about her jar and ewe;
if you ask, the ewe [itself] will confirm it to you.
A barren ewe was brought and for him her milk was flowing,
the pure substance of the ewe's udder, foaming.

Al-Ṭabarī remarks that this is how Abū Hishām recited it, but it should in fact be as follows: "And the ewe's udder flowed for him with the pure substance, foaming."

He left her with Umm Maʿbad as a pledge, for someone [else] to milk
who would lead her time and again to the watering place and back.

When Ḥassān b. Thābit, the Prophet's poet, heard this he composed verses in reply to the voice, saying:[648]

People whose Prophet has left them will fail;
holy are those to whom he travels by morning or night.
He left the people, and their minds lost the trail,
whereas he settled among others, bringing new light.
Through him their Lord guided them after they had gone astray.
He directed them rightly; whoever seeks the Truth shall find
Are they alike, people who erred and foolishly acted blind,
and others who follow the rightly guided one in the right way?

647. Quṣayy was the eponym of the Quraysh.
648. Ḥassān, I, 464–65. The reply is composed in the same rhyme and meter as the verses spoken by the voice.

From Him unto the people of Yathrib came down
the chariots of Truth, bringing the auspicious one,
A Prophet who sees what men around him do not
and reads the book of God in every worshiping spot (*masjid*).

Al-Ṭabarī says: Our version is "in every assembly" (*mashhad*).

[2411] If he sometimes utters an obscure saying,
it is confirmed on the same day or the next morning.
Let Abū Bakr rejoice in his fate, which is felicity;
he will prosper by following one made prosperous by the Almighty.
Let the Banū Kaʿb rejoice in their woman's undertaking
as she stayed there for the believers, waiting.

[Abū Maʿbad] then joined the Prophet and embraced Islam.

According to Ibrāhīm al-Qāriʾ (the Qurʾān reader) Abū Isḥāq al-Kūfī—Bishr b. Ḥasan Abū Aḥmad al-Sukkarī—ʿAbd al-Malik b. Wahb al-Madhḥijī—al-Ḥurr b. al-Ṣayyāḥ al-Nakhaʿī—Abū Maʿbad al-Khuzāʿī: On the night of his Emigration from Mecca to Medina the Prophet left together with Abū Bakr, the latter's client ʿĀmir b. Fuhayrah, and their guide ʿAbdallāh b. Urayqiṭ al-Laythī. They passed by the two tents of Umm Maʿbad al-Khuzāʿiyyah. She was a strong woman, free yet dignified in her discourse with men; she used to sit erect in the court in front of the tent and [order] drink and food to be served. They sought to buy from her meat and dates but did not obtain any of this from her, for [at that time] the people were poor (*murmilūn*), as they were going through a period of drought (*musnitūn*). Umm Maʿbad said [to the visitors] "If we had had anything, offering you food would not have been difficult." The Prophet [then] saw an ewe in the corner of her tent and asked "What is this ewe, O Umm Maʿbad?" She replied "An ewe that was too exhausted [to join] the sheep." He asked "Does she have any milk?" She said "She is too exhausted for this." He asked "Will you permit me to milk her?" She said "Yes, [I swear] by my father and mother, if you think that she has milk, do milk her." The Prophet had the ewe brought before him, passed his hand over her udder, and mentioned the name of God. The ewe parted her legs widely, let the milk flow abundantly, then stood ruminating. The Prophet asked for a vessel [big enough] to sustain the [whole] family and milked into it in a stream until it was [2412] covered with froth. He then gave Umm Maʿbad to drink until her thirst was quenched; then [the rest] were given to drink until they quenched their thirst. The Prophet said "The one who serves drink to the people is the last to drink." They all drank again[649] until they quenched their thirst. Then they[650] milked into the vessel a second time, repeating the first [procedure], whereupon the Prophet left the vessel with Umm Maʿbad [and went away]. Shortly afterward her husband, Abū Maʿbad, came, leading a few ill-fed, lean goats, so exhausted that they tottered as they walked, so thin that there remained no marrow in their bones. When he saw the milk he wondered and asked "Where did you get this, the sheep herding far away and no milking beast being around the tent?" She said "Nay, by God, but a blessed man passed by us, whose story was such-and-so." He said "By God, I think he is the man of the Quraysh we were told about; describe him to me, O Umm Maʿbad." She said: "I saw a radiant man with a luminous face and harmonious build, unspoiled by fleshiness or by small-headedness. He is comely and fine looking, with large black eyes and thick eyelashes. His voice is [like] neighing" (*ṣahl*); al-Ṭabarī says that it should be "rough" (*ṣaḥal*). "[He has] a fair complexion and black eyes, and his brows are fine, arched, and joined. His neck is long and his beard thick." Al-Ṭabarī says: "The [correct word] is *kathāthah*."[651] "When silent he has an air of dignity, and when he speaks he is stately and lustrous. His speech is like strung beads shed from their string, sweet and clear; [he speaks] neither too [2413] little nor too much. He is the finest-looking and handsomest man [when you observe him] from a distance and the nicest and kindest when close to [you]. He is of middle stature; you would not find him loathsome for tallness or offensive to the eye for shortness. He was like a branch that [stands out] between two others, being the most beautiful to look at and the most harmoniously proportioned among the three. He had companions surrounding him

649. Literally, "they all had a second drink after the first one"; the Arabic has a special term for each turn.

650. The verb is in the plural but should refer to the Prophet.

651. The word replaced by al-Ṭabarī is *kathāfah*, a more common word for "thick." The point of replacing it is not clear to me.

who, when he spoke, listened to what he said and, when he commanded, hastened to fulfill his command; they rushed and served him promptly without his being stern or reproachful [to them]." Abū Ma'bad said: "By God, this is the man of Quraysh we were told about. Had I met him I would have sought to become one of his Companions. Indeed, I shall do this if I find a way." Then a loud voice was heard in Mecca; the people heard it and did not know who it was that spoke between heaven and earth. [The voice] said [the following]:

May God the Lord of the people grant the best reward
to the two companions who alighted at the two tents of Umm Ma'bad.
They stopped there as the harbingers of piety; then on they rode.
Happiness is the lot of one who becomes a Companion of Muḥammad.
O come, clan of Quṣayy, [see] how God removed from your midst
leadership and priceless noble deeds.
Ask your sister about her jar and ewe;
if you ask, the ewe [itself] will confirm it to you.
A barren ewe was brought, and for him her milk was flowing,
the pure [substance] of the ewe's udder, foaming.
He left it with her as pledge that someone [else] would milk
abundantly, going to the watering place and back.

In the morning the people missed their Prophet. They followed the way to the two tents of Umm Ma'bad until they caught up with him.[652]

Ḥassān [b. Thābit] answered that voice, saying:

People whose Prophet has left them will fail;
holy are those to whom he travels by morning or night.[653]
[2414] He left the people, and their minds lost the trail,

---

652. It is not clear who are "the people" mentioned here, because the Prophet and Abū Bakr are usually said to have been the last Muslims to emigrate (except for 'Alī b. Abī Ṭālib).

653. Or "Holy are those who travel to him by morning or by night."

whereas he settled among others, bringing new light.
Are they alike, people who erred and foolishly acted blind
and others, who follow him who is guided to what is right,
A Prophet who sees what men around him do not
and reads the book of God in every meeting spot?
If an obscure expression he happens to say,
it is confirmed the same morning or the next day.
Let Abū Bakr rejoice in his fate, which is felicity;
he will prosper by following one made prosperous by the Almighty.
Let the Banū Ka'b rejoice in their woman's undertaking
as she stayed there for the believers, waiting.

Hunaydah b. Khālid al-Khuzā'ī.[654]

According to Muḥammad b. 'Umārah al-Asadī—'Ubaydallāh b. Mūsā—Isrā'īl—Abū Isḥāq—Hunaydah b. Khālid al-Khuzā'ī: The Prophet was fighting when a man came to him and said "O Messenger of God, give me a sword to fight with." The Prophet asked "Perhaps you want to be in the rear rank of the fighters?" and the man replied "No." The Prophet gave him a sword, which he took, reciting the [following] verses:

I am a man who gave an oath to his friend
[there] at the palm trees' feet
That I shall never betray and turn to the rear rank
but shall with the sword of God and the Apostle hit.

He continued to fight until [the enemy] turned to him and killed him.

Numayr al-Khuzā'ī.[655]

According to Muḥammad b. Khalaf al-'Asqalānī and Muḥammad b. 'Awf al-Ṭā'ī, of Ḥimṣ—al-Firyābī—'Iṣām b. Qudāmah—Mālik b. Numayr al-Khuzā'ī—his father: The latter saw the

654. Ibn Ḥajar, *Iṣābah*, III, 612.
655. Khalīfah b. Khayyāṭ, *Ṭabaqāt*, 108.

[2415] Prophet sitting during the prayer, putting his arm on his right thigh, raising his slightly bent forefinger, and praying.[656]

Nāfiʿ b. ʿAbd al-Ḥārith.[657]

According to [Muḥammad] Ibn Bashshār—ʿAbd al-Raḥmān [b. Mahdī]—Sufyān [al-Thawrī]—Ḥabīb—someone—Nāfiʿ b. ʿAbd al-Ḥārith—the Prophet: A spacious home, a good neighbor, and a comfortable means of transport are among the things that make a Muslim happy.

ʿAmr b. Sha's.[658]

According to [Muḥammad] Ibn Ḥumayd—Salamah [b. al-Faḍl]—[Muḥammad] Ibn Isḥāq—Abān b. Ṣāliḥ—ʿĪsā b. al-Faḍl b. Maʿqil b. Sinān al-Ashjaʿī—Abū Burdah b. Niyār b. Mikraz al-Aslamī[659]—his maternal uncle ʿAmr b. Sha's—the Prophet: Whoever harms ʿAlī harms me.

Al-Qaʿqāʿ b. Abī Ḥadrad.[660]

He transmitted [traditions] from the Prophet.

According to Muḥammad b. Ibrāhīm, known as Ibn Ṣudrān, and Yaʿqūb b. Ibrāhīm b. Jubayr al-Wāsiṭī—Ṣafwān b. ʿĪsā—ʿAbdallāh b. Saʿīd—his father—al-Qaʿqāʿ b. Abī Ḥadrad al-Aslamī: The Prophet used to say: Subject yourselves to a hard life, wear coarse clothes, and walk barefoot.

Muʿādh b. Anas al-Juhanī.[661]

According to Abū Kurayb [Muḥammad b. al-ʿAlā']—Saʿīd b. al-Walīd—[ʿAbdallāh] Ibn Mubārak—Yaḥyā b. Ayyūb—ʿAbdallāh b.
[2416] Sulaymān—Ismāʿīl b. Yaḥyā al-Maʿāfirī—Sahl b. Muʿādh b. Anas

---

656. *Wa-huwa yadʿū*, i.e., appeals to God, as distinct from *yuṣallī*, i.e., performs the ritual prayer. See also Ibn Saʿd, VII/1, 42–43.

657. His being a Companion was disputed, but he nevertheless was a respected Muslim and served ʿUmar as governor of Mecca. See Ibn Ḥibbān, *Mashāhīr*, 62; Khalīfah b. Khayyāṭ, *Ta'rīkh*, 127; idem, *Ṭabaqāt*, 109.

658. Ibn Ḥibbān, *Mashāhīr*, 62.

659. That is, the Aslam of Khuzāʿah; see Ibn Ḥazm, *Jamharat*, 240.

660. Khalīfah b. Khayyāṭ, *Ṭabaqāt*, 110–11.

661. He does not belong in this chapter on Khuzāʿīs, being of the Juhaynah and an ally of the Anṣār. See Ibn Ḥibbān, *Mashāhīr*, 95; Khalīfah b. Khayyāṭ, *Ṭabaqāt*, 121.

al-Juhanī—his father—the Prophet: Whoever protects a believer from a Hypocrite's (*munāfiq*) evil tongue, God will send an angel to him who will protect his flesh from hell's fire on the Day of Judgment; and whoever imputes [evil] to a believer wishing to disgrace him, God will detain him on the bridge of hell until he rejects what he said.

The Names of the Ash'arīs Who Transmitted [Traditions] from the Prophet

These are the Banū al-Ash'ar, whose [real] name was Nabt b. Udad b. Zayd b. Yashjub b. 'Arīb b. Zayd b. Kahlān b. Saba' b. Yashjub b. Ya'rub b. Qaḥṭān.[662]

Abū Mūsā, 'Abdallāh and his brother Abū Burdah.[663]

Abū Mālik al-Ash'arī.[664]

According to Yūnus b. 'Abd al-A'lā—['Abdallāh] Ibn Wahb—Mu'āwiyah b. Ṣāliḥ—Ḥātim b. Kurayb—Mālik b. Abī Maryam—'Abd al-Raḥmān b. Ghanm al-Ash'arī—Abū Mālik al-Ash'arī—the Prophet: Indeed, people of my community will drink wine, calling it by other names,[665] and will have musical instruments played before them. God will make the earth swallow them up and will turn them into monkeys and pigs.[666]

---

662. A Yemenī tribe; see Caskel, II, 66; Ibn Ḥazm, *Jamharat*, 397–98; Ibn al-Kalbī, *Nasab ma'add*, 339–42.

663. An eminent Companion who served as a commander during the conquests and a governor of al-Kūfah and al-Baṣrah for 'Umar. See "al-Ash'arī, Abū Musā," *EI²*, I, 695–96 (L. Veccia Vaglieri); Jeffery, 209–11; Ibn Ḥibbān, *Mashāhīr*, 65; Khalīfah b. Khayyāṭ, *Ṭabaqāt*, 132–33. On Abū Burdah, see Khalīfah b. Khayyāṭ, *Ṭabaqāt*, 68, 133; Ibn Ḥibbān, *Mashāhīr*, 167–68; Ibn Ḥajar, *Iṣābah*, IV, 18.

664. Khalīfah b. Khayyāṭ, *Ṭabaqāt*, 68. He is known as a sort of religious guide to his clan. See Ibn Manẓūr, *Mukhtaṣar*, XXIX, 141–45.

665. There is a debate among Muslim scholars about what exactly wine is and whether only grape wine is forbidden or any other alcohol as well; see "Khamr," *EI²*, IV, 994–97 (A. J. Wensinck).

666. Cf. Qur'ān 5:65.

The Names of [the People of] Ḥaḍramawt[667] *Who Transmitted [Traditions] from the Prophet*

Wā'il b. Ḥujr al-Ḥaḍramī.[668]

[2417] 'Abd al-Raḥmān b. 'Ā'ish al-Ḥaḍramī.[669]

According to al-'Abbās b. al-Walīd—his father—Ibn Jābir and al-Awzā'ī—Khālid b. al-Lajlāj—'Abd al-Raḥmān b. 'Ā'ish al-Ḥaḍramī: One morning the Prophet was leading us in prayer, when someone said to him "I never saw your face as radiant as this morning." The Prophet replied:

> The thing with me is, that my Lord appeared before me in the most wonderful way, and said: "O Muḥammad, [do you know] what the celestial council disputes about?" I said: "You know better, my Lord." He put His hand between my shoulders; I felt its coolness in my chest, and I knew what there was in heaven and on earth. He recited the following verse: "Thus do We show Abraham the kingdom of the heavens and the earth, and [it is] so that he may be one of the convinced."[670] He asked [again]: "What does the celestial council dispute about, O Muḥammad?" I said: "About the atonements,[671] my Lord." He asked:

---

667. Ḥaḍramawt, the well-known region in the southern part of the Arabian peninsula, was the dwelling of the royal tribe of Kindah; see "Ḥaḍramawt," *EI*², III, 51–53 (A. F. L. Beeston). Arab genealogists treat the Ḥaḍramawt as a tribal group (cf. Genesis 10:26), and, indeed, Ḥaḍramīs do behave as one (see, e.g., Naṣr b. Muzāḥim, passim). However, the precise place of the Ḥaḍramawt in the genealogical scheme and their relation to other groups, especially the Kindah, are by no means clear. See, e.g., al-Balādhurī, *Ansāb*, I, 9–10; Ibn Ḥazm, *Jamharat*, 460; Muḥammad Ibn Ḥabīb, *Munammaq*, 20; Khalīfah b. Khayyāṭ, *Ṭabaqāt*, 72.

668. A king in Ḥaḍramawt (although not mentioned in al-Ḥimyarī) who embraced Islam and was warmly and generously treated by the Prophet. He later associated with Mu'āwiyah and his governor Ziyād b. Abīhi. See Ibn Ḥibbān, *Mashāhīr*, 77; Ibn Ḥazm, *Jamharat*, 460; al-Dhahabī, *Siyar*, II, 572–73; al-Ṭabarī, *Ta'rīkh*, II, 132–37 (on his role in the Ḥujr b. 'Adī affair).

669. Apparently known only in connection with the tradition recorded here; his being a Companion is disputed. See Ibn Sa'd, VII/2, 150; Ibn Ḥajar, *Iṣābah*, II, 405–6.

670. Qur'ān 6:75, trans. Bell, I, 122; cf. al-Ṭabarī, *Jāmi'*, VII, 247.

671. *Kaffārāt*, sing. *Kaffārah*, a technical term meaning "an expiatory or propitiatory act that grants remission for faults of some gravity"; see "Kaffāra," *EI*², IV, 406–7 (J. Chelhod).

"And what are they?" I said: "Arriving at the Friday prayers by foot, sitting in the mosques after the prayers, and performing the ritual ablution [even] in times of danger." And He said: "Whoever acts in this way will live in virtue and die in virtue and will be [cleansed] from his sins, as [he was] on the day his mother gave birth to him. Feeding [the poor], greeting [one's fellow-Muslim], and praying at night when [other] people are sleeping are among the virtues by which one is raised; ask, and you will be given." The Prophet said: "O God, I ask You that [You lead me to] the good things and keep me away from the forbidden ones; [lead me] to love the poor, and forgive me; if I am tempted to do evil to people, then take me unto You before I fall in the temptation." Learn all this for, by Him Who holds my soul in His hand, they are true.

Of the Kindah

Gharafah b. al-Ḥārith al-Kindī.[672]

According to Ibn Mahdī—['Abdallāh] Ibn al-Mubārak—Ḥarmalah b. 'Imrān—'Abdallāh b. al-Ḥārith al-Azdī—Gharafah [2418]
b. al-Ḥārith al-Kindī: I was present at the Farewell Pilgrimage with the Prophet; when the sacrifice camels were brought he said "Call Abū al-Ḥasan for me." ['Alī b. Abī Ṭālib] was summoned and the Prophet said "Seize the lower part of the javelin." ['Alī did this]; the Prophet seized its upper part, and they stabbed the animals with it. When the Prophet had finished he rode his mule and mounted 'Alī behind him.

'Abdallāh b. Nufayl.[673]

According to 'Abd al-Raḥmān b. al-Walīd—'Umar b. Sa'īd al-Dimashqī—Abū Bakr al-Nahshalī—'Abdallāh b. Salạm—Abū Salamah Sulaymān b. Abī Sulaym—'Abdallāh b. Nufayl al-

672. Ibn Ḥibbān, *Mashāhīr*, 96; Ibn Sa'd, VII/2, 145. According to Ibn Ḥajar, *Iṣābah*, III, 185, he was one of the notables of Egypt and corresponded with the second caliph, 'Umar (al-Ṭabarī does not mention him in the *Annals*).

673. His being a Companion is disputed, and the entry on him in Ibn Ḥajar, *Iṣābah*, II, 376 (quoting also our text) records no biographical details.

Kindī—the Prophet: God has already passed judgment in three matters, so do not violate any of them. Let none of you act wrongfully, for God says "O People, by acting wrongfully you only wrong yourselves";[674] and let none of you deceive [another], for God says "But evil plotting encompasses only those who practice it";[675] and let no one of you break his word, for God says "Whoever breaks faith, to his own hurt he breaks it."[676]

Those Who Transmitted [Traditions] from the Prophet, of the Rest of the Azd

Munīb al-Azdī.[677]

According to Mūsā b. Sahl—Sulaymān b. 'Abd al-Raḥmān al-Dimashqī—'Utbah b. Ḥammād—Munīb b. Mudrik al-Azdī—his father—his grandfather [Munīb al-Azdī]: [Once], in pre-Islamic times, I heard the Prophet say to the people "Say 'There is no God but Allāh,' so that you prosper." At noon a girl came with a bowl of water, and the Prophet washed his face, then said "My girl, rejoice and do not be sad; do not fear that your father will be
[2419] overpowered or humiliated." I asked who it was and was told "Zaynab, his daughter." She was a young girl then.

I was also told this story by 'Abdallāh b. Muḥammad b. 'Amr al-Ghazzī—Isḥāq b. Ibrāhīm al-Ramlī—Sulaymān b. 'Abd al-Raḥmān Abū Ayyūb al-Dimashqī—Abū Khulayd 'Utbah b. Ḥammād al-Ḥakamī—Munīb b. Mudrik al-Azdī—his father—his grandfather [Munīb al-Azdī]: [Once], in pre-Islamic times, I heard the Prophet say to the people "Say 'There is no God but Allāh,' so that you prosper." Some people spat in his face, others threw soil at him, yet others cursed him. At noon a girl came with a bowl of water, and he wahsed his face, then said "My girl, rejoice . . ." The rest of the story is identical with Mūsā b. Sahl's version.

674. Qur'ān 10:24.

675. Qur'ān 35:41, trans. Bell, II, 432.

676. Qur'ān 48:10, trans. Bell, II, 520.

677. Abū Ayyūb al-Azdī al-Ghāmidī, who lived in Syria. See Ibn Ḥajar, *Iṣābah*, III, 465; Ibn Manẓūr, *Mukhtaṣar*, XXV, 275. His house was still known centuries after his death, see Ibn 'Asākir, *Ta'rīkh*, XVII, 250.

Of the Hamdān

[Hamdān] is Asalah b. Mālik b. Zayd b. Asalah b. Rabī'ah b. al-Khiyār b. Mālik b. Zayd b. Kahlān b. Saba'.[678]

'Abd Khayr b. Yazīd al-Khaywānī.[679]

His *kunyah* was Abū 'Umārah; he was contemporaneous with the Prophet.

He reported that a letter from the Prophet had reached [his clan] and that he remembered it.

'Abd Khayr was counted among the companions of 'Alī b. Abī Ṭālib, on whose side he participated in [the battle of] Ṣiffīn.[680]

According to Muḥammad b. Khālid—Mushir b. 'Abd al-Malik b. Sal'—his father: I said to 'Abd Khayr: "O Abū 'Umārah, you are an old man! How many years have you lived?" He replied "One hundred and twenty years." I asked "Do you remember anything about the Barbarians?"[681] He said: "I remember that my mother cooked [something in a] pot for us, and I said 'Give us [something] to eat,' but she replied '[Wait] until your father comes.' My father [2420]
then came and said 'A letter from the Prophet arrived prohibiting carrion meat.' I remember that [the pot] contained carrion meat and [my father] urged us to shun it."

Suwayd b. Hubayrah, an inhabitant of al-Baṣrah.[682]

According to 'Abdallāh b. Isḥāq al-Nāqid al-Wasiṭī and al-Ḥusayn b. 'Alī al-Ṣudā'ī—Rawḥ—Abū Na'āmah al-'Adawī ['Amr b. 'Īsā]—Muslim b. Budayl—Iyās b. Zuhayr—Suwayd b. Hubayrah: I heard the Prophet say: The best property a man can have is a prolific filly (*muhrah ma'mūrah*) or a fruitful palm or-

---

678. A large, powerful Yemenī tribal confederation. Read Awsalah for Asalah. See Ibn Ḥazm, *Jamharat*, 392; "Hamdān," *EI*², III, 122–23 (J. Schleifer [W. M. Watt]); Abū Yāsīn. Note that apparently only the first biography under this rubric is of a Hamdānī.

679. A Kūfan Successor. See al-Dūlābī, II, 37; al-Ṭabarī, *Ta'rīkh*, I, 3152; Ibn Ḥibbān, *Thiqāt*, V, 130–31; Ibn Ḥajar, *Iṣābah*, III, 96, and *Tahdhīb*, VI, 113–14.

680. Naṣr b. Muzāḥim, 136, 342, 353.

681. *Amr al-juhhāl*, "the matter of the Barbarians," that is, pre-Islamic times (the Jāhiliyyah).

682. A Successor; there are various versions of his tribal affiliation. See Ibn Ḥajar, *Iṣābah*, II, 100–1; Khalīfah b. Khayyāṭ, *Ṭabaqāt*, 193.

chard (*sikkah ma'būrah*). Al-Ṣudā'ī's version ends here, whereas al-Nāqid added to his own version: *sikkah* means palm trees, and *muhrah ma'mūrah* means [a filly] foaling many times.

Abū al-Minhāl's father.[683]

According to Zurayq b. al-Sikht—Shabābah b. Sawwār—Salm b. Abī Bilāl—'Abd al-Malik b. Abī Bashīr—Abū al-Minhāl—his father—the Prophet: Sleeping [in the time] between the setting and the rising of the stars is most harmful.

'Umayr b. Wahb, the Prophet's maternal uncle.[684]

He transmitted [traditions] from the Prophet.

According to Muḥammad b. 'Abdallāh al-Hilālī Abū Mas'ūd al-Mukattib—Sa'īd b. Sallām—Hishām b. al-Ghāz—Muḥammad b. Abān—'Umayr b. Wahb, the Prophet's maternal uncle: [Once] the Prophet saw 'Umayr approaching, so he spread his garment for
[2421] him and said "Sit down." ['Umayr] asked "Should I sit on your garment, O Messenger of God?" the Prophet said "Sit down, for one's maternal uncle is [like a] father to one."[685] When he sat down the Prophet said "Shall I teach you the words God teaches those whose happiness He wants, [words] that He does not let them forget until they die?" 'Umayr replied "Certainly, O Messenger of God." The Prophet then said "Say 'O God, I am weak, so strengthen me, with Your consent; take me by the forelock [and lead me] toward what is good; with Your mercy, let me attain Your mercy that I wish for; let Islam be my ultimate goal; make me [find] love with people and a covenant with you.' "[686]

'Abdallāh b. Hilāl.[687]

According to Bishr b. Ādam—Zayd b. al-Ḥubāb—Bishr b. 'Im-

---

683. His identity is unclear; see Ibn Ḥibbān, *Mashāhīr*, 156. Ibn Sa'd mentions two persons by that name with no details. The tradition recorded here is not mentioned in Zaghlūl's *Mawsū'at aṭrāf al-ḥadīth*.

684. That is, brother of the Prophet's mother, Āminah bt. Wahb of the Qurashī clan Zuhrah, not to be confused with 'Umayr b. Wahb of the Qurashī clan Jumaḥ; see Ibn Ḥajar, *Iṣābah*, III, 37. Almost nothing is known about him; he is not mentioned even once in the *Sīrah* of Ibn Hishām and is ignored by Ibn Sa'd.

685. Cf. p. 97, above.

686. Cf. Qur'ān 2:80, 9:7.

687. His identity is unclear. See Ibn Ḥajar, *Iṣābah*, II, 339, 378; Ibn Abī Ḥātim, II/2, 193.

rān—his patron ʿAbdallāh b. Hilāl: My father brought me to the Prophet, who put his hand on my head and blessed me. He seemed to me an old, hairy man, who fasted during daytime and prayed during the night. I remember the coolness of the Prophet's hand on the crown of my head.

Muʿādh b. ʿAbdallāh b. Khubayb's paternal uncle.[688]

According to Muḥammad b. Maʿmar—Abū ʿĀmir—ʿAbdallāh b. Abī Sulaymān, an old man from Medina—Muʿādh b. ʿAbdallāh b. Khubayb—his father—his paternal uncle: The Prophet emerged before us, traces of water on his head, while we were sitting in company. We said "O Messenger of God, we see that you are cheerful," whereupon he said "Indeed." The people then started talking about wealth, and the Prophet said "There is nothing wrong in wealth when a person is God fearing, but health is better than wealth for the God fearing, and cheerfulness is a blessing."

Abū Fāṭimah.[689] [2422]

He transmitted [traditions] from the Prophet.

According to Muḥammad b. ʿAwf—Muḥammad b. Ismāʿīl—his father—Ḍamḍam—Shurayḥ b. ʿUbayd—Kathīr b. Murrah—Abū Fāṭimah, who said to the Prophet "O Messenger of God, tell me about an act that will put me on the right path [if I perform it]."[690] The Prophet said "You should perform the emigration (*hijrah*), for there is nothing like it." I asked [again] "O Messenger of God, tell me about an act that will put me on the right path [if I perform it]." He said "You should fast, for there is nothing like fasting." I said [again] "Tell me, O Messenger of God, about an act that will put me on the right path [if I perform it]." He said "You should perform the prostration before God, for whenever you perform a prostration God raises you by one degree and takes a sin off you."

---

688. His identity is unclear. See Ibn Ḥajar, *Iṣābah*, III, 429; Ibn Abī Ḥatim, IV/1, 426–27.

689. An Egyptian of the Azd. See Khalīfah b. Khayyāṭ, *Ṭabaqāt*, 115; al-Dūlābī, I, 47; Ibn Saʿd, VII/2, 198.

690. Cf. Ibn Abī Shaybah, *Īmān*, 16, where a similar story is attributed to the Companion Muʿādh b. Jabal.

Wahb b. Ḥudhayfah.[691]

According to Abū Kurayb [Muḥammad b. al-ʿAlāʾ]—ʿUthmān b. Saʿīd—Khālid—ʿAmr b. Yaḥyā—his paternal uncle Wāsiʿ b. Ḥabbān—Wahb b. Ḥudhayfah—the Prophet: A man has a right to his seat; if he gets up to fulfill some need or other, then comes back, he has a right to his seat.

Al-Ḥārith b. Mālik.[692]

According to Sahl b. Mūsā al-Rāzī—al-Ḥajjāj b. Muhājir—Ayyūb b. Khūṭ—Layth—Zayd b. Rufayʿ—al-Ḥārith b. Mālik, who said, while with the Prophet "I am truly a believer," whereupon the Prophet said "Be careful with what you say, for every statement has its proper sense."[693] Al-Ḥārith said: "O Messenger of God, I have ordered my soul to turn away from this world, and it [obeyed] calmly; I have abstained from drinking[694] during the daytime and have spent the nights awake. It is as if I look at the
[2423] throne of the Lord and at paradise's dwellers paying visits to one another and at hell's dwellers howling to one another." The Prophet said "You have turned away [from this world], so adhere [to your way]; you have turned away [from this world], so adhere [to your way]."[695] The Prophet then added "Whoever likes to become happy by looking at a servant [of God] whose heart was lit with faith by God, let him look at al-Ḥārith b. Mālik." Al-Ḥārith then asked [the Prophet] "Pray to God that I may die as a *shahīd*!" The Prophet prayed for him, and he fell as a *shahīd*.

Abū al-Ḥamrāʾ.[696]

He transmitted [traditions] from the Prophet.

---

691. Of the Kinānī clan Ghifār or the Muzaynah, a rather insignificant Companion. See Ibn Ḥajar, *Iṣābah*, III, 641; Khalīfah b. Khayyāṭ, *Ṭabaqāt*, 33.

692. An Anṣārī killed during the Prophet's lifetime; see Ibn Ḥajar, *Iṣābah*, I, 289–90.

693. There is a dispute among Muslim scholars as to whether it is permissible to declare oneself a believer or to say "I am a believer if God so wills" or a similar expression. This is connected to the commendable quality of modesty as well as to such theological problems as the true sense of belief, the difference between belief (*īmān*) and Islam, and free will vs. predestination. See, e.g., Ibn Abī Shaybah, *Īmān*, 21–25; idem., *Muṣannaf*, XI, 42–43.

694. Or, "made myself lean," i.e., fasted.

695. Cf. Ibn Abī Shaybah, *Īmān*, 43.

696. Apparently not the Prophet's client mentioned in some sources (al-Dūlābī,

According to ʿAbd al-Aʿlā b. Wāṣil and Sufyān b. Wakīʿ—Abū Nuʿaym al-Faḍl b. Dukayn—Yūnus b. Abī Isḥāq—Abū Dā'ūd—Abū al-Ḥamrā': I lived in Medina for seven months during the Prophet's lifetime; each day at dawn I saw the Prophet come to the door of ʿAlī and Fāṭimah and call "To the prayer, to the prayer; indeed, ʿAllāh simply wishes to take away the foulness from you and to purify you thoroughly.'"[697]

Al-Haddār.[698]

According to Muḥammad b. ʿAwf—his father—Shuqayr, al-ʿAbbās' client: [Shuqayr] heard al-Haddār, the Prophet's Companion, say to al-ʿAbbās, after having seen him eating white bread and other things immoderately "I never saw the Prophet satisfy his hunger with wheat bread until God took him."

Ziyād b. Muṭarrif.[699]

According to Zakariyā' b. Yaḥyā b. Abān al-Miṣrī—Aḥmad b. Ishkāb—Yaḥyā b. Yaʿlā al-Muḥāribī—ʿAmmār b. Zurayq al-Ḍabbī—Abū Isḥāq al-Hamdānī—Ziyād b. Muṭarrif—the Prophet: Whoever wishes to live like me and to die like me and to enter the [2424]
garden some of whose branches God promised to give me, [from trees] He had planted in that garden of eternity, [whoever wishes to attain this], let him befriend ʿAlī b. Abī Ṭālib and his descendants after him, for they will never lead him out through the door of the right path, and never lead him in through the door of error.

I, 25; Ibn Ḥibbān, *Thiqāt*, III, 435–36) or he would not have "lived in Medina for seven months" but would rather have lived there permanently. Ibn Ḥajar, *Iṣābah*, IV, 46, mentions another person by that *kunyah*, of whom he knows only that he participated in Badr and Uḥud.

697. Qur'ān 33:33, trans. Bell, II, 414. This is a version of what is called The Tradition of the Covering (*ḥadīth al-kisā'*), which aims at identifying the *ahl al-bayt*, i.e., the family of the Prophet. The proper identification of the term is directly connected with the political issue of authority, as the Shīʿīs applied it to ʿAlī, Fāṭimah, and their descendants only, whereas the ʿAbbāsids included themselves in it. See Sharon, "Notes"; idem, "Development"; idem, "The Umayyads"; "Ahl al-bayt," *EI*², I, 257–58 (I. Goldziher, C. van Arendonck, and A. S. Tritton). For other versions of the tradition, see Ibn Ḥanbal, *Musnad*, VI, 292; Arazi and Elʿad, 241, 254 no. 39; see also Zaghlūl, III, 555.

698. A Kinānī who lived in Ḥimṣ; see Ibn Ḥajar, *Iṣābah*, III, 600.

699. Apparently known only in connection with the tradition quoted here; see Ibn Ḥajar, *Iṣābah*, I, 559.

Junādah b. Mālik.[700]

According to Abū Kurayb [Muḥammad b. al-'Alā'] and Muḥammad b. 'Umar b. al-Hayyāj al-Hamdānī—Yaḥyā b. 'Abd al-Raḥmān—'Ubaydah b. al-Aswad—al-Qāsim b. al-Walīd—Muṣ'ab b. 'Abdallāh al-Azdī—'Abdallāh b. Junādah—Junādah b. Mālik—the Prophet: There are three features of the people of the Jāhiliyyah never to be given up by the people of Islam—praying to the stars for rain,[701] finding fault with one another's genealogy,[702] and wailing for the dead.[703]

Abū Udhaynah.[704]

According to 'Ubayd b. Ādam b. Abī Iyās—his father—al-Layth b. Sa'd—Mūsā b. 'Ulayy b. Rabāḥ—his father—Abū Udhaynah—the Prophet: The best of your women are those who are prolific, affectionate, obedient, and generous, provided they are God fearing. The worst of your women are those who dress up and are conceited. These are the Hypocrites (*munāfiqāt*); such a one's reaching paradise is [a phenomenon] as rare as a white-footed raven.

Ibn Nuḍaylah.[705]

According to Muḥammad b. 'Abdallāh b. 'Abd al-Ḥakam—Ay-
[2425] yūb b. Suwayd—al-Awzā'ī—Abū 'Ubayd[706]—al-Qāsim b. Mukhaymirah—Ibn Nuḍaylah: A famine befell the people during the Prophet's lifetime, and they appealed to him "O Messenger of

700. Of the tribe of Azd; see al-Bukhārī, *Ta'rīkh*, II, 232–34; Ibn Sa'd, VII/2, 194. He is confused with one Junādah b. Abī Umayyah, and, to add to the confusion, there are two by the latter name, one of them quite well known. See Ibn Ḥajar, *Iṣābah*, I, 247, 245–46; Khalīfah b. Khayyāṭ, *Ta'rīkh*, 159, 216; idem, *Ṭabaqāt*, 116, 305, 309.

701. Prayer for rain (*istisqā'*) was practiced both in pre-Islamic and in Islamic times, naturally with differences arising from paganism vs. monotheism. See Goldziher, *Muslim Studies*, I, 41; "Istisqā'," *EI*², IV, 269–70 (T. Fahd).

702. Genealogy, *nasab* (here *nisbah*), was pivotal in the social life of the Arabs both before and after Islam. Boasting of their own genealogy and degrading that of the others were customary among both tribes and individuals and were strongly repudiated by Islam. See Goldziher, *Muslim Studies*, I, chap. 2.

703. The traditional pre-Islamic way of wailing for the dead, *niyāḥah* or *nawḥ*, was strictly forbidden by Islam; see note 179, above.

704. Apparently known only in connection with the tradition recorded here; see Ibn Ḥajar, *Iṣābah*, I, 4–5. Al-Dūlābī mentions only his name.

705. Apparently known only in connection with the tradition recorded here; see Ibn al-Athīr, *Usd*, V, 331.

706. He was Sulaymān b. 'Abd al-Malik's doorkeeper; see de Goeje, 2424 n. h.

God, announce fixed prices for us." He retorted: "Let not God call me to account for a custom (*sunnah*) I introduced to you without His ordering me to do it. Nay, ask God for His favor."[707]

Abū al-Muʿallā's father.[708]

According to al-Faḍl b. Sahl al-Aʿraj—Muʿallā b. Manṣūr—ʿUbaydallāh b. ʿAmr—ʿAbd al-Malik b. ʿUmayr—Abū al-Muʿallā—his father: The Prophet stood at the pulpit and said "My foot is placed at one of paradise's gates."[709]

Murrah.[710]

According to al-Ḥasan b. ʿArafah—ʿUmar b. ʿAbd al-Raḥmān—Muḥammad b. Juḥādah—Muḥammad b. ʿAjlān—Murrah's daughter—her father—the Prophet: One who acts as guardian of an orphan, whether on his own or someone else's behalf, will be with me in paradise [as close to me as that], if he fears God; and he indicated [it] with his forefinger and middle finger.

ʿUbaydallāh b. Miḥṣan.[711]

According to Ṣāliḥ b. Mismār—Muḥammad b. ʿAbd al-ʿAzīz—Marwān—ʿAbd al-Raḥmān b. Abī Shumaylah al-Anṣārī—Salamah b. ʿUbaydallāh b. Miḥṣan—his father—the Prophet: Whoever of you gets up in the morning safe in his family and property, sound in his body, having food for the day, it is as if he owned this world.

ʿĀṣim b. Ḥadrah.[712]

According to ʿImrān b. Bakkār al-Kalāʿī—Yaḥyā b. Ṣāliḥ—Saʿīd

---

707. *Sunnah* is a term indicating all the customs and practices of the Prophet considered to be the paradigm of a good Muslim's behavior. Here the idea is expressed that not only the Qur'ān, but also the *sunnah*, has a divine origin. See Goldziher, *Muslim Studies*, II, 24–38 and passim.

708. An Anṣārī, known in connection with the tradition recorded here; see Ibn Ḥajar, *Iṣābah*, IV, 182–83.

709. *Turʿah min turaʿ al-jannah. Turʿah* means both the pulpit's flight of steps and a gate or door. The word is here used in both meanings simultaneously, the idea being that this very flight of steps leads to paradise.

710. I could not trace this individual.

711. An Anṣārī, apparently known only in connection with the tradition recorded here; see Ibn Ḥajar, *Iṣābah*, II, 439–40; Ibn Ḥibbān, *Thiqāt*, V, 65.

712. Or Ḥadrad, an Anṣārī known in connection with the tradition recorded here; see Ibn Ḥajar, *Iṣābah*, II, 245.

[2426] b. Bashīr—Qatādah [b. Di'āmah]—al-Ḥasan [al-Baṣrī]: We entered 'Āṣim b. Ḥadrah's [home], and he said to us "The Prophet never ate at a table, never carried a cushion with him, and never had a doorkeeper."

Abū Maryam al-Filasṭīnī.[713]

According to Muḥammad b. Sahl b. 'Askar—Abū Mushir ['Abd al-A'lā b. Mushir]—Ṣadaqah b. Khālid—Yazīd b. Abī Maryam—al-Qāsim b. Mukhaymirah—a man of the people of Filasṭīn whose *kunyah* was Abū Maryam. This man came to see Mu'āwiyah, and the latter asked him to recite a tradition (*ḥadīth*) he had heard from the Prophet. Abū Maryam said: I heard the Prophet say: "Whoever is appointed by God to take care of any of the Muslims' affairs and shuts his eyes to their need and want and poverty, God will shut His eyes to [this ruler's] need and want and poverty on the Day of Judgment.

Rāshid b. Ḥubaysh.[714]

According to [Muḥammad] Ibn Bashshār—Muḥammad b. Bakr—Sa'īd [b. Abī 'Arūbah]—Qatādah [b. Di'āmah]—Muslim b. Yasār—Abū al-Ash'ath al-Ṣan'ānī—Rāshid b. Ḥubaysh: The Prophet visited 'Ubādah b. al-Ṣāmit,[715] who was ill, and said "Do you know the identity of the martyrs (*shuhadā'*) of my community?" The people remained silent; 'Ubādah b. al-Ṣāmit said "Assist me [to sit up]," which they did, and he answered: "Those who bear patiently and seek God's reward." The Prophet then said: "In that case, the martyrs of my community are few. [I say that] to be killed in the path of God counts as martyrdom (*shahādah*), and so do death in a plague, drowning, death by a belly
[2427] disease, and the death of a woman in labor; [such a woman's] child pulls his mother to paradise by the umbilical cord." Abū al-'Aw-

---

713. Of the Azd tribe, al-Dūlābī, I, 53–54; Ibn Sa'd, VII/2, 150. There is, however, a confusion between several persons of that *kunyah*. See Ibn Ḥajar, *Iṣābah*, IV, 179; Khalīfah b. Khayyāṭ, *Ṭabaqāt*, 313; Ibn al-Athīr, *Usd*, V, 295–96.

714. It is disputed whether he was a Companion or a Successor; he is known in connection with the tradition recorded here; see Ibn Ḥajar, *Iṣābah*, I, 494.

715. An eminent Anṣārī and the first judge in Filasṭīn. See Ibn Ḥajar, *Iṣābah*, II, 268–69; Ibn Ḥibbān, *Mashāhīr*, 87–88; al-Ṣafadī, XVI, 618–19.

wwām added: "And the keepers of the temple at Jerusalem (*bayt al-maqdis*) [are martyrs] and also [those who die by] fire or ulceration in the lungs."

Aws b. Shuraḥbīl.[716]

According to ʿAbdallāh b. Aḥmad b. Shabbūyah—Isḥāq b. Ibrāhīm—ʿAmr b. al-Ḥārith—ʿAbdallāh b. Sālim—al-Zabīdī—ʿAyyāsh b. Muʾnis—Abū Nimrān al-Raḥabī—Aws b. Shuraḥbīl, one of the Banū al-Mujammiʿ—the Prophet: He who goes [along] with an unjust [ruler] and supports him, knowing that he is unjust, has forsaken Islam [by this act].[717]

ʿAbd al-Raḥmān b. Khanbash.[718]

According to ʿUbaydallāh b. ʿUmar—Jaʿfar b. Sulaymān al-Ḍubaʿī—Abū al-Tayyāḥ: Someone asked ʿAbd al-Raḥmān b. Khanbash, who was [then] a very old man "O Ibn Khanbash, what used the Prophet to do when the devils plotted against him?" He said: "The devils came down upon the Prophet from the mountains and the valleys, intending [to harm] him. Among them was a devil with a burning piece of wood with which he intended to burn the Prophet. The Prophet was scared when he saw them, [but] Jibrīl came to him and said 'O Muḥammad, repeat after me "I seek refuge in the words of God, which neither the pious nor the sinner can transgress; [I seek refuge] from the evil that He created and made out of nothing and caused to be and from the evil that de- [2428]
scends from the sky and that which ascends it, from the evil that is sown in the earth and that which grows out of it, from the evil of the temptations of night and day, and from the evil of anyone knocking at the door,[719] except one [who brings] good, O Merciful.'"[720] Then the devils' fire was extinguished and they were defeated by God."

---

716. Or Shuraḥbīl b. Aws, a Companion, resident of Ḥimṣ, known in connection with the tradition recorded here; see Ibn Ḥajar, *Iṣābah*, I, 85.

717. This is an antiquietist tradition; but cf. p. 102, above.

718. A Tamīmī, resident of al-Baṣrah; see Ibn Ḥajar, *Iṣābah*, II, 396–97.

719. Or, "the evil of every diviner" (practicing divination by pebbles).

720. Cf. Qurʾān 7:200, 23:97, 41:36, 113, 114; and see note 620, above.

Ibn Ju'dubah.[721]

He transmitted [traditions] from the Prophet.

According to al-'Abbās b. al-Walīd—Sa'īd b. Manṣūr—Ya'qūb b. 'Abd al-Raḥmān and 'Abd al-'Azīz b. Abī Ḥāzim—Abū Ḥāzim [Salamah b. Dīnār]—Muḥammad b. Ka'b—Ibn Ju'dubah—the Prophet: God is pleased with three things and hates three things for you to do: He is pleased that you worship Him without attributing any partner to Him and that you all hold fast to the covenant of God without being at variance with one another and that you obey those whom God has appointed to rule you.[722] He hates you to engage in gossip, to ask too many questions, and to waste money.[723]

Abū Mu'attib b. 'Amr.[724]

According to [Muḥammad] Ibn Ḥumayd—Salamah [b. al-Faḍl]—Muḥammad b. Isḥāq—al-Ḥasan b. Dīnār—'Aṭā' b. Abī Marwān al-Aslamī—his father—Abū Mu'attib b. 'Amr: When the Prophet looked down on Khaybar he said to his Companions, among whom I was [too][725] "Stop!" Then he said: "O God, Lord of the heavens and whatever lies under their shadows, Lord of the earth and whatever it sustains, Lord of the devils and whomever they lead astray, Lord of the winds and whatever they
[2429] scatter! We ask You [to give us] the good of this town and its people and whatever is in it, and we seek refuge in You from its evil and the evil of its people and of whatever is in it; advance, in the name of God." He used to say this for every town he entered.

---

721. Yazīd b. 'Iyāḍ, a Baṣran Successor, of the Kinānī clan the Banū Layth. See Ibn Sa'd, V, 305; Ibn Ḥajar, *Tahdhīb*, XI, 308–9.

722. Unity of the community and obedience to rulers are closely connected. See p. 102 and note 487, above.

723. Or, "property."

724. A Companion, of the Aslam tribe; he is known to have fought in the Muslim army during the apostasy wars. See Ibn Ḥajar, *Iṣābah*, IV, 181; Khalīfah b. Khayyāṭ, *Ṭabaqāt*, 112, 137; al-Dūlābī, I, 55.

725. See al-Wāqidī, 658, where another report about Khaybar is traced back to him (he is called Mu'attib al-Aslamī there).

The Biographies of the Women Who Embraced Islam during the Prophet's Lifetime: Those of Them Who Passed away before the Emigration

Khadījah bt. Khuwaylid b. Asad b. ʿAbd al-ʿUzzā b. Quṣayy.

Her *kunyah* was Umm Hind, after one of her daughters named Hind, whom she bore to ʿAtīq b. ʿĀbid b. ʿAbdallāh b. ʿUmar b. Makhzūm, and [also] after a son of hers called Hind, whom she bore to Abū Hālah b. al-Nabbāsh b. Zurārah b. Waqdān b. Ḥabīb b. Salāmah b. Ghuwayy b. Jirwah b. Usayyid b. ʿAmr b. Tamīm.

According to Ibn ʿUmar [al-Wāqidī]—al-Mundhir b. ʿAbdallāh al-Ḥizāmī—Mūsā b. ʿUqbah—Abū Ḥabībah, al-Zubayr's client—Ḥakīm b. Ḥizām: Khadījah bt. Khuwaylid died in Ramaḍān of the year 10 after [the beginning of] the prophethood,[726] at the age of sixty-five. We carried her from her house to be buried at al-Ḥajūn, and the Prophet descended into her grave.[727] The prayer over the bier was then not yet included in the procedure of funerals. Someone asked [Ḥakīm b. Ḥizām] "When was this [introduced], O Abū Khālid?" [Ḥakīm] replied "Three years or so before the Emigration, shortly after the Banū Hāshim came out of the ravine [where they had been besieged].[728]

Khadījah was the Prophet's first wife, and she bore all his children except Ibrāhīm, son of Māriyah. Her *kunyah* was Umm Hind, after her son from her [former] husband Abū Hālah al-Tamīmī.

Those of Them Who Died during the Prophet's Lifetime after the Emigration [2430]

Of the Prophet's daughters: Ruqayyah, Khadījah's daughter.[729]

Ruqayyah had been married to ʿUtbah b. Abī Lahab b. ʿAbd al-Muṭṭalib before Muḥammad was inspired. When the Prophet was

726. The Muslim era starts with the Emigration, and the Muslims have no concept parallel to that of B.C.. For the years preceding the Emigration various expressions are used. Here the beginning of the prophethood serves as a starting point, although the Muslims differed on the exact date of this event. See al-Sakhāwī's *Iʿlām*, in Rosenthal, *History*, 380.

727. Cf. p. 11, above.

728. That is, after the boycott was removed from them. See p. 55, above.

729. Khalīfah b. Khayyāṭ, *Taʾrīkh*, 24; Ibn Sayyid al-Nās, II, 365.

sent [on his divine mission] and God revealed the verse "The hands of Abū Lahab have perished,"[730] 'Utbah's father said to him "Divorce Muḥammad's daughter, or else all ties between us will be [irreversibly] severed." So 'Utbah divorced Ruqayyah without having consummated the marriage. She embraced Islam when her mother Khadījah did and swore allegiance to the Prophet, together with the other women.[731] 'Uthmān b. 'Affān married her, and she emigrated twice to Abyssinia with him. On the first emigration she miscarried the child she had from 'Uthmān, but later she bore him a son whom he named 'Abdallāh. When the Prophet emigrated [to Medina] she followed suit, after her husband 'Uthmān.

Ruqayyah fell ill when the Prophet was preparing to set out for [the battle of] Badr, so he left 'Uthmān behind [to watch over her].[732] She died in Ramaḍān, seventeen months after the Prophet's Emigration/March 624, while the Prophet was at Badr. Zayd b. Ḥārithah came from Badr with the good news [of the victory], and when he entered Medina the [people] were leveling the earth over her [grave].[733]

Zaynab, the Prophet's daughter.

Her mother was Khadījah. She was the eldest of the Prophet's daughters.

Zaynab's maternal cousin, Abū al-'Āṣ b. al-Rabī', had married her before the Prophet was sent [on his divine mission]. Abū al-'Āṣ's mother was Hālah bt. Khuwaylid b. Asad, Zaynab's maternal aunt. Zaynab bore Abū al-'Āṣ [his children] 'Alī and Umāmah; 'Alī died in infancy, whereas Umāmah remained [to live]. 'Alī b.
[2431] Abī Ṭālib, the Commander of the Faithful, married her after the death of [his wife] Fāṭimah, daughter of the Prophet.

According to Muḥammad b. 'Umar [al-Wāqidī]—Yaḥyā b. 'Abd-

730. Qur'ān 111:4; trans. Bell, II, 684.

731. *Ḥīna bāya'ahu al-nisā'*. This is not to be confused with the so-called *bay'at al-nisā'*, the name given to the first pledge of the Anṣār in the first 'Aqabah meeting; see Ibn Hishām, II, 75; Guillaume, 198–99.

732. This account has a political significance, as 'Uthmān's opponents accused him of cowardice and considered him therefore unqualified to rule. 'Uthmān's supporters justified his absence from the battle of Badr by the permission, or even order, of the Prophet that he should stay behind and watch over the sick Ruqayyah. As for Uḥud, it is claimed that God forgave him. See, e.g., al-Balādhurī, *Ansāb*, I, 326.

733. Ibn Sa'd, VIII, 24.

allāh b. Abī Qatādah—'Abdallāh b. Abī Bakr b. Muḥammad b. 'Amr b. Ḥazm: Zaynab, the Prophet's daughter, died at the beginning of the year 8/the middle of the year 629.

According to al-Ṭabarī: It was reported that the reason for her death was [as follows]. When she left Mecca, intending to reach Medina and join her father, Habbār b. al-Aswad caught up with her. She was [sitting on a camel] in a litter, and he pushed her, whereupon she fell on a rock and, being pregnant, miscarried her child and lost [a lot of] blood. She had this injury and ultimately died of it.

Umm Kulthūm, daughter of the Prophet.

Her mother was Khadījah.

She had been married to 'Utaybah b. Abī Lahab before the Prophet was sent [on his divine mission]. He divorced her for the same reason that his brother 'Utbah divorced her sister Ruqayyah, [even] before the consummation of their marriage,[734] as I mentioned [before].

Umm Kulthūm emigrated to Medina with the [rest of the] Prophet's children. Following the death of Ruqayyah, daughter of the Prophet, he gave Umm Kulthūm in marriage to 'Uthmān b. 'Affān, in Rabī' I 3/September 624. She remained married to him until her death; she bore him no children.

Umm Kulthūm died in Sha'bān 9/November–December 630. Women of the Anṣār, among them Umm 'Aṭiyyah, washed her body, and Abū Ṭalḥah descended into her grave.[735]

The Prophet's Wives Who Died during His Lifetime[736]

Zaynab bt. Khuzaymah b. al-Ḥārith b. 'Abdallāh b. 'Amr b. 'Abd Manāf b. Hilāl b. 'Āmir b. Ṣa'ṣa'ah, named Umm al-Masākīn.[737]

---

734. It is not clear whether or not the text argues that 'Utaybah also divorced Umm Kulthūm before the consummation of their marriage. The argument dulls the edge of the fact that the daughters of the Prophet were already divorced when 'Uthmān married them.

735. See p. 11, above.

736. On the wives of the Prophet, see Morsy, and a critique of the book in Gilliot, "Bulletin d'islamologie", 487–89; al-Ṭabarī, *Ta'rīkh*, I, 1766–82; Ibn Hishām, IV, 293–98; Ibn Isḥāq, *Siyar*, 243–69; Abū Zur'ah, 489–95; Ibn Ḥazm, *Jawāmi' al-sīrah*, 31–38; al-Ṣāliḥī, *Azwāj al-nabiyy*.

737. "Zainab," *EI*[1], IV, 1200 (V. Vacca); al-Balādhurī, *Ansāb*, I, 429; Khalīfah b. Khayyāṭ, *Ta'rīkh*, 26; Ibn Isḥāq, *Siyar*, 258.

[2432] It was reported that she was thus named in pre-Islamic times.

According to Muḥammad b. ʿUmar [al-Wāqidī]—Muḥammad b. ʿAbdallāh—Ibn Shihāb al-Zuhrī: Zaynab bt. Khuzaymah al-Hilāliyyah was called Umm al-Masākīn. She had been married to al-Ṭufayl b. al-Ḥārith b. al-Muṭṭalib b. ʿAbd Manāf, and he divorced her.

According to Ibn ʿUmar [al-Wāqidī]—ʿAbdallāh, that is, Ibn Jaʿfar—ʿAbd al-Wāḥid b. Abī ʿAwn: [Then] ʿUbaydah b. al-Ḥārith married her, and he was killed in [the battle] of Badr as a *shahīd*, leaving her a widow.

According to Ibn ʿUmar [al-Wāqidī]—Kathīr b. Zayd—al-Muṭṭalib b. ʿAbdallāh b. Ḥanṭab, and also Muḥammad b. Qudāmah—his father: The Prophet asked Zaynab bt. Khuzaymah al-Hilāliyyah, Umm al-Masākīn, in marriage, and she entrusted her affairs to him. He let it be known that he gave her twelve and a half ounces [of gold] as bridal gift.[738] The marriage took place in Ramaḍān, thirty-one months after the Emigration/February 625. She stayed with him eight months, then died at the end of Rabīʿ II, thirty-nine months after [the Emigration]/October 626.[739] The Prophet said the prayers over her bier and buried her at al-Baqīʿ.

Ibn ʿUmar [al-Wāqidī] related: I asked ʿAbdallāh b. Jaʿfar who it was that descended into her grave,[740] and he said "three of her brothers." I asked "How old was she when she died?" He said "Thirty years or so."

Rayḥānah bt. Zayd b. ʿAmr b. Khunāfah b. Samʿūn b. Zayd, of the Banū al-Naḍīr.[741]

Rayḥānah had been married to a man of the Banū Qurayẓah named al-Ḥakam; therefore some genealogists traced her pedigree to the Qurayẓah.

According to Muḥammad b. ʿUmar [al-Wāqidī]—ʿAbdallāh b. Jaʿfar—Yazīd b. al-Hād—Thaʿlabah b. Abī Mālik: Rayḥānah bt.

---

738. *Aṣdaqahā*. See "Mahr," *EI*², VI, 78–80 (O. Spies).

739. Although it may seem otherwise, the time here is calculated not from the actual Emigration, which occurred in the third month of the year (Rabīʿ I), but from the first month (Muḥarram) of the year of the Emigration.

740. See p. 11, above.

741. A Jewess captured by the Muslims with the Banū Qurayẓah. See al-Balādhurī, *Ansāb*, I, 453–54; al-Ṭabarī, *Taʾrīkh*, I, 1498.

Zayd b. ʿAmr b. Khunāfah, of the Banū al-Naḍīr, was married to one of the [Banū Qurayẓah] named al-Ḥakam. When the Banū Qurayẓah were taken captive the Prophet took her, set her free, and married her. She was still married to him when she died.[742] [2433]

According to Muḥammad b. ʿUmar [al-Wāqidī]: Rayḥānah remained married to the Prophet until her death on the Prophet's return from the Farewell Pilgrimage; he buried her in al-Baqīʿ. He had married her in Muḥarram 6/May–June 627.

Mulaykah bt. Kaʿb al-Laythī.[743]

According to Ibn ʿUmar [al-Wāqidī]—ʿAbd al-ʿAzīz b. al-Jundaʿī—his father—ʿAṭāʾ b. Yazīd al-Jundaʿī: The Prophet married Mulaykah bt. Kaʿb al-Laythī in Ramaḍān 8/January 630 and consummated the marriage. She was still married to him when she died.

According to Ibn ʿUmar [al-Wāqidī]—Muḥammad b. ʿAbdallāh—[Ibn Shihāb] al-Zuhrī: The same [as the preceding account].

According to Ibn ʿUmar [al-Wāqidī]: Our masters deny this, saying that the Prophet never married a woman of the Kinānah.

According to Ibn ʿUmar [al-Wāqidī]—Abū Maʿshar [Najīḥ b. ʿAbd al-Raḥmān]: The Prophet married Mulaykah bt. Kaʿb, who was famous for her outstanding beauty. ʿĀʾishah went in to her and said "Are you not ashamed to marry the man who killed your father?" Mulaykah said that she sought refuge in God from the Prophet.[744] [On hearing of this] the Prophet divorced her. [People of] her clan came to the Prophet and said "She is small and has no mind of her own; she was beguiled [into saying what she did], so please take her back." But the Prophet refused. They then asked his permission to give her in marriage to a relative of hers, of the Banū ʿUdhrah; The Prophet consented, and the ʿUdhrī married her.

Mulaykah's father was killed in the conquest of Mecca, at Khandamah,[745] by Khālid b. al-Walīd.

742. According to other versions (see the previous note), she refused to marry him and preferred to be his concubine.

743. Of the Kinānī clan al-Layth b. Bakr; see Ibn Ḥazm, *Jamharat*, 180; al-Balādhurī, *Ansāb*, I, 458–59.

744. Cf. pp. 186–89, below.

745. Cf. Ibn Hishām, IV, 49–50.

Sanā bt. al-Ṣalt b. Ḥabīb b. Ḥārithah b. Hilāl b. Ḥarām b. Sammāl b. ʿAwf al-Sulamiyyah.[746]

According to Hishām b. Muḥammad al-Kalbī—someone from [2434] the family of ʿAbdallāh b. Khāzim al-Sulamī:[747] The Prophet married Sanā bt. al-Ṣalt b. Ḥabīb al-Sulamiyyah, but she died before he reached her.

Khawlah bt. al-Hudhayl b. Hubayrah b. Qabīṣah b. al-Ḥārith b. Ḥabīb b. Ḥurqah b. Thaʿlabah b. Bakr b. Ḥubayb b. ʿAmr b. Ghanm b. Taghlib.[748]

Her mother was the daughter of Khalīfah b. Farwah b. Faḍālah b. Zayd b. Imriʾ al-Qays b. al-Khazraj al-Kalbī and the sister of Diḥyah b. Khalīfah.

According to Hishām b. Muḥammad [al-Kalbī]—al-Sharqī b. Quṭāmī: The Prophet married Khawlah bt. al-Hudhayl, but she died on her way, before reaching him. She had been raised by her maternal aunt, Khirniq bt. Khalīfah, Diḥyah b. Khalīfah's sister.[749]

The [Death] Dates[750] of the Prophet's Daughters, Paternal Aunts, and Wives Who Died after Him

Fāṭimah, the Prophet's daughter.

Her mother was Khadījah bt. Khuwaylid. She was born at the time when the Quraysh were building the House,[751] five years before the beginning of the Prophet's mission.

---

746. Called Sanāʾ bt. Asmāʾ in other sources; of the Sulamī clan the Banū Sammāl. See Lecker, *Banū Sulaym*, 84; al-Balādhurī, *Ansāb*, I, 463.

747. A nephew of Sanāʾ. He was a famous warrior and governor of Khurāsān; see Lecker, *Banū Sulaym*, 82.

748. Her father, al-Hudhayl b. Hubayrah, of the Taghlibī clan Thaʿlabah b. Bakr, was a distinguished leader in Mesopotamia in pre-Islamic times. See Ibn al-Kalbī, *Nasab maʿadd*, 93; idem., *Jamharat*, 574; Muḥammad Ibn Ḥabīb, *Muḥabbar*, 249–50; *Naqāʾiḍ*, 473, 703; Caskel, II, 286. One of his daughters, Rayḥānah, was taken captive by the Muslims during the conquests; see al-Ṭabarī, *Taʾrīkh*, I, 2073. On Khawlah, see al-Balādhurī, *Ansāb*, I, 460.

749. Ibn Saʿd, VIII, 114–15.

750. *Dhikr taʾrīkh man māta* . . . etc. *Taʾrīkh* means "date" as well as "history" and "biography," but the chapter deals mainly with deaths and dates. Cf. the next chapter, where it is clear that "dates" are meant in the rubric.

751. That is, the Kaʿbah; see Rubin, "The Kaʿba," 98–104.

According to Muḥammad b. ʿUmar [al-Wāqidī]—Abū Bakr b. ʿAbdallāh b. Abī Sabrah—Yaḥyā b. Shibl—Abū Jaʿfar [Muḥammad b. ʿAlī b. al-Ḥusayn]: Al-ʿAbbās b. ʿAbd al-Muṭṭalib went to see ʿAlī and Fāṭimah [and heard her] say [to ʿAlī] "I am older than you." Al-ʿAbbās said: "You, Fāṭimah, were born at the time when the Quraysh were building the Kaʿbah; the Prophet was then thirty-five years old. As for you, ʿAlī, you were born a few years before that."

According to al-Ṭabarī: ʿAlī married Fāṭimah in Rajab, five months after the Prophet's arrival at Medina/January–February [2435]
623, and consummated the marriage on his return from [the battle of] Badr. She was then eighteen years old. This is so according to Muḥammad b. ʿUmar [al-Wāqidī]—ʿAbdallāh b. Muḥammad b. ʿUmar b. ʿAlī—his father.

Opinions differ concerning the time of her death, although everyone agrees that it occurred after the Prophet's death. According to some, she died six months after the Prophet.

According to Ibn ʿUmar [al-Wāqidī]—Maʿmar [b. Rāshid]—[Ibn Shihāb] al-Zuhrī—ʿUrwah [b. al-Zubayr]—ʿĀʾishah, [the Prophet's wife], and [al-Wāqidī]—Ibn Jurayj [ʿAbd al-Malik b. ʿAbd al-ʿAzīz]—[Ibn Shihāb] al-Zuhrī—ʿUrwah [b. al-Zubayr]: Fāṭimah, daughter of the Prophet, died six months after him. According to Ibn ʿUmar [al-Wāqidī], this is correct. She died on Tuesday night, 3 Ramaḍān 11/November 23, 632, at the age of twenty-nine or so.

According to Ibn ʿUmar [al-Wāqidī]—Ibn Jurayj [ʿAbd al-Malik b. ʿAbd al-ʿAzīz]—ʿAmr b. Dīnār—Abū Jaʿfar [Muḥammad b. ʿAlī b. al-Ḥusayn]: Fāṭimah died three months after the Prophet.

According to Ibn ʿUmar [al-Wāqidī]—ʿUmar b. Muḥammad b. ʿUmar b. ʿAlī—his father—ʿAlī b. al-Ḥusayn—[ʿAbdallāh] Ibn ʿAbbās: Fāṭimah was the first [dead person] for whom a bier was made. Asmāʾ bt. ʿUmays made it for her, after she had seen one made in Abyssinia.

According to Ibn ʿUmar [al-Wāqidī]—ʿAbd al-Raḥmān b. ʿAbd al-ʿAzīz—ʿAbdallāh b. Abī Bakr b. Muḥammad b. ʿAmr b. Ḥazm—ʿAmrah bt. ʿAbd al-Raḥmān: Al-ʿAbbās b. ʿAbd al-Muṭṭalib said the ritual prayer over the bier of Fāṭimah, the Prophet's daughter; he, ʿAlī, and al-Faḍl b. al-ʿAbbās descended into the grave.[752]

---

752. See p. 11, above.

According to Ibn 'Umar [al-Wāqidī]—'Umar b. Muḥammad b. 'Umar b. 'Alī—his father—'Alī b. al-Ḥusayn, who asked Ibn 'Abbās about the time Fāṭimah's burial took place. Al-'Abbās said: "We buried her at night, after a third of it or so had elapsed." ['Alī
[2436] b. al-Ḥusayn] asked who had said the prayer over her bier, and al-'Abbās replied: "'Alī b. Abī Ṭalib".

Ibn 'Umar [al-Wāqidī] said "I asked 'Abd al-Raḥmān b. Abī al-Muwālī 'Some people say that Fāṭimah's grave is at the mosque where the funerary services are held, in al-Baqī.'" 'Abd al-Raḥmān said: "[No], by God, this is the mosque of Ruqayyah"—meaning the woman who had built it—"but Fāṭimah was buried in al-Baqī', in 'Aqīl's place, at the corner next to the dwelling of the Jaḥsh family[753] and opposite the private passageway from the Banū Nubayh's [house], [if you look from the direction] of the Banū 'Abd al-Dār's [house]. Her grave lies seven *dhirā*'s off the road."[754]

According to Ibn 'Umar [al-Wāqidī]—'Abdallāh b. Ja'far—'Abdallāh b. Ḥasan:[755] I [once] found al-Mughīrah b. 'Abd al-Raḥmān[756] standing in al-Baqī', waiting for me at midday in oppressive heat. I said "O Abū Hāshim, what makes you stand [here]?" He replied: "I was waiting for you; it has come to my knowledge that Fāṭimah was buried in this house, in 'Aqīl's place, at the corner next to the dwelling of the Jaḥsh family. I would like you to buy it for me for whatever price, to be buried there." 'Abdallāh said "By God, I shall do that." We tried [to persuade] the 'Aqīl family, but they refused the request of 'Abdallāh b. Ḥasan.[757]

According to 'Abdallāh b. Ja'far, no one doubts that Fāṭimah's grave is in that place.

According to al-Ḥārith—Muḥammad b. Ja'far al-Warkānī—Jarīr b. 'Abd al-Ḥamīd—Yazīd b. Abī Ziyād—'Abdallāh b. al-Ḥārith: Fāṭimah, the Prophet's daughter, passed away eight months after

---

753. A family of bedouin (Asadī) origin, allies of the Quraysh, who joined Muḥammad early in his career; see Kister, "On Strangers and Allies", 137–39.

754. A *Dhirā'* equals 29½ inches.

755. Perhaps the great-grandson of 'Alī b. Abī Ṭālib is meant; see Ibn Qudāmah, 129. See, on him, p. 245, below.

756. One of the rich, generous notables of the Qurashī clan the Makhzūm during Umayyad times; see Ibn Qudāmah, 361–63.

757. There is a shift in the narration here. The story starts with 'Abdallāh b. Ḥasan as the narrator, but from "We tried . . ." until the end the narrator is al-Mughīrah.

him. She became emaciated and complained to Asmā' about the thinness of her body. She asked her "Could you cover me with something?" Asmā' said "I saw the Abyssinians prepare a bedstead for the [dead] women, then fasten the bier to the bedposts." [2437]
So [Fāṭimah] ordered them to do that [when she died].

According to al-Ḥārith—al-Madā'inī—Abū Zakariyyā' al-'Ajlānī: A bier was made for Fāṭimah before she died. She looked at it and said "You have shielded me; may God shield you."

Ṣafiyyah, daughter of 'Abd al-Muṭṭalib b. Hāshim.[758]

Her mother was Hālah bt. Wuhayb b. 'Abd Manāf b. Zuhrah b. Kilāb. She was a sister of Ḥamzah b. 'Abd al-Muṭṭalib from both parents.

Ṣafiyyah was married to al-Ḥārith b. Ḥarb b. Umayyah b. 'Abd Shams in pre-Islamic times and bore him [a child named] Ṣafiyy. She was later married to al-'Awwām b. Khuwaylid b. Asad, to whom she bore al-Zubayr and 'Abd al-Ka'bah.

Ṣafiyyah embraced Islam and gave the Prophet the oath of allegiance. She emigrated to Medina, [where] she died during the caliphate of 'Umar b. al-Khaṭṭāb. Her grave is in al-Baqī', in the courtyard in front of al-Mughīrah b. Shu'bah's dwelling.

According to 'Alī b. Muḥammad [al-Madā'inī]: Ṣafiyyah bt. 'Abd al-Muṭṭalib [once] killed a man in a duel.

The Death Dates of the Prophet's Wives Who Died after Him

Sawdah bt. Zam'ah b. Qays b. 'Abd Wadd b. Naṣr b. Mālik b. Ḥisl b. 'Āmir b. Lu'ayy.[759]

Her mother was al-Shamūs bt. Qays b. 'Amr b. Zayd b. Labīd b. Khidāsh b. 'Āmir b. Ghanm b. 'Adī b. al-Najjār, of the Anṣār. She was married to al-Sakrān b. 'Amr, and they both emigrated to Abyssinia in the second emigration.

According to Ibn 'Umar [al-Wāqidī]—Makhramah b. Bukayr—his father: Al-Sakrān b. 'Amr returned with his wife Sawdah bt.

---

758. Khalīfah b. Khayyāṭ, *Ta'rīkh*, 120; idem, *Ṭabaqāt*, 331; al-Balādhurī, *Ansāb*, III (Dūrī), 313; al-Zubayrī, 17.

759. Of the Qurashī clan 'Āmir b. Lu'ayy. See Khalīfhah b. Khayyāṭ, *Ṭabaqāt*, 335; al-Balādhurī, *Ansāb*, I, 407–9; Ibn Isḥāq, *Siyar*, 254.

Zamʿah from Abyssinia to Mecca, where he died, leaving her a widow. When it was lawful for her [to marry again][760] the Prophet sent her a message, asking her to marry him. She said "O Mes-
[2438] senger of God, I entrust my affairs to you." The Prophet said "Ask a man of your clan to give you in marriage." She asked Ḥāṭib b. ʿAmr b. ʿAbd Shams b. ʿAbd Wadd, and he gave her [to the Prophet] in marriage. She was the first woman the Prophet married after Khadījah's [death].[761]

According to Ibn ʿUmar [al-Wāqidī]—Muḥammad b. ʿAbdallāh b. Muslim—his father: The Prophet married Sawdah in Ramaḍān, in the tenth year after the [beginning of] his prophethood. This was after Khadījah's death and before his marriage to ʿĀʾishah. He consummated the marriage in Mecca, then emigrated to Medina.

Sawdah bt. Zamʿah died in Medina in Shawwāl 54/September–October 674, during the caliphate of Muʿāwiyah b. Abī Sufyān. According to Ibn ʿUmar [al-Wāqidī], this is the correct version.

According to Hishām b. Muḥammad [al-Kalbī]—his father—Abū Ṣāliḥ [Bādhām]—[ʿAbdallāh] Ibn ʿAbbās: Sawdah bt. Zamʿah was married to al-Sakrān b. ʿAmr, brother of Suhayl b. ʿAmr. [Once] she dreamed that the Prophet walked until he trod on her neck. She told her husband about it and he said "By your father's life, if your dream is true, then I shall die, and Muḥammad will marry you." She said "[God] forbid!" According to Hishām, [she said] this by way of banishing the [idea]. Another night she dreamed that a moon fell down from the sky on her while she was lying down. She told her husband, and he said "By your father's life, it shall not be long before I die and you will be given in marriage to [the Prophet]." Since that day al-Sakrān suffered from some complaint; it was not long before he died and the Prophet married Sawdah.

According to al-Ḥārith—Dāʾūd b. al-Muḥabbar—ʿAbd al-Ḥamīd b. Bahrām—Shahr [b. Ḥawshab?]—[ʿAbdallāh] Ibn ʿAbbās: The Prophet asked to be given in marriage a woman of his tribe by

---

760. According to the Muslim law, a widow or divorced woman should wait for a certain period before remarrying (in order to see whether she is pregnant by her former husband); see "ʿIdda," *EI*², III, 1010–13 (Y. Linant de Bellefonds).

761. The Prophet never married another woman during Khadījah's lifetime.

the name of Sawdah. She had [already] five or six small children from her [former] husband, who was dead by then. The Prophet asked her "What is it that prevents you from [marrying] me?" She [2439] replied "O Prophet of God, nothing prevents me from [marrying] you but that you are the most beloved person to me and I respect you [too much to let] these little children squeal around your head all the time." The Prophet asked "Is there anything else that prevents you from [marrying] me?" She replied "No, by God." The Prophet said to her "The best women ever to have ridden the backs of camels[762] are the virtuous women of the Quraysh, who are the most affectionate toward small children and the most excellent in doing good to their husbands when they [the women] are wealthy.[763]

ʿĀ'ishah, daughter of Abū Bakr.[764]

Her mother was Umm Rūmān bt. ʿUmayr b. ʿĀmir, of the Banū Duhmān b. al-Ḥārith b. Ghanm b. Mālik b. Kinānah.[765]

The Prophet married ʿĀ'ishah in Shawwāl in the tenth year after the [beginning of his] prophethood, three years before the Emigration. He consummated the marriage in Shawwāl, eight months after the Emigration. On the day he consummated the marriage with her she was nine years old.

According to Ibn ʿUmar [al-Wāqidī]—Mūsā b. Muḥammad b. ʿAbd al-Raḥmān—Rayṭah—ʿAmrah [bt. ʿAbd al-Raḥmān b. Saʿd]:[766] ʿĀ'ishah was asked when the Prophet consummated his marriage with her, and she said:

> The Prophet left us and his daughters behind when he emigrated to Medina. Having arrived at Medina, he sent

---

762. That is, Arab women.

763. *Aḥnāhu ʿalā waladin fī ṣigharihi wa-arʿāhu ʿalā baʿlin fī dhāt yadin.* The root *ḥ-n-w* specifically denotes widows who remain unmarried in order to devote themselves to their children. Cf. al-Wāqidī, 867, where the text says "and the most generous with their property towards their husbands." The context of the tradition in al-Wāqidī is, however, different. See also p. 197, below.

764. The Prophet's most beloved wife and the only one involved in politics after his death. See "ʿĀ'isha bint Abī Bakr," *EI*², I, 307–8; al-Balādhurī, *Ansāb*, I, 409–22; Ibn Qudāmah, 73–74; Ibn Isḥāq, *Siyar*, 255–56.

765. Ibn Ḥazm, *Jamharat*, 188.

766. Al-Balādhurī, *Ansāb*, I, 269–70.

Zayd b. Ḥārithah and his client Abū Rāfi' for us. He gave them two camels and 500 dirhams he had taken from Abū Bakr to buy [other] beasts they needed. Abū Bakr sent with them 'Abdallāh b. Urayqiṭ al-Dīlī, with two or three camels. He wrote to [his son] 'Abdallāh b. Abī Bakr to take his wife Umm Rūmān, together with me and my sister Asmā', al-Zubayr's wife, [and leave for Medina]. They all left [Medina] together, and when they arrived at Qudayd[767] Zayd b. Ḥārithah bought three camels with those 500 dirhams. All of them then entered Mecca, where
[2440] they met Ṭalḥah b. 'Ubaydallāh on his way to leave town, together with Abū Bakr's family.[768] So we all left: Zayd b. Ḥārithah, Abū Rāfi', Fāṭimah, Umm Kulthūm, and Sawdah bt. Zam'ah. Zayd mounted Umm Ayman and [his son] Usāmah b. Zayd on a riding beast; 'Abdallāh b. Abī Bakr took Umm Rūmān and his two sisters, and Ṭalḥah b. 'Ubaydallāh came [too]. We all went together,[769] and when we reached Bayḍ in Tamannī[770] my camel broke loose. I was sitting in the litter together with my mother, and she started exclaiming "Alas, my daughter, alas [you] bride"; then they caught up with our camel, after it had safely descended the Lift.[771] We then arrived at Medina, and I stayed with Abū Bakr's children, and [Abū Bakr] went to the Prophet.[772] The latter was then busy building the mosque and our homes around it,[773] where he [later] housed his wives. We stayed in Abū Bakr's house for a few days; then Abū Bakr asked [the Prophet] "O Messenger of

767. A place near Mecca, see Yāqūt, *Mu'jam al-buldān*, IV, 42. Note that the story temporarily reverts from the first to the third person.

768. Ṭalḥah and Abū Bakr belonged to the same Qurashī clan, the Banū Taym.

769. The text (and Cairo, 601, and Dār al-Fikr, 604) has "the two of them went together" (*wa-iṣṭaḥabā*), which makes no sense here. The difference between the two words is one character, *n* (*wa-iṣṭaḥabnā*), which can easily be overlooked in a manuscript.

770. See Yāqūt, *Mu'jam al-buldān*, I, 795, 874.

771. A wadi between Mecca and Medina; see Yāqūt, *Mu'jam al-buldān*, I, 360–61.

772. De Goeje interprets *nazala ilā* here not as "went" but as "stayed" or "lived with," the agent of the verb being, according to him, Usāmah b. Zayd; see 2440 n. c.

773. See al-Samhūdī, II, 322–40.

> God, what prevents you from consummating the marriage with your wife?" The Prophet said "The bridal gift (*ṣadāq*)." Abū Bakr gave him the bridal gift, twelve and a half ounces [of gold], and the Prophet sent for us.[774] He consummated our marriage in my house, the one where I live now and where he passed away.[775]

The Prophet made a door in the mosque for his own use, opposite the door of 'Ā'ishah.

['Ā'ishah said]: The Prophet consummated his marriage with Sawdah in one of these houses that are next to mine; he used to stay with her.

'Ā'ishah died in Ramaḍān 58/June–July 678.

Those who hold this view. According to Ibn 'Umar [al-Wāqidī]—'Abd al-Raḥmān b. 'Abd al-'Azīz—'Abdallāh b. Abī Bakr b. Muḥammad b. 'Amr b. Ḥazm: Abū Hurayrah said the prayer [2441] over 'Ā'ishah's bier in Ramaḍān 58/June-July 678. She died after the night prayer.[776]

According to Muḥammad b. 'Umar [al-Wāqidī]: 'Ā'ishah died on Tuesday night, the 17th of Ramaḍān 58/July 13, 678, and was buried the same night after the night prayer. She was then sixty-six years old.

According to Ibn 'Umar [al-Wāqidī]—Ibn Abī Sabrah—Mūsā b. Maysarah—Sālim Sabalān: 'Ā'ishah died the night of the 17th of Ramaḍān, after the night prayer. She had ordered that she should be buried the same night. The Anṣār gathered and attended [the funeral], and no other night was ever seen that was more crowded than that one. [Even] the people of the villages outside Medina (*al-'awālī*) came. She was buried in al-Baqī'.

According to Ibn 'Umar [al-Wāqidī]—Ibn Jurayj ['Abd al-Malik b. 'Abd al-'Azīz]—Nāfi' [client of 'Abdallāh b. 'Umar]: I was pres-

---

774. It is not clear whether Abū Bakr pays this sum as dowry or gives the Prophet the money to pay the bridal gift because the Prophet was short of cash. See also p. 189, below.

775. See al-Samhūdī, II, 458–60, 540–42.

776. *Ītār* or *witr*, a prayer consisting of an odd number of prayer units (*rak'ahs*) performed at night; see "Witr," *EI*[1], IV, 1139–40 (A. J. Wensinck).

ent [at 'Ā'ishah's funeral when] Abū Hurayrah said the prayer over her bier; ['Abdallāh] b. 'Umar was in the crowd and did not condemn it.[777] Marwān had gone on a lesser pilgrimage (*'umrah*) that year and appointed Abū Hurayrah vice-governor.

Ḥafṣah, daughter of 'Umar b. al-Khaṭṭāb.[778]

Her mother was Zaynab bt. Maẓ'ūn, sister of 'Uthmān b. Maẓ'ūn.[779]

According to Ibn 'Umar [al-Wāqidī]—Usāmah b. Zayd b. Aslam—his father—his grandfather—'Umar: Ḥafṣah was born while the Quraysh were building the Ka'bah, five years before the Prophet was sent on his divine mission.

According to [Ibn 'Umar al-Wāqidī]—Abū Bakr b. 'Abdallāh b. Abī Sabrah—Ḥusayn b. Abī Ḥusayn: The Prophet married Ḥafṣah in Sha'bān, thirty months after [the Emigration]/February–March 625, before the battle of Uḥud.

According to Ibn 'Umar [al-Wāqidī]: Ḥafṣah died in Sha'bān 45/October–November 665 during the caliphate of Mu'āwiyah. She was then sixty years old.

According to Ibn 'Umar [al-Wāqidī]—Ma'mar [b. Rāshid]—[Ibn Shihāb] al-Zuhrī—Sālim [b. 'Abdallāh b. 'Umar b. al-Khaṭṭāb]—his father: Ḥafṣah died, and Marwān b. al-Ḥakam, who was then the governor of Medina, said the prayer over her bier.

[2442] According to [Ibn 'Umar al-Wāqidī]—'Alī b. Muslim—[Sa'īd b. Abī Sa'īd] al-Maqbarī—his father: I saw Marwān carrying her bier, holding it between the two posts, from the Ḥazm family's to al-Mughīrah b. Shu'bah's house; Abū Hurayrah carried her from al-Mughīrah's house to her grave.

According to [Ibn 'Umar al-Wāqidī]—'Abdallāh b. Nāfi'—his father: [The people who] descended into Ḥafṣah's grave[780] were

777. It is not clear what was condemnable here; perhaps that it was not the governor, Marwān b. al-Ḥakam, who held the funeral service, as stated in the next sentence. See also below.

778. "Ḥafṣa," *EI*², III, 63–65; Jeffery, 212–13; al-Balādhurī, *Ansāb*, I, 422–28; Khalīfah b. Khayyāṭ, *Ṭabaqāt*, 334; Ibn Qudāmah, 75–76; Ibn Isḥāq, *Siyar*, 257.

779. A member of the Qurashī clan the Jumaḥ and an early convert, known for his asceticism; see Ibn Qudāmah, 444–45.

780. See p. 11, above.

'Abdallāh and 'Āṣim, sons of 'Umar, and Sālim, 'Abdallāh, and Ḥamzah, sons of 'Abdallāh b. 'Umar.

Umm Salamah, whose [real] name was Hind bt. Abī Umayyah, whose [real] name was Suhayl Zād al-Rakb[781] b. al-Mughīrah b. 'Abdallāh b. 'Umar b. Makhzūm.[782]

Her mother was 'Ātikah bt. 'Āmir b. Rabī'ah b. Mālik b. Jadhīmah b. 'Alqamah Jidhl al-Ṭi'ān b. Firās b. Ghanm b. Mālik b. Kinānah.[783]

Umm Salamah was married to Abū Salamah, whose [real] name was 'Abdallāh b. 'Abd al-Asad b. Hilāl.[784] Both of them participated in the two emigrations to Abyssinia, where Umm Salamah bore Zaynab bt. Abī Salamah. She later [also] bore her husband Salamah, 'Umar, and Durrah, sons of Abī Salamah.

According to Ibn 'Umar [al-Wāqidī][785]—'Umar b. 'Uthmān—'Abd al-Malik b. 'Ubayd—Sa'īd b. 'Abd al-Raḥmān b. Yarbū'—'Umar b. Abī Salamah: My father participated in the battle of Uḥud, and Abū Usāmah al-Jushamī shot him in the arm with an arrow. He stayed a month treating his injury, which eventually healed. The Prophet then sent my father to Qaṭan,[786] in Muḥarram, thirty five months [after the Emigration]/June 625. He was away for twenty-nine days, then returned to Medina, on the [2443]
eighth of Ṣafar 4/July 21, 625; by then his wound had reopened. He died from it on the eighth of Jumādā II 4/November 15, 625. My mother observed the legal period of waiting before remarrying (*'iddah*) and became lawful [for marriage] on the 20th of Shawwāl 4/March 25, 626. The Prophet married her at the end of Shawwāl 4/March 626.[787] She died in Dhū al-Qa'dah 59/September–October 679.

---

781. See p. 78, above.

782. Khalīfah b. Khayyāṭ, *Ṭabaqāt*, 334; al-Balādhurī, *Ansāb*, I, 429–32; Ibn Isḥāq, *Siyar*, 260–61. See also Jeffery, 235.

783. 'Alqamah and other members of the Firās family were famous warriors; see Ibn Ḥazm, *Jamharat*, 188.

784. The Prophet's milk brother and an early convert. He died of an injury he received in one of the early Muslim raids; see Ibn Ḥajar, *Iṣābah*, II, 335.

785. Ibn Sa'd, VIII, 60–61.

786. A place in the territory of the bedouin tribe Banū Asad; see Landau-Tasseron, "Asad," 8–11.

787. Al-Ṭabarī, *Ta'rīkh*, I, 1460.

According to Ibn 'Umar [al-Wāqidī]—Kathīr b. Zayd—al-Muṭṭalib b. 'Abdallāh b. Ḥanṭab: The Widow of the Arabs went in to the Lord of the Muslims as a bride early in the evening and got up at the end of the night to mill.

He meant Umm Salamah.[788]

According to Ibn 'Umar [al-Wāqidī]—Ma'mar [b. Rāshid]—[Ibn Shihāb] al-Zuhrī—Hind bt. al-Ḥārith al-Firāsiyyah: The Prophet said "'Ā'ishah has a part in me occupied by no one else." When he married Umm Salamah the Prophet was asked "O Messenger of God, what about that part?" The Prophet remained silent, and it was known that Umm Salamah occupied [a place in] his [heart].[789]

According to Ibn 'Umar [al-Wāqidī]: Umm Salamah died in Shawwāl 59/July–August 679.

According to Ibn 'Umar [al-Wāqidī]—'Abdallāh b. Nāfi'—his father: Abū Hurayrah said the prayer over Umm Salamah's bier in al-Baqī'. The governor [of Medina] was al-Walīd b. 'Utbah b. Abī Sufyān,[790] [but] he had gone on business to al-Ghābah[791] and appointed Abū Hurayrah to lead the prayers, so the latter [also] prayed over Umm Salamah's bier. [The narrator] said: He went away only because she had requested that the governor would not say the prayer over her bier, and he did not want to be present while someone else performed the service, so he left on purpose, appointing Abū Hurayrah [to replace him].

According to al-Ḥārith [b. Muḥammad]—Ibn Sa'd, in another place[792]—al-Wāqidī: Umm Salamah died at the beginning of the year 59/678, during the caliphate of Mu'āwiyah. Her brother's son 'Abdallāh b. 'Abdallāh b. Abī Umayyah said the prayer over her bier.

According to al-Ḥārith—Muḥammad b. Suhayl—Abū 'Ubay-
[2444] dah Ma'mar b. al-Muthannā: The Prophet married Umm Salamah, that is, Hind bt. Abī Umayyah b. al-Mughīrah b. 'Abdallāh b.

---

788. Ibn Sa'd, VIII, 64.

789. Ibn Sa'd, VIII, 66.

790. Cousin of the caliph Mu'āwiyah. He served in administrative posts, as did his father before him. See Ibn Qudāmah, 207–8; al-Zubayrī, 132–33.

791. A well-watered area north of Medina. Residents of the town had cultivated plots of lands there. See Yāqūt, *Mu'jam al-buldān*, III, 767; al-Samhūdī, 1275–76.

792. Ibn Sa'd, VIII, 67. The version here is different from al-Ṭabarī's.

'Umar b. Makhzūm, in Medina in the year 2 of the [Muslim] era/ 624, before the battle of Badr.

According to Abū Ma'shar [Najīḥ b. 'Abd al-Raḥmān]: Zaynab was the first of the Prophet's wives to die, and Umm Salamah was the last.

Umm Ḥabībah, whose [real] name was Ramlah bt. Abī Sufyān b. Ḥarb.[793]

Her mother was Ṣafiyyah bt. Abī al-'Āṣ b. Umayyah b. 'Abd Shams, 'Uthmān b. 'Affān's paternal aunt.

'Ubaydallāh b. Jaḥsh b. Ri'āb, Ḥarb b. Umayyah's ally (*ḥalīf*),[794] had married Umm Ḥabībah. She bore him Ḥabībah, after whom she was named. Ḥabībah was [later] married to Dā'ūd b. 'Urwah b. Mas'ūd al-Thaqafī.[795]

'Ubaydallāh b. Jaḥsh emigrated to Abyssinia in the second emigration, taking Umm Ḥabībah with him. He apostatized and converted to Christianity, then died in Abyssinia, whereas Umm Ḥabībah remained faithful to her religion, Islam, and to her [status] as an Emigrant.

Umm Ḥabībah had taken her daughter Ḥabībah bt. 'Ubaydallah when emigrating to Abyssinia, then brought her back with her to Mecca.

According to Ibn 'Umar [al-Wāqidī]—'Abdallāh b. Ja'far—'Uthmān b. Muḥammad al-Akhnasī: Umm Ḥabībah bt. Abī Sufyān had given birth to Ḥabībah, her daughter from 'Ubaydallāh b. Jaḥsh, in Mecca, before she emigrated to Abyssinia.

According to Ibn 'Umar [al-Wāqidī]—Abū Bakr b. Ismā'īl b. Muḥammad b. Sa'd—his father: Umm Ḥabībah had left Mecca while pregnant and bore her daughter in Abyssinia.

According to Ibn 'Umar [al-Wāqidī]—'Abdallāh b. 'Amr b. Zuhayr—Ismā'īl b. 'Amr b. Sa'īd b. al-'Āṣ—Umm Ḥabībah: I dreamed that 'Ubaydallāh b. Jaḥsh, my husband, was in the worst and most deformed shape. I was frightened and said [to myself]

---

793. Khalīfah b. Khayyāṭ, *Ta'rīkh*, 41; al-Balādhurī, *Ansāb*, I, 200, 438–39, 440; Ibn Qudāmah, 80–82; Ibn Isḥāq, *Siyar*, 259.

794. See note 116, above.

795. Son of 'Urwah b. Mas'ūd, an outstanding leader of the Thaqīf, who was assassinated because of his conversion to Islam; see Ibn Ḥajar, *Iṣābah*, I, 478, II, 477–78.

"By God, he has changed." And, lo and behold, when he got up in the morning he said: "O Umm Ḥabībah, I have contemplated the
[2445] [matter] of religion, and I see no religion better than Christianity. I had professed it [before], then embraced Muḥammad's religion, and now I am going back to Christianity." I said "By God, you have not been blessed," and I told him about my dream about him, but he paid no attention to it and went on drinking wine until he died.[796] Afterward I dreamed that someone came to me and said "O Mother of the Faithful."[797] I was frightened and interpreted it [as a sign] that the Prophet would marry me. And, indeed, the moment my legal waiting period (*'iddah*) elapsed, before I knew [anything], a messenger from the negus[798] was at my door, asking permission to come in. It was a slave girl of his, called Abrahah, whose task was to look after his clothes and balm. She came in and said "The king sends a message to you: 'The Prophet wrote to me, asking to give you to him in marriage.'"[799] I said "May God send glad tidings to you." She went on "The king says to you 'Appoint someone to give you in marriage.'" Umm Ḥabībah sent for Khālid b. Sa'īd b. al-'Āṣ[800] and appointed him [for the task]. She gave Abrahah two silver bracelets and two anklets she had worn on her feet and silver rings she had had on her toes, out of joy at the tidings the girl had brought her. In the evening the negus requested [the presence of] Ja'far b. Abī Ṭālib and the other Muslims who were there, so they came before him. The negus delivered a speech, saying:[801] "God be praised, the King, the Holy, the Perfect, the Faithful to His promises, the Watcher, the Almighty, the Forceful. I testify that there is no God but Allāh and Muḥammad is His servant and messenger and the [prophet] whose [coming]

796. Drinking wine is here used to indicate the difference between Muslims and Christians. It is also related to the dream, in which Umm Ḥabibah saw her husband deformed. Cf. Qur'ān 5:59–61.

797. A designation of the wives of the Prophet.

798. That is, the Abyssinian ruler.

799. As the Muslims who emigrated to Abyssinia were supposed to be under the negus' protection, the story makes the Prophet address him in the matter of the marriage. See also below, and al-Ṭabarī, *Ta'rīkh*, I, 1570–71.

800. A relative of hers, one of the very few early Umayyad converts. See Ibn Ḥajar, *Iṣābah*, I, 406–7; Ibn Qudāmah, 187–90.

801. Cf. Qur'ān 59:23.

was prophesied by Jesus, son of Mary.[802] Now, the Messenger of God wrote to me, asking that I give him Umm Ḥabībah bt. Abī Sufyān in marriage. I comply with the Prophet's wish and give 400 dinars for her bridal gift (*ṣadāq*)." He then poured the dinars in front of the people. Khālid b. Sa'īd then spoke and said: "God be praised; I praise Him and ask His help and assistance and testify [2446]
that there is no God but Allāh and Muḥammad is His servant and messenger. 'He it is who hath sent His messenger with the guidance and the religion of truth in order that He may set it above all (other) religion, though averse are the polytheists.'[803] Now I comply with the Prophet's wish and give him Umm Ḥabībah bt. Abī Sufyān in marriage; may God bless His messenger." The negus gave Khālid b. Sa'īd the dinars, and he took them. The people then wanted to go away, but the negus said "Sit down, for the prophets' custom (*sunnah*) when marrying is to serve food on the occasion of the marriage." So he ordered that food be brought, and they ate and then dispersed.

Umm Ḥabībah narrated: When the money reached me I sent to Abrahah, who had brought me the news, and said to her: "On that day I gave you what I did because I had no money with me. Here are fifty gold coins (*mithqāl*s); take them and benefit from them." She took out a box containing everything I had given her and gave it back to me, saying: "The king asked me not to take anything from you, being [his servant] who looks after his clothes and balm. I have followed the religion of the Prophet and submitted to God. The king has ordered his wives to send to you all the perfumes they have." The next day Abrahah brought me a great quantity of aloes, saffron, ambergris, and civet perfume. I [later] took all this with me to the Prophet, and he used to see me wearing and having it and never disaproved.[804] Then Abrahah said "The favor I ask from you is that you greet the Prophet with peace on my behalf and tell him that I have followed his religion." She was very gentle with me; she was the one who prepared me [for the journey], and whenever she came in she said "Do not forget the favor I asked

---

802. The negus in fact embraces Islam by uttering these words. On the negus legend in Islamic tradition, see Raven; Wansbrough, 38–41.

803. Qur'ān 9:33, 61:9; trans. Bell, I, 177.

804. The permissibility of perfume, as well as other luxuries, was much debated among Muslim scholars.

from you." When we came to the Prophet I told him about the
[2447] betrothal [ceremony] and about Abrahah and her conduct with me, and he smiled. I greeted him on her behalf, and he said "Peace be with her, too, and God's mercy."

According to Ibn 'Umar [al-Wāqidī]—Isḥāq b. Muḥammad—Ja'far b. Muḥammad—his father: The Prophet sent 'Amr b. Umayyah al-Ḍamrī[805] to the negus, asking him to give him in marriage Umm Ḥabībah bt. Abī Sufyān, who had been married to 'Ubaydallāh b. Jaḥsh. The negus gave her to him in marriage and contributed a bridal gift of 400 dinars from his own [pocket], on behalf of the Prophet.

According to Ibn 'Umar [al-Wāqidī]—Muḥammad b. Ṣāliḥ—'Āṣim b. 'Umar b. Qatādah, and also [Ibn 'Umar al-Wāqidī]—'Abd al-Raḥmān b. 'Abd al-'Azīz—'Abdallāh b. Abī Bakr b. Ḥazm: The man who gave Umm Ḥabībah in marriage and from whom the negus asked her was Khālid b. Sa'īd b. al-'Āṣ; this occurred in the year 7/628–29. She was thirty-odd years old when she was brought to Medina.

Umm Ḥabībah died in the year 44/April 4, 664–March 24, 665, during the caliphate of Mu'āwiyah.

Zaynab bt. Jaḥsh b. Ri'āb, sister of 'Abd al-Raḥmān b. Jaḥsh.[806] Her mother was Umaymah bt. 'Abd al-Muṭṭalib b. Hāshim.[807]

According to Ibn 'Umar [al-Wāqidī]—'Umar b. 'Uthmān al-Jaḥshī—his father: Zaynab bt. Jaḥsh, who was a beautiful woman, was among those who emigrated [to Medina] with the Prophet. When the Prophet arrived at Medina he asked that she be given to [his adopted son] Zayd b. Ḥārithah in marriage, but she said "O Messenger of God, I cannot give my consent, for I am the widow of the Quraysh."[808] The Prophet replied "But I give my consent that you should [marry him]." So Zayd b. Ḥārithah married her.

According to Ibn 'Umar [al-Wāqidī]—'Abdallāh b. 'Āmir al-Aslamī—Muḥammad b. Yaḥyā b. Ḥabbān: The Prophet came to

---

805. A famous warrior and Companion, of the Kinānah tribe; see Ibn Ḥajar, *Iṣābah*, II, 524.

806. Of the Jaḥsh family, see p. 168, above; "Zainab bint Jaḥsh," *EI*[1], IV, 1199 (V. Vacca); Khalīfah b. Khayyāṭ, *Ta'rīkh*, 122; al-Balādhurī, *Ansāb*, I, 433–37; Ansari.

807. That is, the Prophet's paternal aunt.

808. Perhaps she considers herself unworthy, having been married before, or Zayd, a former slave, is unworthy of her. See note 853, below.

Zayd b. Ḥārithah's house looking for him. Zayd was [at that time] called only Zayd b. Muḥammad, and the Prophet sometimes [2448] would miss him [after] a time and would say "Where is Zayd?" [Once] he went to Zayd's house but did not find him [there]. Zaynab rose toward him and said "Come here, O Messenger of God," but he turned away, muttering something unintelligible, except the words "Praised be God the Great, praised be God, who turns the hearts." When Zayd came home his wife told him that the Prophet had come to his house. Zayd asked "Didn't you ask him to come in?" She said "I proposed it to him but he declined." Zayd asked "Did you hear him say anything?" She said: "When he turned away I heard him say something I did not understand, and I heard him say 'Praised be God the Great, praised be God who turns the hearts.'" Zayd left [his house] and went to the Prophet. He said: "O Messenger of God, I heard that you came to my house. Why didn't you come in? O Messenger of God, may my father and mother be your ransom! Perhaps [the problem is] that you like Zaynab? In that case, I shall divorce her." The Prophet said "Keep your wife." [But] Zayd could not touch her [after that]. He would come to the Prophet and tell him [about it], and the latter would say "Keep your wife," and Zayd would say "O Messenger of God, I shall divorce her," and the Prophet would say "Keep your wife." Zayd divorced her [all the same] and abstained from her, and she became lawful [for remarriage]. [One day], while talking to 'Ā'ishah, the Prophet fainted. On regaining consciousness he smiled and said "Who will go to Zaynab to bring her the glad tidings that God from above gave her to me in marriage?" The Prophet [then] recited "(Recall) when thou wert saying to him upon whom Allah bestowed favor and upon whom thou didst bestow favor."[809] 'Ā'ishah narrated: I was upset by both near and remote troubles, having heard of Zaynab's beauty. What was more, the greatest and noblest of all things happened to her, as God from heaven gave her in marriage. I said [to myself] "She is going to boast of it to us." Salmā, the Prophet's servant, then went quickly and told [Zaynab] about it. [Zaynab] gave her silver orna- [2449]
ments for this [service].[810]

809. Qur'ān 33:37; trans. Bell, II, 415.
810. Or; "ornaments she had worn" ('*alayhā*).

According to ʿUmar b. ʿUthmān b. ʿAbdallāh al-Jaḥshī—his father: The Prophet married Zaynab bt. Jaḥsh on the first of Dhū al-Qaʿdah 5/April 24, 627.

According to ʿUmar b. ʿUthmān al-Jaḥshī—his father: Zaynab bt. Jaḥsh did not leave behind [when she died even] a dīnār or a dirham, for she used to give [to the needy] everything she could and to give hospitality to the poor. She left [only] her house, which was [later] sold to al-Walīd b. ʿAbd al-Malik,[811] when he pulled the mosque down, for 50,000 dirhams.

According to ʿUmar b. ʿUthmān al-Jaḥshī—Ibrāhīm b. ʿAbdallāh b. Muḥammad—his father: ʿUkāshah b. Miḥṣan's mother was asked how old Zaynab bt. Jaḥsh was when she died, to which she replied "She was thirty-odd years old when we emigrated to Medina, and she died in the year 20/December 21,640–December 9, 641.

According to ʿUmar b. ʿUthmān—his father: Zaynab bt. Jaḥsh died at the age of fifty-three.

According to al-Ḥārith: I was present in the circle [of people around] ʿAlī b. ʿĀṣim, who was relating traditions (*ḥadīths*).[812] He related on the authority of Dā'ūd b. Abī Hind—ʿĀmir [b. Shuraḥbīl al-Shaʿbī]: Zaynab used to say to the Prophet "I have the greatest claim on you from among your wives, for I am the best of them in respect of the way I was married [to you], the noblest lady,[813] and the closest [to you] in terms of kinship." She would say "I was given to you in marriage by the Merciful from above His throne, and [the angel] Jibrīl was the go-between in this matter; I am the daughter of your paternal aunt, and you have no kin among your wives but me."

Juwayriyyah bt. al-Ḥārith b. Abī Ḍirār b. Ḥabīb b. ʿĀ'idh b. Mālik b. Jadhīmah al-Muṣṭaliq, of the Khuzāʿah.[814]

---

811. The sixth Umayyad caliph, reigned 86–96/705–15.

812. A famous scholar of Tradition from Wāsiṭ (d. 200/815–16), often accused of making mistakes and even telling lies; see Ibn Ḥajar, *Tahdhīb*, VII, 302–5.

813. *Akramuhunna sitran*; see Kazimirski, s.v. *str*.

814. Khalīfah b. Khayyāṭ, *Ta'rīkh*, 42, 212; Ibn Ḥibbān, *Thiqāt*, III, 66; al-Balādhurī, *Ansāb*, I, 341, 441–42; al-Ṭabarī, *Ta'rīkh*, I, 1516–17, 1772; Ibn Isḥāq, *Siyar*, 263.

Juwayriyyah had been married to Musāfiʿ b. Ṣafwān Dhū al-Shufr b. Abī Sarḥ b. Mālik b. Jadhīmah, who was killed in the battle of al-Muraysīʿ. [2450]

According to Ibn ʿUmar [al-Wāqidī]—Yazīd b. ʿAbdallāh b. Qusayṭ—his father—Muḥammad b. ʿAbd al-Raḥmān b. Thawbān—ʿĀʾishah: The Prophet took prisoner some women of the Banū al-Muṣṭaliq. He set aside the legal fifth [of the booty] (*khums*) and divided [the rest] among the people, giving the cavalrymen two shares and the footsoldiers one share [each]. Juwayriyyah bt. al-Ḥārith b. Abī Ḍirār fell in the lot of Thābit b. Qays b. Shammās al-Anṣārī. She had been married to a cousin of hers named Ṣafwān b. Mālik b. Jadhīmah Dhū al-Shufr, who was killed, leaving her a widow. Thābit made a contract with her to free her against the sum of nine ounces [of gold]. She was a sweet woman; everyone who just saw her fell for her. Now, the Prophet was staying with me when Juwayriyyah came in, asking his help in that contract of freedom. By God, the moment I saw her I resented her entering upon the Prophet, knowing that he would see in her the same as I did. She said: "O Messenger of God, I am Juwayriyyah, daughter of al-Ḥārith, chief of his clan. You know what I have been going through; I fell in the lot of Thābit b. Qays, and he made a contract to free me against the sum of nine ounces [of gold]. Help me to free myself." The Prophet said "How about a better arrangement?" She asked "What is it?" He said "I will pay your contract on your behalf, then marry you." She said "Yes, O Messenger of God, I accept this." The news spread among the people, and they said "Shall the Prophet's brothers-in-law be enslaved?" So they set free the prisoners they held of the Banū al-Muṣṭaliq. A hundred men, women, and children were freed on the occasion of the Prophet's marriage to Juwayriyyah, and I know no [2451]
woman who was more helpful to her people than she. All this took place on the Prophet's return from the battle of Muraysīʿ.

According to Ibn ʿUmar [al-Wāqidī]—ʿAbdallāh b. Abī al-Abyaḍ, Juwayriyyah's client—his father: The Prophet took [some of the] Banū al-Muṣṭaliq prisoner. Juwayriyyah was among them, and her father came [to Medina] and ransomed her. He gave her to the Prophet in marriage at a later stage.

According to [Ibn ʿUmar al-Wāqidī]—Isḥāq b. Yaḥyā b. Ṭalḥah—[Ibn Shihāb] al-Zuhrī—Mālik b. Aws—ʿUmar: The Prophet obligated Juwayriyyah to veil herself and allotted to her the same [sums and goods] as to his [other] wives.[815]

According to [Ibn 'Umar al-Wāqidī]—'Abdallāh b. 'Abd al-Raḥmān—Zayd b. Abī 'Attāb—Muḥammad b. 'Amr—'Aṭā'—Zaynab bt. Abī Salamah—Juwayriyyah bt. al-Ḥārith: Juwayriyyah's name had been Barrah, and the Prophet changed it to Juwayriyyah, for he resented that people would say "He came out of Barrah's place."[816]

According to [Ibn 'Umar al-Wāqidī]—'Abdallāh b. Abī al-Abyaḍ—his father: Juwayriyyah bt. al-Ḥārith, the Prophet's wife, died in Rabī' I 56/January–February 676, during the caliphate of Mu'āwiyah b. Abī Sufyān. Marwān b. al-Ḥakam, then governor of Medina, said the prayer over her bier.

According to [Ibn 'Umar al-Wāqidī]—Muḥammad b. Yazīd—his grandmother, who was a client of Juwayriyyah bt. al-Ḥārith—Juwayriyyah: I was twenty years old when the Prophet married me.

[According to Juwayriyah's client]: Juwayriyyah died in the year 50/December 21, 670–December 17, 671, at the age of sixty-five; Marwān b. al-Ḥakam said the ritual prayer over her bier.

According to Ibn 'Umar [al-Wāqidī]—Ḥizām b. Hishām—his
[2452] father—Juwayriyyah: Three days before the Prophet arrived I dreamed that the moon came from Yathrib and fell in my bosom. I hated to tell anybody about it; then the Prophet arrived. When we were taken prisoner I feared the dream, and when he freed and married me, and, by God, I did not speak with him about my people, but the Muslims freed them [of their own volition]; before I knew anything, a girl of my relatives came to inform me about it. Then I praised God.

Ṣafiyyah bt. Ḥuyayy b. Akhṭab b. Sa'yah b. 'Āmir b. 'Ubayd b. Ka'b b. Abī al-Khazraj b. Abī Ḥabīb b. al-Naḍīr b. al-Naḥḥām b.

---

815. The veil, *ḥijāb*, was obligatory only on the Prophet's wives. See Qur'ān 33:53; al-Wāḥidī, 241–43; 'Abd al-Malik Ibn Ḥabīb, *Ta'rīkh*, 87; "Ḥidjāb," *EI*², III, 359–61 (J. Chelhod). The point of discussion here is whether Juwayriyyah was the Prophet's wife or concubine.

816. See note 234, above. According to Lane's lexicon, Barrah as a proper name means "obedience."

Tanḥūm, of the Children of Israel, one of the tribe of Hārūn b. 'Imrān.[817]

Her mother was Barrah bt. Samaw'al, sister of Rifā'ah b. Samaw'al, of the Banū Qurayẓah, brother tribe of al-Naḍīr.

Ṣafiyyah had been married to Sallām b. Mishkam al-Quraẓī, who divorced her, whereupon she was married to Kinānah b. al-Rabī' b. Abī al-Ḥuqayq al-Naḍarī. The latter was killed in the battle of Khaybar, leaving her a widow.

Ibn 'Umar [al-Wāqidī]—Kathīr b. Zayd—al-Walīd b. Rabāḥ—Abū Hurayrah: While the Prophet was lying with Ṣafiyyah Abū Ayyūb stayed the night at his door. When he saw the Prophet in the morning he said "God is the Greatest." He had a sword with him; he said to the Prophet "O Messenger of God, this young woman had just been married, and you killed her father, her brother and her husband, so I did not trust her [not to harm] you." The Prophet laughed and said "Good."

According to Muḥammad b. Mūsā—'Umarah b. al-Muhājir—Āminah bt. Abī Qays al-Ghifāriyyah: I was one of the women who [2453]
led Ṣafiyyah as a bride to the Prophet. I heard her say: I was not even seventeen, or I was just seventeen, the night I entered the Prophet's [room].

Ṣafiyyah died in the year 52/January 8, 672–December 26, 672, during the caliphate of Mu'āwiyah, and was buried in al-Baqī'.

Maymūnah bt. al-Ḥārith b. Ḥazn al-Hilālī.[818]

Her mother was Hind bt. 'Awf b. Zuhayr b. al-Ḥārith b. Ḥamāṭah b. Jurash.

In pre-Islamic times Maymūnah had been married to Mas'ūd b. 'Amr b. 'Umayr al-Thaqafī. He divorced her, and she was married to Abū Ruhm b. 'Abd al-'Uzzā b. Abī Qays, of the Banū Mālik b. Ḥisl b. 'Āmir b. Lu'ayy. He died, leaving her a widow, and the Prophet married her. It was al-'Abbās b. 'Abd al-Muṭṭalib who gave her in marriage, [because] he was her guardian, as she was the full

817. Khalīfah b. Khayyāṭ, *Ta'rīkh*, 49; idem, *Ṭabaqāt*, 343; al-Balādhurī, *Ansāb*, I, 442–44; Ibn Isḥāq, *Siyar*, 264–65.

818. Of the Hilāl, a clan of the Banū 'Āmir b. Ṣa'ṣa'ah. See Khalīfah b. Khayyāṭ, *Ta'rīkh*, 49; idem, *Ṭabaqāt*, 338; al-Balādhurī, *Ansāb*, I, 444–47; Ibn Isḥāq, *Siyar*, 266–67.

sister of his concubine (*umm walad*) [Lubābah al-Kubrā] bt. al-Ḥārith al-Hilāliyyah, the mother of his son al-Faḍl.

The Prophet married Maymūnah in Sarif, [a place] ten miles from Mecca.[819] She was the last woman he married, in the year 7/628, during the lesser pilgrimage of the Consummation (*'umrat al-qaḍiyyah*).

According to Ibn 'Umar [al-Wāqidī]—['Abd al-Malik b. 'Abd al-'Azīz] Ibn Jurayj—Abū al-Zubayr—'Ikrimah: Maymūnah bt. al-Ḥārith gave herself to the Prophet.

According to [Ibn 'Umar al-Wāqidī]—Mūsā b. Muḥammad b. 'Abd al-Raḥmān—his father: 'Amrah [bt. 'Abd al-Raḥmān], when told that Maymūnah gave herself to the Prophet, [denied it, saying]: The Prophet married her for 500 dirhams paid as bridal gift;[820] al-'Abbās b. 'Abd al-Muṭṭalib was in charge of giving her in marriage to the Prophet.

According to Ibn 'Umar [al-Wāqidī]: Maymūnah died in the year 61/October 1, 680–September 19, 681, during the caliphate of
[2454] Yazīd b. Mu'āwiyah. She was the last of the Prophet's wives to die, and her age was then eighty or eighty-one. She had been [a] strong [woman].

Al-Kilābiyyah,[821] about whose name opinions differ.

Some [scholars] say that she was Fāṭimah bt. al-Ḍaḥḥāk b. Sufyān al-Kilābī. Others, that she was 'Āliyah bt. Ẓabyān b. 'Amr b. 'Awf b. Ka'b b. 'Abd b. Abī Bakr b. Kilāb, and yet another opinion is that she was Sanā bt. Sufyān b. 'Awf b. Ka'b b. 'Abd b. Abī Bakr b. Kilāb. [Furthermore], some hold that there was only one woman of the Kilāb [married to the Prophet], about whose name opinions differ, whereas others believe that all of the [aforementioned] were [wives of the Prophet], each having her own story.

Ibn 'Umar [al-Wāqidī]—Muḥammad b. 'Abdallāh—[Ibn Shihāb] al-Zuhrī—'Urwah [b. al-Zubayr]—'Ā'ishah: The Prophet married a Kilābī woman, and when she entered his [room] and he ap-

---

819. Yāqūt, *Mu'jam al-buldān*, III, 77.

820. *Mahr*, identical with *ṣadāq* according to Spies. See note 738, above, and note 830 below.

821. That is, of the Kilāb, a clan of the 'Āmir b. Ṣa'ṣa'ah. See Ibn Ḥazm, *Jamharat*, 282–84; al-Ṭabarī, *Ta'rīkh*, I, 1686; al-Balādhurī, *Ansāb*, I, 454–55; Khalīfah b. Khayyāṭ, *Ta'rīkh*, 56.

proached her she said "I seek God's protection against you,"[822] whereupon the Prophet said "You have asked the protection of a mighty one; go [back] to your family."

According to ʿAbdallāh b. Jaʿfar—ʿAbd al-Wāḥid b. Abī ʿAwn—Ibn Mannāḥ: She uttered the formula "I seek God's protection" (*aʿūdhu bi-Allāh*) against the Prophet, for she had been dumbfounded and had lost her mind. [Later], whenever she asked permission to enter and see the Prophet's wives, she would say "I am the miserable one" and "I have been cheated."

According to Muḥammad b. ʿAbdallāh—[Ibn Shihāb] al-Zuhrī: It was Fāṭimah bt. al-Ḍaḥḥāk b. Sufyān, who uttered the formula [2455] "I seek God's protection" against the Prophet, and he divorced her. [Afterward], she used to collect camel dung and say "I am the miserable one."

The Prophet had married [the Kilābiyyah] in Dhū al-Qaʿdah 8/February–March 630. She died in the year 60/October 13, 679–September 30, 680.

According to ʿAbdallāh b. Sulaymān—ʿAmr b. Shuʿayb—his father—his grandfather: The Prophet had already consummated his marriage with her, but when he gave his wives the option [to leave him][823] she opted for her clan, so he divorced her. [Afterward], she used to collect camel dung and say "I am the miserable one."

According to ʿAbdallāh b. Jaʿfar—Mūsā b. Saʿīd and Ibn Abī ʿAwn: The Prophet divorced her only because she had leprosy.[824]

According to ʿAbdallāh b. Jaʿfar, Ibn Abī Sabrah, and ʿAbd al-ʿAzīz b. Muḥammad—[Yazīd] Ibn al-Hād—Thaʿlabah b. Abī Mālik—Ḥusayn b. ʿAlī: The Prophet married a woman of the Banū ʿĀmir who would peep at the people in the mosque[825] whenever he went out. The Prophet's wives informed him about it, and he said "You lie about her," but they said "We will show her to you while she is peeping." He said "Agreed." They showed her to him while she was peeping, and he divorced her. Ibn ʿUmar [al-Wāqidī] said: I told this story to ʿUbaydallāh b. Saʿīd b. Abī Hind, and he

---

822. See p. 165, above.
823. Cf. Qur'ān, 33:28–29.
824. Cf. Ibn Isḥāq, *Siyar*, 268.
825. See p. 172, above.

told me on the authority of his father: She uttered the formula "I seek God's protection against you," so he returned her [to her family].

The Prophet married no other woman of the Banū ʿĀmir; also he never married anyone of the Kindah, except the Jawniyyah.

According to Ibn ʿUmar [al-Wāqidī]—Ibrāhīm b. Wathīmah—Abū Wajzah [Yazīd b. ʿUbayd]: The Prophet married her in Dhū al-Qaʿdah 8/February–March 630, on returning from al-Jiʿrānah.

According to Abū Muṣʿab Ismāʿīl b. Muṣʿab—an old man from her clan: She died in the year 60/679–80.

[2456] According to Hishām b. Muḥammad [al-Kalbī]—al-ʿArzamī—Nāfiʿ [client of ʿAbdallāh b. ʿUmar]—[ʿAbdallāh] Ibn ʿUmar: Among the Prophet's wives was one Sanā bt. Sufyān b. ʿAwf b. Kaʿb b. Abī Bakr b. Kilāb.[826]

[Hishām b. Muḥammad citing ʿAbdallāh] Ibn ʿUmar: The Prophet sent Abū Usayd [Mālik b. Rabīʿah] al-Sāʿidī[827] to ask a woman of the Banū ʿĀmir in marriage on his behalf. Her name was ʿAmrah bt. Yazīd b. ʿUbayd b. Ruwās b. Kilāb. The Prophet married her; then it came to his knowledge that she had leprosy, so he divorced her.

Hishām [b. Muḥammad]—a man of the Banū Abī Bakr b. Kilāb: The Prophet married al-ʿĀliyah bt. Ẓabyān b. ʿAmr b. ʿAwf b. Kaʿb b. ʿAbd b. Abī Bakr b. Kilāb. She stayed with him for a while; then he divorced her.

Asmāʾ bt. al-Nuʿmān b. Abī al-Jawn al-Aswad b. al-Ḥārith b. Sharāḥīl b. al-Jawn b. Ākil al-Murār al-Kindī.[828]

According to Ibn ʿUmar [al-Wāqidī]—Muḥammad b. Yaʿqūb b. ʿUtbah—ʿAbd al-Wāḥid b. Abī ʿAwn al-Dawsī: Al-Nuʿmān b. Abī al-Jawn al-Kindī used to dwell with his clan in Najd, near al-Sharabbah.[829] When he came to the Prophet to declare his conversion to Islam he said to him: "O Messnger of God, shall I give you in marriage the most beautiful among the Arab widows? She had

826. See al-Ṣāliḥī, 246, 250, 254, 255.

827. An Anṣārī of the Khazrajī clan Banū Sāʿidah, who was the standard bearer of his clan on the day of the conquest of Mecca; see Ibn Ḥajar, *Iṣābah*, III, 344.

828. Of the noble Kindah tribe, see al-Balādhurī, *Ansāb*, I, 456–58.

829. A region in Najd (central part of the Arabian Peninsula); see Yāqūt, *Muʿjam al-buldān*, III, 272.

been married to a relative of hers, but he died, and she lost her way. Her heart inclines to you, and she wants [to marry] you." The Prophet [agreed to] marry her [and pay] twelve and a half ounces [of gold]. Al-Nu'mān said "O Messenger of God, do not show contempt for her by [being stingy] with the bridal gift." The Prophet said "I never gave more than that as bridal gift for any of my wives, [2457]
and I never give any of my daughters more than that as dowry."[830] Al-Nu'mān said: "It is you who set the example; O Messenger of God, send for your wife! I shall go with your messenger and send your wife [to you] with him." The Prophet sent Abū Usayd al-Sā'idī [with al-Nu'mān]. When they came to her she was sitting in her tent and gave him permission[831] to come in. Abū Usayd then said "The Prophet's wives should not be seen by men." Abū Usayd [later] related "This was after the verse of the Veil (*ḥijāb*) was revealed."[832] She sent to Abū Usayd a message, saying "Show me the right thing to do." He said "[Put] a veil between yourself and the men you talk with, except those who are your close relatives."[833] She did that. Abū Usayd related: I stayed there for three days, then left carrying a woman in a litter on a camel. I brought her to Medina and lodged her with the Banū Sā'idah. The women of the clan, glad about her [coming], went in to greet her. They came out talking about her beauty, and the news of her arrival spread in Medina. I went to the Prophet, who was staying with the Banū 'Amr b. 'Awf, and told him [about it]. [Meanwhile], a woman came in to see her, having heard [from the other women] about her beauty, of which they knew. She was one of the most beautiful of all women. [That] woman said to her "You are of royal blood,[834] and, if you want to gain favor with the Prophet, utter the formula 'I seek God's protection from you'; in this way you will gain his favor, and he will like you."[835]

---

830. The term used in both cases is *ṣadāq*. Obviously there is no distinction here between bridal gift paid by the groom and the dowry given to the bride by her family. See pp. 164, 186, and notes 738, 820, above.

831. The text shifts to the singular because the following issue, that of the Prophet's women talking to strangers, obviously does not concern al-Nu'mān, the woman's father.

832. Qur'an 33:53; see note 813, above.

833. That is, those unattainable to you in marriage.

834. The Āl al-Jawn were the kings of Kindah.

835. See p. 165, above.

According to ʿAbdallāh b. Jaʿfar—[ʿAbd al-Wāḥid] Ibn Abī ʿAwn:
[2458] The Prophet married the Kindī woman in Rabīʿ I 7/July–August 628.

According to ʿAbd al-Raḥmān b. Abī al-Zinād—Hishām b. ʿUrwah—his father [ʿUrwah b. al-Zubayr], who told him that [the caliph] al-Walīd b. ʿAbd al-Malik wrote to him, asking whether or not the Prophet had married al-Ashʿath b. Qays's sister. He was asked this question and replied: "The Prophet never married her or any other Kindī woman, except the one of the Banū al-Jawn. She was his wife, but when she arrived at Medina and was brought before him [for the first time] he looked at her and divorced her without consummating the marriage."

According to Maʿmar [b. Rāshid]—[Ibn Shihāb] al-Zuhrī: The Prophet never married a Kindī woman, except the one of the Banū al-Jawn, but he divorced her before consummating the marriage.

According to Hishām b. Muḥammad [al-Kalbī]—Ibn al-Ghusayyil—Ḥamzah b. Abī Usayd al-Sāʿidī—his father, who was one of the participants in [the battle of] Badr: The Prophet married Asmāʾ bt. al-Nuʿmān al-Jawniyyah and sent me [to fetch her]. When I brought her Ḥafṣah [the Prophet's wife] said to ʿĀʾishah [the Prophet's wife] or vice versa "Put the dye on her, and I shall comb her hair." So they did; then one of them said to her "The Prophet likes a woman brought before him to say 'I seek God's protection from you.'" So, when she entered his [room] and he locked the door, let down the curtain, and reached out to her, she said "I seek God's protection from you." He held his sleeve to his face, covering himself with it, and said "You indeed have sought protection." He said this three times. Abū Usayd related: The Prophet then came out and said to me "O Abū Usayd, give her two white garments, that is, of cotton, and take her to her clan." [Afterward] she used to say "Call me the wretched one."

According to Hishām—Zuhayr b. Muʿāwiyah al-Juʿfī: She died of sorrow.

According to Ibn ʿUmar [al-Wāqidī]—Sulaymān b. al-Ḥārith—ʿAbbās b. Sahl—Abū Usayd al-Sāʿidī: When I arrived at the camp with her the [people] shouted to one another and said [to her]:
[2459] "You are not blessed! What came over you?" She said "I was beguiled; they told me such-and-so," and [she told them] what was said to her. The members of her clan said "You have made us

notorious among the Arabs." She called Abū Usayd and said "What happened happened; what shall I do now?" He answered: "Stay in your home and keep yourself veiled, except in the presence of your close relatives. No one should want [to marry] you after the Prophet, for you are one of the Mothers of the Faithful." She stayed [like that], no one wishing [to marry] her and no one seeing her except her close relatives, until she died at her family's place in Najd, during the caliphate of ʿUthmān b. ʿAffān.

According to Hishām b. Muḥammad [al-Kalbī]—Zuhayr b. Muʿāwiyah al-Juʿfī: She died of sorrow.

According to al-Ḥārith—Muḥammad b. Suhayl—Abū ʿUbaydah Maʿmar b. al-Muthannā: The Prophet married a Yemenī woman by the name of Asmāʾ bt. al-Nuʿmān b. al-Jawn b. Sharāhīl b. al-Nuʿmān, of the Kindah. When he went to see her and invited her [to approach] him she said "[No], you approach me!" She refused to approach him, so he divorced her.

According to others: She was the most beautiful of all women, and the Prophet's wives were afraid that she would gain precedence with him over them, so they told her "We think that, when he approaches you, you should say 'I seek God's protection from you.'" So when he approached her she said "I seek the Merciful's protection from you, if you are God fearing." He said "You sought protection in a [good] Protector; anyone who seeks God's protection should be granted it, and God indeed protects you from me." So he divorced her and ordered al-Sāqiṭ b. ʿAmr al-Anṣārī to equip her; then he sent her to her clan. She used to call herself "the wretched one."

Biographies of the Women Whose Death Dates Are Known, of the Emigrants, Anṣār, and Others Who Were the Prophet's Contemporaries, Believed in Him, and Followed Him

Umm Ayman, the Prophet's client and nurse.[836] [2460]

Her name was Barakah.

836. A black slave girl who took care of the Prophet as a child. See Khalīfah b. Khayyāṭ, *Ṭabaqāt*, 331; al-Balādhurī, *Ansāb*, I, 471–72, 476.

It was reported that the Prophet bequeathed to Umm Ayman five camels and a herd of sheep. He had freed her when he married Khadījah, whereupon she was married to 'Ubayd b. Zayd, of the Banū al-Ḥārith b. al-Khazraj, and bore him Ayman, who was [later] killed as a *shahīd* in the battle of Ḥunayn.

Zayd b. Ḥārithah had belonged to Khadījah, and she gave him to the Prophet. The latter freed him and gave him Umm Ayman in marriage. This was after the [beginning of] the prophethood. Umm Ayman bore Zayd Usāmah b. Zayd.

According to Muḥammad b. 'Umar [al-Wāqidī]—Yaḥyā b. Sa'īd b. Dīnār—an old man of the Banū Sa'd b. Bakr:[837] The Prophet used to call Umm Ayman "mother" and when looking at her he would say "She is the remainder of my family."

According to Ibn 'Umar [al-Wāqidī]: Umm Ayman died at the beginning of the caliphate of 'Uthmān b. 'Affān.

According to Ibn 'Umar [al-Wāqidī]: Ibn Abī al-Furāt, Usāmah b. Zayd's client, quarreled with al-Ḥasan b. Usāmah b. Zayd. Ibn Abī al-Furāt said during his discourse "O Ibn Barakah," meaning Umm Ayman. Al-Ḥasan said [to the people present] "Be my witness." He brought the case to Abū Bakr b. Muḥammad b. 'Amr b. Ḥazm,[838] then judge of Medina, or 'Umar b. 'Abd al-'Azīz, governor of Medina, and told him the story. Abū Bakr asked Ibn Abī al-Furāt "What did you mean when you said to him 'O Ibn Barakah?'" He replied "I called her by her name." [Abū Bakr] said: "Nay, indeed you wanted to belittle her by this, while her standing in Islam is what it is. The Prophet used to call her 'mother' and 'Umm Ayman.' May God not forgive me if I forgive you"; so he flogged him seventy times.

Arwā bt. Kurayz b. Rabī'ah b. Ḥabīb b. 'Abd Shams.[839]

She embraced Islam, emigrated to Medina, and died during the caliphate of 'Uthmān.

---

837. The clan of the Prophet's milk mother, of the Hawāzin confederation; see Ibn Ḥazm, *Jamharat*, 265.

838. A descendant of the eminent Anṣārī 'Amr b. Ḥazm; see Ibn Ḥajar, *Iṣābah*, II, 532. His son Muḥammad b. Abī Bakr was also judge in Medina; see Wakī', I, 135–48, 175–78. The family is associated with transmission of historical traditions and legal material; see F. Sezgin, I, 284.

839. Of the Qurashī clan the Banū 'Abd Shams. She was 'Uthmān b. 'Affān's mother; see Ibn Qudāmah, 227.

Asmā' bt. Abī Bakr.[840] [2461]

Her mother was Qutaylah bt. 'Abd al-'Uzzā b. 'Abd As'ad b. Jābir b. Mālik b. Ḥisl b. 'Āmir b. Lu'ayy. She was a full sister of 'Abdallāh b. Abī Bakr.

Asmā' embraced Islam in Mecca at an early stage and gave the Prophet the oath of allegiance. She was married to al-Zubayr b. al-'Awwām and bore him 'Abdallāh, 'Urwah, 'Āṣim, al-Muhājir, Khadījah al-Kubrā, Umm al-Ḥasan, and 'Ā'ishah, children of al-Zubayr.

According to al-Ḥārith—Dā'ūd b. al-Muḥabbar—Ḥammād b. Salamah—Hishām b. 'Urwah [b. al-Zubayr]—Asmā' bt. Abī Bakr, who related that during the governorate of Sa'īd b. al-'Āṣ [in Medina], while the internal war (*fitnah*) was on,[841] she took a dagger and put it under her pillow. She was asked what she intended to do with it, and replied "If a brigand breaks into my [place] I will rip up his belly." [The narrator] added that she was blind.

Asmā' died a few days after her son 'Abdallāh b. al-Zubayr, on Tuesday, 17 Jumādā I 73/October 6, 692.[842]

Māriyah, the Prophet's concubine and the mother of his son, Ibrāhīm.

Al-Muqawqas,[843] lord of Alexandria, gave her with her sister Sīrīn and other things as present to the Prophet.

According to Ibn 'Umar [al-Wāqidī]—Ya'qūb b. Muḥammad b. Abī Ṣa'ṣa'ah—'Abdallāh b. 'Abd al-Raḥmān b. Abī Ṣa'ṣa'ah:[844] In the year 7/May 11, 628–April 30, 629, al-Muqawqas, lord of Alexandria, sent to the Prophet Māriyah, her sister Sīrīn, a thousand gold coins, twenty fine robes, his mule Duldul, and his donkey 'Ufayr, or Ya'fur. With them was Māriyah's brother, a very old

---

840. An early convert, daughter of the Prophet's closest Companion. See Ibn Qudāmah, 316; "Asmā' bint Abī Bakr," *EI*², I, 713–14 (H. A. R. Gibb).

841. That is, the first so-called civil war, in the aftermath of 'Uthmān's murder (36/656). Sa'īd (b. al-'Āṣ b. Sa'īd b. al-'Āṣ b. Umayyah) was a member of the Umayyad family who served 'Uthmān and Mu'āwiyah as governor of al-Kūfah and Medina, respectively. He died during the caliphate of Mu'āwiyah. "Sa'īd b. al-'Āṣ," *EI*², VIII, 853 (C. E. Bosworth); al-Zubayrī, 176–78; Ibn Ḥajar, *Iṣābah*, II, 47–48.

842. October 6 was a Sunday, according to Cattenoz' tables.

843. The Arabic name given to the patriarch of Alexandria; see "al-Muqawqas," *EI*², III, 511–13 (K. Öhrenberg).

844. Al-Ṭabarī, *Ta'rīkh*, I, 1591; al-Balādhurī, *Ansāb*, I, 448–51.

[2462] eunuch called Mābūr. Al-Muqawqas sent all this [to the Prophet] with Ḥāṭib b. Abī Balta'ah. The latter suggested to Māriyah that she embrace Islam and made her wish to do so; thus she and her sister were converted, whereas the eunuch adhered to his religion until he was [also] converted later in Medina, while the Prophet was [still] alive.

The Prophet admired Umm Ibrāhīm, who was fair-skinned and beautiful. He lodged her in al-'Āliyah, at the property nowadays called the *mashrabah* of Umm Ibrāhīm. He used to visit her there and ordered her to veil herself, [but] he had intercourse with her by virtue of her being his property.[845] When she became pregnant [and her time was due] she gave birth there, the midwife being Salmā, the Prophet's client. Abū Rāfi', Salmā's husband, brought the Prophet the news of Ibrāhīm's [birth], and the Prophet gave him a slave as a present. This occurred in Dhū al-Ḥijjah 8/March–April 630.

The Anṣār argued among themselves about who would [mind] Ibrāhīm, because they wanted Māriyah to have her hands free for the Prophet, knowing how he loved her.

According to Ibn 'Umar [al-Wāqidī]: Māriyah was from Ḥafn, from the Anṣinā district.[846]

According to Usāmah b. Zayd al-Laythī—al-Mundhir b. 'Ubayd—'Abd al-Raḥmān b. Ḥassān b. Thābit—his mother Sīrīn, Māriyah's sister, whom the Prophet had given to Ḥassān b. Thābit, and she bore him 'Abd al-Raḥmān. She said: "I saw the Prophet when Ibrāhīm died. I was crying loudly and my sister [too], and he never forbade us to cry loudly.[847] Al-Faḍl b. al-'Abbās washed Ibrāhīm's body while the Prophet and al-'Abbās were seated. I then saw the Prophet at the grave's edge, al-'Abbās [stand-
[2463] ing] beside him. Al-Faḍl and Usāmah b. Zayd [b. Ḥārithah] descended into the grave.[848] The sun was eclipsed that day, and people said "The sun is eclipsed because of Ibrāhīm's death," but the

845. That is, Māriyah was ordered to veil herself as did the Prophet's wives, but he did not marry her. Cf. p. 184, above.

846. In Upper Egypt, see Yāqūt, *Mu'jam al-buldān*, I, 381.

847. The issue alluded to here is mourning customs, debated in the Muslim community. See p. 156 and note 179, above.

848. See p. 11, above.

Prophet said "The sun will not be eclipsed for anyone's death or life."

The Prophet saw an opening in the grave and ordered that it be stopped up. He was asked about it and said: "It does neither harm nor good, but the living are pleased [when it is done]. When a man does something, God prefers that he do it properly."

According to Ibn 'Umar [al-Wāqidī]—Mūsā b. Muḥammad b. 'Abd al-Raḥmān—his father: Abū Bakr supported Māriyah until his death; then 'Umar during his caliphate did the same until she died.[849]

According to Ibn 'Umar [al-Wāqidī]: Māriyah, mother of Ibrāhīm, son of the Prophet, died in Muḥarram 16/February 637. 'Umar was seen assembling people to attend her [funeral]; then he said the prayer over her bier. Her grave is in al-Baqī'.

Names of the Hāshimī Women Believers Who Outlived the Prophet, Transmitted Traditions from Him, and Had [Their] Knowledge Transmitted from Them

Fāṭimah, daughter of the Prophet.

She outlived [her father], and traditions were transmitted from her, among them the following. According to 'Imrān b. Mūsā—'Abd al-Wārith—Layth—'Abdallāh b. al-Ḥasan—his mother Fāṭimah—his grandmother Fāṭimah al-Kubrā (senior): The Prophet used to enter the mosque and utter the formula "May God bless the Prophet,"[850] then say "God, forgive me my sins and open the doors of Your benevolence for me."

According to Muḥammad b. 'Ubayd al-Muḥāribī—al-Muṭṭalib b. Ziyād—Layth—'Abdallāh b. al-Ḥasan—Fāṭimah al-Ṣughrā (junior)—Fāṭimah al-Kubrā (senior): The Prophet used to enter the [2464]
mosque and say "In the name of God, O God, bless Muḥammad and his family, forgive my sins, and open the doors of Your mercy for me." Going out he used to say "In the name of God, forgive my sins, and open the doors of Your benevolence for me."

849. The Prophet's wives were entitled to regular pensions, but not Māriyah, who was not married to him.

850. *Idhā dakhala al-masjid ṣallā 'alā al-nabiyy.* See note 379, above.

According to Ya'qūb b. Ibrāhīm and al-Faḍl b. al-Ṣabbāḥ—Ismā'īl b. 'Ulayyah—Layth—'Abdallāh b. Ḥasan b. Ḥasan—his mother, Fāṭimah bt. al-Ḥusayn—her grandmother Fāṭimah daughter of the Prophet: The Prophet used to enter the mosque and utter the formula "May God bless Muḥammad and give him peace," then say "O God, forgive my sins and open the doors of Your mercy for me." On going out he used to utter the formula "May God bless Muḥammad and give him peace," then say "O God, forgive my sins, and open the doors of Your benevolence for me."

According to al-Rabī' b. Sulaymān—Asad [b. Mūsā]—Qays b. al-Rabī'—'Abdallāh b. al-Ḥasan—Fāṭimah bt. al-Ḥusayn—Fāṭimah al-Kubrā (senior): The Prophet used to enter the mosque and say "O God, bless Muḥammad, and give him peace; O God, forgive my sins, and open the doors of Your mercy for me." On going out of the mosque he used to say "O God, bless Muḥammad, and give him peace; O God, forgive my sins, and open the doors of Your benevolence for me."

Umm Hāni' bt. Abī Ṭālib b. 'Abd al-Muṭṭalib b. Hāshim b. 'Abd Manāf.[851]

Her name was Fākhitah, but, according to Hishām b. al-Kalbī, it was Hind. Her mother was Fāṭimah bt. Asad b. Hāshim b. 'Abd Manāf.

It was reported that before he was inspired the Prophet had asked Abū Ṭālib to give her to him in marriage, and the same was
[2465] done by Hubayrah b. Abī Wahb b. 'Amr b. 'Ā'idh b. 'Imrān b. Makhzūm.[852] Abū Ṭālib gave her to Hubayrah, and the Prophet said "O Uncle, you gave her in marriage to Hubayrah and left me out," to which Abū Ṭālib replied "O Nephew, we became related to them [by marriage] because [of the principle that] the noble is another noble's equal."[853]

---

851. Sister of 'Alī and cousin of the Prophet. See Khalīfah b. Khayyāṭ, *Ṭabaqāt*, 330; Ibn Qudāmah, 138; al-Balādhurī, *Ansāb*, I, 459.

852. A poet and warrior who never embraced Islam but ran away when Mecca was conquered and died in Najrān as an infidel. See Ibn Qudāmah, 397; Muḥammad Ibn Ḥabīb, *Munammaq*, 419.

853. The principle of marrying someone of the same social status, wealth, and the like (*kafā'ah*) was maintained in pre-Islamic times and continued afterward as

Umm Hāni' later embraced Islam, a fact that separated her from Hubayrah.[854] The Prophet asked her to marry him, but she said "By God, I used to love you in the Jāhiliyyah, so I certainly do so in Islam, but I have young children, and I hate to [see them] bothering you." The Prophet said: "The best women ever to have ridden camels are the women of the Quraysh. They are the most affectionate toward their small children and the most excellent in doing good to their husbands when they [the women] are wealthy."[855]

Umm Hāni' outlived the Prophet and transmitted traditions from him, among them the following. According to Abū Kurayb [Muḥammad b. al-'Alā']—'Ubaydallāh—Isrā'īl—al-Suddī [Ismā'īl b. 'Abd al-Raḥmān]—Abū Ṣāliḥ [Bādhām]—Umm Hāni': The Prophet asked me to marry him, but I excused myself, and he accepted my excuse. God later revealed the verse "We have made allowable for thee thy wives to whom thou hast given their hires . . . those who have emigrated with thee,"[856] so I became unlawful to him because I did not emigrate with him. I was one of those who were converted to Islam against their will (*ṭulaqā'*).[857]

Ḍubā'ah bt. al-Zubayr b. 'Abd al-Muṭṭalib b. Hāshim.[858]

The Prophet gave this [woman], Ḍubā'ah bt. al-Zubayr, to al-Miqdād b. 'Amr in marriage, and she bore him 'Abdallāh and Karīmah. 'Abdallāh was killed in the battle of the Camel [fighting on the side of] 'Ā'ishah. 'Alī [b. Abī Ṭālib] passed by his body and said "What an evil sister's son this is!"[859]

Ḍubā'ah transmitted traditions from the Prophet.

According to [Muḥammad] Ibn Bashshār—'Abd al-Ṣamad b.

---

well. See "Kafā'ah," *EI*², IV, 404 (Y. Linant de Bellefonds); Shukri, 34–42.

854. See p. 15, above.

855. Cf. p. 171, above.

856. See Qur'ān 33:49; trans. Bell, II, 416.

857. *Ṭulaqā'* is a designation of the Meccans who were converted after the conquest of the town, having opposed the Prophet until then; see Kister, "On Strangers and Allies," 153. Umm Hāni's statement is inconsistent with the former story, in which the Prophet asked for her in marriage after she had embraced Islam and left her pagan husband.

858. Paternal cousin of the Prophet. See Khalīfah b. Khayyāṭ, *Ṭabaqāt*, 331; Ibn Qudāmah, 141.

859. Ḍubā'ah was not in fact 'Alī's sister but a cousin.

'Abd al-Wārith—Hammām b. Yaḥyā—Qatādah [b. Di'āmah]—Isḥāq b. 'Abdallāh b. al-Ḥārith—his grandmother Umm al-Ḥakam—her sister Ḍubā'ah bt. al-Zubayr, who related that she had brought the Prophet [a piece of] meat and he nibbled at it, then prayed without performing ablution.

[2466] Umm al-Ḥakam bt. al-Zubayr b. 'Abd al-Muṭṭalib b. Hāshim.[860]
She was married to Rabī'ah b. al-Ḥārith b. 'Abd al-Muṭṭalib and bore him Muḥammad, 'Abbās, 'Abd Shams, 'Abd al-Muṭṭalib, Umayyah, and Arwā al-Kubrā (senior).

Umm al-Ḥakam transmitted [traditions] from the Prophet.

According to [Muḥammad] Ibn Bashshār—Mu'ādh b. Hishām—his father—Qatādah—Isḥāq b. 'Abdallāh b. Nawfal—Umm al-Ḥakam bt. al-Zubayr, who reported that she had handed the Prophet a [piece] of shoulder meat; he ate some of it, then prayed.

Umm Ḥakīm bt. 'Abd al-Muṭṭalib.[861]
She is the one called al-Bayḍā' (the white one). She did not live to see Islam.

Umm Ḥakīm was 'Āmir b. Kurayz's mother and 'Uthmān b. 'Affān's maternal grandmother.

Kurayz b. Rabī'ah had married Umm Ḥakīm al-Bayḍā', who bore him 'Āmir, Arwā, Ṭalḥah, and Umm Ṭalḥah. 'Affān b. Abī al-'Āṣ b. Umayyah b. 'Abd Shams b. 'Abd Manāf married Arwā bt. Kurayz, who bore him 'Uthmān b. 'Affān. She later married 'Uqbah b. Abī Mu'ayṭ and bore him al-Walīd, Khālid, and Umm Kulthūm, children of 'Uqbah b. Abī Mu'ayṭ.[862]

Ṣafiyyah bt. 'Abd al-Muṭṭalib b. Hāshim.
Her mother was Hālah bt. Wuhayb b. 'Abd Manāf b. Zuhrah b. Kilāb.

Ṣafiyyah was a half-sister of Ḥamzah b. 'Abd al-Muṭṭalib, on

---

860. Sometimes called Umm Ḥakīm. See Khalīfah b. Khayyāṭ, *Ṭabaqāt*, 331; Ibn Qudāmah, 141; Ibn Ḥajar, *Iṣābah*, IV, 442–43.

861. Twin sister of 'Abdallāh, the Prophet's father. See al-Balādhurī, *Ansāb*, I, 88, III (Dūrī), 311; Ibn Qudāmah, 173.

862. A member of the Umayyad family and an enemy of the Prophet. He was one of the two Qurashī captives who were executed by Muḥammad after the battle of Badr; see Ibn Qudāmah, 210.

their mother's side. In pre-Islamic times she had been married to al-Ḥārith b. Ḥarb b. Umayyah b. 'Abd Shams and bore him Ṣufayy. She was later married to al-'Awwām b. Khuwaylid b. Asad and bore him al-Zubayr, al-Sā'ib, and 'Abd al-Ka'bah.

Ṣafiyyah embraced Islam and gave the Prophet the oath of allegiance. She emigrated to Medina and lived after the Prophet's death, to the caliphate of 'Umar b. al-Khaṭṭāb.

Umāmah bt. Ḥamzah b. 'Abd al-Muṭṭalib b. Hāshim.[863] [2467]

Her mother was Salmā bt. 'Umays b. Ma'd b. Taym b. Mālik b. Quḥāfah b. Khath'am, Asmā' bt. 'Umays' sister. [Umāmah] is the name by which Hishām b. Muḥammad [al-Kalbī] refers to her, whereas others say that it was 'Umārah bt. Ḥamzah. According to Hishām, 'Umārah was a man, a son of Ḥamzah, after whom he was called.

Umāmah outlived the Prophet and transmitted [traditions] from him.

Clients [of the Banū Hāshim]

Umm Ayman, the Prophet's client.

According to al-Ḥusayn b. 'Alī al-Ṣudā'ī—Shabābah—Abū Mālik al-Nakha'ī—'Abd al-Malik b. Ḥusayn—al-Aswad b. Qays—Fulayḥ al-'Anazī—Umm Ayman: [One] night the Prophet got up and urinated in the corner of the house into an earthenware vessel. During the night I got up, and, being thirsty, I drank what was in that vessel, not noticing [anything]. When the Prophet got up in the morning he said "O Umm Ayman, take that earthenware vessel and pour away its content." I said "By God, I drank what was in it." The Prophet laughed until his molar teeth showed, then said "After this you will never have a bellyache."

Salmā, the Prophet's client.[864]

She outlived the Prophet and transmitted traditions from him.

According to 'Alī b. Shu'ayb al-Simsār—Ma'n b. 'Īsā—Fā'id, the client of 'Ubaydallāh b. 'Alī b. Abī Rāfi'—'Ubaydallāh b. 'Alī b.

863. Ibn Qudāmah, 148; Ibn Ḥajar, *Iṣābah*, IV, 235–36.
864. Khalīfah b. Khayyāṭ, *Ṭabaqāt*, 332; al-Balādhurī, *Ansāb*, I, 485.

Abī Rāfiʿ—his grandmother Salmā: The Prophet used to apply henna to wounds and the like.

[2468] Maymūnah bt. Saʿd, the Prophet's client.[865]

She transmitted [traditions] from him.

According to Abū Kurayb [Muḥammad b. al-ʿAlāʾ]—ʿUbaydallāh—Isrāʾīl—Zayd b. Jubayr—Abū Zayd al-Ḍabbī—Maymūnah bt. Saʿd: The Prophet was asked about a child born of adultery and replied "A pair of shoes I wear while exerting myself in the path of God is preferable to me than the freeing of a child born of adultery."

Umaymah, the Prophet's client.[866]

She transmitted [traditions] from him.

According to Abū Kurayb [Muḥammad b. al-ʿAlāʾ]—Yūnus b. Bukayr—Yazīd b. Sinān Abū Farwah al-Ruhāwī—Abū Yaḥyā al-Kalāʿī—Jubayr b. Nufayr: I came to see Umaymah, the Prophet's client, and asked her "Tell me something you heard from the Prophet." She said: "One day I was pouring [water] on his hands for his ablution, when a man came in and said 'O Messenger of God, I want to go back to my family, so instruct me with something I shall remember.' The Prophet said: 'Never attribute a partner to God, even if your [limbs] be torn and you be burned in fire. Never disobey your parents; even if they tell you to give up your family and [everything pertaining to] this world, do it. Never deliberately neglect to perform the prayer, for whoever deliberately neglects to perform one, forfeits the protection of God and His messenger. Never drink wine, for it is the mother of all sins. Do not expand beyond the boundaries of [your] land, lest you come on the Day of Judgment with the equivalent of seven [tracts] of land tied to your neck. Never run away on a battle day, for whoever runs away on a battle day arouses the wrath of God, and hell would be his shelter; what a wretched end this is![867] Spend on your family from your wealth, but do not lift your rod off them. Make them fear God.'"

---

865. Khalīfah b. Khayyāṭ, *Ṭabaqāt*, 331; al-Balādhurī, *Ansāb*, I, 485.

866. Ignored in most of the sources I have used. Ibn Ḥajar, *Iṣābah*, IV, 243, records the same tradition as here, referring it to several sources.

867. Cf. Qurʾān 8:16.

Arab Women [Married into the Quraysh][868] *Who Outlived the Prophet and Transmitted [Traditions] from Him, Having Given Him the Oath of Allegiance and Embraced Islam during His Lifetime* [2469]

Umm al-Faḍl, that is, Lubābah al-Kubrā (senior) bt. al-Ḥārith b. Ḥazn b. Bujayr b. al-Huzam b. Ruwaybah b. ʿAbdallāh b. Hilāl b. ʿĀmir b. Ṣaʿṣaʿah b. Muʿāwiyah b. Bakr b. Hawāzin b. Manṣūr b. ʿIkrimah b. Khaṣafah b. Qays b. ʿAylān b. Muḍar.[869]

Her mother was Hind, that is Khawlah bt. ʿAwf b. Zuhayr b. al-Ḥārith b. Ḥamāṭah b. Jurash, who belonged to Ḥimyar.

It was reported that Umm al-Faḍl was the first woman to embrace Islam in Mecca after Khadījah bt. Khuwaylid. The Prophet used to visit her and take siestas in her house.

Umm al-Faḍl's sisters were Maymūnah, the Prophet's wife, her full sister, Lubābah al-Ṣughrā (junior), that is, al-ʿAṣmāʾ bt. al-Ḥārith b. Ḥazn, her half-sister, from her father; Huzaylah bt. al-Ḥārith b. Ḥazn, also a half-sister, from her father; and ʿAzzah, her [half]-sister from her father.

Her brothers and sisters from her mother were Maḥmiyah b. Jazʾ al-Zubaydī, ʿAwn, Asmāʾ, and Salmā, children of ʿUmays b. Maʿd b. al-Ḥārith, of the Khathʿam.[870]

Al-ʿAbbās b. ʿAbd al-Muṭṭalib married Umm al-Faḍl bt. al-Ḥārith, and she bore him al-Faḍl, ʿAbdallāh, ʿUbaydallāh, Maʿbad, Qutham, ʿAbd al-Raḥmān, and Umm Ḥabīb.

ʿAbdallāh b. Yazīd al-Hilālī said:[871]

Never has a Bactrian she-camel borne a stallion
    the like of the six coming from Umm al-Faḍl's womb.
What a noble woman she is, and he [what a noble] man!

---

868. *Wa-min gharāʾib nisāʾ al-ʿarab. Gharībah*, literally, "stranger," is a woman who enters the clan by exogamic marriage. That the Quraysh are meant here is clear from the following biographical details.

869. A member of the ʿĀmirī clan the Banū Hilāl. See al-Balādhurī, *Ansāb*, I, 447, III (Dūrī), 1–2; Khalīfah b. Khayyāṭ, *Ṭabaqāt*, 338 (who seems to confuse her with her sister); Muḥammad Ibn Ḥabīb, *Muḥabbar*, 107, 455.

870. A tribe believed by some to be of northern, by others of southern, descent. See "Khathʿam," *EI*², IV, 1105–6 (G. Levi Della Vida); Ibn al-Kalbī, *Nasab maʿadd*, 356–61; Ibn Ḥazm, *Jamharat*, 390–92.

871. Ibn Saʿd, IV/1, 2, VIII, 203. I found a few persons with the name of ʿAbdallāh b. Yazīd, but none seemed to me to fit the present context. The only "al-Hilālī" was a rather obscure governor of Armenia; see Ibn ʿAbd Rabbihi, II, 468.

According to Ibn ʿUmar [al-Wāqidī]: Umm al-Faḍl bt. al-Ḥārith emigrated to Medina after al-ʿAbbās b. ʿAbd al-Muṭṭalib's conversion to Islam.

[2470] Lubābah al-Ṣughrā (junior), that is, al-ʿAṣmāʾ bt. al-Ḥārith.[872] Her mother was Fākhitah bt. ʿĀmir b. Muʿattib b. Mālik al-Thaqafī.

Lubābah had been married to al-Walīd b. al-Mughīrah b. ʿAbdallāh b. ʿUmar b. Makhzūm in Mecca and bore him Khālid b. al-Walīd. She embraced Islam after the Emigration and gave the Prophet the oath of allegiace.

Asmāʾ bt. ʿUmays b. Maʿd.[873]

Her mother was Hind, that is, Khawlah bt. ʿAwf b. Zuhayr b. Jurash.

According to al-Ḥārith—Khālid b. Khidāsh—Ḥammād b. Zayd—Ayyūb—Muḥammad: Asmāʾ bore Jaʿfar [b. Abī Ṭālib] [his son] Muḥammad, and she bore Abū Bakr [his son] Muḥammad.[874]

Asmāʾ's full sister was Salmā bt. ʿUmays, an early convert to Islam. She was married to Ḥamzah b. ʿAbd al-Muṭṭalib[875] and bore him his daughter ʿUmārah. Ḥamzah was killed in the battle of Uḥud and Salmā bt. ʿUmays became a widow. Shaddād b. [Usāmah b. ʿAmr, that is,] al-Hād al-Laythī then married her, and she bore him ʿAbdallāh b. Shaddād, a half-brother of Ḥamzah's daughter [ʿUmārah], from her mother. He is [also] a maternal cousin of al-ʿAbbās b. ʿAbd al-Muṭṭalib's children and of Khālid b. al-Walīd b. al-Mughīrah.[876]

Asmāʾ bt. ʿUmays outlived the Prophet for a while and transmitted traditions from him.

---

872. Sister of the aforementioned Lubābah al-Kubrā. See al-Balādhurī, *Ansāb*, I, 447–48; Ibn Ḥajar, *Iṣābah*, IV, 398–99.

873. Of the Khathʿam tribe. See Khalīfah b. Khayyāṭ, *Ṭabaqāt*, 342; al-Balādhurī, *Ansāb*, I, 447–48.

874. According to Ibn Ḥajar, *Iṣābah*, IV, 231, she was also married to ʿAlī b. Abī Ṭālib.

875. An uncle of the Prophet, an early convert, and a close Companion. See *EI*², III, 152–53 (G. M. Meredith-Owens); Ibn Qudāmah, 144–47.

876. Salmā was half-sister of Lubābah al-Kubrā, wife of al-ʿAbbās, and of Lubābah al-Ṣughrā, mother of Khālid b. al-Walīd; see p. 201, above. On Shaddād, see al-Ṣafadī, XVI, 124; al-Mizzī, *Tahdhīb*, XII, 405–7.

ʿAbdallāh b. Masʿūd's mother, that is, Umm ʿAbd bt. ʿAbd Wadd b. Sawāʾ b. Quraym b. Ṣāhilah b. Kāhil b. al-Ḥārith b. Tamīm b. Saʿd b. Hudhayl b. Mudrikah b. al-Yās b. Muḍar.[877]

Her mother was Hind bt. ʿAbd b. al-Ḥārith b. Zuhrah b. Kilāb.

Umm ʿAbd embraced Islam and gave the Prophet the oath of allegiace. She transmitted from him the following [tradition]. Ac- [2471] cording to Muḥammad b. Muʿāwiyah al-Anmāṭī—ʿAbbād b. al-ʿAwwām—Abān—Ibrāhīm—ʿAlqamah [b. Qays al-Nakhaʿī]—ʿAbdallāh [b. Masʿūd]—his mother, who related that she [once] spent the night with them and the Prophet got up [in the night] and prayed. She said "I saw him standing long in [that night] prayer (*witr*) before prostrating himself."

Zaynab bt. Abī Muʿāwiyah al-Thaqafiyyah, ʿAbdallāh b. Masʿūd's wife.[878]

Zaynab embraced Islam and gave the Prophet the oath of allegiance. She transmitted traditions from him, among them the following. According to al-Rabīʿ b. Sulaymān—Asad b. Mūsā—[ʿAbdallāh] Ibn Lahīʿah—Bukayr—Busr b. Saʿīd—Zaynab, ʿAbdallāh's wife—the Prophet: Whoever comes to the mosque from among you should not wear perfume.

Umm Sinān al-Aslamiyyah.[879]

She transmitted [traditions] from the Prophet.

According to Muḥammad b. ʿUmar [al-Wāqidī][880]—ʿAbdallāh b. Abī Yaḥyā—Thubaytah bt. Ḥanẓalah al-Aslamiyyah—her mother, Umm Sinān al-Aslamiyyah: I came to the Prophet when he intended to set out for Khaybar and said "O Messenger of God, I shall set out with you in this enterprise of yours, to see about drinking water and to take care of the sick and wounded if there are any, and, if there are not, I shall assist the men." The Prophet said: "Go, with God's blessing. There are [also] friends of yours, both from your clan and others, who approached me [about this], and I have permitted it. You can go with your clan if you like or

877. Ibn Saʿd, VIII, 212. The tribe's name is Hudhayl.
878. Khalīfah b. Khayyāṭ, *Ṭabaqāt*, 337.
879. Ibn Ḥajar, *Iṣābah*, IV, 462–63. Almost no biographical details are given.
880. Al-Wāqidī, 685, 686–87; Wellhausen, *Muḥammad*, 284.

with us." She said[881] "With you." He said "So go with my wife Umm Salamah." She related: So I was with Umm Salamah.[882]

[2472] The daughter of Abū al-Ḥakam, al-Ghifāriyyah.[883]

She transmitted [traditions] from the Prophet.

According to Muḥammad b. Bashshār and Muḥammad b. al-Muthannā—Muḥammad b. Abī 'Awn—Muḥammad b. Isḥāq—Sulaymān b. Suḥaym—his mother, daughter of Abū al-Ḥakam, al-Ghifāriyyah—the Prophet: One may come at a cubit's distance from paradise,[884] then say such a word as will remove him from it to a distance farther than [that between here and] Ṣan'ā'.

Umm Sharīk.[885]

She transmitted [traditions] from the Prophet.

According to 'Amr b. Baydaq—Sufyān—'Abd al-Ḥamīd b. Jubayr b. Shaybah—Sa'īd b. al-Musayyab—Umm Sharīk: The Prophet had ordered her to kill lizards.[886]

According to Yūnus [b. 'Abd al-A'lā]—['Abdallāh] Ibn Wahb—['Abd al-Malik] Ibn Jurayj—'Abd al-Ḥamīd b. Jubayr b. Shaybah—Sa'īd b. al-Musayyab—Umm Sharīk, a woman of the Banū 'Āmir b. Lu'ayy who related that she had asked the Prophet's opinion about the killing of lizards, and he had ordered her to kill them.

According to Abū Kurayb [Muḥammad b. al-'Alā']—'Ubaydallāh b. Mūsā—['Abd al-Malik] Ibn Jurayj—'Abd al-Ḥamīd b. Jubayr b. Shaybah—Sa'īd b. al-Musayyab—Umm Sharīk, who related that the Prophet had ordered to kill lizards, saying: "They used to blow on [the Patriarch] Ibrāhīm."

---

881. There is a shift here from the first to the third person.

882. The legal issue raised here is the permissibility of the participation of women in war; see, e.g., al-Fazārī, 299–300.

883. Āminah bt. al-Ḥakam or Abī al-Ḥakam, mentioned as a source of traditions for her son Sulaymān b. Suḥaym; see Ibn Ḥajar, *Tahdhīb*, IV, 169. Ibn Ḥajar, *Iṣābah*, IV, 224 promises to supply details on her in another place but fails to do so.

884. *Qubbat dhirā'*. De Goeje's manuscript had *q-b-h*, which he edited as *qubbat* but prefers to read as *qaby*. See 2472 n. b; GLOSSARIUM, s.v. *q-b-w*. Cairo, 624, and Dār al-Fikr, 629, also have *qubbat*.

885. A member of the Qurashī clan 'Āmir b. Lu'ayy. She was one of the women who offered themselves to the Prophet in marriage. See Ibn Isḥāq, *Siyar*, 269, cf. 284; Ibn Qudāmah, 489–90; Khalīfah b. Khayyāṭ, *Ṭabaqāt*, 335; al-Balādhurī, *Ansāb*, I, 422.

886. On the issue of killing and eating lizards, see note 587, above; Cook, "Dietary Law," 220–31; Kister, "Locust's Wing," 349.

Umm Marthad.[887]

She transmitted [traditions] from the Prophet.

According to Ibrāhīm b. Sa'īd al-Jawharī—Muḥammad b. Wahb b. Abī Karīmah al-Ḥarrānī—Muḥammad b. Maslamah—Abū 'Abd al-Raḥīm b. al-'Alā'—Muḥammad b. 'Abdallāh b. Abī Ṣa'ṣa'ah—his father—Umm Khārijah bt. Sa'd b. al-Rabī'—Umm Marthad, who was one of those who gave the Prophet the oath of allegiance: We [once] went out with the Prophet, and he said "The first to meet you [on the way] will be one of the dwellers in paradise." 'Alī [b. Abī Ṭālib] met us. [2473]

Umm al-Dardā'.[888]

She transmitted traditions from the Prophet, among them the following. According to Sa'd b. 'Abdallāh b. al-Ḥakam—Abū Zur'ah [al-Dimashqī]—Abū Ḥaywah [Shurayḥ b. Yazīd]—Abū Ṣakhr—'Īsā, father of Mūsā, a client of Ja'far b. Khārijah al-Asadī—Umm al-Dardā': The Prophet met her one day and asked her "Where do you come from, O Umm al-Dardā'?" She replied "From the public bath." He said "By He Who holds my soul in His hand, a woman who takes off her clothes anywhere but in her home disgraces herself before God."[889]

According to al-Rabī' [b. Sulaymān]—Asad b. Mūsā—['Abdallāh] Ibn Lahī'ah—Zabbān b. Fā'id—Sahl b. Mu'ādh—his father—Umm al-Dardā': I came out of the public bath and met the Prophet, who asked me "Where do you come from, O Umm al-Dardā'?" I replied "From the public bath," whereupon he said "By He Who holds my soul in His hand, a woman who takes off her clothes anywhere but in the house of her mother or grandmother[890] utterly disgraces herself before the Merciful."

---

887. Ibn Ḥajar, *Iṣābah*, IV, 496; hardly any details are given Cf. 446 (under Umm Khārijah).

888. Khayrah bt. Abī Ḥadrad, known as a pious and wise woman, a source of traditions for several Successors. See Ibn Isḥāq, *Siyar*, 141, where she is depicted as actively engaged in seeking knowledge. There is, however, a confusion between two women of the same name. See Ibn Ḥajar, *Iṣābah*, IV, 295; Abū Zur'ah, 378; Ibn Manẓūr, *Mukhtaṣar*, VIII, 103.

889. Literally, "tears the veil separating God and herself."

890. Literally, "in the house of one of her mothers."

[2474] Umm al-Mundhir bt. Qays b. ʿAmr b. ʿUbayd b. ʿĀmir b. ʿAdī b. ʿĀmir b. Ghanm b. ʿAdī b. Ghanm b. al-Najjār.[891]

She was a full sister of Salīṭ b. Qays, who had participated in the battle of Badr and was later killed as a *shahīd* in the battle of the Bridge, commanded by Abū ʿUbayd.[892]

Umm al-Mundhir gave the Prophet the oath of allegiance. She transmitted from him the following [tradition]. According to Abū Kurayb [Muḥammad b. al-ʿAlāʾ]—Zayd b. Ḥubāb al-ʿUklī—Fulayḥ b. Sulaymān al-Madanī—Ayyūb b. ʿAbd al-Raḥmān al-Anṣārī—Yaʿqūb b. Abī Yaʿqūb—Umm al-Mundhir al-Anṣāriyyah, who was one of the Prophet's maternal aunts: The Prophet came [to visit] me together with ʿAlī, who was recovering from an illness. There were dates in the house, hung up [somewhere], and the Prophet ate from them while standing, and so did ʿAlī. The Prophet said "This is not good for you," so he stopped [eating]. I cooked some beets and barley for the Prophet and served them to him, and he said "O ʿAlī, eat from this; it is better for you."

The Death Dates of Successors and People of the Following Generations, of [Our] Deceased Forefathers Who Had Been Scholars and Transmitters of Traditions

Successors Who Died in the Year 32 (August 12, 652–August 1, 653)

Kaʿb al-Aḥbār b. Mātiʿ.[893]

His *kunyah* was Abū Isḥāq. He belonged to the Ḥimyar, to the family of Dhū Ruʿayn.[894]

Kaʿb al-Aḥbār lived in Ḥims, where he died in the year 32/652–53, during the caliphate of ʿUthmān b. ʿAffān.

---

891. Her name was Salmā; she was an Anṣārī of the Banū ʿAdī b. al-Najjār (Khazraj). See Khalīfah b. Khayyāṭ, *Ṭabaqāt*, 335; Ibn Ḥajar, *Iṣābah*, IV, 332.

892. A battle during the conquest of Iraq, near al-Ḥīrah, in 13/634, where the Muslims suffered a sound defeat; see Donner, *Early Islamic Conquests*, 174–75.

893. A famous Jewish convert to Islam, the oldest authority on Judeo-Islamic traditions. See "Kaʿb al-Aḥbār," *EI²*, IV, 316–17 (M. Schmitz); Khalīfah b. Khayyāṭ, *Ṭabaqāt*, 308; Ibn Ḥibbān, *Mashāhīr*, 190; al-Dībaʿ, 59–60; Ibn Manẓūr, *Mukhtaṣar*, XXI, 180–88; Ben Ze'ev.

894. A large Ḥimyarī tribe with a royal tradition. See Caskel, II, 67, 237; al-Ḥimyarī, 169, 180; Ibn Ḥazm, *Jamharat*, 433; Ibn Saʿīd, 93.

According to al-ʿAlāʾī—[Yaḥyā] Ibn Maʿīn: [His pedigree was] Kaʿb b. Mātiʿ b. Dhī Hajan al-Ḥimyarī. [2475]

According to al-ʿAbbās—Yaḥyā: Kaʿb al-Aḥbār died during the caliphate of ʿUthmān in the year 34/July 22, 654–July 10, 655, a year before ʿUthmān's murder.

According to [Muḥammad] Ibn al-Muthannā—Aḥmad b. Mūsā—Dāʾūd—a paternal cousin of Kaʿb: Kaʿb learned the Sūrah of the Cow from one of the Prophet's Companions. When they reached the words "Then if ye slip after that the evidences have come to you, know that Allāh is sublime, wise,"[895] Kaʿb said "I do not know of such a thing in any of God's books, that He should prohibit sinning and at the same time promise to forgive it." The man refused to take back his words, and Kaʿb refused to learn [the verse]. One of the Prophet's Companions then passed by them, and [Kaʿb's teacher] asked him "Do you know [by heart] the Sūrah of the Cow?" The man answered in the affirmative. [Kaʿb and his teacher] began to recite "Then if ye slip after that the evidences have come to you," and the man continued "know that Allāh is sublime, wise." He said "Yes, this is how it should be."

Uways b. al-Khulayṣ al-Qaranī.[896]

So it was mentioned by Ḍamrah b. Rabīʿah—ʿUthmān b. ʿAṭāʾ al-Khurāsānī—his father [who said]: I was telling [Uways'] story when I heard a man of my clan, that is, Uways' clan, [asking] "O Abū ʿUthmān, do you know the name of Uways' father?" I said "No." He said "Uways b. al-Khulayṣ." However, according to Yaḥyā b. Saʿīd al-Qaṭṭān—Yazīd b. ʿAṭāʾ—ʿAlqamah b. Marthad, [2476] [the name was] Uways b. Unays al-Qaranī.

Opinions differ as regards the time of his death. Some say that he was killed [fighting] on ʿAlī's side at Ṣiffīn.

According to Muḥammad b. Abī Manṣūr—al-Ḥimmānī—Sharīk—Yazīd b. Abī Ziyād—ʿAbd al-Raḥmān b. Abī Laylā: On

895. Qurʾān 2:205; trans. Bell I, 29.

896. A famous Successor, known as one of the first ascetics and a close companion of ʿAlī; he never met the Prophet, but the latter had foreknowledge of him. See Abū Nuʿaym, II, 162; al-Kashshī, 91–93; al-Quhpāʾī, I, 241–43, II, 249; al-Amīn, XIII, 106–31; Khalīfah b. Khayyāṭ, *Ṭabaqāt*, 146; Ibn Ḥibbān, *Mashāhīr*, 161; *Uways al-Qaranī*. His father's name is usually said to be ʿĀmir or ʿAmr, notwithstanding the versions here. His clan, the Qaran, belonged to the southern tribe Murād; see Ibn Ḥazm, *Jamharat*, 407.

the Day of Ṣiffīn ʿAlī's herald called out "Look for Uways al-Qaranī among the dead." They looked and found him. [This is the report] or some other version of the same meaning.

Those Who Died in the Year 81 (February 26, 700–February 14, 701)

Suwayd b. Ghafalah.[897]

Muḥammad b. ʿAlī al-Akbar b. Abī Ṭālib.[898]

His mother was the Ḥanafiyyah,[899] Khawlah bt. Jaʿfar b. Qays b. Maslamah b. Thaʿlabah b. Yarbūʿ b. Thaʿlabah b. al-Dūl b. Ḥanīfah b. Lujaym b. Ṣaʿb b. ʿAlī b. Bakr b. Wāʾil. It was reported that she had been one of the prisoners [taken by the Muslims] in the battle of Yamāmah and was given to ʿAlī.

According to Ibn ʿUmar [al-Wāqidī][900]—ʿAbd al-Raḥmān b. Abī al-Zinād—Hishām b. ʿUrwah [b. al-Zubayr]—Fāṭimah bt. al-Mundhir—Asmāʾ bt. Abī Bakr: I saw Muḥammad b. al-Ḥanafiyyah's mother, who was a black woman from Sind. She was not descended from the Banū Ḥanīfah but was a slave among them. Khālid b. al-Walīd's treaty with the Banū Ḥanīfah applied only to the slaves, not to tribesmen of pure descent.[901]

Muḥammad b. al-Ḥanafiyyah's *kunyah* was Abū al-Qāsim. He was virtuous, religious, God fearing, and erudite.

---

897. A Kūfan jurist and a *ḥāfiẓ* (expert on tradition), a companion of ʿAlī, of the southern tribe Juʿfī. See al-Amīn, XXXV, 419–20; Khalīfah b. Khayyāṭ, *Ṭabaqāt*, 147; Ibn al-Kalbī, *Nasab maʿadd*, 315; al-Quhpāʾī, III, 176; al-Sayrawān, 99–100.

898. Son of ʿAlī by a wife other than Fāṭimah, daughter of the Prophet. While he stayed in the Ḥijāz a revolt was led on his behalf in al-Kūfah by al-Mukhtār b. Abī ʿUbayd, in the years 685–87. "Muḥammad b. al-Ḥanafiyya," *EI*², VII, 402–3 (F. Buhl); Sharon, *Black Banners*, 104–9, 112–19 and passim; Ibn Ḥibbān, *Mashāhīr*, 103; al-Balādhurī, *Ansāb*, III (Dūrī), 53–54, (Maḥmūdī) 276–96.

899. That is, of the Banū Ḥanīfah tribe, dwellers in al-Yamāmah, in the central eastern part of the Arabian Peninsula.

900. Ibn Saʿd, V, 66.

901. There is nothing to support this claim in the version of the treaty recorded by al-Ṭabarī himself, where the Muslims received as booty "half the prisoners" (obviously releasing the other half), regardless of their origin; see al-Ṭabarī, *Taʾrīkh*, I, 1954. Needless to say, the woman's pedigree as recorded here does not support this claim either.

We have related the account of [what happened with] him and Ibn al-Zubayr during the time of al-Mukhtār b. Abī ʿUbayd in our book entitled *The Supplemented* (*al-Mudhayyal*).[902]

Those Who Died in the Year 83 (February 4, 702–January 23, 703) [2477]

Abū al-Bakhtarī al-Ṭāʾī, a client of the Banū Nabhān of Ṭayyiʾ.[903]

There are different versions of his name. According to Ibn al-Madyanī it was Saʿīd b. Abī ʿImrān, whereas Yaḥyā b. Maʿīn holds that it was Saʿīd b. Jubayr and that Jubayr's *kunyah* was Abū ʿImrān. Still others say that [the name] was Saʿīd b. ʿImrān.

Abū al-Bakhtarī was a Shīʿī.

ʿAbdallāh b. Nawfal b. al-Ḥārith b. ʿAbd al-Muṭṭalib b. Hāshim.[904]

ʿAbdallāh was born during the Prophet's lifetime, and it was said that he resembled him.

According to ʿAlī b. Muḥammad [al-Madāʾinī]: ʿAbdallāh b. Nawfal b. al-Ḥārith died in the year 84/January 24, 703–January 13, 704.

According to Muḥammad b. ʿUmar [al-Wāqidī]—ʿAbd al-ʿAzīz b. Muḥammad and Abū Bakr b. ʿAbdallāh b. Abī Sabrah—ʿUthmān b. ʿUmar—Abū al-Ghayth: When Marwān b. al-Ḥakam became governor of Medina on behalf of Muʿāwiyah b. Abī Sufyān for the first time, in the year 42/April 26, 662–April 14, 663, he appointed ʿAbdallāh b. Nawfal b. al-Ḥārith b. ʿAbd al-Muṭṭalib a judge in Medina. I heard Abū Hurayrah say "This is the first judge I saw in Islam."[905]

According to [Muḥammad] Ibn Saʿd[906]—Muḥammad b. ʿUmar [al-Wāqidī]: Our authorities are unanimous that ʿAbdallāh b.

---

902. Al-Ṭabarī, *Taʾrīkh*, II, 693–95.

903. One of the active participants in the revolt of Ibn al-Ashʿath (see note 990, below). He was killed in the battle of Maskan, fought between the governor al-Ḥajjāj and the rebels; see al-Ṭabarī, *Taʾrīkh*, II, 1088–1100. See also al-Dūlābī, I, 125–26; Ibn Saʿd, VI, 204–5.

904. Ibn Ḥibbān, *Mashāhīr*, 114; al-Balādhurī, *Ansāb*, III (Dūrī), 297–99; Ibn Qudāmah, 102; al-ʿAskarī, 243.

905. Al-Suyūṭī, *Wasāʾil*, 117.

906. Ibn Saʿd, V, 13.

Nawfal b. al-Ḥārith was the first judge in Medina, on behalf of Marwān b. al-Ḥakam. His family, however, deny this; they deny that either he or anyone of the Banū Hāshim [ever] held the office of judge in Medina.[907] They [also] say that he died during the caliphate of Muʿāwiyah, but we hold that he outlived Muʿāwiyah
[2478] for a while and died in the year 84/703, during the caliphate of ʿAbd al-Malik b. Marwān.

Saʿīd b. Wahb al-Hamdānī, of the Banū Yaḥmid b. Mūhib b. Ṣādiq b. Yanāʿ b. Dūmān; these are the Yanāʿūn of Hamdān.[908]

Saʿīd obtained knowledge from Muʿādh b. Jabal[909] in the Yemen before emigrating [to Medina] during the Prophet's lifetime. He was one of ʿAlī b. Abī Ṭālib's close companions, whence his nickname the Tick (*al-qurād*). He lived in al-Kūfah.

No one doubts Saʿīd's truthfulness and faithfulness in the traditions he reported and transmitted.

He died in the year 86/January 2, 705–December 22, 705, during the caliphate of ʿAbd al-Malik. Al-Ṭabarī remarks: His name was mentioned with those who died in the year 76/April 21, 695–April 9, 696 and repeated here, because of the disagreement over his death date.

ʿAlī b. al-Ḥusayn b. ʿAlī b. Abī Ṭālib.[910]

---

907. In view of the enmity between the Hāshimī and the Umayyad clans, it is conceivable that the descendants of ʿAbdallāh denied that he held office on behalf of the Umayyads.

908. Appointed over the Hamdān on behalf of ʿAlī. See Naṣr b. Muzāḥim, 105; Ibn Ḥibbān, *Mashāhīr*, 166; idem, *Thiqāt*, IV, 291; al-Amīn, XXXV, 122–23; Ibn Saʿd, VI, 118. I could not find his clan in any of the genealogical and historical sources (including the Yemenī ones); except for Ibn Saʿd, and al-Zabīdī, *Tāj al-ʿarūs*, V, 566, all the sources trace him to Khaywān, a known tribe of the Hamdān (read Khaywān for Khayrān, as erroneously recorded in several sources). See also pp. 151, above, 237, below.

909. A much-admired member of the Khazraj (Anṣār) and a close Companion of the Prophet, who sent him as his representative to the Yemen. Vast knowledge of religious law is imputed to him; see Ibn Ḥajar, *Iṣābah*, III, 427.

910. The fourth Shīʿī Imām, Zayn al-ʿĀbidīn, who survived the massacre of Karbalāʾ and fathered the next generations of the imāms. He was nevertheless on good terms with the Umayyad al-Walīd b. ʿAbd al-Malik. See Jafrī, 242–47; al-Ṭabāṭabāʾī, 75, 201–2; Ibn Qudāmah, 131–33; Khalīfah b. Khayyāṭ, *Ṭabaqāt*, 238–39; Ibn Ḥibbān, *Mashāhīr*, 104; al-Balādhurī, *Ansāb*, III (Maḥmūdī), 146–47, 273 and passim; Ibn Saʿd, V, 156–64.

His mother was Ghazālah, who was a concubine (*umm walad*). After Ḥusayn's [death] Zubayd, his client, took Ghazālah, and she bore him ʿAbdallāh b. Zubayd, half-brother of ʿAlī b. al-Ḥusayn.

This ʿAlī b. al-Ḥusayn is the progenitor of the descendants in [the line of] al-Ḥusayn [b. ʿAlī]. This is ʿAlī al-Aṣghar (junior) b. Ḥusayn. [His brother] ʿAlī al-Akbar (senior) b. al-Ḥusayn was killed with his father at the canal[911] of Karbalāʾ, having had no offspring.

ʿAlī al-Aṣghar b. al-Ḥusayn participated with his father in the event of Karbalāʾ. He was then twenty-three years old. [As] he was ill, he was sleeping on a mat, and when al-Ḥusayn was killed Shamir b. Dhī al-Jawshan[912] said "Kill this one [too]." One of his companions then said to him "God be praised, should we kill a young man who is ill and did not take part in the fighting?" ʿUmar [2479] b. Saʿd [b. Abī Waqqāṣ][913] then came and said: "Do not harm these women or this sick man."

ʿAlī related: When I was brought before [ʿUbaydallāh] Ibn Ziyād he asked "What is your name?" I said "ʿAlī b. Ḥusayn." He said "Has God not killed ʿAlī?" I said "I had an elder brother called ʿAlī, who was killed by [your] people." Ibn Ziyād said "Nay, it was God who killed him." I said "God [does not kill but] takes the souls when [people] die."[914] Ibn Ziyād ordered that ʿAlī be killed, whereupon Zaynab bt. ʿAlī cried "O Ibn Ziyād, you had enough of our blood. I beseech you in the name of God, if you kill him, kill me together with him." So Ibn Ziyād left him alone.

ʿAlī b. al-Ḥusayn's *kunyah* was Abū al-Ḥusayn.

According to ʿAlī b. Muḥammad [al-Madāʾinī]—Saʿīd b. Khālid—[Saʿīd b. Abī Saʿīd] al-Maqbarī: Al-Mukhtār b. Abī ʿUbayd

911. Or, "stream."

912. He was notorious for his role in killing al-Ḥusayn b. ʿAlī at Karbalāʾ, yet he was considered a Successor, and traditions were transmitted from him. See Ibn Manẓūr, *Mukhtaṣar*, X, 331–34; al-Ṣafadī, XVI, 180. He is also included in the list of "the noble tribal leaders who were infected by leprosy"; see Muḥammad Ibn Ḥabīb, *Muḥabbar*, 301.

913. A general under ʿUbaydallāh b. Ziyād, governor of al-Kūfah. ʿUmar was in charge of the force that carried out the massacre of Karbalāʾ and was later killed by al-Mukhtār b. Abī ʿUbayd in retaliation. See Ibn Saʿd, V, 125; Ibn Manẓūr, *Mukhtaṣar*, XI, 60–68; al-Dhahabī, *Siyar*, IV, 349–50; al-Ṭabarī, *Taʾrīkh*, II, 308–12.

914. Qurʾān 39:42. Cf. al-Ṭabarī, *Taʾrīkh*, II, 372–73; al-Balādhurī, *Ansāb*, III (Maḥmūdī), 207.

sent ʿAlī b. al-Ḥusayn 100,000 [dirhams]. He hated to accept it but was afraid to send it back, so he kept it. When al-Mukhtār was killed ʿAlī b. al-Ḥusayn wrote to ʿAbd al-Malik b. Marwān [the following]: "Al-Mukhtār had sent me 100,000 which I did not want to return or take, so it is with me. Send someone to collect it." ʿAbd al-Malik wrote back to him "O cousin, take it, for I have made it lawful to you."

According to ʿAlī b. Muḥammad [al-Madāʾinī]—Yazīd b. ʿIyāḍ: [Ibn Shihāb] al-Zuhrī had killed someone unintentionally, so he left his family, went out, and pitched a tent, saying "No roof of a house should provide shade for me." ʿAlī b. al-Ḥusayn passed by and said: "O Ibn Shihāb, your despairing is worse than your sin. Fear God, ask His forgiveness, send the blood money to the deceased's family, and go back to your family." [Later], al-Zuhrī
[2480] used to say "Among all the people ʿAlī b. al-Ḥusayn did me the greatest favor."

According to ʿAlī b. Muḥammad [al-Madāʾinī]—ʿAlī b. Mujāhid—Hishām b. ʿUrwah [b. al-Zubayr]: ʿAlī b. al-Ḥusayn used to go to Mecca and back on his riding beast, without [ever] beating it.

According to [Muḥammad] Ibn Saʿd[915]—Mālik b. Ismāʿīl—Sahl b. Shuʿayb al-Nihmī, who was living among the [Nihm], acting as their leader in prayer—his father—al-Minhāl, that is, Ibn ʿAmr: I came to ʿAlī b. al-Ḥusayn and asked him: "How are you? May God keep you in good state." Whereupon he said:

> I never thought that a city notable like you would ignore our condition. Since you do not realize it or know, I shall tell you. We became among our people like the Children of Israel among the people of Pharaoh, as the latter used to kill the sons of the former and let their women live. It has become so that favor is curried with our enemy by cursing or swearing at our leader and master on the pulpits.[916] The Quraysh have come to think that they are superior to the [rest of the] Arabs because Muḥammad descends from

---

915. Ibn Saʿd, V, 162–63.

916. During Umayyad times the governors used to curse the ʿAlids at the Friday sermon, a practice temporarily stopped by the caliph ʿUmar b. ʿAbd al-ʿAzīz.

> them; it is only because of him that they impute merit to themselves, and the [rest of the] Arabs have come to acknowledge it. The Arabs have come to think that they are superior to the non-Arabs because Muḥammad belongs to them; it is only because of him that they impute merit to themselves, and the non-Arabs have come to acknowledge it. If the Arabs are right that they are superior to the non-Arabs and if the Quraysh are right that they are superior to the [rest of the] Arabs because Muḥammad descends from them, then we, the members of [the Prophet's] family (*ahl al-bayt*), are superior to the [rest of the] Quraysh, because Muḥammad descends from us. [But] [2481]
> they have usurped our right and deny us all rights. This is how we are, if you do not know.

Al-Minhāl related: I thought that he wanted those present in the house to hear [this].

According to Muḥammad b. ʿUmar [al-Wāqidī][917]—Ibn Abī Sabrah—Sālim, Abū Jaʿfar's client: Hishām b. Ismāʿīl[918] used to taunt ʿAlī b. al-Ḥusayn and his family, making speeches to this effect on the pulpit and insulting ʿAlī [b. Abī Ṭālib]. When al-Walīd b. ʿAbd al-Malik ascended the throne he removed Hishām from office and ordered that he be stationed in a public place [to be abused by those previously abused by him]. Hishām [later] related: "Nay, by God, no one worried me more than ʿAlī b. al-Ḥusayn. I thought that he was an important man,[919] one to whom people listen." So [Hishām b. Ismāʿīl] was exposed [to the people] in a public place. [But] ʿAlī b. Ḥusayn gathered his offspring and friends and forbade them to abuse Hishām. ʿAlī b. Ḥusayn passed by [him] in the morning on his way to some business and did not chastise him. Hishām b. Ismāʿīl called out to him saying "God knows best where to place His missions."[920]

---

917. Ibn Saʿd, V, 163. Cf. al-Ṭabarī, *Taʾrīkh*, II, 1184.
918. ʿAbd al-Malik's governor of Medina in 83–86/702–705; see al-Ṭabarī, *Taʾrīkh*, II, 1085, 1127, 1182.
919. *Rajul ṣāliḥ*. See GLOSSARIUM, s.v. *ṣlḥ*.
920. Cf. Qurʾān 2:12.

According to Muḥammad b. ʿUmar[921]—ʿAbd al-Ḥakīm b. ʿAbdallāh b. Abī Farwah: ʿAlī b. al-Ḥusayn died in Medina and was buried in al-Baqīʿ in the year 94/October 7, 712–September 25, 713. This year is called "the Year of the Jurists" because of the great number of jurists who died then.

According to Ibn Saʿd[922]—ʿAbd al-Raḥmān b. Yūnus—Sufyān—Jaʿfar b. Muḥammad: ʿAlī b. al-Ḥusayn died at the age of fifty-eight. This proves that ʿAlī b. Ḥusayn was with his father[923] at the age of twenty-three or twenty-four and was not a small boy whose
[2482] pubic hair had not yet grown, as [some] say. It is because he was ill that day that he did not fight. How could he have been [a boy] whose pubic hair had not yet grown, when he had already fathered Abū Jaʿfar Muḥammad b. ʿAlī, and had met Jābir b. ʿAbdallāh and transmitted [traditions] from him? [It should be noted that] Jābir died in the year 78/March 30, 697–March 19, 698.

According to Isḥāq b. Abī Isrāʾīl—Jarīr—Shaybah b. Naʿāmah: ʿAlī b. Ḥusayn was considered miserly. When he died the fact came to light that he had secretly supported 100 families in Medina.

Among [those who died in the year 83/702–703 was], according to ʿAmr b. ʿAlī, Abū ʿUthmān al-Nahdī.

His name was ʿAbd al-Raḥmān b. Mall b. ʿAmr b. ʿAdī b. Wahb b. Rabīʿah b. Saʿd b. Jadhīmah b. Kaʿb b. Rifāʿah b. Mālik b. Nahd b. Zayd b. Layth b. Sūd b. Aslum b. al-Ḥāf b. Quḍāʿah.[924]

According to al-ʿAbbās b. Muḥammad—al-Faḍl b. Dukayn—Abū Ṭālib ʿAbd al-Salām b. Shaddād: I saw Abū ʿUthmān, [in his capacity as] a member of the police guard, come and take mushrooms from a mushroom seller.[925]

---

921. Ibn Saʿd, V, 163–64.

922. Ibid., 164.

923. That is, at Karbalāʾ.

924. His clan's name is Nahd b. Zayd, of the Quḍāʿah confederation; see Ibn Ḥazm, *Jamharat*, 446–47. He lived in pre-Islamic times and embraced Islam only in ʿUmar's time. See Khalīfah b. Khayyāṭ, *Ṭabaqāt*, 205; Ibn Ḥibbān, *Mashāhīr*, 159; idem, *Thiqāt*, V, 75.

925. *Yaʾkhudhu min ṣāḥib al-kamaʾah al-kamaʾah.* Cf. Ibn Saʿd, VII/1, 70: *Yaʾkhudhu min ṣāḥib al-kumāh*, which is probably erroneous, *kumāh* signifying "brave people." I am not sure about the meaning of this in either version.

According to [Muḥammad] Ibn Sa'd[926]—Abū Ghassān Mālik b. Ismā'īl al-Nahdī: Abū 'Uthmān al-Nahdī lived in al-Kūfah, where he had a place among the Banū Nahd. When al-Ḥusayn was killed he moved to al-Baṣrah, saying "I shall not live in a town where the son of the Prophet's daughter was killed."

Khālid b. Ma'dān al-Kalā'ī.[927]

According to [Muḥammad] Ibn Sa'd:[928] [The scholars] are unanimous that Khālid b. Ma'dān died in the year 103/July 1, 721–June 20, 722, during the caliphate of Yazīd b. 'Abd al-Malik.

According to 'Abd al-Quddūs b. al-Ḥajjāj—Ṣafwān b. 'Amr— [2483] Khālid b. Ma'dān: I was contemporaneous with seventy of the Prophet's Companions.

According to al-Ḥārith—al-Ḥajjāj—Abū Ja'far al-Ḥuddānī—Muḥammad b. Dā'ūd—'Īsā b. Yūnus: Khālid b. Ma'dān was in charge of the *shurṭah* of [the caliph] Yazīd b. Mu'āwiyah.[929]

Khālid was not suspected [of fraud] concerning the religious traditions he transmitted and related.

It was reported that he died while fasting. He had lived in Syria, where he [also] died.

Those Who Died in the Year 105 (June 10, 723–May 28, 724)

'Ikrimah, the client of 'Abdallāh b. 'Abbās b. 'Abd al-Muṭṭalib.[930]

His *kunyah* was Abū 'Abdallāh.

According to [Muḥammad] Ibn Sa'd[931]—'Āmir b. Sa'īd Abū

926. Ibn Sa'd, VII/1, 70.

927. A famous Syrian jurist of Ḥimyarī (southern) origin. See Ibn al-Kalbī, *Nasab ma'add*, 540; Khalīfah b. Khayyāṭ, *Ṭabaqāt*, 310; Ibn Ḥibbān, *Mashāhīr*, 183; Abū Zur'ah, 243, 350–51; Ibn Manẓūr, *Mukhtaṣar*, VII, 394–97. Donner, "Problem," 7–9; 'Aṭwān, 97–98; al-Sayrawān, 83–84.

928. Ibn Sa'd, VII/2, 162.

929. Donner, however, doubts that Khālid ever occupied this post; "The *Shurṭa*," 253. The *shurṭah*, usually translated as "police," was a special elite unit some of whose tasks resembled those of modern police forces. See Donner, "The Shurṭa"; Lecker, "*Shurṭat al-khamīs*," 276–80.

930. One of the main transmitters from 'Abdallāh b. 'Abbās, highly appreciated by some but accused of lies by others. See "'Ikrima," *EI*², II, 1081–82 (J. Schacht); Ibn Ḥibbān, *Mashāhīr*, 134; al-Sayrawān 128–29.

931. Ibn Sa'd, V, 212.

Ja'far—Hishām b. Yūsuf, the judge of Ṣan'ā'—Muḥammad b. Rāshid: 'Ikrimah was still a slave when Ibn 'Abbās died. Khālid b. Yazīd b. Mu'āwiyah[932] bought him from 'Alī b. 'Abdallāh b. al-'Abbās for 4,000 dinars. On hearing of this 'Ikrimah went to 'Alī and asked "Did you sell me for 4,000 dinars?" He replied affirmatively, whereupon 'Ikrimah said "Indeed, you did not profit [by this, for] you have sold your father's knowledge for 4,000 dinars." 'Alī went to Khālid and asked him to cancel the transaction, and Khālid agreed, whereupon 'Alī set 'Ikrimah free.

No one who knew 'Ikrimah denied his erudition in religious law, the Qur'ān and its interpretation, as well as his numerous transmissions of traditions.

According to al-Ṣarrār b. Muḥammad b. Ismā'īl—Ismā'īl—Ibrāhīm b. Sa'd—his father: Sa'īd b. al-Musayyab used to say to his
[2484] client Burd "O Burd, do not lie about me, as did 'Ikrimah about Ibn 'Abbās."[933] [To other people he used to say] "Any tradition Burd transmits to you from me, and you do not recognize it nor does anyone else transmit it but he, is a lie."

According to [Muḥammad] Ibn Ḥumayd—Jarīr [b. 'Abd al-Ḥamīd]—Yazīd b. Abī Ziyād: I went into 'Alī b. 'Abdallāh b. 'Abbās' place, and there was 'Ikrimah, tied to the door of the privy. I asked "What is the matter with this one?" He said "He lied about my father."

According to Yaḥyā b. Ma'īn—someone—Ḥammād b. Zayd: I heard Ayyūb [al-Sakhtiyānī] say, when asked about 'Ikrimah "Had I not considered him reliable (*thiqah*) I would not have written down traditions transmitted by him."[934] Others think that a tradition transmitted by 'Ikrimah should not be adduced as proof in legal matters. However, they make the following observation: "We object not to the traditions transmitted by 'Ikrimah but to his

---

932. Grandson of the caliph Mu'āwiyah and brother of Mu'āwiyah II. When the latter died Khālid was considered too young to rule, and Marwān b. al-Ḥakam headed the clan and ascended the throne; see "Khālid b. Yazīd," *EI*², IV, 929–30 (M. Ullmann).

933. That is, by falsely ascribing traditions to him.

934. The permissibility of writing down the Prophetic Tradition was debated among Muslim scholars. See Goldziher, *Muslim Studies*, II, 181–88; Sprenger; and cf. p. 256, below.

creed." They said that he adhered to the Ṣufriyyah, a Khārijī sect.[935] It was reported that he imputed this conviction to Ibn 'Abbās, and this was his lie about him.

According to Muṣ'ab al-Zubayrī: 'Ikrimah adhered to the beliefs of the Khawārij. The governor of Medina sought him out, so he hid at Dā'ūd b. al-Ḥusayn's place, where he died.[936]

According to Yaḥyā b. Ma'īn: Mālik b. Anas did not quote 'Ikrimah only because the latter adhered to the beliefs of the Ṣufriyyah.

There is disagreement over 'Ikrimah's time of death. Some say that it occurred in the year 105. According to Muḥammad b. 'Umar [al-Wāqidī][937]—'Ikrimah's daughter: 'Ikrimah died in the year 105 at the age of eighty.

According to Ibn 'Umar [al-Wāqidī][938]—Khālid b. al-Qāsim al-Bayāḍī: 'Ikrimah and the poet Kuthayyir 'Azzah[939] died on the same day in the year 105. I saw both their funeral services held at the same place, that is, the funeral place, in the afternoon. People [2485] said "The best expert on religious law and the best poet died today."

People other than Khālid b. al-Qāsim said: People wondered at the fact that 'Ikrimah and Kuthayyir met in death, whereas [in life] their views were [so] different.[940] 'Ikrimah was thought to believe in the Khārijī creed and to consider the delaying of judgment[941] as

935. A Khārijī sect that differed from the rest of the Khawārij in that they rejected execution of the women and children of sinners; see al-Baghdādī, *Farq*, 54.

936. Ibn Sa'd, V, 216.

937. Ibid.

938. Ibid.

939. A Ḥijāzī bedouin classical poet, whose poetry was mainly dedicated to his love for 'Azzah, on one hand, and to his Shī'ī convictions, on the other; see "Kuthayyir b. 'Abd al-Raḥmān," *EI²*, V, 551–53 (I. 'Abbās).

940. The only point of this sentence is the play on words contained in it. The Arabic word for "met" also means "agreed," so that "met" and "were different" are in fact antonyms (*ijtimā'* and *ikhtilāf*).

941. *Naẓrah.* The reference is to the theological discussion of sin. The Khawārij saw it as their duty to fight and kill sinners, whereas others held that judgment should be postponed to Judgment Day. The latter are better known as Murji'ah. See Madelung, "The Early Murji'a"; Givon, "The Murji'a"; 'Athāminah, "The Early Murji'a"; Cook, *Early Dogma*, 23–47; Lambton, 21–27, 32–35.

unbelief, whereas Kuthayyir was a Shīʿī, who believed in the return [of the *imām* in hiding].[942]

According to Yaḥyā b. ʿUthmān b. Ṣāliḥ al-Sahmī—[Yūnus] Ibn Bukayr—[ʿAbd al-ʿAzīz b. Muḥammad] al-Durāwardī: ʿIkrimah and the poet Kuthayyir ʿAzzah died in Medina on the same day. Their biers were carried only by blacks.

According to Abū Nuʿaym al-Faḍl b. Dukayn: ʿIkrimah died in the year 107/May 19, 725–May 7, 726.

According to Yaḥyā b. Maʿīn: ʿIkrimah died in the year 115/February 21, 733–February 9, 734.

ʿIkrimah used to travel much around the countries [of Islam].[943] He went to al-Baṣrah, where the people learned [traditions] from him, and to al-Kūfah, where many people studied with him. He went to the Yemen, where many wrote down [the traditions] he dictated, and to the Maghrib, where some heard [traditions] from him. He [also] went to the eastern [centers], where he dictated [traditions].

According to Yaḥyā b. ʿUthmān b. Ṣāliḥ—Nuʿaym b. Ḥammād—ʿAbd al-Muʾmin b. Khālid al-Ḥanafī: ʿIkrimah came to us in Khurāsān, and I asked him "Why did you come to our country?" He replied "I came to take from the dinars and dirhams of your governors." But, according to Abū Tumaylah—ʿAbd al-ʿAzīz b. Abī Rawwād: I said to ʿIkrimah "You have left the two holy cities [Mecca and Medina] to come to Khurāsān?" He said "To earn a living for my daughters." ʿIkrimah, however, died in [Medina], the city of the Prophet.

According to Ibrāhīm b. Khālid—Umayyah b. Shibl—Maʿmar—Ayyūb: ʿIkrimah came to us, and people gathered around him until he was forced to climb to the roof of a house.[944]

[2486] ʿĀmir b. Sharāḥīl b. ʿAbd al-Shaʿbī.[945]

---

942. *Rajʿah.* On this creed, see Sachedina, 151, 166–73. I thank my colleague, Dr. Meir Bar-Asher, for this reference.

943. Traveling around the centers of scholarship (*al-riḥlah fī ṭalab al-ʿilm*) was very common among medieval Muslim scholars; see Eickelman and Piscatori. The purpose was usually to study with famous teachers, but here the emphasis is on ʿIkrimah's teaching, not learning.

944. Ibn Saʿd, V, 213.

945. A famous Kūfan jurist and traditionist. See Schacht, *Origins*, 230–31 and

According to Ibn Sa'd:[946] He belonged to the Ḥimyar but was registered as one of the Hamdān.[947]

According to [Ibn Sa'd]—'Abdallāh b. Muḥammad b. Murrah al-Sha'bānī—old men of the Sha'bān, among them Muḥammad b. Abī Umayyah, who was a knowledgeable man: [Once a lot of] rain fell in the Yemen, and the stream hollowed out a vault, which had a stone door. People broke the lock and went in to find a great spacious [room] with a golden bed placed in it; there lay a man on it. [The narrator] said: We measured him, and he was twelve *shibrs*.[948] He was wearing a silk gown embroidered with gold; a golden staff was at his side and a red ruby on his head. There he was, a white-headed and white-bearded man, wearing two plaits. At his side lay a tablet inscribed in Ḥimyaritic: "In your name, O God, Lord of Ḥimyar. I am Ḥassān b. 'Amr, the king; indeed, there is no king but God. I had lived in hope and died in due course, during the Time of the Fearful Plague.[949] Twelve thousand kings had died then, and I was the last of them. I had come to the mountain of Dhū Sha'bayn to seek protection from death, but it betrayed me."[950] At the man's side a sword was placed, inscribed in Ḥimyaritic "I am a gravedigger; by me is blood revenge taken."

According to 'Abdallāh b. Muḥammad b. Murrah al-Sha'bānī: This was Ḥassān b. 'Amr b. Qays b. Mu'āwiyah b. Jusham b. 'Abd Shams b. Wā'il b. Ghawth b. Qaṭan b. 'Arīb b. Zuhayr b. Ayman b. al-Hamaysa' b. Ḥimyar, that is, Ḥassān Dhū al-Sha'bayn.[951] Dhū al-Sha'bayn is a mountain in the Yemen where Ḥassān and his

---

passim; Khalīfah b. Khayyāṭ, *Ṭabaqāt*, 157; Ibn Ḥibbān, *Mashāhīr*, 163; al-Sayrawān, 105–6; Ibn Manẓūr, *Mukhtaṣar*, XI, 249–64.

946. Ibn Sa'd, VI, 171–78.

947. See note 444, above.

948. A measure of length, about 8 inches.

949. Vocalized *ayyām wakhzahīd*, which I suggest should be read as *ayyāma wakhzi haydin* "the time of the fearful plague." *Wakhz* means plague, and the root *h-y-d* denotes great fear. Ibn Durayd, 524, explains that "hayd was a plague which occurred in ancient times," in which case the rendering will be "the plague of Hayd." See Ibn al-Kalbī, *Nasab ma'add*, 537 n. 4, cf. Ibn Manẓūr, *Lisān*, III, 442, s.v. *h-y-d*. The variants adduced by de Goeje, in Ṭabarī, *Ta'rīkh*, 2486 n. c, suggest that the expression was not very well understood. Note especially Ibn Sa'd's *wa-mā wakhzahīd* "what is *wakhzahīd* anyway?" apparently an addition by a transmitter or a scribe.

950. Cf. Ibn al-Kalbī, *Nasab ma'add*, 536–37.

951. Cf. al-Ḥimyarī, 165, where the genealogy varies.

offspring dwelled and where Ḥassān was buried. He and his off-
[2487] spring were called after this mountain, and those [of them] who lived in al-Kūfah were called Sha'biyyūn, among them 'Āmir al-Sha'bī. Those [of them] who lived in Syria were called Sha'bāniyyūn, whereas those who remained in the Yemen were called Āl Dhī Sha'bayn. [Still others] lived in Egypt and the Maghrib, and they were called al-Ash'ūb. These are all the offspring of Ḥassān b. 'Amr Dhū al-Sha'bayn.[952]

The clan of 'Āmir b. Sharāḥīl b. 'Abd al-Sha'bī was the Banū 'Alī b. Ḥassān b. 'Amr. They had joined the Aḥmūr of the Hamdān in the Yemen and were registered as part of them.[953] The Aḥmūr[954] included the Khārif, al-Ṣā'idiyyūn, Āl Dhī Bāriq, al-Sabī', Āl Dhī Juddān, Āl Dhī Raḍwān, Āl Dhī La'wah, Āl Dhī Marrān, and the bedouin of the Hamdān, that is, 'Udhar, Yām, Nihm, Shākir, and Arḥab.

Many tribal groups of the Ḥimyar joined the Hamdān, among them the offspring of Dhī Ḥawāl, who had been the commander of Tubba''s military vanguard.[955] To this clan belongs Ya'fur b. al-Ṣabbāḥ, the present lord of Ṣan'ā''s provinces.[956]

Al-Sha'bī's *kunyah* was Abū 'Amr; he was a thin, lean person. He was skilled in Muslim law and knowledgeable [in general], a transmitter of poetry, traditions, and accounts of battles.

Ṭāwūs b. Kaysān.[957]
His *kunyah* was Abū 'Abd al-Raḥmān.

---

952. See Ibn Ḥazm, *Jamharat*, 433.

953. "Joined," *dakhalū fī*, is a term reflecting the fluctuating structure of the Arab tribal system. Often a group left its own tribe and joined another. Only when such groups retained their original genealogy and identity could this term be used. See also note 444, above.

954. De Goeje has doubts about the vocalization of the name. According to Hamdānī, *Iklīl* II (ed. Muḥammad al-Akwa'), 247 (as quoted by al-Akwa', "Al-af'ūl," 322) the name is Akhmūr, and the confederation ceased to exist at some point. This confederation is not recorded by Ibn al-Kalbī or by Ibn Ḥazm and other later genealogists, although they mention some of the constituent groups.

955. Tubba' was the name of the Himyaritic kings.

956. "Present" applies not to al-Ṭabarī's time but to that of Ibn Sa'd (d. 230/845); see Ibn Sa'd, VI, 172. The reference is to Ya'fur b. 'Abd al-Raḥmān, founder of the local Yemeni Ya'furid dynasty in the time of the caliph al-Mu'taṣim (218–27/833–42); see Kay, 141, 185, 223–26.

957. An early Qur'ān reader and authority on exegesis. See al-Sayrawān, 104; Ibn al-Jazarī, 341; al-Rāzī, 318–59, 562, and passim; al-Amīn, XXXVI, 325.

Ṭāwūs was skilled in Muslim law and knowledgeable [in general], pious, God fearing, and meritorious.

According to Abū Kurayb [Muḥammad b. al-ʿAlāʾ]—Yaḥyā [b. Saʿīd al-Qaṭṭān]—Zuhayr—Layth—Ṭāwūs: Seventy *shaykhs* from [2488] the Prophet's Companions were still alive in my lifetime.[958]

According to Yaḥyā b. Maʿīn—al-Muʿtamir b. Sulaymān: My father said "Why doesn't Khālid al-Ḥadhdhāʾ[959] do like Ṭāwūs?" [I] asked "And what did Ṭāwūs do?" He said "He used to sit, and, if someone brought him something, he would accept it; if not, he would keep silent." Yaḥyā said "I say Ṭāwūs was appointed over the tithe, and so was Khālid al-Ḥadhdhāʾ."

According to ʿAlī b. al-Madyanī—Yaḥyā b. Saʿīd—Sufyān b. Saʿīd: Ṭāwūs was a Shīʿī.

According to Ibn ʿUmar [al-Wāqidī]—Sayf b. Sulaymān: Ṭāwūs died in Mecca one day before the Tarwiyah.[960] Hishām b. ʿAbd al-Malik, then caliph, performed the pilgrimage that year, that is, 106/May 29, 724–May 18, 725, so he said the prayer over Ṭāwūs' bier. He was seventy-odd years old when he died.

According to al-Ḥārith—Surayj b. Yūnus—Yaḥyā b. Sulaymān: It came to my knowledge that Ṭāwūs had said to Mujāhid[961] "If your shortness had been applied to my tallness and my tallness to your shortness, we would have made two middle-sized men."

According to Zayd b. Ḥubāb—Ibrāhīm b. Nāfiʿ: Ṭāwūs died in the year 106/May 29, 724–May 18, 725.

According to Ibn ʿUmar [al-Wāqidī]: Ṭāwūs was a client of Baḥīr b. Raysān al-Ḥimyarī and lived in al-Janad.[962]

Al-Ḥasan b. Abī al-Ḥasan.[963]

---

958. Cf. p. 215, above.

959. Khālid b. Mihrān, a Baṣran traditionist of the early second century, who was also appointed to collect the tithe; see Ibn Ḥajar, *Tahdhīb*, III, 105.

960. That is, the Day of Providing Water, the eighth of Dhū al-Ḥijjah, when the pilgrims in Mecca prepare for the journey to Minā.

961. A famous traditionist, jurist, and Qurʾān interpreter of the first century. See a very detailed biography in Mujāhid, 39–53.

962. A town and a large province in the Yemen. See Yāqūt, *Muʿjam al-buldān*, II, 127–29. Kay, 354.

963. One of the earliest theologians and a highly esteemed traditionist. See "Ḥasan al-Baṣrī," *EI*², III, 247–49 (H. Ritter); Ibn Saʿd, VII/1, 114–29; al-Sayrawān, 74.

The name of Abū al-Ḥasan [al-Ḥasan's father] was Yasār. It is related that he was taken prisoner [by the Muslims] at Maysān,[964] brought to Medina, and bought by al-Rubayyiʿ bt. al-Naḍir, Anas b. Mālik's paternal aunt.

According to ʿAlī b. Muḥammad [al-Madāʾinī]: The father of al-Ḥasan b. Abī al-Ḥasan al-Baṣrī was one of the prisoners of Maysān.
[2489] His mother was a servant of Umm Salamah, the Prophet's wife.

According to al-Aṣmaʿī—Ḥammād b. Salamah—ʿAlī b. Zayd b. Judʿān, who knew al-Ḥasan better than anyone: Al-Ḥasan was born a slave.

According to Yaḥyā b. Maʿīn: Al-Ḥasan b. Abī al-Ḥasan's mother was called Khayrah.

According to ʿAlī b. Muḥammad [al-Madāʾinī]—Salamah b. ʿUthmān—[ʿAbdallāh] Ibn ʿAwn—al-Ḥasan: I was fourteen years old when [the caliph] ʿUthmān was killed.

Al-Ḥasan was knowledgeable, skilled in Islamic law, virtuous, and an expert on the readings of the Qurʾān (*qārī*). No one doubts his truthfulness in the matter of [the traditions] he related and transmitted, but he transmitted many traditions in which the chain of authority (*isnād*) did not reach up to the Prophet.[965] He [also] transmitted many [traditions] from unknown people, as well as from written records (*ṣuḥuf*) that came to his hands. These records reached him either directly [from the compilers] or through transmitters.[966]

According to Muḥammad b. Hārūn al-Ḥarbī—Nuʿaym—Sufyān—Musāwir al-Warrāq: I asked al-Ḥasan al-Baṣrī "From whom do you transmit these traditions?" He said "From a written record (*kitāb*) that I have; I have heard it from someone."[967]

---

964. Ibn Saʿd, VII/1, 114. Maysān is a town in southern Iraq taken by the Muslims during the conquests; see Donner, *Early Islamic Conquests*, 213–14.

965. *Marāsīl*, sing. *mursal*. Such a tradition was considered inferior to one with a full chain of transmission.

966. *Akhadhahā minhum wa-ʿanhum*, literally, "that he received from them and on their authority." As a rule, the earlier Muslim scholars preferred direct personal contact between master and pupil and were suspicious of those who cited written records; see Schoeler.

967. That is, he wrote it down from dictation, a procedure that made the use of written records acceptable. The *kitāb* of this period is not "a book" in the modern sense of the word but any written record.

According to 'Amr b. 'Alī—'Affān—Wuhayb—Ayyūb: Al-Ḥasan did not learn traditions [directly] from Abū Hurayrah.

According to 'Amr b. 'Alī—Abū Qutaybah—Shu'bah: I asked Yūnus "Did al-Ḥasan hear [traditions] from Abū Hurayrah?" He said "No, not one word."

According to Ibn Sa'd[968]—Yaḥyā b. Sa'īd al-Qaṭṭān, concerning the traditions of Samurah [b. Jundab] which al-Ḥasan transmitted: They were taken from written records.

Some people impute to al-Ḥasan Qadarī convictions,[969] whereas others deny this.

According to [Muḥammad] Ibn Ḥumayd—Jarīr [b. 'Abd al-Ḥamīd]—Mughīrah [b. Miqsam]: The most knowledgeable in matters of blood money, judiciary, and battles was ['Āmir b. Sharāḥīl] [2490]
al-Sha'bī. The best expert on prayer, legal alms, and lawful and unlawful practices was Ibrāhīm al-Nakha'ī.[970] The best expert in matters of rites was 'Aṭā' b. Abī Rabāḥ. The most knowledgeable in the field of Qur'ān interpretation was Sa'īd b. Jubayr.[971] The best expert in matters of trade and money was Ibn Sīrīn. But al-Ḥasan al-Baṣrī was the master of them all.

According to Ibn Sa'd[972]—Mūsā b. Ismā'īl—Ḥammād b. Zayd—'Amr b. 'Ubayd: We learned from al-Ḥasan only in times of anger.[973]

According to 'Alī b. Sahl—al-Walīd [b. Muslim]—Khulayd: Someone asked al-Ḥasan about a certain issue. Al-Ḥasan discussed it, and the man said "O Abū Sa'īd, the scholars disagree with you." Al-Ḥasan said: "May your mother be bereft of you! [Where] did you see a scholar? By God, the scholars of all the cities are gone. The last of them to have died were Jābir b. 'Abdallāh in Medina and 'Abdallāh b. 'Umar, or 'Amr, in Mecca. Al-Ṭabarī re-

---

968. Ibn Sa'd, VII/1, 115.

969. Belief in the freedom of the human will as opposed to belief in predestination. See "Ḳadariyya," *EI*², V, 370. (J. van Ess); Lambton, 33–36; Obermann; Alavi; Cook, *Early Muslim Dogma*; Watt, *Free Will*; note 981, below.

970. A famous Kūfan Successor. See Schacht, *Origins*, 233–37 and passim; al-Mizzī, *Tahdhīb*, II, 233–40; Ibn Ḥibbān, *Mashāhīr*, 163; al-Sayrawān, 49.

971. A famous Kūfan Successor. See al-Mizzī, *Tahdhīb*; X, 358–76; al-Sayrawān, 95.

972. Ibn Sa'd, VII/1, 124.

973. The meaning of this is not clear to me. The parallel in Ibn Sa'd, VII/1, 124, is identical; the dictionaries, and GLOSSARIUM provide no clue.

marks: The doubt is mine. In my notes I have Ibn 'Umar. [The last scholar to have died] in al-Baṣrah was Anas b. Mālik, in al-Kūfah 'Abdallāh b. Abī Awfā, and in Damascus Abū Umāmah [al-Bāhilī, Ṣudayy b. 'Ajlān]."

According to 'Alī b. Muḥammad [al-Madā'inī]—Abū Isḥāq—al-Ḥasan: I went to see al-Ḥajjāj, and he said: "O Ḥasan, what makes you so impertinent to me? In addition [to everything else] you sit in our mosque to give legal opinions!" I said "The covenant by which God pledged mankind." Al-Ḥajjāj then said "And what do you think about Abū Turāb?" meaning 'Alī b. Abī Ṭālib. I said "What can I say, except what God says?" He retorted "And what does God say?" I answered: "'We appointed the *qiblah*, which thou hast been observing, only that We might know those who would follow the messenger from those who would turn on their heels, though it was a big thing except to those whom Allāh guided'[974] and 'Alī was one of those directed by God to the right
[2491] way." Al-Ḥajjāj raged and bent down, striking the ground. I went out, and no one stood in my way. Then I went into hiding until he died.

Al-Ḥasan was in hiding nine years.

According to al-Ḥārith—Dā'ūd b. al-Muḥabbar—al-Rabī' b. Ṣubayḥ—al-Ḥasan: The [interdiction] of slander does not apply in cases of transgressors openly declaring their transgression or people following devious doctrines[975] or unjust rulers.

According to al-Ḥārith—al-'Abbās b. al-Faḍl al-'Abdī—[Sufyān] Ibn 'Uyaynah—Abū Mūsā: When al-Ḥasan left al-Ḥajjāj he said: "I come from a little squinting man, a short [person] wagging the few hairs he has and pointing at me with short fingers that rarely knew [the touch of] reins [of the horses led to] holy war. By God, even though they ride non-Arabian horses[976] and climb the pulpits, the dishonor of sin is pendant from their necks. God refuses to do anything but disgrace those who disobey Him; He will not cease

974. Qur'ān 2:138; trans. Bell, I, 20.

975. *Ahl al-ahwā' wa-l-bida'* "the people of passions/[evil] inclinations and innovations" is the name commonly used by Orthodox Islam to depict the sects.

976. *Barādhīn*, sing. *birdhawn*. According to Lane, these are horses of mean breed. Notwithstanding, they appear to have been a status symbol. Among other things, they are counted among the luxuries 'Umar refused to use; see Ibn al-Jawzī, *Ta'rīkh*, 110.

to teach them lessons [by afflicting] their persons and to use them as examples for the believers. O God, kill him as he killed Your *sunnah*."[977]

According to al-Ḥārith—Khālid b. Khidāsh—'Umarah b. Zādhān al-Ṣaydalānī: I saw al-Ḥasan wearing an 'Adanī garment, streaky and marked with crosses, with an Egyptian shirt from Shaṭāh and sandals like those used by people belonging to the *futuwwah* orders.[978]

According to al-Ḥārith—'Alī b. Muḥammad—'Abdallāh b. Muslim: Some sweetmeat was brought to al-Ḥasan, and he said to his son Sa'īd "Come, my son, eat from it." Sa'īd said "I am afraid of the consequences," whereupon al-Ḥasan replied "O my son, [this is] the best wheat [mixed] with bees' honey and pure butter; no bad consequence can ever result from this," or [perhaps] he said "no evil can ever result from this."

According to Yūnus—Mūsā—Sahl b. Ḥuṣayn b. Muslim al- [2492]
Bāhilī: I sent [a message] to 'Abdallāh b. al-Ḥasan b. Abī al-Ḥasan, saying: "Send me the writings of your father." He sent me [a reply] saying: "When al-Ḥasan had fallen ill he told me 'Collect [my writings] for me.' I did this, not knowing what he would do with them, and brought them to him. He then told the maid to kindle the oven and ordered [the writings] to be burned, except one notebook." ['Abdallāh b. al-Ḥasan] sent me that [notebook].[979] I later met him, and he told me personally the same [story] the messenger had conveyed to me on his behalf.

According to 'Alī b. Sahl—Ḍamrah b. Rabī'ah—Ibn Shawdhab: Al-Ḥasan died in the year 110/April 16, 728-April 4, 729, whereas Ibn Sīrīn died a hundred days later.

---

977. On the "killing" of the *Sunna*, i.e., the customs and practices of the Prophet, see Goldziher, *Muslim Studies*, II, 31–37.

978. Cf. Ibn Sa'd, VII/1, 126. *Ḥadhw al-fityān* could also mean "sandals like those used by young people." For the orders, widespread in medieval Muslim urban communities, see "*Futuwwah*," *EI²*, II, 961–65 (C. Cahen).

979. "Notebook" is my rendering of *ṣaḥīfah*, whereas "writings" is my translation of *kutub* (sing. *kitāb*), normally rendered as "books"; see note 965, above. This passage, like many others describing the burning or effacing of early writings, is pertinent to the discussion about the existence of early writings; see Landau-Tasseron, "Reconstruction" and the bibliography there; and on *ṣaḥīfah*, Goldziher, *Muslim Studies*, II, 22–24; Aḥmad, 256–69, 318–26; "Ṣaḥīfa," *EI²*, VIII, 834–35 (A. Ghēdira).

According to Abū al-Sā'ib—Ibn Idrīs—Shu'bah: Al-Ḥasan died in the year 110; there were a hundred days between his and Ibn Sīrīn's death, and al-Ḥasan died first.

According to Ibn Sa'd[980]—Mu'ādh b. Mu'ādh: Al-Ḥasan was ten years older than Muḥammad b. Sīrīn.

According to 'Alī b. Muslim al-Ṭūsī—Sa'īd b. 'Āmir: Al-Ḥasan was born in the year 21/December 10, 641–November 29, 642, and died in the year 110. A Syrian by the name of al-Naḍr b. 'Amr, who was in charge of the prayers, said the prayer over his bier. He reached the age of eighty-nine years.

According to [Sufyān] Ibn Wakī'—his father—Ḥammād b. Zayd—Ayyūb: I quarreled with al-Ḥasan about predestination (*al-qadar*) to the point that I threatened to [denounce] him to the authorities.

According to Abū 'Uthmān al-Muqaddamī—al-Farawī: I heard Mālik say: "We hold Ibn Sīrīn in higher esteem than al-Ḥasan." I asked: "O Abū 'Abdallāh, for what reason?" He said: "Al-Ḥasan was led astray by the doctrine of [free will held by the] Qadariyyah."[981]

[2493] According to [Muḥammad] Ibn Ḥumayd—al-Ḥakam b. Bashīr—Zakariyyā' b. Sallām: Someone came to al-Ḥasan and told him that he had divorced his wife [by uttering the formula "you are divorced"] three times. Al-Ḥasan said "You have disobeyed your Lord and alienated your wife." The man said "God had decreed this for me." Al-Ḥasan, who was eloquent, said "God had not decreed (*qaḍā*)," that is, "God had not ordered [this]," whereupon he recited the following verse: "Your Lord had ordered (*qaḍā*) that you worship no one but Him."[982]

According to Ismā'īl b. Mas'ūd al-Jaḥdarī—al-Mu'tamir b. Sulaymān—Qurrah b. Khālid—Abū Rabāḥ b. 'Abīdah: As far as I

980. Ibn Sa'd, VII/1, 129.

981. The term Qadariyyah, derived from *qadar* "predestination," was applied by the holders of the determinist view to their opponents, i.e., the supporters of the doctrine of free will, among whom al-Ḥasan al-Baṣrī was counted. Nondeterminists applied the term to determinists. Eventually the term came to refer to the doctrine of free will. It is commonly assumed that the doctrine favored by the authorities of the time, the Umayyads, was that of the *Murji'ah*, hence the threat to denounce al-Ḥasan to the authorities. See Cook, *Early Dogma*, 107–52; note 969, above.

982. Qur'ān 17:24. The verb *qaḍā* means both "to decree" and "to order."

am concerned, the most worrying thing about al-Ḥasan is his view about predestination, by which he brings discord among the people.

Muḥammad b. Sīrīn.[983]

His *kunyah* was Abū Bakr, and he was a client of Anas b. Mālik. It was reported that he was deaf.

According to Ibn Sa'd[984]—Khālid b. Khidāsh—Ḥammād b. Zayd—Anas b. Sīrīn: Muḥammad b. Sīrīn was born two years before the end of 'Uthmān's caliphate, whereas I was born one year later.

According to Bakkār b. Muḥammad: Muḥammad b. Sīrīn fathered thirty children, all of them from the same woman, but none survived except 'Abdallāh b. Muḥammad.

Wahb b. Munabbih b. Kāmil b. Sayj.[985]

He was a descendant of [one of] the Persians who had been dispatched by Khusraw to the Yemen to fight the Abyssinians who ruled there (*al-abnā'*). [These Persians] ousted the Abyssinians and governed the Yemen and its provinces.

Wahb's *kunyah* was Abū 'Abdallāh. He was one of those who read the books of the prophets and knew the history of the ancients.

Wahb lived in Ṣan'ā', as did also his brothers.[986] [2494]

According to Muḥammad b. 'Umar [al-Wāqidī] and 'Abd al-Mun'im b. Idrīs:[987] Wahb died in Ṣan'ā' in the year 110/April 16,

---

983. "Ibn Sīrīn," *EI*², III, 947–48 (T. Fahd); Khalīfah b. Khayyāṭ, *Ta'rīkh*, 354; idem, *Ṭabaqāt*, 210; Ibn Ḥibbān, *Mashāhīr*, 143.

984. Ibn Sa'd, VII/1, 140.

985. Of Persian-Yemeni origin, one of the earliest storytellers and historians whose writings have come down to us, author of a biography of the Prophet preceding that of Ibn Isḥāq. He is said to have met many Companions and to have been closely associated with 'Abdallāh b. 'Abbās for many years. See Khoury, *Wahb*, I, 189–316; Krenkow, "The Two Oldest Books," 230–34; Duri, *Rise of Historical Writing*, 122–35 and passim; al-Rāzī, 367–68, 372–411, 609; al-Ja'dī, 57; Nuwayhiḍ, II, 721.

986. Wahb had several brothers, the most famous being Hammām b. Munabbih. Also known to the Yemeni biographer al-Rāzī are Ma'qil the jurist and Ghaylān; see al-Rāzī, 370–71, 415–17, 421, 585, 601, 607; Duri, *Rise of Historical Writing*, 134; p. 322, below.

987. A descendant of Wahb and transmitter of his material; see Khoury, *Wahb*, I, 184–88, 291–92 and passim.

728–April 4, 729, at the beginning of the caliphate of Hishām b. ʿAbd al-Malik b. Marwān. According to others he died in the year 114/March 3, 732–February 20, 733.

Those Who Died in the Year 111 (April 5, 729–March 25, 730)

ʿAṭiyyah b. Saʿd b. Junādah al-ʿAwfī, of the Jadīlah of Qays.[988]

His *kunyah* was Abū al-Ḥasan.

According to Ibn Saʿd[989]—Saʿīd b. Muḥammad b. al-Ḥasan b. ʿAṭiyyah: Saʿd b. Junādah came to ʿAlī b. Abī Ṭālib in al-Kūfah and said [to him] "O Commander of the Faithful, a son was born to me; [please] give him a name." ʿAlī said "This is God's gift," so the boy was called ʿAṭiyyah (that is, "a gift").

His mother was Greek.

ʿAṭiyyah participated in the revolt of Ibn al-Ashʿath[990] then fled to Fārs. Al-Ḥajjāj wrote to Muḥammad b. al-Qāsim al-Thaqafī[991] [the following instructions]: "Send for ʿAṭiyyah; if he curses ʿAlī b. Abī Ṭālib, [fine];[992] if not, flog him 400 times and shave his head and beard." Muḥammad b. al-Qāsim sent for ʿAṭiyyah and read al-Ḥajjāj's letter to him. ʿAṭiyyah refused to do [as requested], so Muḥammad had him flogged 400 times and had his head and beard shaven.

When Qutaybah b. Muslim[993] became governor of Khurāsān ʿAṭiyyah went to him and stayed in Khurāsān until ʿUmar b.

---

988. Mentioned as a Shīʿī transmitter, al-Quhpāʾī, IV, 141, and a Qurʾān interpreter; Nuwayhiḍ, I, 347; Khalīfah b. Khayyāṭ, *Taʾrīkh*, 366. Jadīlah was the name of several tribal groups, one of them belonging to the northern confederation of Qays ʿAylān; see Caskel, II, 252, and p. 276, below.

989. Ibn Saʿd, VI, 212–13.

990. A grandson of the Kindī chief al-Ashʿath b. Qays. ʿAbd al-Raḥmān b. Muḥammad b. al-Ashʿath was one of the tribal nobles (*ashrāf*), governor of Sīstān, and an army general. He led a revolt against the Umayyads during the years 700–3. See Hawting, *First Dynasty*, 67–70; Crone, *Slaves*, 110–11, no. 21; "Ibn al-Ashʿath," *EI²*, III, 715–19 (L. Veccia-Vaglieri); Sayed.

991. One of al-Ḥajjāj's relatives, appointed by him as a military commander and governor of Sind. See al-Ṭabarī, *Taʾrīkh*, II, 1200, 1257, 1271, 1275; Crone, *Slaves*, 135 no. 25.

992. See p. 212, above. Here the curse is used as a test of loyalty to the Umayyads.

993. A Syrian of northern descent, appointed governor of Rayy and later of Khurāsān, by al-Ḥajjāj b. Yūsuf. He was killed in an attempt to rebel against the

Hubayrah[994] was appointed governor of Iraq. ʿAṭiyyah then wrote to ʿUmar, asking permission to return, and was granted it. ʿAṭiyyah went to al-Kūfah, where he remained until his death in the year 111.

ʿAṭiyyah transmitted many traditions; he was reliable, if God so wills.

Those Who Died in the Year 112 (March 26, 730–March 14, 731)

ʿAbd al-Raḥmān b. Abī Saʿīd al-Khudrī.[995]

Abū Saʿīd's name was Saʿd b. Mālik b. Sinān.

There is disagreement over ʿAbd al-Raḥmān's *kunyah*. According to Muḥammad b. ʿUmar [al-Wāqidī], it was Abū Muḥammad. [2495]

According to Ibn ʿUmar [al-Wāqidī]: ʿAbd al-Raḥmān b. Abī Saʿīd died in Medina in the year 112, at the age of seventy-seven. He had transmitted [traditions] from his father.

Abū Jaʿfar Muḥammad b. ʿAlī b. Ḥusayn b. ʿAlī b. Abī Ṭālib.[996]

His mother was Umm ʿAbdallāh bt. Ḥasan b. ʿAlī b. Abī Ṭālib.

According to Ibn ʿUmar [al-Wāqidī]—ʿAbd al-Raḥmān b. ʿAbd al-ʿAzīz—Ḥakīm b. Ḥakīm b. ʿAbbād b. Ḥunayf: I saw Abū Jaʿfar leaning on a folded Persian mantle in the mosque.[997] Ibn ʿUmar [al-Wāqidī] said: The noble and virtuous among us, who frequent the mosque, still practice this. They lean on folded Persian mantles other than the mantles and cloaks they wear.

According to ʿAbd al-Raḥmān b. Yūnus—Sufyān b. ʿUyaynah—Jaʿfar b. Muḥammad: I heard Muḥammad b. ʿAlī mention to

---

Umayyad caliph Sulaymān. See Crone, *Slaves*, 136–38 no. 33; "Ḳutayba b. Muslim," *EI²*, V, 541–42 (C. E. Bosworth).

994. Of the northern tribe of Fazārah, a branch of the confederation of Ghaṭafān. See "Fazāra," *EI²*, II, 873 (W. M. Watt); Ibn Ḥazm, *Jamharat*, 255–59. He was an army general and governor of Iraq and Khurāsān under the Marwānids; see Crone, *Slaves*, 107.

995. Son of the eminent Anṣārī Abū Saʿīd al-Khudrī. See Khalīfah b. Khayyāṭ, *Taʾrīkh*, 357; idem, *Ṭabaqāt*, 253; Ibn Ḥibbān, *Mashāhīr*, 117.

996. That is, Muḥammad al-Bāqir, the fifth imām according to the Imāmī and Ismāʿīlī Shīʿah. See "Muḥammad b. ʿAlī al-Bāqir," *EI²*, VII, 397–400 (E. Kohlberg); Jafrī, 248–55; Ṭabāṭabāʾī, 202–3; Ibn Ḥibbān, *Mashāhīr*, 103.

997. On the importance of the mantle, *ṭaylasān*, see al-Suyūṭī, *al-Aḥādīth al-ḥisān*.

Fāṭimah, daughter of Ḥusayn, some [property] of the Prophet's bequest,[998] saying "This one yields for me fifty-eight [. . .]"[999]

According to Ibn 'Umar [al-Wāqidī]: According to our version, he died in the year 117/January 31, 735–January 19, 736, at the age of seventy-three.

According to Muḥammad b. Ismā'īl—Abū Nu'aym [al-Faḍl b. Dukayn]: Muḥammad b. 'Alī Abū Ja'far died in the year 114/ March 3, 732–February 20, 733.

According to 'Alī b. Muḥammad al-Madā'inī: Abū Ja'far Muḥammad b. 'Alī b. Ḥusayn died in the year 117 at the age of sixty-three.

[2496] According to Yaḥyā b. Ma'īn: Abū Ja'far Muḥammad b. 'Alī b. Ḥusayn died in the year 118/January 20, 736–January 7, 737.

According to Muḥammad b. 'Abdallāh al-Ḥaḍramī—Suwayd b. Sa'īd—Mufaḍḍal b. 'Abdallāh—Abān b. Taghlib—Abū Ja'far [Muḥammad b. 'Alī]: Jābir b. 'Abdallāh came to me at school and told me "Uncover your belly." I uncovered my belly, and he kissed it, saying "The Prophet told me to convey his greetings to you."

Al-Ḥakam b. 'Utaybah.[1000]

Opinions about his *kunyah* differ. Some say it is Abū Muḥammad. However, according to Ibn Sa'd[1001]—al-Faḍl b. Dukayn—Abū Isrā'īl: Al-Ḥakam b. 'Utaybah's *kunyah* was Abū 'Abdallāh.

There is also disagreement over [the tribe] to which he was affiliated [as client]. According to Ibn Sa'd he was a client of the Kindah. 'Alī b. Muḥammad [al-Madā'inī] said: Al-Ḥakam b.

---

998. *Ṣadaqat al-nabī.* The status of the property left behind by the Prophet was disputed. Whereas his family demanded that it should be considered as inheritance, the rulers insisted that prophets do not leave inheritance and that their property should become *waqf* or *ṣadaqah* to be used for charitable purposes. The discussion had political implications for authority after the Prophet's death; see Goldziher, *Muslim Studies*, II, 102.

999. *Hādhihi tuwaffī lī thamāniyan* (sic) *wa-khamsīn wa-māta lahā.* The text (also Dār al-Fikr, 648, Cairo, 641) is obviously garbled, as are the variants in Ibn Sa'd, V, 238, and Ibn Ḥajar, *Tahdhīb*, IX, 312. In the latter this confusion led to a further misunderstanding. Perhaps the text should read *wa-mā talāhā* "and what follows," in the sense of "and more." Such a copyist's error is possible if the *alif* was at some point written above, rather than after, the *lām* (as in the word *hādhā*).

1000. Not to be confused with the judge al-Ḥakam b. 'Uyaynah. See Ibn Ḥajar, *Tahdhīb*, II, 372; Khalīfah b. Khayyāṭ, *Ṭabaqāt*, 162.

1001. Ibn Sa'd, VI, 231.

'Utaybah was a Kindī, but some say he was an Asadī, that is, a client of that tribe.

Al-Ḥakam b. 'Utaybah was erudite [especially in] religious law and transmitted many traditions.

According to 'Abd al-Raḥmān b. Ṣāliḥ—Nūḥ b. Darrāj—Ibn Abī Laylā: I was visiting al-Ḥakam when Dā'ūd al-Awdī came to him and said "People allege that you denigrate Abū Bakr and 'Umar." He retorted "I do not, but I contend that 'Alī is better than they are."[1002]

According to Abū al-Sā'ib—['Abd al-Mun'im] Ibn Idrīs—Shu'bah [b. al-Ḥajjāj]: Al-Ḥakam b. 'Utaybah died in the year 115/February 21, 733–February 9, 734.

According to Muḥammad b. Ismā'īl—Abū Nu'aym al-Faḍl b. Dukayn: Al-Ḥakam b. 'Utaybah died in the year 115.

Sa'īd b. Yasār Abū al-Ḥubāb.[1003]

He was a client of al-Ḥasan b. 'Alī. He lived in Medina and died there in the year 117/January 31, 735–January 19, 736.

Muḥammad b. Ka'b b. Ḥayyān b. Salīm b. Asad al-Quraẓī.[1004]

He was an ally of the Aws. His *kunyah* was Abū Ḥamzah. [2497]

Opinions differ as to the time of his death. According to Muḥammad b. Ismā'īl—Abū Nu'aym al-Faḍl b. Dukayn: He died in the year 108/May 8, 726–April 27, 727.

[Muḥammad b. Ka'b] was knowledgeable, virtuous, and acceptable. He transmitted many [traditions].

Qatādah b. Di'āmah al-Sadūsī.[1005]

1002. The evaluation of the first two caliphs, Abū Bakr and 'Umar, versus the fourth caliph, the Prophet's cousin 'Alī b. Abī Ṭālib, played a crucial role in the debate between Sunnīs and Shī'īs around the legitimacy of rulers in Islam. Cf. al-Ṭabarī, *Ṣarīḥ al-sunnah*, 23–24; al-Lālikā'ī, VII, 1363–72; al-Ash'arī, *Maqālāt*, 74–75; al-Khallāl, *al-Sunnah*, 371–410.

1003. Khalīfah b. Khayyāṭ, *Ta'rīkh*, 363; Ibn Ḥibbān, *Mashāhīr*, 118.

1004. A convert of a Medinan Jewish tribe annihilated by the Prophet, the Banū Qurayẓah. Khalīfah b. Khayyāṭ, *Ta'rīkh*, 363; idem, *Ṭabaqāt*, 264; Ibn Ḥibbān, *Mashāhīr*, 107; F. Sezgin, I, 32.

1005. A Baṣran of the Sadūs, a branch of the Shaybān tribe; see Ibn Ḥazm, *Jamharat*, 317–18. He was considered an expert on religious law and the Qur'ān. See "Ḳatāda b. Di'āma," *EI*², IV, 748 (C. Pellat); Khalīfah b. Khayyāṭ, *Ta'rīkh*, 363; idem, *Ṭabaqāt*, 213; Ibn Ḥibbān, *Mashāhīr*, 154; al-Sayrawān, 266; Ibn al-Jazarī, II, 25.

His *kunyah* was Abū al-Khaṭṭāb. He was blind.

Qatādah was a *ḥāfiẓ*[1006] and a clever person.

According to Ibn Ma'īn: Qatādah died in the year 117/January 31, 735–February 19, 736.

'Alī b. 'Abdallāh b. 'Abbās b. 'Abd al-Muṭṭalib.[1007]

His mother was Zur'ah bt. Mishraḥ b. Ma'di-Karib b. Walī'ah b. Shuraḥbīl b. Mu'āwiyah b. Ḥujr al-Qird b. al-Ḥārith al-Wallādah b. 'Amr b. Mu'āwiyah b. al-Ḥārith b. Mu'āwiyah b. Thawr b. Murattiʿ b. Thawr, that is, Kindah.[1008]

His *kunyah* was Abū Muḥammad.

It was reported that he was born the night 'Alī b. Abī Ṭālib, the Commander of the Faithful, was killed, in Ramaḍān 40/February 661. He therefore was given both the name and the *kunyah* of ['Alī b. Abī Ṭālib], that is, Abū al-Ḥasan. 'Abd al-Malik b. Marwān said to him: "By God, I shall not tolerate it that you would use both the name and the *kunyah* [of 'Alī b. Abī Ṭālib]." So he changed his *kunyah* and made it Abū Muḥammad.[1009]

This 'Alī b. 'Abdallāh was the youngest of his father's sons. It was reported that he was the most comely and handsome man in the Quraysh. He was [also] the one most dedicated to prayer among them and was nicknamed al-Sajjād (the habitual prostrator or the worshiper) because of his piety.

Opinions differ as to the time of his death. According to Muḥammad b. 'Umar [al-Wāqidī]: 'Alī b. 'Abdallāh b. 'Abbās died in the year 118/January 20, 736–January 7, 737.

1006. A technical term denoting a high degree of knowledge in the prophetic tradition. Definitions of the term vary; see al-Sayrawān, 37–38.

1007. Head of the 'Abbāsid movement in his time and ancestor of the 'Abbasid caliphs. See Sharon, *Black Banners*, 86–87, 159–61; Khalīfah b. Khayyāṭ, *Ṭabaqāt*, 239; Ibn Ḥibbān, *Mashāhīr*, 107; al-Balādhurī, *Ansāb*, III (Dūrī), 70–71; Ibn Qudāmah, 160; *Akhbār al-dawlah*, 134–48.

1008. The text (as well as Ibn Sa'd, V, 229) has *wa-huwa kindī*, but the reading must be *wa-huwa kindah*, because Thawr, the tribe's eponym, was nicknamed Kindah; see Ibn Ḥazm, *Jamharat*, 425.

1009. Al-Ṭabarī, *Ta'rīkh*, II, 1592. And see note 113, above. The matter of genealogy and family relations within the Quraysh was of crucial importance in Umayyad propaganda, which is reflected in the stance taken by 'Abd al-Malik; see Sharon, "The Umayyads."

Ḥammād b. Abī Sulaymān.[1010]

His *kunyah* was Abū Ismā'īl.

Ḥammād was a client of Ibrāhīm b. Abī Mūsā al-Ash'arī. He was one of the people sent by Mu'āwiyah to Abū Mūsā at Dūmat al-Jandal.[1011] [2498]

Ḥammād was an expert on religious law.

According to Abū al-Sā'ib—['Abd al-Mun'im] Ibn Idrīs—Shu'bah [b. al-Ḥajjāj]: Ḥammād b. Abī Sulaymān died in the year 120/December 29, 737–December 17, 738.

Zayd b. 'Alī b. al-Ḥusayn b. 'Alī b. Abī Ṭālib.[1012]

Zayd's mother was a concubine (*umm walad*).

I have told the story of Zayd's death in my book entitled *the Supplemented* (*al-Mudhayyal*).

According to al-Ḥārith [b. Muḥammad]—Muḥammad b. Sa'd[1013]—Muḥammad b. 'Umar [al-Wāqidī]—'Abdallāh b. Ja'far: Zayd b. 'Alī came to Hishām b. 'Abd al-Malik[1014] and brought forward the matter of his many debts, as well as [other] needs. Hishām did not fulfill any of his needs. [Moreover], he was sulky with him and spoke harsh words to him. 'Abdallāh b. Ja'far related: Sālim, Hishām's client and chamberlain, told me that Zayd b. 'Alī came out of Hishām's presence twisting his moustache with his hand, and saying "No one ever loved [this] life without having to be humiliated [for it]." He then departed, heading for al-Kūfah, where he rose in rebellion. Yūsuf b. 'Umar al-Thaqafī[1015] was at that time governor of Iraq on behalf of Hishām b. 'Abd al-Malik.

1010. Khalīfah b. Khayyāṭ, *Ta'rīkh*, 365; idem, *Ṭabaqāt*, 162; Ibn Ḥibbān, *Mashāhīr*, 178.

1011. The reference is to the arbitration following the battle of Ṣiffīn between 'Alī and Mu'āwiyah, in the year 36/657.

1012. The fifth imām according to the Zaydī Shī'ah and the eponym of the sect. See van Arendonck, 28–33 and passim; Jafri, 247–48, 251–54; Ṭabāṭabā'i, 76–77; al-Ṭabarī, *Ta'rīkh*, II, 1668–88, 1698–1715; Ibn Ḥibbān, *Mashāhīr*, 104–5; al-Amīn, XXXIII, 37–132; Ḥasan.

1013. Ibn Sa'd, V, 239.

1014. The tenth Umayyad caliph (105–25/724–43); see Hawting, *First Dynasty*, 81.

1015. Governor of Iraq under the Marwānids. He was a relative (not "a parent," as stated by Zetterstéen) of the famous general and statesman al-Ḥajjāj b. Yūsuf. See "Yūsuf b. 'Omar," *EI*[1], IV, 1177–78 (K. V. Zetterstéen); al-Dhahabī, *Siyar*, V, 442–44.

Yūsuf sent troops to fight Zayd b. ʿAlī, and those who had rebelled in support of Zayd deserted him during the fighting. Zayd was killed and crucified.

Sālim reported: I later told Hishām about Zayd's statement the day he had come out of his presence, and Hishām said: "May your mother be bereft of you! Why didn't you tell me this before? A mere 500,000 dirhams would have satisfied him, and this would have been easier for us than what became of him."[1016]

[2499] According to Muḥammad b. ʿUmar [al-Wāqidī]: When the ʿAbbāsids came to power ʿAbdallāh b. ʿAlī b. ʿAbdallāh b. ʿAbbās[1017] resolved upon [doing something about] Hishām b. ʿAbd al-Malik. He gave the order, and Hishām was dug out of his grave. ʿAbdallāh had him crucified and said "This is [done] in retaliation for what he did to Zayd b. ʿAlī."[1018]

Zayd was killed on Monday, 2 Ṣafar 120/January 29, 738 or 122/740, at the age of forty-two, as was reported. He had lived in Medina and was killed in al-Kūfah.

Salamah b. Kuhayl al-Ḥaḍramī.[1019]

Salamah was an inhabitant of al-Kūfah, where he died on the last day of the year 121/December 6, 739. Some say that he died in the year 122, when ʿAlī b. Zayd was killed.[1020]

Muḥammad b. Muslim b. ʿUbaydallāh b. ʿAbdallāh al-Aṣghar b. Shihāb b. ʿAbdallāh b. al-Ḥārith b. Zuhrah b. Kilāb b. Murrah.[1021]

1016. The report has an obvious anti-Zaydī bias. Zayd, who was out to fight the oppressors (i.e., the Umayyads) and retrieve the rights of the family of the Prophet, is here portrayed as a wordly, venal figure.

1017. Uncle of the first and second ʿAbbāsid caliphs and commander of the ʿAbbasid army. He rose in rebellion against his nephew al-Manṣūr, claiming the caliphate for himself, but was defeated; see Sharon, *Revolt*, 235–38, 280, 287–88.

1018. On the ʿAbbāsids as patrons of the ʿAlids, see Sharon, *Revolt*, 135–37 and passim; note 113, above.

1019. Of the southern group, the Ḥaḍramawt. See Khalīfah b. Khayyāṭ, *Ṭabaqāt*, 163; Ibn Ḥibbān, *Mashāhīr*, 77.

1020. Ibn Saʿd, VI, 221.

1021. Known as Ibn Shihāb al-Zuhrī (died 124/742), an early Medinan scholar and transmitter of prophetic tradition and historical reports, mainly about the Prophet. See Horovitz, 1928, 33–50; Duri, "al-Zuhrī"; idem, *Rise of Historical Writing*, 95–121; Abdur Rahman; al-Ḍāri; Lecker, "Biographical Notes"; Muṣṭafā, I, 157–58.

His mother was 'Ā'ishah bt. 'Abdallāh al-Akbar b. Shihāb, and his *kunyah* was Abū Bakr.

Muḥammad b. Muslim al-Zuhrī was an expert on the campaigns (*maghāzī*) of the Prophet and the history of the Quraysh and the Anṣār. He was a transmitter (*rāwiyah*) of traditions from the Prophet and his Companions.[1022]

Muḥammad b. 'Alī b. 'Abdallāh b. al-'Abbās b. 'Abd al-Muṭṭalib.[1023]

His mother was al-'Āliyah bt. 'Ubaydallāh b. al-'Abbās b. 'Abd al-Muṭṭalib.

The offspring of Muḥammad b. 'Alī are the following: 'Abdallāh al-Aṣghar, that is, Abū al-'Abbās, the [first] 'Abbāsid caliph;[1024] Dā'ūd b. Muḥammad; 'Ubaydallāh; and Rayṭah, who died without having been married.[1025] Their mother was Rayṭah bt. 'Ubaydallāh b. 'Abdallāh b. 'Abd al-Madān b. al-Dayyān, of the [2500] Banū al-Ḥārith b. Ka'b.[1026]

[Muḥammad b. 'Alī's children from other women are] (1) 'Abdallāh al-Akbar, that is, Abū Ja'far al-Manṣūr, who ascended the caliphate after his brother Abū al-'Abbās[1027] and whose mother was a concubine; (2) Ibrāhīm b. Muḥammad, that is, al-Imām, whom the members of the 'Abbāsid movement used to frequent and whose instructions they used to follow,[1028] his mother was a concubine; (3) Yaḥyā b. Muḥammad and (4) al-'Āliyah bt. Muḥammad, whose mother was Umm al-Ḥakam bt. 'Abdallāh b. al-Ḥārith b. Nawfal b. al-Ḥārith b. 'Abd al-Muṭṭalib; (5) Mūsā b.

1022. Or, "A transmitter of accounts of the life of the Prophet and his Companions."

1023. The initiator of the 'Abbāsid movement and founder of the dynasty. See Sharon, *Black Banners*, 123–28, 134 and passim; Ibn Qudāmah, 160–61; al-Balādhurī, *Ansāb*, III (Dūrī), 71–72, 80–87; Ibn Ḥibbān, *Mashāhīr*, 207; Khalīfah b. Khayyāṭ, *Ta'rīkh*, 372; idem, *Ṭabaqāt*, 312.

1024. Named al-Saffāḥ, reigned between 132–36/749–54. See "Abū al-'Abbās," *EI*², I, 103 (S. M. Moscati); Kennedy, 128.

1025. See GLOSSARIUM, s.v. *b-r-z*.

1026. A large confederation of Yemeni tribes, prominent in the 'Abbāsid revolution in al-Kūfah; see Sharon, *Black Banners*, 142–43.

1027. Considered the real founder of the 'Abbāsid state, reigned 36–58/754–75; see "Al-Manṣūr," *EI*², VI, 427–28 (H. Kennedy).

1028. See Sharon, *Black Banners*, 86, 174, and passim; idem, *Revolt*, 52, 140, 225, and passim.

Muḥammad, whose mother was a concubine; (6) al-ʿAbbās b. Muḥammad, whose mother was a concubine; (7) Ismāʿīl; (8) Yaʿqūb, that is, Abū al-Asbāṭ; and (9) Lubābah bt. Muḥammad, who was married to Jaʿfar b. Sulaymān b. ʿAlī and died without children. All these were born to various mothers.

According to al-ʿAbbās b. Muḥammad: Muḥammad b. ʿAlī b. [ʿAbdallāha b.] al-ʿAbbās died in al-Sharāt[1029] in Syria in the year 125/November 4, 742–October 24, 743, during the caliphate of al-Walīd b. Yazīd b. ʿAbd al-Malik b. Marwān,[1030] at the age of sixty.

Abū Hāshim ʿAbdallāh b. Muḥammad b. al-Ḥanafiyyah had chosen Muḥammad b. ʿAlī as his heir and handed his books over to him, so that Muḥammad b. ʿAlī was Abū Hāshim's heir (*waṣiyy*). Abū Hāshim said to him: "This matter [of the caliphate] will remain among your descendants only." Consequently, the Shīʿah who used to frequent Abū Hāshim and attend his presence transferred [their allegiance] to Muḥammad b. ʿAlī.[1031]

Thābit al-Bunānī b. Aslam.[1032]

His *kunyah* was Abū Muḥammad, and he belonged to the Saʿd b. Luʾayy b. Ghālib. According to Hishām [Ibn al-Kalbī]—his father: Bunānah was the clan's ancestress.[1033]

According to ʿAlī b. Muḥammad [al-Madāʾinī]: Thābit al-Bunānī died in the year 127/October 13, 744–October 2, 745. He had lived in al-Baṣrah, where he [also] died. He was reliable (*thiqah*) and transmitted many traditions.

1029. The mountainous area south of the Dead Sea, where the ʿAbbāsid family settled toward the end of the eighth century. From their dwelling place in the village of Ḥumaymah they conducted the ʿAbbāsid movement; see Sharon, *Black Banners*, 120.

1030. The eleventh Umayyad caliph, 125–26/743–44; see Hawting, *First Dynasty*, 90–94.

1031. Abū Hāshim was the leader of the Hāshimiyyah movement after the death of his father Muḥammad b. al-Ḥanafiyyah. This account served as the basis of the ʿAbbāsid claim to rule, see Sharon, *Black Banners*, 82–98, 121–40. The books mentioned here apparently symbolize the knowledge that, according to the Shīʿah, ʿAlī inherited from the Prophet and that now lawfully passes into the hands of the ʿAbbāsids. Alternatively the word could be read *kitāb* (assuming a pendant *alif* above the *tāʾ*), referring to Abū Hāshim's testament.

1032. Khalīfah b. Khayyāṭ, *Ṭabaqāt*, 214; Ibn Ḥibbān, *Mashāhīr*, 45. He was considered an expert on tradition (*ḥāfiẓ*); see al-Sayrawān, 69.

1033. Saʿd b. Luʾayy was a clan attributed, though hesitantly, to the Quraysh. See Ibn Ḥazm, *Jamharat*, 172–73; Ibn Qudāmah, 492.

'Abdallāh b. Dīnār.[1034]
He was a client of 'Abdallāh b. 'Umar b. al-Khaṭṭāb.
His *kunyah* was Abū 'Abd al-Raḥmān. He died in the year 127. [2501]
He had lived in Medina, where he [also] died. He transmitted many traditions and was reliable (*thiqah*).

Wahb b. Kaysān.[1035]
His *kunyah* was Abū Nu'aym. He was a client of 'Abdallāh b. al-Zubayr b. al-'Awwām. He died in the year 127.

Bukayr b. 'Abdallāh b. al-Ashajj.[1036]
He was a client of al-Miswar b. Makhramah al-Zuhrī.[1037] His *kunyah* was Abū 'Abdallāh. He died in the year 127 in Medina.

Mālik b. Dīnār.[1038]
His *kunyah* was Abū Yaḥyā. He was a client of a woman of the Banū Sāmah b. Lu'ayy.[1039]
According to Ibn 'Ā'ishah: Mālik b. Dīnār's origins were in Kābul.[1040] He was a pious man, an expert on the prophetic tradition (*ḥāfiẓ*), and a Qur'ān reader. He used to make Qur'ān copies [for a living].

Jābir b. Yazīd al-Ju'fī.[1041]
He had Shī'ī inclinations. He lived in al-Kūfah, where he died in the year 128/October 3, 745–September 21, 746.[1042]

1034. Considered a *ḥāfiẓ* (an expert on the prophetic tradition). See Khalīfah b. Khayyāṭ, *Ṭabaqāt*, 263; Ibn Ḥibbān, *Mashāhīr*, 129; al-Sayrawān, 116.

1035. Khalīfah b. Khayyāṭ, *Ta'rīkh*, 398; idem, *Ṭabaqāt*, 260; Ibn Ḥibbān, *Mashāhīr*, 130.

1036. Khalīfah b. Khayyāṭ, *Ta'rīkh*, 369, 403; idem, *Ṭabaqāt*, 263; Ibn Ḥibbān, *Mashāhīr*, 299.

1037. Perhaps he was rather a client of the family, not of al-Miswar himself, who died in 64/683.

1038. "Mālik b. Dīnār," *EI*², VI, 266–67 (C. Pellat); Khalīfah b. Khayyāṭ, *Ta'rīkh*, 418; idem, *Ṭabaqāt*, 216; Ibn Ḥibbān, *Mashāhīr*, 147; Ibn al-Jazarī, II, 36.

1039. A clan said to be of Qurashī origin; see Ibn Ḥazm, *Jamharat*, 172–74.

1040. The region in eastern Afghanistan. Mālik's father came from there as a prisoner; see Ibn Ḥajar, *Tahdhīb*, X, 13.

1041. The tribe Ju'fiyy belonged to the southern confederation Sa'd al-'Ashīrah; see Ibn Ḥazm, *Jamharat*, 409. Jābir was a traditionist accused by Shī'īs and Sunnīs alike of telling lies. See Ibn Ḥazm, 410; Khalīfah b. Khayyāṭ, *Ta'rīkh*, 398; idem, *Ṭabaqāt*, 163; al-Quhpā'ī, II, 7–11; al-Kashshī, 169–74.

1042. Ibn Sa'd, VI, 240.

According to Sa'īd b. 'Uthmān al-Tanūkhī—Ibrāhīm b. Mahdī al-Maṣṣīṣī—Ismā'īl b. 'Ulayyah—Shu'bah: Jābir and Muḥammad b. Isḥāq were most reliable (*ṣadūq*).[1043]

According to 'Abd al-Raḥmān b. Bishr al-Naysābūrī—Sufyān b. 'Uyaynah: Jābir al-Ju'fī believed in the Return [of the hidden Imam] (*raj'ah*).

According to Yaḥyā b. Ma'īn: Jābir al-Ju'fī died in the year 132/August 20, 749–August 8, 750.

According to al-'Abbās al-Dūrī—Abū Yaḥyā al-Ḥimmānī 'Abd al-Ḥamīd b. Bashmīr[1044]—Abū Ḥanīfah al-Nu'mān b. Thābit: I never saw a greater liar than Jābir al-Ju'fī.

According to al-'Abbās—Yaḥyā b. Ya'lā al-Muḥāribī—Zā'idah: Jābir al-Ju'fī was a liar who believed in the Return.

[2502] 'Āṣim b. Abī al-Najūd al-Asadī, that is, 'Āṣim b. Bahdalah.[1045]

He was a client of the Banū Jadhīmah b. Mālik b. Naṣr b. Qu'ayn b. Asad.[1046]

According to Abū Nu'aym al-Faḍl b. Dukayn—Abū al-Aḥwaṣ: his *kunyah* was Abū Bakr.[1047]

'Āṣim was the Qur'ān teacher of al-Kūfah after Yaḥyā b. Waththāb.

He was a reliable [transmitter] (*thiqah*), but he erred a lot.[1048]

He lived in al-Kūfah where he died in the year 128/October 3, 745–September 21, 746.

Abū Isḥāq al-Sabī'ī.[1049]

1043. Ibn Isḥāq's reliability was a matter of dispute. See Landau-Tasseron, "Sayf," 8, and p. 252, below.

1044. The Dār al-Fikr edition, 653, has "Bashīr"; see also de Goeje, p. 2501 n. *d*.

1045. Khalīfah b. Khayyāṭ, *Ta'rīkh*, 398; idem, *Ṭabaqāt*, 159; Ibn Ḥibbān, *Mashāhīr*, 261.

1046. A tribe of northern origin. See 'Alī; Landau-Tasseron, "Asad."

1047. Ibn Sa'd, VI, 224.

1048. That is, he did not intend to lie, which is enough to classify him as a reliable transmitter (*thiqah*).

1049. A famous Kūfan jurist of the southern tribe al-Sabī', a branch of the Hamdān confederation. See Ibn Ḥazm, *Jamharat*, 395; Khalīfah b. Khayyāṭ, *Ṭabaqāt*, 162; Ibn Ḥibbān, *Mashāhīr*, 178; Ibn al-Jazarī, I, 602; F. Sezgin, I, 283.

His name was 'Amr b. 'Abdallāh b. 'Alī b. Aḥmad b. Dhī Yaḥmad b. al-Sabī' b. Sabu' b. Ṣa'b b. Mu'āwiyah b. Kathīr b. Mālik b. Jusham b. Ḥāshid b. Jusham b. Khaywān b. Nawf b. Hamdān.[1050]

According to al-Aswad b. 'Āmir—Sharīk: Abū Isḥāq al-Sabī'ī was born during the caliphate of 'Uthmān. Sharīk may have said: Three years before its end. Abū Isḥāq transmitted many traditions and was most reliable (*ṣadūq*). He was [also] a Qur'ān reader.

According to Abū Nu'aym: Abū Isḥāq reached the age of ninety-eight or ninety-nine and died in the year 128.

Abū Isḥāq al-Shaybānī.[1051]

His name was Sulaymān b. Abī Sulaymān, a client of the Banū Shaybān.

According to Muḥammad b. 'Umar [al-Wāqidī]:[1052] He lived in al-Kūfah, where he died in the year 129/September 22, 746–September 10, 747.

Maṭar b. Ṭahmān al-Warrāq.[1053]

He was from Khurāsān, a client of 'Ilbā' al-Sulamī.[1054]

Some hold that he was a weak [transmitter]. His *kunyah* was Abū Rajā'.

According to Ja'far b. Sulaymān: Maṭar b. Ṭahmān died in the year 125/November 4, 742–October 24, 743.

Yaḥyā b. Abī Kathīr al-Ṭā'ī.[1055] [2503]

His *kunyah* was Abū Naṣr.

1050. Ibn Sa'd, VI, 219, has Khayrān, but the correct form is Khaywān, as indicated by an anonymous hand on the manuscript (see de Goeje, 2502 n. *b*) and recorded in many other sources; see Ibn al-Kalbī, *Nasab ma'add*, 514; the manuscripts of Ibn Ḥazm (erroneously corrected by the editor; see 392, n. 7); al-Sam'ānī, II, 433. See also p. 151 and note 908, above.

1051. Khalīfah b. Khayyāṭ, *Ta'rīkh*, 445; idem, *Ṭabaqāt*, 165; Ibn Ḥibbān, *Mashāhīr*, 178. Shaybān was a name of several branches of the large northern confederation of Bakr b. Wā'il (Rabī'ah), see Ibn Ḥazm, *Jamharat*, 317, 321.

1052. Ibn Sa'd, VI, 241.

1053. Khalīfah b. Khayyāṭ, *Ta'rīkh*, 411; idem, *Ṭabaqāt*, 215; Ibn Ḥibbān, *Mashāhīr*, 153.

1054. Much effort was spent in tracing this individual but to no avail.

1055. A Baṣran traditionist of the southern tribe Ṭayyi', who settled in al-Yamāmah. See Khalīfah b. Khayyāṭ, *Ṭabaqāt*, 215; Ibn Ḥibbān, *Mashāhīr*, 304.

According to 'Alī b. al-Madyanī—Yaḥyā b. Sa'īd [al-Qaṭṭān]—Shu'bah [b. al-Ḥajjāj]: The traditions [transmitted by] Yaḥyā b. Abī Kathīr are better than those [transmitted by Ibn Shihāb] al-Zuhrī.

According to 'Abd al-Razzāq—Ma'mar [b. Rāshid]: Yaḥyā b. Abī Kathīr was requested to swear allegiance to the Umayyad caliph [of the time], but he refused, whereupon he was whipped and treated like Sa'īd b. al-Musayyab.

Yaḥyā b. Abī Kathīr made extensive use of *tadlīs*.[1056]

It was reported that Yaḥyā b. Abī Kathīr died in the year 129/September 22, 746–September 10, 747. He had lived in al-Yamāmah, where he [also] died.

Muḥammad b. al-Munkadir b. 'Abdallāh b. al-Hudayr b. 'Abd al-'Uzzā b. 'Āmir b. Ḥārithah b. Sa'd b. Taym b. Murrah.[1057]

His mother was a concubine, and his *kunyah* was Abū 'Abdallāh.

Muḥammad b. al-Munkadir fathered 'Umar, 'Abd al-Malik, al-Munkadir, 'Abdallāh, Yūsuf, Ibrāhīm, and Dā'ūd, whose mother was a concubine.

Some trace Muḥammad's genealogy as follows: Muḥammad b. al-Munkadir b. 'Abdallāh b. al-Hudayr b. Muḥriz b. 'Abd al-'Uzzā.

It was reported that Muḥammad b. al-Munkadir died in Medina, where he had lived, in the year 130/September 11, 747–August 30, 748 or 131/August 31, 748–August 19, 749.

Abū al-Ḥuwayrith.[1058]

His name was 'Abd al-Raḥmān b. Mu'āwiyah. [Sufyān] Ibn 'Uyaynah transmitted [traditions] from him.

According to Yaḥyā: He was a Medinan and a reliable transmitter (*thiqah*).

According to Muḥammad b. Bakkār—Abū Ma'shar [Najīḥ b. 'Abd al-Raḥmān]—Abū al-Ḥuwayrith 'Abd al-Raḥmān b. Mu'āwi-

---

1056. A term referring to various kinds of tampering with the chains of transmission (*isnād*) of traditions, e.g., hiding the name of one's source, citing someone without having directly heard him, or changing the name of a source in the chain; see al-Ḥākim al-Naysābūrī, 103–12.

1057. Of the Qurashī clan the Banū Taym, known for both piety and generosity. See Khalīfah b. Khayyāṭ, *Ta'rīkh*, 418; idem, *Ṭabaqāt*, 268; Ibn Ḥibbān, *Mashāhīr*, 107; 'Abd al-Malik Ibn Ḥabīb, 161–62.

1058. Khalīfah b. Khayyāṭ, *Ta'rīkh*, 422; al-Dūlābī, I, 160–61.

yah: God spoke to Moses within the measure that was endurable to him. Had God spoken all His words, Moses would not have endured it. Moses stayed forty nights; no one saw him but was struck dead by the light of the Lord of the Universe.[1059]

Abū al-Ḥuwayrith lived in Medina, where he died in the year 130.

Yazīd b. Rūmān.[1060] [2504]

He was a client of al-Zubayr b. al-ʿAwwām's family.

Yazīd was knowledgeable on the campaigns (*maghāzī*) of the Prophet and a reliable transmitter (*thiqah*). He was an inhabitant of Medina, where he died in the year 130.

Shuʿayb b. al-Ḥabḥāb.[1061]

He was an inhabitant of al-Baṣrah, where he died in the year 130. His *kunyah* was Abū Ṣāliḥ. He was one of the clients of the Banū Rāfid, a clan of the Maʿāwil who belonged to the Azd [confederation].[1062]

Manṣūr b. Zādhān.[1063]

He lived in al-Mubārak, [a place] situated nine *farsakhs*[1064] away from Wāsiṭ.

Manṣūr used to read fast and could not slow down, [even when] he wanted to do so.

According to Muḥammad b. ʿUmar [al-Wāqidī]: Manṣūr b. Zādhān died in the year 129/September 22, 746–September 10, 747, [but] according to Yaḥyā b. Maʿīn it was in the year 127/October 13, 744–October 2, 745.

1059. In Muslim tradition Moses is said to have been the only prophet to whom God spoke directly, because of which he was nicknamed *kalīm allāh* "the one spoken to by God." See "Mūsā," *EI*², VII, 638–40 (D. B. MacDonald).

1060. A traditionist and Qurʾān reader. See Khalīfah b. Khayyāṭ, *Taʾrīkh*, 418; idem, *Ṭabaqāt*, 260; Ibn Ḥibbān, *Mashāhīr*, 216; Ibn al-Jazarī, II, 381.

1061. Khalīfah b. Khayyāṭ, *Taʾrīkh*, 418; Ibn Ḥibbān, *Mashāhīr*, 156.

1062. Ibn Saʿd, VII/2, 18, has Zāfir instead of Rāfid. See al-Samʿānī, V, 335, for the Maʿāwil.

1063. A client of a Thaqafī, known for his piety and asceticism, reportedly mourned not only by Muslims but also by Jews, Christians, and Magians. See Khalīfah b. Khayyāṭ, *Ṭabaqāt*, 217; Ibn Ḥibbān, *Mashāhīr*, 279; Abū Nuʿaym, III, 57–62.

1064. That is, about twenty-seven miles.

Manṣūr b. al-Mu'tamir al-Sulamī.[1065]

His *kunyah* was Abū 'Attāb. He was a meritorious person, godly, religious, reliable, and trustworthy.

According to [Muḥammad] Ibn Ḥumayd—Jarīr [b. 'Abd al-Ḥamīd]: [Once], Manṣūr fasted sixty [days] and prayed the nights, until he fell ill.[1066]

According to Ibn Ḥumayd—Jarīr: Manṣūr used to wear shabby clothes and skins. You could perceive the water running down inside his chest when he was drinking during illness.

According to Ibn Ḥumayd—Jarīr: Manṣūr was seen [by someone] in a dream after he had died. He was asked "O Abū 'Attāb, how are you?" He answered "I almost met God, for [I had] acted as a prophet."[1067]

According to Ibn Ḥumayd—Jarīr: ['Umar] Ibn Hubayrah[1068] wanted to appoint Manṣūr as judge, but he refused. Ibn Hubayrah put him under arrest for two months, then released him and presented him with a gift, which Manṣūr accepted.[1069]

[2505] Manṣūr performed the pilgrimage together with his son, he and al-Qāsim.

According to al-Ḥusayn b. 'Alī al-Ṣudā'ī—Khalaf b. Tamīm—Zā'idah: Manṣūr b. al-Mu'tamir fasted a whole year, praying the nights and fasting the days. He used to weep in the nights, and his mother would ask him "My son, did you murder anybody?" and he would reply "I know better than anyone what I have myself done." In the morning he would make up his eyes with kohl, anoint his head, and shine his lips with oil and go out to meet people.

Yūsuf b. 'Umar, governor of al-Kūfah, wanted to appoint him as

---

1065. A Kūfan jurist, ascetic, and Qur'ān reader of the northern tribe Sulaym. See Khalīfah b. Khayyāṭ, *Ta'rīkh*, 429; idem, *Ṭabaqāt*, 164; Ibn Ḥibbān, *Mashāhīr*, 263; Ibn al-Jazarī, II, 314–15. For the tribe, see Lecker, *Banū Sulaym*.

1066. Ibn Sa'd, VI, 235.

1067. Or, "I almost met God with prophetic acts [to my credit]." The question of meeting God or seeing Him in the hereafter was debated by Muslim theologians; see, e.g., al-Lālikā'ī, III, 454–523.

1068. A general and governor under the Marwānids; see Crone, *Slaves*, 107.

1069. Pious men are often reported to have refused official nominations because of the iniquity associated with government. See note 323, above. According to another version, however, Manṣūr accepted the appointment but was soon dismissed; see Wakī', III, 145–48.

judge, but Manṣūr refused. Yūsuf sent for him [someone] with shackles, and he bound him [and brought him to Yūsuf]. Someone said to Yūsuf "Even if you scatter this old man's limbs he will not accept an office." Two litigants came, sat down, and spoke, but Manṣūr never replied. At that Yūsuf exempted Manṣūr and freed him.

Manṣūr was an inhabitant of al-Kūfah, where he died in the year 132/August 20, 749–August 8, 750. He was a Shīʿī.

Muḥammad b. Abī Bakr b. Muḥammad b. ʿAmr b. Ḥazm.[1070]

His mother was Fāṭimah bt. ʿUmārah b. ʿAmr b. Ḥazm, and his *kunyah* was Abū ʿAbd al-Malik. He was a judge in Medina.

According to [Muḥammad] Ibn Saʿd[1071]—Maʿn b. ʿĪsā—Saʿīd b. Muslim: I saw Muḥammad b. Abī Bakr b. Muḥammad b. ʿAmr b. Ḥazm act as judge in the mosque.

According to [Ibn Saʿd]—Muṭarrif b. ʿAbdallāh al-Yasārī—Mālik b. Anas: Muḥammad b. Abī Bakr b. Muḥammad b. ʿAmr b. Ḥazm held the office of judge in Medina. Sometimes he would issue a verdict that contradicted [Muḥammadan] tradition (*ḥadīth*) and would go home. His brother ʿAbdallāh b. Abī Bakr, who was a virtuous man,[1072] would say to him "O Brother, you decreed today such-and-so in the [issue of] such-and-so." Muḥammad would say "Yes, brother." ʿAbdallāh would say: "Where is tradition then, Brother? Is tradition too sparse to pass judgment according to it?"[1073] Muḥammad would retort "Yes, but what about practice?"
meaning the practice as commonly agreed upon in Medina. Ac- [2506]
cording to their opinion, the commonly accepted practice was more valid than tradition.[1074]

1070. Of an aristocratic Anṣārī family, the Banū Ḥazm, a branch of the Banū al-Najjār. He succeeded his father as governor or judge, or both, of Medina and was killed in the battle of al-Ḥarrah between the Medinans and the Syrian army in the year 64/683. See Ibn Ḥazm, *Jamharat*, 348; Khalīfah b. Khayyāṭ, *Taʾrīkh*, 384, 429; idem, *Ṭabaqāt*, 237; Ibn Ḥibbān, *Mashāhīr*, 207; Wakīʿ, I, 175–78.

1071. Ibn Saʿd, *al-Qism al-mutammim*, 282.

1072. A traditionist, jurist, and historian. See F. Sezgin, I, 284; Horovitz, 1928, 22–31.

1073. *ʿAzza al-ḥadīth an yuqḍā bihi?* Alternatively, "Is Tradition too exalted to pass judgment according to it?"

1074. See also Wakīʿ, I, 176. This tradition supports Schacht's view that in the early period it was not prophetic tradition but rather agreed practice (the "living

According to Muḥammad b. 'Umar [al-Wāqidī]: Muḥammad b. Abī Bakr b. Muḥammad b. 'Amr b. Ḥazm died in the year 132, at the beginning of the 'Abbāsid regime, at the age of seventy-two.

Ṣafwān b. Sulaym.[1075]
He was a client of Ḥumayd b. 'Abd al-Raḥmān b. 'Awf al-Zuhrī,[1076] and his *kunyah* was Abū 'Abdallāh. Originally he belonged to the 'Ibād,[1077] [but] he lived in Medina, where he died in the year 132. He was a reliable [transmitter of traditions] (*thiqah*), if God so wills.

'Abdallāh b. Abī Najīḥ.[1078]
His *kunyah* was Abū Yasār, and he was a client of the Thaqīf tribe. He lived in Mecca, where he [also] died. There is disagreement over the time of his death. According to Muḥammad b. 'Umar [al-Wāqidī], he died in Mecca in the year 132, whereas, according to 'Abd al-Raḥmān b. Yūnus—Sufyān, Ibn Abī Najīḥ died before the plague; the plague was in the year 131/August 31, 748–August 19, 749.[1079]

According to 'Alī b. al-Madyanī–Yaḥyā b. Sa'īd: Ibn Abī Najīḥ was a Mu'tazilī.[1080] Yaḥyā reported that Ayyūb said: "What a man they corrupted!"

Ibn Abī Najīḥ was the *muftī* in Mecca after 'Amr b. Dīnār.[1081]

---

sunna") that served as the basis for religious law. See Schacht, "A Revaluation"; idem, *Origins.* See also Wakī', 143–44; 'Abd al-Malik Ibn Ḥabīb, 161.

1075. Khalīfah b. Khayyāṭ, *Ta'rīkh*, 429; idem, *Ṭabaqāt*, 261. He was a Qur'ān reader according to Ibn Ḥibbān, *Mashāhīr*, 216 (not recorded by Ibn al-Jazarī) and considered a *ḥāfiẓ* by al-Suyūṭī; see al-Sayrawān, 103.

1076. Son of a famous Companion of the Prophet, 'Abd al-Raḥmān b. 'Awf. See al-Mizzī, *Tahdhīb*, VII, 378–81; Ibn Sa'd, V, 114–15; Ibn Ḥibbān, *Mashāhīr*, 113.

1077. The 'Ibād (whose name means "worshipers of God") were the Christian Arabs of the kingdom of al-Ḥīrah, which flourished between A.D. the third and seventh centuries in southern Iraq. The Arab genealogists, however, fitted this group into the genealogical scheme; see Ibn Ḥazm, *Jamharat*, 422.

1078. Khalīfah b. Khayyāṭ, *Ta'rīkh*, 421; idem, *Ṭabaqāt*, 282; Ibn Qutaybah, 206 (who adds that he was a Qadarī).

1079. Ibn Sa'd, V, 355.

1080. The Mu'tazilah was a theological movement founded in al-Baṣrah in the second/eighth century; see "Mu'tazila," *EI*², VII, 783–93 (D. Gimaret).

1081. That is, the jurist in charge of giving opinions in legal issues addressed to him; see "Fatwa," *EI*², II, 866 (E. Tyan).

Rabī'ah b. Abī 'Abd al-Raḥmān, nicknamed Rabī'ah of Personal Opinion (Rabī'at al-ra'y).[1082]

The name of his father, Abū 'Abd al-Raḥmān, was Farrūkh.

His *kunyah* was Abū 'Uthmān. He was a client of the family of al-Hudayr of the Banū Taym b. Murrah.

Rabī'ah lived in Medina, where he died in the year 136/July 7, 753–June 26, 754, at the end of Abū al-'Abbās' reign.[1083]

'Abdallāh b. Ḥasan b. Ḥasan b. 'Alī b. Abī Ṭālib.[1084]

His *kunyah* was Abū Muḥammad. He was a pious man, dignified, eloquent, and articulate, a man of distinction. The Umayyad caliphs honored him and acknowledged his eminence. When the 'Abbāsids came to power he went to see Abū al-'Abbās [2507]
[al-Saffāḥ] in al-Anbār.[1085]

According to Muḥammad b. 'Umar [al-Wāqidī]—Ḥafs b. 'Umar: 'Abdallāh b. Ḥasan came to Abū al-'Abbās in al-Anbār. Abū al-'Abbās honored him, presented him [with gifts], and treated him as his companion. [The caliph] behaved toward 'Abdallāh as he never did toward anyone else. He used to spend nights in pleasant conversation with him. Once the caliph spent [the night] in conversation with 'Abdallāh until the middle of the night. Abū al-'Abbās then ordered a basket full of pearls to be brought before him, opened it, and said "O Abū Muḥammad, these, by God, are the pearls that had been the property of the Umayyads and came to my possession." Abū al-'Abbās shared the pearls with 'Abdallāh, giving him half of them. The other half he sent to his wife Umm Salamah with the message "I commit these to you as a trust."

1082. The nickname refers to his use of reasoning as a source of religious law; see p. 000, below. Rabī'ah was a Medinan *ḥāfiẓ* and jurist, one of the teachers of Mālik b. Anas, founder of the Mālikī school of law. See Khalīfah b. Khayyāṭ, *Ta'rīkh*, 441; idem, *Ṭabaqāt*, 268; Ibn Ḥibbān, *Mashāhīr*, 131–32; Ibn Qutaybah, 217; al-Sayrawān, 89; Ibn Ḥajar, *Tahdhīb*, III, 223–24.

1083. That is, the first 'Abbāsid caliph, al-Saffāḥ (132–36/749–54).

1084. An eminent member of the 'Alid family in Medina, father of Muḥammad al-Nafs al-Zakiyyah and his brother Ibrāhīm, who led a Shī'ī revolt against the caliph al-Manṣūr in Medina and al-Kūfah in the years 144–45/761–62. See van Arendonck, 46–50; Khalīfah b. Khayyāṭ, *Ta'rīkh*, 448; idem, *Ṭabaqāt*, 258; Ibn Ḥibbān, *Mashāhīr*, 205; al-Balādhurī, *Ansāb* III (Maḥmūdī), 81–91, III (Dūrī), 90, 150, 165–66, 234–35.

1085. A city in Iraq on the Euphrates, about 60 km. west of Baghdad; see "al-Anbār," *EI*², I, 484–85 (M. Streck [A. A. Duri]).

Then they talked again for an hour [until] Abū al-'Abbās dozed off and then his head bobbed, whereupon 'Abdallāh recited the following verses:[1086]

Did you not see the big-bellied one
 building palaces for the benefit of Nutaylah's sons?[1087]
He hopes like Noah to be given a long life,
 but every night God's decree may strike.

Abū al-'Abbās woke up and grasped 'Abdallāh's meaning, whereupon he said "O Abū Muḥammad, you recite such verses in my [palace], having seen that I treated you [so well] and that I never withheld anything from you?" 'Abdallāh said: "O Commander of the Faithful, this was a lapse by which I meant no harm. These were just verses that occurred to me, so I recited them. If the Commander of the Faithful sees it appropriate to tolerate my deed, let him do so." Abū al-'Abbās said "I do [forgive you]."

[2508] 'Abdallāh returned to Medina. When Abū Ja'far [al-Manṣūr] came to power he insisted on seeking out 'Abdallāh's two sons, Muḥammad and Ibrāhīm. Now Abū al-'Abbās [al-Saffāḥ] had asked 'Abdallāh about his two sons, and he had replied "They are in the desert; [God] made them so that they like being in solitude."[1088] Abū Ja'far sought them out in the desert and was upset by their absence. He therefore wrote to his governor of Medina, Riyāḥ b. 'Uthmān, ordering him to detain their father, 'Abdallāh b. Ḥasan, and his brothers. So they were arrested and brought to al-Hāshimiyyah,[1089] where they were kept in prison. 'Abdallāh b. Ḥasan died in prison at the age of seventy-two in the year 145/April 1, 762–March 20, 763.

According to al-Qāsim b. Dīnār al-Qurashī—Isḥāq b. Manṣūr—Abū Bakr b. 'Ayyāsh—Sulaymān b. Qarm: I asked 'Abdallāh b. al-

1086. Al-Ṭabarī, *Ta'rīkh*, III, 153.

1087. That is, the 'Abbāsids. Nutaylah was the mother of al-'Abbās, the eponymous ancestor of the dynasty. See p. 24, above; Ibn Ḥazm, *Jamharat*, 301.

1088. This description of the two Shī'ī leaders is deliberately reminiscent of the descriptions of the Prophet before he was endowed with the prophecy, for which see Kister, *"al-Taḥannuth."*

1089. The name of several places in Iraq that served the 'Abbāsids as capital before the building of Baghdad; see "al-Hāshimiyyah," *EI*², III, 265–66 (J. Lassner).

Ḥasan "Are there infidels among those who pray facing toward Mecca?" He replied "Yes, the Rāfiḍah."[1090]

Muḥammad b. al-Sā'ib b. Bishr b. 'Amr b. al-Ḥārith b. 'Abd al-Ḥārith b. 'Abd al-'Uzzā b. Imri' al-Qays b. 'Āmir b. al-Nu'mān b. 'Āmir b. 'Abd Wadd b. 'Awf b. Kinānah b. 'Udhrah b. Zayd al-Lāt b. Rufaydah b. Thawr b. Kalb.[1091]

Muḥammad b. al-Sā'ib's *kunyah* was Abū al-Naḍr. His grandfather Bishr b. 'Amr and his sons al-Sā'ib, 'Ubayd, and 'Abd al-Raḥmān [sons of Bishr] participated in the battles of the Camel and Ṣiffīn on the side of the Commander of the Faithful, 'Alī b. Abī Ṭālib.

Al-Sā'ib b. Bishr was killed [fighting] on the side of Muṣ'ab b. al-Zubayr.[1092] He is the one about whom Ibn Warqā' al-Nakha'ī recited the following verses:[1093]

Who will inform 'Ubayd in my name
  that I struck his brother with a sharp Indian sword?
If you wish some knowledge of him to obtain, [2509]
  he lies by the two monasteries, no pillow beneath his head.
Purposely did I strike his head with a sharp one,
  making Sufyān and Muḥammad bereaved.

Sufyān and Muḥammad were sons of al-Sā'ib.

1090. Among Sunnī Muslims it is commonly agreed that anyone praying toward the *qiblah* and formally professing Islam cannot be considered an infidel, be his opinions and conduct as they may; see Lewis, chap. 16. Not all the sects share this attitude. The Rāfiḍah is a term reflecting schisms within the Shī'ah; it refers either to the early Shī'ah, the Twelver Shī'ah, or to various other Shī'ī sects. See "al-Rāfiḍa," *EI*[2], VIII, 386–89, (E. Kohlberg).

1091. One of the earliest Kūfan historians, genealogists, and Qur'ān interpreters, known as "al-Kalbī" (of the southern Kalb confederation); he was a Shī'ī. See Conrad, "al-Kalbī"; Duri, *Rise of Historical Writing*, 51, 146; F. Sezgin, I, 34; Muṣṭafā, 190; al-Sayrawān, 276.

1092. Brother of the rival caliph 'Abdallāh b. al-Zubayr and governor of al-Kūfah on his behalf in the years 64–71/683–91.

1093. Ibn Sa'd, VI, 249–50; al-Ṭabarī, *Ta'rīkh*, II, 731. The author of the verses is either 'Abdallāh b. Warqā' b. 'Āzib, or Warqā' himself, a Kūfan who served as commander in the Umayyad *shurṭah* (quasi police force); see al-Ṭabarī, II, 644, 645–46, 648.

Muḥammad b. al-Sā'ib participated in the battle of [Dayr] al-Jamājim, [fighting] on the side of 'Abd al-Raḥmān b. Muḥammad b. al-Ash'ath.[1094]

Muḥammad b. al-Sā'ib was knowledgeable about Qur'ān exegesis, genealogy, and Arabian tales. He died in al-Kūfah, where he had lived, in the year 146/March 21, 763–March 9, 764, during the caliphate of Abū Ja'far [al-Manṣūr]. All this was reported by Ibn Sa'd on the authority of Hishām b. Muḥammad b. al-Sā'ib, who had informed him of all this.[1095]

Sulaymān b. Mihrān al-A'mash.[1096]

He was a client of the Banū Kāhil, of [the tribe of] Asad. His *kunyah* was Abū Muḥammad.

Al-A'mash lived among the Banū 'Awf of the Banū Sa'd and used to pray at the mosque of the Banū Ḥarām of the Banū Sa'd.[1097]

Mihrān, father of al-A'mash, originated in Ṭabaristān. Al-A'mash [himself] lived in al-Kūfah, where he died in the year 148/February 27, 765–February 15, 766 at the age of eighty-two. He had been born on the day of 'Āshurā' in Muḥarram 60/October 681, the day when al-Ḥusayn b. 'Alī was killed.[1098]

Ja'far b. Muḥammad b. 'Alī b. Ḥusayn b. 'Alī b. Abī Ṭālib.[1099]

His mother was Umm Farwah bt. al-Qāsim b. Muḥammad b. Abī Bakr al-Ṣiddīq.

Ja'far b. Muḥammad's children were the following: Ismā'īl al-A'raj;[1100] 'Abdallāh and Umm Farwah, whose mother was Fāṭimah bt. al-Ḥusayn al-Athram b. Ḥasan b. 'Alī b. Abī Ṭālib;

1094. On the battle of Dayr al-Jamājim between al-Ḥajjāj and the rebel Ibn al-Ash'ath, see "Dayr al-Djamādjim," *EI*², II, 196–97 (Ṣāliḥ A. el-'Alī); al-Ṭabarī, *Ta'rīkh*, II, 1070–77.

1095. Ibn Sa'd, VI, 249–50.

1096. A Kūfan traditionist, a *ḥāfiẓ* and Qur'ān reader. See "al-A'mash," *EI*², I, 431 (C. Brockelmann [C. Pellat]); Khalīfah b. Khayyāṭ, *Ta'rīkh*, 452; idem, *Ṭabaqāt*, 164; Ibn Ḥibbān, *Mashāhīr*, 179; Ibn al-Jazarī, I, 315–16; al-Sayrawān, 99.

1097. That is, Sa'd b. Zayd Manāh, an important lineage of the confederation of Tamīm; see Ibn Ḥazm, *Jamharat*, 215.

1098. That is, the massacre of Karbalā'.

1099. The sixth imām according to the Ismā'īlī and Twelver Shī'ah. See "Dja'far al-Ṣādiḳ," *EI*², II, 374–75 (M. G. S. Hodgson); Ṭabāṭabā'ī, 203–5; Jafri, 259–60 and passim.

1100. The seventh and last imām according to the Ismā'īlī Shī'ah and the eponymous founder of the sect. See Daftary, 97–99; al-Amīn, XII, 299–304.

Mūsā b. Ja'far,[1101] who was imprisoned by Hārūn al-Rashīd[1102] in Baghdad with al-Sindī[1103] and died in prison; Isḥāq; Muḥammad; Fāṭimah, who was married to Muḥammad b. Ibrāhīm b. Muḥammad b. 'Alī b. 'Abdallāh b. 'Abbās[1104] and died while being married to him (the mother of [Isḥāq, Muḥammad, and Fāṭimah] was a concubine); Yaḥyā b. Ja'far, al-'Abbās, Asmā', and Fāṭimah al-Ṣughrā (junior), who were born to various mothers. [2510]

Muḥammad b. 'Umar [al-Wāqidī] related: I heard Ja'far b. Muḥammad say to his young slave Mu'attib "Go to Mālik b. Anas and ask him about such-and-so; then come back and tell me [what he said]."

According to Muḥammad: Abū Ja'far al-Manṣūr seized this Mu'attib and had him flogged a thousand lashes, until he died.

Ja'far b. Muḥammad transmitted many traditions (*ḥadīth*); he was a reliable [transmitter] (*thiqah*). This was, reportedly, Yaḥyā b. Ma'īn's opinion.

It was reported that [Yaḥyā b. Sa'īd] al-Qaṭṭān[1105] was asked "Whom do you prefer, Mujālid b. Sa'īd or Ja'far b. Muḥammad?" Al-Qaṭṭān replied "I prefer Mujālid to Ja'far."

Ja'far lived in Medina, where he [also] died in the year 148/February 27, 765–February 15, 766, during the caliphate of Abū Ja'far [al-Manṣūr], according to al-Wāqidī and al-Madā'inī.

Ja'far b. Muḥammad's *kunyah* was Abū 'Abdallāh.

Al-'Abbās b. Muḥammad said: I heard Yaḥyā say "Ja'far b. Muḥammad is a reliable transmitter."

1101. Mūsā al-Kāẓim, the seventh imām according to the Twelver Shī'ah; see "Mūsā al-Kāẓim," *EI*[2], VII, 645–48 (E. Kohlberg).

1102. One of the most famous 'Abbāsid caliphs. He ruled between 170–93/786–809, and his reign is considered the golden era of the caliphate; see Kennedy, 141–48.

1103. Al-Sindī b. Shāhak, a client of the caliph al-Manṣūr, who served the 'Abbāsids in several offices. Among other things he was in charge of the guard and prison in Baghdad. See al-Sam'ānī, III, 320; al-Ṣafadī, XV, 487–88; Ibn Manẓūr, *Mukhtaṣar*, X, 210.

1104. That is, the nephew of the first and second 'Abbāsid caliphs. This marriage between the daughter of the sixth Shī'ī imām and a member of the 'Abbāsid family points to an attempt at reconciling the Shī'īs with the new regime.

1105. A highly regarded Baṣran traditionist and expert on *rijāl*, i.e., the biographies and evaluation of transmitters of tradition. He died in 198/812; see Ibn Ḥajar, *Tahdhīb*, XI, 190–93.

Those Who Died in the Year 150 (February 6, 767–January 25, 768)

Abū Ḥanīfah al-Nuʿmān b. Thābit.[1106]

He was a client of Taym Allāh b. Thaʿlabah of the Bakr b. Wāʾil.

According to Abū Hishām al-Rifāʿī—his paternal uncle Kathīr b. Muḥammad: I heard a man of the Banū Qafal, of the noblest of the Banū Taym Allāh, say to Abū Ḥanīfah "What are you but a client of mine?" whereupon [Abū Ḥanīfah] retorted "I bring you more honor than you do me."

According to al-Walīd b. Shujāʿ—ʿAlī b. al-Ḥasan b. Shaqīq: ʿAbdallāh b. al-Mubārak used to say "If these two agree on something, I adhere to that opinion," meaning [Sufyān b. Saʿīd] al-Thawrī and Abū Ḥanīfah.

According to Sulaymān b. Abī Shaykh: Abū Saʿīd al-Rānī[1107] firmly opposed the Kūfan [jurists] and supported the Medinan [school].[1108] One of the Kūfans composed satirical verses against him, calling him Shirshīr and saying "[There is] a small dog in hell
[2511] whose name is Shirshīr."[1109] [The Kūfan] composed [the following verses]:[1110]

1106. A theologian and the eponymous founder of one of the law schools, the Ḥanafiyyah. See "Abū Ḥanīfa," *EI²*, I, 123–24 (J. Schacht); Ibn ʿAbd al-Barr, *al-Intiqāʾ*, 122–75; al-Suyūṭī, *Tabyīḍ al-ṣaḥīfah*; al-Sayrawān, 82; Abū Zahrah; al-Dhahabī, *Manāqib al-Imām Abī Ḥanīfah.*

1107. Or al-Rādhānī, al-Walīd b. Kathīr, a traditonist who transmitted from Rabīʿah al-Raʾy among others. See al-Samʿānī, III, 21, 31; Ibn al-Athīr, *Lubāb*, II, 10; Ibn Ḥajar, *Tahdhīb*, XI, 130; al-Dhahabī, *Mushtabih*, 208, 210; al-Mizzī, *Tahdhīb*, XXXI, 71–73. He is recorded, usually very briefly, in many other biographical sources. He would have been of no special interest, had my assistant, Ṭāriq Abū Rajab, not unearthed the following unique information: The man was "a poet, a learned man, and practiced *kalām* (i.e. theological discussions) in the time of al-Ṭabarī. He had some original views"; see Ibn Ḥajar, *Nuzhat*, 178 (note that the text is garbled but the meaning clear). This is the only biographical source to mention one of the verses recorded here by al-Ṭabarī.

1108. On the schools of law and their rivalry, see Schacht, *Origins.*

1109. This nickname is problematic. It is the name of a small bird; see Ibn Khallikān, III, 92. The verb *sharshara* means "to bite," and according to the lexicographer al-Layth, explaining a certain verse, *shirshīr* means a dog. The lexicographer al-Azharī, however, argues that al-Layth was mistaken: *shirshīr* is the name of a certain desert shrub. I fail to see how a shrub can be confused with a dog. See Ibn Manẓūr, *Lisān*, IV, 403.

1110. Ibn ʿAbd Rabbihi, V, 303; al-Jāḥiẓ, I, 148–49 (read al-Rānī for al-Raʾy; the editor could not identify Abū Saʿīd).

These are issues no Shirshīr can master
    or his friends, when asked [their opinion].
Only Ḥanafīs, dwellers in al-Kūfah,
    do we know to grasp this religion.
Do not ask a Medinan, turning him thereby into an infidel,[1111]
    about anything but the cords of the lute [of a musician].

A variant is *wa-al-muthannā aw al-zīr.*[1112]

According to Sulaymān—Abū Sa'īd: I wrote to Medina [informing the people there] "You have been mocked with this and that, so respond to it." So one of the Medinans responded:

I wonder at this erring one, though by fate he is led,
    for everything that is ordained is ordained.
He says that in Medina there is nothing
    but musical instruments and singing.
You lie, by God, for there you can find
    the graves of the Prophet and the best of mankind.

According to Sulaymān—'Amr b. Sulaymān al-'Aṭṭār: I was in al-Kūfah, where I associated with Abū Ḥanīfah, when Zufar[1113] got married. Abū Ḥanīfah was present [at the wedding], and Zufar asked him to speak. Abū Ḥanīfah then delivered a speech, saying "Here is Zufar b. al-Hudhayl, one of the Muslims' [religious] leaders and a prominent figure, a man of noble descent, dignity, and knowledge." Some of Zufar's clan said "We are pleased that it was Abū Ḥanīfah who spoke and no other," as Abū Ḥanīfah mentioned Zufar's qualities and praised him. But other people of Zufar's clan resented this and said to Zufar "Your relatives and the clan's chiefs are present, and you ask Abū Ḥanīfah to deliver a speech!"[1114] Zufar said "Had my father been present I would have

---

1111. *Fa-tukfirahu* (with *fā' al-sababiyyah*) is a better reading than the present *wa-tukfiruhu*; see 2511 n. *a*. The idea is that one can cause someone else to become an infidel by asking him questions (on religious matters) to which he does not know the answer.

1112. Instead of "*wa-al-mathnāh wa-al-zīr,*" names of different strings of the instrument.

1113. A jurist and a friend of Abū Ḥanīfah. See al-Ṣafadī, XIV, 200–1; Ibn Sa'd, VI, 270; al-Dhahabī, *Mīzān*, I, 348.

1114. Zufar belonged to the 'Anbar clan of the tribe of Tamīm, whereas Abū Ḥanīfah was a client of Taymallāh of the Bakr confederation, traditional enemies of the Tamīm; see Jād al-Mawlā et al., 170–228.

preferred Abū Ḥanīfah to him." Zufar b. al-Hudhayl belonged to the Banū al-'Anbar, [a clan] of the Tamīm.

According to Ibrāhīm b. Bashshār al-Ramādī—[Sufyān] Ibn 'Uyaynah: I never saw anyone more insolent toward God than Abū Ḥanīfah. A man from Khurāsān came to him with a hundred thousand issues and said to him "I want to ask you about all this," whereupon Abū Ḥanīfah said "Ask!" Sufyān [Ibn 'Uyaynah] said:
[2512] Have you seen a greater insolence toward God?

According to 'Abdallāh b. Aḥmad b. Shabbawayh—his father—'Alī b. al-Ḥusayn b. Wāqid—his paternal uncle al-Ḥakam b. Wāqid: I saw Abū Ḥanīfah [sit] to give legal opinions from early in the day until midday. When the crowds around him decreased I approached him and said "O Abū Ḥanīfah, had Abū Bakr and 'Umar been with us in this session and had they been presented with the same arduous issues, they would have avoided some of the answers, and they would have stopped [at some point]." Abū Ḥanīfah looked at me and said "Are you seized with fever?"

According to Aḥmad b. Khālid al-Khallāl—al-Shāfi'ī[1115]: Mālik [b. Anas] was once asked [to give his opinion about] al-Battī[1116] and said "He was of a middling sort." He was [also] asked about ['Abdallāh] Ibn Shubrumah[1117] and said "He was of a middling sort." "What about Abū Ḥanīfah?" he was asked. Mālik said "Had he approached these [stone] columns of yours [in the mosque] and argued with you on the basis of analogy (*qiyās*), he would have made them [turn into] wood."[1118]

Muḥammad b. Isḥāq b. Yasār.[1119]

1115. Founder of one of the schools of law (*madhāhib*) and systematizer of the method of deriving the religious law from its sources. He died in 204/819. See Schacht, *Origins*, passim; Halm; Landau-Tasseron, "Cyclical Reform," 101, n. 96.

1116. Apparently the reference is to the Baṣran jurist 'Uthmān b. Muslim al-Battī; see al-Dhahabī, *Siyar*, VI, 148; al-Mizzī, *Tahdhīb*, XIX, 492–94.

1117. A famous Kūfan judge, who died in 144/761. See Juynboll, *Muslim Tradition*, 87–88; al-Dhahabī, *Siyar*, VI, 347; Ibn Ḥibbān, *Mashāhīr*, 265; al-Ṣafadī, XVII, 207; Wakī', passim, especially vol. III, where there is hardly a page on which his name is not mentioned.

1118. The use of analogy in establishing religious laws was a point of debate between Abū Ḥanīfah (who supported it) and al-Shāfi'ī (who had reservations about it). Here al-Shāfi'ī (quoting Mālik) admires Abū Ḥanīfah's method, at least as far as it is persuasive; see Landau-Tasseron, "Cyclical Reform," 101, 106.

1119. Known as Ibn Isḥāq (d. 150/767), a famous early historian and biographer of the Prophet. The biography he wrote (*sīrah*) was widely known and cited, and

He was a client of ʿAbdallāh b. Qays b. Makhramah b. al-Muṭṭalib b. ʿAbd Manāf b. Quṣayy. His *kunyah* was Abū ʿAbdallāh.

According to Muḥammad b. ʿUmar [al-Wāqidī]: He was a client of Qays b. Makhramah. His grandfather Yasār was a captive, among others, from ʿAyn al-Tamr.[1120] These were the first captives to arrive at Medina from Iraq.

Ibn Isḥāq transmitted [traditions] from his father Isḥāq b. Yasār and from his paternal uncles Mūsā and ʿAbd al-Raḥmān, sons of Yasār. He was an expert on the campaigns of the Prophet (*maghāzī*), [as well as] on the battles of the Arabs, their history, and genealogies. He was a transmitter of Arab poetry (*rāwiyah*), [as well as] many traditions. His erudition was immense; he was a seeker of knowledge and a first-rate scholar. In all [these fields] he was reliable.[1121]

According to Saʿīd b. ʿUthmān al-Tanūkhī—Ibrāhīm b. Mahdī al-Maṣṣīṣī—Ismāʿīl b. ʿUlayyah—Shuʿbah: Muḥammad b. Isḥāq [2513]
and Jābir [b. Yazīd] al-Juʿfī are reliable.

According to Ibn Saʿd[1122]—a son of Muḥammad b. Isḥāq: My father died in Baghdad in the year 150/February 6, 767–January 25, 768 and was buried in the cemetery of al-Khayzurān.

Misʿar b. Kidām b. Zuhayr al-Hilālī, a genuine member of the Banū Hilāl.[1123]

His *kunyah* was Abū Salamah.

According to Abū al-Sāʾib—Abū Nuʿaym—Misʿar: I came to see Abū Jaʿfar [al-Manṣūr] and said [to him] "O Commander of the Faithful, I am your maternal uncle." He said "Which one of them

---

together with the work of al-Wāqidī constituted the foundation of all subsequent research on Muḥammad's life. See "Ibn Isḥāk," *EI*[1], III, 389–90 (C. Brockelmann); *EI*[2], III, 810–11 (J. M. B. Jones); Suhayl Zakkār, introduction to Ibn Isḥāq, *Siyar*; Conrad, "Ibn Isḥāq"; Muṣṭafā, I, 160–62; Duri, 33–37; al-Samūk; Ḥamīdullah, "Muḥammad ibn Isḥāq."

1120. One of the first places in Iraq to be raided by the Muslims in the year 12/63. See al-Ṭabarī, *Taʾrīkh*, I, 2062–69. Donner, *Early Islamic Conquests*, 180.

1121. Al-Ṭabarī himself drew heavily on Ibn Isḥāq. Nevertheless, the latter's reliability was not beyond dispute. See Kister, "Massacre," 74–80; Landau-Tasseron, "Sayf," 8.

1122. Ibn Saʿd, VII/2, 67 (without mention of the source).

1123. That is, not a client. The Banū Hilāl were a branch of the northern great confederation of ʿĀmir b. Ṣaʿṣaʿah. On Misʿar, see Khalīfah b. Khayyāṭ, *Taʾrīkh*, 455; idem, *Ṭabaqāt*, 168; Ibn Ḥibbān, *Mashāhīr*, 267.

are you?" I said "I am a member of the Banū Hilāl." Abū Ja'far said "I have no ancestress I like better than the one who was a member of your clan."[1124] I said "O Commander of the Faithful, do you know what the poet said about us and you?" He asked "What did he say?" whereupon I recited:

With the Quraysh we share both piety and kinship;
this is a specific partnership[1125]
Through the offspring of the women of the Banū Hilāl,
as well as the women of the Banū Abān.[1126]

I then said "O Commander of the Faithful, my family has sent me to buy something with some money, then refused to accept it." Abū Ja'far said: "What a bad treatment you received from your family! Take these ten thousands and dole it out."

Opinions differ as to the time of Mis'ar's death. According to Ibn Sa'd[1127]—Muḥammad b. 'Abdallāh al-Asadī: Mis'ar died in al-Kūfah in the year 152/January 14, 769–January 3, 770, during the caliphate of Abū Ja'far [al-Manṣūr]. [But], according to Muḥammad b. Ismā'īl—Abū Nu'aym al-Faḍl b. Dukayn, Mis'ar b. Kidām died in the year 156/December 2, 772–November 20, 773.

Ḥamzah b. Ḥabīb al-Zayyāt.[1128]

He was a client of the Banū Taymallāh.[1129]

Ḥamzah was one of the Qur'ān readers, who excelled in learning the Qur'ān by heart. He transmitted few traditions and was reliable (*thiqah*).

[2514] Ḥamzah was an inhabitant of al-Kūfah. He died in the year 156.

1124. The reference is to Umm al-Faḍl, wife of al-'Abbās b. 'Abd al-Muṭṭalib and mother of 'Abdllāh b. al-'Abbās, great-grandfather of al-Manṣūr; see Ibn Ḥazm, *Jamharat*, 18. Al-Manṣūr's own mother was a concubine.

1125. *Shirk* (read *shirkat*) *al-'inān*, a partnership in a particular thing to the exclusion of the rest of the partners' property.

1126. The reference is to the offspring of Āminah bt. Abān of the Banū Kulayb b. Rabī'ah b. 'Āmir b. Ṣa'ṣa'ah, who was married to Umayyah b. 'Abd Shams; see Ibn Ḥazm, *Jamharat*, 280. The verse was composed by the poet al-Nābighah al-Ja'dī. See Ibn Manẓūr, *Lisān*, XIII, 292–93 (s.v. '*nn*); Nallino, 119.

1127. Ibn Sa'd, VI, 253.

1128. Ibn Ḥibbān, *Mashāhīr*, 266; Ibn al-Jazarī, I, 261–63; al-Ṣadr, 15, 20, 21; F. Sezgin, I, 9 (erroneously attributed to the tribe of Tamīm instead of the Taymallāh).

1129. Taymallāh b. Tha'labah of the Rabī'ah confederation; see al-Sam'ānī, I, 499.

According to Muḥammad b. Manṣūr al-Ṭūsī—Ṣāliḥ b. Ḥammād—an authority whom he named—Ḥamzah al-Zayyāt: I saw the Prophet in a dream. I presented to him twenty traditions [for inspection], and he recognized two of them.[1130]

'Abd al-Raḥmān b. 'Amr.[1131]

His *kunyah* was Abū 'Amr, and he was called al-Awzā'ī. He was a Saybānī by virtue of his living among [that clan].[1132] According to Hishām b. Muḥammad al-Kalbī—his father: Al-Awzā'ī, 'Abd al-Raḥmān b. 'Amr, belonged to the Awzā', [a group including] Mālik and Marthad, sons of Zayd b. Shadad b. Zur'ah. Shadad was the husband of Bilqīs, friend of King Solomon.[1133]

Al-Awzā'ī lived in Beirut, a coastal city in Syria. He was one of the *muftī*s and transmitters of tradition of that locality in his time and one of the excellent [people there].

Al-Awzā'ī died in Beirut in the year 157/November 21, 773–November 10, 774, toward the end of the caliphate of Abū Ja'far [al-Manṣūr], at the age of seventy. This information is given by Muḥammad b. 'Umar [al-Wāqidī].

Shu'bah b. al-Ḥajjāj b. Ward.[1134]

He was from the Azd, a freed slave and client of the Ashāqir.[1135] His *kunyah* was Abū Bisṭām. He was ten years older than [Sufyān] al-Thawrī.

1130. Ḥamzah here refers to the procedure of the authorization and authentication of transmitted traditions, initiated in order to prevent fabrications; see F. Sezgin, I, 59. As for the role of dreams, see Kinberg, especially 230–31 (on Ḥamzah).

1131. A jurist, the main representative of the ancient Syrian school of religious law. See "Al-Awzā'ī," *EI*², I, 772–73 (J. Schacht); F. Sezgin, I, 516–17; Khalīfah b. Khayyāṭ, *Ṭabaqāt*, 315–16; Ibn Ḥibbān, *Mashāhīr*, 285–86; Abū Zur'ah, 261–67 and passim.

1132. The Saybān b. al-Ghawth was a Yemeni clan. According to Ibn Ḥazm, *Jamharat*, 435, 437, al-Awzā'ī originated with this clan and was called Awzā'ī only because he lived among the Awzā', another Yemeni clan. According to Ibn Ḥibbān, however, al-Awzā' was the name of a village near Damascus.

1133. Ibn al-Kalbī, *Nasab ma'add*, II, 546–47. Bilqīs is the Arabic name for the Queen of Sheba, see "Bilḳīs," *EI*², I, 1219–20 (E. Ullendorff).

1134. Khalīfah b. Khayyāṭ, *Ta'rīkh*, 459; idem, *Ṭabaqāt*, 222; Ibn Ḥibbān, *Mashāhīr*, 280; al-Sam'ānī, IV, 153–54; al-Sayrawān, 101.

1135. Of the group called Ghassān; see Ibn Ḥazm, *Jamharat*, 381, 474.

According to Aḥmad b. al-Walīd—al-Rabīʿ b. Yaḥyā: I heard Sufyān al-Thawrī say: There has remained on earth no one like Shuʿbah and Ḥammād b. Salamah.[1136]

Al-Ṭabarī said: I was told by Muḥammad b. Isḥāq al-Ṣāghānī—Abū Qaṭan: Shuʿbah said to me: There is nothing that makes me more afraid of entering hell than tradition.[1137]

Shuʿbah was an inhabitant of al-Baṣrah, where he died in the beginning of the year 160/October 19, 776–October 8, 777, at the age of seventy-five.

[2515] Baḥr b. Kanīz al-Saqqāʾ al-Bāhilī.[1138]

His *kunyah* was Abū al-Faḍl. He lived in al-Baṣrah, where he died in the year 160, during the caliphate of al-Mahdī.[1139] His transmission [of traditions] was not trustworthy.

Al-Aswad b. Shaybān.[1140]

An inhabitant of al-Baṣrah, a meritorious man and a reliable [transmitter] (*thiqah*).

According to ʿAlī b. Muḥammad [al-Madāʾinī], al-Aswad died in the year 160 in al-Baṣrah.

Zāʾidah b. Qudāmah al-Thaqafī.[1141]

1136. A famous Baṣran traditionist and jurist, client of the Tamīm. See Ibn Ḥajar, *Tahdhīb*, III, 11–14; Ibn al-Nadīm, I, 549, II, 993.

1137. Cf. Ibn Saʿd, VII/2, 38. This may be interpreted in two ways. First, pious Muslim scholars sometimes express the fear of failing in the task of faithfully transmitting the Prophet's traditions. Second, certain Muslim scholars of the second century held that writing down prophetic traditions was unlawful. See Sprenger; Goldziher, *Muslim Studies*, II, 181–88. For a critique of these two scholars, see F. Sezgin, II, 53–81.

1138. The name may be Kunayz. He was a Baṣran, a client of the Bāhilah, not trusted because of his bad memory and arbitrary additions to the traditions. See Ibn Ḥibbān, *Majrūḥīn*, I, 192–94; Ibn ʿAdī, II, 482–87.

1139. The third ʿAbbāsid caliph, 158–69/775–85; see Kennedy, 137–39.

1140. Khalīfah b. Khayyāṭ, *Ṭabaqāt*, 221, see also 224; Ibn Ḥibbān, *Thiqāt*, VIII, 129–30.

1141. He died in the year 161/777–78. See Khalīfah b. Khayyāṭ, *Taʾrīkh*, 468; idem, *Ṭabaqāt*, 169; Ibn Ḥibbān, *Mashāhīr*, 269. He cannot be identical with Zāʾidah b. Qudāmah al-Thaqafī, who was associated with al-Mukhtār b. Abī ʿUbayd, not only because the latter was a Shīʿī whereas "our" Zāʾidah opposed the Shīʿah, but also because of the time gap between the two. See, e.g., al-Ṭabarī, *Taʾrīkh*, II, 605, 926.

He was a genuine member of the Thaqīf.[1142] His *kunyah* was Abū al-Ṣalt.

Zā'idah opposed 'Alī b. Abī Ṭālib.[1143]

Those Who Died in the Year 161 (October 9, 777–September 27, 778)

Sufyān b. Sa'īd b. Masrūq b. Ḥabīb b. Rāfi' b. 'Abdallāh b. Mawhibah b. Ubayy b. 'Abdallāh b. Munqidh b. Naṣr b. al-Ḥārith b. Tha'labah b. 'Āmir b. Milkān b. Thawr b. 'Abd Manāh b. Udd b. Ṭābikhah b. al-Yās b. Muḍar.[1144]

His *kunyah* was Abū 'Abdallāh.

According to Muḥammad b. 'Umar [al-Wāqidī]: Sufyān was born in the year 97/September 5, 715–August 24, 716. He was learned, knowledgeable, pious, God fearing, ascetic, a transmitter of many traditions, reliable, and trustworthy in what he transmitted from the Prophet and from others who transmitted [traditions] on religious matters.[1145]

According to Muḥammad b. Khalaf—Ya'qūb b. Isḥāq al-Ḥaḍramī—Shu'bah b. al-Ḥajjāj—Sufyān b. Sa'īd al-Thawrī—'Alī b. al-Aqmar—Abū Juḥayfah—the Prophet: As for me, I do not eat while leaning back.

According to Muḥammad b. Ismā'īl al-Ḍirārī—Abū Nu'aym [al- [2516]
Faḍl b. Dukayn]—Sufyān: There is no deed more frightening than this. When I was ill I never thought of anything else, and I wished that I was completely saved from it. He meant [the transmission of] traditions.[1146]

According to 'Abdallāh b. Aḥmad b. Shabbawayh—his father—Abū 'Īsā al-Zāhid—Ma'dān: Sufyān al-Thawrī was my colleague.

1142. That is, not a client.

1143. That is, he opposed the Shī'ah, not 'Alī personally, for 'Alī died a hundred years before him. Cf. Ibn Sa'd, VI, 283, where he is said to be "one of the consensus" (*ṣāḥib sunnah wa-jamā'ah*), i.e., "orthodox."

1144. Commonly known as Sufyān al-Thawrī, a very famous traditionist, *ḥāfiẓ*, and jurist; see *EI*[1], IV, 500–2 (M. Plessner); F. Sezgin, I, 518–19; Schacht, *Origins*, 242; al-Sayrawān, 96–97; Khalīfah b. Khayyāṭ, *Ta'rīkh*, 468; idem, *Ṭabaqāt*, 168; Ibn Ḥibbān, *Mashāhīr*, 268; 'Abd al-Malik Ibn Ḥabīb, 177; al-Kashshī, 336–40. The tribe, Thawr, was a rather obscure one, see Ibn Ḥazm, *Jamharat*, 201.

1145. Or, "others who left their mark on the religion." This translation is possible as far as the language is concerned but it does not seem right to me.

1146. Cf. p. 256, above.

When we left al-Kūfah he said to me "O Ma'dān, I did not leave behind me anyone I trust, nor am I heading for anyone I trust." He meant trust in religious matters.

According to Zayd b. Ḥubāb: 'Ammār b. Ruzayq al-Ḍabbī, Sulaymān b. Qarm al-Ḍabbī, Ja'far b. Ziyād al-Aḥmar, and Sufyān al-Thawrī were all students of tradition. They all showed a leaning toward the Shī'ah. As for Sufyān, he left for al-Baṣrah, where he met ['Abdallāh] Ibn 'Awn and Ayyūb [al-Sakhtiyānī].[1147] He then abandoned his Shī'ī views.

Sufyān died in al-Baṣrah in the year 161/October 9, 777–September 27, 778, during the caliphate of al-Mahdī.

Al-Ḥasan b. Ṣāliḥ, also called Ḥayy.[1148]

Ḥasan's *kunyah* was Abū 'Abdallāh. He was a pious, virtuous man, skilled in religious law and inclined to love the family of the Prophet (*ahl bayt rasūl Allāh*). He adhered to the principle that one ought to protest against evil by all the means available to one.[1149] He transmitted many traditions and was reliable (*thiqah*).

It was reported that al-Ḥasan gave his daughter in marriage to 'Īsā b. Zayd b. 'Alī b. al-Ḥusayn.[1150] [The caliph] al-Mahdī gave an

---

1147. See Ibn Ḥajar, *Tahdhīb*, I, 348, V, 303.

1148. There is some confusion about this Ḥayy, a name sometimes considered to belong to al-Ḥasan's grandfather, rather than being another name for his father. In addition, Ḥayy had a twin brother; note the confusion in Ibn Ḥazm, *Jamharat*, 396. Al-Ḥasan belonged to the southern tribe Bakīl of the Hamdān confederation and was an ascetic and an important Zaydī leader. The Zaydī schism of al-Ṣāliḥiyyah (also called Batriyyah; see note 1256, below) is attributed to him. See Ibn Ḥazm, *Jamharat*, 396; al-Shahrastānī, 120–21; van Arendonck, 83–86; Ṣubḥī, 98–100; Ibn al-Kalbī, *Nasab ma'add*, 523; al-Quhpā'ī, II, 116; Khalīfah b. Khayyāṭ, *Ta'rīkh*, 470; idem, *Ṭabaqāt*, 168; Ibn Ḥibbān, *Mashāhīr*, 268. In spite of his political importance, al-Ṭabarī never mentions him in the *Annals*.

1149. The precept *al-amr bi-al-ma'rūf wa-al-nahy 'an al-munkar* "enjoining what is good and prohibiting (or, protesting against) what is evil," is based on several Qur'ānic verses (3:104, 3:110, 3:114, 7:157, 9:67, 9:71, 9:112, 22:41, 31:17). It was variously interpreted and applied by diverse sects, movements, and persons, among them indeed the Zaydīs. See "Amr be-Ma'rūf," *Encyclopaedia Iranica*, I, 92–95 (W. Madelung); Crone and Hinds, 62; al-Khallāl; Ṣubḥī, 147; Ibn al-Murtaḍā, V, 464–66; al-Ghazālī, VII, 1186–1275.

1150. Son of the eponymous founder of the Zaydī Shī'ah. He participated in the revolt of Muḥammad b. 'Abdallāh al-Nafs al-Zakiyyah against al-Manṣūr and continued to be considered a menace by the next caliph, al-Mahdī. See van Arendonck, 61, 83; al-Ṭabarī, *Ta'rīkh*, III, 258, 448, 503.

order to seek out [and arrest] both ʿĪsā and al-Ḥasan. He exerted his efforts in pursuing them.

According to Ibn Saʿd[1151]—al-Faḍl b. Dukayn: I saw al-Ḥasan b. Ṣāliḥ attending the Friday prayer with everyone else; then he went into hiding [the next] Sunday, [remaining thus] until his death. Al-Mahdī could not capture him or ʿĪsā b. Zayd. Al-Ḥasan hid together with ʿĪsā b. Zayd in the same place for seven years. The latter died six months before al-Ḥasan.

Ḥasan b. Ḥayy was an inhabitant of al-Kūfah, where he died in [2517] the year 167/August 5, 783–July 23, 784 at the age of sixty-two or [sixty]-three.

According to Yaḥyā b. Maʿīn: Al-Ḥasan b. Ṣāliḥ b. Ḥayy was born in the year 100/August 3, 718–July 23, 719.

According to al-ʿAbbās—Yaḥyā: Al-Ḥasan b. Ṣāliḥ is Ḥasan b. Ṣāliḥ b. Ṣāliḥ b. Muslim b. Ḥayyān. People call [him] Ibn Ḥayy, but it is Ibn Ḥayyān.

Jaʿfar b. Ziyād al-Aḥmar.[1152]

He was the client of Muzāḥim b. Zufar of the Taym al-Ribāb.[1153]

He was an inhabitant of al-Kūfah, where he died in the year 167. He was a Shīʿī and transmitted many traditions.

ʿUbaydallāh b. al-Ḥasan b. al-Ḥuṣayn b. Mālik b. Mālik b. al-Khashkhāsh b. Ḥubāb b. al-Ḥārith b. Khalaf b. Mujfir b. Kaʿb b. al-ʿAnbar b. ʿAmr b. Tamīm.[1154]

He was a jurist and counts among the educated and clever people of al-Baṣrah. He was appointed judge of al-Baṣrah after Sawwār b. ʿAbdallāh.[1155]

1151. Ibn Saʿd, VI, 261.

1152. A companion of the sixth Shīʿī imām, Jaʿfar al-Ṣādiq. See al-Ṭūsī, 161; Ibn ʿAdī, II, 564–66.

1153. One of the tribal chiefs (*ashrāf*) in al-Kūfah, of the Taym b. ʿAbd Manāh, one of the constituents of the northern confederation al-Ribāb. See Ibn Ḥazm, *Jamharat*, 199; Ibn Ḥajar, *Tahdhīb*, X, 100–1.

1154. The tribe's name is the Banū al-ʿAnbar. See Khalīfah b. Khayyāṭ, *Taʾrīkh*, 457, 462, 470, 472–73; Ibn Ḥibbān, *Mashāhīr*, 251; Wakīʿ, II, 88–123.

1155. The reference here is not to the famous judge whose biography is recorded in Wakīʿ, II, 57–88, and many other sources but to his grandfather who bore the same name and was also a judge. See al-Mizzī, *Tahdhīb*, XII, 238; Ibn Ḥajar, *Tahdhīb*, IV, 236–37.

According to 'Alī b. Muḥammad [al-Madā'inī]: 'Ubaydallāh b. al-Ḥasan was born in the year 100 or 106/May 29, 724–May 18, 725 and was appointed judge in the year 157/November 21, 773–November 10, 774.

According to Ibn Sa'd[1156]—Aḥmad b. Makhlad, who heard 'Ubaydallāh b. al-Ḥasan al-'Anbarī recite on the pulpit [in the mosque] of al-Baṣrah:

Where are the kings, [who were] heedless of their fate
until the cup of death was given them to taste?
Our riches for inheritors we accumulate;
our houses we build for time to lay waste.

[2518] According to Muḥammad b. 'Umar [al-Wāqidī]: 'Ubaydallāh b. al-Ḥasan al-'Anbarī died in Dhū al-Qa'dah 168/May–June 784.

According to Fuḍayl b. 'Abd al-Wahhāb—Mu'ādh b. Mu'ādh: I came to visit 'Ubaydallāh b. al-Ḥasan, the judge of al-Baṣrah, and said "I see that you are well today, God be praised." He replied:

In the evening [I look] healthy, but do not be deceived.
Dawn will bring death, [and I shall be deceased].

At dawn I heard the cry [announcing his death].

Ḥasan b. Zayd b. Ḥasan b. 'Ali b. Abī Ṭālib.[1157]

Al-Ḥasan b. Zayd's *kunyah* was Abū Muḥammad.

He fathered [many children]: Muḥammad; al-Qāsim; Umm Kulthūm bt. al-Ḥasan, who was married to the caliph Abū al-'Abbas [al-Saffāḥ] and bore him two children, both of whom died young; 'Ali; Zayd; Ibrāhīm; 'Īsā; Ismā'īl; Isḥāq al-A'war (the one-eyed); and 'Abdallāh.

Ḥasan b. Zayd was a pious man. Abū Ja'far [al-Manṣūr] appointed him governor of Medina, a position he held for five years. Al-Manṣūr then found fault with [al-Ḥasan] and became angry

1156. Not in Sachau's edition or *al-Qism al-mutammim*; cf. the short biography of this 'Ubaydallāh, in Ibn Sa'd, VII/2, 42.

1157. He collaborated with the 'Abbāsid caliph al-Manṣūr against the other members of the Ḥāshimī family, in particular his cousins, the rebels Muḥammad al-Nafs al-Zakiyyah and Ibrāhīm, sons of 'Abdallāh b. al-Ḥasan. See al-Ṭabarī, *Ta'rīkh*, III, 144–45, and also 149, where he appears to be double-crossing the caliph; Khalīfah b. Khayyāṭ, *Ta'rīkh*, 466; idem, *Ṭabaqāt*, 272; al-Balādhurī, *Ansāb*, III (Dūrī), 269.

with him. He dismissed him [from office], confiscated all his property, and sold it, then imprisoned him. Muḥammad al-Mahdī [b. al-Manṣūr], who was his father's heir apparent, wrote secretly to ʿAbd al-Ṣamad b. ʿAlī:[1158] "Beware! beware!"

Al-Ḥasan remained in prison until Abū Jaʿfar's death. Al-Mahdī then freed al-Ḥasan, brought him to his [court], and returned to him all the property he had lost.[1159] Al-Ḥasan remained with al-Mahdī until the latter set out for the pilgrimage, in the year 168/July 785.

Al-Ḥasan b. Zayd came along with him. Water was scarce on the way, and al-Mahdī feared thirst for his companions, so he returned and did not perform the pilgrimage that year. Al-Ḥasan b. Zayd, however, continued [the journey] in the direction of Mecca but fell ill for a few days, then died in al-Ḥājir[1160] and was buried there. This occurred in the year 168/785.

Mālik b. Anas b. Mālik b. Abī ʿĀmir b. ʿAmr b. al-Ḥārith b. [2519]
Ghaymān b. Khuthayl b. ʿAmr b. al-Ḥārith, that is, Dhū Aṣbaḥ of the Ḥimyar.[1161]

As a pension recipient, he counted as one of the Taym b. Murrah of the Quraysh;[1162] [his name was attached to that of] ʿAbd al-Raḥmān b. ʿUthmān b. ʿUbaydallāh al-Taymī.[1163]

Mālik's *kunyah* was Abū ʿAbdallāh. He was the *muftī* and traditionist (*muḥaddith*) of his town in his time.[1164]

According to al-ʿAbbas b. al-Walīd—Ibrāhīm b. Ḥammād al-Zuhrī al-Madīnī—Mālik: [The caliph] al-Mahdī said to me "O Abū ʿAbdallāh, prepare a book [of law], and I shall make the community adhere to it." Mālik replied: "O Commander of the Faith-

---

1158. Al-Manṣūr's paternal uncle, as well as his governor in Mecca and al-Ṭaʾif; see al-Ṭabarī, *Taʾrīkh*, III, 359, 377.

1159. Cf. al-Ṭabarī, III, 377, 454.

1160. See Yāqūt, *Muʿjam al-buldān*, II, 182.

1161. On the clan the Dhū Aṣbaḥ, offspring of al-Ḥārith b. Mālik b. Zayd of the Ḥimyar; see al-Ḥimyarī, 164–65. On Mālik, for whom the Mālikī school of law was named, see "Mālik b. Anas," *EI²*, VI, 262–65 (J. Schacht); Schacht, *Origins*, passim; Ibn Ḥibbān, *Mashāhīr*, 223; Ibn ʿAbd al-Barr, *al-Intiqāʾ*, 9–63.

1162. See p. 92, above.

1163. The only Qurashī bearing this name and recorded by Ibn Qudāmah, 330, died in the year 73/692. See also Ibn al-Athīr, *Usd al-ghābah*, III, 308–9; al-Ṣafadī, XVIII, 184.

1164. That is, in Medina, or, country, i.e., the Ḥijāz.

ful, as for that quarter, I can accomplish that"; he was pointing toward the Maghrib. "As for Syria, you know who lives among them"; he meant al-Awzāʿī. "And, as for the people of Iraq, they are the people of Iraq."[1165]

As for Muḥammad b. ʿUmar [al-Wāqidī], he related this story about Mālik in a way different from the version of al-ʿAbbas–Ibrāhīm b. Ḥammād. Muḥammad b. ʿUmar's account runs as follows. According to al-Ḥārith [b. Muḥammad]—Ibn Saʿd[1166]—Muḥammad b. ʿUmar [al-Wāqidī]—Mālik b. Anas: When Abū Jaʿfar al-Manṣūr performed the pilgrimage he summoned me. I went in to see him and conversed with him. He was asking me questions, and I replied. Then he said: "I have decided to take the books you have written"—meaning the *Muwaṭṭa'*—"and have several copies made of them. I shall then send a copy to every Islamic city and order the people to act according to what is written in this book, not to turn from it to any other, and to abandon everything else of this science [of religious law], which is innovation. For I have come to realize that the authentic knowledge [of religious law] is that possessed and transmitted by the people of Medina." I said: "O Commander of the Faithful, do not do this, for [various] views and traditions (*aḥādīth*) have already reached the public, and people have transmitted material in various ways. Every community adheres to those of the different opinions and
[2520] lessons that have reached it first; it follows these and holds them. It is difficult to make people renounce their beliefs, so leave them as they are, and let the people of every city choose for themselves." Al-Manṣūr said "Upon my soul, had you agreed with me in this, I would have ordered it."

According to Ibn Saʿd—Ibn Abī Uways: Mālik b. Anas was ill for a few days [before he died]. I asked people of our family about what he said on the brink of death, and they replied that he uttered the words "There is no god but Allāh and Muḥammad is His Mes-

1165. That is, nothing can be done about them. This anecdote reflects the actual [but later] distribution of certain schools of law over the Islamic provinces. The Mālikī school became prevalent in the Maghrib.

1166. Ibn Saʿd, *al-Qism al-mutammim*, 440–41; cf. the short biography of Mālik in Ibn Saʿd, VII/1, 140. The next two references to Ibn Saʿd in al-Ṭabarī's text are in *al-Qism al-mutammim*, 443, 444.

senger," then recited "The affair belongs to Allāh before and after."[1167] He died in the morning of Rabīʿ I 14, 179/June 7, 795, during the caliphate of Hārūn [al-Rashīd]. ʿAbdallāh b. Muḥammad b. Ibrāhīm b. Muḥammad b. ʿAlī b. ʿAbdallāh b. al-ʿAbbās, son of Zaynab bt. Sulaymān b. ʿAlī, said the prayer over his bier. [This ʿAbdallāh] was known by his mother's name, that is, ʿAbdallāh b. Zaynab, and was governor of Medina at the time.[1168] ʿAbdallāh said the prayer over Mālik at the funeral place; then Mālik was buried in al-Baqīʿ.[1169]

Mālik was eighty-five years old when he died.

Ibn Saʿd said: I mentioned this to Muṣʿab b. ʿAbdallāh al-Zubayrī, and he said: "I know better than anyone else about Mālik's death. He died in Ṣafar 179/April–May 795.

ʿAbdallāh b. al-Mubārak.[1170]

His *kunyah* was Abū ʿAbd al-Raḥmān. He was a pursuer and transmitter of knowledge, and his erudition in the fields of religious law, philology, history, and poetry was great.[1171] Moreover, he was an ascetic and a generous person.

Ibn al-Mubārak was born in the year 118/January 20, 736–January 7, 737, and lived in Khurāsān. He died in Hīt[1172] on his way back from a raid against the Byzantines in the year 181/March 5, 797–February 21, 798, at the age of sixty-three.

According to ʿAbdallāh b. Aḥmad b. Shabbawayh—ʿAlī b. al- [2521]
Ḥasan—Ibn al-Mubārak: We transmit what the Jews and the

1167. Qur'ān 30:3; trans. Bell, II, 393.

1168. According to al-Ṭabarī, *Ta'rīkh*, III, 739, he was governor of Mecca. See also Ibn Ḥazm, *Jamharat*, 31.

1169. See al-Samhūdī, III, 920, on Mālik's tomb.

1170. A famous jurist and traditionist of Persian origin, a client of the northern Tamīmī tribe the Banū Ḥanẓalah. He was a *ḥāfiẓ* and an ascetic, known for his enthusiasm in the matter of *jihād*. See F. Sezgin, I, 95; Bonner, 19–28; al-Sayrawān, 119, 243; Khalīfah b. Khayyāṭ, *Ṭabaqāt*, 323; Ibn Ḥibbān, *Mashāhīr*, 309; Ibn al-Nadīm, I, 552, II, 936.

1171. I have translated *adab* as philology, following Lane's lexicon, even though Ibn al-Mubārak is not usually considered a philologist. The other possibility, "belles lettres," seemed to me less feasible. It should also be noted that Sezgin omits to mention his poetry, but see Ibn al-Nadīm, I, 552, II, 936.

1172. A town in Iraq on the right bank of the Euphrates; see *EI*², III, 510 (M. Streck).

Christians say, but we cannot transmit what the Jahmiyyah say.[1173]

According to ʿAbdallāh b. Aḥmad b. Shabbawayh—ʿAlī b. al-Ḥasan: We asked ʿAbdallāh b. al-Mubārak "What do you know of our Lord?" He said: "He is above seven heavens, on the throne, separated from His creation by a partition. We do not believe, like the Jahmiyyah, that He is found here"; [he said this] pointing with his hand to the ground.[1174]

Muḥammad b. al-Ḥasan.[1175]

His *kunyah* was Abū ʿAbdallāh, and he was a client of the Shaybān.

Muḥammad's origin was in the Jazīrah.[1176] His father, who had been enlisted in the Syrian army, came to Wāsiṭ,[1177] where Muḥammad was born in the year 132/August 20, 749–August 8, 750. He grew up in al-Kūfah and became a student of tradition, attending lectures [on the subject]. He later participated in Abū Ḥanīfah's assembly and studied from him. The latter's school [of law] became the predominant one as far as Muḥammad b. al-Ḥasan was concerned, and he was known as a Ḥanafī.

Muḥammad settled in Baghdad, where people studied [traditions] from him. He later moved to al-Raqqah[1178] when the caliph, Hārūn al-Rashīd, was staying there.[1179] Hārūn appointed him

---

1173. Muslim scholars debated the permissibility of transmitting from Jews as well as Christians; see Kister, "*Ḥaddithū*'." On the Jahmiyyah, an early and somewhat obscure sect, see "Djahmiyya," *EI*², II, 388 (W. M. Watt).

1174. The theological issue here is apparently that of anthropomorphism, vehemently rejected by the Jahmiyyah in all its forms. Their argument here would be that God is found everywhere, not seated on a throne in Heaven. See, e.g., al-Ashʿarī, *Ibānah*, 59–64; al-Lālikāʾī, I, 30–31.

1175. Known as al-Shaybānī, author of several law books, among them *al-Siyar al-kabīr*, dealing with the law of war and translated by Majid Khadduri as *The Islamic Law of Nations* (Baltimore, 1966). See Khalīfah b. Khayyāṭ, *Taʾrīkh*, 494; idem, *Ṭabaqāt*, 328; Ibn Qutaybah, *Maʿārif*, 219. Although a judge, his biography is not recorded by Wakīʿ.

1176. That is, Mesopotamia.

1177. A city in the center of Iraq built by the Umayyad governor al-Ḥajjāj b. Yūsuf, to accomodate the Syrian troops stationed in Iraq. "Wāsiṭ," *EI*¹, IV, 1128–32 (M. Streck).

1178. Ancient Kallinikos, a city in the Jazīrah on the left bank of the Euphrates; see "al-Raḳḳa," *EI*², VIII, 410–14 (M. Meinecke).

1179. See al-Ṭabarī, *Taʾrīkh*, III, 1180.

judge of al-Raqqah but later dismissed him, so he returned to Baghdad. When Hārūn left for al-Rayy the first time[1180] he ordered Muḥammad to accompany him, which he did. Muḥammad then died in al-Rayy in the year 189/December 8, 804–November 26, 805.

Yūsuf b. Ya'qūb b. Ibrāhīm al-Qāḍī (the Judge).[1181]

He learned tradition and studied the [method of] analogy (*ra'y*).[1182] He held the office of judge in west Baghdad while his father was still alive and acted as the leader of prayer on Fridays in the city of Abū Ja'far[1183] by order of Hārūn [al-Rashīd]. He remained judge there until his death in Rajab 193/April–May 808.

Sufyān b. 'Uyaynah b. Abī 'Imrān.[1184]

His *kunyah* was Abū Muḥammad; he was a client of the Banū 'Abdallāh b. Ruwaybah, [a clan of] the Banū Hilāl b. 'Āmir b. Ṣa'ṣa'ah.

Sufyān's father, 'Uyaynah, was a functionary of Khālid b. 'Abdallāh al-Qasrī.[1185] When Khālid was dismissed from [his office as governor of] Iraq and replaced by Yūsuf b. 'Umar al-Thaqafī, the latter pursued Khālid's functionaries, so they fled from him. 'Uyaynah b. Abī 'Imrān went away and settled in Mecca. [2522]

According to Ibn Sa'd[1186]—Muḥammad b. 'Umar [al-Wāqidī]: Sufyān b. 'Uyaynah told me that he was born in the year 107/May

---

1180. See al-Ṭabarī, *Ta'rīkh*, III, 704–5.

1181. An Arab of the tribe of Bajīlah, commonly known as Yūsuf b. Abī Yūsuf, his father being the famous jurist and judge Abū Yūsuf, who served the caliph al-Mahdī and his son Hārūn al-Rashīd. See "Abū Yūsuf," *EI²*, I, 164–65 (J. Schacht); Wakī', III, 254–64. For Yūsuf himself, see Wakī', III, 256, 282.

1182. *Ra'y*, literally, "[personal] opinion," is a term referring to the use of human reasoning as a source of religious law. The opponents of this method advocated the use of tradition instead; see "Aṣḥāb al-ra'y," *EI²*, I, 692 (J. Schacht)

1183. That is, in Baghdad; cf. Wakī', III, 282. The office of judge in Baghdad was divided between two officials from the days of the fourth 'Abbāsid caliph, al-Hādī; see Wakī', III, 254.

1184. A famous Kūfan jurist, Qur'ān interpreter, and *ḥāfiẓ*. See F. Sezgin, I, 96; Khalīfah b. Khayyāṭ, *Ta'rīkh*, 351, 505; idem, *Ṭabaqāt*, 284; Ibn Ḥibbān, *Mashāhīr*, 235–36; al-Quhpā'ī, III, 133–34; al-Sayrawān, 97, 234. Wakī', in his *Akhbār al-quḍāh*, records many legal decisions transmitted by him.

1185. Governor of Iraq under the Umayyad caliph Hishām. See *EI²*, IV, 925–27 (G. Hawting); Hawting, *First Dynasty*, 81–88; Leder, 141–95 (including a literary analysis of the reports).

1186. Ibn Sa'd, V, 364, but note the difference in the text.

19, 725–May 7, 726. He had pursued knowledge at an early [age] and become a *ḥāfiẓ*. He lived a long life, until his peers died and he outlived them.

Sufyān related: I went to the Yemen in the years 150/February 6, 767–January 25, 768, and 152/January 14, 769–January 3, 770, while Maʿmar [b. Rāshid] was still alive. [Sufyān] al-Thawrī preceded me [there] by a year.

According to Ibn Saʿd[1187]—al-Ḥasan b. ʿImrān b. ʿUyaynah, Sufyān's nephew: I was with my uncle on the last pilgrimage he made [to Mecca], in the year 197/(August) 813. When he was at Jamʿ,[1188] having prayed, he lay on his mat and said to me: "I have arrived at this place for seventy years, and each time I said 'O Lord, do not make this the last time that I visit this place.' I feel embarrassed before God about asking Him this so many times." Sufyān returned [from his pilgrimage] and died the next year, on Saturday, the 1st of Rajab 198/February 25, 814. He was buried at al-Ḥajūn. He was ninety-one years old [when he died].

Uways al-Qaranī.

He was of the Murād, that is, Yuḥābir b. Mālik, who belonged to the Madhḥij. His [genealogy] is as follows: Uways b. ʿĀmir b. Jazʾ b. Mālik b. ʿAmr b. Saʿd b. ʿUṣwān b. Qaran b. Radmān b. Nājiyah b. Murād; that is, Yuḥābir b. Mālik.

[2523] Uways was a pious, virtuous man. It was reported that he was killed in [the battle of] Ṣiffīn.

According to [Muḥammad b. al-ʿAlāʾ] Abū Kurayb—Abū Bakr—Hishām—al-Ḥasan—the Prophet: [Many people, in numbers] as many as [the whole of] Rabīʿah and Muḍar, will enter paradise thanks to the intercession of one man of my community. According to Hishām—Ḥawshab—[al-Ḥasan]:[1189] That is Uways al-Qaranī.

Ḥuḍayn b. al-Mundhir al-Raqāshī.[1190]

1187. Ibn Saʿd, V, 365.

1188. Another name for Muzdalifah, where certain rituals of the Pilgrimage are held; see Yāqūt, *Muʿjam al-buldān*, II, 118.

1189. See Ibn Ḥajar, *Iṣābah*, I, 116 s.v. Uways.

1190. A minor tribal chief in al-Baṣrah, of the Raqāshiyyūn, a branch of the

His *kunyah* was Abū Muḥammad. In battle his *kunyah* was Abū Sāsān.

According to al-Ḥārith—'Alī b. Muḥammad [al-Madā'inī]—'Alī b. Mālik al-Jushamī: Al-Ḥuḍayn b. al-Mundhir was mentioned in the presence of al-Aḥnaf [b. Qays], and people said "He had become a chieftain before his beard was fully grown." Al-Aḥnaf retorted "Leadership [is befitting] the blackness [of the hair] before one becomes white haired."

Ḥuḍayn b. al-Mundhir was carrying the banner of [the confederation of] Rabī'ah in the battle of Ṣiffīn.[1191]

I think that 'Alī b. Abī Ṭālib was referring to al-Ḥuḍayn when he recited the following verse:

Who is he who holds the black banner, with its fluttering
  shadow?
  When called "Advance, Ḥuḍayn," he [bravely] does so.[1192]

According to Muḥammad b. Ma'mar—Rawḥ—'Alī b. Suwayd b. Manjūf: We came to Ḥuḍayn b. al-Mundhir, Abū Sāsān, and he said "Welcome to a visitor who is not boring."

Sa'd b. al-Ḥārith b. al-Ṣimmah b. 'Amr b. 'Atīk b. 'Amr b. Mabdhūl, that is, 'Āmir b. Mālik, b. al-Najjār.[1193]

Sa'd b. al-Ḥārith was killed in [the battle of] Ṣiffin, [fighting] on the side of 'Alī b. Abī Ṭālib.[1194]

Al-Ḥārith al-A'war (the one-eyed) b. 'Abdallāh b. Ka'b b. Asad b. [2524]
Yakhlud b. Ḥūth, that is, 'Abdallāh b. Sabu' b. Ṣa'b b. Mu'āwiyah

---

northern Banū Shaybān. He was one of 'Alī's commanders in the battle of Ṣiffīn and served as governor of Iṣṭakhr. He died in the year 99/717–18. See Crone, *Slaves*, 113; Ibn Ḥazm, *Jamharat*, 317; Naṣr b. Muzāḥim, 205 and passim; Ibn Ḥajar, *Tahdhīb*, II, 340–41; Khalīfah b. Khayyāṭ, *Ṭabaqāt*, 200, 204; Ibn Ḥibbān, *Mashāhīr*, 157; idem, *Thiqāt*, IV, 191; al-Balādhurī, *Ansāb*, IVa, 22, 93.

1191. See Hinds, "Banners and Battle-Cries."

1192. A part of a poem; see Naṣr b. Muzāḥim, 289–90.

1193. An Anṣārī Companion of the Prophet and a supporter of 'Alī. See Ibn Ḥajar, *Iṣābah*, II, 23; Ibn al-Athīr, *Usd*, II, 372; Ibn Sa'd, V, 59, gives only his genealogy.

1194. Not recorded by Naṣr b. Muzāḥim or al-Quhpā'ī.

b. Kathīr b. Mālik b. Jusham b. Ḥāshid b. Jusham b. Khaywān b. Nawf b. Hamdān.[1195]

Ḥūth is the brother of Sabīʿ, Abū Isḥāq al-Sabīʿī's clan.

Al-Ḥārith was one of ʿAlī [b. Abī Ṭālib]'s prominent companions. He worshipped God by [studying] the religious law, the science of the division of inheritances,[1196] and arithmetic.

According to Zakariyā' b. Yaḥyā—Aḥmad b. Yūnus—Zā'idah—al-Aʿmash [Sulaymān b. Mihrān]—Ibrāhīm—al-Ḥārith: I learned reading in one year and the Revelation in three years.[1197]

[Muḥammad] Ibn Ḥumayd—Yaḥyā b. Wāḍiḥ—Ismāʿīl—Makhlad—Abū Isḥāq: Al-Ḥasan b. ʿAlī [b. Abī Ṭālib] wrote to al-Ḥārith [the following] "Indeed, you used to hear from ʿAlī things I did not hear." So [al-Ḥārith] sent to him a camel load [of written material].

Abū al-Sā'ib—Ibn Fuḍayl—Mujālid [b. Saʿīd]—[ʿĀmir b. Shuraḥbīl] al-Shaʿbī: I learned from al-Ḥārith al-Aʿwar the science of inheritances and arithmetic. He was the best of all people at arithmetic.

Yaḥyā b. Maʿīn claimed that al-Ḥārith died in the year 65/August 18, 684–August 7, 685. All the historians agree that al-Ḥārith's death occurred during the time when ʿAbdallāh b. Yazīd al-Anṣārī acted as governor of al-Kūfah on behalf of ʿAbdallāh b. al-Zubayr. ʿAbdallāh b. Yazīd said the prayer over al-Ḥārith's bier in his time [as governor of] al-Kūfah.[1198]

Al-Ḥārith was an inhabitant of al-Kūfah, where he [also] died. He had belonged to the Shīʿah of the Commander of the Faithful ʿAlī b. Abī Ṭālib.

[2525] ʿAmr b. Salimah b. ʿAbdallāh b. Salimah b. ʿAmīrah b. Muqātil b. al-Ḥārith b. Kaʿb b. ʿAlwā b. ʿAlyān b. Arḥab b. Duʿām, of the [tribe of] Hamdān.[1199]

1195. The clan's name is Ḥūth. See Ibn Ḥajar, *Tahdhīb*, II, 126–28; Khalīfah b. Khayyāṭ, *Ṭabaqāt*, 149–50 (only his genealogy); al-Khashshī, 81–83; al-Amīn, XVIII, 293–320; Naṣr b. Muzāḥim, 121.

1196. *ʿIlm al-farā'iḍ*. See Lane, s.v. *f.r.ḍ*.

1197. *Taʿallamtu al-qur'āna fī sanatin wa-l-waḥya fī thalāthi sinīna. Waḥya* ("inspiration") must refer to the Qur'ān, so the word *qur'ān* must be used here in its original meaning, i.e., "reading."

1198. On ʿAbdallāh, see al-Balādhurī, *Ansāb*, V, 190, 207–9, 273–74.

1199. The clan's name is Arḥab. See Ibn Ḥazm, *Jamharat*, 396, 476; Ibn Ḥibbān, *Mashāhīr*, 165.

ʿAmr was a tribal noble (*sharīf*).[1200] Al-Ḥasan b. ʿAlī sent him, together with Muḥammad b. al-Ashʿath b. Qays, [as go-between] in the matter of the agreement between himself and Muʿāwiyah [b. Abī Sufyān].[1201] Muʿāwiyah admired ʿAmr's appearance and eloquence and asked him "Are you a Muḍarī?" ʿAmr replied "No," then recited [the following verses]:

I belong to people whose glory lies in God's apostle,
    [superior to] all people, both nomad and settled.
Our fathers are men of excellence, raised to glory
    by the noble origins of their ancestry.
Our mothers, what women! noble [and fine];
    nobility is inherited in their line.
They gathered camphor, musk, and ambergris,[1202]
    but you, son of Hind, are a gatherer of the gum of trees.

[ʿAmr then said]: "I am a man of Hamdān, of the tribe of Arḥab."

Abū ʿAbd al-Raḥmān al-Sulamī.[1203]

His name was ʿAbdallāh b. Ḥabīb.

According to Ibn Saʿd[1204]—Ḥajjāj b. Muḥammad—Shuʿbah [b. al-Ḥajjāj]: Abū ʿAbd al-Raḥmān did not hear [traditions] from ʿUthmān [b. ʿAffān], but he did hear from ʿAlī [b. Abī Ṭālib].

Abū ʿAbd al-Raḥmān was a companion of ʿAlī [b. Abī Ṭālib] and a resident of al-Kūfah.[1205] He died there during the time when Bishr b. Marwān was governor of Iraq.[1206]

1200. Tribal nobles (*ashrāf*) played a pivotal role in the politics of the Umayyad period. They first formed a link between the government and the tribesmen, then lost this position. Although many of them continued to serve the rulers, others tended to initiate or join rebellions. However, they never formed a definite party, and each acted in his own interest; see Crone, *Slaves*.

1201. See al-Ṭabarī, *Taʾrīkh*, II, 1–4; al-Balādhurī, *Ansāb*, III (Maḥmūdī), 40–43, 51–52.

1202. The reference is to Yemeni perfume production.

1203. Of the tribe of Sulaym. See Khalīfah b. Khayyāṭ, *Taʾrīkh*, 271; idem, *Ṭabaqāt*, 153; Ibn Ḥibbān, *Mashāhīr*, 164. Considered a *ḥāfiẓ* and a Qurʾān reader by al-Suyūṭī; al-Sayrawān, 116; Ibn al-Jazarī, I, 413–14. He was a supporter of ʿAlī according to al-Ṣadr, 24.

1204. Ibn Saʿd, VI, 119.

1205. According to a report in al-Ṭabarī, *Taʾrīkh*, I, 3319, Abū ʿAbd al-Raḥmān participated in the battle of Ṣiffīn, but cf. Naṣr b. Muzāḥim, 288, where the phrasing suggests that he was not present there.

1206. In the years 71–73 or 74/691–93 or 694; see al-Ṭabarī, *Taʾrīkh*, II, 816, 834, 852.

According to [Muḥammad] Ibn Ḥumayd—Jarīr [b. 'Abd al-Ḥamīd]—'Aṭā' [b. al-Sā'ib]: Someone asked Abū 'Abd al-Raḥmān: "I beseech you in the name of God, [tell me] when it was that you [began] to hate 'Alī? Was it not when he doled out allowances in al-Kūfah and omitted to give you any or your family?" Abū 'Abd al-Raḥmān replied "If you beseech me in the name of God [to tell you], the answer is yes."

[2526] Kumayl b. Ziyād b. Nahīk b. Haytham b. Sa'd b. Mālik b. al-Ḥārith b. Ṣuhbān b. Sa'd b. Mālik b. al-Nakha', of the Madhḥij.[1207]

Kumayl participated in [the battle of] Ṣiffīn on the side of 'Alī [b. Abī Ṭālib]. He was a tribal chief (*sharīf*), and his people obeyed him.[1208]

When al-Ḥajjāj [b. Yūsuf] came to al-Kūfah he ordered that Kumayl be brought before him and had him executed.

According to Abū Kurayb [Muḥammad b. al-'Alā']—Abū Bakr—al-A'mash [Sulaymān b. Mihrān]: Al-Ḥajjāj said to al-'Uryān [b. al-Haytham b. al-Aswad]:[1209] "O 'Uryān, what became of Kumayl? Did he not participate in the revolt against us in [the battle of] al-Jamājim?"[1210] 'Uryān replied; [al-A'mash] mentioned the exchange, then [continued the story]: Al-Ḥajjāj waited until [one day] Kumayl came to collect his pension (*'aṭā'*). Al-Ḥajjāj seized him and said to him "You are the one who treated [the caliph] 'Uthmān in such-and-such a manner," and he said [other] things [as well].[1211] Kumayl retorted: "Do not put so much blame on me, and do not pour a mountain of sand on me.[1212] It was only that the

---

1207. One of the tribal nobles of al-Kūfah (*ashrāf*), of the Nakha'. Kumayl was involved in the uprising against 'Uthmān and even went to Medina to kill him himself, but his plan failed, and he had only an exchange of blows with the caliph. After the murder of 'Uthmān he joined 'Alī's camp. See al-Ṭabarī, *Ta'rīkh*, I, 2908, 2917, 2921, 3034–35; Khalīfah b. Khayyāṭ, *Ṭabaqāt*, 148.

1208. This is especially noted because obedience to tribal leaders was not a matter of course, nor did these leaders have any institutionalized coercive power. It is perhaps worthy of note that he is not mentioned by Naṣr b. Muzāḥim in *Waq'at Ṣiffīn*.

1209. Of the same tribe as Kumayl, al-Nakha'. He was chief of the *shurṭah* in the time of Yazīd II. See al-Ṭabarī, *Ta'rīkh*, II, 672–73, 1407, 1655; Ibn Manẓūr, *Mukhtaṣar*, XVII, 31–32; Ibn al-Kalbī, *Nasab ma'add*, 297.

1210. Cf. al-Ṭabarī, *Ta'rīkh*, II, 1076–77.

1211. Cf. al-Ṭabarī, *Ta'rīkh*, I, 3036, II, 1097.

1212. Cf. Qur'ān 73:14.

man had slapped me, then asked me to be patient, and I forgave him, so which one of us was the evil one?" Al-Ḥajjāj gave the order, and Kumayl was put to death.

Kumayl had participated in [the battle of] al-Qādisiyyah.

ʿUmar al-Akbar (Senior) b. ʿAlī b. Abī Ṭālib b. ʿAbd al-Muṭṭalib b. Hāshim.[1213]

His mother was al-Ṣahbāʾ, that is, Umm Ḥabīb bt. Bujayr b. al-ʿAbd b. ʿAlqamah b. al-Ḥārith b. ʿUtbah b. Saʿd b. Zuhayr b. Jusham b. Bakr b. Ḥubayb b. ʿAmr b. Ghanm b. ʿUthmān b. Taghlib b. Wāʾil. She was a war captive, taken by Khālid b. al-Walīd during his raid on the Banū Taghlib at ʿAyn al-Tamr.

ʿUbaydallāh b. ʿAlī b. Abī Ṭālib.[1214]

His mother was Laylā bt. Masʿūd b. Khālid b. Mālik b. Ribʿī b. Sulmā b. Jandal b. Nahshal b. Dārim.[1215] [2527]

ʿUbaydallāh was killed at al-Madhār in the battle between the followers of Muṣʿab b. al-Zubayr and the followers of al-Mukhtār. He was in Musʿab's camp.[1216]

Abū Naḍrah.[1217]

His name was al-Mundhir b. Mālik b. Qiṭʿah.

He was of the ʿAwaqah, a clan of the ʿAbd al-Qays.[1218]

According to ʿAlī b. Muḥammad [al-Madāʾinī]: Abū Naḍrah participated in the revolt of Ibn al-Ashʿath. He belonged to the Shīʿah of ʿAlī.

1213. A son of ʿAlī by a Taghlibī woman, apparently more involved in family disputes over inheritance than in politics. See al-Balādhurī, *Ansāb*, III (Maḥmūdī), 230–32, 268; al-Ṭabarī, *Taʾrīkh*, I, 3472; Ibn Qudāmah, 137; Khalīfah b. Khayyāṭ, *Taʾrīkh*, 260; idem, *Ṭabaqāt*, 230.

1214. Khalīfah b. Khayyāṭ, *Taʾrīkh*, 225; Ibn Qudāmah, 137.

1215. An important branch of the Tamīm; see Ibn Ḥazm, *Jamharat*, 229–33.

1216. See al-Ṭabarī, *Taʾrīkh*, II, 721; al-Balādhurī, *Ansāb*, V, 260, 271.

1217. A Baṣran Successor. See Ibn al-Kalbī, *Jamharah*, 590; Khalīfah b. Khayyāṭ, *Taʾrīkh*, 352; idem, *Ṭabaqāt*, 209; Ibn Ḥibbān, *Mashāhīr*, 155.

1218. Called ʿAwq by Ibn al-Kalbī; see *Jamharah*, 590. The ʿAbd al-Qays was a large tribe of the northern confederation of Rabīʿah; see Ibn Ḥazm, *Jamharat*, 295–96.

Nawf al-Bikālī, that is, Nawf b. Faḍālah, the son of Ka'b's wife.[1219]

Nawfal b. Musāḥiq b. 'Abdallāh b. Makhramah b. 'Abd al-'Uzzā b. Abī Qays b. 'Abd Wadd b. Naṣr b. Mālik b. Ḥisl b. 'Āmir b. Lu'ayy.[1220]

Al-Ashtar.[1221]

His name was Mālik b. al-Ḥārith b. 'Abd Yaghūth b. Maslamah b. Rabī'ah b. al-Ḥārith b. Jadhīmah b. Sa'd b. Mālik b. al-Nakha', of the Madhḥij.

According to Isḥāq b. Ibrāhīm b. Ḥabīb b. al-Shahīd—Abū Bakr b. 'Ayyāsh—'Alqamah:[1222] I said to al-Ashtar "You had opposed the murder of 'Uthmān, so what made you go out [to fight on 'Alī's side] in al-Baṣrah?"[1223] Al-Ashtar replied: "These people[1224] had given 'Alī the oath of allegiance, then broke it. It was ['Abdallāh] b. al-Zubayr who incited 'Ā'ishah to participate in the revolt (*khurūj*).[1225] I had prayed to God that I should meet him, and indeed we met in combat. As my arm is strong, I was not satisfied until I raised myself in my saddle and hit him so that he fell." ['Alqamah] said: I asked "Is he the one who exclaimed 'Kill me

---

1219. That is, Ka'b al-Aḥbār. Nawf was of the tribe of Ḥimyar and lived in Egypt and Damascus. He was a storyteller (*qāṣṣ*, see p. 276, n. 1251, below) and a traditionist and acted as prayer leader (imām) in Damascus. See Khalīfah b. Khayyāṭ, *Ṭabaqāt*, 308; Ibn Ḥibbān, *Mashāhīr*, 196; Ibn Ḥajar, *Tahdhīb*, X, 436–37; al-Sam'ānī, I, 382; Ibn Manẓūr, *Mukhtaṣar*, XXVI, 220–23; Ibn Sa'd, VII/2, 160.

1220. One of the notables of the Qurashī clan 'Āmir b. Lu'ayy, associated with the Umayyad caliph al-Walīd b. 'Abd al-Malik. See al-Zubayrī, 427; Ibn Qudāmah, 483; Ibn Ḥibbān, *Mashāhīr*, 64.

1221. One of the most fervent supporters of 'Alī b. Abī Ṭālib; he died on his way to Egypt to assume the post of governor on behalf of 'Alī. See "al-Ashtar," *EI*², I, 704 (L. Veccia Vaglieri); Khalīfah b. Khayyāṭ, *Ta'rīkh*, 174, 177, 184, 186; idem, *Ṭabaqāt*, 148; al-Kashshī, 61–63; Naṣr b. Muzāḥim, passim; al-Kindī, 25–28.

1222. Al-Ṭabarī, *Ta'rīkh*, I, 3200.

1223. The reference is to the battle of the Camel. Al-Ashtar is said to have come to Medina with 'Uthmān's opponents but to have kept himself uninvolved in the murder of the caliph. See al-Ṭabarī, *Ta'rīkh*, I, 2954, 2999, but see also 'Abd al-Malik Ibn Ḥabīb, 113.

1224. That is, Ṭalḥah b. 'Ubaydallāh and al-Zubayr b. al-'Awwām; see 'Abd al-Malik Ibn Ḥabīb, 114.

1225. *Khurūj* is here used in both its senses simultaneously (to go out and to rebel), referring to the revolt against 'Alī, and to the fact that the rebels left Medina in order to rally support in al-Baṣra. On the role played by 'Abdallāh b. al-Zubayr, see al-Ṭabarī, *Ta'rīkh*, I, 3109, 3126, 3200. The report clearly reflects an 'Alid argument, refuting as it does the allegation that 'Alī's supporters were 'Uthmān's murderers.

together with Mālik?' " Al-Ashtar replied: "No, I left him, and I do not remember anything [of the sort]. That one was 'Abd al-Raḥmān b. 'Attāb b. Asīd.[1226] We met, we exchanged two blows, and we both fell, whereupon he started calling 'Kill me together with Mālik,' but they did not know who Mālik was; had they known, they would have killed me." Abū Bakr b. 'Ayyāsh then said: This is [as vivid] as though you witnessed it yourself;[1227] it was told to me by al-Mughīrah—Ibrāhīm—'Alqamah, [who said]: I said to al-Ashtar [etc.]. [2528]

Shabath b. Rib'ī b. Ḥuṣayn b. 'Uthaym b. Rabī'ah b. Zayd b. Riyāḥ b. Yarbū' b. Ḥanẓalah, of the tribe of Tamīm.[1228]

His *kunyah* was Abū 'Abd al-Quddūs.

According to Ibn Sa'd[1229]—al-Faḍl b. Dukayn—Ḥafṣ b. Ghiyāth—al-A'mash [Sulaymān b. Mihrān]: I was present at Shabath's funeral. The slaves, the slave girls, the noblemen, the she camels (*nūq*)—[al-A'mash] mentioned other sorts as well—all were divided into separate respective groups. I saw them wailing for him and beating their faces with grief.[1230]

According to Ibn 'Abd al-A'lā—al-Mu'tamir—his father—Anas—Shabath: I am the first who led the Ḥarūriyyah.[1231] Someone said: "This is nothing to be proud of."

Al-Musayyab b. Najabah b. Rabī'ah b. Riyāḥ b. 'Awf b. Hilāl b. Shamkh b. Fazārah.[1232]

1226. A member of the Umayyad family, who was killed in the battle of the Camel. See Ibn Qudāmah, 199; al-Zubayrī, 193. Note the circumstances of his death: He receives a blow aimed at 'Abdallāh b. al-Zubayr; see Ibn Ḥajar, *Iṣābah*, III, 72.

1227. *Hādhā ka-annaka shāhiduhu.* The version in al-Ṭabarī, *Ta'rīkh*, I, 3200, does not make much sense.

1228. The clan's name is Banū Riyāḥ b. Yarbū'. Shabath was a chieftain of his clan in his time. He showed extreme fickleness in his political behavior, having joined and deserted almost every possible camp and persuasion. See Crone, *Slaves*, 118; Khalīfah b. Khayyāṭ, *Ṭabaqāt*, 153.

1229. Ibn Sa'd, VI, 150.

1230. These are in fact practices prohibited by Islam. See p. 156, above.

1231. That is, the first Khawārij. When the fourth caliph, 'Alī b. Abī Ṭālib, decided to comply with Mu'āwiyah's request for arbitration, many of his supporters opposed his decision and deserted his camp. They encamped at Ḥarūrā', hence the name Ḥarūriyyah, and this group later became the Khārijī sect. See al-Ṭabarī, *Ta'rīkh*, I, 3341, 3362–63; al-'Irāqī, 10.

1232. Of the northern tribe Fazārah. See Ibn Ḥibbān, *Mashāhīr*, 174; al-Balādhurī, *Futūḥ* (de Goeje), 247, 352.

He took part in [the battle of] Qādisiyyah and fought on the side of 'Alī [b. Abī Ṭālib] in his battles.

Al-Musayyib was killed in the battle of 'Ayn al-Wardah with the Repenters (*tawwābūn*). These [people] had repented having forsaken al-Ḥusayn [b. 'Alī].[1233] Al-Huṣayn b. Numayr[1234] sent the [detached] head of al-Musayyib b. Najabah to [the governor], 'Ubaydallah b. Ziyād,[1235] at the hand of Adham b. Muḥriz al-Bāhili. 'Ubaydallāh b. Ziyād sent it to [the caliph], Marwān b. al-Ḥakam, and he set it up [in public] in Damascus.

[2529] Ḥujr b. 'Adī b. Jabalah b. 'Adī b. Rabī'ah b. Mu'awiyah al-Akramīn b. al-Ḥārith b. Mu'āwiyah b. al-Ḥārith b. Mu'āwiyah b. Thawr b. Muratti' b. Kindiyy (sic).[1236]

He is [called] Ḥujr al-Khayr (the good one). His father was 'Adī al-Adbar (the sore backed), [thus nicknamed] because he had been stabbed after having turned his back [to the enemy].

Ḥujr b. 'Adī lived both in pre-Islamic and Islamic times. Some scholars mention that he came to the Prophet together with his brother Hāni' b. 'Adī.[1237] He was the one who conquered Marj 'Adhrā'.[1238]

Ḥujr's pension was 2,500 [dirhams per year].[1239] He was a companion of 'Alī [b. Abī Ṭālib] and fought on his side in [the battles of] the Camel and Ṣiffīn.[1240]

1233. See pp. 50–51, above.

1234. A general of the Sufyānids. See "al-Ḥuṣayn b. Numayr," *EI²*, III, 620–21 (H. Lammens and V. Cremonesi); Crone, *Slaves*, 97.

1235. One of the important governors of Iraq for the Sufyānids, son of the previous governor and adopted brother of Mu'āwiyah, Ziyād b. Abīhi (= b. Abī Sufyān); see Hawting, *First Dynasty*, 41, 50, 53, 55.

1236. The tribe's name is Kindah, not as written here. Ḥujr was a Kindī leader in al-Kūfah, charged as an instigator of opposition to the Umayyads. He was executed by Mu'awiyah in the year 51/671. See "Ḥudjr b. 'Adī," *EI²*, III, 545 (H. Lammens); Hasson, 133–39; Hawting, *First Dynasty*, 41; al-Ṭabarī, *Ta'rīkh*, II, 112–155; al-Balādhurī, *Ansāb*, IVa, 211–36; Ibn Ḥibbān, *Mashāhīr*, 144; al-Kashshī, 94; al-Quhpā'ī, II, 85–86; al-Ḍabbī, 20; al-Amīn, XX, 141–227; Ibn Sa'd, VI, 151–54.

1237. This makes him a Companion (*ṣaḥābī*). Certain historians, however, deny him the title; see Lammens, "Ḥudjr b. 'Adī."

1238. A village 15 miles away from Damascus, conquered by Khālid b. al-Walīd; see al-Ṭabarī, *Ta'rīkh*, I, 2103. Ḥujr is not mentioned here among the conquerors, and Yāqūt, *Mu'jam al-buldān*, III, 625, treats this information cautiously. Marj 'Adhrā' was the place where Ḥujr was imprisoned, executed, and buried. See Yāqūt, III, 625; al-Ṭabarī, II, 137. The translation in Blankenship, 103, is erroneous.

1239. This was the highest pension, called *sharaf al-'aṭā'*.

1240. See, e.g., Naṣr b. Muzāḥim, 103–4, 117, and passim.

Ṣaʿṣaʿah b. Ṣūḥān.[1241]
He died in al-Kūfah during the caliphate of Muʿāwiyah.

ʿAbd Khayr b. Yazīd al-Khaywānī, of the Hamdān.
His *kunyah* was Abū ʿUmārah. He participated on ʿAlī's side in [the battle of] Ṣiffin, where he excelled.

Al-Aṣbagh b. Nubātah b. al-Ḥārith b. ʿAmr b. Fātik b. ʿĀmir b. Mujāshiʿ b. Dārim.[1242]
He was the commander of the *shurṭah* for ʿAlī [b. Abī Ṭālib].
Al-Aṣbagh belonged to the party (*shīʿah*) of ʿAlī.

Ḥajjār b. Abjar b. Jābir b. Bujayr b. ʿĀʾidh b. Shurayṭ b. ʿAmr b. Mālik b. Rabīʿah b. ʿIjl.[1243]
He was a tribal noble (*sharīf*).

Muslim b. Nudhayr al-Saʿdī, of the Saʿd b. Zayd Manāh b. Tamīm.[1244]
He too belonged to the Shīʿah.

Abū ʿAbdallāh al-Jadalī.[1245]
His name was ʿAbadah b. ʿAbd b. ʿAbdallāh b. Abī Yaʿmur b. Ḥabīb b. ʿĀʾidh b. Mālik b. Wāʾilah b. ʿAmr b. Nāj b. Yashkur b. [2530]
ʿAdwān—whose [real] name was al-Ḥārith—b. ʿAmr b. Qays b. ʿAylān b. Muḍar.
ʿAdwān (the aggressor) was thus nicknamed because he had acted most aggressively against his brother Fahm b. ʿAmr and killed him.

1241. Of the ʿAbd al-Qays; see Ibn Ḥazm, *Jamharat*, 297. He was an important companion of ʿAlī b. Abī Ṭālib. See Khalīfah b. Khayyāṭ, *Ṭabaqāt*, 144; al-Kashshī, 64–65; al-Quhpāʾī, III, 212–14; al-Ḍabbī, 29; Naṣr b. Muzāḥim, passim.

1242. A member of the Mujāshiʿ family, a part of the Tamīmī clan Dārim. See Khalīfah b. Khayyāṭ, *Taʾrīkh*, 184; al-Quhpāʾī, I, 232–33; Ibn Ḥazm, *Jamharat*, 231.

1243. The tribe is ʿIjl b. Lujaym of the Bakr b. Wāʾil, and the family of Bujayr was a leading one. Ḥajjār was a tribal leader in al-Kūfah; see Ibn Ḥazm, *Jamharat*, 314. He was associated with the Umayyads, but during the second civil war he joined the Zubayrid party; see al-Balādhurī, *Ansāb*, IVa, 144, 22, V, 174, 225, 232, 296.

1244. Ibn Saʿd, VI, 159; Ibn Ḥibbān, *Thiqāt*, V, 398.

1245. A member of the Jadīlah of Qays. His name is variously given as ʿAbd al-Raḥmān, ʿUbayd, and ʿAbadah. See Khalīfah b. Khayyāṭ, *Taʾrīkh*, 259; idem, *Ṭabaqāt*, 143; Ibn Saʿd, VI, 159; al-Kashshī, 85–87; al-Quhpāʾī, IV, 114–15.

The mother of ʿAdwān and Fahm was Jadīlah bt. Murr b. Ṭābikhah, a sister of Tamīm b. Murr,[1246] and the [members of these tribes] were called after her.

Abū ʿAbdallāh al-Jadalī belonged to ʿAlī's party. He was the commander of the 800 [troops] sent by al-Mukhtār [to the Ḥijāz] to protect Muḥammad b. al-Ḥanafiyyah from [ʿAbdallāh] Ibn al-Zubayr when the latter wanted to kill him.[1247]

Abū al-Mutawakkil al-Nājī.[1248]
His name was ʿAlī b. Du'ād.

Abū al-Ṣiddīq al-Nājī.[1249]
His name was Bakr b. ʿAmr. He was a reliable [transmitter] (*thiqah*).

Dharr b. ʿAbdallāh b. Zurārah b. Muʿāwiyah b. ʿAmīrah b. Munabbih b. Ghālib b. Waqsh b. Qāsim b. Murhibah, of the Hamdān.[1250]

Dharr was an eminent storyteller (*qāṣṣ*)[1251] and a Murji'. He was one of the Qur'an readers (*qurrā'*) who participated in the revolt of ʿAbd al-Raḥmān b. Muḥammad b. al-Ashʿath against al-Ḥajjāj.[1252]

1246. That is, the eponym of the tribal confederation of Tamīm.

1247. See Sharon, *Black Banners*, 112–14; al-Ṭabarī, *Ta'rīkh*, II, 693–95. Abū ʿAbdallāh also acted as imām for al-Mukhtār; see al-Balādhurī, *Ansāb*, V, 267.

1248. Of the Banū Sāmah b. Lu'ayy, an obscure group claiming descent from the Quraysh; part of them were called after the ancestress Nājiyah. See Ibn Ḥazm, *Jamharat*, 173; Khalīfah b. Khayyāṭ, *Ta'rīkh*, 352; idem, *Ṭabaqāt*, 206; Ibn Ḥibbān, *Mashāhīr*, 148; al-Dūlābī, II, 105.

1249. A Baṣran *ḥāfiẓ* of the same tribe as the previous one. See Khalīfah b. Khayyāṭ, *Ta'rīkh*, 352; idem, *Ṭabaqāt*, 206; Ibn Ḥibbān, *Mashāhīr*, 150; Ibn Ḥajar, *Tahdhīb*, I, 426. According to Ibn Saʿd, VII/1, 164, he was not a trustworthy transmitter.

1250. A traditionist of the Murhibah, a branch of the southern Hamdān. See Ibn Ḥazm, *Jamharat*, 396; Ibn Ḥajar, *Tahdhīb*, III, 189.

1251. On the storytellers and their role in spreading traditions see "Ḳiṣṣa," *EI*², V, 185–87 (C. Pellat); Pedersen; Bosworth, *Medieval*, I, 27; Juynboll, *Muslim Tradition*, 11–12; Ṭahā al-Najm; al-Zubur; al-Suyūṭī, *Taḥdhīr al-khawāṣṣ*; Ibn al-Jawzī, *al-Quṣṣāṣ*; Muṣṭafā, II, 145–47.

1252. Dharr is not included in the list of the Qurrā' who supported Ibn al-Ashʿath given in Khalīfah b. Khayyāṭ, *Ta'rīkh*, I, 286. It is not certain that in the context of Ibn al-Ashʿath's revolt *qurrā'* meant Qur'ān readers. See Shaban, 50–54, 67–68, and passim; Sayed; Juynboll, "The Qurrā'."

According to Ibn Sa'd[1253]—al-Faḍl b. Dukayn—Abū Isrā'īl—al-Ḥakam: I heard Dharr say during [the battle of] al-Jamājim "Is it anything but the coolness of iron in the hand of an unbeliever [who is going to be] burned [in hell]?"

Ṭalḥah b. 'Abdallāh b. Khalaf b. As'ad, of the Banū Mulayḥ b. 'Amr b. Rabī'ah, of the Khuzā'ah.[1254] [2531]

His father, 'Abdallāh b. Khalaf, was killed in the battle of the Camel, [fighting] on the side of 'Ā'ishah and Ṭalḥah.

This Ṭalḥah was the one called Ṭalḥah of the Ṭalḥahs. He was the most generous Arab of his time.

Ṭalḥah's mother was Ṣafiyyah bt. al-Ḥārith b. Ṭalḥah b. Abī Ṭalḥah b. 'Abd al-'Uzzā b. 'Uthmān b. 'Abd al-Dār b. Quṣayy. His father's mother was Ḥumaynah bt. Abī Ṭalḥah b. 'Abd al-'Uzzā.[1255] He was called Ṭalḥah of the Ṭalḥahs because both Ṭalḥah and Abū Ṭalḥah were [among] his ancestors.

Sālim b. Abī Ḥafṣah.[1256]

His *kunyah* was Abū Yūnus.

He was an ultra-Shī'ī. When the Banū Hāshim came to power[1257] Dā'ūd b. 'Alī[1258] led the pilgrimage that year, that is, the year 132/749. Sālim b. Abī Ḥafṣah performed the pilgrimage that same year. He entered Mecca uttering the *talbiyah* formula thus "Here I am at your service, O God, here I am, O Annihilator

1253. Ibn Sa'd, VI, 205.

1254. A Baṣran tribal noble of a leading family. He was governor of Sijistān under the Umayyads, and his father, 'Abdallāh, had run the *dīwān* of al-Baṣrah for the caliphs 'Umar and 'Uthmān. See Khalīfah b. Khayyāṭ, *Ta'rīkh*, 245; Muḥammad Ibn Ḥabīb, *Muḥabbar*, 156, 306, 356, 377; Ibn Qudāmah, 117, 222.

1255. Both the mother and grandmother of Ṭalḥah were Qurashīs of the 'Abd al-Dār clan.

1256. He was a Kūfan client of the Banū 'Ijl, said to be a Murji' and a Zaydī of the Batriyyah/Ṣāliḥiyyah, for which see note 1148, above. See Ibn Sa'd, VI, 234; al-Kashshī, 202–4 (read "al-Ḥasan b. Ṣāliḥ b. Ḥayy" instead of "al-Ḥasan b. Ṣāliḥ b. Yaḥyā"), 249; al-Quhpā'ī, III, 89–92; al-Amīn, XXXIII, 377–85; Ibn Ḥibbān, *Majrūḥīn*, I, 343.

1257. That is, the 'Abbasids, in the year 132/749.

1258. Son of 'Abdallāh b. al-'Abbās and the most respected uncle of the first 'Abbasid caliphs, al-Saffāḥ and al-Manṣūr. He died in the year 133/750–51. See Lassner, 141, 144, 146; al-Dhahabī, *Siyar*, V, 444–45; al-Balādhurī, *Ansāb*, III (Dūrī), 87–89; Ibn Manẓūr, *Mukhtaṣar*, VIII, 149–52; Ibn al-Athīr, *Kāmil*, V, 409–16.

of the Banū Umayyah." Now Sālim was a loud-spoken person. Dā'ūd b. 'Alī heard him and asked "Who is this?" Someone replied "Sālim b. Abī Ḥafṣah." Dā'ūd was then informed about Sālim and his convictions.[1259]

According to Ibn Sa'd[1260]—'Alī b. 'Abdallāh—Sufyān—Sālim b. Abī Ḥafṣah: Whenever ['Āmir b. Shuraḥbīl] al-Sha'bī saw me he would recite the following:

O God's police, fall down and away
like a grain of barley.[1261]

Al-Khalīl b. Aḥmad, who founded the science of prosody, al-Farāhīdī.[1262]

He was of the 'Atīk.[1263]

According to Hishām b. Muḥammad [al-Kalbī]—Isḥāq b. Ibrāhīm b. Ḥabīb b. al-Shahīd—Quraysh b. Anas—al-Khalīl b.
[2532] Aḥmad, the founder of the science of grammar: When a book is copied three times it becomes [as if it were written] in Persian. Abū Ya'qūb commented: He meant that faults proliferate in it.

Qurashī [Women], [Younger] Contemporaries of Companions of the Prophet, from Whom Knowledge Was Transmitted

Fāṭimah bt. 'Alī b. Abī Ṭālib.[1264]

She transmitted traditions from her father, among them [the following]. According to Muḥammad b. al-Ḥusayn—al-Faḍl b.

1259. Al-Ṣafadī, XIII, 478–79.

1260. Ibn Sa'd, VI, 234, see also al-Amīn, XXXIII, 383.

1261. Al-Dhahabī, *Mīzān*, I, 367, adds that this was said in mockery. Al-Amīn, XXXIII, 383, explains that the reference is to the forces of al-Mukhtār (supposedly supported by Sālim); cf. Al-Balādhurī, *Ansāb*, V, 260.

1262. A Baṣran philologist of the Farāhīd, a branch of the Azd. He was the first Arab scholar to write a dictionary and set rules for prosody. See "al-Khalīl b. Aḥmad," *EI²*, IV, 962–64 (R. Sellheim); al-Sam'ānī, IV, 357; Ibn al-Nadīm, I, 93–96, II, 1030.

1263. A branch of the southern confederation of Azd. According to Ibn Ḥazm, however, al-Khalīl's clan, the Farāhīd, belonged to a different branch within the Azd; see Ibn Ḥazm, *Jamharat*, 367–71, 380.

1264. Her mother was a concubine, and it was reported that she knew no tradition from her father. According to a certain anecdote, she threw ashes in the face of a man who glorified her father. See Ibn Sa'd, VIII, 341–42; al-Amīn, XLII, 254–55.

Dukayn—Ibn Abī Nu'm; that is, al-Ḥakam b. 'Abd al-Raḥmān b. Abī Nu'm—Fāṭimah bt. 'Alī—her father—the Prophet: Whoever sets free a Muslim or a believer [slave], God will protect from hellfire every limb of his, in exchange for every limb of that [slave].

Umm Kulthūm bt. 'Alī b. Abī Ṭālib.[1265]

Fāṭimah bt. al-Ḥusayn b. 'Alī b. Abī Ṭālib.
She transmitted traditions from her father and others, among them the following. According to Muḥammad b. 'Ubayd al-Muḥāribī—Ṣāliḥ b. Mūsā al-Ṭalḥī—'Abdallāh b. al-Ḥasan—his mother Fāṭimah bt. al-Ḥusayn—her father—'Alī: The Prophet used to say, on entering the mosque: "O God, open the gates of Your mercy for me." Walking out he would say: "O God, open the gates of Your livelihood for me."

Umm Kulthūm bt. al-Zubayr b. al-'Awwām.[1266]
She transmitted the following. According to al-'Abbās b. al-Walīd—his father—al-Awzā'ī—Umm Kulthūm bt. Asmā' bt. Abī Bakr al-Ṣiddīq[1267]—'Ā'ishah, the Prophet's wife: The Prophet was at home when 'Alī b. Abī Ṭālib came [one day] and entered. When [2533]
he saw the Prophet praying he stood by his side, praying [too]. A scorpion emerged and reached the Prophet, then left him and approached 'Alī. When 'Alī saw it he hit it with his shoe. The Prophet did not find fault with 'Alī for killing it.

Umm Ḥumayd bt. 'Abd al-Raḥmān.[1268]
She transmitted the following. According to Sa'īd b. Yaḥyā al-Umawī—his father—['Abd al-Malik] Ibn Jurayj—'Abd al-Malik b.

1265. Daughter of Fāṭimah (Muḥammad's daughter) and wife of the second caliph, 'Umar. See Ibn Sa'd, VIII, 339–41; al-Zubayrī, 349; Ibn Ḥazm, *Jamharat*, 37, 38, 152; Ibn Qudāmah, 134–35.

1266. I could not trace her, not even in the works of the descendants of the family, al-Zubayrī's *Nasab quraysh* and al-Zubayr b. Bakkār's *Muwaffaqiyyāt*.

1267. That is, daughter of al-Zubayr, whose wife was Asmā'.

1268. Her identity is in fact unknown. See Ibn Ḥajar, *Tahdhīb*, XII, 492; al-Bandārī and Ḥasan, IV, 478. The identity of 'Abd al-Malik, son of Umm Ḥumayd, is not clear either; see Ibn Ḥajar, *Tahdhīb*, VI, 160. There was, however, a Companion bearing this name, wife of the Anṣārī Companion Abū Ḥumayd; see Ibn Ḥajar, *Iṣābah*, IV, 445.

ʿAbd al-Raḥmān—his mother Umm Ḥumayd bt. ʿAbd al-Raḥmān: I asked ʿĀʾishah about the middle prayer (*al-ṣalāh al-wusṭā*), and she said: During the Prophet's lifetime we used to read it in the first mode of reading, thus: "Keep the prayers, the middle prayer and the afternoon prayer, and stand [praying] in obedience to God."[1269]

According to ʿAbbās b. Muḥammad—Ḥajjāj [b. Muḥammad]—[ʿAbd al-Malik b. ʿAbd al-ʿAzīz] Ibn Jurayj—ʿAbd al-Malik b. ʿAbd al-Raḥmān—his mother, Umm Ḥumayd bt. ʿAbd al-Raḥmān, who asked ʿĀʾishah about the middle prayer mentioned by God [in the Qurʾān], and she replied: During the Prophet's lifetime we used to read it according to the first mode of reading, thus: "Keep the prayers, the middle prayer and the afternoon prayer, and stand [praying] in obedience to God."

Āminah.[1270]

She transmitted the following: According to al-Rabīʿ—Asad—Ḥammād b. Salamah—ʿAlī b. Zayd—Āminah, who asked ʿĀʾishah about the following verse: "Whether you reveal what is within you or conceal it, Allāh will reckon with you for it [and will forgive whom He willeth] and punish whom He willeth."[1271] ʿĀʾishah replied: "No one asked me about this verse since I had asked the Prophet, who said: 'O ʿĀʾishah, this is how God reckons with His servants, by striking them with fever, or misfortunes, or
[2534] pestilence. Even a piece of merchandise one puts in one's hand, loses, worries about, then finds under one's arm, [even that is an

1269. Qurʾān 2:238. The canonical reading omits the words "and the afternoon prayer." According to ʿĀʾishah's reading as recorded here, the "middle prayer" cannot be identical with the afternoon prayer. However, in the *Jamiʿ*, II, 555, al-Ṭabarī ascribes to ʿĀʾishah a reading that makes these two prayers identical. See the whole discussion in al-Ṭabarī, *Jamiʿ*, II, 553–68; and the various readings in Jeffery, 30, 122, 196, 214, 232, 235, 237.

1270. Perhaps Āminah bt. ʿAbdallāh; see note 1271, below.

1271. Qurʾān 2:285; trans. Bell, I, 41. According to al-Ṭabarī, *Jāmiʿ*, III, 149, ʿAlī b. Zayd transmitted this tradition from his mother, whose name is not mentioned. In ʿAlī's biography, Ibn Ḥajar, *Tahdhīb*, VII, 283, one Āminah bt. ʿAbdallāh is mentioned as one of ʿAlī's sources. I could not trace this Āminah. ʿAlī b. Zayd was a Baṣran, Qurashī transmitter who died in the year 127/744–45 (there are other versions). According to al-Zubayrī, 293, his mother was a concubine. See also Ibn Ḥibbān, *Majrūḥīn*, II, 103–4.

act of God]. So that the believer eventually emerges out of his sins like red gold dust emerging from the blacksmith's bellows.'"

The Following Are Names and Kunyahs *Mentioned in the* History[1272]

Abū Bakr.

Opinions differ as to his name. Most of the scholars hold that it was 'Abdallāh b. Abī Quḥāfah. Others say that it was 'Atīq. As for Abū Quḥāfah, there is no disagreement over his name. It was 'Uthmān b. 'Āmir b. Ka'b b. Sa'd b. Taym b. Murrah.

Abū 'Ubaydah.[1273]
His name was 'Āmir b. 'Abdallāh b. al-Jarrāḥ.

Abū al-Arqam.[1274]
His name was 'Abd Manāf b. Asad b. 'Abdallāh al-Makhzūmī.

Abū Marthad al-Ghanawī.
He was an ally of 'Abd al-Muṭṭalib,[1275] and his name was Kannāz b. al-Ḥuṣayn or Kināz b. al-Ḥuṣayn.

1272. It is not clear whether or not the title applies only to this chapter or to the subsequent ones as well. In any case, in what follows al-Ṭabarī records *kunyahs*, nicknames, and names of people, regardless of whether or not they were already mentioned in the *Dhayl al-mudhayyal.* Moreover, he sometimes mentions the same person twice in one chapter, e.g., Tamīm al-Dārī (pp. 298, 302). Despite the chapter heading, some of these people are not mentioned in the *Ta'rīkh*, e.g., Abū al-Arqam (*Dhayl*, 2534); others figure there only once, e.g., 'Abdallāh b. Zayd 2539 = al-Ṭabarī, *Ta'rīkh*, I, 2894. Many, however, such as 'Alī b. Abī Ṭālib or al-Zubayr, occupy many pages in various places of the *Ta'rīkh.* I saw no point in overloading the footnotes with references. The reader is invited to use de Goeje's index or the indexes to the other volumes of the translation. On the other hand, I supply some details wherever al-Ṭabarī mentions none at all. Where no details are adduced, it means either that the person's biography was recorded before or that I could not trace the person.

1273. A close Companion of the Prophet and one of the army commanders during the conquests. He died in the plague of 'Amwās in Palestine in the year 18/639. See "Abū 'Ubayda b. al-Djarrāḥ," *EI*², 158–59 (H. A. R. Gibb); al-Balādhurī, *Ansāb*, I, 223–24; Ibn Ḥibbān, *Mashāhīr*, 27; Khalīfah b. Khayyāṭ, *Ṭabaqāt*, 27–28, 300.

1274. Of the Qurashī clan Makhzūm, father of al-Arqam who gave the Prophet shelter in the beginning of his career. According to Ibn Ḥajar, *Iṣābah*, IV, 5, he was not a Companion, having apparently died before Islam. See also Ibn Qudāmah, 306, 388.

1275. That is, the Prophet's grandfather.

Abū Mūsā al-Ash'arī.
His name was 'Abdallāh b. Qays, and he was an ally of Abū Uḥayḥah Sa'īd b. al-'Āṣ.

Abū Maḥdhūrah, the muezzin.
His name was Aws b. Mi'yar or Samurah b. 'Umayr. [Yaḥyā] Ibn Ma'īn said: It is Samurah b. Ma'īn.[1276]

Abū al-'Āṣ b. al-Rabī'.
[He was] the Prophet's son-in-law, [as] he was married to his daughter Zaynab. His name was Miqsam.

[2535] Abū Dharr.
Opinions differ as to his name. All experts on genealogy hold that it was Jundab b. Junādah, but, according to Abū Ma'shar Najīḥ, it was Burayr b. Jundab.

Abū Umāmah, Ṣudayy b. 'Ajlān al-Bāhilī.

Abū Bakrah, Nufay' b. Masrūḥ.[1277]
According to another view, his name was Masrūḥ.

Abū Laylā, Bilāl b. Bulayl b. Uḥayḥah b. al-Julāḥ.[1278]

1276. Probably Mi'yar, not Ma'īn, as in Ibn al-Athīr, *Usd al-ghābah* (see al-Ṭabarī, *Dhayl*, 2534 n. *f*). The two names are very similar graphically. Cairo, 669, and Dār al-Fikr, 679, also have Ma'īn.

1277. A slave from Ṭā'if, freed by the Prophet upon converting to Islam. He was half-brother of the governor of Iraq, Ziyād b. Abīhi (= b. Abī Sufyān). He lived in al-Baṣrah and died in the year 54/674. His children, having attained high positions under their uncle Ziyād, claimed descent from a respected, genuine Thaqafī. See Khalīfah b. Khayyāṭ, *Ṭabaqāt*, 54; al-Balādhurī, *Ansāb*, I, 367, 489–506, IVa, 163–65, 183–84, 194–95; Ibn Ḥibbān, *Mashāhīr*, 66–67; Ibn Qutaybah, *Ma'ārif*, 125–26.

1278. There are many versions of his name: Bilāl, Bulayl, Yasār, Dā'ūd, etc.; see p. 310, below. It is noteworthy that most, if not all, of these names are typical of slaves or foreign clients, and the uncertainty about Abū Laylā's name may arise from the debate between his grandson Muḥammad b. 'Abd al-Raḥmān b. Abī Laylā and his enemies over his own Arab descent; see Ibn Qutaybah, *Ma'ārif*, 216, and 320, below. However, it is generally accepted that Abū Laylā was an Anṣārī (Awsī) Companion who settled in al-Kūfah, supported 'Alī b. Abī Ṭālib, and participated in Ṣiffīn (though not recorded by Naṣr b. Muzāḥim). He died in the year 83/702–3 during the revolt of Ibn al-Ash'ath. See Khalīfah b. Khayyāṭ, *Ṭabaqāt*, 85, 135, 150; Ibn Ḥazm, *Jamharat*, 335; Ibn Ḥibbān, *Mashāhīr*, 82, 164; Ibn Ḥajar, *Iṣābah*, IV, 169–70; al-Dūlābī, I, 51; al-Mizzī, *Tahdhīb*, XXXIV, 238–39.

Abū Burdah b. Niyār.[1279]
He originated in the Quḍā'ah confederation, but he became an ally of the Banū Ḥārithah of the Aws.

Abū al-Dardā', 'Uwaymir b. Zayd, of the Banū al-Ḥārith b. al-Khazraj.[1280]

Abū 'Amrah, Bashīr b. 'Amr b. Miḥṣan.
He was the father of 'Abd al-Raḥmān b. Abī 'Amrah.

Abū Ayyūb al-Anṣārī, Khālid b. Zayd b. Kulayb.

Abū Qatādah.[1281]
Opinions differ as to his name. According to Ibn Isḥāq, it was al-Ḥārith b. Rib'ī, whereas others maintain that it was 'Amr b. Rib'ī. According to al-Wāqidī, it was al-Nu'mān b. Rib'ī.

Abū al-Yasar, Ka'b b. 'Amr.

Abū Hurayrah.[1282]
According to Hishām [b. Muḥammad al-Kalbī], his name was 'Umayr b. 'Āmir b. 'Abd Dhī al-Sharā, but al-Wāqidī says that it was 'Abd Shams and that he was renamed 'Abdallāh [upon embracing] Islam.[1283] Yet others hold that his name was 'Abd Nuhm or Sukayn or 'Abd Ghanm.

1279. An Anṣārī Companion and a supporter of 'Alī (not mentioned by Naṣr b. Muzāḥim) who died in Medina in the year 45/665–66. See Khalīfah b. Khayyāṭ, *Ta'rīkh*, 190; idem, *Ṭabaqāt*, 118; Ibn Ḥibbān, *Mashāhīr*, 49; Ibn Ḥajar, *Isābah*, IV, 18–19.

1280. A Companion of the Prophet, who lived in Syria and died in the year 32/652–53. See Khalīfah b. Khayyāṭ, *Ṭabaqāt*, 95; Ibn Ḥibbān, *Mashāhīr*, 84; al-Balādhurī, *Ansāb*, I, 271; al-Shayyāl, 14–31.

1281. An Anṣārī of the Banū Salimah (Khazraj), an eminent Companion of the Prophet, and a horseman, who died in the year 54/674. See Khalīfah b. Khayyāṭ, *Ta'rīkh*, 64, 70, 185, 211; idem, *Ṭabaqāt*, 102; Ibn Ḥibbān, *Mashāhīr*, 33–34.

1282. A close Companion of the Prophet of humble origins of the tribe of Daws, a branch of the southern Azd; see Ibn Ḥazm, *Jamharat*, 379. He was one of the most prolific traditionists, thousands of traditions being connected with his name (not all genuine, of course). See "Abū Hurayra," *EI*², I, 129 (J. Robson); Juynboll, *Authenticity*, chap. 7; Khalīfah b. Khayyāṭ, *Ṭabaqāt*, 114; Ibn Ḥibbān, *Mashāhīr*, 35; Muḥammad al-Khaṭīb.

1283. See note 234, above.

Abū Usayd al-Sā'idī, Mālik b. Rabī'ah.[1284]

Abū Ḥadrad al-Aslamī, Salāmah b. 'Umayr b. Abī Salāmah.[1285] Others say: 'Abd b. 'Umayr.

[2536] Abū Sa'īd al-Khudrī, Sa'd b. Mālik b. Sinān.

Abū Barzah al-Aslamī.[1286]
According to Hishām [b. Muḥammad al-Kalbī]: This is Naḍlah b. 'Abdallāh. Others say Naḍlah b. 'Ubayd b. al-Ḥārith, whereas, according to al-Wāqidī, it is 'Abdallāh b. Naḍlah.

Abū Zayd al-Anṣārī, Thābit b. Zayd b. Qays.[1287]
He belonged to the Banū al-Ḥārith b. al-Khazraj. He was one of the six who collected the Qur'ān.[1288]

Abū Wadā'ah al-Ḥārith b. Ḍubayrah b. Su'ayd, father of al-Muṭṭalib b. Abī Wadā'ah al-Sahmī.[1289]

1284. An Anṣārī Companion of the Prophet, of the Banū Sā'idah (Khazraj), who died in the year 40/660–61. See Khalīfah b. Khayyāṭ, *Ta'rīkh*, 142, 242; idem, *Ṭabaqāt*, 97; Ibn Ḥibbān, *Mashāhīr*, 44.

1285. He, his two sons, and his daughter Umm al-Dardā' were Companions of the Prophet, of the northern Aslam, a branch of Muḍar. See Ibn Ḥazm, *Jamharat*, 241–42. Khalīfah b. Khayyāṭ, *Ṭabaqāt*, 110.

1286. A Companion, of the Aslam tribe, who lived in al-Baṣrah and died after the year 64/683–84 in a raid to Khurāsān. See Khalīfah b. Khayyāṭ, *Ṭabaqāt*, 109, 187, 322; Ibn Ḥibbān, *Mashāhīr*, 68; Ibn Qutaybah, *Ma'ārif* 146.

1287. There are several Companions bearing this *kunyah*, many of them Anṣārīs. Oddly, the "one who collected (or, knew by heart) the Qur'ān" is not better known than the rest. See note 1288, below.

1288. See p. 22, above. Note that the *kunyah* of Sa'd al-Qāri' is also Abū Zayd. Apparently there is a confusion among several people. According to Ibn Ḥajar, *Iṣābah*, IV, 78, the "Abū Zayd who collected the Qur'ān" was called Qays b. al-Sakan, but he adduces other versions too, including "Sa'd b. 'Ubayd"; see also Ibn Ḥajar, III, 250; and p. 294, below, on the famous collector of the Qur'ān, Zayd b. Thābit.

1289. A rich Meccan merchant, of the Qurashī clan the Banū Sahm, a contemporary of the Prophet who embraced Islam after the Conquest of Mecca and transmitted a few traditions. See Ibn Ḥajar, *Iṣābah*, III, 425; al-Ṭabarī, *Ta'rīkh*, I, 1343, 1369; Ibn Ḥazm, *Jamharat*, 164.

Abū Līnah, 'Abdallāh b. Abī Karib, of the Banū Mu'āwiyah al-Akramīn.[1290]

Abū Sabrah, Yazīd b. Mālik b. 'Abdallāh b. Ju'fī.[1291]
He was the grandfather of Khaythamah b. 'Abd al-Raḥmān,[1292] the companion of [Sulaynān b. Mihrān] al-A'mash.

Abū al-Ḥamrā', Hilāl b. al-Ḥārith.

Abū Juḥayfah, Wahb al-Suwā'ī.[1293]

Abū Jum'ah, Ḥabīb b. Sibā'.[1294]

Abū al-A'war al-Sulamī, 'Amr b. Sufyān.[1295]

Abū 'Ayyāsh al-Zuraqī, Zayd b. al-Ṣāmit.[1296]

1290. Mentioned as a Companion. According to Ibn Ḥajar his son 'Iyāḍ was a companion of 'Alī b. Abī Ṭālib and apparently more famous than his father. Al-Ṭabarī, however, *Ta'rīkh*, II, 903, 908, mentions 'Iyāḍ as a commander in al-Ḥajjāj's army; see Ibn Ḥajar, *Iṣābah*, II, 362.

1291. Of the southern tribe Ju'fiyy. He came to the Prophet and received from him license to claim possession of the wadi of Ju'fiyy. See Ibn Ḥazm, *Jamharat*, 409–10; Ibn Sa'd, VI, 32; Ibn Ḥajar, *Iṣābah*, II, 399, s.v. 'Abd al-Raḥmān b. Abī Sabrah.

1292. A Kūfan jurist of the second century. See Ibn Sa'd, VI, 200–1; Ibn Ḥibbān, *Mashāhīr*, 166; al-Ṣafadī, XIII, 443; Ibn Ḥajar, *Tahdhīb*, III, 154.

1293. A Companion of the Prophet, of the Suwā'ah, a branch of the northern 'Āmir b. Ṣa'ṣa'ah; see Ibn Ḥazm, *Jamharat*, 273. He died in the year 74/693–94. See Khalīfah b. Khayyāṭ, *Ṭabaqāt*, 57, 132; Ibn Ḥibbān, *Mashāhīr*, 80.

1294. A Companion of the Prophet. There is disagreement both over his name and his genealogy. See Ibn Ḥajar, *Iṣābah*, IV, 33; Khalīfah b. Khayyāṭ, *Ṭabaqāt*, 124, 307; Ibn Ḥibbān, *Mashāhīr*, 94.

1295. A member of the tribe of Sulaym, a contemporary of the Prophet, but it is doubtful whether he was a Companion. The family was allied to the Umayyads in pre-Islamic times. Abū al-A'war later excelled as governor and army commander in the service of 'Umar, 'Uthmān, and Mu'āwiyah b. Abī Sufyān. See Lecker, *Banū Sulaym*, 118, 136–40, and passim; Ibn Ḥazm, *Jamharat*, 263–64; Khalīfah b. Khayyāṭ, *Ta'rīkh*, 175, 178; idem, *Ṭabaqāt*, 51, 308.

1296. An Anṣārī (Khazrajī) Companion of the Prophet, one of the famous horsemen. There is, however, disagreement over his name. See Khalīfah b. Khayyāṭ, *Ṭabaqāt*, 100; Ibn Ḥibbān, *Mashāhīr*, 38; Ibn Ḥajar, *Iṣābah*, IV, 142–43.

Abū Mas'ūd al-Anṣārī, 'Uqbah b. 'Amr.[1297]

[2537] Abū Lubābah, Rifā'ah b. 'Abd al-Mundhir.[1298]

Abū Ḥumayd al-Sā'idī, 'Abd al-Raḥmān b. Sa'd.[1299]

Abū Umāmah al-Anṣārī, As'ad b. Zurārah.[1300]

Abū Dujānah, Simāk b. Kharashah.[1301]

Abū al-Haytham b. al-Tayyihān, Mālik b. al-Tayyihān.[1302]

The Women Contemporary with the Prophet Who Gave Him the Oath of Allegiance and Are Known by Their Kunyahs

Umm Salamah bt. Abī Umayyah b. al-Mughīrah.

Her name was Hind bt. Suhayl b. al-Mughīrah; she was [one of the] Prophet's wives.

Umm Hāni' bt. Abī Ṭālib b. 'Abd al-Muṭṭalib.

1297. An Anṣārī (Khazrajī) Companion of the Prophet who took part in the 'Aqabah meeting. He was governor of al-Kūfah for 'Alī and died during his, or Mu'āwiyah's, caliphate. See Khalīfah b. Khayyāṭ, *Ta'rīkh*, 186; idem, *Ṭabaqāt*, 96; Ibn Ḥibbān, *Mashāhīr*, 75; al-Balādhurī, *Ansāb*, I, 245; al-Quhpā'ī, IV, 144.

1298. An eminent Anṣārī Companion of the Prophet, of the Awsī clan the Banū 'Amr b. 'Awf, said to have been one of the twelve leaders appointed by Muḥammad at the 'Aqabah meeting (*nuqabā'*, see note 1375, below), and the standard bearer of his clan in the conquest of Mecca. Nevertheless, there is disagreement over his name (Rifā'ah, Bashīr, Marwān). He died after the murder of 'Uthmān. See Khalīfah b. Khayyāṭ, *Ṭabaqāt*, 84; Ibn Ḥibbān, *Mashāhīr*, 37; Ibn Ḥajar, *Iṣābah*, IV, 168.

1299. An Anṣārī (Khazrajī) Companion of the Prophet and a Qur'ān reader who died in Medina at the end of Mu'āwiyah's caliphate. See Ibn Ḥibbān, *Mashāhīr*, 41; Khalīfah b. Khayyāṭ, *Ta'rīkh*, 216.

1300. One of the twelve leaders appointed by Muḥammad at the 'Aqabah meeting. He died before the Prophet arrived at Medina or shortly afterward. See Khalīfah b. Khayyāṭ, *Ta'rīkh*, 12–13; idem, *Ṭabaqāt*, 90–91; al-Balādhurī, *Ansāb*, I, 243, 252; al-A'ẓamī, *Kuttāb al-nabī*, 32–33.

1301. An eminent Anṣārī (Khazrajī) Companion of the Prophet, known for his courage and horsemanship, who was killed in the battle of al-Yamāmah. See Ibn Ḥibbān, *Mashāhīr*, 85; Ibn Sa'd, III/2, 101.

1302. An ally of the Khazrajī clan the Banū 'Abd al-Ashhal and a highly regarded Anṣārī Companion who died in the year 20 or 21/642. See Khalīfah b. Khayyāṭ, *Ta'rīkh*, 122; idem, *Ṭabaqāt*, 78; Ibn Ḥibbān, *Mashāhīr*, 32.

According to the transmitters of traditions and reports, her name was Fākhitah, but it was reported that, according to Hishām b. Muḥammad al-Kalbī, it was Hind.

Umm Ḥabībah bt. Abī Sufyān.
Her name was Ramlah.

Umm Sharīk.
Her name was Ghaziyyah bt. Jābir b. Ḥakīm.

Umm Ayman.
Her name was Barakah, and she was a client of the Prophet.

Umm al-Faḍl, Lubābah al-Kubrā bt. al-Ḥārith b. Ḥazn.
She was married to al-ʿAbbās b. ʿAbd al-Muṭṭalib.

Umm Maʿbad.
Her name was ʿĀtikah bt. Khālid b. Khulayf, of the Khuzāʿah. She is the one of whom it was reported that the Prophet passed by her [place] and she gave him hospitality and described him to her husband.

Umm al-Dardā' al-Kubrā, Khayrah bt. Abī Ḥadrad al-Aslamī. [2538]

Umm Bishr b. al-Barā' b. Maʿrūr, Khulaydah bt. Qays b. Thābit.[1303]

Umm al-Ḥakam bt. al-Zubayr b. ʿAbd al-Muṭṭalib b. Hāshim.

Umm Kulthūm bt. ʿUqbah b. Abī Muʿayṭ.[1304]

The Kunyahs *of People Who Outlived the Prophet and Were Known by Their Names, Not by Their* Kunyahs

The Commander of the Faithful, ʿAlī b. Abī Ṭālib.

1303. Wife of the Anṣārī al-Barā' b. Maʿrūr, one of the twelve leaders (*nuqabā'*) appointed by Muḥammad at the ʿAqabah meeting; see n. 1375 below. She herself belonged to the Ashjaʿ, a northern tribe whose territory lay near Medina. See Ibn Ḥazm, *Jamharat*, 249–50; al-Balādhurī, *Ansāb*, I, 246.

1304. An early convert of the Umayyad family. She was married to Zayd b. Ḥārithah and later to al-Zubayr b. al-ʿAwwām, ʿAbd al-Raḥmān b. ʿAwf, and ʿAmr b. al-ʿĀṣ. See Ibn Ḥajar, *Iṣābah*, IV, 491; Ibn Qudāmah, 212–13.

His *kunyah* was Abū al-Ḥasan after his son al-Ḥasan.

Ṭalḥah b. ʿUbaydallah.
His *kunyah* was Abū Muḥammad after his son Muḥammad.

Al-Zubayr b. al-ʿAwwām.
His *kunyah* was Abū ʿAbdallāh after his son ʿAbdallāh.

Saʿd b. Abī Waqqāṣ.
His *kunyah* was Abū Isḥāq after his son Isḥāq.

Saʿd b. Zayd.
His *kunyah* was Abū al-Aʿwar.[1305]

ʿAbdallāh b. al-ʿAbbās.
His *kunyah* was Abū al-ʿAbbās after his son al-ʿAbbās.

ʿUbaydallāh b. al-ʿAbbās, the latter's brother.
His *kunyah* was Abū Muḥammad after his son Muḥammad.

Al-Faḍl b. Al-ʿAbbās.
His *kunyah* was Abū Muḥammad after his son Muḥammad.

Al-Ḥusayn b. ʿAlī [b. Abī Ṭālib].
His *kunyah* was Abū ʿAbdallāh after his son ʿAbdallāh. The latter was killed together with his father, al-Ḥusayn.[1306]

ʿAbdallāh b. Jaʿfar b. Abī Ṭālib.
His *kunyah* was [Abū Jaʿfar] after his son Jaʿfar al-Akbar (senior).

Rabīʿah b. al-Ḥārith b. ʿAbd al-Muṭṭalib.
His *kunyah* was Abū Arwā after his daughter Arwā.

ʿAqīl b. Abī Ṭālib.
His *kunyah* was Abū Yazīd after his son Yazīd.

1305. The reference is to the famous Companion Saʿīd b. Zayd. Read Saʿīd for Saʿd; Cairo, 672, and Dār al-Fikr, 682, also have Saʿd. See Ibn Ḥajar, *Iṣābah*, IV, 9; al-Dūlābī, I, 11–12.

1306. In Karbalāʾ, in the year 61/680. See p. 50, above.

Zayd al-Ḥibb b. Ḥārithah. [2539]
His *kunyah* was Abū Usāmah after his son Usāmah.

Usāmah al-Ḥibb b. Zayd b. Ḥārithah.
His *kunyah* was Abū Muḥammad after his son Muḥammad.

'Ammār b. Yāsir, Abū al-Yaqẓān.

'Abdallāh b. Mas'ūd.
His *kunyah* was Abū 'Abd al-Raḥmān after his son 'Abd al-Raḥmān.

Al-Miqdād b. al-Aswad, of the Bahrā'.
His *kunyah* was Abū Ma'bad.

Khabbāb b. al-Aratt b. Jandalah b. Sa'd b. Zayd Manāh b. Tamīm.
His *kunyah* was Abū 'Abdallāh after his son 'Abdallāh.

Ḥāṭib b. Abī Balta'ah of the Lakhm.[1307]
He was an ally of al-Zubayr b. al-'Awwām. According to al-Wāqidī, his *kunyah* was Abū Muḥammad, whereas Yaḥyā holds that it was Abū Yaḥyā.

Al-Arqam b. Abī al-Arqam, of the Makhzūm.
His *kunyah* was Abū 'Abdallāh. Abū al-Arqam's name was 'Abd Manāf.

Ubayy b. Ka'b.[1308]
His *kunyah* was Abū al-Mundhir.

1307. A tribe of southern origin, from which the royal clan of al-Ḥīrah was also descended; see Ibn Ḥazm, *Jamharat*, 422–23. Ḥāṭib was an ally of a certain family in Mecca, where he lived, and was an early convert. He died in the year 30/650–51. See Khalīfah b. Khayyāṭ, *Ṭabaqāt*, 70; Ibn Ḥibbān, *Mashāhīr*, 42; al-Balādhurī, *Ansāb*, I, 323; Ibn Ḥajar, *Iṣābah*, I, 300.

1308. An Anṣārī Companion and secretary of the Prophet, credited with knowledge of the ancient scriptures and said to have participated in the collection of the Qur'ān; he died in Medina in the year 32/652–53. See Watt, *Bell's Introduction*, 37, 45, 49, 55; Jeffery, 114–16; Ibn al-Jazarī, I, 31; Khalīfah b. Khayyāṭ, *Ta'rīkh*, 143; idem, *Ṭabaqāt*, 88–89; Ibn Ḥibbān, *Mashāhīr*, 31; al-Sayrawān, 49; al-A'ẓamī, *Kuttāb al nabī*, 42–44.

'Abdallāh b. Zayd b. 'Abd Rabbihi.[1309]
He was the one who was shown in a dream [how] the call to prayer [should be performed].
His *kunyah* was Abū Muḥammad after his son Muḥammad.

Rifā'ah b. Rafi' b. Mālik.[1310]
His *kunyah* was Abū Mu'ādh after his son Mu'ādh.

Sa'd b. 'Ubādah b. Dulaym.[1311]
His *kunyah* was Abū Thābit.

Buraydah b. al-Ḥuṣayb b. 'Abdallāh.
His *kunyah* was Abū 'Abdallāh after his son 'Abdallāh. According to al-'Abbās—Yaḥyā: Buraydah al-Aslamī's [*kunyah*] was Abū Sahl.

Bilāl b. Rabāḥ, the muezzin.[1312]
His *kunyah* was Abū 'Abdallāh.

Thābit b. al-Ḍaḥḥāk, Abū Zayd.[1313]

1309. An Anṣārī Companion of the Prophet, who died in Medina in the year 32/652–53. See Khalīfah b. Khayyāṭ, *Ta'rīkh*, 143; idem, *Ṭabaqāt*, 96; Ibn Ḥibbān, *Mashāhīr*, 40; al-Balādhurī, *Ansāb*, I, 244, 273. These sources call him 'Abdallāh b. Zayd b. Tha'labah b. 'Abd Rabbihi.

1310. An Anṣārī Companion of the Prophet, of the Banū Zurayq (Khazraj), whose father was one of the twelve leaders (*nuqabā'*) appointed at the 'Aqabah meeting; see note 1375, below. He died in Medina during the caliphate of Mu'āwiyah. See Ibn Ḥibbān, *Mashāhīr*, 43; Khalīfah b. Khayyāṭ, *Ṭabaqāt*, 100, 250; al-Balādhurī, *Ansāb*, I, 245.

1311. One of the closest Anṣārī Companions of the Prophet, leader of the Khazraj and one of the twelve leaders (*nuqabā'*) appointed at the 'Aqabah meeting. After the Prophet's death the Anṣār attempted, but failed, to elect him leader of the community. He died in Syria during the caliphate of Abū Bakr or 'Umar. See "Sa'd b. 'Ubāda," *EI*[1], IV, 30–31 (K. V. Zettersteen); Khalīfah b. Khayyāṭ, *Ṭabaqāt*, 97 (note the difference in the *kunyah*), 303; Ibn Ḥibbān, *Mashāhīr*, 28–29; al-Balādhurī, *Ansāb*, 250, 252, 254, 580–82; Ibn Manẓūr, *Mukhtaṣar*, IX, 235–46.

1312. An Abyssinan slave bought and freed by Abū Bakr to save him from the tortures his master inflicted upon him for being a Muslim. He served as the Prophet's muezzin and crier and died in Syria in the year 20 or 21/642. See "Bilāl b. Rabāḥ," *EI*[2], I, 1215 (W. 'Arafat); al-Balādhurī, *Ansāb*, I, 184–93; Ibn Ḥibbān, *Mashāhīr*, 85; Khalīfah b. Khayyāṭ, *Ṭabaqāt*, 19, 298.

1313. There were two Anṣārīs bearing this name, apparently confused by Ibn Ḥazm, *Jamharat*, 354; cf. Ibn Ḥajar, *Iṣābah*, I, 193–94. Here the reference apparently is to Thābit b. al-Ḍaḥḥāk b. Khalīfah of the 'Abd al-Ashhal, Abū Zayd, who died in the year 45/665–66; see Ibn Ḥibbān, *Mashāhīr*, 68.

'Uthmān b. Ḥunayf. [2540]
His *kunyah* was Abū 'Abdallāh.

Ḥassān b. Thābit.
His *kunyah* was Abū al-Walīd.

Jābir b. 'Abdallāh b. Ḥarām.
His *kunyah* was Abū 'Abdallāh.

Ka'b b. Mālik, the poet.[1314]
His *kunyah* was Abū 'Abdallāh.

Jubayr b. Muṭ'im.
His *kunyah* was Abū 'Abdallāh after his son 'Abdallāh.

'Abd al-Raḥmān b. Abī Bakr.[1315]
His *kunyah* was Abū 'Abdallāh after his son 'Abdallāh.

Khālid b. al-Walīd b. al-Mughīrah.
His *kunyah* was Abū Sulaymān after his son Sulaymān.

'Amr b. al-'Āṣ.[1316]
His *kunyah* was Abū 'Abdallāh after his son 'Abdallāh.

Wāthilah b. al-Asqa'.[1317]

1314. An eminent Anṣārī (Khazrajī) Companion of the Prophet, a poet, and one of the twelve leaders (*nuqabā'*) appointed by Muḥammad at the 'Aqaba meeting. He died in the year 50/670 (there are other versions). See "Ka'b b. Mālik," *EI*², IV, 315–16 (W. M. Watt); Khalīfah b. Khayyāṭ, *Ṭabaqāt*, 102–3; Ibn Ḥibbān, *Mashāhīr*, 38; al-Balādhurī, *Ansāb*, I, 248.

1315. Son of the first caliph and brother of the Prophet's wife 'Ā'ishah, with whom he participated in the battle of the Camel; he died in the year 58/677–78. See Khalīfah b. Khayyāṭ, *Ṭabaqāt*, 18, 189; Ibn Ḥibbān, *Māshāhīr*, 34–35.

1316. A Meccan Companion of the Prophet, of the Qurashī clan the Banū Sahm. Although he was not an early convert, the Prophet entrusted him with important tasks, and he later played a major role in the conquests in Syria and Egypt. He was governor of Egypt until his dismissal by the third caliph, 'Uthmān, then received the post again from Mu'āwiyah as a reward for his support. He died in Egypt in the year 42 or 43/663–64. See "'Amr b. al-'Āṣ," *EI*², I, 451 (A. J. Wensinck); Khalīfah b. Khayyāṭ, *Ṭabaqāt*, 25–26; Ibn Ḥibbān, *Mashāhīr*, 93; al-Balādhurī, *Ansāb*, I, 168–74; Naṣr b. Muzāḥim, passim; Ibn Manẓūr, *Mukhtaṣar*, XIX, 232–54; al-Waqā.

1317. A poor Companion of the Prophet, of the Kinānī clan the Banū Layth, who died in the year 83/702. See Khalīfah b. Khayyāṭ, *Ta'rīkh*, 292; idem, *Ṭabaqāt*, 31; Ibn Ḥibbān, *Mashāhīr*, 86; al-Balādhurī, *Ansāb*, I, 272, IVa, 61.

His *kunyah* was Abū Qirṣāfah, but some hold that it was Abū al-Asqa', whereas Abū Qirṣāfah was [the *kunyah* of] Jandarah b. Khayshanah.[1318]

Ma'qil b. Yasār.[1319]
His *kunyah* was Abū 'Abdallāh. The canal Nahr Ma'qil in al-Baṣrah is called after him.[1320]

Qurrah b. Iyās, Abū Mu'āwiyah.[1321]

Ṣafwān b. al-Mu'aṭṭal.[1322]
His *kunyah* was Abū 'Amr.

Al-'Irbāḍ b. Sāriyah, Abū Najīḥ.[1323]

Al-Mughīrah b. Shu'bah.
His *kunyah* was Abū 'Abdallāh.

'Imrān b. Ḥuṣayn.[1324]

1318. Of the Kinānī clan the Banū Layth. He belonged to the Ahl al-Ṣuffah, that is, the group of poor Companions. He lived in al-Baṣrah and died in Syria in the year 83/702–3. See Khalīfah b. Khayyāṭ, *Ta'rīkh*, 292; idem, *Ṭabaqāt*, 174–75; Ibn Ḥibbān, *Mashāhīr*, 86; al-Balādhurī, *Ansāb*, I, 272. See also Ibn Ḥazm, *Jamharat*, 189; al-Dūlābī, I, 49; al-Mizzī, *Tahdhīb*, V, 149–50.

1319. A Companion of the Prophet, of the Muzaynah tribe. He lived in al-Baṣrah, where he was associated with the governor of Iraq Ziyād b. Abīhi and died during the caliphate of Mu'āwiyah. See Ibn Ḥazm, *Jamharat*, 202; Khalīfah b. Khayyāṭ, *Ta'rīkh*, 246; idem, *Ṭabaqāt*, 37; Ibn Ḥibbān, *Mashāhīr*, 66; Ibn Qutaybah, *Ma'ārif*, 129.

1320. See Yāqūt, *Mu'jam al-buldān*, IV, 845; Ibn Qutaybah, *Ma'ārif*, 129; al-Balādhurī, *Futūḥ* (Riḍwān), 352.

1321. A Companion of the Prophet, of the tribe of Muzaynah, who was killed in al-Baṣrah in a battle against the Khawārij in the year 64/683–84. See Khalīfah b. Khayyāṭ, *Ṭabaqāt*, 37, 176; Ibn Ḥibbān, *Mashāhīr*, 72.

1322. A Companion of the Prophet, of the tribe of Sulaym. He was accused of a liaison with the Prophet's wife 'Ā'ishah, but Qur'ānic verses exonerated 'Ā'ishah (the *ḥadīth al-ifk*). He lived in al-Baṣrah and was killed in a raid in the Jazīrah in the year 19/640. See Lecker, *Banū Sulaym*, 91–92; Khalīfah b. Khayyāṭ, *Ta'rīkh*, 216; idem, *Ṭabaqāt*, 51; Ibn Ḥibbān, *Mashāhīr*, 59; al-Balādhurī, *Ansāb*, I, 342, 452.

1323. A Companion of the Prophet, of the Sulaym, said to have been appointed by Muḥammad as tax collector of his clan. He later lived in Syria and died in the year 75/694–95 or before. See Lecker, *Banū Sulaym*, 94–98, 156; Khalīfah b. Khayyāṭ, *Ṭabaqāt*, 52; Ibn Ḥibbān, *Mashāhīr*, 87.

1324. A Companion of the Prophet, of the Khuzā'ah. He lived in al-Baṣrah and officiated as governor there and died in the year 52/672. See Khalīfah b. Khayyāṭ, *Ta'rīkh*, 49, 106, 128, 217; idem, *Ṭabaqāt*, 106; Ibn Ḥibbān, *Mashāhīr*, 66.

His *kunyah* was Abū Nujayd.

Sulaymān b. Ṣurad.
His *kunyah* was Abū Muṭarrif. His name had been Yasār, and the Prophet renamed him Sulaymān when he embraced Islam.[1325]

Salamah b. al-Akwaʿ.[1326]
His *kunyah* was Abū Iyās after his son Iyās. According to Yaḥyā, it was Abū Muslim.

ʿAbdallāh b. Abī Awfā.[1327]
His *kunyah* was Abū Muʿāwiyah.

ʿAbdallāh b. Abī Ḥadrad.[1328]
His *kunyah* was Abū Muḥammad.

ʿUqbah b. ʿĀmir al-Juhanī.[1329] [2541]
His *kunyah* was Abū ʿAmr, according to al-Wāqidī. According to al-ʿAbbās—Yaḥyā: His *kunyah* was Abū Ḥammād, but in another place he said Abū Asad.

Zayd b. Khālid al-Juhanī.[1330]
His *kunyah* was Abū Ṭalḥah.

1325. See n. 234, above.

1326. Or, Salamah b. ʿAmr b. al-Akwaʿ, a Companion of the Prophet, of the Aslam, known as a brave warrior and a very swift runner(!). He lived in Medina where he died in the year 74/693–94. See Ibn Ḥajar, *Iṣābah*, II, 66–67; Khalīfah b. Khayyāṭ, *Taʾrīkh*, 268; idem, *Ṭabaqāt*, 111; Ibn Ḥibbān, *Mashāhīr*, 42.

1327. A Companion of the Prophet, of the Aslam. He lived in al-Kūfah, where he died in the year 86/705. See Khalīfah b. Khayyāṭ, *Ṭabaqāt*, 110; Ibn Ḥibbān, *Mashāhīr*, 83; al-Balādhurī, *Ansāb*, I, 248.

1328. A Companion of the Prophet, of the Aslam. See Khalīfah b. Khayyāṭ, *Taʾrīkh*, 48, 265; idem, *Ṭabaqāt*, 110–11; Ibn Ḥibbān, *Mashāhīr*, 49.

1329. A famous Companion of the Prophet, of the Juhaynah tribe, known as a Qurʾān reader. He is said to have had his own version of the Qurʾān; cf. Watt, *Bell's Introduction*, 45; and p. 22, above. ʿUqbah was governor of Egypt for Muʿāwiyah and died in the year 58/677–78. See Khalīfah b. Khayyāṭ, *Taʾrīkh*, 181, 214; idem, *Ṭabaqāt*, 221, 292; Ibn Ḥibbān, *Mashāhīr*, 94; Ibn Ḥajar, *Iṣābah*, II, 489; al-Sayrawān, 128; al-Kindī, 35–36.

1330. An early Companion, apparently of some importance, as he was one of the standard bearers of his tribe in the conquest of Mecca. See Ibn Ḥajar, *Iṣābah*, I, 565; Ibn Ḥibbān, *Mashāhīr*, 36.

Ma'bad b. Khālid, Abū Raw'ah al-Juhanī.[1331]

Al-Barā' b. 'Āzib.[1332]
His *kunyah* was Abū 'Umārah.

Usayd b. Ẓuhayr.[1333]
His *kunyah* was Abū Thābit.

Thābit b. Wadī'ah.[1334]
His *kunyah* was Abū Sa'd.

Khuzaymah b. Thābit.
His *kunyah* was Abū 'Umārah.

Zayd b. Thābit.[1335]
His *kunyah* was Abū Sa'īd after his son Sa'īd.

'Amr b. Ḥazm.[1336]

1331. An early Companion said, like the previous one, to have been one of the standard bearers of the Juhaynah in the conquest of Mecca. See Ibn Ḥajar, *Iṣābah*, III, 439; Khalīfah b. Khayyāṭ, *Ṭabaqāt*, 211. Note that other persons bear the same name.

1332. An Anṣārī (Awsī) Companion of the Prophet and conqueror of al-Rayy. He supported 'Alī b. Abī Ṭālib in the first civil war. He lived in al-Kūfah and died during the governorship of Muṣ'ab b. al-Zubayr (64–72/683–91). See Ibn Ḥajar, *Iṣābah*, I, 142–43; Khalīfah b. Khayyāṭ, *Ta'rīkh*, 132, 205; Ibn Ḥibbān, *Mashāhīr*, 76; al-Quhpā'ī, I, 251–52; al-Kashshī, 45–46. But see Naṣr b. Muzāḥim, 448, where he is included in a group cooperating with Mu'āwiyah.

1333. Counted among the Anṣārī Companions. Ibn Ḥajar, *Iṣābah*, I, 49, knows of only one tradition transmitted by him.

1334. Or, Thābit b. Yazīd, counted among the Anṣārī Companions. See Ibn Ḥibbān, *Mashāhīr*, 80; Ibn Ḥajar, *Iṣābah*, I, 196, 197.

1335. An eminent Anṣārī Companion (Khazrajī), one of the Prophet's scribes, expert on the Qur'ān and religious law. According to a certain tradition, he was the first to collect the Qur'ān already in Abū Bakr's lifetime. He lived in Medina; various versions of the year of his death are given, in the period 42-55/662–74. See Watt, *Bell's Introduction*, 40–56, and passim; "Ḳur'ān," *EI*², V, 404–6 (A. T. Welch); Jeffery, 223–25; F. Sezgin, I, 401–2; al-A'ẓamī, *Kuttāb al-nabī*, 65–67; al-Sayrawān, 92–93; Wakī', I, 107–10; 'Abd al-Malik Ibn Ḥabīb, 156, 157; Ibn al-Jazarī, I, 296; Ibn al-Nadīm, I, 47–48.

1336. An eminent Anṣārī Companion reputed to have been in possession of a document in which the Prophet wrote the details of the legal alms, blood money, and other precepts. He was appointed by the Prophet to administer Najrān and died during 'Umar's caliphate or after the year 50/670. See Ibn Ḥajar, *Iṣābah*, II, 532; Ibn Ḥibbān, *Mashāhīr*, 45; al-Balādhurī, *Ansāb*, I, 529; Muṣṭafā, I, 155.

His *kunyah* was Abū al-Ḍaḥḥāk.

Shaddād b. Aws b. Thābit.[1337]
His *kunyah* was Abū Ya'lā after his son Ya'lā.

Mu'ādh b. al-Ḥārith, of the Banū al-Najjār of the Anṣār.[1338]
He was called "the Reader." His *kunyah* was Abū al-Ḥārith.

Anas b. Mālik.[1339]
His *kunyah* was Abū Ḥamzah.

Zayd b. Arqam.[1340]
His *kunyah* was Abū Sa'd, according to al-Wāqidī, whereas others hold that it was Abū Unaysah.

Al-Nu'mān b. Bashīr.[1341]

1337. An Anṣārī (Khazrajī) Companion, nephew of the Prophet's poet Ḥassān b. Thābit. He lived in Filasṭīn; versions of his death date vary between 41/661–62 and 64/683–84(!). See Ibn Ḥajar, *Iṣābah,* II, 140; Khalīfah b. Khayyāṭ, *Ta'rīkh,* 216; idem, *Ṭabaqāt,* 88; Ibn Ḥibbān, *Mashāhīr,* 85.

1338. There were at least three Anṣārīs bearing this name. Confusion prevails mainly between Mu'ādh b. al-Ḥārith, whose mother was named 'Afrā', and Mu'ādh b. al-Ḥārith b. al-Arqam, the only one of the three called "the reader" (but his *kunyah* is Abū Ḥalīmah, not as recorded by al-Ṭabarī). See the Cairo edition, index s.vv. Mu'ādh b. al-Ḥārith, Mu'ādh, b. 'Afrā', Mu'ādh b. al-Ḥārith al-Qāri' (de Goeje's index mentions only one Mu'ādh b. al-Ḥārith); al-Ṭabarī, *Ta'rīkh,* I, 2182; Ibn Ḥajar, *Iṣābah,* 427–28; Ibn al-Jazarī, II, 301–2; al-Mizzī, *Tahdhīb,* XXVIII, 117.

1339. Of the Anṣār (Khazraj); his mother gave him to the Prophet as a servant, and he became a close Companion and one of the most prolific traditionists (naturally, not all the traditions ascribed to him are authentic). He was also one of Muḥammad's scribes (not recorded by al-A'ẓamī). He lived in al-Baṣrah, where he acted as prayer leader (imām) for 'Abdallāh b. al-Zubayr during the latter's rule. Anas died in the year 93/711–12 (there are other versions). See "Anas b. Mālik," *EI²*, I, 482 (A. J. Wensinck and J. Robson); Jeffery, 214; Khalīfah b. Khayyāṭ, *Ta'rīkh,* 64, 73, 254–55, 262, 309; idem, *Ṭabaqāt,* 91; Ibn Ḥibbān, *Mashāhīr,* 65.

1340. A Companion of the Prophet, of the Anṣār (Khazraj), who participated in the battle of Ṣiffīn on 'Alī's side and died later in al-Kūfah in the year 66/685–86. See Ibn Ḥajar, *Iṣābah,* I, 560; Khalīfah b. Khayyāṭ, *Ṭabaqāt,* 94; Ibn Ḥibbān, *Mashāhīr,* 80. But see Naṣr b. Muzāḥim, 448, where he appears to be cooperating with Mu'āwiyah; cf. the biography of al-Barā' b. 'Āzib, above.

1341. A famous Anṣārī (Khazrajī) Companion of the Prophet, who was governor for Mu'āwiyah in al-Kūfah, later in Ḥimṣ, and a judge in Damascus. In the second civil war he supported 'Abdallāh b. al-Zubayr; Marwān b. al-Ḥakam fought him and killed him, in the year 64/683–84 or 65/684–85. See Khalīfah b. Khayyāṭ, *Ta'rīkh,* 247; idem, *Ṭabaqāt,* 94; Ibn Ḥibbān, *Mashāhīr,* 87; al-Balādhurī, *Ansāb,* V, 127–28, 132, 147; Wakī', III, 201; Ibn Manẓūr, *Mukhtaṣar,* XXVI, 160–64.

His *kunyah* was Abū ʿAbdallāh after his son ʿAbdallāh.

Saʿd b. ʿUbādah, Abū Thābit, according to Yaḥyā.

Qays b. Saʿd b. ʿUbādah.[1342]
His *kunyah* was Abū ʿAbd al-Malik.

Sahl b. Saʿd al-Sāʿidī.[1343]
His *kunyah* was Abū al-ʿAbbās after his son al-ʿAbbās.

[2542] ʿAbdallāh b. Salām.[1344]
His *kunyah* was Abū Yūsuf. His name had been al-Ḥuṣayn, but the Prophet renamed him ʿAbdallāh when he embraced Islam.[1345]

ʿAbdallāh b. al-Zubayr b. al-ʿAwwām.
His *kunyah* was Abū Bakr after his son Bakr. According to another version, his *kunyah* was Abū Khubayb.

Al-Miswar b. Makhramah.
His *kunyah* was Abū ʿAbd al-Raḥmān after his son ʿAbd al-Raḥmān.

ʿUmar b. Abī Salamah b. ʿAbd al-Asad.
His *kunyah* was Abū Ḥafṣ.

ʿAmr b. Ḥurayth.
His *kunyah* was Abū Saʿīd.

Ḥāṭib b. Abī Baltaʿah.

1342. Son of the Khazrajī leader Saʿd b. ʿUbādah, a Companion of the Prophet, and supporter of ʿAlī, who appointed him chief of the *shurṭah* (quasi-police) and governor of Egypt. See Ibn Ḥibbān, *Mashāhīr*, 101; al-Kashshī, 102–3; Ibn Ḥajar, *Iṣābah*, III, 249; Naṣr b. Muzāḥim, passim; al-Kindī, 23–25.

1343. A Companion of the Prophet, of the Anṣār (Khazraj), and the last Companion to die in Medina, in the year 88/707 or 91/709–10. See Khalīfah b. Khayyāṭ, *Ṭabaqāt*, 98; Ibn Ḥibbān, *Mashāhīr*, 48.

1344. A Jewish convert and Companion of the Prophet credited with deep knowledge of the ancient scriptures and Islamic religious law. He died in the year 43/663–64. See "ʿAbd Allāh b. Salām," *EI²*, I, 52 (J. Horovitz); F. Sezgin, I, 304; Ibn al-Nadīm, I, 42, II, 937; Khalīfah b. Khayyāṭ, *Ṭabaqāt*, 8; Ibn Ḥibbān, *Mashāhīr*, 36; al-Balādhurī, *Ansāb*, I, 266.

1345. See note 234, above.

His *kunyah* was Abū ʿAbd al-Raḥmān.

Muḥammad b. Ḥāṭib.[1346]
His *kunyah* was Abū Ibrāhīm.

Muʿāwiyah b. Abī Sufyān.[1347]
His *kunyah* was Abū ʿAbd al-Raḥmān.

Al-Walīd b. ʿUqbah b. Abī Muʿayṭ.[1348]
His *kunyah* was Abū Wahb.

Makhramah b. Nawfal.
[His *kunyah* was] Abū Ṣafwān after his son Ṣafwān.

Qabīṣah b. al-Mukhāriq.[1349]
His *kunyah* was Abū Bishr.

Jābir b. Samurah b. Junādah.[1350]
His *kunyah* was Abū ʿAbdallāh.

ʿAdī b. Ḥātim al-Jawād (the generous), al-Ṭāʾī.
His *kunyah* was Abū Ṭarīf.

1346. A Companion of the Prophet, of the Qurashī clan the Banū Jumaḥ, who was a supporter of ʿAlī and died in the year 74/693–94 in al-Kūfah or in Mecca. See Khalīfah b. Khayyāṭ, *Ṭabaqāt*, 25, 278; Ibn Ḥibbān, *Mashāhīr*, 81; Ibn Qudāmah, 324, 449; al-Balādhurī, *Ansāb*, V, 10.

1347. The founder of the Umayyad dynasty. See "Muʿāwiya b. Abī Sufyān," *EI*², VII, 263–68 (M. Hinds), *EI*¹, VI, 617–21 (H. Lammens); Hawting, *First Dynasty*, 21–45; Hasson, *Recherches*; Khalīfah b. Khayyāṭ, *Ṭabaqāt*, 10, 139, 297–98; Ibn Ḥibbān, *Mashāhīr*, 85–86; al-Balādhurī, *Ansāb*, IVa, 11–138; Ibn Manẓūr, *Mukhtaṣar*, XXIV, 399–405, XXV, 5–93; al-Munajjid, 167–74.

1348. A Companion of the Prophet, a late convert, of the aristocratic Umayyad family. He was governor of al-Kūfah for ʿUthmān but was dismissed and flogged for drinking wine. See Ibn Qudāmah, 210–11; Khalīfah b. Khayyāṭ, *Ṭabaqāt*, 11, 126, and passim; Ibn Ḥibbān, *Mashāhīr*, 78; al-Balādhurī, *Ansāb*, V, 29–35.

1349. A Companion of the Prophet, of the northern Hilāl, apparently of a noble family, as his son Qaṭan counted as a tribal noble and became governor of Sijistān (according to Crone, *Slaves*, 136, of al-Baṣrah). See Ibn Ḥajar, *Iṣābah*, III, 222; Khalīfah b. Khayyāṭ, *Ṭabaqāt*, 56, 184; Ibn Ḥibbān, *Mashāhīr*, 70.

1350. A Companion of the Prophet, originally of the northern, ʿĀmirī clan Suwāʾah and an ally of the Qurashī clan Zuhrah. He lived in al-Kūfah and died in the year 74/693–94. See Ibn Ḥajar, *Iṣābah*, I, 212; Khalīfah b. Khayyāṭ, *Ṭabaqāt*, 56–57, 131–32; Ibn Ḥibbān, *Mashāhīr*, 81.

Al-Ash'ath b. Qays.
His *kunyah* was Abū Muḥammad after his son Muḥammad.

Tamīm al-Dārī, that is, Tamīm b. Aws b. Khārijah.[1351]
His *kunyah* was Abū Ruqayyah.

'Amr b. Ma'dī-karib.[1352]
His *kunyah* was Abū Thawr.

Hāni' b. Yazīd, the father of Shurayḥ b. Hāni'.[1353]
His *kunyah* was Abū Shurayḥ.
It was reported that in pre-Islamic times his *kunyah* was Abū al-Ḥakam (father of the arbitrator), because he used to act as arbitrator among his people. When he embraced Islam the Prophet gave him the *kunyah* Abū Shurayḥ.[1354]

[2543] Jarīr b. 'Abdallāh al-Bajalī.[1355]
According to al-Wāqidī, His *kunyah* was Abū 'Abdallāh, but we hold that it was Abū 'Amr. A verse attributed to him runs as follows:

I am Jarīr; my *kunyah* is Abū 'Amr.

1351. A Christian convert to Islam, and a famous Companion, of the southern Banū al-Dār (a branch of the Lakhm); see Ibn Ḥazm, *Jamharat*, 422. He was an ascetic and a storyteller (*qāṣṣ*; see note 1251, above) and so much identified with the *qaṣaṣ* that he was considered by some to have introduced it to Islam. He lived in Filasṭīn, where the Prophet (allegedly?) granted him lands. See "Tamīm al-Dārī," *EI*¹, VIII, 646–48 (G. Levi Della Vida); Gil, 129–30; Khalīfah b. Khayyāṭ, *Ta'rīkh*, 335; idem, *Ṭabaqāt*, 70, 305; Ibn Ḥibbān, *Mashāhīr*, 89; Ibn Manẓūr, *Mukhtaṣar*, V, 307–23; al-Ghayṭī; Ibn al-Jawzī, *Kitāb*, 77–78, 87, 107; Sharāb.

1352. A famous warrior, poet, and tribal chief among the Yemeni tribe Zubayd. He embraced Islam in the year 9/630, apostatized, returned to Islam, and died in the battle of al-Qādisiyyah (there are other versions of his death date). See Ibn Ḥazm, *Jamharat*, 411; Khalīfah b. Khayyāṭ, *Ṭabaqāt*, 74; al-Rāzī, 37, 583; Abū al-Faraj al-Iṣfahānī, XIV, 24–40; Ibn Nubātah, 306–12.

1353. A Companion of the Prophet, of the Yemeni tribe al-Ḥārith b. Ka'b; see Ibn Ḥazm, *Jamharat*, 417. His son Shurayḥ was a jurist and a supporter of 'Alī, who entrusted him with certain offices. See Ibn Ḥibbān, *Mashāhīr*, 82; Ibn Ḥajar, *Iṣābah*, III, 597. For Shurayḥ, see Ibn Ḥajar, *Iṣābah*, II, 166; al-Dhahabī, *Siyar*, IV, 107–9; Ibn Manẓūr, *Mukhtaṣar*, X, 303–4.

1354. Cf. note 234, above. The previous *kunyah* was perhaps improper because al-Ḥakam is an epithet of God; see Ibn Ḥajar, *Iṣābah*, III, 597.

1355. An early convert, a tribal noble (*sharīf*), unifier and leader of the Bajīlah, who died in the year 51/671. See Crone, *Slaves*, 114–15; Khalīfah b. Khayyāṭ, *Ṭabaqāt*, 116–17, 138, 318; Ibn Ḥibbān, *Mashāhīr*, 76; Ibn Ḥanbal, *Faḍā'il*, 891–93.

I hit with my sword while Sa'd is in the citadel.[1356]

Fayrūz al-Daylamī.
His *kunyah* was Abū 'Abdallāh after his son 'Abdallāh.
Some transmitters refer to him as al-Daylamī al-Ḥimyarī. This is so because he lived [in the Yemen] among the Ḥimyar. [Actually] he was one of the descendants of the Persians (*abnā'*) who had been sent by the Persian ruler Khusraw to the Yemen to fight the Abyssinians there.

Safīnah, Umm Salamah's client.[1357]
According to al-'Abbās—Yaḥyā: His *kunyah* was Abū 'Abd al-Raḥmān.

Uhbān b. Ṣayfī.[1358]
According to [al-'Abbās] (?): His *kunyah* was Abū Muslim.

Al-Miqdām b. Ma'dī-Karib.[1359]
His *kunyah* was Abū Karīmah.

Ya'lā b. Murrah.[1360]
According to Yaḥyā, his *kunyah* was Abū al-Marāzim, but al-Wāqidī holds that Abū al-Marāzim was the *kunyah* of Ya'lā b. Umayyah.

Labīd b. Rabī'ah, the poet.
His *kunyah* was Abū 'Aqīl.

1356. The reference is to Sa'd b. Abī Waqqāṣ, and the occasion was the battle of al-Qādisiyyah; see al-Ṭabarī, *Ta'rīkh*, I, 2357, 2361.

1357. Or the Prophet's client; he was of Persian, or bedouin, origin. There are twenty-one versions of his name. See Khalīfah b. Khayyāṭ, *Ṭabaqāt*, 22, 190; Ibn Ḥibbān, *Mashāhīr*, 71; al-Balādhurī, *Ansāb*, I, 480; Ibn Ḥajar, *Iṣābah*, II, 58.

1358. A Companion of the Prophet, of the northern tribe Ghifār, resident of al-Baṣrah. See Khalīfah b. Khayyāṭ, *Ṭabaqāt*, 33, 175; Ibn Ḥibbān, *Mashāhīr*, 72.

1359. Counted among the Companions, although some doubted that he had ever seen the Prophet. He was a Kindī, lived in Ḥimṣ, and died in the year 87/706 or, according to Ibn Sa'd, VII/2, during the caliphate of 'Abd al-Malik. According to Abū Zur'ah, 237, 240, he was associated with al-Walīd b. 'Abd al-Malik. See Khalīfah b. Khayyāṭ, *Ṭabaqāt*, 72, 304; Ibn Ḥibbān, *Mashāhīr*, 91; Ibn Ḥajar, *Iṣābah*, III, 455; Ibn Manẓūr, *Mukhtaṣar*, XXV, 222–24.

1360. A Companion of the Prophet, of the Thaqīf, resident of al-Baṣrah. See Khalīfah b. Khayyāṭ, *Ṭabaqāt*, 53, 131; Ibn Ḥibbān, *Mashāhīr*, 78.

Qarazah b. Ka'b.[1361]
His *kunyah* was Abū 'Amr.

Ḥuwayṭib b. 'Abd al-'Uzzā b. Abī Qays.
His *kunyah* was Abū Muḥammad.

Mālik b. al-Ḥuwayrith al-Laythī.[1362]
His *kunyah* was Abū Sulaymān.

Ḥudhayfah b. al-Yamān.
His *kunyah* was Abū 'Abdallāh.

Those of the Prophet's Companions Who Were Known by [the Names of] Their Patrons or Brothers or by Their [Own] Nicknames or by Their Grandfathers, Instead of Their Actual Fathers

[2544] Sālim b. Ma'qil, called Sālim the client of Abū Ḥudhayfah.[1363]
He was known as Abū Ḥudhayfah's client but was [actually] a slave of an Awsī woman called Thubaytah bt. Ya'ār, who was married to Abū Ḥudhayfah b. 'Utbah. She set Sālim free, renouncing all claim to his services.[1364] Sālim then attached himself to Abū Ḥudhayfah by clientage, and the latter adopted him.

Al-Miqdād b. al-Aswad.

1361. An Anṣārī Companion of the Prophet who lived in al-Kūfah and commanded the force that conquered al-Rayy (but cf. p. 294, above; al-Barā' b. 'Āzib). He was later appointed governor of the town by 'Alī and died during the caliphate of 'Alī or Mu'āwiyah. See al-Ṭabarī, *Ta'rīkh*, I, 2650, 3173; Khalīfah b. Khayyāṭ, *Ṭabaqāt*, 94–95; Ibn Ḥibbān, *Mashāhīr*, 82.

1362. A Companion of the Prophet of the northern, Kinānī clan the Banū Layth; he lived in al-Baṣrah and died in the year 74/693–94. See Khalīfah b. Khayyāṭ, *Ṭabaqāt*, 30; Ibn Ḥibbān, *Mashāhīr*, 70.

1363. An early convert and a famous Qur'ān reader reputed for his courage in the battle of al-Yamāmah against Musaylimah, where he was killed. See Jeffery, 234; Khalīfah b. Khayyāṭ, *Ta'rīkh*, 77; idem, *Ṭabaqāt*, 12; Ibn Ḥibbān, *Mashāhīr*, 45–6; al-Balādhurī, *Ansāb*, I, 264; Ibn al-Jazarī, I, 301. His patron, Abū Ḥudhayfah, was a Qurashī of the Umayyad clan.

1364. That is, as opposed to freeing a slave on condition that he stays in the household, which involved rights and obligations for both the freedman and his patron. See Crone, *Roman, Provincial and Islamic Law*, 67–68; Ibn Qutaybah, *Ma'ārif*, 118–19.

He was the son of 'Amr b. Bahrā' b. 'Amr b. al-Ḥāf b. Quḍā'ah but became an ally of al-Aswad b. 'Abd Yaghūth al-Zuhrī in pre-Islamic times. Al-Aswad adopted him, so he was called al-Miqdād b. al-Aswad. When the Qur'ānic verse "Call them by their fathers' names" was revealed al-Miqdād was again called by the name of his real father, 'Amr.

Dhū al-Shimālayn (the one with two left hands), sometimes also called Dhū al-Yadayn (the one with two hands), because he was, it was reported, ambidexterous; he could work with both his hands.

His name was 'Umayr b. 'Abd 'Amr b. Naḍlah b. 'Amr b. Ghubshān, of the Khuzā'ah.[1365] He was killed in the battle of Badr as a *shahīd* with the other Muslims who were killed there.

As for the second one, his name was al-Khirbāq.[1366] He outlived the Prophet for a while and transmitted a few traditions from him.

Suhayl b. Bayḍā'.[1367]

He is known by the name of his mother, al-Bayḍā', whose name was Da'd bt. Jaḥdam b. 'Amr. Suhayl was the son of Wahb b. Rabī'ah b. Hilāl, of the Banū al-Ḥārith b. Fihr.

His brother was Ṣafwān b. Bayḍā'.[1368]

Ḥudhayfah b. al-Yamān.

He was known by the name of his great-grandfather's grandfather. He was [actually] the son of Ḥusayl b. Jābir b. Rabī'ah b. 'Amr b. Jirwah b. al-Ḥārith b. Quṭay'ah b. 'Abs b. Baghīḍ. Jirwah b. al-Ḥārith is the Yamān who fathered Ḥudhayfah. He was thus

---

1365. He was an ally of the Banū Zuhrah of the Quraysh. See al-Balādhurī, *Ansāb*, I, 295; Ibn Qutaybah, *Ma'ārif*, 140–41.

1366. His identity is uncertain, except that he was of the Sulaym, and the identification between him and Dhū al-Yadayn is uncertain as well; see Ibn Ḥajar, *Iṣābah*, I, 422–23; cf. Ibn Qutaybah, *Ma'ārif*, 140–41. Note that at the beginning of the entry al-Ṭabarī takes Dhū al-Shimālayn and Dhū al-Yadayn to be one and the same person.

1367. A Qurashī Companion who died in the year 9/630 (before the Prophet); see Ibn Ḥajar, *Iṣābah*, II, 91–92.

1368. A rather obscure Companion, counted by some scholars among those killed at Badr, according to others he died in the year 30/650–51 or 38/658–59. See Ibn Ḥajar, *Iṣābah*, II, 191–92 s.v. Ṣafwān b. Wahb; Ibn Sa'd, III/1, 303; Khalīfah b. Khayyāṭ, *Ta'rīkh*, 18; al-Balādhurī, *Ansāb*, I, 225.

[2545] called because he had murdered someone of his own tribe, so he fled to Medina and became an ally of the Banū ʿAbd al-Ashhal. His family was then called al-Yamān (the southerners), because they were allied to a Yemenī clan.[1369]

Yaʿlā b. Siyābah.
Siyābah was his mother, and his father was Murrah, so he was [actually] Yaʿlā b. Murrah.

Yaʿlā b. Munyah.
Munyah was his mother, and his father was Umayyah, so he was [actually] Yaʿlā b. Umayyah.

Nābighah of the Banū Jaʿdah, the poet.
He was known by his nickname [Nābighah] (the copious),[1370] but his [real] name was Qays b. ʿAbdallāh b. ʿUdas b. Rabīʿah b. Jaʿdah.

Al-Ashʿath b. Qays b. Maʿdī-Karib.
Al-Ashʿath (the shaggy-haired one) was a nickname by which he was known. His real name was Maʿdī-Karib, but he received that nickname because he was always shaggy-haired, or so it was reported.

Tamīm al-Dārī.
He was known by the name of al-Dār b. Hāniʾ, [a clan] of the Lakhm. He was the son of Aws b. Khārijah al-Dārī.

Al-Hulb b. Yazīd al-Ṭāʾī.[1371]
He was known by his nickname [al-Hulb] (the hairy one),[1372] but his [real] name was Salāmah, father of Qabīṣah b. Hulb.[1373] He was thus nicknamed because he was bald, and when he came to

1369. The ʿAbd al-Ashhal, a part of the Aws, originated in the southern (Yemenī) confederation of al-Azd.

1370. The nickname is a reference to his creative poetic talent.

1371. There are various versions of his name. See Khalīfah b. Khayyāṭ, *Ṭabaqāt*, 69; Ibn Ḥajar, *Iṣābah*, III, 607.

1372. *Hulb* is in fact a noun meaning "hair" or "bristle," the adjective is *halib*, and indeed some scholars vocalize the name that way; see Ibn Ḥajar, *Iṣābah*, 609.

1373. See Ibn Ḥajar, *Tahdhīb*, VIII, 350–51; Ibn Saʿd, VI, 206.

the Prophet and embraced Islam, as it was reported, the Prophet stroked his head with his hand, and [Salāmah]'s head grew hair, so he was called Hulb after his bristles.

The Names of the Successors Who Were Known by Their Kunyahs

Abū Umāmah b. Sahl b. Ḥunayf.[1374]

His name was As'ad.

It was reported that the Prophet called him thus and gave him his *kunyah.* This was because his mother was Ḥabībah, daughter of Abī Umāmah As'ad b. Zurārah b. 'Udas, the leader who was responsible (*naqīb*) for the Banū al-Najjār.[1375] When she gave birth [2546]
to Abū Umāmah he was given the name and *kunyah* of her father.

Abū Sa'īd al-Maqbarī.[1376]

This is the father of Sa'īd b. Abī Sa'īd al-Maqbarī.[1377] His [real] name was Kaysān, and he was a client of Banū Jundu' of the clan Layth b. Bakr.

Abū Ja'far al-Qāri' (the reader).[1378]

His name was Yazīd b. al-Qa'qā', a client of ['Abdallāh] Ibn 'Ayyāsh.[1379]

1374. An Anṣārī Companion, son and grandson of Companions, who died in the year 100/718–19. See Ibn Sa'd, V, 59–60; Ibn Ḥajar, *Tahdhīb*, I, 231; cf. *Iṣābah*, IV, 9.

1375. When the Medinans, at the 'Aqabah meeting, agreed to shelter the Prophet and the Muslims in Medina, the Prophet appointed twelve leaders, *nuqabā'*, to take charge of the Medinans' affairs. See Ibn Hishām, II, 86–89; Guillaume, 204. On As'ad b. Zurārah, said to have been one of the earliest converts to Islam in Medina, see Muir, 117, n. 119; Ibn Ḥajar, *Iṣābah*, I, 34–35.

1376. He lived in Medina and died in the year 100/718–19. See Khalīfah b. Khayyāṭ, *Ṭabaqāt*, 248; Ibn Ḥibbān, *Mashāhīr*, 117; idem, *Thiqāt*, V, 340; al-Sam'ānī, V, 361–62.

1377. A transmitter who settled on the frontier (and participated in the *jihād* there); he died in the year 117/735 (there are other versions). See Ibn Ḥajar, *Tahdhīb*, IV, 34–35; Ibn Manẓūr, *Mukhtaṣar*, X, 6–8.

1378. One of the most famous Qur'ān readers and an ascetic, who died in the year 130/747–48 or 132/749–50. See Khalīfah b. Khayyāṭ, *Ta'rīkh*, 429; idem, *Ṭabaqāt*, 262; Ibn Ḥibbān, *Mashāhīr*, 124; Ibn al-Jazarī, II, 382–84; Ibn Qutaybah, *Ma'ārif*, 230.

1379. A Qurashī Companion, of the Banū Makhzūm, who lived in Medina; see Ibn Sa'd, V, 18.

Abū Maymūnah, a client of Umm Salamah, the Prophet's wife.[1380]
He was the reader of the people of Medina in his time. It was with him that Nāfi' b. Abī Nu'aym[1381] studied.

Abū Ṣāliḥ al-Sammān, that is, al-Zayyāt (the oil seller), a client of the Ghaṭafān or, according to another version, of a woman of the Qays named Juwayriyyah.[1382]
He is also known as Abū Suhayl, and his name was Dhakwān.

Abū Ṣāliḥ Bādhām, a client of Umm Hāni', daughter of Abū Ṭālib.[1383]
Al-Kalbī and Ismā'īl b. Abī Khālid transmitted from him.

Abū Ṣāliḥ Sumay'.[1384]
He transmitted from ['Abdallāh] b. 'Abbās.

Abū Ṣāliḥ, a client of [the caliph] al-Saffāḥ.[1385]
His name was 'Ubayd. Busr b. Sa'īd[1386] transmitted from him.

1380. Ibn Sa'd, V, 219.

1381. Of Persian origin, a client of the Kinānī clan the Banū Layth. He was one of the leading Qur'ān readers in Medina, where he died in the year 169 or 170/786–87; see Ibn Qutaybah, *Ma'ārif*, 230. Ibn al-Jazarī, II, 330–34, does not mention Abū Maymūnah, among Nāfi''s teachers or otherwise.

1382. Also called al-Zayyāt, which signifies the same; see al-Mizzī, *Tahdhīb*, VIII, 513. He lived in Medina, frequented al-Kūfah, and died in the year 101/719–20. See Khalīfah b. Khayyāṭ, *Ta'rīkh*, 332; idem, *Ṭabaqāt*, 248; Ibn Ḥibbān, *Mashāhīr*, 122–23; Ibn Sa'd, V, 222. Ibn Qutaybah, *Ma'ārif*, 210, says he died during the caliphate of al-Manṣūr (136–58/754–75), but this is unlikely if he were a companion of Abū Hurayrah (the Prophet's Companion), as stated by Abū Zur'ah, 479.

1383. He could not read the Qur'ān well but engaged in exegesis, a fact that aroused anger in some scholars. Al-Sha'bī reprimanded him, and al-Kalbī claimed that he was a liar (yet transmitted from him). See Ibn Ḥajar, *Tahdhīb*, I, 364–65; Ibn Qutaybah, *Ma'ārif*, 210; also Abū Zur'ah, 478.

1384. A Kūfan, also called al-Zayyāt (the oil seller) but, oddly, he tends to be confused, not with Abū Ṣāliḥ al-Sammān/al-Zayyāt (see above), but with Abū Ṣāliḥ al-Ḥanafī (see below). See al-Mizzī, *Tahdhīb*, XXXIII, 417; Ibn Sa'd, V, 222; Abū Zur'ah, 479.

1385. Ibn Sa'd, V, 223. According to Abū Zur'ah, 479, his name was Numayr.

1386. The only one I found bearing this name is a Medinan transmitter, a client of the Ḥaḍramī family, who died in the year 100/718–19. He was thus perhaps too old to have transmitted from a client of al-Saffāḥ. See Ibn Ḥajar, *Tahdhīb*, IV, 383; Ibn Qutaybah, *Ma'ārif*, 197; Khalīfah b. Khayyāṭ, *Ṭabaqāt*, 255.

Abū Ṣāliḥ al-Ḥanafī.[1387]

His name was 'Abd al-Raḥmān b. Qays, brother of Ṭulayq b. Qays al-Ḥanafī.[1388] According to Yaḥyā his name was Māhān.

Abū Ṣāliḥ al-Ghifārī.[1389]

Abū Ṣāliḥ Maysarah.[1390]

Abū Ṣāliḥ from whom the people of Filasṭīn transmitted [traditions].[1391] [2547]

[His name was] Rudayḥ.

Abū Ṣāliḥ, the one from whom Yaḥyā b. Abī Kathīr[1392] transmitted.

His name was Qaylūh.[1393]

Abū Ṣāliḥ.[1394]

1387. Ibn Sa'd VI, 158; Ibn Qutaybah, *Ma'ārif*, 210; al-Mizzī, *Tahdhīb*, XVII, 360–63. He figures in yet other sources, but only Ibn Ḥibbān, *Thiqāt*, V, 458, has the information that he was a Kūfan and a Shī'ī, executed by the governor al-Ḥajjāj. According to Dodge, in Ibn al-Nadīm, II, 1091, he was a genealogist; Dodge refers to Ibn al-Nadīm, I, 205, but there is no way of identifying the genealogist Abū Ṣāliḥ mentioned there. Abū Zayd's *Ṭabaqāt al-nassābīn* records no genealogist named Abū Ṣāliḥ.

1388. A Kūfan traditionist; see al-Mizzī, *Tahdhīb*, XIII, 462–65.

1389. His name was Sa'īd b. 'Abd al-Raḥmān, and apparently he was a client. See Ibn Sa'd, V, 223; al-Mizzī, *Tahdhīb*, X, 538.

1390. A Kūfan, client of the Kindah, who was with 'Alī in the battle of Nahrawān, against the Khawārij. See al-Mizzī, *Tahdhīb*, XXIX, 197–98; Ibn Sa'd, V, 223.

1391. Rudayḥ b. 'Aṭiyyah of the Quraysh, said to be the muezzin of [the mosque in] Jerusalem (*mu'adhdhin bayt al-maqdis*). See Ibn Ḥajar, *Tahdhīb*, III, 234–35; Abū Zur'ah, 448; Ibn Ḥibbān, *Mashāhīr*, 292; Ibn Abī Ḥātim, I/2, 518. His *kunyah* was also Abū al-Walīd; cf. al-Wāsiṭī, 14, 36, and passim.

1392. A client of the Ṭayyi' who lived in al-Baṣrah and later in al-Yamāmah and died in the year 129/746–47; see Ibn Sa'd, V, 404.

1393. Al-Dūlābī, II, 10 has Qaylūbah. Ibn Sa'd, VII/1, 165, and Abū Zur'ah, 479: Qaylūyah.

1394. A Baṣran and a Shī'ī, who studied Qur'ān exegesis from 'Abdallāh Ibn 'Abbās; he died after the turn of the first century. See Abū Zur'ah, 479; Ibn Ḥibbān, *Thiqāt*, V, 458; al-Ṣadr, 23.

Khālid al-Ḥadhdhā' and al-Taymī transmitted from him.[1395]
[His name was] Mīzān.

Abū Ṣāliḥ, a client of 'Uthmān b. 'Affān.[1396]
His name was Burkān.[1397]

Abū Wā'il.[1398]
His name was Shaqīq b. Salamah al-Asadī.

Abū 'Amr al-Shaybānī.[1399]
His name was Sa'd b. Iyās.

Abū 'Abd al-Raḥmān al-Sulamī.
His name was 'Abdallāh b. Ḥabīb.

Abū Fākhitah Sa'īd b. 'Ilāqah.[1400]

Abū al-Sha'thā' al-Muḥāribī.[1401]
His name was Sulaym b. al-Aswad.

Abū 'Abdallāh al-Jadalī.

1395. For Khālid, see p. 221, above. By al-Taymī Sulaymān al-Taymī is meant; see Ibn Ḥibbān, *Thiqāt*, V, 458. Several traditionists bore this name, the most famous being Sulaymān b. Ṭarkhān, father of al-Mu'tamir. See Ibn Ḥajar, *Tahdhīb*, IV, 170, 176, 181, 187; al-Sam'ānī, I, 498–501.

1396. Ibn Sa'd, V, 222.

1397. According to Abū Zur'ah, 478: Turkān. For the version al-Ḥārith, see al-Mizzī, *Tahdhīb*, XXXIII, 420–22.

1398. He was born in the Prophet's lifetime but embraced Islam after the Prophet's death and died in the year 83/702–3. See Khalīfah b. Khayyāṭ, *Ṭabaqāt*, 155; Ibn Ḥibbān, *Mashāhīr*, 159; Ibn Ḥajar, *Iṣābah*, II, 167–68; Ibn Qutaybah, *Ma'ārif*, 198.

1399. Of the northern Shaybān, a branch of the Bakr b. Wā'il. He lived in the time of the Prophet but embraced Islam after the Prophet's death and died in the year 101/719–20 (there are other versions). See Khalīfah b. Khayyāṭ, *Ṭabaqāt*, 156; Ibn Ḥibbān, *Mashāhīr*, 160; Ibn Sa'd VI, 70. He should not be confused with the philologist bearing the same *kunyah*.

1400. Or Sa'īd b. Juhmān. He was a client of Umm Hāni', sister of 'Alī, and a supporter of 'Alī who died during the caliphate of 'Abd al-Malik or his son al-Walīd. See Ibn Ḥajar, *Tahdhīb*, IV, 63; al-Quhpā'ī, I, 302–4 (s.v. Thuwayr).

1401. A Kūfan jurist of the northern Qaysī tribe Muḥārib; see Ibn Ḥazm, *Jamharat*, 259–60. He was a supporter of 'Alī and died during the caliphate of 'Abd al-Malik (there are other versions). See Ibn Ḥajar, *Tahdhīb*, IV, 145; al-Dhahabī, *Siyar*, IV, 179.

His name was ʿAbdah b. ʿAbd b. ʿAbdallāh.

Abū Burdah b. Abī Mūsā.[1402]
His name was ʿĀmir b. ʿAbdallāh b. Qays.

Abū ʿUthmān al-Nahdī.
His name was ʿAbd al-Raḥmān b. Mall.

Abū al-Aswad al-Dīlī.[1403]
His name was Ẓālim b. ʿAmr.

Abū al-ʿĀliyah al-Riyāḥī.[1404]
His name was Rufayʿ.

Abū Umayyah, a client of ʿUmar b. al-Khaṭṭāb.[1405]
His name was ʿAbd al-Raḥmān; he was the grandfather of Mubārak b. Faḍālah b. Abī Umayyah.[1406]

Abū Rajāʾ al-ʿUṭāridī.[1407]

1402. Son of the Companion Abū Mūsā al-Ashʿarī, called after his uncle ʿĀmir, cf. p. 147, above. He was a judge in al-Kūfah under al-Ḥajjāj and died in the year 103/721–22 (there are other versions). See Ibn Saʿd, VI, 187; Ibn Ḥajar, *Tahdhīb*, XII, 21–22; Wakīʿ, II, 408–11.

1403. Read al-Duʾilī, of the northern clan al-Duʾil, a branch of the Kinānah; see Ibn Ḥazm, *Jamharat*, 184–85. He was a supporter of ʿAlī and held certain offices in his time, dying at al-Baṣrah in the year 69/688. He is considered to be the first Arab philologist, but, according to Fück, this claim is unwarranted. It is also claimed that he was the first to vocalize the Qurʾānic text. See "Abū al-Aswad al-Duʾalī," *EI*², I, 106–7 (J. W. Fück); al-Ṣadr, 20, 122–28; Khalīfah b. Khayyāṭ, *Taʾrīkh*, 184; Ibn Ḥibbān, *Mashāhīr*, 152; Ibn Qutaybah, *Maʿārif*, 197.

1404. Rufayʿ b. Mihrān. He was a client of a Riyāḥī woman (a family of the Tamīmī clan the Yarbūʿ) in al-Baṣrah, who died in the year 93/711–12. See Ibn Ḥibbān, *Mashāhīr*, 153 no. 697; cf. p. 308, below; Ibn Manẓūr, *Mukhtaṣar*, VIII, 326–32; Ibn ʿAdī, III, 1022–31.

1405. A slave freed by ʿUmar who lived in Iraq. It seems that his main importance lies in the story of his release from slavery; see Ibn Saʿd, VII/1, 85–86.

1406. A Baṣran traditionist, a client of ʿUmar's family who died in the year 165/781–82 (there are other versions). See Ibn Saʿd, VII/2, 35; Ibn Ḥajar, *Tahdhīb*, X, 27–29; Ibn Ḥibbān, *Mashāhīr*, 249; al-Dhahabī, *Siyar*, VII, 281–85.

1407. Of the Tamīmī clan, the ʿUṭārid; see Ibn Ḥazm, *Jamharat*, 218. He was born in the Prophet's lifetime but embraced Islam only after the Prophet's death. He died in al-Baṣrah in the year 105/723–24 (there are other versions). According to Ibn Qutaybah, *Maʿārif*, 189, he died at the age of 128. See Khalīfah b. Khayyāṭ, *Taʾrīkh*, 344; idem, *Ṭabaqāt*, 196; Ibn Ḥibbān, *Mashāhīr*, 142.

His name was ʿImrān b. Taym; according to another version, ʿImrān b. Milḥān.

[2548] Abū al-Mutawakkil al-Nājī.
His name was ʿAlī b. Du'ād.

Abū al-Ṣiddīq al-Nājī.
His name was Bakr b. ʿAmr.

Abū al-Zinbāʿ.[1408]
His name was Ṣadaqah b. Ṣāliḥ.

[Abū Ayyūb al-ʿAtakī].[1409]
According to al-ʿAlā'ī—Yaḥyā b. Maʿīn: Abū Ayyūb al-ʿAtakī's name was Yaḥyā b. al-Mundhir.

Abū al-ʿĀliyah al-Barrā'.[1410]
His name was Ziyād b. Fayrūz.

Abū ʿImrān al-Jawnī.[1411]
His name was ʿAbd al-Malik b. Ḥabīb al-Azdī.

Abū Muslim al-Khawlānī.[1412]
His name was ʿAbdallāh b. Thuwab.

1408. Al-Dūlābī, I, 184; Ibn Saʿd, VI, 218, VII/1, 165, only mentions his name among the Kūfan Successors.

1409. The ʿAtīk was a tribe of the southern confederation of the Azd; see al-Samʿānī, IV, 153. Abū Ayyūb was a Baṣran who died after the year 80/699–700. See Ibn Ḥajar, *Tahdhīb*, XII, 19; Ibn Abī Ḥātim, IV/2, 190; al-Dūlābī, I, 102; cf. Ibn Saʿd, VII/1, 164. There are several versions of his name and tribal affiliation, among them Yaḥyā b. Mālik. See also p. 310, below.

1410. A client of a Riyāḥī woman (of the Yarbūʿ of the Tamīm) who died in the year 90/708–9. See Ibn Ḥibbān, *Mashāhīr*, 153, biography no. 698; cf. Abū al-ʿĀliyah mentioned on p. 307, above.

1411. A Baṣran traditionist who was either a Kindī, an Azdī, or a Kinānī and supported ʿAbdallāh b. al-Zubayr in the second civil war, dying in the year 128/745–46 (there are other versions). See Khalifah b. Khayyāṭ, *Ta'rīkh*, 403; idem, *Ṭabaqāt*, 215; Ibn Ḥibbān, *Mashāhīr*, 154–55; Ibn Ḥajar, *Tahdhīb*, VI, 346.

1412. Khawlān was a branch of the southern Saba' or of the Quḍāʿah; see al-Samʿānī, II, 419. Abū Muslim was a Syrian ascetic and Qur'ān reader who, during the caliphate of Muʿāwiyah, embraced Islam and died. See Khalīfah b. Khayyāṭ, *Ṭabaqāt*, 307; Ibn Ḥibbān, *Mashāhīr*, 181; Ibn Qutaybah, *Maʿārif*, 194; Abū Zurʿah, 226, 227 (= 690); Ibn Manẓūr, *Mukhtaṣar*, XII, 55–67; Abū Nuʿaym, II, 122–31.

Abū al-Ẓāhiriyyah al-Ḥaḍramī.[1413]
His name was Ḥudayr b. Kurayb. According to another version, he was a Ḥimyarī.

Abū Ja'far al-Madā'inī.[1414]
His name was 'Abdallāh b. al-Miswar b. Muḥammad b. Ja'far b. Abī Ṭālib.

Abū Ḥāzim, who transmitted [traditions] to Ismā'īl b. Abī Khālid.[1415]
[His name was] Nabtal.

Abū al-Ḥuwayrith, 'Abd al-Raḥmān b. Mu'āwiyah.

Abū Ḥāzim al-Ashja'ī, Salmān.[1416]

Abū al-Sha'thā', Jābir b. Zayd.[1417]

Abū al-Sha'thā', who transmitted [traditions] to Ḥumayd al-Ṭawīl.[1418]

1413. Another version of his name is Ja'far b. Kurayb. He was a Syrian Successor whose death date is variously given in the years 100/718–19, 127/744–45, before 86/705, and so on. Such variations between versions are unusual. See Khalīfah b. Khayyāṭ, *Ṭabaqāt*, 311; al-Balādhurī, *Ansāb*, I, 10; Ibn Manẓūr, *Mukhtaṣar*, VI, 245–46; Abū Zur'ah, 214; Ibn Ḥibbān, *Mashāhīr*, 184, 284.

1414. A Qurashī of the Hāshimī clan and a descendant of the Prophet's uncle Abū Ṭālib, known as a weak transmitter if not an outright forger. See Khalīfah b. Khayyāṭ, *Ṭabaqāt*, 325; al-Dhahabī, *Mīzān*, III, 78; Ibn 'Adī, IV, 1483–84.

1415. According to al-Dūlābī, I, 141, he was a client of Ibn 'Abbās. However, the authors of the great biographical works (Ibn Ḥajar, al-Mizzī, Ibn Sa'd, Ibn 'Adī, among others) do not mention him.

1416. Or Sulaymān, sometimes confused with Salamah b. Dīnār; see al-Dūlābī, I, 141. He was a client of an Ashja'ī woman (from a branch of the northern Qays 'Aylān) and died during the caliphate of 'Umar II. See Ibn Ḥibbān, *Mashāhīr*, 174; Ibn Ḥajar, *Tahdhīb*, IV, 123; Ibn Sa'd, VI, 205.

1417. An Azdī, resident of al-Baṣrah, a *ḥāfiẓ*, and an expert on the Qur'ān and religious law who died in the year 93/711–12 (not 73 as recorded in some sources, for he died the same week as Anas b. Mālk). See Khalīfah b. Khayyāṭ, *Ṭabaqāt*, 210; Ibn Ḥibbān, *Mashāhīr*, 144; al-Sayrawān, 70.

1418. According to al-Dūlābī, II, 5, he was a client of 'Umar b. 'Ubaydallāh b. Ma'mar, a Qurashī Medinan notable, officiating as judge in al-Baṣrah for Hārūn al-Rashīd; see Ibn Ḥajar, *Tahdhīb*, VII, 424 (s.v. 'Umar b. 'Uthmān). Ḥumayd al-Ṭawīl's name was Ḥumayd b. Ṭarkhān; he was a client of Ṭalḥah al-Ṭalḥāt (= Ṭalḥah b. 'Abdallāh). He died in the year 142/759–60; see Ibn Qutaybah, *Ma'ārif*, 211.

[He was] the client of 'Umar b. 'Abd al-'Azīz.
[His name was] Fayrūz.

[2549] Abū Jamrah, the companion of Ibn 'Abbās.[1419]
[Ḥis name was] 'Imrān b. 'Aṭā'.

Abū Ja'far al-Bajalī, who transmitted [traditions] to Mu'tamir b. Sulaymān.[1420]
[His name was] Mūsā b. al-Musayyib.

Abū Balj, Yaḥyā b. Sulaym, or Yaḥyā b. Abī Sulaym. According to another version, Yaḥyā b. Abī al-Aswad.[1421]

Abū al-'Udhāfir, Dā'ūd b. Dīnār.[1422]

[Abū Laylā].[1423]
It was reported on the authority of Ibn al-Muthannā: The name of Abū Laylā, father of 'Abd al-Raḥmān b. Abī Laylā, was Dā'ūd.

Abū Ayyūb, who transmitted [traditions] to Qatādah.
[His name was] Yaḥyā b. Ayyūb.[1424]

1419. Abū Ḥamrah, Naṣr b. 'Imrān, in Ibn Qutaybah, *Ma'ārif*, 206. He was a Baṣran of the northern tribe Ḍubay'ah, a branch of the Rabī'ah; see Ibn Ḥazm, *Jamharat*, 292–93; he died in the year 124/741–42. See Khalīfah b. Khayyāṭ, *Ta'rīkh*, 372; Ibn Ḥibbān, *Mashāhīr*, 151.

1420. A Kūfan of the northern Thaqīf tribe. See al-Dūlābī, I, 134; Ibn Ḥibbān, *Thiqāt*, VII, 456; Ibn Ḥajar, *Tahdhīb*, X, 332. Al Mu'tamir died in the year 187/803.

1421. Of the northern tribe Fazārah. He fought on 'Alī's side in the battle of Nahrawān and later lived in Wāsiṭ. See Khalīfah b. Khayyāṭ, *Ṭabaqāt*, 325; al-Dūlābī, I, 130; Ibn Sa'd, VII/2, 60; al-Mizzī, *Tahdhīb*, XXXIII, 162.

1422. In all probability the reference is to Dā'ūd b. Abī Hind, although this person's *kunyah* is usually given as Abū Bakr or Abū Muḥammad. Abū Hind's name was Dīnār b. 'Udhāfir, the latter being quite a rare name. See p. 328, below.

1423. See p. 282, above. It is not clear whether there are two different Abū Laylās or only one whose name is not certain.

1424. Al-Ṭabarī probably made a mistake here. According to all the sources I examined, the Abū Ayyūb from whom Qatādah (b. Di'āmah) transmitted was Yaḥyā b. Mālik. There seems, however, to be a confusion between Abū Ayyūb al-Marāghī Yaḥyā b. Mālik, associated with Qatādah (al-Mizzī, *Tahdhīb*, XXXIII, 60–61; Ibn Ḥibbān, *Thiqāt*, V, 529; al-Dūlābī, I, 103), and Abū Ayyūb al-'Atakī, also called Yaḥyā b. Mālik by Ibn Ma'īn (al-Dūlābī, I, 103). The latter is called Yaḥyā b. al-Mundhir by al-Ṭabarī, see p. 308, above. Al-Sam'ānī, V, 245, records Abū Ayyūb, Yaḥyā b. Mālik, under al-Marāghī but no Abū Ayyūb under al-'Atakī.

Abū Khabṭah, who transmitted [traditions] to Mālik b. Mighwal.[1425]
[His name was] Ḥakīm al-Ḥadhdhā'.

Abū Sufyān, the companion of Jābir [b. 'Abdallāh].[1426]
[His name was] Ṭalḥah b. Nāfi'.

Abū Sufyān, who transmitted [traditions] to Abū Mu'āwiyah and Ḥafṣ b. Ghiyāth.[1427]
[His name was] Ṭarīf al-Sa'dī.

Abū Ḥayyān al-Ashja'ī.[1428]
His name was Mundhir.

Abū Ḥudhayfah, Salamah b. Ṣuhayb.[1429]
'Alī b. al-Aqmar transmitted [traditions] from him.[1430]

Abū Bisṭām, who transmitted [traditions] to al-Fazārī.[1431]

1425. The manuscript has Ḥanṭah; see 2549, n. *e*. There seems to be no person with the *kunyah* Abū Khabṭah. The closest I could reach was one of Mālik's informants named al-Ḥakam (not Ḥakīm) b. 'Utaybah b. al-Nahhās b. Ḥanṭab. The last is a rather unusual name and could easily be garbled. Al-Ḥakam b. 'Utaybah, however, was a famous judge, not known as a traditionist, and, in addition, his *kunyah* is usually given as Abū Muḥammad and not Abū Ḥanṭab (but many people had more than one *kunyah*). He died in the year 115/733–34; see Ibn Ḥajar, *Tahdhīb*, II, 374. For Mālik b. Mighwal, a Kūfan traditionist who died in the year 158/774–75, see Ibn Ḥajar, ibid., X, 20–21; Ibn Ḥibbān, *Mashāhīr*, 267.

1426. A client of the Quraysh, of the second half of the first/seventh century, resident of Wāsiṭ. See Khalīfah b. Khayyāṭ, *Ṭabaqāt*, 155; Ibn Ḥibbān, *Mashāhīr*, 175; Ibn 'Adī, IV, 1432; Ibn Ḥajar, *Tahdhīb*, V, 24 (read Nāfi' for Nafa').

1427. Abū Sufyān Ṭarīf b. Shihāb of the Tamīm, a Baṣran traditionist; see Ibn 'Adī, IV, 1436–38; al-Mizzī, *Tahdhīb*, XIII, 377–80. Abū Mu'āwiyah mentioned here is Muḥammad b. Khāzim, a Kūfan client of the Tamīmī group, the Banū Sa'd, who died in the year 195/810–11. He was a *ḥāfiẓ* but held Murji'ī views; see al-Mizzī, *Tahdhīb*, XXV, 123–33.

1428. A companion of 'Abdallāh b. Mas'ūd; see al-Dūlābī, I, 161.

1429. A Kūfan of the southern tribe Arḥab, a branch of Hamdān, who lived in the second half of the first/seventh century. See Ibn Ḥibbān, *Mashāhīr*, 176; al-Mizzī, *Tahdhīb*, XI, 291–95.

1430. A Kūfan Hamdānī traditionist. See Ibn Ḥajar, *Tahdhīb*, VII, 250–51; al-Dhahabī, *Siyar*, V, 313; al-Mizzī, *Tahdhīb*, XX, 323–25.

1431. Al-Dūlābī, I, 127; al-Dhahabī, *Mīzān*, III, 296. Al-Fazārī was the *ḥāfiẓ* Marwān b. Mu'āwiyah, a descendant of the leading family of the Fazārah. He lived in al-Kūfah, Mecca, and Damascus and died in the year 194/809–10 (there are other versions). See al-Sam'ānī, IV, 380; Ibn Manẓūr, *Mukhtaṣar*, XXIV, 224–26.

[His name was] Yaḥyā b. ʿAbd al-Raḥmān al-Tamīmī.

Abū Maryam, ʿAbd al-Ghaffār b. al-Qāsim.[1432]

Abū al-Muʿallā al-ʿAṭṭār.[1433]
His name was Yaḥyā b. Maymūn.

[2550] Abū Bakr al-Hudhalī, Sulmā b. ʿAbdallāh b. Sulmā.[1434]

Abū Bakkār, al-Ḥakam b. Farrūkh al-Ghazzāl.[1435]

Abū al-Tayyāḥ, Yazīd b. Ḥumayd.[1436]

Abū Hilāl al-Rāsibī, Muḥammad b. Sulaym.[1437]

Abū al-Muʿallā, Zayd b. Murrah.[1438]

Abū Ḥamzah al-Sukkarī, Muḥammad b. Maymūn.[1439]

Abū Isḥāq al-Ṣāʾigh, Ibrāhīm b. Maymūn.[1440]

1432. A Kūfan, of Anṣārī origin. According to Ibn ʿAdī, V, 1964–65, he was an ultra-Shīʿī and used to invent traditions; Shīʿī sources mention him as a trustworthy transmitter and author of a book. There is, however, a confusion between him and his brother ʿAbd al-Muʾmin; see al-Quhpāʾī, IV, 99, 109.

1433. A Kūfan of the northern Ḍabbah tribe who died after the year 130/747–48. See Khalīfah b. Khayyāṭ, *Taʾrīkh*, 429; idem, *Ṭabaqāt*, 217; Ibn Abī Ḥātim, IV/2, 188.

1434. A Baṣran who specialized in Qurʾān interpretation and history (*ayyām* "the history of battle days"). He was a companion of al-Ḥasan (al-Baṣrī? d. 110/728–29). See Ibn ʿAdī, III, 1167–72; al-Dhahabī, *Mīzān*, I, 408.

1435. A Baṣran traditionist who transmitted from ʿIkrimah (died 107/72–26). See al-Dūlābī, I, 124; Ibn Abī Ḥātim, I/2, 126; al-Mizzī, *Tahdhīb*, VII, 130–31.

1436. A Baṣran jurist of the northern Sulaym tribe who died in the year 130/747–48. See Khalīfah b. Khayyāṭ, *Taʾrīkh*, 418; idem, *Ṭabaqāt*, 216; Ibn Ḥibbān, *Mashāhīr*, 155; Ibn Qutaybah, *Maʿārif*, 206.

1437. A Baṣran traditionist, a client of the (pseudo-)Qurashī clan the Banū Sāmah or the Banū Ḥayyah. He died in the year 165/781–82. See Ibn Qutaybah, *Maʿārif*, 223; al-Samʿānī, III, 25; Ibn ʿAdī, VI, 2218–21; Ibn Saʿd, VII/2, 36.

1438. Also called Zayd b. Abī Laylā; see al-Dūlābī, I, 124.

1439. A *ḥāfiẓ*, a resident of Marw, who died in the year 167 or 168/784–85. See Khalīfah b. Khayyāṭ, *Ṭabaqāt*, 324; Ibn Ḥibbān, *Mashāhīr*, 311; al-Sayrawān, 169.

1440. Originally from Iṣfahān, he later settled in Khurāsān. He was associated with Abū Muslim, but when the latter openly spread ʿAbbasid propaganda Abū Isḥāq expressed objections and was therefore executed, in the year 131/748–49. See Ibn Saʿd, VII/2, 103; al-Mizzī, *Tahdhīb*, II, 223–24; Ibn Ḥibbān, *Mashāhīr*, 309.

Abū Sinān al-Rāzī, Sa'īd b. Sinān.[1441]

Abū Salām al-Ḥanafī, 'Abd al-Malik b. Salām al-Madā'inī.[1442]

Abū al-Azhar al-Shāmī, Farwah b. al-Mughīrah.[1443]

Abū Ḥamzah, who transmitted [traditions] to al-A'mash.[1444] [His name was] Sa'd b. 'Ubādah.

Abū Kathīr al-Zubaydī, 'Abdallāh b. Mālik.[1445]

Abū Hilāl al-Ṭā'ī, Yaḥyā b. Ḥayyān.[1446]

Abū Khālid al-Wālibī, Hurmuz.[1447]

Abū Mu'āwiyah al-Bajalī, 'Ammār al-Duhnī.[1448]

Abū al-Mu'tamir, Yazīd b. Ṭahmān.[1449]

1441. Abū Sinān al-Aṣghar, of the northern Shaybān, a jurist of the second century, originally a Kūfan, who settled in al-Rayy. See Ibn Ḥibbān, *Mashāhīr*, 260; Ibn Sa'd, VII/2, 109; al-Mizzī, *Tahdhīb*, X, 492–95.

1442. According to al-Mizzī, *Tahdhīb*, XVIII, 415–16, and al-Dhahabī, *Mīzān*, II, 153: 'Abd al-Malik b. Muslim b. Salām, a Kūfan transmitter of the generation of Sufyān al-Thawrī (d. 161/777–78). Some say he was a Shī'ī.

1443. A Syrian, counted among the Companions. According to Abū Zur'ah, 695, his name was al-Mughīrah b. Farwah. He died before the year 113/731–32. See also Abū Zur'ah, 327; Ibn Ḥajar, *Iṣābah*, IV, 6.

1444. A Kūfan of the northern Sulaym tribe who was a Khārijī but renounced the creed later in life. He died during the second quarter of the eighth century. See Ibn Sa'd, VI, 208; al-Mizzī, *Tahdhīb*, X, 290–91.

1445. A Kūfan Successor of the southern tribe Zubayd of whose name there are several versions. He died during the caliphate of 'Abd al-Malik. See al-Dhahabī, *Mīzān*, III, 377 (Abū Kabīr); al-Mizzī, *Tahdhīb*, X, 219–20.

1446. A transmitter of the first half of the eighth century who originated in Khurāsān and lived in al-Madā'in. See al-Dūlābī, II, 154; Ibn 'Adī, VII, 2704; al-Dhahabī, *Mīzān*, III, 285–86; cf. 309, where he is called Yazīd b. Ḥayyān (read Ḥayyān for Ḥibbān).

1447. A slave, or client, of the Banū Asad in al-Kūfah, who died in the year 100/718–19. See Khalīfah b. Khayyāṭ, *Ṭabaqāt*, 158; Ibn Ḥibbān, *Mashāhīr*, 176; Ibn Sa'd, VI, 88.

1448. There are several versions of the name. He was a Kūfan, some say, a Shī'ī, who died in the year 133/750–51. See Khalīfah b. Khayyāṭ, *Ṭabaqāt*, 163; al-Mizzī, *Tahdhīb*, XXXIV, 303; al-Dhahabī, *Mīzān*, III, 382.

1449. A Baṣran traditionist of the first half of the eighth century who belonged to the Raqāsh, a group from the northern Qays 'Aylān. See al-Mizzī, *Tahdhīb*, XXXII, 166–67; al-Sam'ānī, III, 81.

Abū al-Hayyāj, who transmitted [traditions] to ʿĀmir b. Sharāḥīl al-Shaʿbī and Saʿīd b. Jubayr.[1450]
[His name was] ʿAmr b. Mālik al-Azdī.

[2551] Abū Maryam al-Asadī, who transmitted [traditions] to Ashʿath b. Abī al-Shaʿthāʾ.[1451]
His name was ʿAbdallāh b. Ziyād.

Abū Idrīs, who transmitted [traditions] from al-Musayyib b. Najabah.[1452]
His name was Sawād.

Abū al-Haytham, the reed seller.[1453]
His name was ʿAmmār.

The Kunyahs *of the Successors Who Were Known by Their Names, Rather than by Their* Kunyahs

ʿAbd al-Raḥmān b. al-Ḥārith b. Hishām.[1454]
His *kunyah* was Abū Muḥammad.

1450. He is not recorded in the lists of informants of al-Shaʿbī and Ibn Jubayr. He belonged to the northern Asad, not to the southern Azd as recorded here (the southern Azd are sometimes called Asd, so that an Azdī may be called Asdī, but not the reverse) and was among those entrusted by Saʿd b. Abī Waqqāṣ (or ʿUmar b. al-Khaṭṭāb) with the planning of al-Kūfah. See Yāqūt, *Muʿjam al-buldān*, IV, 324; al-Mizzī, *Tahdhīb*, VII, 471–72 (his name is given as Ḥayyāh b. al-Ḥuṣayn); al-Balādhurī, *Futūḥ* (de Goeje), 276; Ibn Ḥazm, *Jamharat*, 194; Khalīfah b. Khayyāṭ, *Ṭabaqāt*, 141; al-Ṭabarī, *Taʾrīkh*, I, 2369, 2488, 2491.

1451. Abū Maryam was a Kūfan traditionist and a companion of ʿAbdallāh b. Masʿūd; see Ibn Ḥibbān, *Thiqāt*, V, 58. Al-Ashʿath was the son of Sulaym b. al-Aswad, mentioned above, a Kūfan traditionist who died in the year 125/741–42. See Ibn Ḥibbān, *Thiqāt*, VI, 62; al-Ṣafadī, IX, 275.

1452. A Kūfan of the southern Hamdān confederation of the second half of the seventh century; he was a Shīʿī. His name was Sawwār or Musāwir (b. Muṣʿab?). See al-Mizzī, *Tahdhīb*, XXXIII, 21; Ibn Ḥibbān, *Thiqāt*, IV, 338; idem, *Majrūḥīn*, I, 356; al-Quhpāʾī, III, 175.

1453. *Ṣāḥib al-qaṣab*, which can also mean "the sugarcane seller." A Kūfan transmitter. See al-Dūlābī, II, 156; Ibn Ḥibbān, *Thiqāt*, VII, 660. It is recorded that Ibrāhīm al-Nakhaʿī (d. 96/714) transmitted from him.

1454. A Medinan, one of the notables of the Quraysh, of the Makhzūm clan. He was born in the Prophet's lifetime and died in the year 43/663–64. See Ibn Ḥajar, *Iṣābah*, III, 66; Ibn Ḥibbān, *Mashāhīr*, 109; idem, *Thiqāt*, III, 253.

Muḥammad b. Rabī'ah b. al-Ḥārith b. 'Abd al-Muṭṭalib.[1455]
His *kunyah* was Abū Ḥamzah after his son Ḥamzah.

'Abdallāh b. al-Ḥārith b. Nawfal b. al-Ḥārith b. 'Abd al-Muṭṭalib.
His *kunyah* was Abū Muḥammad, and his nickname was Babbah.

Marwān b. al-Ḥakam.[1456]
His *kunyah* was Abū 'Abd al-Malik.

Muḥammad b. Ṭalḥah b. 'Ubaydallāh.[1457]
His *kunyah* was Abū Sulaymān after his son Sulaymān.

'Abdallāh b. 'Utbah b. Mas'ūd.[1458]
His *kunyah* was Abū 'Abd al-Raḥmān.

Muḥammad b. al-Ash'ath b. Qays.[1459]
His *kunyah* was Abū al-Qāsim.

1455. A Qurashī of the Hāshimī clan, a jurist. See Khalīfah b. Khayyāṭ, *Ṭabaqāt*, 231; al-Balādhurī, *Ansāb*, III, (Dūrī), 295.

1456. The fourth Umayyad caliph, founder of the Marwānid branch of the Umayyads, reigned 64–65/684–85. See "Marwān b. al-Ḥakam," *EI*², VI, 621–23 (C. E. Bosworth); Strayer, *Dictionary*, s.v. "Marwān (I) ibn al-Ḥakam" (L. Conrad); Hammarneh; al-Balādhurī, *Ansāb*, V, 125–60; al-Munajjid, 158–59.

1457. Another version of his *kunyah* is Abū al-Qāsim; he thus bears both the name and *kunyah* of the Prophet. He was the son of the close Companion of the Prophet Ṭalḥah b. 'Ubaydallāh and known for his piety. He was killed in the battle of the Camel on 'Ā'ishah's side. See Ibn Qudāmah, 322–24; Khalīfah b. Khayyāṭ, *Ṭabaqāt*, 233; Ibn Ḥibbān, *Mashāhīr*, 45; Ibn Sa'd, V, 37–39.

1458. Of the Hudhayl, nephew of the Companion 'Abdallāh b. Mas'ūd. He acted as the leader of prayer (imām) and a judge in al-Kūfah and died in the year 73/692–93 or 74/693–94. See Khalīfah b. Khayyāṭ, *Ta'rīkh*, 266, 271; idem, *Ṭabaqāt*, 141–42; Ibn Ḥibbān, *Mashāhīr*, 166; Wakī', II, 402–4.

1459. A son of the Kindī prince al-Ash'ath b. Qays and father of the rebel 'Abd al-Raḥmān b. Muḥammad. He was a leader of the Kindah and governor of Ṭabaristān for 'Ubaydallāh b. Ziyād, then of Mosul for 'Abdallāh b. al-Zubayr. He fell in battle against al-Mukhtār in the year 67/686–87. See Crone, *Slaves*, 110; "al-Ash'ath b. Ḳays," *EI*², VII, 400–1 (G. R. Hawting). al-Balādhurī, *Ansāb*, V, 241, 251–54, 259–60; Khalīfah b. Khayyāṭ, *Ṭabaqāt*, 146; Ibn Ḥibbān, *Mashāhīr*, 166. He must not be confused with the early 'Abbāsid general, Muḥammad b. al-Ash'ath b. 'Uqbah al-Khuzā'ī.

'Umārah b. Khuzaymah b. Thābit.[1460]
His *kunyah* was Abū Muḥammad.

Muḥammad b. Ubayy b. Ka'b.[1461]
His *kunyah* was Abū Mu'ādh.

Sa'īd b. al-Musayyab, Abū Muḥammad.[1462]

Al-Muhallab b. Abī Ṣufrah.[1463]
His *kunyah* was Abū Sa'īd.

Zurārah b. Awfā al-Ḥarashī.[1464]
His *kunyah* was Abū Ḥājib.

[2552] Yazīd b. 'Abdallāh b. al-Shikhkhīr.[1465]
His *kunyah* was Abū al-'Alā'.

Jāriyah b. Qudāmah al-Sa'dī, of the [Banū] Sa'd of Tamīm.[1466]

1460. Another version of his *kunyah* is Abū 'Abdallāh. He was a son of the Anṣārī (Awsī) Companion Khuzaymah b. Thābit, and died in Medina in the year 105/723–24. See Khalīfah b. Khayyāṭ, *Ta'rīkh*, 344; idem, *Ṭabaqāt*, 248; Ibn Ḥibbān, *Mashāhīr*, 115.

1461. A Medinan, son of the Anṣārī Companion Ubayy b. Ka'b. He was born in the Prophet's lifetime and died in the battle of al-Ḥarrah in the year 63/683. See Ibn Ḥajar, *Iṣābah*, III, 471–72; Ibn Sa'd, V, 55; Khalīfah b. Khayyāṭ, *Ṭabaqāt*, 237–38.

1462. A famous, most highly regarded Medinan jurist, *ḥāfiẓ*, historian, and genealogist of the Qurashī clan the Makhzūm. He was put in prison for refusing to give allegiance to al-Walīd and Sulaymān, sons of the caliph 'Abd al-Malik, and died in the year 94/712–13. See F. Sezgin, I, 276; Ibn Sa'd, V, 88–106; Khalīfah b. Khayyāṭ, *Ṭabaqāt*, 244; Ibn Ḥibbān, *Mashāhīr*, 105; al-Sayrawān, 96; 'Abd al-Malik Ibn Ḥabīb, 160–61, 170; Abū Zayd, *Ṭabaqāt al-nassābīn*, 26.

1463. Of the southern confederation the Azd. A general and governor of Khurāsān under al-Ḥajjāj, founder of the Muhallabī family and the Azdī power in Khurāsān, father of the rebel Yazīd b. al-Muhallab. He died in the year 83/703. See Hawting, *First Dynasty*, 66, 73; "al-Muhallab b. Abī Ṣufra," *EI*[2], VII, 357 (P. Crone); Khalīfah b. Khayyāṭ, *Ṭabaqāt*, 201; Ibn Qutaybah, *Ma'ārif*, 175.

1464. Of the clan Banū al-Ḥarīsh, a branch of the northern 'Āmir b. Ṣa'ṣa'ah. He was a prayer leader (imām) and judge in al-Baṣrah, who died in the year 73/692–93 (there are other versions). See Khalīfah b. Khayyāṭ, *Ta'rīkh*, 303, 306; idem, *Ṭabaqāt*, 197; Ibn Ḥibbān, *Mashāhīr*, 153–54; idem, *Thiqāt*, IV, 266; Wakī', I, 292–97.

1465. A Baṣran of the Banū al-Ḥarīsh (see note 1464, above). He died in the year 108/726–27 or 111/729–30. Khalīfah b. Khayyāṭ, *Ta'rīkh*, 352; idem, *Ṭabaqāt*, 208; Ibn Ḥibbān, *Thiqāt*, V, 532.

1466. A Companion, tribal leader, and supporter of 'Alī, which did not hinder him from visiting Mu'āwiyah at his court. He lived in al-Baṣrah. See Khalīfah b. Khayyāṭ, *Ṭabaqāt*, 44; Ibn Ḥibbān, *Mashāhīr*, 71; al-Ḍabbī, 35, 41–42; Naṣr b. Muzāḥim, 24–25, 205.

His *kunyah* was Abū Ayyūb.

Al-Ḥasan b. Abī al-Ḥasan al-Baṣrī.
Abū al-Ḥasan's name was Yasār. [Al-Ḥasan's] *kunyah* was Abū Saʿīd.

Jābir b. Zayd, Abū al-Shaʿthāʾ al-Azdī.

ʿUqbah b. ʿAbd al-Ghāfir.[1467]
His *kunyah* was Abū Nahār al-Azdī.

Qatādah b. Diʿāmah al-Sadūsī.
His *kunyah* was Abū al-Khaṭṭāb.

Thābit al-Bunānī.
His *kunyah* was Abū Muḥammad and his [full] name Thābit b. Aslam.

Kaʿb b. Mātiʿ, that is, Kaʿb al-Aḥbār.
His *kunyah* was Abū Isḥāq, and he belonged to Ḥimyar.

ʿAṭāʾ b. Yasār, the client of Maymūnah, the Prophet's wife.[1468]
His *kunyah* was Abū Muḥammad.

Qabīṣah b. Dhuʾayb.[1469]
His *kunyah* was Abū Isḥāq or, according to another version, Abū Saʿīd.

1467. A Baṣran of the Azd confederation who participated in the revolt of ʿAbd al-Raḥmān Ibn al-Ashʿath and was killed in battle. See Khalīfah b. Khayyāṭ, *Taʾrīkh*, 281, 286; idem, *Ṭabaqāt*, 205; Ibn Ḥibbān, *Mashāhīr*, 149; idem, *Thiqāt*, V, 224.

1468. A jurist, traditionist, storyteller (*qāṣṣ*), and judge who lived in Medina and Syria. (It is not certain that he was a judge: The sources sometimes confuse *qāḍī*, with *qāṣṣ*, the two words being graphically similar, and he was not recorded by Wakīʿ.) He died in Alexandria in the year 103/721–22 (there are other versions). See Khalīfah b. Khayyāṭ, *Taʾrīkh*, 354; idem, *Ṭabaqāt*, 247; Ibn Ḥibbān, *Mashāhīr*, 114; ʿAbd al-Malik Ibn Ḥabīb, 174; al-Sayrawān, 128; Ibn Manẓūr, *Mukhtaṣar*, XVII, 80–83.

1469. Of the Khuzāʿah; a jurist and traditionist, responsible for the postal (and spying) services (*barīd*), as well as the seal (*khātam*), under the caliph ʿAbd al-Malik b. Marwān. He died in the year 86/705 (there are other versions). See Ibn Ḥazm, *Jamharat*, 236; Khalīfah b. Khayyāṭ, *Taʾrīkh*, 293, 302; idem, *Ṭabaqāt*, 309; Ibn Ḥibbān, *Mashāhīr*, 106–7; al-Balādhurī, *Ansāb*, V, 356; Abū Zurʿah, 405, 408; Ibn Manẓūr, *Mukhtaṣar*, XXI, 63–64.

'Urwah b. al-Zubayr.[1470]
His *kunyah* was Abū 'Abdallāh.

His full brother, al-Mundhir b. al-Zubayr.[1471]
His *kunyah* was Abū 'Uthmān.

Muṣ'ab b. al-Zubayr.[1472]
His *kunyah* was Abū 'Abdallāh.

Muḥammad b. Jubayr b. Muṭ'im.[1473]
His *kunyah* was Abū Sa'īd.

'Abd al-Malik b. Marwān.[1474]
His *kunyah* was Abū al-Walīd.

1470. Son of the Companion al-Zubayr and brother of 'Abdallāh b. al-Zubayr. He was one of the most highly regarded traditionists and jurists. Traditions concerning the Prophet's life were transmitted in his name, and some scholars credit him with a book on the campaigns (*maghāzī*) of the Prophet. He lived in Medina and died in the year 93/711–12 (there are other versions). See Horovitz, I, 542–52; Duri, *Rise of Historical Writing*, 76–95; Landau-Tasseron, "Reconstruction"; al-A'ẓamī, *Maghāzī*; Ibn Ḥibbān, *Mashāhīr*, 105.

1471. Counted among the noble and courageous Qurashīs. He was associated with Mu'āwiyah (and his governor Ziyād) but later supported his brother 'Abdallāh and was killed during the first Syrian siege of Mecca (64/683). See al-Ṭabarī, *Ta'rīkh*, II, 132, 224, 402–3, 528; Ibn Qudāmah, 266–67; al-Zubayrī, 244–45.

1472. Brother of the previous two, one of the noblemen and horsemen of the Quraysh. He governed Iraq on behalf of his brother 'Abdallāh and was killed by the Umayyad caliph 'Abd al-Malik in the year 72/691. See "Muṣ'ab b. al-Zubayr," *EI²*, VII, 649–50 (C. Pellat); Ibn Ḥibbān, *Mashāhīr*, 111; al-Balādhurī, *Ansāb*, V, 251–65, 278–90, 294–97, 331–51; Ibn Qudāmah, 268–69 and passim.

1473. Son of the Qurashī nobleman and Companion Jubayr b. Muṭ'im, of the Nawfal clan. He transmitted traditions, was an expert on Qurashī history, and associated with the caliph 'Abd al-Malik. He died during the caliphate of 'Umar II (99–101/717–20). See Khalīfah b. Khayyāṭ, *Ṭabaqāt*, 241; Ibn Ḥibbān, *Mashāhīr*, 118; al-Balādhurī, *Ansāb*, IVa, 105; Ibn Qudāmah, 239.

1474. One of the most important Umayyad rulers; he unified the Islamic community after a long crisis, centralized the government while emphasizing its "Arabness," and built the Dome of the Rock in Jerusalem, an early, magnificent articulation of the Islamic faith. He died in the year 86/705. See "'Abd al-Malik b. Marwān," *EI²*, I, 76–77 (H. A. R. Gibb); Hawting, *First Dynasty*, 58–66; Strayer, *Dictionary*, s.v. "'Abd al-Malik ibn Marwān" (L. Conrad); al-Balādhurī, *Ansāb*, V, passim; Ibn Manẓūr, *Mukhtaṣar*, XV, 219–34; al-Munajjid, 112–16; al-Rayyis.

ʿAbd al-ʿAzīz b. Marwān.[1475]
His *kunyah* was Abū al-Aṣbagh.

Iyās b. Salamah b. al-Akwaʿ.[1476]
His *kunyah* was Abū Salamah.

Rifāʿah b. Rāfiʿ b. Khadīj.
His *kunyah* was Abū Khadīj.

ʿAbd al-Raḥmān b. Abī Saʿīd al-Khudrī.
According to al-Wāqidī, his *kunyah* was Abū Muḥammad, whereas, according to ʿAbdallāh b. Muḥammad b. ʿUmārah, it was Abū Ḥafṣ.

Ḥamzah b. Abī Usayd al-Sāʿidī.[1477] [2553]
His *kunyah* was Abū Mālik.

Al-Mundhir b. Abī Usayd al-Sāʿidī.[1478]
His *kunyah* was Abū Saʿīd.

Saʿīd b. Yasār, Abū al-Ḥubāb, the client of al-Ḥasan b. ʿAlī.

Salmān al-Agharr, Abū ʿAbdallāh.[1479]

1475. Brother of the caliph ʿAbd al-Malik and father of the caliph ʿUmar II. He served his father and ʿAbd al-Malik as governor of Egypt, where he died in the year 82 or 83/702–3. See Khalīfah b. Khayyāṭ, *Ṭabaqāt*, 240–41; Ibn Ḥibbān, *Mashāhīr*, 193; al-Balādhurī, *Ansāb*, V, 183–84; al-Kindī, 44–51.

1476. A Medinan Successor, son of the Aslamī Companion Salamah b. al-Akwaʿ; he died in the year 119/737. See Khalīfah b. Khayyāṭ, *Ṭabaqāt*, 249; Ibn Ḥibbān, *Mashāhīr*, 116; idem, *Thiqāt*, IV, 35.

1477. A Medinan Successor, of the Khazraj. He died during the caliphate of al-Walīd I (86–96/705–15; there are other versions). See Khalīfah b. Khayyāṭ, *Ṭabaqāt*, 254; Ibn Ḥibbān, *Mashāhīr*, 125; al-Mizzī, *Tahdhīb*, VII, 311–13.

1478. Brother of the just-mentioned Ḥamzah. He is sometimes considered a Companion, having been born in the Prophet's lifetime. See Khalīfah b. Khayyāṭ, *Ṭabaqāt*, 253; Ibn Ḥibbān, *Thiqāt*, V, 419–20; Ibn Saʿd, V, 201.

1479. A storyteller (*qāṣṣ*) who lived in Medina in the second half of the seventh century. His origin was in Iṣfahān, and he was a client of the northern tribe Juhaynah. See Khalīfah b. Khayyāṭ, *Ṭabaqāt*, 265; Ibn Saʿd, V, 210; Ibn Ḥibbān, *Thiqāt*, IV, 333.

'Ikrimah, the client of Ibn 'Abbās.
His *kunyah* was Abū 'Abdallāh.

Shu'bah, the client of 'Abdallāh b. 'Abbās.[1480]
His *kunyah* was Abū 'Abdallāh.

Miqsam, the client of 'Abdallāh b. al-Ḥārith b. Nawfal b. al-Ḥārith b. 'Abd al-Muṭṭalib.[1481]
He is considered the client of Ibn 'Abbās because he was close to him. His *kunyah* was Abū al-Qāsim.

Nabhān, the client of Umm Salamah.[1482]
His *kunyah* was Abū Yaḥyā.

Nā'im b. Ujayl, the client of Umm Salamah.[1483]
His *kunyah* was Abū Qudāmah.

Suwayd b. Ghafalah, Abū Umayyah.

'Abd al-Raḥmān b. Abī Laylā.[1484]
His *kunyah* was Abū 'Īsā.

Zirr b. Ḥubaysh.[1485]

1480. Shu'bah b. Dīnār; he lived in Medina and died around the year 100/718–19 (there are other versions). See Khalīfah b. Khayyāṭ, *Ṭabaqāt*, 280; Ibn Sa'd, V, 217; al-Mizzī, *Tahdhīb*, XII, 497–500.

1481. He died in the year 101/719–20. See Khalīfah b. Khayyāṭ, *Ta'rīkh*, 332; idem, *Ṭabaqāt*, 281.

1482. A Medinan of the second half of the seventh century. See Ibn Ḥibbān, *Thiqāt*, V, 486; Khalīfah b. Khayyāṭ, *Ṭabaqāt*, 246.

1483. An early Egyptian transmitter and, according to Ibn Ḥajar, *Tahdhīb*, X, 360, also a jurist (although *faqīh* may mean "intelligent"), who died in the year 80/699–700. See Ibn Sa'd, V, 219; Ibn Ḥibbān, *Thiqāt*, V, 485.

1484. A *ḥāfiẓ*, a descendant of the Aws (Anṣār), of some standing in al-Kūfah (but see Ibn Qutaybah, *Ma'ārif*, 216, where rivals of his son refute the genealogy, and see p. 282, above). He died in the year 83/702–3, participating in the revolt of 'Abd al-Raḥmān b. Muḥammad b. al-Ash'ath. See Khalīfah b. Khayyāṭ, *Ṭabaqāt*, 150; Ibn Ḥibbān, *Mashāhīr*, 164; al-Balādhurī, *Ansāb*, IVa, 232; Ibn Ḥazm, *Jamharat*, 335; al-Sayrawān, 110.

1485. A member of the northern tribe Asad, who lived in pre-Islamic times and embraced Islam only after the Prophet's death; he became a supporter of 'Alī b. Abī Ṭālib. In addition to transmitting traditions, he was an expert on the Arabic language. He died during the revolt of Ibn al-Ash'ath, in the year 82/701–2. See Ibn Ḥajar, *Iṣābah*, I, 577; al-Kashshī, I, 241, III, 25; Khalīfah b. Khayyāṭ, *Ṭabaqāt*, 140; Ibn Ḥibbān, *Mashāhīr*, 161; idem, *Thiqāt*, IV, 269.

His *kunyah* was Abū Maryam.

Shurayḥ, the judge, that is, Shurayḥ b. al-Ḥārith b. Qays.[1486]
His *kunyah* was Abū Umayyah.

Al-Rabīʿ b. Khuthaym, Abū Yazīd.[1487]

Ṣilah b. Zufar al-ʿAbdī, Abū al-ʿAlāʾ.[1488]

Shabath b. Ribʿī.
His *kunyah* was Abū ʿAbd al-Quddūs.

ʿAbd Khayr b. Yazīd al-Khaywānī. [2554]
His *kunyah* was Abū ʿUmārah.

ʿAṭāʾ b. Abī Rabāḥ.[1489]
His *kunyah* was Abū Muḥammad.

Rajāʾ b. Ḥaywah.[1490]
His *kunyah* was Abū Naṣr.

1486. A *ḥāfiẓ* and judge, counted as one of the Ḥimyar. It was reported that he was appointed judge of al-Kūfah by ʿUmar and held the post for seventy-five years (!) He died in 80/699–700. See Ibn Qutaybah, *Maʿārif*, 191–92; Khalīfah b. Khayyāṭ, *Ṭabaqāt*, 145; Ibn Ḥibbān, *Mashāhīr*, 160; Wakīʿ, II, 189–398; al-Sayrawān, 101.

1487. A Kūfan jurist and ascetic of the rather obscure, northern tribe Thawr, who died in the year 63/682–83. See Ibn Ḥazm, *Jamharat*, 201; Khalīfah b. Khayyāṭ, *Ṭabaqāt*, 141; Ibn Ḥibbān, *Mashāhīr*, 160; Abū Nuʿaym, II, 105–19.

1488. A Kūfan, of the northern tribe ʿAbs, who died around the year 70/689–90. See Khalīfah b. Khayyāṭ, *Ṭabaqāt*, 143; Ibn Ḥibbān, *Mashāhīr*, 169.

1489. A client of a Qurashī clan. He was black, crippled, blind, and a highly regarded *ḥāfiẓ* and jurist. He lived in Mecca, where he died in the year 115/733–34 or 116/734–35. See Khalīfah b. Khayyāṭ, *Taʾrīkh*, 361; idem, *Ṭabaqāt*, 280; Ibn Ḥibbān, *Mashāhīr*, 133; al-Jaʿdī, 58–59; al-Sayrawān, 127–28.

1490. A Kindī or a client of the Kindah. He was a Syrian, a highly-regarded jurist, very influential at the Umayyad court. He died in the year 112/730–31. See Bosworth, "Rajāʾ ibn Ḥaywa." Gil, 121 (I thank Amikam Elʿad for these two references). Hawting, *First Dynasty*, 72; Khalīfah b. Khayyāṭ, *Ṭabaqāt*, 310; Ibn Ḥibbān, *Mashāhīr*, 189; Abū Zurʿah, 335, 336, 337, 370, 623, 711; Ibn ʿAsākir, *Taʾrīkh*, VI, 230–40.

Maymūn b. Mihrān.[1491]
His *kunyah* was Abū Ayyūb.

Mishraḥ b. ʿĀhān, Abū Muṣʿab.[1492]

Wahb b. Munabbih.
His *kunyah* was Abū ʿAbdallāh.

His brother, Hammām b. Munabbih.[1493]
His *kunyah* was Abū ʿUtbah.

Maʿqil b. Munabbih, their brother.[1494]
His *kunyah* was Abū ʿUqayl.

ʿAlī b. ʿAbdallāh b. al-ʿAbbās b. ʿAbd al-Muṭṭalib.
His *kunyah* was Abū Muḥammad after his son Muḥammad.

Al-Ḥasan b. Muḥammad b. al-Ḥanafiyyah.[1495]
His *kunyah* was Abū Muḥammad.

1491. A client of the northern tribe Naṣr b. Muʿāwiyah of the Hawāzin; see Ibn Ḥazm, *Jamharat*, 269 (there are other versions of the tribe). He was a *ḥāfiẓ*, a leading jurist in the Jazīrah (Mesopotamia), and collector of the Kharāj tax for ʿUmar II. He died in the year 117/735 (there are other versions). See Khalīfah b. Khayyāṭ, *Ṭabaqāt*, 319; Ibn Ḥibbān, *Mashāhīr*, 190; Ibn Qutaybah, *Maʿārif*, 198; al-Sayrawān, 178; ʿAbd al-Malik Ibn Ḥabīb, 174.

1492. The spelling in most of the sources is Hāʿān. He was an early Egyptian transmitter and a source of information for ʿAbdallāh b. Lahīʿah and al-Layth b. Saʿd, among others. See Khalīfah b. Khayyāṭ, *Ṭabaqāt*, 293; Ibn Ḥibbān, *Thiqāt*, V, 452; al-Mizzī, *Tahdhīb*, XXVIII, 7–8; Ibn Ḥajar, *Tahdhīb*, X, 141; Ibn ʿAdī, VI, 2460.

1493. A famous Yemenī traditionist. He had reportedly a written collection of traditions (*ṣaḥīfah*). His death date is variously given as 101/719–20, 102/720–21, 132/749–50, etc. (unusually large disparities among the versions). See Khalīfah b. Khayyāṭ *Ṭabaqāt*, 287; Ibn Ḥibbān, *Mashāhīr*, 198–99; Ibn Saʿd, V, 396; al-Mizzī, *Tahdhīb*, XXX, 298–300; al-Jaʿdī, 57. See also note 986, above.

1494. The least known of the Banū Munabbih, usually mentioned only as "brother of Wahb and Hammām." See Khalīfah b. Khayyāṭ, *Ṭabaqāt*, 287; Ibn Saʿd, V, 396; al-Jaʿdī, 57. See also note 986, above.

1495. In spite of his ancestry, he was not a Shīʿī, and perhaps this is why Sunnī sources state that he was superior to his brother Abū Hāshim (leader of the Hāshimiyyah movement). He is said to have been the first to discuss Murjiʾī views and to put them in writing. He lived in Medina and died in the year 99 or 100/718–19. See F. Sezgin, I, 594–95; Ibn Ḥibbān, *Thiqāt*, IV, 122; Ibn Saʿd, V, 241; al-Dhahabī, *Siyar*, IV, 130; al-Shahrastānī, 106.

Nāfi', the client of ['Abdallāh] Ibn 'Umar.[1496]
His *kunyah* was Abū 'Abdallāh.

Al-Ḍaḥḥāk b. Muzāḥim.[1497]
His *kunyah* was Abū al-Qāsim.

Nawf al-Bikālī, Nawf b. Faḍālah.
His *kunyah* was Abū Yazīd or Abū al-Rashīd.

Sa'īd b. Abī 'Arūbah.[1498]
His *kunyah* was Abū al-Naḍr, and the name of Abū 'Arūbah was Mihrān.

Ismā'īl b. Ibrāhīm, Ibn 'Ulayyah.[1499]
His *kunyah* was Abū Bishr.

Al-Mu'tamir b. Sulaymān al-Taymī.[1500]
His *kunyah* was Abū Muḥammad.

1496. A famous jurist and *ḥāfiẓ* of Persian origin who lived in Medina and died in the year 119/737 (there are other versions). See "Nāfi'," *EI*², VII, 127–28 (G. H. A. Juynboll); Khalīfah b. Khayyāṭ, *Ta'rīkh*, 191; idem, *Ṭabaqāt*, 256; Ibn Ḥibbān, *Mashāhīr*, 129; al-Sayrawān, 179.

1497. A member of the northern tribe Hilāl who is variously said to have lived in Khurāsān, al-Kūfah, and other places. He was an expert on the Qur'ān and a teacher and died in the year 105/723–24 (there are other versions). See F. Sezgin, I, 29–30; Ibn al-Nadīm, I, 75, II, 977; Khalīfah b. Khayyāṭ, *Ṭabaqāt*, 311; Ibn Ḥibbān, *Mashāhīr*, 308; Ibn Qutaybah, *Ma'ārif*, 201–2. Ibn al-Jazarī, I, 337; al-Sayrawān, 239; Nuwayhiḍ, I, 237.

1498. A client of the northern Banū Yashkur, a branch of Bakr b. Wā'il; see Ibn Ḥazm, *Jamharat*, 308. He was a Baṣran jurist and a Qadarī and died in the year 156/772–73 (there are other versions). See Khalīfah b. Khayyāṭ, *Ta'rīkh*, 457; idem, *Ṭabaqāt*, 220; Ibn Ḥibbān, *Mashāhīr*, 149; al-Sayrawān, 96; Ibn Qutaybah, *Ma'ārif*, 222.

1499. A Baghdādī, client of the northern tribe Banū Asad. He was appointed over the court of grievances (*maẓālim*) in Baghdād, and died in the year 194/809–10. See Khalīfah b. Khayyāṭ, *Ta'rīkh*, 503; idem, *Ṭabaqāt*, 224, 328; Ibn Ḥibbān, *Mashāhīr*, 255; Ibn Qutaybah, *Ma'ārif*, 221.

1500. Son of the Baṣran traditionist and historian and client of the Sulaym (or Murrah) Sulaymān b. Ṭarkhān (or Ṭahmān; but this version is due perhaps to a confusion between him and another Abū al-Mu'tamir, Yazīd b. Ṭahmān, see p. 313, above). See Khalīfah b. Khayyāṭ, *Ta'rīkh*, 493; idem, *Ṭabaqāt*, 224–25; Ibn Ḥibbān, *Mashāhīr*, 253; Ibn Qutaybah, *Ma'ārif*, 209; al-Sayrawān, 175; Ibn Sa'd, VII/2, 45.

Mu'ādh b. Mu'ādh.[1501]
His *kunyah* was Abū al-Muthannā.

Hawdhah b. Khalīfah.[1502]
His *kunyah* was Abū al-Ashhab.

'Abbād b. Ṣuhayb al-Kulaybī.[1503]
His *kunyah* was Abū Bakr.

[2555] Musaddad b. Musarhad.[1504]
His *kunyah* was Abū al-Ḥasan.

'Amr b. Murrah, Abū 'Abdallāh.[1505]

'Amr b. Dīnār, Abū Muḥammad al-Athram, the client of Bādhām, or Bādhān, Khusraw's governor of the Yemen.[1506]

Sulaymān b. Arqam, Abū Mu'ādh.[1507]

1501. A Baṣran jurist, *ḥāfiẓ*, and judge of the Tamīmī clan the Banū al-'Anbar. See Khalīfah b. Khayyāṭ, *Ta'rīkh*, 480, 495, 501, 503; idem, *Ṭabaqāt*, 226; Ibn Ḥibbān, *Mashāhīr*, 253; Wakī', II, 137–43.

1502. A descendant of Abū Bakrah who lived in al-Baṣrah and Baghdād and died in the year 215/830–31 or 210/825–26. See Ibn Qutaybah, *Ma'ārif*, 226; Ibn Ḥibbān, *Mashāhīr*, 257.

1503. A Baṣran of the Tamīmī clan Kulayb b. Yarbū; see Ibn Ḥazm, *Jamharat*, 225. He held Qadarī views. He died around the year 212/827–28. See al-Dhahabī, *Mīzān*, II, 10; Ibn 'Adī, IV, 1652–53.

1504. A Baṣran *ḥāfiẓ*, of the Asad tribe, who died in the year 228/842–43. See Khalīfah b. Khayyāṭ, *Ṭabaqāt*, 229; Ibn Qutaybah, *Ma'ārif*, 229; Ibn Sa'd, VII/2, 57; al-Sayrawān, 172.

1505. A Kūfan jurist of the southern tribe Murād who died in the year 118/736; see Ibn al-Kalbī, *Nasab ma'add*, 333.

1506. There are several persons by the name 'Amr b. Dīnār. The one meant here was a jurist and *muftī* in Mecca who died in the year 126/743–44. See Khalīfah b. Khayyāṭ, *Ṭabaqāt*, 281; Ibn Ḥibbān, *Mashāhīr*, 137; al-Rāzī, 582; Ibn Sa'd, V, 353–54; al-Ja'dī, 59–60; Bādhām or Bādhān, who had been governor of the Yemen for Khusraw and later for the Prophet, was killed during the latter's lifetime; see Ibn Ḥajar, *Iṣābah*, I, 170.

1507. A Baṣran of Anṣārī origin, apparently of the first half of the eighth century; see Ibn 'Adī, III, 1100–5. Al-Dhahabī, *Mīzān*, I, 409, records an odd piece of information: "He was a client of the Qurayẓah and al-Naḍīr"; both were Jewish Medinan tribes, the former exterminated, the latter exiled from Medina by the Prophet more than a century before Sulaymān's time. Perhaps the reference is to former ties of his family with the Jews in Medina.

Yazīd b. Abī Ziyād.[1508]
His *kunyah* was Abū 'Abdallāh.

Abū Isḥāq al-Sabī'ī.
According to Yaḥyā [b. Ma'īn], his name was 'Amr, and his father [was] Abū 'Amr.

Al-Ma'rūr b. Suwayd, Abū Umayyah.[1509]

Qays b. Abī Ḥāzim, Abū 'Abdallāh.[1510]

Sayyār b. Abī Sayyār, who transmitted [traditions] from Qays b. Abī Ḥāzim.[1511]
His *kunyah* was Abū Ḥamzah.

'Ubaydallāh b. al-Akhnas.[1512]
His *kunyah* was Abū Mālik.

Ḥabīb b. Abī Thābit.[1513]
His *kunyah* was Abū Yaḥyā.

Yazīd b. Kaysān, Abū Munīr.[1514]

1508. A client of the Hāshimī 'Abdallāh b. al-Ḥārith who lived in al-Kūfah and died in the year 136/753–54. According to al-Dhahabī, *Siyar*, VI, 129–33, he was a Shī'ī. See also idem, *Mīzān*, III, 310–11; Khalīfah b. Khayyāṭ, *Ta'rīkh*, 441; Ibn Sa'd, VI, 237; al-Sayrawān, 189.

1509. A Kūfan Successor, of the northern Asad tribe. He is said to have been associated with 'Umar b. al-Khaṭṭāb. See Khalīfah b. Khayyāṭ, *Ta'rīkh*, 287; idem, *Ṭabaqāt*, 152; Ibn Ḥibbān, *Mashāhīr*, 175; Ibn Sa'd, VI, 80–81.

1510. A famous Successor and a member of the Bajīlah tribe who lived in al-Kūfah and died in the year 94/712–13 (there are other versions). See Khalīfah b. Khayyāṭ, *Ta'rīkh*, 321; idem, *Ṭabaqāt*, 151–52; Ibn Ḥibbān, *Mashāhīr*, 164.

1511. A Kūfan transmitter. He is often confused with another person by the same name whose *kunyah* was Abū al-Ḥakam. See Ibn Ḥibbān, *Thiqāt*, VI, 421; al-Mizzī, *Tahdhīb*, XII, 315–17.

1512. A client of the Azd (there are other versions), a Kūfan of the mid-eighth century. See Ibn Ḥibbān, *Thiqāt*, VII, 147; Ibn Abī Ḥātim, II/2, 307.

1513. A client of the Banū Asad in al-Kūfah who died in the year 119/737. See Khalīfah b. Khayyāṭ, *Ta'rīkh*, 364; idem, *Ṭabaqāt*, 159; Ibn Ḥibbān, *Mashāhīr*, 174.

1514. Read Munayn for Munīr. An alternative *kunyah*: Abū Ismā'īl. His tribal affiliation is given as Yashkurī or Aslamī, and he was a Kūfan. See Ibn Ḥibbān, *Thiqāt*, VII, 628; cf. 627: there is probably a confusion between two persons here. See also Ibn 'Adī, VII, 2736–37; al-Mizzī, *Tahdhīb*, XXXII, 230–32.

Jabalah b. Suḥaym, Abū Suwayrah.[1515]

Ismā'īl b. Abī Khālid, Abū 'Abdallāh.[1516]

Yazīd al-Faqīr, Abū 'Uthmān.[1517]

Al-Walīd b. Muslim.[1518]
Khālid al-Ḥadhdhā' transmitted [traditions] from him. [His *kunyah* was] Abū Bishr.

[2556] Dā'ūd b. Abī Hind, Abū Bakr.[1519]

Ja'far b. Maymūn, Abū al-'Awwām.[1520]

'Āṣim al-Jaḥdarī, Abū al-Mujashshir.[1521]

Iyās b. Mu'āwiyah, Abū Wāthilah.[1522]

1515. A client of the Shaybān, a branch of the Bakr b. Wā'il. He lived in Iraq and died during the caliphate of Hishām. See Khalīfah b. Khayyāṭ, *Ta'rīkh*, 386; idem, *Ṭabaqāt*, 161; Ibn Ḥibbān, *Mashāhīr*, 170.

1516. An important traditionist, a client of the Bajīlah, who died in al-Kūfah in the year 145/762–63. Khalīfah b. Khayyāṭ, *Ta'rīkh*, 450; idem, *Ṭabaqāt*, 167; Ibn Ḥibbān, *Mashāhīr*, 178; Ibn Qutaybah, *Ma'ārif*, 211; al-Ṣafadī, IX, 115.

1517. Yazīd b. Ṣuhayb al-Kūfī. An early transmitter of the first half of the eighth century. See Ibn Sa'd, VI, 213; al-Dūlābī, II, 28; Ibn Ḥibbān, *Thiqāt*, V, 535.

1518. A Baṣran Successor of the Tamīmī clan the Banū al-'Anbar, of the first half of the eighth century. He must not be confused with the much more famous person of the same name, whose *kunyah* was Abū al-'Abbās (see Muṣṭafā, I, 129). See Ibn Ḥibbān, *Thiqāt*, VII, 554; al-Dhahabī, *Mīzān*, III, 276.

1519. A client of the northern Qushayr; see Ibn Ḥazm, *Jamharat*, 289. He was of Khurāsānī origin, a *ḥāfiẓ*, Qur'ān reader and commentator, and a *muftī*. He lived in Sarakhs and al-Baṣrah and died in the year 138/755–56 (there are other versions). See Ibn Sa'd, VII/2, 20; Ibn Ḥajar, *Tahdhīb*, III, 177; Khalīfah b. Khayyāṭ, *Ta'rīkh*, 445; idem, *Ṭabaqāt*, 218; Ibn Ḥibbān, *Mashāhīr*, 238; Ibn al-Nadīm, I, 75, II, 979; Ibn Qutaybah, *Ma'ārif*, 211; al-Sayrawān, 86, 229; Nuwayhiḍ, I, 181–82.

1520. Or, Abū 'Alī. A Baṣran Tamīmī transmitter of the first half of the eighth century. See Ibn 'Adī, II, 562; Ibn Ḥajar, *Tahdhīb*, II, 93; Ibn Ḥibbān, *Thiqāt*, VI, 135.

1521. 'Āṣim b. al-'Ajjāj or b. Abī al-Ṣabāḥ (there are other versions of the name); a Baṣran Qur'ān reader who died in the year 129/746–47. See Khalīfah b. Khayyāṭ, *Ta'rīkh*, 411; idem, *Ṭabaqāt*, 214; Ibn Ḥibbān, *Mashāhīr*, 152; al-Dhahabī, *Mīzān*, II, 4; Ibn al-Jazarī, I, 349.

1522. Of the northern Muzaynah tribe; see Ibn Ḥazm, *Jamharat*, 203. He was judge of al-Baṣrah for 'Umar II and died after the year 120/738. See Khalīfah b. Khayyāṭ, *Ta'rīkh*, 330–31; idem, *Ṭabaqāt*, 212; Ibn Ḥibbān, *Mashāhīr*, 241; Wakī', I, 312–74.

Abū al-Qamūṣ, Zayd b. ʿAlī.[1523]

ʿAmr b. Shuʿayb.[1524]
His *kunyah* was Abū Ibrāhīm.

ʿAṭāʾ b. al-Sāʾib.[1525]
His *kunyah* was Abū Zayd.

Hārūn b. ʿAntarah, Abū ʿAmr.[1526]

Misʿar [b. Kidām], Abū Salamah.

Al-Aswad b. Qays, Abū Qays.[1527]

Ḥafṣ b. Ghiyāth, Abū ʿUmar.[1528]

ʿImrān b. ʿUyaynah, Abū Muḥammad.[1529]

Al-Naḍr b. Abī Maryam, Abū Labīd.[1530]

1523. There are various versions of his tribal affiliation (ʿAbd al-Qays, Jarm, or Kindah). He was a Successor and must not be confused with the fifth Shīʿī imām. See Ibn Ḥibbān, *Thiqāt*, IV, 249; al-Mizzī, *Tahdhīb*, X, 100–1.

1524. A descendant of the Qurashī Companion and statesman ʿAmr b. al-ʿĀṣ, who died in the year 118/736 in al-Ṭāʾif. See Khalīfah b. Khayyāṭ, *Taʾrīkh*, 363; idem, *Ṭabaqāt*, 286; al-Zubayrī, 411.

1525. His *kunyah* is variously given as Abū Zayd, Abū Yazīd, and Abū al-Sāʾib. Some call him a Kūfan, whereas according to others he originated in Medina and lived in Marw. He was a client of the northern tribe Thaqīf, a *ḥāfiẓ*, and a Qurʾān reader and died in the year 136/753–54. See Ibn Ḥibbān, *Thiqāt*, VII, 251–52; al-Dhahabī, *Siyar*, VI, 110–14; Ibn al-Jazarī, I, 513; al-Sayrawān, 128; Khalīfah b. Khayyāṭ, *Ṭabaqāt*, 164; Nuwayhiḍ, I, 346.

1526. Or Abū ʿAbd al-Raḥmān or Abū Wakīʿ. He was a Kūfan traditionist, accused of lying and inventing traditions. See al-Mizzī, *Tahdhib*, XXX, 100–2; al-Dhahabī, *Mīzān*, III, 247.

1527. A Kūfan transmitter of the first half of the eighth century. See Ibn Ḥibbān, *Thiqāt*, IV, 32; Ibn Ḥajar, *Tahdhīb*, I, 298.

1528. Of the Nakhaʿ tribe. A *ḥāfiẓ* and judge in al-Kūfah and Baghdad who died in the year 194/809–10 (there are other versions). See Khalīfah b. Khayyāṭ, *Taʾrīkh*, 501; idem, *Ṭabaqāt*, 170; Ibn Ḥibbān, *Mashāhīr*, 272; al-Sayrawān, 80; Ibn Qutaybah, *Maʿārif*, 222–23; Wakīʿ, III, 184–88.

1529. A Kūfan of the middle or late eighth century, brother of the famous traditionist Sufyān b. ʿUyaynah, of the northern Hilāl tribe. See Ibn Ḥibbān, *Thiqāt*, VII, 240; Ibn Ḥajar, *Tahdhīb*, VIII, 120–21; al-Dhahabī, *Mīzān*, II, 278 (read ʿUyaynah for ʿAyyah).

1530. Read Līnah for Labīd. He apparently lived in the first half of the eighth century; see Ibn Abī Ḥātim, IV/1, 476.

[He was] a Kūfan, and the name of his father, Abū Maryam, was Ṭahmān.

'Ubayd b. Nuḍaylah, Abū Mu'āwiyah.[1531]

Dā'ūd b. Abī Hind.
His *kunyah* was Abū Bakr, and the name of his father, Abū Hind, was Dīnār.

'Āṣim b. Sulaymān al-Aḥwal.[1532]
His *kunyah* was Abū 'Abd al-Raḥmān, and he was a client of the Banū Tamīm.

Al-Nahhās b. Qahm.[1533]
His *kunyah* was Abū al-Khaṭṭāb.

[2557] Ḥaywah b. Shurayḥ.[1534]
His *kunyah* was Abū Yazīd al-Tujībī.

Thawr b. Yazīd.[1535]
His *kunyah* was Abū Khālid.

1531. Or b. Naḍlah. He was a Kūfan Qur'ān reader of the Khuzā'ah who died in the year 74/693–94. See Ibn Ḥibbān, *Mashāhīr*, 171; Khalīfah b. Khayyāṭ, *Ta'rīkh*, 271; idem, *Ṭabaqāt*, 150; Ibn al-Jazarī, I, 498.

1532. A client of the Tamīm, a *ḥāfiẓ*, who was overseer of measures and scales (*muḥtasib*) in al-Kūfah for the caliph al-Manṣūr, then a judge in al-Madā'in. He died in the year 141 or 142/759–60. See Khalīfah b. Khayyāṭ, *Ṭabaqāt*, 218, 325; Ibn Ḥibbān, *Mashāhīr*, 57; Wakī', III, 132; al-Sayrawān, 105; Ibn Qutaybah, *Ma'ārif*, 222.

1533. A Baṣran transmitter and storyteller (*qāṣṣ*), of the mid-eighth century. See Ibn 'Adī, VII, 2522–23; al-Dhahabī, *Mīzān*, III, 243.

1534. An Egyptian *ḥāfiẓ*, of the Kindī group Tujīb (called after the ancestress), see Ibn Ḥazm, *Jamharat*, 429–30. He died in the year 158/774–75 (there are other versions). See Khalīfah b. Khayyāṭ, *Ṭabaqāt*, 296; Ibn Ḥibbān, *Mashāhīr*, 298; al-Sayrawān, 82. His *kunyah* is given in all these sources as Abū Zur'ah.

1535. A Ḥimyarī (Kalā'ī) who lived in Ḥimṣ. He was considered trustworthy by some, but others accused him of being a Qadarī, and there is a report that he was driven out of Ḥimṣ. He died in Jerusalem in the year 153/770. See Abū Zur'ah, 359–60, 398, 712–13; Khalīfah b. Khayyāṭ, *Ṭabaqāt*, 315; Ibn Qutaybah, *Ma'ārif*, 220–21. He must not be confused with Thawr b. Zayd; see al-Ṭabarī, *Ta'rīkh*, I, 1329, n. *d*.

Al-Layth b. Sa'd.[1536]
His *kunyah* was Abū al-Ḥārith.

Rishdīn b. Sa'd.[1537]
His *kunyah* was Abū al-Ḥajjāj.

'Īsā b. Yūnus b. Abī Isḥāq al-Sabī'ī.[1538]
His *kunyah* was Abū 'Amr.

Muḥammad b. Yūsuf al-Firyābī.[1539]
His *kunyah* was Abū 'Abdallāh.

Ādam b. Abī Iyās.[1540]
His *kunyah* was Abū al-Ḥasan.

'Abd al-Majīd b. 'Abd al-'Azīz b. Abī Rawwād.[1541]
His *kunyah* was Abū 'Abd al-Ḥamīd.

Sufyān b. 'Uyaynah.
His *kunyah* was Abū Muḥammad.

1536. A client of the rather insignificant northern tribe Fahm; see Ibn Ḥazm, *Jamharat*, 243. He was one of the leading jurists in Egypt and died in the year 175/791–92. See Khoury, "al-Layth b. Sa'd"; idem, *'Abd Allah Ibn Lahī'a*, 173–77; Khalīfah b. Khayyāṭ, *Ṭabaqāt*, 296; Ibn Ḥibbān, *Mashāhīr*, 303; al-Sayrawān, 145; Shiḥāṭah.

1537. An Egyptian transmitter, of the Quḍa'ah confederation, also known as Abū al-Ḥajjāj al-Miṣrī, who died in the year 188/804. See Khalīfah b. Khayyāṭ, *Ta'rīkh*, 386; idem, *Ṭabaqāt*, 297; al-Dūlābī, I, 144; al-Dhahabī, *Mīzān*, I, 338–39.

1538. A Kūfan, grandson of the famous jurist Abū Isḥāq of the southern Sabī' (a branch of the Hamdān); he died in the year 191/806–7. See Khalīfah b. Khayyāṭ, *Ṭabaqāt*, 317–18; Ibn Ḥibbān, *Mashāhīr*, 295.

1539. A client of the Ḍabbah who originated in Firyāb, a village near Balkh and moved to Caesarea in Palestine, where he died in the year 212/827–28. He was associated with Sufyān al-Thawrī. See al-Sam'ānī, IV, 376; al-Dhahabī, *Mīzān*, III, 151; Abū Zur'ah, 26, 280; Ibn Manẓūr, *Mukhtaṣar*, XXIII, 371–74.

1540. A client of the Tamīm who originated in Khurāsān then settled in Baghdād, later in Palestine, and died in the year 220/835. See Ibn Ḥibbān, *Thiqāt*, VIII, 134; Ibn Sa'd, VII/2, 186.

1541. A client of the Azd (or of the Azdī chief al-Muhallab b. Abī Ṣufrah), who lived in Mecca and died in the year 206/821–22. He is said to have been a Murji' and a forger of Prophetic traditions. See Khalīfah b. Khayyāṭ, *Ṭabaqāt*, 284; Ibn Sa'd, V, 367; al-Dhahabī, *Mīzān*, II, 145–47; idem, *Siyar*, IX, 434–36.

Al-Fuḍayl b. 'Iyāḍ.[1542]
His *kunyah* was Abū 'Alī.

'Abdallāh b. Ja'far b. 'Abd al-Raḥmān b. al-Miswar b. Makhramah.[1543]
His *kunyah* was Abū Ja'far.

Ḥusayn b. Zayd b. 'Alī b. Ḥusayn b. 'Alī b. Abī Ṭālib.[1544]
His *kunyah* was Abū 'Abdallāh.

Hilāl b. Khabbāb.[1545]
His *kunyah* was Abū al-'Alā'.

Al-Ḥasan b. Qutaybah, Abū 'Alī.[1546]

[2558] 'Abbād b. 'Abbād al-Muhallabī.[1547]
His *kunyah* was Abū Mu'āwiyah.

1542. Of the Tamīmī clan Yarbū', an ascetic and *ḥāfiẓ*. He originated in Samarqand and lived in al-Kūfah and later in Mecca, where he died in the year 187/803. His tomb became a place of pilgrimage. See Khalīfah b. Khayyāṭ, *Ta'rīkh*, 493; idem, *Ṭabaqāt*, 284; Ibn Ḥibbān, *Mashāhīr*, 235; Ibn Sa'd, V, 366; Abū Nu'aym, VIII, 84–140; al-Sayrawān, 139–40.

1543. A descendant of the Qurashī Companion al-Miswar. He was a jurist, *muftī*, and expert on the campaigns of Muḥammad (*maghāzī*). Al-Wāqidī obtained information from him; see al-Wāqidī, 1. He lived in Medina, participated in the revolt of Muḥammad al-Nafs al-Zakiyyah in the year 145/762, and died in the year 170/786–87. See Khalīfah b. Khayyāṭ, *Ṭabaqāt*, 275; al-Dhahabī, *Mīzān*, II, 28; idem, *Siyar*, VII, 328–30.

1544. Son of the fifth Shī'ī imām (according to the Zaydiyyah), who lived in Medina and apparently later in al-Kūfah. He participated in the revolt of Muḥammad al-Nafs al-Zakiyyah but, it seems, was reconciled with the 'Abbasids, judging by the fact that his daughter was married to the caliph al-Mahdī (d. 169/785). See van Arendonck, 61 n. 4; al-Ṭabarī, *Ta'rīkh*, III, 258; al-Amīn, XXVI, 81–91; al-Ṣafadī, XII, 367.

1545. A client of Zayd b. Ṣūḥān, who was a Companion of the Prophet from the 'Abd al-Qays tribe. Hilāl was a Kūfan or Baṣran but settled in al-Madā'in, where he died in the year 144/761–62. See Khalīfah b. Khayyāṭ, *Ṭabaqāt*, 325; al-Dhahabī, *Mīzān*, III, 259–60; Ibn 'Adī, VII, 2580–81.

1546. A transmitter from al-Madā'in, of the second half of the eighth century. See Ibn Abī Ḥātim, I/2, 33–34; Ibn 'Adī, II, 739.

1547. A grandson of al-Muhallab b. Abī Ṣufrah, the Azdī leader. He originated in al-Baṣrah, settled in Baghdād, and died in the year 177/793–94 (there are other versions). See Ibn Ḥibbān, *Mashāhīr*, 254; idem, *Thiqāt*, VII, 161; Ibn Ḥajar, *Tahdhīb*, V, 84; al-Dhahabī, *Siyar*, VIII, 294–96. According to Ibn Sa'd, VII/2, 71, he practiced medicine.

Faraj b. Faḍālah.[1548]
His *kunyah* was Abū Faḍālah.

Ismā'īl b. Ja'far b. Abī Kathīr al-Madanī.[1549]
His *kunyah* was Abū Ibrāhīm.

Muḥammad b. al-Ḥasan, the companion of Abū Ḥanīfah.
His *kunyah* was Abū 'Abdallāh.

'Alī b. al-Ja'd.[1550]
His *kunyah* was Abū al-Ḥasan.

Surayj b. al-Nu'mān, the pearl trader.[1551]
His *kunyah* was Abū al-Ḥusayn.

Bishr b. al-Ḥārith al-'Ābid (the ascetic).[1552]
His *kunyah* was Abū Naṣr.

Al-Haytham b. Khārijah.[1553]
His *kunyah* was Abū Aḥmad.

Yaḥyā b. Yūsuf al-Zimmī.[1554]

1548. A Ḥimṣī traditionist, who was appointed head of the treasury (*bayt al-māl*) during al-Mahdī's caliphate and died in the year 176/792–93. See Khalīfah b. Khayyāṭ, *Ta'rīkh*, 474; idem, *Ṭabaqāt*, 316; al-Mizzī, *Tahdhīb*, XXXIII, 155–64; Ibn Manẓūr, *Mukhtaṣar*, XX, 263–64. See also El'ad, n. 152.

1549. A *ḥāfiẓ* and Qur'ān reader of Anṣārī descent who died in the year 108/726–27. See Khalīfah b. Khayyāṭ, *Ṭabaqāt*, 327; Ibn Ḥibbān, *Mashāhīr*, 224; al-Sayrawān, 65.

1550. A client of the Banū Hāshim or of the caliph Abū al-'Abbās' wife, Umm Salamah. He was a *ḥāfiẓ* and died in Baghdād in the year 230/844–45. See Khalīfah b. Khayyāṭ, *Ṭabaqāt*, 329; Ibn Qutaybah, *Ma'ārif*, 229; al-Sayrawān, 131.

1551. A Khurāsānī who lived in Baghdād and died in the year 217/832–33. See Ibn Ḥibbān, *Thiqāt*, VIII, 306–7; al-Dhahabī, *Mīzān*, I, 270; idem, *Siyar*, X, 219–20.

1552. A famous Baghdādī ascetic, also known as Bishr al-Ḥāfī (the barefooted), who died in the year 227/841–42. See Ibn Sa'd, VII/2, 83; al-Qummī, II, 152–55; al-Dhahabī, *Siyar*, X, 469–77; Abū Nu'aym, VIII, 336–60.

1553. He originated in Khurāsān, then lived in Baghdād and in Syria, and died in the year 227/841–42. See Ibn Sa'd, VII, 83; al-Khaṭīb al-Baghdādī, XIV, 58–59.

1554. He originated in Zimm, a village in Khurāsān, and lived in Baghdād, where he died in the year 225/839–40 (there are other versions). See Ibn Sa'd, VII/2, 87 (read al-Zimmī for al-Raqqī); al-Khaṭīb al-Baghdādī, XIV, 166–67; al-Mizzī, *Tahdhīb*, XXXII, 60–62.

His *kunyah* was Abū Zakariyā'.

Khalaf b. Hishām.[1555]
His *kunyah* was Abū Muḥammad.

Sulaymān b. Mihrān al-A'mash.
His *kunyah* was Abū Muḥammad.

Ismā'īl b. Abī Khālid.
His *kunyah* was Abū 'Abdallāh.

Mujālid b. Sa'īd.[1556]
His *kunyah* was Abū 'Uthmān.

Layth b. Abī Sulaym.[1557]
His *kunyah* was Abū Bakr.

[2559]

The Kunyahs *of People of Subsequent Generations Who Were Known by Their Names, Rather than by Their* Kunyahs

'Umar b. 'Abd al-'Azīz b. Marwān b. al-Ḥakam.[1558]
His *kunyah* was Abū Ḥafṣ.

1555. A transmitter and one of the ten most famous Qur'ān readers. He lived in Baghdād and died in the year 229/843–44, reportedly while in hiding from the Jahmī sect. See Ibn Sa'd, VII/2, 87; Ibn al-Jazarī, I, 272–74; Ibn Qutaybah, *Ma'ārif*, 231; al-Sayrawān, 228 (read Hishām for Hāshim).

1556. A transmitter of traditions, historical reports, and genealogies who died in the year 143 or 144/761–62. See Khalīfah b. Khayyāṭ, *Ta'rīkh*, 447; idem, *Ṭabaqāt*, 166; Ibn Sa'd, VI, 243; Abū Zayd, 31.

1557. A client of [the family of] Mu'āwiyah's brother 'Anbasah who lived in al-Kūfah and died in the year 143/760–61. See Khalīfah b. Khayyāṭ, *Ta'rīkh*, 447; idem, *Ṭabaqāt*, 166–67; Ibn Sa'd, VI, 243; Ibn 'Adī, VI, 2105–8.

1558. The eighth Umayyad caliph (99–101/717–20), reputed for his piety and just reforms, the only Umayyad recognized as *rāshid*, i.e., a just ruler following in the footsteps of the four first caliphs. See Hawting, *First Dynasty*, 76–81. "'Omar b. 'Abd al-'Azīz," *EI*[1], VI, 977–79 (K. V. Zettersteen); Gibb, "Fiscal Rescript"; Ibn Ḥibbān, *Mashāhīr*, 283; al-Ājurrī; Ibn al-Jawzī, *Sīrat*; Ibn Manẓūr, *Mukhtaṣar*, XIX, 98–128.

Ḥamzah b. ʿAbdallāh b. al-Zubayr.[1559]
His *kunyah* was Abū ʿUmārah after his son ʿUmārah.

ʿĀmir b. ʿAbdallāh b. al-Zubayr.[1560]
His *kunyah* was Abū al-Ḥārith.

Muḥammad b. Kaʿb al-Quraẓī.
His *kunyah* was Abū Ḥamzah.

Yaʿqūb b. Abī Salamah, the client of the family of al-Munkadir, of the [Qurashī clan] Taym b. Murrah.[1561]
His *kunyah* was Abū Yūsuf. He is the [one called] al-Mājishūn, and his brother and offspring were thus called after him. The name of his father, Abū Salamah, was Dīnār.

Muḥammad b. Muslim b. ʿUbaydallāh b. ʿAbdallāh b. Shihāb.[1562]
His *kunyah* was Abū Bakr.

His brother ʿAbdallāh b. Muslim.[1563]
His *kunyah* was Abū Muḥammad.

Muḥammad b. al-Munkadir.
His *kunyah* was Abū ʿAbdallāh.

1559. Renowned for his generosity but also for his weakness and stupidity. His father, the rival caliph ʿAbdallāh b. al-Zubayr, appointed him governor of al-Baṣrah but dismissed him after a short while. See al-Zubayrī, 240; Muḥammad Ibn Ḥabīb, *Munammaq*, 381; al-Balādhurī, *Ansāb*, V, 256–58 and passim; Ibn Ḥibbān, *Mashāhīr*, 119.

1560. Another son of ʿAbdallāh b. al-Zubayr, known for his piety, generosity, and knowledge of tradition and religious law, who lived in Medina and died in the year 121/739. See Ibn Ḥibbān, *Mashāhīr*, 110; Ibn Qudāmah, 260; Khalīfah b. Khayyāṭ, *Taʾrīkh*, 368; idem, *Ṭabaqāt*, 258.

1561. A famous jurist who lived in Baghdād and died in the year 164/780–81; the caliph al-Mahdī himself said the ritual prayer over his bier. See Khalīfah b. Khayyāṭ, *Ṭabaqāt*, 268; Ibn Ḥibbān, *Mashāhīr*, 130; Ibn Qutaybah, *Maʿārif*, 203.

1562. That is, al-Zuhrī.

1563. He lived in Medina and died before the year 124/741–42. See Khalīfah b. Khayyāṭ, *Ṭabaqāt*, 261; Ibn Ḥibbān, *Thiqāt*, V, 59–60; al-Mizzī, *Tahdhīb*, XVI, 129–30.

Ismā'īl b. 'Amr b. Sa'īd b. al-'Āṣ.[1564]
His *kunyah* was Abū Muḥammad.

'Abdallāh b. 'Urwah b. al-Zubayr b. al-'Awwām.[1565]
His *kunyah* was Abū Bakr.

Yaḥyā b. 'Urwah b. al-Zubayr.[1566]
His *kunyah* was Abū 'Urwah.

Hishām b. 'Urwah b. al-Zubayr.[1567]
His *kunyah* was Abū al-Mundhir.

'Abdallāh b. Ḥasan b. Ḥasan b. 'Alī b. Abī Ṭālib.
His *kunyah* was Abū Muḥammad.

'Abdallāh b. Muḥammad b. 'Aqīl b. Abī Ṭālib.[1568]
His *kunyah* was Abū Muḥammad.

'Abāyah b. Rifā'ah b. Rāfi' b. Khadīj.[1569]
His *kunyah* was Abū Rifā'ah.

1564. Of the Umayyad family, son of 'Amr b. Sa'īd al-Ashdaq, who rebelled against and was killed by the caliph 'Abd al-Malik; see al-Ṭabarī, *Ta'rīkh*, II, 783–89. Ismā'īl participated in that event, then lived in Medina, shunning politics, and died at the beginning of the 'Abbāsid caliphate. See Ibn Qudāmah, 196–97; Ibn Manẓūr, *Mukhtaṣar*, IV, 373–74.

1565. A grandson of the close Companion of the Prophet al-Zubayr b. al-'Awwām. 'Abdallāh lived in Medina and died toward the end of the Umayyad caliphate. He was reputed for feeding the poor during years of drought. See Khalīfah b. Khayyāṭ, *Ṭabaqāt*, 267; Ibn Qudāmah, 264–65; al-Mizzī, *Tahdhīb*, XV, 294–95.

1566. Brother of the aforementioned 'Abdallāh and one of the most distinguished among 'Urwah's sons. See Khalīfah b. Khayyāṭ, *Ṭabaqāt*, 267; Ibn Qudāmah, 265; Ibn Ḥibbān, *Thiqāt*, VII, 593; al-Mizzī, *Tahdhīb*, XXXI, 466–71.

1567. Brother of the aforementioned Yaḥyā and 'Abdallāh, a jurist and *ḥāfiẓ*, one of the leading religious figures in Medina. He moved to Baghdad, where he died in the year 146/763–64; the caliph al-Manṣūr himself said the ritual prayer over his bier. See F. Sezgin, I, 88–89; Ibn al-Nadīm, II, 1005; Ibn Qudāmah, 265; Khalīfah b. Khayyāṭ, *Ta'rīkh*, 365, 451; idem, *Ṭabaqāt*, 267; Ibn Ḥibbān, *Mashāhīr*, 130–31; al-Sayrawān, 182.

1568. A member of the Hāshimī family, he lived in Medina and died after the year 140/757–58, or before 145/762. See Khalīfah b. Khayyāṭ, *Ṭabaqāt*, 258; al-Dhahabī, *Mīzān*, II, 68; Ibn 'Adī, IV, 1466–68.

1569. A grandson of the Anṣārī Companion, Rāfi', who lived in Medina. See Khalīfah b. Khayyāṭ, *Ṭabaqāt*, 258; Ibn Ḥibbān, *Thiqāt*, V, 281; al-Mizzī, *Tahdhīb*, XIV, 268–69.

Bukayr b. ʿAbdallāh b. al-Ashajj, the client of al-Miswar b. Makhramah.
His *kunyah* was Abū ʿAbdallāh.

His brother Yaʿqūb b. ʿAbdallāh b. al-Ashajj.[1570]
His *kunyah* was Abū Yūsuf.

Wahb b. Kaysān. [2560]
His *kunyah* was Abū Nuʿaym; he was the client of ʿAbdallāh b. al-Zubayr.

Zayd b. Aslam.[1571]
His *kunyah* was Abū Usāmah.

His brother Khālid b. Aslam.[1572]
His *kunyah* was Abū Thawr.

Dā'ūd b. al-Ḥuṣayn, the client of ʿAmr b. ʿUthmān b. ʿAffān.[1573]
His *kunyah* was Abū Sulaymān.

Rabīʿah b. Abī ʿAbd al-Raḥmān.
The name of his father, Abū ʿAbd al-Raḥmān, was Farrūkh. The *kunyah* of Rabīʿah was Abū ʿUthmān.

Ṣafwān b. Sulaym.
His *kunyah* was Abū ʿAbdallāh.

1570. A client of the Qurashī clan Makhzūm (or of the Ashjaʿ), who lived in Medina and Egypt and died in a maritime raid in the year 122/740. Al-Dhahabī, *Siyar*, VIII, 174, says he was a jurist. See Ibn Ḥibbān, *Mashāhīr*, 298; idem, *Thiqāt*, VII, 641; Ibn Ḥajar, *Tahdhīb*, XI, 342.

1571. A client of [the family of] ʿUmar b. al-Khaṭṭāb, a Qur'ān reader, and interpreter, said to have used his personal judgment (*ra'y*) in his interpretations. He died in the year 136/753–54. He must not be confused with the Companion of the Prophet of the same name. See Ibn Ḥibbān, *Mashāhīr*, 130; al-Dhahabī, *Mīzān*, I, 361; Ibn al-Jazarī, I, 296; al-Sayrawān, 232.

1572. Also a client of [the family of] ʿUmar b. al-Khaṭṭāb who lived in Medina and transmitted to Ibn Shihāb al-Zuhrī (d. 124/741–42), among others. See Ibn Ḥibbān, *Thiqāt*, IV, 198; al-Mizzī, *Tahdhīb*, VIII, 28–29.

1573. A jurist who lived in Medina and died in the year 135/752–53. He was suspected of holding Khārijī or Qadarī views. See Khalīfah b. Khayyāṭ, *Ta'rīkh*, 437; idem, *Ṭabaqāt*, 259; Ibn Ḥibbān, *Mashāhīr*, 215; al-Dhahabī, *Mīzān*, I, 317; idem, *Siyar*, VI, 106.

Ṣāliḥ b. Kaysān.[1574]
His *kunyah* was Abū Muḥammad.

Muḥammad b. Abī Ḥarmalah.[1575]
His *kunyah* was Abū ʿAbdallāh; he was a client of the Banū ʿĀmir b. Luʾayy.

Yaḥyā b. Saʿīd al-Anṣārī.[1576]
His *kunyah* was Abū Yazīd.

Mūsā b. ʿUqbah.[1577]
His *kunyah* was Abū Muḥammad.

Asīd b. Abī Asīd, the client of Abū Qatādah al-Anṣārī.[1578]
His *kunyah* was Abū Ibrāhīm.

Ṣāliḥ b. Muḥammad b. Zāʾidah al-Laythī, a genuine member of the Layth.[1579]
His *kunyah* was Abū Wāqid.

1574. A client of the northern Banū ʿAmir (there are other versions) and an important Medinan jurist. He served as instructor to Umayyad princes and died after the year 140/757–58. See Ibn Ḥibbān, *Mashāhīr*, 216; Khalīfah b. Khayyāṭ, *Ṭabaqāt*, 263; Muḥammad Ibn Ḥabīb, *Muḥabbar*, 477; al-Sayrawān, 103.

1575. A client of the Qurashī family of Ḥuwayṭib b. ʿAbd al-ʿUzzā who lived in Medina and died after the year 130/747–48. See Ibn Ḥibbān, *Thiqāt*, V, 365; al-Mizzī, *Tahdhīb*, XXV, 47–48.

1576. Many people bore this name, but only one Anṣārī. His *kunyah* was, however, Abū Saʿīd (none of these people bore the *kunyah* Abū Yazīd; see al-Bandārī and Ḥasan, IV, 208–9). He was a *muftī* and judge in Medina for the Umayyads, then in al-Hāshimiyyah for the second ʿAbbasid caliph, al-Manṣūr. He died in the year 144/761–62. See al-Khaṭīb al-Baghdādī, XIV, 101–7; al-Dhahabī, *Siyar*, V, 468–81.

1577. A client of the Zubayr family, a *ḥāfiẓ*, and one of the earliest historians. He lived in Medina and died in the year 141/758–59 (there are other versions). See F. Sezgin, I, 286–87; Duri, *Rise of Historical Writing*, 32–33 (and n. *j*); Krenkow, "Note"; Muṣṭafā, I, 158–59; al-Sayrawāh, 177; Khalīfah b. Khayyāṭ, *Ṭabaqāt*, 267; Ibn Ḥibbān, *Mashāhīr*, 131.

1578. According to Ibn Ḥajar, *Tahdhīb*, I, 300, his *kunyah* was Abū Ayyūb, and he died during the caliphate of al-Manṣūr (136–58/754–75). There is a confusion between him and another man of the same name, nicknamed al-Barrād; see also Khalīfah b. Khayyāṭ, *Ṭabaqāt*, 253.

1579. That is, not a client or a confederate. He was a Medinan, also known as Abū Wāqid al-Laythī, who took part in the *jihād* in Syria (against the Byzantines) and died after the year 145/762–63. See al-Dhahabī, *Mīzān*, I, 459; Ibn Manẓūr, *Mukhtaṣar*, XI, 38.

'Abd al-Raḥmān b. Ḥarmalah al-Aslamī.[1580]
His *kunyah* was Abū Ḥarmalah.

Isḥāq b. 'Abdallāh b. Abī Farwah.[1581]
His *kunyah* was Abū Sulaymān. It was reported that the name of this Abū Farwah was Aswad b. 'Amr.

His brother 'Abd al-Ḥakīm b. 'Abdallāh b. Abī Farwah.[1582]
His *kunyah* was Abū 'Abdallāh.

'Amr b. Abī 'Amr, the client of al-Muṭṭalib b. 'Abdallāh [b. al-Muṭṭalib] b. Ḥanṭab al-Makhzūmī.[1583]
His *kunyah* was Abū 'Uthmān, and the name of his father, Abū 'Amr, was Maysarah.

Al-Muhājir b. Yazīd, a client of the family of Abū Dhi'b al- [2561]
'Āmirī.[1584]
His *kunyah* was Abū 'Abdallāh.

Bukayr b. Mismār.[1585]
His *kunyah* was Abū Muḥammad.

'Abdallāh b. Yazīd b. Qanṭash al-Hudhalī.[1586]

1580. A Medinan scholar of the northern tribe Aslam who died in the year 145/762–63. See Ibn Ḥibbān, *Mashāhīr*, 218; Khalīfah b. Khayyāṭ, *Ṭabaqāt*, 270.

1581. A client of [the family of] 'Uthmān b. 'Affān or al-Zubayr who lived in Medina and died in the year 144/761–62. See Khalīfah b. Khayyāṭ, *Ta'rīkh*, 448; idem, *Ṭabaqāt*, 266; Ibn Ḥibbān, *Majrūḥīn*, I, 131–32.

1582. A client of [the family of] 'Uthmān who died in the year 156/772–73. See Khalīfah b. Khayyāṭ, *Ta'rīkh*, 457; idem, *Ṭabaqāt*, 272; Ibn Ḥibbān, *Mashāhīr*, 212.

1583. A Medinan transmitter who died during the caliphate of al-Manṣūr (136-58/754–75). See Khalīfah b. Khayyāṭ, *Ṭabaqāt*, 266; Ibn 'Adī, V, 1768–69; Ibn Ḥajar, *Tahdhīb*, VIII, 723. Ḥanṭab was one of the leading noble Qurashī families in Medina; see Ibn Qudāmah, 390.

1584. I could not trace this person. The family of Abū Dhi'b was Qurashī, of the clan 'Āmir b. Lu'ayy; see Ibn Qutaybah, *Ma'ārif*, 213.

1585. A client of (the family of) Sa'd b. Abī Waqqāṣ, a Medinan transmitter who died in the year 153/770. He is confused with a person of the same name. See Khalīfah b. Khayyāṭ, *Ta'rīkh*, 455; idem, *Ṭabaqāt*, 270; Ibn Ḥibbān, *Mashāhīr*, 210; idem, *Thiqāt*, VI, 105; idem, *Majrūḥīn*, I, 108, 194; al-Dhahabī, *Mīzān*, I, 163.

1586. A Medinan accused of unbelief (*zandaqah*); see al-Dhahabī, *Mīzān*, II, 88. Ibn 'Adī, IV, 1550 has Qanṭas.

His *kunyah* was Abū Yazīd. He transmitted [traditions] from Anas b. Mālik and [Sa'īd] b. al-Musayyab.

End of the excerpts from the book The Supplement to the Supplemented, *Praise be to God, Lord of the Heavens and the Earth, may He bless His Messenger, our master Muḥammad, and his family*

Bibliography of Cited Works

Abdur Raḥmān, Ḥāfiẓ. "*The Life of az-Zuhrī and His Scholarship in Quranic Sciences and Hadith and Sunna.*" Doctoral thesis, University of Edinburgh, 1977.

Abū Dā'ūd, Sulaymān b. al-Ash'ath. *Sunan Abī Dā'ūd.* 2 vols. Cairo, 1292/1875.

Abū al-Layth al-Samarqandī, Naṣr b. Muḥammad. *Bustān al-'ārifīn.* Ms. 8322. W. Ahlwardt, *Die Handschrifen-Verzeichnisse der Königlichen Bibliothek zu Berlin.* 10 vols. Berlin, 1887–99.

Abū al-Naṣr, Muḥammad Aḥmad, *'Abdallāh b. 'Abbās: Ḥabr al-ummah wa-turjumān al-qur'ān,* Beirut, 1412/1992.

Abū Nu'aym, Aḥmad b. 'Abdallāh. *Ḥilyat al-awliyā' wa-ṭabaqāt al-aṣfiyā'.* 10 vols. Cairo, 1932–38.

Abū 'Ubayd al-Qāsim b. Sallām. *Kitāb al-amwāl.* Beirut, 1981.

Abū Yāsīn, Ḥasan 'Īsā. *Shi'r hamdān wa-akhbāruhā fī al-jāhiliyyah wa-al-islām.* Riyadh, 1983.

Abū Yūsuf, Ya'qūb b. Ibrāhīm. *al-Radd 'alā siyar al-Awzā'ī.* Hyderabad, 1938.

Abū Zahrah, Muḥammad. *Abū Ḥanīfah, ḥayātuhu wa-'aṣruhu, ārā'uhu wa-fiqhuhu.* Cairo, 1947, 1976.

Abū Zayd, Bakr. *Ṭabaqāt al-nassābīn.* Riyadh, 1987.

Abū Zayd al-Qurashī, Muḥammad b. al-Khaṭṭāb. *Jamharat ash'ār al-'arab fī al-jāhiliyyah wa-al-islām,* ed. Muḥammad 'Alī al-Hāshimī. 3 vols. Riyadh, 1981.

Abū Zur'ah al-Dimashqī, 'Abd al-Raḥmān b. 'Amr. *Ta'rīkh,* ed. Shukr Allāh b. Ni'mat Allāh al-Qawjānī. Damascus, 1980.

Aḥmad, Imtiyāz. *Dalā'il al-tawthīq al-mubakkar lil-sunnah wa-al-ḥadīth.* Cairo 1990.

al-Ājurrī, Muḥammad b. al-Ḥasan. *Akhbār Abī Ḥafṣ 'Umar b. 'Abd al-'Azīz*. Beirut, 1980.

Akhbār al-Dawlah al-'Abbāsiyyah, ed. 'Abd al-'Azīz al-Dūrī. Beirut, 1971.

Akram, A. I. *The Sword of Allah*. Karachi and Dacca, 1970.

al-Akwa', Ismā'īl b. 'Alī. "al-Af'ūl." *Majallat majma' al-lughah al-'arabiyyah bi-Dimashq* (1406/1986): 305–47.

Alavi, Muḥammad Badrudīn. *Fatalism, Free Will and Acquisition*. Lahore, 1956.

'Alī, Muḥammad 'Uthmān. *Shu'arā' Banī Asad*. Beirut, 1986.

al-'Alī, Ṣāliḥ Aḥmad. *al-Tanẓīmāt al-ijtimā'iyyah wa-al-iqtiṣādiyyah fī al-Baṣrah fī al-qarn al-awwal al-hijrī*. Baghdad, 1953.

al-Amīn, Muḥsin, al-'Āmilī. *A'yān al-shī'ah*, 60 vols. Beirut, 1369/1950.

Ansari, G. "The Prophet's Marriage to Zainab." *Basheer* 4, nos. 3–4 (1976): 8–16.

Arazi, A., and El'ad, A. "*al-Ināfa fī rutbat al-xilāfa* de Ǧalāl al-Dīn al-Suyūṭī." *IOS* 8 (1978): 230–65.

van Arendonck, C. *Les debuts de l'imamat zaidite au Yemen*. Leiden, 1960.

'Armūsh, Aḥmad Rātib. *al-Fitnah wa-waq'at al-jamal*. Beirut 1977.

al-Ash'arī, Abū al-Ḥasan. *al-Ibānah 'an uṣūl al-diyānah*. Riyadh, 1400/1980.

———. *Maqālāt al-islāmiyyīn wa-ikhtilāf al-muṣallīn*, ed. H. Ritter. Istanbul, 1929.

al-'Askarī, Abū Hilāl. *al-Awā'il*. Beirut, 1987.

'Athāminah, K. "The Early Murji'a: Some Notes." *JSS* 35 (1990): 109–30.

———. "The 'Ulamā' in the Opposition: The 'Stick and Carrot' Policy in Early Islam." *IQ* 36 (1992): 153–78.

'Aṭwān, Ḥusayn. *al-Riwāyah al-ta'rīkhiyyah fī bilād al-Shām fī al-'aṣr al-umawiyy*. Amman, 1986.

Auchterlonie, P. *Arabic Biographical Dictionaries: A Summary Guide and Bibliography*. Durham, N.C., 1987.

al-A'ẓamī, Muḥammad Muṣṭafā. *Kuttāb al-nabī*. Riyadh, 1981.

———. *Maghāzī rasūl allāh li-'Urwah b. al-Zubayr* ((*al- Nuskhah al-mustakhrajah*), ed. Muḥammad Muṣṭafā al-A'ẓamī. Riyadh, 1981.

al-Azraqī, Muḥammad b. 'Abdallāh. *Akhbār Makkah al-musharrafah*, ed. F. Wüstenfeld. 3 vols. Göttingen, 1275/1858.

al-Baghdādī. See al-Khaṭīb, al-Baghdādī.

al-Baghdādī, 'Abd al-Qāhir b. Ṭāhir. *al-Farq bayna al-firaq*, ed. Ṭahā 'Abd al-Ra'ūf Sa'd. Cairo, n.d.

al-Baghdādī, Ismā'īl Bāshā b. Muḥammad. *Hadiyyat al-'ārifīn asmā' al-mu'allifīn wa-āthār al-muṣannifīn*. 2 vols. Istanbul, 1955.

al-Balādhurī, Aḥmad b. Yaḥyā. *Ansāb al-ashrāf*, vol. I, ed. Muḥammad

Ḥamīd Allāh. Cairo, 1959; vol. III, ed. Muḥammad Bāqir al-Maḥmūdī, Beirut, 1977; vol. III, ed. 'Abd al-'Azīz al-Dūrī, Beirut and Wiesbaden, 1978; vol. IVa, ed. M. Schloessinger and M. J. Kister, Jerusalem, 1971; vol. V, ed. S. D. F. Goitein, Jerusalem, 1936; vol. VI, ed. Khalīl 'Athāminah, Jerusalem, 1993.

———. *Futūḥ al-buldān*, ed. M. de Goeje. Leiden 1866. Ed. Riḍwān Muḥammad Riḍwān. Beirut, 1978.

al-Bandārī, 'Abd al-Ghaffār Sulaymān, and Ḥasan, Sayyid Kisrawī. *Mawsū'at rijāl al-kutub al-tis'ah*. 4 vols. Beirut, 1993.

Bashear, S. "The Mission of Diḥya al-Kalbī and the Situation in Syria." *JSAI* 14 (1991): 84–114.

———. "On the Origins and Development of the Meaning of *Zakāt* in Early Islam." *Arabica* 40 (1993): 84–113.

———. "The Title *fārūq* and Its Association with 'Umar I." *SI* 72 (1990): 47–70.

Bat Ye'or. *The Dhimmī*. Rev. and enl. English ed. Rutherford N.J., 1985.

Ben Shemesh, A., ed. and trans. *Taxation in Islam*. 3 vols. Leiden and London, 1958–69.

Ben Ze'ev, Israel (Abū Dhu'ayb, Isrā'īl). *Ka'b al-Aḥbār*. Jerusalem, 1976 [in Hebrew and Arabic].

Blankenship, K. Y., tr., *The Challenge to the Empires*. The History of al-Ṭabarī XI. Albany, N.Y., 1993.

Blochet, E. *Catalogue de la collection de manuscrits orienteaux arabes, persans et turcs formée par M. Charles Schefer*. Paris, 1900.

Bonner, M. "Some Observations Concerning the Early Development of *Jihād* on the Arab-Byzantine Frontiers." *SI* 75 (1992): 5–31.

Bosworth, C. E. *The Medieval Islamic Underworld*. Leiden, 1976.

———. "Rajā' ibn Ḥaywa al-Kindī and the Umayyad Caliph." *IQ* 14 (1972): 36–80.

al-Bukhārī, Ismā'īl b. Ibrāhīm. *al-Ta'rīkh al-kabīr*. 9 vols. Hyderabad, 1360/1941.

———. *al-Jāmi' al-ṣaḥīḥ*, ed. L. Krehl. 4 vols. Leiden, 1864.

Burton, J. *The Collection of the Qur'ān*. Cambridge, 1977.

Caetani, L. *Annali dell'Islam*. 10 vols. Milan, 1905–26.

Cameron, A. J. *Abū Dharr al-Ghifārī*. London, 1973; rev. ed., London, 1982.

Caskel, W. *Ğamharat an-Nasab, das genealogische Werk des Hišam Ibn Muḥammad al-Kalbī*. 2 vols. Leiden, 1966.

Cattenoz, H. G. *Tables de concordances des ères chrétienne et hégirienne*. Rabat, 1954.

Conrad, L. I. "Abraha and Muḥammad: Some Observation Apropos of Chronology and Literary *Topoi* in the Early Arabic Historical Tradition." *BSOAS* 50 (1987): 225–40.

———. "Ibn Isḥāq." In J. S. Meisami and P. Starkey, eds., *Encyclopedia of Arabic Literature.* London, 1998 (in press). Pp. 336.

———. "al-Kalbī." In J. S. Meisami and P. Starkey, ed., *Encyclopedia of Arabic Literature,* London, 1998 (in press). Pp. 340.

———. "The Plague in the Early Medieval Near East." Doctoral dissertation, Princeton University. Princeton, N.J., 1981.

Cook, M. A. "Early Muslim Dietary Law." *JSAI* 7 (1986): 217–75.

———. *Early Muslim Dogma.* Cambridge and London, 1981.

——— and Crone, P. *Hagarism.* Cambridge, 1980.

Coulson, N. J. *A History of Islamic Law.* Edinburgh, 1964.

Crone, P., *Meccan Trade and the Rise of Islām.* Princeton, N.J., 1987.

———. "On the Meaning of the 'Abbāsid Call to al-*Riḍā.*" In *The Islamic World from Classical to Modern Times: Essays in Honor of Bernard Lewis,* ed. C. E. Bosworth, Charles Issawi, Roger Savory, and A. L. Udovitch. Princeton, N.J., 1989.

———. *Roman, Provincial and Islamic Law.* Cambridge and London, 1987.

———. *Slaves on Horses.* Cambridge and London, 1974.

——— and Hinds, M. *God's Caliph: Religious Authority in the First Centuries of Islam.* Cambridge and London, 1986.

al-Ḍabbī, al-'Abbās b. Bakkār. *Akhbār al-wāfidīn min al-rijāl min ahl al-Baṣrah wa-al-Kūfah 'alā Mu'āwiyah b. Abī Sufyān,* ed. Sukaynah al-Shihābī. Beirut, 1984.

Daftary, F. *The Ismā'īlis: Their History and Doctrines.* Cambridge and New York, 1990.

al-Dāraquṭnī, 'Alī b. 'Umar. *al-Mu'talif wa-al-mukhtalif,* ed. Muwaffaq b. 'Abd Allāh. 5 vols. Beirut, 1406/1986.

al-Ḍārī, al-Ḥārith Sulaymān. *al-Imām al-Zuhrī wa-atharuhu fī al-sunnah.* Mosul, 1985.

Dennett, M. *Conversion and the Poll-Tax in Early Islam.* Cambridge, Mass., 1950.

al-Dhahabī, Muḥammad b. Aḥmad. *Manāqib al-Imām Abī Ḥanīfah,* ed. M. Z. al-Kawtharī and Abū al-Wafā al-Afghānī. Hyderabad, n.d. after 1367/1948.

———. *Mīzān al-i'tidāl fī naqd al-rijāl,* ed. Muḥammad Badr al-Dīn al-Na'sānī. 3 vols. Cairo, 1325–1907. The same, ed. al-Bijāwī, 1962.

———. *al-Mushtabih fī asmā' al-rijāl,* ed. P. de Jong. Leiden, 1863.

———. *Siyar a'lām al-nubalā',* ed. Shu'ayb al-Arna'ūṭ et al. 25 vols. Beirut, 1982–88.

———. *Ta'rīkh al-islām wa-wafayāt al-mashāhīr wa-al-a'lām,* ed. 'Umar 'Abd al-Salām Tadmurī. 45 vols. Beirut, 1987–1990.

al-Dība', 'Abd al-Raḥmān b. 'Alī al-Zabīdī. *Tuḥfat al-zaman fī faḍā'il ahl al-Yaman,* ed. Sayyid Kisrawī Ḥasan. Beirut, 1992.

Djaït, H. *Al-Kūfa: Naissance de la ville islamique.* Paris, 1986.
———. "Les yamanites á Kufa au 1re siècle de l'Hégire." *JESHO* 19 (1976): 148–81.
Donner, F. M. *The Early Islamic Conquests.* Princeton, N.J., 1981.
———. "The Problem of Early Arabic Historiography in Syria." In *Proceedings of the Second Symposium on the History of Bilād al-Shām During the Early Islamic Period up to 40 A.H./640 A.D.*, vol. I, ed. Muḥammad A. al-Bakhīt and Iḥsān 'Abbās. Amman, 1987.
———. "The *Shurṭa* in Early Umayyad Syria." In *Proceedings of the Third Symposium on the History of Bilād al-Shām During the Umayyad Period*, vol. II, ed. Muḥammad A. al-Bakhīt and Robert Schick. Amman, 1989.
———. "Tribal Settlement in Basra During the First Century A.H." In *Land Tenure and Social Transformation in the Middle East*, ed. Tarif Khalidi. Beirut, 1984.
al-Dūlābī. *al-Kunā wa-al-asmā'.* Hyderabad, 1322/1904.
Duri, A. A. *The Rise of Historical Writing among the Arabs*, ed. and trans. L. I. Conrad. Princeton, N.J., 1983.
———. "Al-Zuhri—A Study on the Beginning of Historical Writing in Islam." *BSOAS* 19 (1957): 1–12.
Eickelman, D., and Piscatori, J., eds. *Muslim Travellers: Pilgrimage, Migration and the Religious Imagination.* Berkeley, Calif., 1990.
El'ad, A. "Aspects of the Transition from the Umayyad to the 'Abbāsid caliphate." *JSAI* 19, (1995): 89–132.
van Ess, J. *Theologie und Gesellschaft im 2. and 3. Jahrhundert Hidschra. Eine Geschichte des religiösen Denkens im frühen Islam.* Berlin and New York, vol. I, 1991; vols. II–III, 1992; vol. V, 1993; vol. VI, 1995.
Fahd, T. *La divination arabe: études religieuse, sociologique et folkloriques sur le milieu natif de l'Islam.* Leiden, 1966.
Farah, C., *The Dhayl in Medieval Arabic Historiography*, American Oriental Series no. 6, ed. E. Bender. New Haven, Conn., 1967.
Fattal, A. *Le statut legal de non-musulmans en pays de l'Islam.* Beirut, 1958.
al-Fazārī, Abū Isḥāq. *Kitāb al-siyar*, ed. Fārūq Ḥamādah. Beirut, 1987.
Friedmann, Y. "Finality of Prophethood in Sunnī Islām." *JSAI* 7 (1986): 177–215.
———. "The Temple of Multān, a Note on Early Muslim Attitudes to Idolatry." *IOS* 2 (1972): 176–82.
Fück, Johann. *Muḥammad ibn Isḥāq: Literarhistorische Untersuchungen.* Frankfurt am Main, 1925.
al-Ghayṭī, Najm al-Dīn Muḥammad b. Aḥmad. *al-Jawāb al-qawīm 'an al-su'āl al-muta'alliq bi-iqṭā' al-Sayyid Tamīm*, ed. Ḥasan 'Abd al-Raḥmān Salwādī. Jerusalem, 1986.

al-Ghazālī, Abū Ḥāmid. *Iḥyā' 'ulūm al-dīn*. 4 vols. Cairo n.d.
Gibb, H. A. R. "The Fiscal Rescript of 'Umar II." *Arabica* 2 (1955): 1–16.
———. "Islamic Biographical Literature." In B. Lewis and P. M. Holt, eds., *Historians of the Middle East*, Oxford, 1962. Pp. 54–58.
Gil, M. *A History of Palestine 637–1090*. 3 vols. Cambridge and New York, 1992.
Gil-'adi, Avner. "Some Notes on *Taḥnīk* in Medieval Islam." *JNES* 47 (1988): 175–79.
Gilliot, C., "Bulletin d'islamologie et d'études arabes." *Revue des Sciences Philosophique et Théologiques* 64 (1990): 477–505.
———. "Les oeuvres de Tabari (m. 310/923)." *MIDEO* 19 (1989): 49–90.
Givon, J. "*The Murji'a and the School of Abū Ḥanīfa*. Doctoral dissertation, University of Edinburgh, 1977.
Glassé, C. *The Concise Encyclpaedia of Islām*. London, 1989.
Goitein, S. D. "Attitudes Towards Government in Islam and Judaism." In *Studies in Islamic History and Institutions*. Leiden, 1966. Pp. 197–213.
Goldziher, I. "Die literarische Thätigkeit des Ṭabari nach Ibn 'Asâkir." *WZKM* 9 (1895): 359–71.
———. *Muslim Studies*, trans. and ed. C. R. Barber and S. M. Stern. 2 vols. London, 1967–71.
Guillaume, A. *The Life of Muḥammad: A Translation of Isḥāq's sīrat rasūl allāh*. London, 1955.
al-Hādī, Ṣalāḥ al-Dīn. *al-Shammākh b. Ḍirār al-Dhubyānī, Ḥayātuhu wa-shi'ruhu*. Cairo, 1968.
Hafsi, I. "Recherches sur le genre 'Ṭabaqāt' dans la littérature arabe." *Arabica* 23 (1976): 227–65; 24 (1977): 1–41, 150–86.
al-Ḥākim al-Naysābūrī, Muḥammad b. 'Abdallāh. *Ma'rifat 'ulūm al-ḥadīth*, ed. Mu'aẓẓam Ḥusayn. Beirut, 1980.
al-Ḥalabī, 'Alī b. Burhān al-Dīn. *Insān al-'uyūn fī sīrat al-amīn al-ma'mūn* (*al-Sīrah al-ḥalabiyyah*). 7 vols. Cairo, 1320/1902.
Halm, H. *Ausbreitung der šafitischen Rechtschule*. Wiesbaden, 1974.
Hamidullah (Ḥamīd Allāh), Muḥammad. *The Battlefields of the Prophet Muḥammad*. Woking, U.K., 1953.
———. *Majmū'at al-wathā'iq al-siyāsiyyah fī al-'ahd al-nabawī wa-al-khilāfah al-rāshidah*. Cairo, 1941.
———. "Muḥammad ibn Isḥāq, the Biographer of the Holy Prophet." *JPHS* 15, no. 2 (1967): 77–100.
Hammarneh, S. "Marwān b. al-Ḥakam and the Caliphate." *Der Islam* 65 (1988): 200–25.
Ḥasan, Nājī. *Thawrat Zayd b. 'Alī*. Baghdad, 1386/1966.
Ḥassān b. Thābit. *Dīwān of Ḥassān b. Thābit*, ed. Walid N. Arafat, the Gibb Memorial Series 26. London, 1971.

Hasson, I. "Contribution à l'étude des Aws et des Ḫazraǧ." *Arabica* 36 (1989): 1–35.
———. *Recherches sur Mu'āwiya Ibn Abī Sufyān, sa politique tribale, militaire et agraire.* Doctoral thesis, Jerusalem, Hebrew University, 1982 [in Hebrew, abstract in French].
Hawting, G. R. "The Development of the Biography of al-Ḥārith ibn Kalada and the Relationship Between Medicine and Islām." In *The Islamic World, from Classical to Modern Times: Essays in Honor of Bernard Lewis*, ed. C. E. Bosworth, C. Issawi, R. Savory, and A. L. Udovitch. Princeton, N.J., 1989.
———. *The First Dynasty of Islam.* London and Sydney, 1986.
———. "Ḥudaybiyya and the Conquest of Mecca: Reconsideration of the Tradition About the Muslim Takeover of the Sanctuary." *JSAI* 8 (1986): 1–23.
———. "The *Tawwābūn*, Atonement and 'Āshurā'," *JSAI* 17 (1994): 166–81.
al-Ḥillī, Abū al-Baqā' Hibat Allāh. *al-Manāqib al-mazyadiyyah fī akhbār al-mulūk al-asadiyyah*, ed. Ṣāliḥ Mūsā Darādikah and Muḥammad 'Abd al-Qādir Khuraysāt. Amman, nd.
al-Ḥimyarī, Nashwān b. Sa'īd. *Mulūk Ḥimyar wa-aqyāl al-Yaman*, ed. Ismā'īl b. Aḥmad al-Jarāfī and 'Alī b. Ismā'īl al-Mu'ayyad. Beirut and Ṣan'ā, 1978.
Hinds, M. "The Banners and Battle-Cries of the Arabs at Ṣiffīn (657 A.D.)." *al-Abḥāth* 24 (1971): 3–33.
———. "The Ṣiffīn Arbitration Agreement." *JSS* 17 (1972): 93–129.
Horovitz, J. "The Earliest Biographies of the Prophet and Their Authors." *IC* 1 (1927): 535–59; 2 (1928): 22–50, 164–82, 495–526.
al-Ḥuṭay'ah. *Dīwān*, ed. Nu'mān Amīn Ṭahā. Cairo, n.d.
Ibn ' Abd al-Barr, Yūsuf b. 'Abdallāh al-Namarī al-Qurṭubī. *al-Intiqā' fī faḍā'il al-thalāthat al-a'immah al-fuqahā'.* Cairo, 1350/1931.
———. *al-Istī'āb fī ma'rifat al-aṣḥāb.* Printed on the margins of Ibn Ḥajar, *al-Iṣābah fī tamyīz al-ṣaḥabah.* Cairo, 1328/1910.
Ibn 'Abd Rabbihi. *al-'Iqd al-farīd*, ed. A. Amīn, A. al-Zayn, and I. al-Abyārī. 7 vols. Cairo, 1940–53.
Ibn Abī Ḥātim al-Rāzī, 'Abd al-Raḥmān. *Kitāb al-jarḥ wa-al-ta'dīl.* 4 vols. Hyderabad, 1952–53.
Ibn Abī Shaybah, 'Abdallāh b. Muḥammad. *Kitāb al-īmān*, ed. Muḥammad Nāṣir al-Dīn al-Albānī. 7 vols. Beirut, 1983.
———. *Muṣannaf*, ed. Sa'īd al-Laḥḥām. 9 vols. Beirut, 1989.
Ibn 'Adī, Abū Aḥmad al-Jurjānī. *al-Kāmil fī ḍu'afā' al-rijāl.* 7 vols. Beirut, 1404/1984.
Ibn al-'Arabī, Muḥī al-Dīn. *al-Nafaḥāt al-nūrāniyyah fī al-ṣalāh 'alā khayr al-bariyyah.* Cairo, 1323/1906.

Ibn 'Asākir, 'Alī b. al-Ḥasan. *Tahdhīb ta'rīkh Ibn 'Asākir*, ed. 'Abd al-Qādir b. Aḥmad b. Badrān and Aḥmad 'Ubayd. 7 vols. Damascus, 1329–49/1911–30.

———. *Ta'rīkh madīnat Dimashq*, facsimile edition. 19 vols. Cairo, 1989.

Ibn A'tham, Aḥmad al-Kūfī. *Kitāb al-futūḥ*, ed. Na'īm Zarzūr. 8 vols. Beirut, 1986.

Ibn al-Athīr, 'Izz al-Dīn. *al-Kāmil fī al-ta'rīkh*. 13 vols. Beirut, 1965.

———. *al-Lubāb fī tahdhīb al-ansāb*. Beirut n.d.

———. *Usd al-ghābah fī ma'rifat al-ṣaḥābah*. 5 vols. Cairo 1280–86/1863–69.

Ibn Durayd, Muḥammad b. al-Ḥasan. *Kitāb al-ishtiqāq*, ed. 'Abd al-Salām Muḥammad Hārūn. Cairo, 1958.

Ibn al-Farrā', Abū Ya'lā Muḥammad b. al-Ḥusayn. *al-Aḥkām al-sulṭāniyyah*, ed. Muḥammad Ḥāmid al-Faqī. Beirut, 1974.

Ibn Ḥabīb, 'Abd al-Malik. *Kitāb al-Ta'rīkh (La Historia)*, ed. J. Aguadé. Madrid, 1991.

Ibn Ḥabīb, Abū Ja'far Muḥammad. *Asmā' al-mughtālīn min al-ashrāf fī al-jāhiliyyah wa-al-islām: Nawādir al-Makhṭūṭāt*. Vol. II/5, ed. 'Abd al-Salām Hārūn. Cairo, 1373/1954.

———. *Kitāb al-muḥabbar*, ed. I. Lichtenstadter. Hyderabad, 1947.

———. *al-Munammaq fī akhbār Quraysh*, ed. Khurshīd Aḥmad Fāriq. Hyderabad, 1965.

Ibn Ḥajar, Aḥmad b. 'Alī al-'Asqalānī. *al-Iṣābah fī tamyīz al-ṣaḥābah*. 4 vols. Cairo, 1382.

———. *Nuzhat al-albāb fī al-alqāb*. Beirut, 1991/1411.

———. *Lisān al-mīzān*. 8 vols. Beirut, 1988.

———. *Tahdhīb al-tahdhīb*. 14 vols. Beirut, 1404–9/1313/1984–88.

Ibn Ḥanbal, Aḥmad. *Faḍā'il al-ṣaḥābah*, ed. Waṣiyy Allāh 'Abbās. Mecca, 1983.

———. *Musnad*. 6 vols. Cairo, 1313/1895.

Ibn Ḥazm, 'Alī b. Aḥmad. *Jamharat ansāb al-'arab*, ed. 'Abd al-Salām Muḥammad Hārūn. Cairo, 1962.

———. *Jawāmi' al-sīrah*, ed. Iḥsān 'Abbās, Nāṣir al-Dīn al-Asad, Aḥmad Muḥammad Shākir. Cairo, n.d.

Ibn Ḥibbān, Muḥammad al-Bustī. *Kitāb al-majrūḥīn min al-muḥaddithīn wa-al-ḍu'afā' wa-al-matrūkīn*, ed. Maḥmūd Ibrāhīm Zāyid. 3 vols. Aleppo, 1396/1976.

———. *Kitāb al-thiqāt*. 8 vols. Hyderabad, 1973–82.

———. *Mashāhīr 'ulamā' al-amṣār*, ed. Marzūq 'Alī Ibrāhīm. Cairo, 1991.

Ibn Hishām, 'Abd al-Malik. *al-Sīrah al-nabawiyyah*, 4 vols. Cairo, 1936.

Ibn Ḥubaysh, 'Abd al-Raḥmān b. Muḥammad. *Kitāb al-ghazawāt*, ed. Suhayl Zakkār. 2 vols. Beirut, 1992.

Ibn Hudhayl. *Tuḥfat al-anfus wa-shi'ār sukkān al-Andalus*, ed. and trans. L. Mercier as *L'ornement des ames et la devise des habitants d'el-Andalus: Traité de guerre sainte islamique*. Paris, 1936.

Ibn Isḥāq, Muḥammad. *Kitāb al-siyar wa-al-maghāzī*, ed. Suhayl Zakkār. Beirut, 1978.

———. *Sīrat Ibn Isḥāq*, ed. Muḥammad Ḥamīdullāh. Rabat, 1396/1976.

Ibn al-Jawzī, 'Abd al-Raḥmān b. 'Alī. *Kitāb al- quṣṣāṣ wa-al-mudhakkirīn*, ed. Qāsim al-Sāmarrā'ī. Riyadh, 1403/1983.

———. *al-Muntaẓam fī ta'rīkh al-mulūk wa-al-umam*, ed. Muḥammad and Muṣṭafā 'Abd al-Qādir 'Aṭā. 18 vols. Beirut, 1412/1992.

———. *Sīrat 'Umar b. 'Abd al-'Azīz*. Cairo, 1331.

———. *Ta'rīkh 'Umar b. al-Khaṭṭāb*. Cairo, 1930.

Ibn al-Jazarī. *Ghāyat al-nihāyah fī ṭabaqāt al-qurrā'*, ed G. Bergsträsser and O. Pretzl. 3 vols. Leipzig, 1933–35.

Ibn al-Kalbī, Hishām b. Muḥammad. *Jamharat al-nasab*, ed. Nājī Ḥasan. Beirut, 1986.

———. *Nasab Ma'add wa-al-Yaman al-kabīr*, ed. Nājī Ḥasan. Beirut, 1988.

Ibn Khallikān. *Wafayāt al-a'yān wa-anbā' abnā' al-zamān*, ed. Iḥsān 'Abbās. 8 vols. Beirut, 1968–72.

Ibn Khayr al-Ishbīlī. *Fahrasah*, ed. F. Codera. Saragossa, 1894.

Ibn Ma'īn. See Sayf.

Ibn Manẓūr, Muḥammad b. Makram. *Lisān al-'arab*. 15 vols. Beirut, 1374/1955.

———. *Mukhtaṣar ta'rīkh Dimashq*, ed. Ibrāhīm Zībaq. 25 vols. Damascus, 1408/1988.

Ibn al-Murtaḍā, Aḥmad b. Yaḥyā. *al-Baḥr al-zakhkhār al-jāmi' li-madhāhib 'ulamā' al-amṣār*, ed. 'Abdallāh b. 'Abd al-Karīm al-Jarāfī. Ṣan'ā, 1947.

Ibn al-Nadīm, Muḥammad. *The Fihrist of al-Nadīm*, ed. and trans. B. Dodge. 2 vols. New York and London, 1970.

Ibn Nubātah, Muḥammad b. Muḥammad. *Sarḥ al-'uyūn sharḥ risālat Ibn Zaydūn*. Cairo, 1321/1903.

Ibn Qayyim al-Jawziyyah, Muḥammad b. Bakr. *Zād al-ma'ād fī hadyi khayr al-'ibād*. 4 vols. Beirut, 1379/1959.

Ibn Qudāmah, 'Abdallāh b. Aḥmad al-Maqdisī. *al-Tabyīn fī ansāb al-Qurashiyyīn*, ed. Muḥammad Nā'if al-Dalīmī. Beirut, 1988.

Ibn Qutaybah, 'Abdallāh b. Muslim. *al-Awā'il*, ed. Muḥammad Badr al-Dīn al-Qahwajī. Damascus and Beirut, 1987.

———. *al-Ma'ārif*, ed. Muḥammad Ismā'īl 'Abdallāh al-Ṣāwī. Beirut, 1970.

Ibn Sa'd, Muḥammad. *Kitāb al-ṭabaqāt al-kabīr*, ed. E. Sachau et al. 3 vols. Leiden, 1904–40.

———. *al-Ṭabaqāt al-kubrā al-qism al-mutammim*, ed. Ziyād Muḥammad Manṣūr. Medina, 1987.

Ibn Sa'īd, al-Andalusī. *Nashwat al-ṭarab fī ta'rīkh jāhiliyyat al-'arab*, ed. Naṣrat 'Abd al-Raḥmān. Amman, 1982.

Ibn Sayyid al-Nās, Muḥammad b. Muḥammad. *'Uyūn al-athar fī funūn al-maghāzī wa-al-shamā'il wa-al-siyar*. 2 vols. Beirut, 1980.

Ibn al-Zubayr, al-Rashīd. *Kitāb al-dhakhā'ir wa-al-tuḥaf*, ed. Muḥammad Ḥamīdullāh and Ṣalāḥ al-Dīn al-Munajjid. Kuwait, 1959.

Imru' al-Qays. See al-Sandūbī.

al-'Irāqī, 'Uthmān b. 'Abdallāh. *al-Firaq al-muftaraqah bayna ahl al-zaygh wa-al-zandaqah*, ed. Yasar Kultuay. Ankara, 1961.

al-Iṣfahānī, Abū al-Faraj. *Kitāb al-aghānī*, ed. Aḥmad al-Shanqīṭī. 21 vols. and indexes, Cairo, n.d.

al-Iṣfahānī, Ḥamzah. *Ta'rīkh sinī mulūk al-arḍ wa-al-anbiyā'*. Beirut, n.d.

Jabbūr, Jibrā'īl. *'Umar ibn Abī Rabī'ah*. Beirut, 1979.

Jād al-Mawlā Bek, 'Alī Muḥammad al-Bijāwī, and Muḥammad Abū al-Faḍl Ibrāhīm. *Ayyām al-'arab fī al-jāhiliyyah*. Cairo, n.d.

al-Ja'dī, 'Umar b. 'Alī b. Samurah. *Ṭabaqāt fuqahā' al-Yaman*, ed. Fu'ād Sayyid. Cairo, 1957.

Jafrī, S. H. M. *The Origins and Early Development of Shī'a Islam*. London and New York, 1979.

al-Jāḥiẓ, 'Amr b. Baḥr. *al-Bayān wa-al-tabyīn*, ed 'Abd al-Salām Muḥammad Hārūn. 4 vols. Cairo, Beirut and Kuwait, 1388/1968.

Jarrār, Māhir. "Some Light on an Early Zaydite Manuscript: *Akhbār fakhkh wa-khabar Yaḥyā b. 'Abdallāh*." *Asiatische Studien/Etudes Asiatiques*, 47, no. 2 (1993): 279–97.

Jeffery, A. *Materials for the History of the Text of the Qur'ān, the Old Codices*. Leiden, 1937.

Juynboll, G. H. A. *The Authenticity of the Tradition Literature*. Leiden, 1969.

———. *Muslim Tradition: Studies in the Chronology, Provenance and Authorship of Early Hadith*. Cambridge and London, 1983.

———. "The Qurrā' in Early Islamic History." *JESHO* 16 (1973): 113–29.

al-Kalā'ī, Sulaymān b. Mūsā. *Ḥurūb al-riddah*, ed. Aḥmad Ghunaym. Cairo, 1981.

Kamāl, Aḥmad 'Ādil. *al-Qādisiyyah*. Beirut, 1977.

al-Kashshī, Muḥammad b. 'Umar b. 'Abd al-'Aziz. *Rijāl*, ed. Aḥmad al-Ḥusaynī. Karbalā', n.d.

al-Kattānī, Muḥammad b. Ja'far. *al-Risālah al-mustaṭrafah*. Beirut, 1332/1913–14.

Kay, H. C., ed. and trans. *Yaman, Its Early Medieval History, by Najm al-Dīn 'Omārah al-Ḥakamī*. London, 1892.

Kazimirski, A. de Biberstein. *Dictionnaire arabe-français*, Paris, 1860.

Kennedy, H. *The Prophet and the Age of the Caliphates.* London and New York, 1986.
Khalīfah b. Khayyāṭ al-'Uṣfurī. *Ṭabaqāt al-rijāl wa-al-nisā'*, ed. Akram Ḍiyā' al-'Umarī. Baghdad, 1967.
———. *Ta'rīkh*, ed. Akram Ḍiyā' al-'Umarī. Najaf, 1967.
al-Khallāl, Abū Bakr. *al-Amr bi-al-ma'rūf wa-al-nahy 'an al-munkar*, ed. 'Abd al-Qādir Aḥmad 'Aṭā. Cairo, 1974.
———. *al-Sunnah*, ed. 'Aṭiyyah al-Zahrānī. Riyadh, 1410–1989.
al-Kharbūṭalī, 'Alī Ḥasan. *'Abdallāh b. al-Zubayr.* Cairo, 1965.
al-Khaṭīb al-Baghdādī, Aḥmad b. 'Alī. *Ta'rīkh Baghdād.* 14 vols. Cairo and Baghdad, 1349–1931.
al-Khaṭīb, Muḥammad 'Ajjāj. *Abū Hurayrah rāwiyat al-Islām.* Cairo, 1963.
Khoury, R. G. *'Abd Allāh Ibn Lahī'a (97–174/715–790): Juge et grand maitre de l'école égyptienne.* Wiesbaden, 1986.
———. "Al-Layth ibn Sa'd (94/713–175/791), grand maitre et mécène de l'Egypte vu a travers quelques documents islamiques anciens." *JNES* 40 (1981): 189–202.
———. *Wahb b. Munabbih: Der heidelberger Papyrus PSR Heid Arab 23.* Wiesbaden, 1972.
al-Khū'ī, Abū al-Qāsim al-Mūsawī. *Mu'jam rijāl al-ḥadīth.* 23 vols. Beirut, 1409/1989.
Kinberg, Lea. "The Standardization of Qur'ān-Readings: The Testimonial Value of Dreams." *Proceedings of the Colloquium on Arabic Grammer*, ed. K. Dévényi and T. Ivényi. The Arabist: Budapest Studies in Arabic 3–4 Budapest, 1991 Pp. 223–38.
al-Kindī, Muḥammad b. Yūsuf. *Wulāt Miṣr.* Beirut, 1987.
Kister, M. J. "Call Yourselves by Graceful Names." In *Lectures in Memory of Professor Martin M. Plessner.* Jerusalem, 1975. Pp. 3–25.
———. "The Campaign of Ḥulubān." *Le Muséon* 78 (1965): 425–36.
———. "The Expedition of Bīr Ma'ūna." In *Arabic and Islamic Studies in Honor of Hamilton A. R. Gibb*, Pp. 337–57. Leiden, 1965.
———. " '*Ḥaddithū 'an Banī Isrā'īl wa-lā ḥaraj*', a Study of an Early Tradition." *IOS* 2 (1972): 215–39.
———. " '. . . *Illā biḥaqqihi* . . .' A Study of an Early *Ḥadīth.*" *JSAI* 5 (1984): 33–52.
———. "Khuzā'a" *EI*², V, 76–80.
———. "Ḳuḍā'a" *EI*², V, 315–18.
———. " '*Labbayka, allahumma labbayka* . . .' On a Monotheistic Aspect of a Jāhiliyya Practice." *JSAI* 2 (1980), 33–58.
———. "Land Property and *Jihād*: A Discussion of Some Early Traditions." *JESHO* 34 (1992): 270–311.
———. "The Locust's Wing: Some Notes on Locust in the Ḥadith." *Le Muséon* 106 (1993): 347–59.

———. "The Massacre of the Banū Qurayẓa." *JSAI* 8 (1986): 61–96.
———. "Mecca and Tamīm." *JESHO* 3, no. 2 (1965): 113–62.
———. "'O God, Tighten Thy Grip on Muḍar . . .' Some Socio-Economic and Religious Aspects of an Early *Ḥadīth*." *JESHO* 24 (1981): 242–73.
———. "On Strangers and Allies in Mecca." *JSAI* 13 (1990): 113–54.
———. "The Papyrus Account of the 'Aqaba Meeting." *Le Muséon* 76 (1963): 403–17.
———. "Social and Religious Concepts of Authority in Islam." *JSAI* 18 (1994): 84–127.
———. "Some Reports Concerning al-Ṭā'if." *JSAI* 1 (1979): 1–18.
———. "Some Reports Concerning Mecca, from Jāhiliyya to Islām." *JESHO* 15 (1972): 61–93.
———. "The Sons of Khadīja." *JSAI* 16 (1993): 59–95.
———. "*Al-taḥannuth*: An Inquiry into the Meaning of a Term." *BSOAS* 31, no. 2 (1968): 223–36.
Krenkow, F. "Note on the *Kitāb al-maghāzī* of Mūsā b. 'Uqbah." *IC* 2, no. 4 (1928): 645.
———. "The Two Oldest Books on Arabian Folklore." *IC* 2 (1928): 55–89, 204–36.
al-Lālikā'ī, Hibat Allāh b. al-Ḥasan. *Sharḥ uṣūl i'tiqād ahl al-sunnah wa-al-jamā'ah*, ed. Aḥmad Sa'd Ḥamdān. 8 vols. Riyadh, 1982.
Lambton, A. K. S. *State and Government in Medieval Islam*. Oxford, 1981.
Lammens, H., *Etudes sur le règne du calife omaiyade Mo'awiyah Ier*, Beirut, 1906.
Landau-Tasseron, E. "Asad from Jāhiliyya to Islam." *JSAI* 6 (1985): 1–28.
———. "The Cyclical Reform: A Study of the *Mujaddid* Tradition." *SI* 70 (1989): 79–117.
———. "F. McG. Donner, *The Early Islamic Conquests*." *JSAI* 6 (1985): 493–512.
———. "Murra." *EI*², VII, 628–31.
———. "On the Reconstruction of Lost Sources." In *History and Historiography in Early Islamic Times: Studies and Perspectives*, ed. L. I. Conrad. Princeton, N.J., 1998 forthcoming.
———. "The Participation of Ṭayyi' in the *Ridda*." *JSAI* 5 (1984): 53–72.
———. "Processes of Redaction: The Case of the Tamīmite Delegation to the Prophet Muḥammad." *BSOAS* 69, no. 2 (1986): 253–70.
———. "Sayf Ibn 'Umar in Medieval and Modern Scholarship." *Der Islam* 67 (1990): 1–26.
———. "The Sinful Wars: Religious, Social and Historical Aspects of *ḥurūb al-fijār*." *JSAI* 8 (1986): 37–60.
———. "The Biographical Work of al-Ṭabarī." In *Al-Ṭabarī: A Medieval Muslim Historian and His Work*, ed. Hugh Kennedy, Princeton, N.J. (forthcoming).

———. "The Waning of the Umayyads: Notes on Ṭabarī's History Translated, vol. XXVI." *Der Islām* 49 (1992): 81–109.

Lane, E. W. *Arabic-English Lexicon.* New York, 1863.

Lassner, J. *The Shaping of the 'Abbāsid Rule.* Princeton, N.J., 1980.

Lecker, M. *The Banū Sulaym: A Contribution to the Study of Early Islam.* Jerusalem, 1989.

———. "Biographical Notes on Ibn Shihāb al-Zuhri." *JSS* 41 (1996): 21–63.

———. "The Ḥudaybiyya-Treaty and the Expedition Against Khaybar." *JSAI* 5 (1984): 1–12.

———. "Judaism among Kinda and the *Ridda* of Kinda." *JAOS* 115, no. 4 (1995): 635–50.

———. "Kinda on the Eve of Islam and During the *Ridda.*" *JRAS* (1994) third series. vol. 4, 333–356.

———. "*Shurṭat al-khamīs* and Other Matters: Notes on the Translation of Ṭabarī's *Ta'rīkh.*" *JSAI* 14 (1991): 276–89.

Leder, S. *Das Korpus al-Haiṯam ibn 'Adī (st. 207/822): Herkunft, Überlieferung, Gestalt früher Texte der aḫbār Literatur.* Frankfurt am Main, 1991.

Lewis, B. *Islam in History: Ideas People and Events in the Middle East.* Chicago, 1993.

Lings, Martin. *Muhammad: His Life Based on the Earliest Sources.* New York, 1983.

Loth, O. "Über eine Ṭabarī-Handschrift." *ZDMG* 32 (1878): 581–83.

Madelung, W. "The Early Murji'a in Kurāsān and Transoxania and the Spread of Ḥanafism." *Der Islam* 59 (1982): 32–39.

———. "The Hāshimiyyāt of al-Kumayt and Hāshimī Shī'ism." *SI* 70 (1989): 5–26.

Mālik b. Anas. *al-Muwaṭṭ'.* Cairo, 1279/1862.

al-Manbijī, Agapius b. Constantine. *al-Muntakhab min ta'rīkh al-manbijī,* ed. 'Umar 'Abd al-Salām Tadmurī. Tripoli, Lebanon, 1986.

al-Marzubānī, Muḥammad b. 'Imrān. *Mu'jam al-shu'arā',* ed. F. Krenkow. Cairo, 1354/1935.

Meisami, J. S., and P. Starkey, eds. *Companion to Arabic Literature.* London, 1995.

al-Mizzī, Jamāl al-Dīn Yūsuf b. 'Abd al-Raḥmān. *Tahdhīb al-kamāl fī asmā' al-rijāl,* ed. Bashshār 'Awwād Ma'rūf. 35 vols. Beirut, 1985–92.

———. *Tuḥfat al-ashrāf bi-ma'rifat al-aṭrāf,* ed. 'Abd al-Ṣamad Sharaf al-Dīn. 14 vols. Beirut, 1974.

Morony, M. *Iraq after the Muslim Conquest.* Princeton, N.J., 1984.

Morsy, M. *Les femmes du Prophète.* Paris, 1989.

Motzki, H. "The Muṣannaf of 'Abd al-Razzāq al-Ṣan'ānī as a Source of Authentic *Aḥādīth* of the First Century A.H." *JNES* 50 (1991): 1–21.

Mu'arrij b. 'Amr al-Sadūsī. *Kitāb ḥadhf min nasab Quraysh*, ed. Ṣalāḥ al-Dīn al-Munajjid. Beirut, 1976.
al-Mubarrad, Abū al-'Abbās. *al-Kitāb al-kāmil*, ed. W. Wright. Leipzig, 1864.
Muir, Sir William. *The Life of Moḥammad from Original Sources*, ed. T. H. Weir. Edinburgh, 1923.
Mujāhid b. Jabr. *Tafsīr*, ed. 'Abd al-Raḥmān al-Ṭāhir b. Muḥammad al-Sūratī. Beirut, n.d.
al-Munajjid, Ṣalāḥ al-Dīn. *Mu'jam Banī Umayyah*. Beirut, 1970.
Muslim b. al-Ḥajjāj. *Ṣaḥīḥ*, ed. Muḥammad Fu'ād 'Abd al-Bāqī. 5 vols. Cario, 1955.
———. *Ṭabaqāt*, ed. Mashhūr b. Ḥasan. Riyadh, 1991.
Muṣṭafā, Shākir. *al-Ta'rīkh al-'arabī wa-al-mu'arrikhūn*, vol. I, Beirut, 1978.
Nallino, Maria. *La poésie di an-Nābigah al-Ga'dī: Raccolta, critica dei testi, traduzione e note.* Rome, 1953.
Naqā'id Ed. A. A. Bevan, *The Naḳā'iḍ of Jarīr and al-Farazdaḳ*. 3 vols. Leiden, 1908–12.
Naṣr b. Muzāḥim. *Waq'at Ṣiffīn*. Cairo, 1981.
Nuwayhiḍ, 'Ādil. *Mu'jam al-mufassirīn min ṣadr al-islām ḥattā al-'aṣr al-ḥāḍir*. Beirut, 1983–84.
Obermann, J. "Political Theology in Early Islam: Ḥasan al-Baṣrī's Treatise on *Qadar*." *JAOS* 60 (1935): 138–62.
Pedersen, J. "The Islamic Preacher: *Wā'iẓ, mudhakkir, qāṣṣ*." In S. Löwinger and J. Somogyi, eds. *Ignace Goldziher Memorial Volume*. Vol. I. Budapest, 1948. Pp. 226–51.
Petersen, E. L. "'Alī and Mu'āwiya: The Rise of the Umayyad Caliphate 656–661." *AO* 23 (1959): 157–96.
Puin, G. R. "*Der Dīwān von 'Umar ibn al-Ḫaṭṭāb.*" Doctoral dissertation, University of Bonn, 1970.
al-Quhpā'ī, 'Ināyatullāh 'Alī. *Majma' al-rijāl*, ed. Ḍiyā' al-Dīn al-'Allāmah al-Iṣfahānī. 7 vols. Isfahan, 1384/1964.
al-Qummī, 'Abbās. *al-Kunā wa-al-alqāb*. 3 vols. Najaf, 1376/1956.
al-Qurṭubī, Muḥammad b. Aḥmad. *al-Jāmi' li-aḥkām al-qur'ān*. 8 vols. Cairo, n.d.
al-Rāshid, Saad al-Dīn bin 'Abd al-'Azīz. *al-Rabadha: A portrait of Early Islamic Civilization in Saudi Arabia*. Riyadh, 1986.
Raven, W. "Some Early Islamic Texts on the Negus of Abyssinia." *JSS* 33 (1988): 197–218.
al-Rayyis, Ḍiyā' al-Dīn. *'Abd al-Malik b. Marwān, muwaḥḥid al-dawlah al-'arabiyyah*. Cairo, 1962.
al-Rāzī, Aḥmad b. 'Abdallāh. *Ta'rīkh madīnat Ṣan'ā'*, ed. Ḥusayn b. 'Abdallāh al-'Umarī. Ṣan'ā', 1974.

Robson, J. "Blessings on the Prophet." *MW* 26 (1936): 365–71.
Rosenthal, F. *A History of Muslim Historiography.* Leiden, 1968.
———. *General Introduction and From the Creation to the Flood.* The History of al-Ṭabarī I. Albany, N.Y., 1989.
Rotter, G. *Die Umayyaden und der Zweite Bürgerkrieg in Islam.* Wiesbaden, 1970.
Rubin, U. "Abū Lahab and Sūra CXI." *BSOAS* 42, no. 1 (1979): 13–28.
———. "The Great Pilgrimage of Muḥammad: Some Notes on *Sūra* IX." *JSS* 27 (1982): 241–60.
———. "*Ḥanīfiyya* and Ka'ba: An Inquiry into the Arabian Pre-Islamic Background of *Dīn Ibrāhīm.*" *JSAI* 13 (1990): 85–112.
———. "The Īlāf of Quraysh." *Arabica* 31 (1984): 165–88.
———. "The Ka'ba: Aspects of Its Ritual Functions and Position in Pre-Islamic and Early Islamic Times." *JSAI* 8 (1986): 97–132.
———. "Morning and Evening Prayers in Early Islam." *JSAI* 10 (1987): 40–64.
Sachedina, 'Abd al-'Azīz. *Islamic Messianism: The Idea of Mahdi in Twelver Shī'ism.* New York, 1981.
al-Ṣadr, al-Sayyid Ḥasan. *al-Shī'ah fī funūn al-islām.* Beirut, n.d.
al-Ṣafadī, Khalīl b. Aybak. *al-Wāfī bi-l-wafayāt, Das Biographische Lexicon des Ṣalāḥaddīn Ḫalīl Ibn Aybak Aṣ-Ṣafadī,* ed. Helmut Ritter et al. 22 vols. Wiesbaden, 1931–93.
al-Sakhāwī, Muḥammad b. 'Abd al-Raḥmān. *al-I'lān bi-l-tawbīkh li-man dhamma al-ta'rīkh,* ed. and tr. Ṣāliḥ Aḥmad al-'Alī, annotated by F. Rosenthal. Beirut, n.d.
al-Ṣāliḥī, Muḥammad b. Yūsuf al-Dimashqī. *Azwāj al-nabī,* ed. Muḥammad Niẓām al-Dīn al-Futayyiḥ. Medina, 1992.
al-Sam'ānī, 'Abd al-Karīm b. Muḥammad. *al-Ansāb,* ed. 'Abdallāh 'Umar al-Bārūdī. 5 vols. Beirut, 1988.
al-Samhūdī, 'Alī b. Aḥmad. *Wafā' al-wafā bi-akhbār dār al-muṣṭafā,* ed. Muḥammad Muḥyī al-Dīn 'Abd al-Ḥamīd. 4 vols. Beirut, 1955.
al-Samūk, S. M. *Die historischen Überlieferungen nach Ibn Isḥāq, eine synoptische Untersuchung.* Doctoral dissertation, University of Frankfurt, 1978.
al-Sandūbī, Ḥasan. *Sharh dīwān Imri' al-Qays wa-ma'ahu akhbār al-marāqisah wa-ash'āruhum fī al-jāhiliyyah wa ṣadr al-islām wa-yalīhi akhbār al-nawābigh wa-āthāruhum fī al-jāhiliyyah wa-ṣadr al-islam.* Cairo, n.d.
Sayed, R. *Die Revolte des Ibn al-Aš'aṯ und die Koranleser.* Freiburg, 1977.
Sayf, Aḥmad Muḥammad Nūr. *Yaḥyā b. Ma'īn wa-kitābuhu al-ta'rīkh.* Mecca, 1979.
al-Sayrawān, 'Abd al-'Azīz 'Izz al-Dīn. *Mu'jam ṭabaqāt al-ḥuffāẓ wa-al-*

mufassirīn ma'a dirāsah 'an al-Imām al-Suyūṭī wa-mu'allafātihi. Beirut, 1984.

Schacht, J. *The Origins of Muḥammadan Jurisprudence.* Oxford, 1950.

———. "A revaluation of Islamic Tradition." *JRAS* (1949): 143–54.

Schoeler, G. "Die Frage der schriftlichen oder mündlichen Überlieferung der Wissenschaften in frühen Islam." *Der Islam* 62 (1985): 201–30.

Sezgin, F. *Geschichte des arabischen Schrifttums,* vol. I. Leiden, 1967.

Sezgin, U. *Abū Miḫnaf, ein Beitrag zur Historiographie der umayyadischen Zeit.* Leiden, 1971.

Shaban, M. A. *Islamic History* A.D. *600–750* (A.H. *132*)*: A New Interpretation.* Cambridge, 1971.

al-Shahrastānī. *Book of Religious and Philosophical Sects (al-Milal wa-al-niḥal),* ed. W. Cureton. London, 1846.

al-Shammākh. *Dīwān al-Shammākh b. Ḍirār,* ed. Aḥmad b. al-Amīn al-Shanqīṭī. Cairo, 1327.

Sharon, M., *Black Banners from the East.* Jerusalem and Leiden, 1983.

———. "The development of the Debate Around the Legitimacy of Authority in Early Islam." *JSAI* 5 (1984): 121–42.

———. "Notes on the Question of the Legitimacy of Government in Islam." *IOS* 10 (1980): 116–23.

———. *Revolt: The Social and Military Aspects of the 'Abbasid Revolution.* Jerusalem, 1990.

———. "The Umayyads as *Ahl al-Bayt.*" *JSAI* 14 (1991): 115–52.

al-Shayyāl, Jamāl al-Dīn. *A'lām al-Iskandariyyah fī al-'aṣr al-islāmī.* Cairo, 1965.

Shiḥāṭah, 'Abdallāh Maḥmūd. *al-Imām al-miṣrī al-Layth b. Sa'd.* Cairo, 1965.

Shoufani, E. S. *Al-Riddah and the Muslim Conquest of Arabia.* Toronto and Beirut, 1972.

Shukri, Ahmed. *Muhammedan Law of Marriage and Divorce.* New York, 1917.

Shurrāb, Muḥammad Muḥammad Ḥasan. *Tamīm ibn Aws al-Dārī Rāhib ahl 'aṣrihi wa-'ābid ahl Filasṭīn.* Damascus, 1990.

Simon, R. *Meccan Trade and Islām: Problems of Origin and Structure.* Budapest, 1989.

———. "Sur l'institution de la Mu'ākhāh—entre le tribalisme et l'Umma." *AOH* 27 (1973): 333–43.

Sprenger, A. "On the Origin and Progress of Writing down Historical Facts Among the Musalmans." *JASB* 25 (1857): 303–29, 376–81.

Strayer, J. R. ed. *Dictionary of the Middle Ages,* 14 vols. New York, 1987–89.

Ṣubḥī, Aḥmad Maḥmūd. *al-Zaydiyyah.* Alexandria, 1984.

al-Suyūṭī, Jalāl al-Dīn. *al-Aḥādīth al-ḥisān fī faḍl al-ṭaylasān,* ed. A. Arazi. Jerusalem, 1983.

———. *Tabyīḍ al-ṣaḥīfah bi-manāqib Abī Ḥanīfah*, ed. Maḥmūd Muḥammad Ḥasan Naṣṣār. Beirut, 1990.

———. *Taḥdhīr al-khawāṣṣ min akādhīb al-quṣṣāṣ*, ed. Muḥammad al-Sabbāgh. Beirut and Damascus, 1972.

———. *al-Thughūr al-bāsimah fī manāqib Fāṭimah*. Tanta, 1991.

———. *al-Wasā'il ilā ma'rifat al-awā'il*, ed. 'Abd al-Raḥmān al-Jūzū. Beirut, 1988.

al-Ṭabarānī, Sulaymān b. Aḥmad. *al-Mu'jam al-awsaṭ*, ed. Muḥammad al-Ṭaḥḥān. 3 vols. Riyadh, 1985.

———. *al-Mu'jam al-kabīr*, ed. al-Salafī. 7 vols. Baghdad, 1980–85.

al-Ṭabarī, Muḥammad b. Jarīr. *Jāmi' al-bayān 'an ta'wīl āy al-qur'ān* (=*Tafsīr al-Ṭabarī*). 30 vols. Cairo, 1954.

———. *al-Muntakhab min kitāb dhayl al-dhayl* (sic!). In *Ṣilat wa-takmilat wa-dhayl ta'rīkh al-umam wa-al-mulūk*. Beirut, 1987.

———. *al-Muntakhab min kitāb dhayl al-mudhayyal*. In *Dhuyūl ta'rīkh al-Ṭabarī*, ed. Muḥammad Abū al-Faḍl Ibrāhīm. Cairo, 1977.

———. *Ṣarīḥ al-sunnah*, ed. Badr b. Yūsuf al-Ma'tūq. Kuwait, 1985.

———. *Ta'rīkh al-rusul wa-al-mulūk*, ed. M J. de Goeje et al. Leiden, 1879–1901.

Ṭabāṭabā'ī, 'Allāmah Sayyid Muḥammad Ḥusayn. *Shī'ite Islam*. Albany, N.Y., 1975.

Ṭahā al-Najm, Wadī'ah. "*al-Qaṣaṣ, nash'atuhu fī al-Islām wa-taṭawwuruhu.*" *Majallat Kulliyat al-Ādāb bi-Baghdād* 10: 166–78.

Tuetey, C. G. *Imrulkais of Kinda, Poet, circa* A.D. *500–535*. London, 1977.

al-Ṭūsī, Muḥammad b. al-Ḥasan. *al-Rijāl*, ed. Muḥammad Ṣādiq Āl Baḥr al-'Ulūm. Najaf, 1961.

al-'Ujaymī, Ḥasan b. 'Alī. *Ihdā' al-laṭā'if min akhbār al-Ṭā'if*, ed. Yaḥyā Maḥmūd Sā'ātī. Taif, 1980.

'Umar b. Shabbah. *Ta'rīkh al-Madīnah al-munawwarah*, ed. Fahīm Muḥammad Shaltūt. N.p., n.d.

Uways al-Qaranī wa-qiṣṣatuhu ma'a al-Khalīfah 'Umar b. al-Khaṭṭāb wa-al-imām 'Alī b. Abī Ṭālib. Damascus, 1990 (this book was unavailable to me; it is recorded in *'Ālam al-kitāb* 35 [July–September 1992]: 180, without the author's name).

al-Wāḥidī, 'Alī b. Aḥmad. *Asbāb al-nuzūl*. Cairo, 1968.

Wakī', Muḥammad b. Khalaf. *Akhbār al-quḍāh*. 3 vols. Beirut, n.d.

Wansbrough, J. *Quranic Studies*. Oxford, 1977.

al-Waqā, Naẓmī. *'Amr ibn al-'Āṣ*. Cairo, 1970.

al-Wāqidī, Muḥammad b. 'Umar. *Kitāb al-maghāzī*, ed. M. Jones. 3 vols. London, 1966.

al-Wāsiṭī, Muḥammad b. Aḥmad. *Faḍā'il al-bayt al-muqaddas*, ed. I. Hasson. Jerusalem, 1979.

Watt, W. M. *Bell's Introduction to the Qur'ān*. Edinburgh, 1970.
———. "The Expedition of al-Ḥudaybiyya Reconsidered." *Hamdard Islamicus*, 8, no. 1 (1985): 3–6.
———. *Free Will and Pre-Destination in Early Islam*. London, 1948.
———. *Muhammad at Mecca*. Oxford, 1953.
———. *Muhammad at Medina*. Oxford, 1956.
al-Wazīr Ibn al-Maghribī, al-Ḥusayn b. ʿAlī. *al- Īnās bi-ʿilm al-ansāb*, ed. Ibrāhīm al-Abyārī. Cairo and Beirut, 1980.
Wellhausen, J. *Muḥammad in Medina*. Berlin, 1882 (a translation of al-Wāqidī's *Kitāb al-maghāzī*).
———. *The Arab Kingdom and Its Fall*. Calcutta, 1927.
Yaḥyā b. Maʿīn. See Sayf.
al-Yaʿqūbī, Aḥmad b. Abī Yaʿqūb. *Ta'rīkh*. 2 vols. Beirut, 1960.
Yāqūt al-Rūmī. *Irshād al-arīb li-maʿrifat al-adīb* (= *Muʿjam al-udabā'*), ed. Iḥsān ʿAbbās. 7 vols. Beirut, 1993.
———. *Muʿjam al-buldān*. 6 vols. Leipzig, 1866–73.
Yūsuf b. Yaḥyā al-Sulamī. *ʿAqd al-durar fī akhbār al-muntaẓar*, ed. Muhīb b. Ṣāliḥ al-Būrīnī. al-Zarqā', 1989.
al-Zabīdī, al-Murtaḍā. *Tāj al-ʿarūs min jawāhir al-qāmūs*. Cairo, 1306–7/1888–89.
Zaghlūl, Muḥammad. *Mawsūʿat aṭrāf al-ḥadīth al-nabawī al-sharīf*. 11 vols. Beirut, 1989.
al-Zamakhsharī, Jār Allāh Muḥammad b. ʿUmar. *al-Mustaqṣā fī amthāl al-ʿarab*. Hyderabad, 1962.
al-Zubayr b. Bakkār. *al-Akhbār al-muwaffaqiyyāt*, ed. Sāmī Makkī al-ʿĀnī. Baghdad, n.d.
al-Zubayrī, al-Muṣʿab b. ʿAbd al-Raḥmān. *Kitāb nasab Quraysh*, ed. E. Lévi-Provençal. Cairo, n.d.
al-Zubur, Muḥammad b. Ḥasan. *al-Qaṣaṣ fī al-ḥadīth al-nabawī*. Jidda, 1985.

Index

The index includes all names of persons, places, and groups, as well as technical terms, legal issues, and titles of books mentioned in the text. Genealogical chains are not included.

Bold numbers indicate the places of the main entries, or definitions, of the terms. Where a name or topic occurs in both the text and footnotes on the same page, only the page number is given. An asterisk (*) indicates a figure who is mentioned in the text only as a transmitter.

*The definite article (*al-*, the) and the abbreviations* b bt. *(son of, daughter of) are disregarded for the purpose and of alphabetization.*

A

Abān * 203
Abān (tribal group) 254
Abān b. Ṣāliḥ * 146
Abān b. Taghlib * 230
Abān b. 'Uthmān 59
Abān b. 'Uthmān * 60
'Abāyah b. Rifā'ah b. Rāfi' **334**
'Abbād b. 'Abbād al-Muhallabī **330**
'Abbād b. 'Abdallāh * 13
'Abbād b. al-'Awwām * 203
'Abbād b. Ṣuhayb al-Kulaybī **324**
'Abbād b. Tamīm * 132
al-'Abbās * 259, 293, 299
al-'Abbās b. 'Abdallāh b. al-'Abbās 54
al-'Abbās b. 'Abd al-Muṭṭalib 19, 20, 21, **24–25**, 60, 62, 66, **95**, 97, 98, 99, 111, 155, 167, 185, 186, 194, 201, 202, 246 n. 1087, 254 n. 1124, 287
al-'Abbās b. 'Abd al-Muṭṭalib * 64
al-'Abbās b. Abī Ṭālib * 128, 131
al-'Abbās b. al-Faḍl al-'Abdī * 224
al-'Abbās b. Ja'far b. Muḥammad 249
al-'Abbās b. Mirdās 82
al-'Abbās b. Muḥammad * 214, 236, 249, 280
al-'Abbās b. Muḥammad b. 'Alī 236
al-'Abbās b. Rab'īah b. al-Ḥārith 198
al-'Abbās b. Sahl * 190
al-'Abbās b. al-Walīd * 160, 261, 279
al-'Abbās b. al-Walīd al-Bayrūtī * 132, 148
al-'Abbās al-Dūrī * 238
'Abbāsid army 234 n. 1017
'Abbāsid movement 232 n. 1007, 235 nn. 1023, 1026, 236 n. 1029

'Abbāsid period xvi
'Abbāsid propaganda 234 n. 1018, 236 n. 1031, 312 n. 1440
'Abbāsids, 'Abbāsid dynasty 24 n. 106, 25 n. 113, 54 n. 242, 56 n. 241, 74, 98 n. 468, 155 n. 697, 234, 235, 236 n. 1031, 245, 246 nn. 1087, 1089, 249 nn. 1103, 1104, 277 n. 1257, 330 n. 1544, 334 n. 1564
'Abd al-Akram * 138
'Abd al-A'lā b. Mushir. *See* Abū Mushir. *See* Abū Mushir
'Abd al-A'lā b. Wāṣil * 155
'Abd al-Ashhal (a clan of the Aws) 30 n. 138, 133, 136, 286 n. 1302, 290 n. 1313, 302
'Abd al-'Azīz b. Abī Ḥāzim * 160
'Abd al-'Azīz b. Abī Rawwād * 218
'Abd al-'Azīz b. al-Junda'ī * 165
'Abd al-'Azīz b. Marwān **319**
'Abd al-'Azīz b. Muḥammad * 187, 209
'Abd al-'Azīz b. Muḥammad. *See* al-Durāwardī
'Abd al-'Azīz b. 'Ubaydallāh * 133
'Abd al-'Azīz b. 'Uqbah * 58
'Abd al-Dār b. Qu'sayy (a clan of the Quraysh) 67 n. 309, 79, 95 n. 461, 106, 168, 277 n. 1255
'Abd al-Ḥakīm b. 'Abdallāh b. Abī Farwah * 214
'Abd al-Ḥamīd b. 'Abdallāh b. Abī Farwah **337**
'Abd al-Ḥamīd b. Bahrām * 170
'Abd al-Ḥamīd b. Bashmīr * 238
'Abd al-Ḥamīd b. Bayān al-Qannād * 114
'Abd al-Ḥamīd b. 'Imrān * 116
'Abd al-Ḥamīd b. Jubayr b. Shaybah * 204
'Abd al-Ḥārith b. Zuhrah, (a family of the Quraysh) **110**
'Abd al-Ka'bah b. al-'Awwām 169, 199
'Abd Khayr b. Yazīd al-Khaywānī **151, 275, 321**
'Abd al-Majīd b. 'Abd al-'Azīz **329**
'Abd al-Malik b. 'Abd al-'Azīz. *See* Ibn Jurayj
'Abd al-Malik b. 'Abd al-Raḥmān * 279, 280
'Abd al-Malik b. Abī Bashīr * 152
'Abd Malik b. Abī Maḥdhūrah 48
'Abd al-Malik b. al-Ḥusayn * 199
'Abd al-Malik b. Marwān, the caliph 51 n. 227, 59 n. 263, 60, 95, 105 n. 499, 113, 210, 212, 213 n. 918, 232, 299 n. 1359, 306 nn. 1400, 1401, 313 n. 1445, 317 n. 1469, **318**, 319 n. 1475, 334 n. 1564
'Abd al-Malik b. Muslim 313 n. 1442
'Abd al-Malik b. Muḥammad b. al-Munkadir 240
'Abd al-Malik b. Sal' * 151
'Abd al-Malik b. 'Ubayd * 175
'Abd al-Malik b. 'Umayr * 108, 114, 157
'Abd al-Malik b. Wahb al-Madhḥijī * 152
'Abd al-Malik b. Zayd * 38
'Abd Manāf (a clan of the Quraysh) 78
'Abd al-Mu'min b. Khālid al-Ḥanafī * 218
'Abd al-Mu'min b. al-Qāsim 312 n. 1432
'Abd al-Mun'im * 94
'Abd al-Mun'im b. Idrīs * 226, **227**, 231, 233
'Abd al-Muṭṭalib 25, **41**, 106, 137, 281
'Abd al-Muṭṭalib (a clan of the Quraysh) 95
'Abd al-Muṭṭalib b. Rabī'ah b. al-Ḥārith **63, 97**, 198
'Abd Nuhm (tribal group) 92, **93 n. 449**
'Abd Qays (tribe) **271**, 275 n. 1241, 327 n. 1523, 330 n. 1545
'Abd al-Quddūs b. al-Ḥajjāj * 215
'Abd al-Raḥmān * 125
'Abd al-Raḥmān b. al-'Abbās 201
'Abd al-Raḥmān b. 'Abd al-'Azīz * 4, 36, 167, 173, 180, 229
'Abd al-Raḥmān b. 'Abdallāh b. 'Abd al-Ḥakam * 131

'Abd al-Raḥmān b. 'Abdallāh b. Muḥayrīz * 118
'Abd al-Raḥmān b. 'Abdallāh b. 'Uthmān. *See* Ibn Umm al-Ḥakam
'Abd al-Raḥmān b. Abī 'Amrah 35, 283
'Abd al-Raḥmān b. Abī Bakr **291**
'Abd al-Raḥmān b. Abī Laylā **310, 320**
'Abd al-Raḥmān b. Abī Laylā * 207
'Abd al-Raḥmān b. Abī al-Muwālī 168
'Abd al-Raḥmān b. Abī Sa'īd al-Khudrī **229, 319**
'Abd al-Raḥmān b. Abī Sa'īd al-Khudrī * 57
'Abd al-Raḥmān b. Abī Shumaylah * 157
'Abd al-Raḥmān b. Abī al-Zinād. *See* Ibn Abī al-Zinād
'Abd al-Raḥmān b. 'Ā'ish al-Ḥaḍramī **148**
'Abd al-Raḥmān b. 'Ā'ish al-Ḥaḍramī * 148
'Abd al-Raḥmān b. 'Amr. *See* al-Awzā'ī
'Abd al-Raḥmān b. al-Aswad 67 n. 308
'Abd al-Raḥmān b. 'Attāb b. Asīd **273**
'Abd al-Raḥmān b. 'Awf 42, 51, **107**, 244 n. 1076, 287 n.1304
'Abd al-Raḥmān b. Azhar **108**
'Abd al-Raḥmān b. Azhar * 108
'Abd al-Raḥmān b. Bishr 247
'Abd al-Raḥmān b. Bishr al-Naysābūrī * 238
'Abd al-Raḥmān b. Ghanm al-Ash'arī * 147
'Abd al-Raḥmān b. al-Ḥārith b. Hishām **314**
'Abd al-Raḥmān b. Ḥarmalah al-Aslamī **337**
'Abd al-Raḥmān b. Ḥassān b. Thābit * 194
'Abd al-Raḥmān b. Isḥāq * 134
'Abd al-Raḥmān b. Khanbash **159**
'Abd al-Raḥmān b. al-Mahdī * 101, 124, 146, 149
'Abd al-Raḥmān b. Mall. See Abū 'Uthmān al-Nahdī
'Abd al-Raḥmān b. Mu'āwiyah * 134
'Abd al-Raḥmān b. Muḥammad b. al-Ash'ath. *See* Ibn al-Ash'ath
'Abd al-Raḥmān b. Ṣāliḥ * 231
'Abd al-Raḥmān b. 'Ubaydallāh b. al-'Abbās 74
'Abd al-Raḥmān b. 'Uthmān 261
'Abd al-Raḥmān b. al-Walīd * 149
'Abd al-Raḥmān b. al-Walīd al-Jurjānī * 122
'Abd al-Raḥmān b. Yasār 253
'Abd al-Raḥmān b. Yazīd * 101
'Abd al-Raḥmān b. Yūnus * 214, 229, 244
'Abd al-Razzāq b. Hammām * 112, 240
'Abd al-Ṣamad b. 'Abd al-Wārith * 197
'Abd al-Ṣamad b. 'Alī **261**
'Abd Shams (a clan of the Quraysh) **13 n. 50, 23 n. 104**, 76 nn. 362–63, 192 n. 839
'Abd Shams b. al-Ḥārith 19
'Abd Shams b. Rabī'ah b. al-Ḥārith 198
'Abd Shams b. Sulay' 93
'Abd al-Wahhāb b. 'Abd al-Majīd al-Thaqafī * 103, 114, 121
'Abd al-Wāḥid b. Abī Awn. *See* Ibn Abī 'Awn
'Abd al-Wāḥid b. Wāṣil * 124
'Abd al-Wārith * 195
'Abd al-Wārith b. Sa'īd * 69
'Abdah b. Ḥazn 122 n. 563
'Abdallāh b. al-'Abbās. *See* Ibn 'Abbās
'Abdallāh b. 'Abd Asad. *See* Abū Salamah
'Abdallāh b. 'Abd al-Muṭṭalib, father of the Prophet **41**, 106, 198 n. 861
'Abdallāh b. 'Abd al-Raḥmān * 184
'Abdallāh b. 'Abd al-Raḥmān b. Abī Ṣa'ṣa'ah * 193
'Abdallāh b. 'Abdallāh b. Abī Umayyah 176
'Abdallāh b. 'Abdallāh b. 'Umar 175
'Abdallāh b. Abī al-Abyaḍ * 183, 184
'Abdallāh b. Abī Awfā 224, **293**
'Abdallāh b. Abī Bakr 172, 193

'Abdallāh b. Abī Bakr * 15
'Abdallāh b. Abī Bakr b. Ḥazm. *See* 'Abdallāh b. Abī Bakr b. Muḥammad
'Abdallāh b. Abī Bakr b. Muḥammad **243**
'Abdallāh b. Abī Bakr b. Muḥammad * 163, 167, 173, 180
'Abdallāh b. Abī Ḥadrad **293**
'Abdallāh b. Abī Mulaykah * 103
'Abdallāh b. Abī Najīḥ **244**
'Abdallāh b. Abī Rabī'ah **114**
'Abdallāh b. Abī Ṣa'ṣa'ah * 205
'Abdallāh b. Abī Sulaymān * 153
'Abdallāh b. Abī 'Ubaydah b. Muḥammad * 31, 33
'Abdallāh b. Abī Umayyah **112**
'Abdallāh b. Abī Yaḥyā * 203
'Abdallāh b. 'Adī b. Ḥamrā' **109**
'Abdallāh b. 'Adī b. Ḥamrā' * 109
'Abdallāh b. Aḥmad b. Shabbūyah (or Shabbawayh) * 159, 252, 257, 263, 264
'Abdallāh b. 'Alī b. 'Abdallāh b. al-'Abbās 234
'Abdallāh b. 'Alqamah. *See* Abū Nabiqah
'Abdallāh b. 'Āmir al-Aslamī * 180
'Abdallāh b. 'Āmir b. Kurayz **63,** 76
'Abdallāh b. 'Amir, Abū Ma'mar * 69
'Abdallāh b. 'Amr b. Zuhayr * 91, 177
'Abdallāh b. al-Arqam **109**
'Abdallāh b. al-Arqam * 109
'Abdallāh b. 'Awn. *See* Ibn 'Awn
'Abdallāh b. Aws 73
'Abdallāh b. 'Ayyāsh 112, 303
'Abdallāh b. Budayl b. Warqā' **34**
'Abdallāh b. Dīnār **237**
'Abdallāh b. Ḍumayrah * 100
'Abdallāh b. al-Faḍl b. 'Ayyāsh * 55
'Abdallāh b. Fuḍālah * 120, 121
'Abdallāh b. Ḥakīm b. Ḥizām 41, 106
'Abdallāh b. Ḥanẓalah al-Rāhib **131**
'Abdallāh b. al-Ḥārith * 12, 31, 60, 97, 168
'Abdallāh b. al-Ḥārith al-Azdī * 149
'Abdallāh b. al-Ḥārith b. 'Abd al-Muṭṭalib **62**
'Abdallāh b. al-Ḥārith b. Nawfal 63, **96, 315,** 325 n. 1508
'Abdallāh b. al-Ḥārith b. Nawfal * 19, 96, 97
'Abdallāh b. al-Ḥasan al-Baṣrī 225
'Abdallāh b. al-Ḥasan b. al-Ḥasan b. 'Alī 168, **245–47, 334**
'Abdallāh b. al-Ḥasan b. al-Ḥasan b. 'Alī * 195, 196, 279
'Abdallāh b. al-Ḥasan b. Zayd 260
'Abdallāh b. Ḥazn al-Naṣrī * 122
'Abdallāh b. Hilāl **152**
'Abdallāh b. Hilāl * 153
'Abdallāh b. al-Ḥusayn b. 'Alī 49
'Abdallāh b. 'Imrān * 125
'Abdallāh b. 'Imrān al-Iṣbahānī * 128
'Abdallāh b. Isḥāq al-Nāqid * 151
'Abdallāh b. Ja'far b. 'Abd al-Raḥmān **330**
'Abdallāh b. Ja'far b. 'Abd al-Raḥmān * 30, 32, 39, 43, 51, 52, 164, 168, 177, 187, 190, 233
'Abdallāh b. Ja'far b. Abī Ṭālib **59,** 96, **288**
'Abdallāh b. Ja'far b. al-Miswar, *see also* 'Abdallāh b. Ja'far b. 'Abd al-Raḥmān * 108
'Abdallāh b. Ja'far b. Muḥammad 248
'Abdallāh b. Jubayr **13**
'Abdallāh b. Junādah * 156
'Abdallāh b. Khalaf 277
'Abdallāh b. Khāzim al-Sulamī * **166**
'Abdallāh b. Khubayb * 153
'Abdallāh b. Lahī'ah. *See* Ibn Lahī'ah
'Abdallāh b. Maslamah b. Qa'nab * 27
'Abdallāh b. Mas'ūd 27, 105, **110,** 139 n. 638, **289,** 311 n. 1428, 314 n. 1451, 315 n. 1458
'Abdallāh b. Mas'ūd * 203
'Abdallāh b. Mas'ūd's mother. *See* Umm 'Abd bt. 'Abd Wadd
'Abdallāh b. Miqdād 197
'Abdallāh b. al-Mubārak 250, **263–64**
'Abdallāh b. al-Mubārak * 101, 146, 149

'Abdallāh b. Muḥammad * 5, 182
'Abdallāh b. Muḥammad b. 'Amr al-Ghazzī * 150
'Abdallāh b. Muḥammad b. 'Aqīl **334**
'Abdallāh b. Muḥammad b. Ibrāhīm 263
'Abdallāh b. Muḥammad b. 'Imrān * 131
'Abdallāh b. Muḥammad b. al-Munkadir 240
'Abdallāh b. Muḥammad b. Murrah al-Sha'bānī * 220
'Abdallāh b. Muḥammad b. Sīrīn 227
'Abdallāh b. Muḥammad b. 'Umar * 38
'Abdallāh b. Muḥammad b. 'Umar b. 'Alī * 167
'Abdallāh b. Muḥammad b. 'Umārah 319
'Abdallāh b. Muḥayrīz * 118
'Abdallāh b. Muslim **333**
'Abdallāh b. Muslim * 170, 225
'Abdallāh b. al-Muṭā' 111
'Abdallāh b. Nāfi' * 30, 174, 176
'Abdallāh b. Nawfal b. al-Ḥārith **209–210**
'Abdallāh b. Nufayl **149–50**
'Abdallāh b. Nufayl * 150
'Abdallāh b. Qays b. Makhramah **77**, 253
'Abdallāh b. Qusayṭ * 183
'Abdallāh b. Rabī'ah b. al-Ḥārith * 98
'Abdallāh b. Ruwaybah (tribal group) 265
'Abdallāh b. Sa'd b. Abī Sarḥ **81**
'Abdallāh b. al- Sā'ib **115**
'Abdallāh b. Sa'īd * 146
'Abdallāh b. Salām **296**
'Abdallāh b. Salām * 149
'Abdallāh b. Sālim * 159
'Abdallāh b. al-Ṣāmit * 122
'Abdallāh b. Sarjis al-Muzanī **125**
'Abdallāh b. Sarjis al-Muzanī * **125**
'Abdallāh b. Shaddād b. al-Hādi 202
'Abdallāh b. Shaddād b. al-Hādi * 121
'Abdallāh b. Shaqīq * 125
'Abdallāh b. Sulaym 94
'Abdallāh b. Sulaymān * 146, 187
'Abdallāh b. Sulaymān b. Ukaymah * 120
'Abdallāh b. Thābit 34
'Abdallāh b. 'Ubaydallāh b. al-'Abbās 55
'Abdallāh b. 'Umar. *See* Ibn 'Umar
'Abdallāh b. Urayqiṭ 138, 142, 172
'Abdallāh b. 'Urwah b. al-Zubayr **334**
'Abdallāh b. 'Utbah b. Mas'ūd **315**
'Abdallāh b. Wahb. *See* Ibn Wahb
'Abdallāh b. Warqā'. *See* Ibn Warqā'
'Abdallāh b. Yāsir 29
'Abdallāh b. Yazīd al-Anṣārī 268
'Abdallāh b. Yazīd al-Hilālī 201
'Abdallāh b. Yazīd al-Hudhalī * 81
'Abdallāh b. Yazīd b. Qanṭash **337–38**
'Abdallāh b. Yūnus al-Jubayrī * 109
'Abdallāh b. Zam'ah **76**
'Abdallāh b. Zayd b. 'Abd Rabbihi 281 n. 1272, **290**
'Abdallāh b. Zayd b. Tha'labah 290 n. 1309
'Abdallāh b. Zaynab. *See* 'Abdallāh b. Muḥammad b. Ibrāhīm
'Abdallāh b. Zubayd 211
'Abdallāh b. al-Zubayr 52, 95, **105**, 193, 209, 237, 247 n. 1092, 268, 272, 273 n. 1226, 276, 295 nn. 1339, 1341, **296**, 308 n. 1411, 315 n. 1459, 318 nn. 1470, 1471, 1472, 333 nn. 1559, 1560, 335
'Abdallāh b. al-Zubayr * 17
Abjar 57
abnā' (of the Yemen) 94, 227, 299
Abrahah, the Abyssinian **24 n. 108**
Abrahah, the slave girl 178–80
Abraham, the patriarch 37 n. 171, 43 n. 195, 148, 204
'Abs (tribe) 30 n. 138, 133, 321 n. 1488
al-Arqam **281**
Abū 'Ayyāsh al-Zuraqī, Zayd b. al-Ṣāmit **285**
Abū al-'Abbās. *See* al-Saffāḥ
Abū 'Abdallāh al-Jadalī **275–76, 306–307**
Abū 'Abd al-Raḥīm b. al-'Alā' * 205

Abū 'Abd al-Raḥmān al-Sulamī **269–70, 306**
Abū Aḥmad al-Sukkarī. *See* Bishr b. al-Ḥasan
Abū al-Aḥwaṣ * 238
Abū al-'Āliyah, al-Barrā' **308**
Abū al-Āliyah al-Riyāḥī **307**
Abū 'Āmir * 70, 108, 153
Abū 'Amr al-Shaybānī **306**
Abū 'Amrah, Bashīr b. 'Amr **35, 283**
Abū al-'Āṣ b. al-Rabī' **13–17**, 162, **282**
Abū al-Ash'ath al-Ṣan'ānī * 158
Abū al-Aswad al-Dīlī (al-Du'ilī) **307**
Abū al-A'war al-Sulamī, 'Amr b. Sufyan **285**
Abū 'Awn * 51, 52
Abū al-'Awwām 158
Abū Ayyūb al-Anṣārī **40, 133**, 185, **283**
Abū Ayyūb al-'Atakī, Yaḥyā b. Mālik **308**, 310 n. 1424
Abū Ayyūb al-Azdī. *See* Munīb al-Azdī
Abū Ayyūb al-Marāghī, Yaḥyā b. Mālik 310 n. 1424
Abū Ayyūb, Yaḥyā b. Ayyūb **310**
Abū al-Azhar al-Shāmī **313**
Abū al-Bakhtarī 77
Abū al-Bakhtarī * 119
Abū al-Bakhtarī al-Ṭā'ī **209**
Abū Bakkār, al-Ḥakam b. Farrūkh **312**
Abū Bakr * 266, 270
Abū Bakr b. 'Abdallāh. *See* Ibn Abī Sabrah
Abū Bakr b. 'Abd al-Raḥmān b. al-Ḥārith * 120
Abū Bakr b. 'Ayyāsh * 246, 272, 273
Abū Bakr, the caliph 16, 19, 30 n. 139, 41, 46, 65 nn. 299, 300, 81, 82, 88, 90, **111**, 128 n. 589, 138, 139 n. 638, 140 n. 641, 142, 144 n. 652, 145, 172, 173 n. 774, 195, 202, 231, 252, **281**, 290 nn. 1311–12, 294 n. 1335
Abū Bakr al-Hudhalī **312**
Abū Bakr b. Ismā'īl b. Muḥammad * 23, 177
Abū Bakr b. Kilāb (tribal group) 188
Abū Bakr b. Muḥammad b. 'Amr 192
Abū Bakr al-Nahshalī * 149
Abū Bakrah **29, 282**, 324 n. 1502
Abū Balj **310**
Abū Barzah al-Aslamī **284**
Abū Bisṭām, Yaḥyā b. 'Abd al-Raḥmān **311–12**
Abū Buraydah 69
Abū Burdah, brother of Abū Mūsā al-Ash'arī **147**
Abū Burdah b. Abī Mūsā **307**
Abū Burdah b. Niyār **283**
Abū Burdah b. Niyār * 146
Abū al-Dardā' **283**
Abū Dā'ūd * 155
Abū Dharr al-Ghifārī 45–46, **69–70**, 99, **282**
Abū Dharr al-Ghifārī * 122
Abū Dh'ib (a family of the Quraysh) **337 n. 1584**
Abū Dujānah, Simāk b. Kharashah **286**
Abū Faḍālah al-Anṣārī **35**
Abū Fā'id * 27
Abū Fākhitah, Sa'īd b. 'Ilāqah **306**
Abū Fāṭimah **153**
Abū Fāṭimah * 153
Abū Ghādiyah **31**, 33
Abū Ghassān, Mālik b. Ismā'īl al-Nahdī * 215
Abū al-Ghayth * 209
Abū Ghifār * 124
Abū Ḥabībah, client of al-Zubayr b. al-'Awwām * 17, 41, 106, 161
Abū Ḥadrad al-Aslamī **284**
Abū al-Ḥajjāj al-Miṣrī, *see also* Rishdīn b. Sa'd 329 n. 1537
Abū al-Ḥakam 325 n. 1511
Abū Hālah b. al-Nabbāsh 3, 79, 161
Abū Hālah b. Zurārah. *See* Abū Hālah b. al-Nabbāsh
Abū al-Ḥamrā' **154, 285**
Abū al-Ḥamrā' * 155
Abū Ḥamrah 310 n. 1419
Abū Ḥamzah, Sa'd b. 'Ubādah **313**
Abū Ḥamzah al-Sukkarī **312**

Abū Ḥanīfah xix, 238, **250–52**, 264, 331
Abū Ḥarb * 120, 121
Abū Hāshim b. Muḥammad b. al-Ḥanafiyyah 236, 322 n. 1495
Abū Hāshim b. 'Utbah b. Rabī'ah **76**
Abū al-Haytham, 'Ammār **314**
Abū al-Haytham b. al-Tayyihān, Mālik b. al-Tayyihān **286**
Abū Ḥaywah, Shurayḥ b. Yazīd * 205
Abū al-Hayyāj, 'Amr b. Mālik **314**
Abū Ḥayyān al-Ashja'ī **311**
Abū Ḥāzim, Nabtal **309**
Abū Ḥāzim * 160
Abū Ḥāzim al-Ashja'ī, Salmān **309**
Abū Hilāl al-Rāsibī 312
Abū Hilāl al-Ṭā'ī **313**
Abū Hishām al-Rifā'ī * 250
Abū Hishām, *see also* Muḥammad b. Sulaymān 140
Abū Ḥudhayfah b. al-Mughīrah 29, 117
Abū Ḥudhayfah, Salamah b. Ṣuhayb **311**
Abū Ḥudhayfah b. 'Utbah 300
Abū Ḥumayd al-Sā'idī, 'Abd al-Raḥmān b. Sa'd 279 n. 1268, **286**
Abū Hurayrah 50, 70, 173, 174, 176, 209, 223, **283**, 304 n. 1382
Abū Hurayrah * 185
Abū al-Ḥuṣayn * 81
Abū al-Ḥuwayrith, 'Abd al-Raḥmān b. Mu'āwiyah **240–41, 309**
Abū al-Ḥuwayrith, 'Abd al-Raḥmān b. Mu'āwiyah * 240
Abū Ibrāhīm al-Anṣārī * 136
Abū Ibrāhīm al-Anṣārī's father **136**
Abū Ibrāhīm al-Anṣārī's father * 136
Abū Idrīs * 101
Abū Idrīs, Sawād **314**
Abū 'Imrān al-Jawnī **308**
Abū 'Isā al-Zāhid * 257
Abū Isḥāq * 119, 122, 128, 145, 224, 268
Abū Isḥāq al-Hamdānī * 155
Abū Isḥāq al-Kūfī. *See* Ibrāhīm al-Qāri'
Abū Isḥāq al-Sabī'ī **238–39, 325**, 329 n. 1538
Abū Isḥāq al-Sabī'ī * 115
Abū Isḥāq al-Ṣā'igh **312**
Abū Isḥāq al-Shaybānī **239**
Abū Isrā'īl * 230, 277
Abū Ja'far al-Bajalī **310**
Abū Ja'far al-Ḥuddānī * 215
Abū Ja'far al-Madā'inī **309**
Abū Ja'far, Muḥammad b. 'Alī b. al-Ḥusayn **229–30**
Abū Ja'far, Muḥammad b. 'Alī b. al-Ḥusayn * 12, 25, 37, 39, 167, 214, 230
Abū Ja'far, Muḥammad b. Jarīr. *See* al-Ṭabarī
Abū Ja'far al- Qāri' **303**
Abū Jahl **18 n. 70**, 60, 68 n. 315, 112
Abū Jamrah **310**
Abū Juḥayfah, Wahb al-Suwā'ī **285**
Abū Juḥayfah, Wahb al-Suwā'ī * 257
Abū Juhaym b. al-Ḥārith **35**
Abū Jumaḥ, Ḥabīb b. Sibā' **285**
Abū Jurayy. *See* Sulaym b. Jābir
Abū Kathīr al-Zubaydī **313**
Abū Khabṭah **311**
Abū Khālid al-Wālibī **313**
Abū Kurayb * 97 113, 116, 146, 154, 156, 197, 200, 204, 205, 221, 266, 270
Abū Lahab **64 n. 293**
Abū Laylā, Bilāl b. Bulayl **282, 310**
Abū Līnah, 'Abdallāh b. Abī Karib **285**
Abū Lubābah, Rifā'ah b. 'Abd al-Mundhir **286**
Abū Ma'bad 139, 140, 143, 144
Abū Ma'bad * 142
Abū Maḥdhūrah **48, 118, 181, 282**
Abū Mālik al-Ash'arī **147**
Abū Mālik al-Ash'arī * 147
Abū Mālik al-Nakha'ī * 199
Abū Marthad al-Ghanawī **100, 281**
Abū Marthad al-Ghanawī * 101
Abū Marwān al-Aslamī * 69, 160
Abū Maryam, 'Abd al-Ghaffār **312**
Abū Maryam al-Asadī **314**
Abū Maryam al-Filasṭīnī **158**

Abū Maryam al-Filasṭīnī * 158
Abū Maryam, Mālik b. Rabī'ah **128**
Abū Maryam, Mālik b. Rabī'ah * 128
Abū Maryam, Ṭahmān 328
Abū Ma'shar, Najīḥ xxiv
Abū Ma'shar, Najīḥ * 50, 69, 165, 177, 240, 282
Abū Mas'ūd al-Anṣārī, 'Uqbah b. 'Amr **286**
Abū Maymūnah **304**
Abū Mikhnaf xxiv, **94**
Abū Mikhnaf * 32
Abū al-Minhāl * 152
Abū al-Minhāl's father 152
Abū al-Minhāl's father * 152
Abū al-Mu'allā * 157
Abū al-Mu'allā al-'Aṭṭār **312**
Abū al-Mu'allā, Zayd b. Murrah **312**
Abū al-Mu'allā's father **157**
Abū al-Mu'alla's father * 157
Abū Mu'attib b. 'Amr **160**
Abū Mu'attib b. 'Amr * 160
Abū Mu'āwiyah al-Bajalī **313**
Abū Mu'awiyah, Muḥammad b. Khāzim **311**
Abū al-Muhazzam * 50
Abū Mūsā * 224
Abū Mūsā al-Ash'arī 69, 88, 102 n. 487, **147**, 233, **282**, 307 n. 1402
Abū Mūsā al-Thaqafī * 39
Abū Muṣ'ab, Ismā'īl b. Muṣ'ab * 188
Abū Mushir * 158
Abū Muslim al-Khawlānī **308**
Abū Muslim al-Khurāsāni 312 n. 1440
Abū al-Mu'tamir, Yazīd b. Ṭahmān **313**, 323 n. 1500
Abū al-Mutawakkil al-Nājī **276**, **308**
Abū Na'āmah al-'Adawī * 104, 151
Abū Nabiqah **77**
Abū Naḍrah **271**
Abū Nimrān al-Raḥabī * 159
Abū Nu'aym. *See* al-Faḍl b. Dukayn
Abū Qāmūṣ, Zayd b. 'Alī **327**
Abū Qatādah al-Anṣārī **283**, 336
Abū Qaṭan * 256
Abū Quḥāfah 281
Abū Qutaybah * 223
Abū Rabāḥ b. 'Abīdah * 226
Abū Rabī'ah al-Iyādī * 99
Abū Rāfi' **65–66**, **99**, 172, 194
Abū Rajā' al-'Uṭāridī **307–308**
Abū Ruhm b. 'Abd al-'Uzzā 185
Abū al-Rūm b. 'Umayr **67**
Abū Sabrah, Yazīd b. Mālik **285**
Abū al-Sā'ib * 226, 231, 233, 253, 268
Abū Sa'īd * 251
Abū Sa'īd al-Khudrī **57**, 229 n. 995, **284**
Abū Sa'īd al-Maqbarī **303**
Abū Sa'īd al-Maqbarī * 174
Abū Sa'īd al-Rādhānī. *See* Abū Sa'īd al-Rānī
Abū Sa'īd al-Rānī **250**
Abū Ṣakhr * 205
Abū Salām al-Ḥanafī **313**
Abū Salamah * 136
Abū Salamah b. 'Abd al-Raḥmān * 109
Abū Salamah, 'Abdallāh b. 'Abd al-Asad 113, 175
Abū Salamah, Dīnār 333
Abū Salamah al-Ḥaḍramī * 56
Abū Salamah, Sulaymān b. Abī Sulaym * 149
Abū Ṣāliḥ, Bādhām **304**
Abū Ṣāliḥ, Bādhām * 9, 170, 197
Abū Ṣāliḥ, Burkān **306**
Abū Ṣāliḥ, client of al-Saffāḥ **304**
Abū Ṣāliḥ al-Ghifārī **305**
Abū Ṣāliḥ al-Ḥanafī 304 n. 1384, **305**
Abū Ṣāliḥ, Maysarah **305**
Abū Ṣāliḥ, Mīzān **305–306**
Abū Ṣāliḥ, Qaylūh **305**
Abū Ṣāliḥ, Rudayḥ 305
Abū Ṣāliḥ, scribe of al-Layth * 101
Abū Ṣāliḥ al-Sammān **304**
Abū Ṣāliḥ, Sumay' **304**
Abū Ṣāliḥ al-Zayyāt. *See* Abū Ṣāliḥ al-Sammān
Abū al-Sanābil b. Ba'kak **107**
Abū al-Sha'thā' Fayrūz **309–10**
Abū al-Sha'thā', Jābir b. Zayd **309**
Abū al-Sha'thā' al-Muḥāribī **306**
Abū al-Ṣiddīq al-Nājī **276**, **308**

Abū Sinān * 119
Abū Sinān al-Rāzī **313**
Abū Ṣirmah * 57
Abū Sufyān b. Ḥarb **48–49**
Abū Sufyān b. al-Ḥārith 19, **21**, 62
Abū Sufyān, Ṭalḥah b. Nāfi' **311**
Abū Sufyān, Ṭarīf al-Sa'dī **311**
Abū Suhayl. See Abū Ṣāliḥ al-Sammān
Abū Ṭalḥah, Zayd b. Sahl **12**, 163
Abū Ṭālib 196, 309 n. 1414
Abū Ṭālib, 'Abd al-Salām b. Shaddād * 214
Abū Tamīmah * 124
Abū al-Tayyāḥ * 159
Abū al-Tayyāḥ, Yazīd b. Ḥumayd **312**
Abū Tumaylah * 5, 218
Abū Turāb (nickname of 'Alī b. Abī Ṭālib 224)
Abū 'Ubayd, Sulaymān's doorkeeper **156**
Abū 'Ubayd al-Thaqafī 205
Abū 'Ubaydah b. al-Jarrāḥ 15 n. 56, **281**
Abū 'Ubaydah, Ma'mar b. al-Muthannā xxiv
Abū 'Ubaydah, Ma'mar b. Muthannā * 80, 176, 191
Abū 'Ubaydah b. Muḥammad * 33
Abū 'Udhāfir **310**
Abū Udhaynah **156**
Abū Udhaynah * 156
Abū Uḥayḥah, Sa'īd b. al-'Āṣ 282
Abū Umāmah al-Anṣārī, Asad b. Zurārah **286**
Abū Umāmah al-Bāhilī, Ṣudayy b. 'Ajlān **84**, 224, **282**
Abū Umāmah b. Sahl b. Ḥunayf **303**
Abū Umāmah b. Sahl b. Ḥunayf * 36
Abū Umayyah, client of 'Umar b. al-Khaṭṭāb **307**
Abū Umayyah b. al-Mughīrah **80**, 175
Abū Usāmah al-Jushamī 175
Abū Usayd al-Sā'idī **188**, 189, **284**
Abū Usayd al-Sā'idī * 190
Abū 'Uthmān al-Muqaddamī * 226
Abū 'Uthmān al-Nahdī **214–215**, **307**
Abū Wadā'ah, al-Ḥārith b. Ḍumayrah **284**
Abū Wā'il **306**
Abū Wajzah, Yazīd b. 'Ubayd * 188
Abū Wāqid al-Laythī. *See* Ṣāliḥ b. Muḥammad b. Zā'idah
Abū Yaḥyā al-Ḥimmānī. *see* 'Abd al-Ḥamīd b. Bashmīr
Abū Yaḥyā al-Kalā'ī * 200
Abū Ya'qūb * 278
Abū al-Yasar, Ka'b b. 'Amr **134**, **283**
Abū al-Yasar, Ka'b b. 'Amr * 134
Abū Yūsuf **265 n. 1181**
Abū al-Ẓāhiriyyah al-Ḥaḍramī **309**
Abū Zakariyyā' al-'Ajlānī * 169
Abū Zayd al-Anṣārī, Thābit b. Zayd **284**
Abū Zayd al-Ḍabbī * 200
Abū Zayd who collected the Qur'ān, *see also* Sa'd b. 'Ubayd 22 n. 94, 284 n. 1288
Abū al-Zinbā' **308**
Abū al-Zubayr * 186
Abū Zuhayr al-Anmārī 127 n. 586
Abū Zuhayr al-Numayrī **127**
Abū Zuhayr al-Numayrī * 127
Abū Zur'ah al-Dimashqī xxiv
Abū Zur'ah al-Dimashqī * 131, 205
al-Abwā' **21**
Abyssinia 167, 170, 177
Abyssinia, emigration to **5**, 26, 27, 30, 66, 67, 104, 105, 110, 162, 169, 175, 177, 178 n. 799
Abyssinians 94, 169, 227, 299
Ādam 126
Ādam b. Abī Iyās **329**
Ādam b. Abī Iyās * 156
Ādam b. Rabī'ah 62
al-'Adawiyyah (tribal group) **104 n. 498**
Adham b. Muḥriz 53, 274
'Adī b. 'Amr (tribal group) 34 n. 151, 93
'Adī b. Ḥātim **86**, **297**
'Adī b. Ka'b (a clan of Quraysh) 37 n. 168, 95 n. 461, 117
'Abī b. Rabī'ah (tribal group) 137

'Adnān **7 n. 25**
'Adūl (tribal group) **111**
'Adwān (tribal group) 275
'Affān * 223
'Affān b. Abī al-'Āṣ 198
Afghanistan 237 n. 1040
al-Aghlab al-'Ijlī **94**
ahl al-bayt. See Family of the Prophet
ahl al-dhimmah **23 n. 99**
ahl al-kitāb. See Possessors of the Scriptures
ahl al-ṣuffah **292 n. 1318**
Aḥmad b. 'Abd al-Raḥmān al-Ḥarrānī * 109
Aḥmad b. Ishkāb * 155
Aḥmad b. Khālid al-Khallāl * 252
Aḥmad b. Makhlad * 260
Aḥmad b. Mūsā * 207
Aḥmad b. Shabbūyah (or Shabbawayh) * 252, 257
Aḥmad b. 'Uthmān b. Ḥakīm * 115
Aḥmad b. al-Walīd * 256
Aḥmad b. Yūnus * 268
Aḥmūr (tribal group) 220
al-Aḥnaf b. Qays 123 n. 568, 267
al-Aḥnaf b. Qays * 70
al-Aḥsā'. See Hajar
'Ā'isha bt. 'Abdallāh al-Akbar 235
'Ā'ishah bt Sa'd * 39
'Ā'ishah, wife of the Prophet 22 n. 96, 28 n. 126, 105 n. 499, 165, 170, **171–74,** 176, 181, 190, 198, 272, 277, 280, 291 n. 1315, 292 n. 1322, 315 n. 1457
'Ā'ishah, wife of the Prophet * 12, 13, 167, 183, 279
'Ā'ishah bt. al-Zubayr 193
Ajnādayn **19**
Ajyād **123**
Akhmūr (tribal group) 220 n. 954
al-'Alā'ī * 207, 308
a'lām al-ḥaram, see also *anṣāb al-ḥaram* 93
alcohol 103, 108
Āl Dhī Bāriq (tribal group) 220
Āl Dhī Juddān (tribal group) 220
Āl Dhī La'wah (tribal group) 220
Āl Dhī Marrān (tribal group) 220
Āl Dhī Raḍwān (tribal group) 220
Āl Dhī Sha'bayn (tribal group) 220
Alexandria 193, 317 n. 1468
'Alī b. 'Abdallāh * 278
'Alī b. 'Abdallāh b. al-'Abbās 54, 74, 216, **232, 322**
'Alī b. 'Abdallāh b. Ja'far 54
'Alī b. Abī al-'Āṣ 13, 162
'Alī b. Abī Ṭālib 11, 13, 25, 28 n. 126, 31 n. 141, 32 n. 144, 34, 35, 36, **36–37,** 38–39, 50, 51 n. 228, 53, 60, 65 nn. 299, 302, 66, 72, 74, 75, 77 n. 371, 84, 86, 87 n. 418, 88, 92, 93 n. 453, 96, 99, 104 n. 498, 105 n. 499, 107 n. 566, 113, 117, 128, 138, 144 n. 652, 146, 149, 151, 155, 156, 162, 167, 168, 196 n. 851, 197 n. 859, 198, 202 n. 874, 205, 206, 207, 208, 210, 213, 224, 228, 231, 232, 233 n. 1011, 236 n. 1031, 247, 257, 267, 268, 269, 270, 271 n. 1213, 272, 273 n. 1231, 274, 275, 278, 279, 281 n. 1272, 282 n. 1278, 283 n. 1279, 285 n. 1290, 286 n. 1297, **287,** 294 n. 1332, 295 n. 1340, 296 n. 1342, 297 n. 1346, 298 n. 1353, 300 n. 1361, 305 n. 1390, 306 nn. 1400, 1401, 307 n. 1403, 310 n. 1421, 316 n. 1466, 320 n. 1485
'Alī b. Abī Ṭālib * 279
'Alī al-Aqmar **311**
'Alī al-Aqmar * 257
'Alī b. 'Āṣim 182
'Alī b. al-Ḥasan * 263, 264
'Alī b. al-Ḥasan b. Shaqīq * 250
'Alī b. al-Ḥasan b. Zayd 260
'Alī b. Ḥassān b. 'Amr (tribal group) 220
'Alī b. al-Ḥusayn ('Alī al-Akbar) 48, 211
'Alī b. Ḥusayn ('Alī al-Aṣghar, Zayn al-'Ābidīn) 49, **210–14**
'Alī b. al-Ḥusayn * 167, 168
'Alī b. al-Ḥusayn b. Wāqid * 252
'Alī b. 'Īsā al-Nawfalī * 19, 60, 63, 64

'Alī b. Ja'd **331**
'Alī b. al-Madyanī * 221, 240, 244
'Alī b. Mālik al-Jushamī * 267
'Alī b. Muḥammad. *See* al-Madā'inī
'Alī b. Mujāhid * 51, 212
'Alī b. Mūsā * 101
'Alī b. Muslim * 174, 226
'Alī b. Sahl al-Ramlī * 96, 223, 225
'Alī b. Ṣhuayb al-Simsār * 199
'Alī b. Suwayd b. Manjūf * 267
'Alī b. Yaḥyā * 134
'Alī b. Zayd b. Jud'ān **280 n. 1271**
'Alī b. Zayd b. Jud'ān * 222, 280
'Ali Zayn al-'Ābidīn, *see also* 'Alī b. al-Ḥusayn 54 n. 244
'Alids, 'Alid family 212 n. 916, 234 n. 1018, 245 n. 1084
al-'Āliyah (place) 194
al-'Āliyah bt. Muḥammad b. 'Alī 235
al-'Āliyah bt. 'Ubaydallāh b. al-'Abbās 74, 235
al-'Āliyah bt. Ẓabyān. *See* al-Kilābiyyah
Āl al-Jawn (tribal group) 189 n. 834
Alliances, allies 9 n. 30, **26,** 29, 30, 79, 95, 100, 101, 104, 105, 110, 111, 116, 125 n. 577, 133, 146 n. 661, 177, 199, 231, 281, 282, 283, 285 n. 1295, 286 n. 1302, 289, 297 n. 1350, 301
'Alqamah * 272, 273
'Alqamah b. Marthad * 97, 207
'Alqamah b. Qays al-Nakha'ī * 203
'Alqamah Jidhl al-Ṭi'ān 175
Amānāh b. Qays **89**
al-A'mash. *See* Sulaymān b. Mihrān
Āminah **280**
Āminah * 280
Āminah bt. Abān 254 n. 1126
Āminah bt. Abdallāh 280 n. 1270
Āminah bt. Abī Murrah 48, 49
Āminah bt. Abī Qays al-Ghifāriyyah * 185
Āminah bt. al-Ḥakam. *See* al-Ghifāriyyah
Āminah bt. Wahb, mother of the Prophet 152 n. 684
'Āmir (tribal group) 187, 188
'Āmir b. 'Abdallāh b. al-Zubayr **333**
'Āmir b. Fuhayrah 138, 142
'Āmir b. Kurayz **76,** 198
'Āmir b. Lu'ayy (a clan of the Quraysh) **43,** 44 n. 202, 68 n. 318, 81 n. 384, 95 n. 461, 118, 169 n. 759, 204, 272 n. 1220, 336
'Āmir b. Mālik, Mulā'ib al-Asinnah 73 n. 343
'Āmir b. Mas'ūd **119**
'Āmir b. Mas'ūd al-Jumaḥī **119 n. 550**
'Āmir b. Sa'd b. Abī Waqqāṣ * 115
'Āmir b. Sa'īd, Abū Ja'far * 215
'Āmir b. Ṣa'ṣa'ah (tribe) **54 n. 243,** 73 n. 343, 83 n. 395, 126 n. 581, 185 n. 818, 186 n. 821, 253 n. 1123, 285 n. 1293, 316 n. 1464, 336 n. 1574
'Āmir b. Sharāḥīl see al-Sha'bī
'Āmir b. al-Ṭufayl 73 n. 343
'Āmir b. al-Ḍaḥyān 24 n. 107
'Āmmār b. Ruzayq al-Ḍabbī 258
'Ammār b. Yāsir **28–34, 116, 289**
'Ammār b. Ruzayq al-Ḍabbī * 155
al-amr bi-al-ma'rūf **258 n. 1149**
'Amr * 134
'Amr, brother of Ḥārithah 7
'Amr b. 'Abd al-Raḥmān * 118
'Amr b. Abī 'Amr **337**
'Amr b. Abī Qays * 137
'Amr b. 'Alī * 214, 223
'Amr b. al-'Āṣ 32, 88, 287 n. 1304, **291,** 327 n. 1524
'Amr b. 'Awf (tribal group) 132, 133, 189, 286 n. 1298
'Amr b. Bahrā' 301
'Amr b. Baydaq * 204
'Amr b. Dīnār 244, **324**
'Amr b. Dīnār * 167
'Amr b. al-Ḥamiq **92**
'Amr b. al-Ḥārith (Baḥzaj) 36
'Amr b. al-Ḥārith * 132, 159
'Amr b. al-Ḥārith b. Abī Shamir 30
'Amr b. Ḥazm **192 n. 838, 294–95**
'Amr b. Ḥurayth **59–60, 113, 296**
'Amr b. Ḥurayth * 113, 114

'Amr b. 'Īsā. *See* Abū Na'āmah al-'Adawī
'Amr b. Jahm 67
'Amr b. Ma'dī-karib 91, **298**
'Amr b. Murrah **324**
'Amr b. Murrah * 119
'Amr b. al-Musabbiḥ **86–87**
'Amr b. Qays b. Zā'idah. *See* Ibn Umm Maktūm
'Amr b. al-Rabī' 13
'Amr b. Sa'īd al-Ashdaq 334 n. 1564
'Amr b. Salimah **268–69**
'Amr b. Sha's **146**
'Amr b. Sha's * 146
'Amr b. Shu'ayb **327**
'Amr b. Shu'ayb * 187
'Amr b. Sulaymān al-'Aṭṭār * 251
'Amr b. Thābit * 27
'Amr b. 'Ubayd * 223
'Amr b. Udd (tribe) **125 n. 577**
'Amr b. Umayyah al-Ḍamrī 180
'Amr b. 'Uthmān b. 'Affān 335
'Amr b. Yaḥyā * 154
'Amr b. Yaḥyā al-Māzinī * 133
'Amrah bt. 'Abd al-Raḥmān * 167, 171, 186
'Amwās **95**, 281 n. 1273
Anas * 273
Anas b. Mālik 224, 227, **295**, 309 n. 1417, 338
Anas b. Mālik * 12, 22
Anas b. Sīrīn * 227
al-Anbār **245**
al-'Anbar (tribal group) 124 n. 574, 252, 259 n. 1154, 324 n. 1501, 326 n. 1518
'Anbasah b. Abī Sufyān 332 n. 1557
'Anbasah b. Sa'īd * 128
anṣāb al-ḥaram, see also *a'lām al-ḥaram* 42
Anṣār **11**, 34 n. 155, 35 n. 157, 36 n. 162, 40, **55**, 58, 71 n. 331, 72 nn. 336, 339, 133 n. 616, 146 n. 661, 163, 162 n. 731, 173, 191, 194, 210 n. 909, 235, 290 n. 1311, 294 nn. 1333, 1334, 295 nn. 1339, 1340, 1341, 296 1343, 320 n. 1424, 331 n. 1549
Anṣinā 194
al-'Ansī. See al-Aswad al-'Ansī
apostasy wars 30 n. 139, 78 n. 375, 82, 85, 88, 90 n. 436, 91, 111 n. 523, 133 n. 616, 160 n. 724
'Aqabah meeting **11**, 40, 58, 133, 162 n. 731, 286 nn. 1297–98, 1300, 287 n. 1303, 290 nn. 1310–11, 291 n. 1314, 303 n. 1375
'Aqīl b. Abī Ṭālib 21, **60**, 96, **288**
'Aqīl family 168
al-'Aqīq **38**, 47
'aqr **5 n. 12**
al-'Aqra' b. Ḥābis **82**
Arab, Arabs 3 n. 2, 5 n. 12, 6 n. 19, 13 n. 48, 29 nn. 130, 134, 30 n. 136, 37 nn. 166, 169, 73, 82, 83, 85 n. 405, 87, 90 n. 436, 129 n. 599, 138 n. 637, 148 n. 667, 156 n. 702, 171 n. 762, 175, 18, 191, 201, 212, 213, 220 n. 953, 244 n. 1077, 253, 277, 278 n. 1262, 282 n. 1278, 307 n. 1403
'Arābah b. Aws 71, 72, **73–74**
Arabian Peninsula 30 n. 139, 32 n. 145, 108, 148 n. 667, 188 n. 829, 208 n. 899
'Arafāt 64 n. 295, 98
arbitration **88 n. 422**, 233 n. 1011, 273 n. 1231
Arḥab (tribal group) 220, **268**, 269, 311 n. 1429
Armenia 201 n. 871
al-Arqam b. Abī al-Arqam **46–47**, **289**
al-Arqam b. Abī al-Arqam, house of 5, 38, **47**, 118, 281 n. 1274
Arwā bt. Kurayz **192**, 198
Arwā bt. Rabī'ah b. al-Ḥārith 198
Arwā senior. *See* Arwā bt. Rabī'ah
al-'Arzamī * 188
'aṣabiyyah 17 n. 68
Asad b. 'Abd al-'Uzzā (a clan of Quraysh) 3, 26 n. 122, 40 n. 185, 66 n. 305, 76 n. 360, 77 n. 371, 95 n. 461, 105

Asad (tribe) 9 n. 30, 175 n. 786, 231, 248, 313 n. 1447, 314 n. 1450, 320 n. 1485, 323 n. 1499, 324 n. 1504, 325 nn. 1509, 1513
Asad b. Mūsā * 196, 203, 205, 280
Asad b. Zurārah **303 n. 1375**
Aṣbagh, client of 'Amr b. Ḥurayth * 113, 114
al-Aṣbagh b. Nubātah **275**
asceticism, ascetics 70 n. 323, 174 n. 779, 207 n. 896, 241 n. 1063, 242 n. 1065, 257, 258 n. 1148, 263, 298 n. 1351, 303 n. 1378, 308 n. 1412, 321 n. 1487, 330 n. 1542, 331
al-Ashāqir (tribal group) **255**
al-Ash'ar (tribal group) **147**
al-Ash'ath b. Abī al-Sha'thā' **314**
al-Ash'ath b. Qays **87–88**, 89, 90, 190, 228 n. 990, **298, 302,** 314 n. 1459
Ashja' (tribe) 287 n. 1303, 335 n. 1570
ashrāf. See tribal nobles
al-Ashtar al-Nakha'ī 51 n. 228, **272–73**
al-Ash'ūb (tribal group) 220
'Āshūrā' 248
Asīd b. Abī Asīd, al-Barrād 336 n. 1578
Asīd b. Abī Asīd, client of Abū Qatādah **336**
'Āṣim * 125
'Āṣim al-Aslamī * 70
'Āṣim b. Abī al-Najūd **238**
'Āṣim b. Abī al-Najūd * 51
'Āṣim b. Bahdalah. *See* 'Āṣim b. Abī al-Najūd
'Āṣim b. Ḥadrah **157–58**
'Āṣim b. Ḥadrah * 158
'Āṣim al-Jaḥdarī **326**
'Āṣim b. Sulaymān al-Aḥwal **328**
'Āṣim b. Sulaymān al-Aḥwal * 125
'Āṣim b. 'Ubaydallāh * 96
'Āṣim b. 'Umar 175
'Āṣim b. 'Umar b. Qatādah * 74, 180
'Āṣim b. al-Zubayr 193
Aslam (tribe) 70 n. 326, 122, 146 n. 659, 160 n. 724, 284 nn. 1285, 1286, 293 nn. 1326, 1327, 1328, 325 n. 1514, 337 n. 1580
Aslum (tribe) 130
Asmā' * 134
Asmā' bt. 'Abdallāh b. al-'Abbās 55
Asmā' bt. Abī Bakr 105, 172, **193**
Asmā' bt. Abī Bakr * 208
Asmā' bt. Ja'far b. Muḥammad 249
Asmā' bt. Mukharribah **112**
Asmā' bt. al-Nu'mān **188–91**
Asmā' bt. Salamah b. Mukharribah **112**
Asmā' bt. 'Umays 5, 59, 121, 167, 169, 199, 201, **202**
al-Aṣma'ī * 222
'Aṣmā'. *See* Lubābah al-Ṣughrā
al-Aswad b. 'Āmir * 239
al-Aswad b. 'Abd Yāghūth 10, 26, 110, 301
al-Aswad b. Abī al-Bakhtarī 77
al-Aswad al-'Ansī **81,** 91, 94
al-Aswad b. Nawfal b. Khuwaylid **66–67**
al-Aswad b. Qays **327**
al-Aswad b. Qays * 199
al-Aswad b. Shaybān **256**
'Aṭā' * 184
'Aṭā' b. Abī Marwān * 69, 160
'Aṭā' b. Abī Rabāḥ 223, **321**
'Aṭā al-Khurāsānī * 207
'Aṭā' b. Muslim * 51
'Aṭā' b. al-Sā'ib **327**
'Aṭā' b. al-Sā'ib * 98, 128, 129, 270
'Aṭā' b. Yasār **317**
'Aṭā' b. Yazīd al-Junda'ī * 165
'aṭā'. *See* pensions
'Atīk (tribal group) **278, 308 n. 1409**
'Atīk b. 'Ābid 161
'Atīkah bt. 'Abdallāh b. 'Ankathah 68
'Atīkah bt. 'Abd al-Muṭṭalib 76, 112
'Atīkah bt. 'Āmir 175
'Atīkah bt. 'Awf 42, 51
'Aṭiyyah b. Sa'd b. Junādah **228**
'Aṭṭāf b. Makhramah, 'Aṭṭāf al-Akbar 42
'Aṭṭāf b. Makhramah, 'Aṭṭāf al-Aṣghar 42

'Awaqah (tribal group) **271**
'Awf b. 'Abd 'Awf b. al-Ḥārith 110
'Awf b. 'Amr (a clan of the Aws) **36,** 72 n. 336
'Awf (tribal group) 248
'Awf b. Zurārah 79
'Awn b. 'Umays 201
Aws (tribe) 34 n. 153, 36 n. 162, 71 n. 331, 72 n. 336, 130, 133 n. 614, 231, 283, 302 n. 1369, 320 n. 1484
Aws b. Khārijah al-Dārī 302
Aws b. Mi'yar, *see also* Abū Maḥdhūrah 48
Aws b. Qayẓī **71–72,** 73
Aws b. Shuraḥbīl **159**
Aws b. Shuraḥbīl * 159
Awṭās, battle of **101**
al-'Awwām b. Khuwaylid 169, 199
Awzā' (tribal group) **255**
al-Awzā'ī **255,** 262
al-Awzā'ī * 132, 136, 148, 156, 279
'Ayn al-Tamr **253,** 271
'Ayn al-Wardah 138, 274
'Ayyāsh b. Abī Rabī'ah **68, 112,** 114
'Ayyāsh b. Abī Rabī'ah * 112
'Ayyāsh b. Mu'nis * 159
Ayyūb * 103, 202, 218, 222, 226, 244
Ayyūb b. 'Abd al-Raḥmān al-Anṣārī * 205
Ayyūb b. Abī Tamīmah * 112
Ayyūb b. al-Ḥakam b. Ayyūb * 138
Ayyūb b. Khūṭ * 154
Ayyūb al-Sakhtiyānī 216, 258
Ayyūb b. Suwayd * 156
Azd (tribal group) 52 n. 233, 93 n. 453, 130 n. 600, 150, 153 n. 689, 156 n. 700, 158 n. 713, 241, 255, 277 n. 1263, 283 n. 1282, 302 n. 1369, 308 n. 1409, 309 n. 1417, 314 n. 1450, 316 n. 1463, 317 n. 1467, 325 n. 1512, 329 n. 1541
Azhar b. 'Abd 'Awf **42**
al-Azharī 250 n. 1109
al-Azraq, slave of al-Ḥārith b. Kaladah 29
'Azzah bt. al-Ḥārith 201

B

Babbah 96
Bādhām, governor of Yemen. *See* Bādhān
Bādhān, governor of Yemen **324**
Badr **10,** 11, 13, 18 n. 70, 19, 20, 21 n. 91, 22, 23, 24, 26, 28, 30, 35 n. 161, 36, 38, 40, 44, 47, 48, 57, 58, 60, 62, 66, 69, 71, 73, 76 n. 361, 77, 93 n. 451, 101, 103, 117, 133, 134 n. 620, 135, 136, 155 n. 696, 162, 164, 167, 177, 190, 198 n. 862, 205, 301
Baghdad 246 n. 1089, 249, 253, 264, 265, 323 n. 1499, 324 n. 1502, 327 n. 1528, 329 n. 1540, 330 n. 1547, 331 nn. 1550–54, 332 n. 1555, 333 n. 1560, 334 n. 1567
Bahdalah (tribal group) 82 n. 390
Bāhilah (tribe) 84 n. 403, 256 n. 1138
Baḥīr b. Raysān 221
Bahrā' (tribal group) **26 n. 115**
Baḥr b. Kanīz al-Saqqā' **256**
Baḥzaj. *See* 'Amr b. al-Ḥārith
Bajīlah (tribe) 265 n. 1181, 298 n. 1355, 325 n. 1510, 326 n. 1516
Bakīl 258 n. 1148
Bakkah **140**
Bakkār b. Muḥammad * 227
Bakr b. Wā'il (tribal group) 251 n. 1114, 275 n. 1243, 306 n. 1399, 323 n. 1498, 326 n. 1515
al-Balādhurī xv, xvi
al-Balāṭ 46
bāligh **57 n. 260**
Balkh 329 n. 1539
al-Bāqarḥī, Abū 'Alī, Makhlad b. Ja'far xviii, xix
al-Baqī' **20,** 21, 22, 25, 39, 164, 165, 168, 169, 173, 176, 185, 195, 214, 263
al-Barā' b. 'Āzib **294,** 295 n. 1340, 300 n. 1361
al-Barā' b. Ma'rūr 287 n. 1303
Barakah. *See* Umm Ayman
barīd. See postal services

Barrah bt. Samaw'al 185
Bashīr b. 'Amr. *See* Abū 'Amrah
Bashīr b. Salmān * 109
Bāsil b. Ḍabbah 94 n. 458
Baṣrah, Baṣran 63, **71**, 72, 76, 80, 96, 104, 147 n. 663, 151, 159 n. 718, 160 n. 721, 215, 218, 221 n. 959, 224, 231 n. 1005, 236, 239 n. 1055, 241, 244 n. 1080, 249 n. 1105, 252 n. 1116, 256, 258, 259, 260, 266 n. 1190, 271 n. 1217, 272, 276 n. 1249, 277 n. 1254, 278 n. 1262, 280 n. 1271, 282 n. 1277, 284 n. 1286, 292, 295 n. 1339, 297 n. 1349, 299 nn. 1358, 1360, 300 n. 1362, 305 nn. 1392, 1394 307 nn. 1403–404, 1406–407, 308 nn. 1409, 1411, 309 n. 1418, 310 n. 1419, 311 n. 1427, 312 n. 1434–37, 313 n. 1449, 316 nn. 1464–66, 317 nn. 1467–68, 323 n. 1500, 324 nn. 1501–504, 1507, 326 nn. 1518–22, 328 n. 1533, 330 nn. 1545, 1547, 333 n. 1559
al-Baṭḥā' 46
Batriyyah 258 n. 1148, 277 n. 1256
al-Battī **252**
Bayāḍah b. 'Āmir (tribal group) **135**
bay'at al-nisā' 162 n. 731
Bayḍ **172**
al-Bayḍā', mother of Suhayl 301
al-Bayḍā'. *See* Umm Ḥakīm bt 'Abd al-Muṭṭalib
Bayt Jibrīn 19 n. 74
bayt al-māl. See treasury
bedouin(s), 9 n. 30, 11 n. 41, 18 n. 69, 21 n. 90, 30 n. 138, 101 n. 482, 109 n. 517, 121 n. 558, 217 n. 939, 220, 299 n. 1357
Beirut 255
the Bible 136
Bilāl b. Rabāḥ 44, **290**
Bilāl b. Yasār * 100
Bilqīs 255
Bi'r Ma'ūnah **122 n. 559**
Bishr b. Ādam *152
Bishr b. 'Amr 247
Bishr b. Diḥyah * 125
Bishr al-Ḥāfī. *See* Bishr b. al-Ḥārith
Bishr b. al-Ḥārith **331**
Bishr b. al-Ḥasan * 142
Bishr b. 'Imrān * 152
Bishr b. Marwān **269**
Bishr b. al-Mufaḍḍal * 134, 136
the Black stone 64
blood money 294 n. 1336
blood revenge **61**
bridal gift, *see also* bride price 164, 173, 178, 180, 186, 189
bride price 16 n. 59
the Bridge, battle of 86 n. 409, **205**
Brotherhood (mu'ākhāh) **20**, 27, 30, 40, 105
Budayl b. Maysarah 125
Budayl b. Maysarah * 125
Bujayr family 275 n. 1243
Bukayr * 203
Bukayr b. 'Abdallāh b. al-Ashajj **237, 335**
Bukayr b. Mismār **337**
al-Bukhārī xviii n. 9
Bunānah (tribal group) 236
Burayd b. Abī Maryam * 128
Buraydah b. al-Ḥuṣayb **70–71, 290**
Burayr b. Jundab. *See* Abū Dharr
Burd, client of Sa'īd b. al-Musayyab 216
Busr b. Abī Arṭāh **74**
Busr b. Sa'īd 304
Busr b. Sa'īd * 203
Busr b. 'Ubaydallāh * 101
Buṭḥān **134**
Buwayb, battle of 86 n. 409
Byzantines 6, 40, 65 n. 300, 108, 263, 336 n. 1579

C

Caesaria 329 n. 1539
the Camel, battle of **27**, 28, 31, 86, 94, 105, 113, 138, 198, 247, 272 n. 1223, 273 n. 1226, 274, 277, 291 n. 1315, 315 n. 1457

carrion meat 151
Cemetery of Khayzurān 253
Children of Israel 212
Christian Arabs 244 n. 1077
Christians, *see also* Possessors of the Scriptures 23 n. 99, 129, 136, 241 n. 1063, 264
civil war, first 193, 294 n. 1332
civil war, second **52 n. 230,** 77 n. 371, 95 n. 465, 96 n. 466, 105 n. 499, 119 n. 550, 131 n. 606, 275 n. 1243, 295 n. 1341, 308 n. 1411
client, clients **16,** 25, 26, 31, 33, 66, 98, 99, 110 n. 520, 112, 113, 114, 155, 173, 176, 181, 188, 194, 199, 200, 205, 209, 213, 215, 216, 221, 230, 231, 233, 237, 238, 239, 241, 244, 245, 248, 249 n. 1103, 250, 252, 254, 255, 256 n. 1136, 256 n. 1138, 259, 263 n. 1170, 264, 265, 277 n. 1256, 282 n. 1278, 287, 299, 300, 303, 304, 305 nn. 1389–90, 1392, 306, 307, 308 n. 1410, 309 nn. 1415–16, 1418, 310, 311 n. 1426, 312 n. 1437, 313 n. 1447, 317, 319, 321 nn. 1489–90, 322 n. 1491, 323 nn. 1498–500, 324, 325 nn. 1508, 1512–13, 326 nn. 1515–16, 1519, 327 n. 1525, 328 n. 1532, 329 nn. 1536, 1539–41, 330 n. 1545, 331 n. 1550, 332 n. 1557, 333, 335, 336, 337
Companions of 'Alī b. Abī Ṭālib, see also *shī'ah* 31, 151, 207 n. 896, 208 n. 897, 210, 268, 269, 274, 275 n. 1241, 285 n. 1290
Companions of the Prophet xv, xviii, 10, 12 n. 45, 17, 19 n. 80, 20 n. 88, 21, 26, 27 n. 122, 28 n. 128, 29 n. 135, 30 n. 138, 31 n. 142, 32, 63 n. 286, 64, 66 n. 303, 67 n. 311, 79, 84, 85, 92, 93, 95, 10 n. 476, 105 n. 499, 107 nn. 505, 506, 110 n. 517, 111 n. 524, 115 n. 542, 118, 122 n. 559, 124 n. 574, 125 n. 577, 127, 131, 133 n. 613, 138–144, 146 n. 657, 147 n. 663, 148 n. 669, 149 n. 673, 153 nn. 690–91, 155, 158 n. 714, 159 n. 716, 160, 180 n. 805, 193 n. 840, 202 n. 875, 207, 210 n. 909, 215, 221, 227 n. 985, 235, 244 n. 1076, 267 n. 1193, 274 n. 1237, 278, 279 n. 1268, 281 nn. 1273–74, 282 n. 1278, 283 nn. 1279–82, 284 nn. 1284–87, 285 nn. 1290, 1293–96, 286 nn. 1297–99, 1301, 1302, 28 n. 1305, 289 n. 1308, 290 nn. 1309–11, 291 nn. 1314, 1316–17, 292 nn. 1318–19, 1321–24, 293 nn. 1326–30, 294 nn. 1331–36, 295 nn. 1337–41, 296 nn. 1342–44, 297 nn. 1346, 1348–50, 298 nn. 1351, 1353, 299 nn. 1358–60, 300, 301 nn. 1367–68, 303 nn. 1374, 1379, 313 n. 1443, 315 nn. 1457–58, 316 nn. 1460–61, 316 n. 1466, 319 nn. 1476, 1478, 330 n. 1545, 334 nn. 1565, 1569, 335 n. 1571
Constantinople 40
court of grievances 323 n. 1499

D

Ḍabbah (tribe) **94,** 125, 312 n. 1433, 329 n. 1539
Da'd bt Jaḥdam. *See* al-Bayḍā', mother of Suhayl
Daghsh (tribal group) 87
al-Ḍaḥḥāk b. Muzāḥim **323**
al-Ḍaḥḥāk b. 'Uthmān * 57
al-Dajjāl. *See* the Deceiver
Dallah bt. Manjishān 85
Damascus 15 n. 56, 33 n. 147, 63, 224, 225 n. 1132, 272 n. 1219, 274, 295 n. 1341, 311 n. 1431
Ḍamḍam * 127, 153
Ḍamḍam b. Jaws * 131
Ḍamrah b. Rabī'ah * 207, 225
al-Dār b. Hāni' (tribal group) 298 n. 1351, 302
Dārim (tribal group) 275 n. 1242
Da's (tribal group) 87 n. 416

Dā'ūd (King David) 123
Dā'ūd * 207
Dā'ūd b. 'Abd al-Raḥmān al-Makkī * 133
Dā'ūd b. Abī Hind 310 n. 1422, **326, 328**
Dā'ūd b. Abī Hind * 83, 120, 121, 182
Dā'ūd b. 'Alī b. 'Abdallāh **277–78**
Dā'ūd b. 'Amr al-Ḍabbī * 55
Dā'ūd al-Awdī 231
Dā'ūd b. al-Ḥusayn 217, **335**
Dā'ūd b. al-Ḥusayn * 16
Dā'ūd b. al-Muḥabbar * 170, 193, 224
Dā'ūd b. Muḥammad b. 'Alī 235
Dā'ūd b. Muḥammad b. al-Munkadir 240
Dā'ūd b. Sinān * 39
Dā'ūd b. 'Urwah b. Mas'ūd 177
Daws (tribe) 283 n. 1282
Daylam **94**
Day of Sacrifices 132
Dayr al-Jamājim, battle of **248**, 270, 277
the Dead Sea 236 n. 1029
the Deceiver **108**
al-Dhahabī xxiii, xiv
Dhakwān (tribe) **122**
Dharr b. 'Abdallāh b. Zurārah **276–77**
Dhayl al-mudhayyal, see also *Supplement to the Supplemented* xv, xvi, xvii, xviii, xix, xx, xxii, xxiii, xxiv, xxv, xxvi, xxvii
Dhī Ḥawāl (tribal group) 220
Dhū Aṣbaḥ (tribal group) 261 n. 1160
Dhubyān (tribe) **72 n. 334**
Dhū al-Kalā' **32**
Dhū Ru'ayn (tribal group) 206
Dhū al-Sha'bayn 219
Dhū al-Shimālayn **301**
Dhū al-Yadayn **301**
Diḥyah b. Khalīfah, **71**, 166
al-Dīl (tribal groups of the Rabī'ah) **29**
al-Dīl (tribal group of the Kinānah). *See* al-Du'il
Dīnār b. 'Udhāfir 310 n. 1422, 328
Dirghāmah b. 'Ulaybah * 124
the Ditch, siege of **10**, 11, 22, 26, 30, 36, 38, 40, 47, 57, 62, 66, 69, 73, 133
divorce, rules of 15, 16 n. 59
dīwān, see also pensions **42 n. 192**, 277 n. 1254
the Dome of the Rock 318 n. 1474
dowry, *see also* bridal gift 189 n. 830
Ḍubā'ah bt. al-Zubayr b. 'Abd al-Muṭṭalib **197–98**
Ḍubay'ah (tribe) **310 n. 1419**
duel **23 n. 104**, 33
Duhmān b. al-Ḥārith (tribal group) **171**
al-Du'il (tribal group) **72**, 119 n. 552, **307 n. 1403**
Dūmat al-Jandal 233
Ḍumayrah b. Abī Ḍumayrah **100**
Ḍumayrah b. Abī Ḍumayrah * 100
al-Durāwardī, 'Abd al-'Azīz b. Muḥammad * 218
Durrah b. Abī Salamah 175
Dustūr al-munajjimīn xx n. 18

E

Egypt 32 n. 144, 149 n. 672, 220, 272 nn. 1219, 1221, 291 n. 1316, 293 n. 1329, 296 n. 1342, 319 n. 1475, 328 n. 1534, 329 nn. 1536–37, 335 n. 1570
Elephant, Year of **24**, 41, 106
Emigrants **18**, 51, 69 n. 321, 105 n. 499, 191
Emigration 3, 5, 10 n. 35, 20 n. 83, 40 n. 182, 52, 55, 56, 70, 115 n. 541, 128 n. 589, 138, 142, 153, 163, 161, 164, 171, 174, 175, 182, 202
Euphrates 263 n. 1172, 274 n. 1178
evil eye 134

F

Faḍālah al-Laythī **120**
Faḍālah al-Laythī * 120, 121

al-Faḍl b. al-ʻAbbās 11, 24, **95**, 167, 186, 194, 201, **288**
al-Faḍl b. ʻAbdallāh b. al-ʻAbbās 54
al-Faḍl b. Dukayn * 60, 65, 70, 155, 214, 218, 230, 231, 238, 253, 254, 257, 259, 273, 277, 278
al-Faḍl b. al-Ṣabbāḥ * 196
al-Faḍl b. Sahl al-Aʻraj * 157
Fahm (tribe) 275, **329 n. 1536**
Fā'id, client of ʻUbaydallāh b. ʻAlī b. Abī Rāfiʻ * 199
Fākhitah bt. Abī Ṭālib. *See* Umm Hāni'
Fākhitah bt. ʻĀmir 202
Fakhkh **50**
Family of the Prophet 155 n. 697, 213, 234 n. 1016, 258
Farāhīd (tribal group) 278 n. 1263
Faraj b. Faḍālah **331**
al-Farawī * 226
al-Farazdaq **82**, 123
Fardah **85**
the Farewell Pilgrmage **19**, 55, 92, 128, 149, 165
al-Farghānī, Abū Aḥmad xv
Fārs 113, 228
fatḥ see Mecca, conquest of
Fāṭimah bt. ʻAlī b. Abī Ṭālib **278–79**
Fāṭimah bt. ʻAlī b. Abī Ṭālib * 279
Fāṭimah bt. al-Ḍaḥḥāk. *See* al-Kilābiyyah
Fāṭimah bt. al-Ḥusayn * 195, 196
Fāṭimah bt. al-Ḥusayn al-Athram b. al-Ḥasan 248
Fāṭimah bt. al-Ḥusayn b. ʻAlī 49, 230, **279**
Fāṭimah bt. al-Ḥusayn b. ʻAlī * 279
Fāṭimah bt. Jaʻfar b. Muḥammad 249
Fāṭimah bt. Muḥammad the Prophet **12–13**, 80, 155, 162, **166–69**, 172, **195–96**, 208 n. 898, 279 n. 1265
Fāṭimah bt. Muḥammad the Prophet * 195, 196
Fāṭimah bt. al-Mundhir * 208
Fāṭimah bt. ʻUmārah 243
Fāṭimah junior (al-Sughrā). See Fāṭimah bt. al-Ḥusayn
Fayrūz b. al-Daylamī **94, 299**
Fazārah (tribe) **229 n. 994**, 273 n. 1232, 310 n. 1421, 311 n. 1431
al-Fazārī, Marwān b. Muʻāwiyah **311**
the Fijār wars **41**, 73
Filasṭīn, *see also* Palestine 158 n. 715, 295 n. 1337, 298 n. 1351, 305
Firās family 175
Firyāb 329 n. 1539
al-Firyābī * 145
fitnah, see also civil war 102, 193
Fuḍayl b. ʻAbd al-Wahhāb * 260
Fuḍayl b. ʻIyāḍ **330**
Fulayḥ al-ʻAnazī * 199
Fulayḥ b. Sulaymān al-Madanī * 205

G

genealogy, see also *nasab* **94 n. 459**, 232 n. 1009, 244 n. 1077
al-Ghābah 176
al-Ghamīm **70**
Ghanī (tribe) **101 n. 479**, 102
Gharafah b. al-Ḥārith **149**
Gharafah b. al-Ḥārith * 149
Ghassān **30**, 255 n. 1135
Ghaṭafān (tribe) 229 n. 994, 304
Ghaylān b. Munabbih 227 n. 986
Ghazālah, mother of ʻAlī b. al-Ḥusayn 211
Ghifār (tribe) **69**, 119 n. 552, 122, 154 n. 691, 299 n. 1358
al-Ghifāriyyah bt. Abī al-Ḥakam **204**
al-Ghifāriyyah bt. Abī al-Ḥakam * 204
Gīlān 94 n. 460
de Goeje xvi, xix, xx, xxi, xxii, xxiii, xxvi
the Gospel 136
de Goeje xvi, xix, xx, xxi, xxii, xxiii, xxvi
the Gospel 136
grave, descending into **11**, 38, 161, 163, 164, 167, 174, 194
Greeks. *See* Byzantines

H

Habbār b. al-Aswad 4, **77–79**, 163
Ḥabīb * 146
Ḥabīb b. Abī Thābit **325**
Ḥabībah bt. Abī Umāmah 303
Ḥabībah bt. 'Ubaydallāh 177
Haddār **155**
al- Hādī, the caliph 265 n. 1183
ḥadīth al-ifk 292 n. 1322
ḥadīth al-kisā'. *See* Tradition of the Covering
Ḥaḍramawt 89 n. 431, 135 n. 625, **148**, 234 n. 1019
Ḥaḍramī family 304 n. 1386
ḥāfiẓ **232**, 236 n. 1032, 237, 244 n. 1075, 245 n. 1082, 248 n. 1096, 257 n. 1144, 263 n. 1170, 265, 269 n. 1203, 276 n. 1249, 309 n. 1417, 311 nn. 1427, 1431, 312 n. 1439, 316 n. 1462, 320 n. 1484, 321 nn. 1486, 1489, 322 n. 1491, 323 n. 1496, 324 n. 1501, 324 n. 1504, 326 n. 1519, 327 nn. 1525, 1528–29, 328 nn. 1531, 1534, 330 n. 1542, 331 nn. 1549–50, 334 n. 1567, 336 n. 1577
Ḥafn 194
Ḥafṣ b. Ghiyāth 311, **327**
Ḥafṣ b. Ghiyāth * 273
Ḥafṣ b. Maymūn * 56
Ḥafṣ b. 'Umar * 39, 245
Ḥafṣ b. 'Umar al-Ḥawḍī * 97
Ḥafṣ b. 'Umar al-Shannī * 100
Ḥafṣah bt. Sīrīn * 125
Ḥafṣah bt. 'Umar b. al-Khaṭṭāb **174–75**, 190
Hajar **32**
al-Ḥājir **261**
Ḥajj 129
al-Ḥajjāj * 215
al-Ḥajjāj b. Abī Manī' * 109
al-Ḥajjāj b. al-Muhājir * 154
al-Ḥajjāj b. Muḥammad * 269, 280
al-Ḥajjāj b. Yūsuf **51**, 77 n. 367, 209 n. 903, 224, 228, 233 n. 1015, 248 n. 1094, 264 n. 1177, 270–71, 276 285 n. 1290, 305 n. 1385, 307 n. 1402, 316 n. 1463
Ḥajjār b. Abjar **275**
ḥajjat al-wadā'. *See* the Farewell Pilgrimage
al-Ḥajūn **4**, 161, 266
al-Ḥakam * 277
al-Ḥakam b. 'Abd al-Raḥmān * 279
al-Ḥakam b. 'Amr **122**
al-Ḥakam b. Bashīr * 109, 226
al-Ḥakam b. Mas'ūd al-Najrānī * 102
al-Ḥakam b. Sa'd al-Ashīrah (tribal group) **100**
al-Ḥakam b. 'Utaybah **230–31**
al-Ḥakam b. 'Utaybah b. al-Nahhās **311 n. 1425**
al-Ḥakam b. 'Uyaynah **230 n. 1000**
al-Ḥakam b. Wāqid * 252
Ḥakīm b. Ḥakīm b. 'Abbād * 229
Ḥakīm b. Ḥizām 6, **40–42**, 43, **106**
Ḥakīm b. Ḥizām * 106, 161
Ḥakkām b. Salm * 128
Hālah bt Khuwaylid 13, 162
Hālah bt. Wuhayb b. 'Abd Manāf 169, 198
Ḥalīmah, the Prophet's wetnurse **21**
al-Hamadhānī, Muḥammad b. 'Abd al-Malik xv
Hamdān (tribal group) **151**, 210 n. 908, 219, 220, 238 n. 1049, 248 n. 1148, 268, 275, 276 n. 1250, 277, 311 n. 1429, 314 n. 1452, 329 n. 1538
Ḥammād b. Abī Sulaymān **233**
Ḥammād b. Salamah 50, 256
Ḥammād b. Salamah * 50, 132, 193, 222
Ḥammād b. Zayd * 125, 202, 216, 223, 226, 227
Hammām 97
Hammām b. Munabbih 227 n. 986, **322**
Hammām b. Yaḥyā 198
Ḥamrā al-Asad, raid of **58**
Ḥamzah al-Iṣfahānī xx, xxi

Ḥamzah b. ʿAbd al-Muṭṭalib **19,** 101, 169, 198, 202
Ḥamzah b. ʿAbdallāh b. ʿUmar 175
Ḥamzah b. ʿAbdallāh b. al-Zubayr **333**
Ḥamzah b. Abī Usayd al-Sāʿidī **319**
Ḥamzah b. Abī Usayd al-Sāʿidī * 190
Ḥamzah b. Ḥabīb al-Zayyāt **254–55**
Ḥamzah b. ʿUtbah b. Ibrāhīm * 64
Ḥanafī's 251
Ḥanafī school 250 n. 1106, 264
Ḥanash b. al-Ḥārith * 51, 65
Hāni' b. ʿAdī 274
Hāni' b. Yazīd **298**
ḥanīf **37 n. 169**
Ḥanīfah (tribe) 30 n. 139, 208
Ḥanṭab family **337 n. 1583**
Ḥanẓalah (tribal group) 263 n. 1170
Ḥanẓalah b. Qays * 134
Ḥarām (tribal group) 248
Ḥarām b. Ḥubshiyyah (tribal group) 52 n. 233
Ḥarb b. ʿUbaydallāh **129**
Ḥarb b. ʿUbaydallāh * 129
Ḥarb b. Umayyah 177
al-Ḥarīsh (tribal group) 316 nn. 1464–65
al-Ḥārith * 168, 169, 170, 176, 182, 191, 193, 202, 215, 221, 224, 225, 267, 268
Ḥārithah (a clan of the Aws) 71 n. 331, 283
Ḥārithah b. al-Ḥārith (a clan of the Khazraj) 132
Ḥārithah b. Sharāḥīl 6, 8
Ḥārithah b. Surāqah 90
al-Ḥārith al-Aʿwar b. Abdāllah b. Kaʿb **267–68**
al-Ḥārith b. ʿĀmir 29, 116
al-Ḥārith b. Fihr (a clan of the Quraysh) **41,** 301
al-Ḥārith b. Ḥarb b. Umayyah 169, 199
al-Ḥārith b. Kaʿb (tribal group) **235,** 298 n. 1353
al-Ḥārith b. Kaladah **29**
al-Ḥārith b. Khazraj (a clan of the Khazraj) 192, 283, 284
al-Ḥārith b. Khufāf * 121
al-Ḥārith b. Mālik **154**
al-Ḥārith b. Mālik * 154
al-Ḥārith b. Mālik b. Zayd 261 n. 1161
al-Ḥārith b. Muḥammad * 4, 9, 27, 98, 106, 115, 176, 233, 262
al-Ḥārith b. Nawfal b. ʿAbd Manāf 105
al-Ḥārith b. Nawfal b. al-Ḥārith **63, 96**
al-Ḥārith b. Nawfal b. al-Ḥārith * 96, 97
al-Ḥārith b. Saʿīd b. Qays **89**
al-Ḥārith al-Wallādah (tribal group) **90**
Ḥarmalah b. ʿAbdallāh al-ʿAnbarī **124–125**
Ḥarmalah b. ʿAbdallāh al-ʿAnbarī * 124
Ḥarmalah b. ʿImrān * 149
al-Ḥarrah, battle of 131 n. 606, 243 n. 1070, 316 n. 1461
Hārūn b. ʿAntarah **327**
Hārūn b. ʿImrān (Aaron, son of Amram) 185
Hārūn b. al-Mughīrah * 137
Hārūn al-Rashīd, the caliph **249,** 263, 264, 265, 309 n. 1418
Ḥarūrā' 273 n. 1231
Ḥarūriyyah **273**
al-Ḥasan * 66, 99, 123 266
al-Ḥasan b. ʿAbdallāh b. ʿUbaydallāh 55
al-Ḥasan b. Abī al-Ḥasan. *See* al-Ḥasan al-Baṣrī
al-Ḥasan b. ʿAlī b. Abī Ṭālib **39–40,** 49, 75, 80, 96, 121, 231, 268, 269, 319
al-Ḥasan b. ʿArafah * 133, 157
al-Ḥasan al-Baṣrī **221–27, 317,** 312 n. 1434 (?)
al-Ḥasan al-Baṣrī * 158
al-Ḥasan b. Dīnār * 160
al-Ḥasan b. Ḥayy. *See* al-Ḥasan b. Ṣāliḥ
al-Ḥasan b. ʿImrān b. ʿUyaynah * 266
al-Ḥasan b. Muḥammad b. al-Ḥanafiyyah **322**
al-Ḥasan b. Qazaʿah * 120
al-Ḥasan b. Qutaybah **330**

al-Ḥasan b. Ṣāliḥ **258–59**
al-Ḥasan b. Sawwār * 131
al-Ḥasan b. Usāmah b. Zayd 192
al-Ḥasan b. Yasār. *See* al-Ḥasan al-Baṣrī
al-Ḥasan b. Zayd b. al-Ḥasan **260–61**
Ḥasā. *See* Hajar
Hāshim (the Prophet's clan) 19, 23 n. 103, 25, 39, 55 n. 248, 59 n. 264, 60, 62 n. 285, 64, 95 n. 461, 98, 102 n. 488, 210, 277, 331 n. 1550
Hāshim, Banū, siege of **55**, 103 n. 491, 161, 199
Hāshim b. 'Aṣim al-Aslamī * 70, 71
Hāshim b. 'Utbah al-Mirqāl 31, 32, **35**, 108
Hāshimi family, *see also* Hāshim 260 n. 1157, 309 n. 1414, 315 n. 1455, 334 n. 1568
Hāshimiyyah (movement) 236 n. 1031, 322 n. 1495
Hāshimiyyah (place) 246, 336 n. 1576
Ḥassān b. 'Amr Tubba' 219–20
Ḥassān b. Thābit **49**, 55, **72**, 103, 141, 144, 194, **291**, 295 n. 1337
Ḥassān Dhū al-Sha'bayn. *See* Ḥassān b. 'Amr
Ḥāṭib b. Abī Balta'ah 194, 289, 296–97
Ḥāṭib b. 'Amr b. 'Abd Shams 170
Ḥātim * 114
Ḥātim b. Kurayb * 147
Hawāzin (tribal group) **19**, 106, 192 n. 837, 322 n. 1491
Hawdhah b. Khalīfah **324**
Ḥawshab * 266
Ḥawtharah b. Muḥammad al-Minqarī * 134
al-Haytham b. Khārijah **331**
Ḥaywah b. Shurayḥ **328**
Ḥazawwarah **109**
Ḥazm, family of 243 n. 1070
ḥijāb. *See* veil
Ḥijāz 74 n. 350, 91, 208 n. 898, 261 n. 1164, 276
al-Ḥijr **9**
Hijrah. *See* emigration
Hilāl b. al-'Alā al-Raqqī * 96
Hilāl b. 'Āmir (tribe) 54, 96, 126 n. 584, 185 n. 818, 201 n. 869, 253, 254, 265, 297 n. 1349, 323 n. 1497, 327 n. 1529
Hilāl b. Khabbāb **330**
ḥilf. *See* Alliance
ḥilm **126**
al-Ḥimmānī * 207
Ḥimṣ 53 n. 241, 100, 145, 155 n. 698, 159 n. 716, 206, 295 n. 1341, 299 n. 1359, 328 n. 1535, 331 n. 1548
Ḥimyar (tribe) 32 n. 146, 33, **85**, 94, 201, 206, 220, 261, 272 n. 1219, 299, 317, 321 n. 1486, 328 n. 1535
Hind bt. 'Abd b. al-Ḥārith 203
Hind b. Abī Hālah 3, **79–80**, 161
Hind bt. Abī Ṭālib. *See* Umm Hāni'
Hind bt. Abī Umayyah. *See* Umm Salamah
Hind bt. 'Awf 185, 201
Hind bt. al-Ḥārith al-Firāsiyyah * 176
Hind bt. Khadījah 161
al-Ḥīrah 206 n. 892, 244 n. 1077, 289 n. 1307
al-Hirmās b. Ziyād al-Bāhilī **128–29**
al-Hirmās b. Ziyād al-Bāhilī * 128
Hishām * 266
Hishām b. 'Abd al-Malik, the caliph 82 n. 389, 221, 228, 233, 234, 265 n. 1185, 326 n. 1515
Hishām b. al-Ghāz * 152
Hishām b. Ḥakīm b. Ḥizām 41, 106
Hishām b. Ḥassān * 66, 98
Hishām b. Ḥubaysh * 138
Hishām b. Ismā'īl **213**
Hishām b. Muḥammad. *See* Ibn al-Kalbī
Hishām b. 'Umārah * 79
Hishām b. 'Urwah **334**
Hishām b. 'Urwah * 27, 109, 190, 193, 208, 212
Hishām b. Yūsuf * 216
Hishām al-Dastawā'ī * 136
The History (by al-Ṭabarī) xv–xxvii
Hīt **263**
Ḥizām b. Hishām * 138, 184

Ḥizām b. Khuwaylid 41
Hubayrah b. Abī Wahb 196, 197
Hubayrah al-Makshūḥ 91
Ḥubaysh b. Khālid **138**
Ḥubaysh b. Khālid * 138
Ḥubshī b. Junādah **84, 127–28**
Ḥubshī b. Junādah * 128
Ḥudaybiyyah **10,** 11, 38, 44, 45 n. 203, 107
Ḥuḍayn b. al-Mundhir al-Raqāshī **266–67**
Ḥudayr b. Abī Maḥdhūrah 48
Ḥudayr family 245
Ḥudhayfah b. al-Yamān 30, **133,** 300, **301–302**
Hudhayl (tribe) **61,** 110, 203 n. 877, 315 n. 1458
al-Hudhayl b. Hubayrah **166 n. 748**
Ḥujr b. ʿAdī 148 n. 668, **274**
al-Hulb b. Yazīd al-Ṭāʾī **302–303**
Ḥumayd b. ʿAbd al-Raḥmān b. ʿAwf **244**
Ḥumayd b. Hilāl * 70, 122
Ḥumayd b. Masʿadah al-Sāmī * 134
Ḥumayd b. Ṭarkhān. *See* Ḥumayd al-Ṭawīl
Ḥumayd b. Thawr al-Hilālī **126**
Ḥumayd al-Ṭawīl **309**
Ḥumaymah 236 n. 1029
Ḥumaynah bt. Abī Ṭalḥah 277
Hunaydah b. Khālid al-Khuzāʿī **145**
Hunaydah b. Khālid al-Khuzāʿī * 145
Ḥunayn **11,** 20, 21, 24, 34, 43, 46, 61, 62, 64, 73, 79 n. 376, 82, 101, 105, 106, 108, 112, 115, 127, 192
Ḥuraymilah bt. ʿAbd al-Aswad 67
Ḥurayth b. Yāsir 29
Ḥurayth b. Zayd al-Khayl **85**
al-Ḥurr b. al-Ṣayyāḥ al-Nakhaʿī * 142
Ḥusayl b. Jābir 301
al-Ḥuṣayn b. ʿAbd al-Raḥmān b. ʿAmr * 83
al-Ḥusayn b. ʿAbdallāh b. Ḍumayrah * 100
al-Ḥuṣayn b. ʿAbdallāh b. ʿUbaydallāh 55
al-Ḥusayn b. Abī al-Ḥusayn * 174
al-Ḥusayn b. ʿAlī b. Abī Ṭālib **48–51,** 53, 96, 121, 211, 215, 248, 274, **288**
al-Ḥusayn b. ʿAlī b. Abī Ṭālib * 187, 279
al-Ḥusayn b. ʿAli b. al-Ḥasan 50 n. 224
al-Ḥusayn b. ʿAli al-Ṣudāʾī * 151, 199, 242
al-Ḥuṣayn b. b. al-Ḥārith **24**
al-Ḥuṣayn b. Numayr 53 n. 240, 274
al-Ḥuṣayn b. ʿUbayd **137**
al-Ḥuṣayn b. ʿUbayd * 137
al-Ḥusayn b. Zayd b. ʿAlī b. al-Ḥusayn **330**
al-Ḥusayn al-Muʿallim * 69
Ḥūth 268
Ḥuwayṭib b. ʿAbd al-ʿUzzā 42, **43–46,** 300, 336 n. 1575
Ḥuwayy al-Saksakī **33**
Huzaylah bt. al-Ḥārith 201
Hypocrites **9,** 132 n. 612, 156

I

ʿIbād **244**
Ibn al-ʿAbbās 25, **54–57,** 74, 88, **95,** 111, 215, 216, 217, 227 n. 985, 254 n. 1124, 277 n. 1258, **288,** 304, 305 n. 1394, 309 n. 1415, 310, 320
Ibn al-ʿAbbās * 9, 16, 55, 56, 64, 167, 168, 170
Ibn ʿAbd al-Aʿlā * 273
Ibn ʿAbd al-Barr xxiv
Ibn Abī ʿAwn * 32, 164, 187, 188, 190
Ibn Abī Dhiʾb * 100, 120
Ibn Abī Fudayk * 120
Ibn Abī al-Furāt 192
Ibn Abī Laylā 231
Ibn Abī Nuʿm. *See* al-Ḥakam b. ʿAbd al-Raḥmān
Ibn Abī Qays. *See* ʿAmr b. Abī Qays
Ibn Abī Sabrah * 17, 45, 69, 73, 80, 81, 167, 173, 174, 187, 209, 213
Ibn Abī Uways * 262
Ibn Abī al-Zinād * 42, 46, 55, 190, 208

Ibn ʿĀʾishah * 237
Ibn al-Ashʿath 209 n. 903, **228**, 248, 271, 276, 282 n. 1278, 315 n. 1459, 317 n. 1467, 320 nn. 1484, 1485
Ibn ʿAwn 258
Ibn ʿAwn * 134, 222
Ibn Bashshār * 101, 103, 104, 114, 121, 125, 146, 158, 197, 198, 204
Ibn Buraydah * 99
Ibn Fuḍayl * 97, 268
Ibn Ghusayyil * 190
Ibn Ḥibbān al-Bustī xv, xvi
Ibn Ḥumayd * 5, 13, 14, 98, 109, 119, 128, 129, 137, 146, 160, 216, 223, 226, 242, 268, 270
Ibn Isḥāq xxiv, 227 n. 984, 238, **253**
Ibn Isḥāq * 5, 13, 14, 16, 26, 109, 146, 160, 204, 283
Ibn Jābir * 148
Ibn Jubayr. *See* Saʿīd b. Jubayr
Ibn Juʿdubah **160**
Ibn Juʿdubah * 160
Ibn Jurayj * 12, 167, 173, 186, 204, 279, 280
Ibn al-Kalbī xxiv
Ibn al-Kalbī * 9, 16, 32, 68, 69, 85, 89, 90, 115, 130, 166, 170, 188, 190, 191, 196, 199, 236l, 248, 255, 278, 283, 284, 287
Ibn Khayr al-Ishbīlī xxiii, xiv
Ibn Lahīʿah 322 n. 1492
Ibn Lahīʿah * 203, 205
Ibn al-Madyanī * 209
Ibn al-Mahdī. *See* ʿAbd al-Raḥmān b. al-Mahdī
Ibn Maʿīn * 207, 209, 216, 221, 222, 230, 232, 238, 241, 249, 259, 268, 282, 289, 293, 299, 305, 208, 325
Ibn Mannāḥ * 187
Ibn Muḥayrīz al-Jumaḥī * 57
Ibn al-Muthannā * 124, 136
Ibn Nuḍaylah **156**
Ibn Nuḍaylah * 156
Ibn Numayr * 113
Ibn Saʿd xviii n. 9, xxi, xxiv, xxv
Ibn Saʿd * 4, 9, 19, 23, 26, 27, 48, 60, 63, 65, 69, 70, 83, 98, 106, 115, 176, 209, 212, 214, 215, 219, 223, 226, 227, 228, 230, 233, 243, 248, 253, 254, 259, 260, 262, 263, 265, 266, 269, 273, 277, 278
Ibn Shawdhab * 225
Ibn Shihāb. *See* al-Zuhrī
Ibn Shubrumah 252
Ibn Sinān al-Qazzāz * 132
Ibn Sīrīn 223, 225, 226, **227**
Ibn Ṣudrān. *See* Muḥammad b. Ibrāhīm
Ibn ʿUmar, ʿAbdallāh 38, **117**, 174, 175, 223, 237
Ibn ʿUmar, ʿAbdallāh * 30, 57 (?), 62 (?) 174, 188
Ibn ʿUmar. *See* al-Wāqidī
Ibn Umm al-Ḥakam **92**
Ibn Umm Maktūm **68–69, 118–119**
Ibn Umm Maktūm * 119
Ibn Wahb * 100, 108, 132, 133, 147, 204
Ibn Wakīʿ * 135, 136, 226
Ibn Warqāʾ al-Nakhaʿī 247
Ibn al-Zubayr. *See* ʿAbdallāh b. al-Zubayr
Ibrāhīm. *See* Abraham
Ibrāhīm * 203, 268, 273
Ibrāhīm b. ʿAbdallāh b. al-Ḥasan 245 n. 1084, 246, 260 n. 1157
Ibrāhīm b. ʿAbdallah b. Muḥammad * 182
Ibrāhīm b. Abī Mūsā al-Ashʿarī 233
Ibrāhīm b. ʿĀmir b. Abī Sufyān * 64
Ibrāhīm b. Bashshār al-Ramādī * 252
Ibrāhīm b. Ḥammād al-Zuhrī * 261
Ibrāhīm b. al-Ḥasan b. Zayd 260
Ibrāhīm b. Jaʿfar b. Maḥmūd * 43, 45, 58, 68
Ibrāhīm b. Khālid * 218
Ibrāhīm b. al-Mahdī al-Maṣṣīṣī * 238, 253
Ibrāhīm b. al-Muhājir * 116
Ibrāhīm b. Muḥammad b. al-Munkadir 240
Ibrāhīm b. Muḥammad the Prophet 22, 161, 193, 194

Ibrāhīm b. Muḥammad, Ibrāhīm al-Imām **235**
Ibrāhīm b. Nāfi' * 221
Ibrāhīm al-Nakha'ī 223, 314 n. 1453
Ibrāhīm al- Qāri' al-Kūfī * 142
Ibrāhīm b. Qays **89**
Ibrāhīm b. Sa'd * 23, 216
Ibrāhīm b. Sa'īd al-Jawharī * 205
Ibrāhīm b. Wathīmah * 188
Ibrāhīm b. Yūsuf * 115
'Īd al-Aḍḥā. See the Day of Sacrifices
'iddah **170 n. 760,** 175, 178
iḥrām **103**
iḥtibā' **138 n. 637**
ijāzah xix
'Ijl b. Lujaym (tribe) **275,** 277 n. 1256
'Ikrimah * 186
'Ikrimah b. Abī Jahl **17–19, 115**
'Ikrimah b. 'Ammār * 128, 131
'Ikrimah, client of Ibn 'Abbās **215–18, 320,** 312 n. 1435
'Ikrimah, client of Ibn 'Abbās * 16
al-'Ilbā' al-Sulamī 239
'ilm al-rijāl xvii, xx
'ilm al-farā'iḍ 268 n. 1196
imām, return of 218
īmān 154 n. 693
'Imrān b. Bakkār al-Kalā'ī * 157
'Imrān b. Hind b. 'Abdallāh * 47
'Imrān b. al-Ḥuṣayn 137, **292–93**
'Imrān b. al-Ḥuṣayn * 137
'Imrān b. Mūsā * 195
'Imrān b. 'Uyaynah **327**
Imru' al-Qays **87**
'Iqāl b. Shabbah **82**
Iram 16
Iraq 22 n. 95, 72, 86 nn. 409, 412, 88, 107 n. 506, 129 n. 595, 206 n. 892, 222 n. 964, 229, 233, 244 n. 1077, 246 n. 1089, 253, 262, 263 n. 1172, 264 n. 1177, 265, 269, 274 n. 1235, 282 n. 1277, 292 n. 1319, 307 n. 1405, 318 n. 1472, 326 n. 1515
al-'Irbāḍ b. Sāriyah **292**
'Īsā b. 'Abd Raḥmān * 92
'Īsā b. 'Abdallāh al-Nawfalī * 19, 60
'Īsā, client of Ja'far b. Khārijah 205
'Īsā b. al-Faḍl b. Ma'qil * 146
'Īsā b. al-Ḥasan b. Zayd 260
'Īsā b. Yūnus * 215
'Īsā b. Yūnus al-Sabī'ī **329**
'Īsā b. Zayd b. 'Alī **258,** 259
'Iṣām b. Qudāmah * 145
Iṣfahān 93 n. 453, 312 n. 1440, 319 n. 1479
Isḥāq b. 'Abdallāh b. Abī Farwah 37, **337**
Isḥāq b. 'Abdallāh b. al-Ḥārith * 19, 60, 198
Isḥāq b. 'Abdallāh b. Nawfal * 198
Isḥāq b. Abī Isrā'īl * 214
Isḥāq al-A'war b. al-Ḥasan b. Zayd 260
Isḥāq b. Ibrāhīm * 159
Isḥāq b. Ibrāhīm b. Ḥabīb * 272, 278
Isḥāq b. Ibrāhīm al-Ramlī * 150
Isḥāq b. Ibrāhīm al-Ṣawwāf * 124
Isḥāq b. Ja'far b. Muḥammad 249
Isḥāq b. Manṣūr * 246
Isḥāq b. Muḥammad * 180
Isḥāq b. Shāhīn al-Wāsiṭī * 121
Isḥāq b. Yaḥyā * 56
Isḥāq b. Yaḥyā b. Ṭalḥah * 183
Isḥāq b. Yasār 253
Ismā'īl * 216, 268
Ismā'īl b. Abān * 101
Ismā'īl b. 'Abd al-Raḥmān. *See* al-Suddī
Ismā'īl b. 'Abdallāh b. Zurārah * 98
Ismā'īl b. Abī Khālid 304, 309, **326, 332**
Ismā'īl b. Abī Khālid * 113, 114
Ismā'īl b. 'Amr b. Sa'īd **334**
Ismā'īl b. 'Amr b. Sa'īd * 177
Ismā'īl al-A'raj b. Ja'far al-Ṣādiq **248**
Ismā'īl b. 'Ayyāsh * 133
Ismā'īl b. al-Ḥasan b. Zayd 260
Ismā'īl b. Ibrāhīm Ibn 'Ulayyah **323**
Ismā'īl b. Ibrāhīm, Ibn 'Ulayyah * 196, 238, 253
Ismā'īl b. Ibrāhīm al-Makhzūmī * 114
Ismā'īl b. Ibrāhīm b. al-Muhājir * 114
Ismā'īl b. Ibrāhīm, the patriarch 130
Ismā'īl b. Ja'far b. Abī Kathīr 331

Ismā'īl b. Mas'ūd al-Jaḥdarī * 226
Ismā'īl b. Muḥammad b. 'Alī 236
Ismā'īl b. Muḥammad b. Sa'd * 23, 177
Ismā'īl b. Mūsā al-Suddī * 99, 128
Ismā'īl b. 'Ulayyah. *See* Ismā'īl b. Ibrāhīm, Ibn 'Ulayyah
Ismā'īl b. Yaḥyā al-Ma'āfirī * 146
Ismā'īliyyah. *See* Shī'ah, Ismā'īlī
isnād xxv, xxvii
al-'Īṣ, raid of 14 n. 54
Isrā'īl * 116, 119, 122, 145, 197, 200
Iṣṭakhr 267 n. 1190
'Iyāḍ b. Abī Līnah 285 n. 1290
Iyās b. Mu'āwiyah **326**
Iyās b. Rabī'ah 62
Iyās b. Salamah b. al-Akwa' **319**
Iyās b. Salamah b. al-Akwa' * 58
Iyās b. Zuhayr * 151

J

Jabalah (tribal group) **87 n. 418**
Jabalah b. Ḥārithah 7
Jabalah b. Suḥaym **326**
Jābir b. 'Abdallāh **58–59,** 214, 223, 230, **291,** 311
Jābir b. Samurah **297**
Jābir b. Samurah * 108
Jābir b. Yazīd al-Ju'fī **237–38,** 253
Jābir b. Zayd. *See* Abū al-Sha'thā'
Ja'dah (tribal group) **126**
Jadhīmah b. Mālik (tribal group) **238**
Jadīlah (tribal group) **228 n. 988,** 275 n. 1245
Jadīlah bt. Murr 276
Ja'far b. Abī Sufyān b. al-Ḥārith 21, **62–63**
Ja'far b. Abī Ṭālib **4–6,** 178, 202
Ja'far b. al-Ḥusayn b. 'Alī 49
Ja'far b. Kilāb (tribal group) **83**
Ja'far b. Maḥmūd b. Muḥammad * 43, 45
Ja'far b. Maymūn **326**
Ja'far b. Muḥammad **248–49,** 259 n. 1152
Ja'far b. Muḥammad * 13, 60, 180, 214, 229
Ja'far al-Ṣādiq. *See* Ja'far b. Muḥammad
Ja'far b. Sulaymān * 66, 98, 239
Ja'far b. Sulaymān b. 'Alī 236
Ja'far b. Sulaymān al-Ḍuba'ī * 159
Ja'far b. Ziyād al-Aḥmar 258, **259**
Jafshīsh **90**
al-Jafūl. *See* Mālik b. Nuwayrah
Jāhiliyyah **43,** 72, 73, 116, 151 n. 681, 156, 197
jahl **126**
Jahm b. Qays b. Shuraḥbīl **67**
Jahmiyyah **264,** 332 n. 1555
Jaḥsh b. Ri'āb **9 n. 30**
Jaḥsh family **168,** 180 n. 806
Jalūlā', battle of **88**
Jam' **266**
Jamājim. *See* Dayr al-Jamājim
Jamal (tribal group) 92
Jamīl b. Marthad al-Ṭā'ī * 9
al-Janad 221
al-jarḥ wa-al-ta'dīl xviii
Jarīr * 214
Jarīr b. 'Abd al-Ḥamīd * 98, 128, 129, 168, 216, 223, 242, 270
Jarīr b. 'Abdallāh al-Bajalī **298–99**
Jarīr b. Ḥāzim * 121, 123
Jāriyah b. Qudāmah **316–17**
Jarm (tribal group) 327 n. 1523
Jawn (tribal group) 190
the Jawniyyah, wife of the Prophet 188
Jaydā' 49
Jazīrah, *see also* Mesopotamia 92, 264, 292 n. 1322, 322 n. 1491
Jerusalem 159, 305 n. 1391, 318 n. 1474, 328 n. 1535
Jesus 179
Jews, *see also* Possessors of the Scriptures 23 n. 99, 129, 136, 241 n. 1063, 263, 324 n. 1507
Jibrīl 43 n. 195, 71, 159, 182
Jidh' 11
jihād 263 n. 1170, 303 n. 1377, 336 n. 1579

Ji'rānah **79,** 188
Jirwah b. al-Ḥārith 301
jiwār. See protection
jizyah 129 n. 599
Jubayr b. Muṭ'im * 79
Jubayr b. Muṭ'im **102, 291,** 318 n. 1473
Jubayr b. Nufayr * 200
Juddah **20**
Ju'fīyy (tribe) 208 n. 897, **237 n. 1041,** 285 n. 1291
the Juḥāf, Year of **59**
Juhaym b. al-Ṣalt b. Makhramah **77**
Juhaynah (tribe) 146 n. 661, 293 n. 1329, 293 n. 1331, 319 n. 1479
Julhumah (original name of the tribe of Ṭayyi') 85
Jumaḥ (a clan of the Quraysh) **48 n. 216,** 95 n. 461, 111 n. 522, 118, 152 n. 684, 174 n. 779, 297 n. 1346
Junādah b. Abī Umayyah 156 n. 700
Junādah b. Mālik **156**
Junādah b. Mālik * 156
Junaydah 31 n. 142
Jundab b. Junādah. See Abū Dharr
Jundu' (tribal group) 303
Jurf **26,** 65, 99
Jūthah b. 'Ubayd * 73
Juwayriyyah bt. al-Ḥārith, wife of the Prophet **182–84**

K

Ka'b al-Aḥbār **206–207,** 272 n. 1219, **317**
Ka'b b. Mālik **291**
Ka'b b. Māti'. *See* Ka'b al-Aḥbār
Ka'b b. Rabī'ah (tribal group) 137, 141, 142, 145
Ka'b b. Sharāḥīl 8
the Ka'bah 7 n. 24, 8, 9 n. 29, 37, 51, 64, 106 n. 501, 109 n. 516, 132, 135, 166, 167, 174
Kabāthah b. Aws 73
Kābul 237
kafā'ah **196 n. 843**
kaffārah **148 n. 671**
Kāhil (tribal group) 248
Kalb b. Wabarah (tribe) **6,** 7, 71 n. 330, 88 n. 424
al-Kalbī **247–48,** 304
al-Kalbī * 85, 130, 170, 236, 255
Kannāz b. al-Ḥuṣayn. *See* Abū Marthad
Karbalā' **48 n. 219,** 51 n. 228, 53 n. 236, 210 n. 910, 211, 214 n. 923, 248 n. 1098, 288 n. 1305
Karīmah bt. al-Miqdād 26, 197
Karīmah bt. al-Miqdād * 26
Kathīr b. al-'Abbās **75,** 96
Kathīr b. Muḥammad * 250
Kathīr b. Murrah * 153
Kathīr b. Zayd * 164, 176, 185
Khabbāb b. al-Aratt **110, 289**
Khadījah bt. Khuwaylid, wife of the Prophet **3–4,** 6, 13, 40 n. 185, 66 n. 305, 79, 80 n. 378, **161,** 162, 163, 166, 170, 192
Khadījah bt. al-Zubayr 193
Khalaf b. Hishām **332**
Khalaf b. Tamīm * 242
Khālid * 154
Khālid b. 'Abdallāh b. Ḥarmalah * 121
Khālid b. 'Abdallāh al-Qasrī **265**
Khālid b. Abī 'Imrān * 102
Khālid b. Aslam **335**
Khālid al-Ḥadhdhā' **221,** 306, 326
Khālid b. Ḥakīm b. Ḥizām 41, 106
Khālid b. Khidāsh * 50, 202, 225, 226
Khālid b. al-Lajlāj * 148
Khālid b. Ma'dān al-Kalā'ī **215**
Khālid b. Ma'dān al-Kalā'ī * 215
Khālid b. Mihrān. *See* Khālid al-Ḥadhdhā'
Khālid b. al-Qāsim al-Bayāḍī * 25, 56, 217
Khālid b. Sa'īd b. al-'Āṣ 178, 179, 180
Khālid b. 'Umayr * 104
Khālid b. al-Walīd 15 n. 56, 67 n. 311, 85, 108, **111,** 165, 198, 202, 208, 271, 274 n. 1238, **291**
Khālid b. Yazīd b. Mu'āwiyah 216

Khalīfah b. Farwah 166
Khalīfah b. Khayyāṭ xv, xvi, xviii n. 9
al-Khalīl b. Aḥmad **278**
Khallād b. Rifā'ah b. Rāfi' **134**
Khandamah 165
al-Khandaq. *See* the Ditch
kharāj tax 322 n. 1491
Khārif (tribal group) 220
Khārijah b. al-Ḥārith * 58
Khārijī doctrines xix, 217, 335 n. 1573
Khath'am **201,** 202 n. 873
Khaṭmah (a clan of the Aws) **34**
Khawārij 86 n. 412, 217, 273 n. 1231, 292 n. 1321, 305 n. 1390
Khawlah bt. 'Awf. *See* Hind bt. 'Awf
Khawlah bt. al-Hudhayl **166**
Khawlah bt. Ja'far al-Ḥanafiyyah 208
Khawlān (tribal group) **308 n. 1412**
Khaybar **5** 10, 11, 66, 160, 185, 203
Khayrah 222
Khayrah bt. Abī Ḥadrad. *See* Umm al-Dardā'
Khaythamah b. 'Abd al-Raḥmān **285**
Khaywān (tribal group) 210 n. 908, **239 n. 1050**
Khazraj (tribe) 34 n. 155, 35 n. 157, 40 n. 181, 56 n. 258, 72 n. 339, 130, 133 n. 615, 206 n. 891, 210 n. 909, 283 n. 1281, 284 n. 1284, 290 1310, 1311, 295 nn. 1339, 1340, 1341, 296 n. 1343, 319 n. 1477
al-Khirbāq **301**
Khirniq bt. Khalīfah 166
Khudrah (a clan of the Khazraj) **57**
Khufāf b. Īmā' **121**
Khufāf b. Īmā' * 121
Khulayd * 223
khums **75,** 183
Khurāsān 71, 75, 122 n. 560, 166 n. 747, 218, 228, 229 n. 994, 239, 263, 284 n. 1286, 312 n. 1440, 313 n. 1446, 316 n. 1463, 323 n. 1497, 326 n. 1519, 329 n. 1540, 331 n. 1551, 1553, 1554
Khusraw 94, 227, 299, 324
Khuzā'ah (tribal group) **52 n. 233,** 70 n. 326, 92 n. 445, 93 n. 449, 110, 277, 287, 292 n. 1324, 301 317 n. 1469, 328 n. 1531
Khuzaymah b. Jahm 67
Khuzaymah b. Muḥammad b. 'Umārah * 131
Khuzaymah b. Thābit **34, 131, 294,** 316 n. 1460
Khuzaymah b. Thābit * 131
Khuzaymah b. Thābit's brother **131**
Kilāb (tribal group) 83, 186 n. 821
the Kilābiyyah, wife of the Prphet **186–88**
Kinānah (tribe) 61 n. 276, 69 n. 320, 72 n. 340, 119, 165, 180 n. 805, 307 n. 1403
Kinānah b. al-Rabī' b. Abī al-Ḥuqayq 185
Kindah (tribe) **33 n. 147,** 54 n. 245, 87, 88, 89 n. 431, 90, 111, 148 n. 667, 149, 188, 189 n. 834, 191, 230, 232, 274 n. 1236, 305 n. 1390, 315 n. 1459, 321 n. 1490, 327 n. 1523
Kūfah, Kūfan 22 n. 92, 36, 38 n. 176, 39, 48 n. 219, 51 nn. 227–28, **53,** 60, 65 n. 302, 69, 84, 86, 87 n. 418, 88, 93, 107 n. 506, 113, 114, 119 n. 550, 129 n. 596, 138, 147 n. 663, 151 n. 679, 193 n. 841, 208 nn. 897–98, 210, 211 n. 913, 215, 218, 220, 223 nn. 970–71, 224, 228, 229, 233, 235 n. 1023, 237, 238, 239, 242, 243, 245 n. 1084, 247 nn. 1091–93, 248, 250, 251, 252 n. 1117, 254, 258, 259, 264, 265 n. 1184, 268, 269, 270, 274 n. 1236, 275, 277 n. 1256, 282 n. 1278, 285 n. 1297, 293 n. 1327, 294 n. 1332, 295 n. 1341, 297 nn. 1346, 1348, 1350, 300 n. 1361, 304 nn. 1382, 1384, 305 n. 1387–88, 1390, 306 n. 1401, 307 n. 1402, 308 n. 1408, 310 n. 1420, 311 nn. 1425, 1427, 1429–1431, 312 nn. 1432–33, 313 nn. 1441–42, 1444–45, 1447–48, 314 n. 1450–53, 315 n. 1458, 320 n.

Kūfah, Kūfan *(continued)* 1848, 321 n. 1486–88, 323 n. 1497, 324 n. 1505, 325 nn. 1508–14, 326 n. 1516, 327 nn. 1525–29, 328 nn. 1531–32, 329 n. 1538, 330 nn. 1542, 1544–45, 332 n. 1557
Kulayb b. Rabī'ah (tribal group) 254 n. 1126
Kulayb b. Yarbū' (tribal group) **324 n. 1503**
Kumayl b. Ziyād **270–71**
kunyah **3**
Kurayz b. Rabī'ah 198
Kurz b. 'Alqamah **92–93**
Kuthayyir 'Azzah **217**

L

Labīd b. Rabī'ah **83, 299**
Lakhm (tribe) **289,** 302
Laylā bt. Mas'ūd 271
al-Layth * 97, 154, 195, 196, 221
al-Layth b. Abī Sulaym **332**
al-Layth b. Bakr (tribal group) **61,** 119 n. 552, 138, 160 n. 721, 165 n. 743, 291 n. 1317, 292 n. 1318, 300 n. 1362, 303, 304 n. 1381, 336
al-Layth b. Sa'd 322 n. 1492, **329**
al-Layth b. Sa'd * 101, 156
al-Layth (lexicographer) 250 n. 1109
legal alms 82, 83, 91, 129, 223, 294 n. 1336
Lift (a wādī) **172**
Living Sunnah 243 n. 1074
lizards, killing of **204**
locusts, killing of **127**
Lubābah bt. 'Abdallāh b. al-'Abbās 54
Lubābah bt. al-Ḥārith, Lubābah al-Kubrā 54, 96, 111, 186, **201–202,** 254 n. 1124, **287**
Lubābah bt. al-Ḥārith, Lubābah sl-Ṣughrā 111, **202**
Lubābah bt. Muḥammad b. 'Alī 236
Lu'lu'ah, client of Umm al-Ḥakam * 31, 33
Lūṭ b. Yaḥyā. See Abū Mikhnaf

M

Ma'add **7**
Ma'āwil 241
Ma'bad b. al-'Abbās **75,** 96, 201
Ma'bad b. Khālid **294**
Mābūr, brother of Māriyah 194
al-Madā'in 99, 313 n. 1446, 328 n. 1532, 330 nn. 1545, 1546
al-Madā'in, battle of **88**
al-Madā'inī xxiv
al-Madā'inī * 39, 49, 50, 51, 54, 56, 57, 59, 75, 169, 209, 211, 212, 222, 224, 225, 230, 236, 249, 256, 260, 267, 271
Ma'dān * 257
Ma'dān b. al-Aswad **90**
Madhār 271
Madhḥij (tribal group) **29,** 85, 91, 266, 272
maghāzī 235, 241, 253, 318 n. 1470, 330 n. 1543
al-Maghrib 218, 220, 262
Magians, *see also* Zoroastrians 241 n. 1063
al-Mahdī, the caliph **256,** 258, 260, 265 n. 1181, 330 n. 1544, 331 n. 1548, 333 n. 1560
Maḥmiyyah b. Jaz' al-Zubaydī 201
mahr. See bride price
al-Mājishūn. See Ya'qūb b. Abī Salamah
Makhlad * 268
Makhlad b. Ja'far. See al-Bāqarḥī
Makhramah b. Bukayr * 169
Makhramah b. Nawfal **42–43,** 69, **297**
Makhzūm (a clan of the Quraysh) **17,** 29 n. 132, 47, 59 n. 267, 67 n. 311, 80 n. 380, 95 n. 461, 111, 116, 125 n. 577, 168 n. 756, 281 n. 1274, 303 n. 1379, 314 n. 1454, 316 n. 1462, 335 n. 1570
Mālik b. Abī Maryam * 147
Mālik b. 'Āmir 29, 116
Mālik b. Anas 217, 226, 245 n. 1082, 249, 252, **261–63**
Mālik b. Anas * 55, 132, 243, 261

Mālik al-Ashtar. *Seer al-Ashtar al-Nakha'ī*
Mālik b. A 'ṣur. *See* Bāhilah
Mālik b. Aws * 183
Mālik b. Dīnār **237**
Mālik b. al-Ḥārith. *See* al-Ashtar al-Nakha'ī
Mālik b. Ḥisl (tribal group) 185
Mālik b. Ḥuwayrith **300**
Mālik b. Ismā'īl * 212
Mālik b. Mighwal **311**
Mālik b. Numayr al-Khuzā'ī * 145
Mālik b. Nuwayrah **83**
Mālik b. Udad (tribal group) **29**
Mālik b. Zayd b. Shadad 255
Mālikī school 245 n. 1082
Ma'mar * 218
Ma'mar b. Rāshid * 12, 108, 112, 167, 174, 176, 190, 240, 265
Ma'n (tribal group) 6, 87 n. 416
Ma'n b. 'Īsā al-Qazzāz * 127, 199, 243
Manṣūr * 137
al-Manṣūr, Abū Ja'far, the caliph 234 n. 1017, **235**, 245 n. 1084, 246, 248, 249, 253–54, 255, 258 n. 1150, 260, 261, 262, 277 n. 1258, 304 n. 1382, 328 n. 1532, 334 n. 1567, 336 n. 1576, 337 n. 1583
Manṣūr b. al-Mu'tamir **242**
Manṣūr b. Sa'd * 125
Manṣūr b. Zādhān **241**
Ma'qil b. Munabbih 227 n. 986, **322**
Ma'qil b. Yasār **292**
Māriyah, wife of the Prophet **22**, 161, **193–95**
Marj 'adhrā' **274**
Marthad b. Abī Marthad al-Ghanawī **101**
Marthad b. Abī Marthad al-Ghanawī * 101
Marthad b. Zayd b. Shadad 255
Ma'rūf b. Kharrabūdha * 16
Ma'rūr b. Suwayd **325**
Marw 71, 312 n. 1439, 327 n. 1525
Marwah 47 n. 213
Marwān * 157
Marwān b. al-Ḥakam, the caliph 28, 43, 47, 53, 93, 174, 184, 209, 210, 216 n. 932, 274, 295 n. 1341, **315**
Marwānī faction 96
Marwānids 229 n. 994, 233 n. 1015, 242 n. 1068, 315 n. 1456
mashhad, mashāhid **16 n. 60**, 57, 117
Maskan, battle of 209 n. 903
Maslamah b. 'Alqamah * 120
Maslamah b. Muḥārib * 39
Mas'ūd b. 'Āmir b. 'Umayr 185
al-Mas'ūdī * 108
Maṭar b. Ṭahmān al-Warrāq **239**
mawlā. See client
Mawsū'at aṭrāf al-ḥadīth (by Muḥammad Zaghlūl) xxvi
Mawsū'at rijāl al-kutub al-tis'ah (by al-Bandārī and Ḥasan) xxvi
Maymūn b. Mihrān **322**
Maymūn b. Mihrān * 56
Maymūnah bt. al-Ḥārith, wife of the Prophet 111 **185–86**, 201, 317
Maymūnah bt. Sa'd **200**
Maymūnah bt. Sa'd * 200
Maysān **222**
Maysarah al-Fajr **125**
Maysarah al-Fajr * 125
Maẓālim. See court of grievances
Māzin b. Manṣūr (tribal group) **104**
Mecca 3, 4, 5 n. 14, 7, 8, 9 n. 30, 11 n. 41, 42 n. 195, 15, 16, 19 n. 75, 23 n. 104, 29, 30, 41, 42, 44, 45, 46, 47 n. 213, 48, 52 n. 232, 52, 59, 60, 61 n. 277, 64 n. 295, 65, 66, 67, 68, 70, 75, 78, 79, 81, 93, 105 n. 499, 109, 110, 112, 117, 123 n. 566, 128 n. 589, 138, 140, 142, 144, 146 n. 657, 163, 170, 172, 177, 186, 193, 196 n. 842, 201, 202, 212, 221, 223, 244, 247, 261, 263 n. 1168, 265, 266, 277, 287 n. 1307, 297 n. 1346, 311 n. 1431, 318 n. 1471, 321 n. 1489, 324 n. 1506, 329 n. 1541, 330 n. 1542
Mecca, conquest of **11**, **14**, 17, 18 n. 68, 20, 21, 24, 34, 35, 44, 45, 61, 62, 64, 68 n. 314, 73, 76, 77, 81, 93, 98, 101, 102, 103 n. 493, 106,

Mecca, conquest of *(continued)* 107, 108, 112, 114, 115, 116, 118, 165, 188 n. 827, 197 n. 857 284 n. 1289, 286 n. 1298, 293 n. 1330, 294 n. 1331
Meccans, *see also* Quraysh 13, 45 n. 203
Medina 3, 4, 5, 10, 11 n. 43, 14 n. 52, 16, 18 n. 69, 20 nn. 83, 88, 21, 26, 28, 30 n. 138, 38, 40 n. 182, 42, 43, 45 n. 203, 46 n. 209, 47, 48, 59, 63, 65, 66, 68, 69, 70, 73, 74, 77, 81, 83, 88, 90 n. 436, 91, 99, 102, 105, 106, 113, 128 n. 589, 130 n. 603, 131 n. 606, 134 n. 618, 135, 138, 142, 155, 162, 163, 167, 169, 170-, 171, 172, 173, 174, 175, 176, 177, 180, 182, 184, 189, 190, 192, 193, 194, 199, 201, 202, 209, 210, 213 n. 918, 214, 217, 218, 223, 229, 231, 234, 237, 240, 241, 243, 244, 245, 246, 249, 251, 253, 260, 261 n. 1164, 262, 263, 270 n. 1207, 272 nn. 1223, 1225, 283 n. 1278, 286 nn. 1299, 1300, 287 n. 1303, 289 n. 1308, 290 nn. 1309, 1310, 293 n. 1236, 294 n. 1335, 296 n. 1343, 302, 303 nn. 1376, 1379, 304, 316 n. 1460, 317 n. 1468, 318 n. 1470, 319 n. 1479, 320 n. 1480, 322 n. 1495, 323 n. 1496 324 n. 1507, 327 n. 1525, 330 nn. 1543, 1544, 333 nn. 1560, 1563, 334 nn. 1564, 1565, 1567, 1568, 1569, 335 nn. 1570, 1572, 1573, 336 nn. 1574, 1575, 1576, 1577, 337 nn. 1580, 1581, 1583, 1585, 1586
Medinans, *see also* Anṣār, Aws, Khazraj 303 n. 1375
Merv. *See* Marw
Mesopotamia 166 n. 748
Mihrān, battle of **86**
Mihrān, father of Sulaymān 248
Mikhnaf b. Sulaym **93**
Miknaf b. Zayd al-Khayl **85**
Minā 221 n. 960
al-Minhāl b. ʿAmr * 212
al-Miqdād b. ʿAmr 10, **25–27**, 99, **110**, 197, **289**, **300–301**
al-Miqdād b. al-Aswad. *See* al-Miqdād b. ʿAmr
al-Miqdām b. Maʿdī-Karib **299**
Miqsam. *See* Abū al-ʿĀṣ b. al-Rabīʿ
Miqsam, client of Abdallāh b. al-Ḥārith **320**
al-Mirqāl. See Hāshim b. ʿUtbah
Misʿar b. Kidām **253–54**, **327**
Mishraḥ b. Abān **322**
Mishraḥ b. Maʿdī-Karib **54**
al-Miswar b. Makhramah 42, **51–52**, **107**, 237, **296**, 330 n. 1543, 335
al-Miswar b. Makhramah * 108
Mosul 92 n. 447, 315 n. 1459
Muʿādh b. ʿAbdallāh b. Khubayb * 153
Muʿādh b. ʿAbdallāh's paternal uncle **153**
Muʿādh b. ʿAfrāʾ 295 n. 1338
Muʿādh b. Anas al-Juhanī **146**
Muʿādh b. Anas al-Juhanī * 146
Muʿādh b. al-Ḥārith **295**
Muʿādh b. Hishām * 198
Muʿādh b. Jabal 153 n. 690, 210
Muʿādh b. Muʿādh **324**
Muʿādh b. Muʿādh * 226, 260
muʾākhāh. *See* Brotherhood
al-Muʿallā b. Manṣūr * 157
Muʾammil b. Ismāʿīl * 96
Muʿattib b. Abī Lahab 64
Muʿattib al-Aslamī 160 n. 725
Muʿattib, slave of Jaʿfar b. Muḥammad 249
Muʿāwiyah al-Akramīn (tribal group) 285
Muʿāwiyah b. Abī Sufyān, the caliph 31 n. 141, 32, 33 n. 147, 38 n. 176, 39, 40, 41, 42, 43, 46, 47, 48 n. 220, 61, 63, 65, 70 n. 325, 71, 72, 74 nn. 350, 351, 75, 77, 81, 88 nn. 422, 423, 92 n. 447, 93, 99, 102, 106, 107 n. 506, 122 n. 560, 148 n. 668, 158, 170, 174, 176, 180, 184, 185, 193 n. 841, 209, 210, 216 n. 932, 233, 269, 273 n. 1231, 274 nn. 1235, 1236, 275, 285 n. 1295, 286 nn. 1297, 1299, 290 n. 1310,

291 n. 1316, 292 n. 1319, 293 n. 1329, 294 n. 1332, 295 nn. 1340, 1341, **297**, 300 n. 1361, 308 n. 1412, 316 n. 1466, 318 n. 1471
Mu'āwiyah b. 'Ammār al-Duhnī * 60
Mu'āwiyah b. Ṣakhr 73
Mu'āwiyah b. Ṣāliḥ * 147
Mu'āwiyah II, the caliph 216 n. 932
Mubārak (place) 241
Mubārak b. Faḍālah **307**
Muḍar 34 n. 151, 52 n. 233, **88 n. 424**, 91, 266, 284 n. 1285
al-Mudhayyal, see also *the Supplemented* xx, xxi, xxii, xxiii, 36, 53
al-Mufaḍḍal b. 'Abdallāh * 230
mufākharah **123 n. 564**
muftī **244**, 255, 261, 324 n. 1506, 326 n. 1519, 330 n. 1543, 336 n. 1576
al-Mughīrah * 273
al-Mughīrah b. 'Abd al-Raḥmān 68
al-Mughīrah b. Miqsam * 223
al-Mughīrah b. Shu'bah **38–39**, 84, 169, 174, **292**
al-Muhājir b. Abī Umayyah **80–81**
al-Muhājir b. Mismār * 80
al-Muhājir b. Yazīd **337**
al-Muhājir b. al-Zubayr 193
Muhājirūn. *See* Emigrants
al-Muhallab b. Abī Ṣufrah **316**, 329 n. 1541, 330 n. 1547
Muhallabī family 316 n. 1463
Muḥammad * 202
Muḥammad b. Abān * 152
Muḥammad b. 'Abd al-'Azīz * 157
Muḥammad b. 'Abd al-Raḥmān * 186, 195
Muḥammad b. 'Abd al-Raḥmān b. Abī Laylā 282 n. 1278
Muḥammad b. 'Abd al-Raḥmān b. al-Aswad **67**
Muḥammad b. 'Abd al-Raḥmān b. Thawbān * 183
Muḥammad b. 'Abdallāh, *see also* Ibn Abī Sabrah * 67, 165, 186, 187
Muḥammad b. 'Abdallāh al-Asadī * 27, 254
Muḥammad b. 'Abdallāh b. al-'Abbās 54
Muḥammad b. 'Abdallāh b. 'Abd al-Ḥakam * 120, 156
Muḥammad b. 'Abdallāh b. Abī Ṣa'ṣa'ah * 205
Muḥammad b. 'Abdallāh b. Abī Ya-'qūb * 121
Muḥammad b. 'Abdallāh b. Bazī' * 136
Muḥammad b. 'Abdallāh al-Ḥaḍramī * 230
Muḥammad b. 'Abdallāh b. al-Ḥasan. See Muḥammad al-Nafs al-Zakiyyah
Muḥammad b. 'Abdallāh al-Hilālī * 152
Muḥammad b. 'Abdallāh b. Muslim * 170
Muḥammad b. Abī 'Awn * 204
Muḥammad b. Abī Bakr 202
Muḥammad b. Abī Bakr b. Muḥammad **243–244**
Muḥammad b. Abī Ḥarmalah **336**
Muḥammad b. Abī Manṣūr * 207
Muḥammad b. Abī Mūsā al-Thaqafī * 39
Muḥammad b. Abī Umāmah b. Sahl * 36, 20
Muḥammad b. 'Ajlān * 157
Muḥammad b. al-'Alā'. *See* Abū Kurayb
Muḥammad b. 'Alī b. 'Abdallāh b. al-'Abbās 74, **235–36**
Muḥammad b. 'Alī. *See* Abū Ja'far, Muḥammad b. 'Alī
Muḥammad b. 'Alī. *See* Muḥammad b. al-Ḥanafiyyah
Muḥammad b. 'Amr * 121, 184
Muḥammad b. 'Amr b. 'Abd al-Raḥmān * 118
Muḥammad b. al-Ash'ath b. Qays 269, 315
Muḥammad b. al-Ash'ath b. 'Uqbah 315 n. 1459
Muḥammad b. 'Awf * 153
Muḥammad b. 'Awf * 155
Muḥammad b. 'Awf al-Ṭā'ī * 127, 145

Muḥammad b. Bakkār * 240
Muḥammad b. Bakr * 158
Muḥammad al-Bāqir. *See* Abū Ja'far, Muḥammad b. 'Alī
Muḥammad b. Bashshār. *See* Ibn Bashshār
Muḥammad b. Dā'ūd * 215
Muḥammad b. al-Faḍl b. al-'Abbās * 118
Muḥammad b. al-Ḥanafiyyah 56, **208–209**, 236 n. 1031, 276
Muḥammad b. Hārūn al-Ḥarbī * 222
Muḥammad b. al-Ḥasan b. Usāmah * 10
Muḥammad b. al-Ḥasan b. Zayd 260
Muḥammad b. al-Ḥasan al-Shaybānī **264–65, 331**
Muḥammad b. Ḥāṭib **297**
Muḥammad b. Ḥumayd. See Ibn Ḥumayd
Muḥammad b. al-Ḥusayn * 278
Muḥammad b. Ibrāhīm b. Muḥammad 249
Muḥammad b. Ibrāhīm, Ibn Ṣudrān * 146
Muḥammad b. 'Imrān b. Hind * 47
Muḥammad b. Isḥāq. See Ibn Isḥāq
Muḥammad b. Isḥāq al-Ṣāghānī * 265
Muḥammad b. Ismā'īl * 127, 153, 230, 231, 254
Muḥammad b. Ismā'īl al-Ḍirārī * 257
Muḥammad b. Ismā'īl al-Sulamī * 131
Muḥammad b. Ja'far b. Abī Ṭālib 202
Muḥammad b. Ja'far b. Muḥammad 249
Muḥammad b. Ja'far al-Warkānī * 168
Muḥammad b. Jubayr b. Muṭ'im **318**
Muḥammad b. Jubayr b. Muṭ'im * 79
Muḥammad b. Juḥādah * 157
Muḥammad b. Ka'b * 160
Muḥammad b. Ka'b al-Quraẓī **231, 333**
Muḥammad al-Kalbī * 9, 85
Muḥammad b. Khalaf al-'Asqalānī * 108, 145, 257
Muḥammad b. Khālid * 151
Muḥammad b. Makhramah 42
Muḥammad b. Ma'mar * 153, 267
Muḥammad b. Manṣūr al-Ṭūsī * 255
Muḥammad b. Maslamah * 205
Muḥammad b. Mu'āwiyah al-Anmāṭī * 203
Muḥammad b. al-Munkadir **240, 333**
Muḥammad b. al-Muntashir 33
Muḥammad b. Mūsā * 185
Muḥammad b. Muslim b. 'Ubaydallah. See al-Zuhrī
Muḥammad b. al-Muthannā * 204, 207
Muḥammad al-Nafs al-Zakiyyah 245 n. 1084, 246, 248 n. 1150, 260 n. 1157, 330 nn. 1543, 1544
Muḥammad, the Prophet 3, 4, 5, 6, 8, 9, 10, 11, 12, 13, 14, 15, 16, 17, 18, 19 n. 75, 20, 21, 22, 23, 24, 25 n. 113, 27, 29, 30, 31, 34 n. 154, 36, 37, 38, 40, 41, 44, 45, 46, 47, 49 n. 221, 51, 53 n. 234, 54 n. 245, 55, 56, 57, 58, 60, 61, 62, 63, 64, 65, 66, 68, 69, 70, 71, 72, 73, 74, 75, 76 n. 361, 77 n. 366, 78, 79, 80, 81, 82, 83, 85, 87, 88, 89, 90, 91, 92, 93 n. 449, 95, 96 97, 98, 99, 100, 101, 102, 103, 104, 105, 106, 107, 108, 109, 110, 111, 112, 113, 114, 115, 116, 117, 118, 119, 120, 121, 122, 123, 124, 125, 126, 127, 128, 129, 130 n 603, 131, 132, 133, 134, 135, 136, 137, 138, 139–145, 146, 147, 148, 149, 150, 151, 152, 153, 154, 155, 156, 157, 158, 159, 160, 161, 162, 163, 164, 165, 166, 167, 168, 169, 170, 171, 172, 173, 174, 175, 176, 178, 179, 180–81, 182, 183, 184, 185, 186, 187, 188–90, 191, 192, 193, 194, 195, 196, 197, 198, 199, 200, 201, 202, 203, 204, 205, 206, 207 n. 896, 209, 210, 212, 213, 222, 225 n. 977, 227 n. 985, 230, 231 n. 1004, 234 n. 1021, 235, 236 n. 1031, 241, 246 n. 1088, 251, 252 n. 1119, 253, 255, 256 n. 1138, 257, 266, 274, 278, 279, 280, 281 n. 1274, 282, 285 n. 1291, 286,

287, 289 n. 1308, 290 nn. 1310–12, 291 nn. 1314–15, 292 n. 1323, 293, 294 nn. 1335–36, 295 n. 1339, 298, 299 n. 1359, 301, 303, 306 nn. 1398–99, 307 n. 1407, 314 n. 1454, 315 n. 1457, 316 n. 1461, 318 n. 1470, 319 n. 1478, 320 n. 1485, 324 nn. 1506, 1507
Muḥammad b. al-Qāsim al-Thaqafī **228**
Muḥammad b. Qudāmah * 164
Muḥammad b. Rabī'ah b. al-Ḥārith 198, **315**
Muḥammad b. Rāshid * 216
Muḥammad b. Rifā'ah b. Tha'labah * 56
Muḥammad b. Sa'd. *See* Ibn Sa'd
Muḥammad b. Sahl b. 'Askar * 112, 158
Muḥammad b. al-Sā'ib. See al-Kalbī
Muḥammad b. Ṣāliḥ * 4, 180
Muḥammad b. Sinān al-Qazzāz. *See* Ibn Sinān al-Qazzāz
Muḥammad b. Sīrīn. *See* Ibn Sīrīn
Muḥammad b. Suhayl * 176, 191
Muḥammad b. Sulaymān b. al-Ḥakam * 138
Muḥammad b. Ṭalḥah b. 'Ubaydallāh 28, **315**
Muḥammad b. Thābit b. Qays * 133
Muḥammad b. 'Ubaydallāh b. al-'Abbās 74
Muḥammad b. 'Ubayd al-Muḥāribī * 195, 279
Muḥammad b. Ubayy b. Ka'b **316**
Muḥammad b. 'Umārah al-Asadī * 119, 122, 145
Muḥammad b. 'Umārah b. Khuzaymah * 91, 131
Muḥammad b. 'Umar b. 'Alī * 38, 167, 168
Muḥammad b. 'Umar b. al-Hayyāj * 156
Muḥammad b. 'Umar. See al-Wāqidī
Muḥammad b. 'Uqbah * 56
Muḥammad b. Wahb b. Abī Karīmah al-Ḥarrānī * 205
Muḥammad b. Yaḥyā b. Ḥabbān * 57, 180
Muḥammad b. Ya'qūb b. 'Utbah * 188
Muḥammad b. Yazīd * 114, 184
Muḥammad b. Yazīd al-Ādamī * 127
Muḥammad b. Yūsuf al-Firyābī **329**
Muḥārib (tribe) **306 n. 1401**
muḥtasib 328 n. 1532
Mujāhid * 116
Mujāhid **221**
Mujālid b. Sa'īd 249, **332**
Mujālid b. Sa'īd * 268
Mujammi' (tribal group) 159
Mujammi' b. Jāriyah **132–33**
Mujammi' b. Jāriyah * 133
Mu'jam rijāl al-ḥadīth (by al-Khū'ī) xxvi
Mujāshi' (tribal group) **82 n. 385,** 275 n. 1242
al-Mukhtalis (tribal group) **85**
al-Mukhtār b. Abī 'Ubayd al-Thaqafī **86,** 208 n. 898, 209, 211, 256 n. 1141, 271, 276, 277 n. 1261, 3115 n. 1459
Mulayḥ b. 'Amr (tribal group) 277
Mulayḥ b. Rabī'ah (tribal group) 137
Mulaykah bt Ka'b al-Laythī **165**
Mulaykah bt. Mālik 41
multazam **64**
munāfiqāt. See Hypocrites
munāfiqūn. See Hypocrites
al-Mundhir b. 'Abdallāh al-Ḥizāmī * 41, 106
al-Mundhir b. Abī Usayd al-Sā'idī **319**
al-Mundhir b. Jahm * 45, 71
al-Mundhir b. 'Ubayd * 194
al-Mundhir b. al-Zubayr **318**
Munīb b. Mudrik al-Azdī **150**
Munīb b. Mudrik al-Azdī * 150
al-Munkadir b. Muḥammad b. al-Munkadir 240
al-Munkadir family 333
Munyah bt. Jābir 104
al-Muqawqas **193,** 194

Murād (tribe) 91, 92 n. 444, 266, 324 n. 1505
Muraysī', raid of **10**, 183
Murhibah **276 n. 1250**
Murji'ah, Murji'ī views **217 n. 941**, 226 n. 981, 276, 311 n. 1427, 322 n. 1495, 329 n. 1541
Murrah **157**
Murrah (tribe) **5**
Murrah b. Ṣa'ṣa'ah (tribal group). *See* Salūl
mursal 222 n. 965
Mūsā * 225
Mūsā (Moses) 123, 241
Mūsā b. Abī Kathīr * 116
Mūsā b. Ismā'īl * 100, 121, 132, 223
Mūsā b. Ja'far **249**
Mūsā al-Kāẓim. *See* Mūsā b. Ja'far
Mūsā b. Maysarah * 173
Mūsā b. Muḥammad b. 'Abd al-Raḥmān * 171, 186, 195
Mūsā b. Muḥammad b. 'Alī 235
Mūsā b. Sahl * 150
Mūsā b. Sahl al-Ramlī * 118
Mūsā b. Sa'īd * 187
Mūsā b. Shaybah b. 'Amr * 83
Mūsā b. 'Ubaydah * 69
Mūsā b. 'Ulayy * 156
Mūsā b. 'Uqbah xxiv, **336**
Mūsā b. 'Uqbah * 17, 41, 45, 66, 69, 106, 161
Mūsā b. Ya'qūb * 26
Mūsā b. Yasār 253
Muṣ'ab b. 'Abdallāh al-Azdī * 156
Muṣ'ab b. Miqdām * 116
Muṣ'ab b. 'Umayr **40**, 67
Muṣ'ab b. al-Zubayr **246**, 271, 294 n. 1332, **318**
Muṣ'ab al-Zubayrī * 217, 263
Musaddad b. Musarhad **324**
Musāfi' b. Ṣafwān 183
Musāwir b. al-Warrāq * 222
Musaylimah 30 n. 139, 300 n. 1363
al-Musayyab b. Najabah 53, **273–74**, 314
Mushir b. 'Abd al-Malik * 151
Muslim b. Budayl * 151
Muslim b. al-Ḥajjāj xviii n. 9
Muslim b. Ibrāhīm * 122
Muslim b. Nudhayr **275**
Muslim b. Yasār * 158
Muslims 10 n. 37, 11 n. 41, 15, 18 n. 71, 19, 20, 22 n. 95, 23, 30, 44, 45 n. 203, 53, 55 n. 249, 65 nn. 299, 300, 73, 78 n. 373, 88, 89 n. 431, 127, 129, 133, 158, 161 n. 726, 164 n. 741, 166 n. 748, 176, 178, 184, 206 n. 892, 208, 222, 241 n. 1060, 251, 253 n. 1120, 301, 303 n. 1375
Musliyah 75
mustahzi'ūn **117**
al-Muṣṭaliq, raid of **10 n. 36**, 57, 183
Mu'tah, battle of **4**, 5, 6 n. 17, 60, 65 n. 300
al-Mu'tamir b. Sulaymān 310, **323**
al-Mu'tamir b. Sulaymān * 221, 226, 273
Muṭarrif b. 'Abdallāh al-Ysārī * 243
al-Mu'taṣim, the caliph 220 n. 956
Mu'tazilah **244**
Muṭ'im b. 'Adī 103
al-Muṭṭalib b. 'Abdallāh b. Ḥanṭab * 164, 176
al-Muṭṭalib b. 'Abdallāh b. al-Muṭṭalib 337
al-Muṭṭalib b. Abī Wadā'ah 284
al-Muṭṭalib (a clan of the Quraysh) **23 n. 103**, 55 n. 248, 76 n. 364, 95 n. 461, 102
al-Muṭṭalib b. Ziyād * 195
al-Muwaṭṭa' 262
Muzāḥim b. Zufar 259
Muzaynah (tribe) 31, 125 n. 577, 154 n. 691, 292 nn. 1319, 1321, **326 n. 1522**
Muzdalifah **266 n. 1188**

N

al-Nabbāsh b. Zurārah. *See* Abū Hālah b. Zurārah
Nabhān (tribal group) 85 n. 404, 209

Nabhān, client of Umm Salamah **320**
al-Nābighah al-Ja'dī **126,** 254 n. 1126, **302**
al-Naḍīr (Jewish tribe) 165, 185, 324 n. 1507
al-Naḍr b. Abī Maryam **327–28**
al-Naḍr b. 'Amr 226
Nāfi' b. 'Abd al-Ḥārith **146**
Nāfi' b. 'Abd al-Ḥārith * 146
Nāfi' b. Abī Nu'aym **304**
Nāfi' b. 'Utbah b. Abī Waqqāṣ **108**
Nāfi' b. 'Utbah b. Abī Waqqāṣ * 108
Nāfi', client of Ibn 'Umar **323**
Nāfi', client of Ibn 'Umar * 30, 112, 173, 176, 188
Nafīsah bt. Munyah 105
Nahd (tribal group) **214,** 215
al-Nahhās b. Qahm **328**
Nahrawān, battle of **86,** 305 n. 1390, 310 n. 1421
Nahr Ma'qil 292
Nahshal (tribal group) **112 n. 527**
Najd 6 n. 20, 188, 191
Nājiyah (tribal group) **276 n. 1248**
al-Najjār (a clan of the Khazraj) **34,** 35 n. 157, 40 n. 181, 72 n. 339, 206 n. 891, 243 n. 1070, 303
Najrān 196 n. 842, 294 n. 1336
al-Nakha' (tribe) 51, 89 n. 429, 270 nn. 1207, 1209, 327 n. 1528
names, changing of 19 n. 80, **53 n. 234,** 62, 90 n. 433, 114, 137, 184, 283, 293, 298
al-Namir b. Qāsiṭ (tribe) **24 n. 107**
naqīb pl. *nuqabā'* 286 nn. 1298, 1300, 287 n. 1303, 290 nn. 1310–11, 291 n. 1314, **303**
nasab, see also genealogy 156 n. 702
Naṣr b. 'Abīdah al-Naṣrī **122**
Naṣr b. 'Alī al-Jahḍamī * 125, 138
Naṣr b. Bāb * 83
Naṣr b. Duhmān **89**
Naṣr b. Mu'āwiyah (tribal group) **322 n. 1491**
Nawfal b. 'Abd Manāf (clan of Quraysh) 95 n. 461, 102 n. 488, 104, 318 n. 1473
Nawfal b. al-Ḥārith b. 'Abd al-Muṭṭalib **19,** 21, 60, 62
Nawfal b. Khuwaylid 67
Nawfal b. Mu'āwiyah **72–73, 119–120**
Nawfal b. Mu'āwiyah * 120
Nawfal b. Musāḥiq **272**
Nawf b. Faḍālah. *See* Nawf al-Bikālī
Nawf al-Bikālī **272, 323**
nawḥ. See *niyāḥah*
Negus 178, 179, 180
Nihāwand, battle of **88**
Nihm (tribal group) 212, 220
niyāḥah **39 n. 179,** 68 n. 317, 156 n. 703, 194 n. 847
Nizār **7 n. 25**
Noah 246
Nu'aym * 222
Nu'aym b. 'Abdallāh al-Mujmir * 69
Nu'aym b. Ḥammād * 218
Nu'aymān 103
Nubayh (tribal group) 168
Nūḥ b. Darrāj * 231
Nūḥ b. Qays * 125
Nujayr, battle of **89**
Nukhaylah, **53**
Nukhaylah, battle of **86,** 94
al-Nu'mān b. Abī al-Jawn 188
al-Nu'mān b. Bashīr **295–96**
Numayr (tribe) **127**
Numayr al-Khuzā'ī **145–46**
Numayr al-Khuzā'ī * 145
nuqabā'. See *naqīb*
Nutaylah bt. Janāb 24, 246

P

Palestine, *see also* Filasṭīn 19 n. 74, 95 n. 464, 281 n. 1273, 329 n. 1539–40
partnership **20 n. 84**
pensions, see also *dīwān*, *'aṭā'* 66, 84, 92, 99, 195 n. 849, 270, 274
People of Pharaoh 212
perfumes, wearing of 179, 203
Persia 29 n. 134
Persians 22 n. 95, 108

pilgrimage, lesser 129, 174
the Pilgrimage of the Consummation **44,** 186
police guard 214, **215,** 247 n. 1093, 270 n. 1209, 275, 278, 296 n. 1342
Possessors of the Scriptures **23**
postal services 317 n. 1469
prayer 109, 120, 121, 129, 135, 146, 198, 200, 223, 232, 247, 280, 290
prayer, evening 71, 120
prayer for rains **156 n. 701**
prayer for the Prophet/prophets **80,** 130 n. 602, 136, 195–96
prayer, morning 14, 113, 114, 120, 125
prayer, night **173 n. 776,** 203
prayer, ritual, at burial 11, 20, 21, 22, 25, 27, 26, **47,** 59, 97, 136, 161, 164, 167, 168, 173, 174, 176, 184, 195, 221, 226, 263, 268, 333 n. 1560, 334 n. 1567
the Prophet. *See* Muḥammad
Protection (*amān, jiwār*) **15,** 17, 45, 49 n. 222, 103, 116

Q

Qabīṣah b. Dhu'ayb **317**
Qabīṣah b. Hulb **302**
Qabīṣah b. Mukhāriq **297**
Qadarī doctrines xix, **223,** 324 n. 1503, 328 n. 1535, 335 n. 1573
Qadariyyah 223, **226,** 323 n. 1498
Qādisiyyah, battle of **22,** 69, 85, 86, 88, 271, 274, 298 n. 1352, 299 n. 1356
Qafal (tribal group) 250
Qaḥṭān **6,** 130
Qanṭas 337 n. 1586
al-Qa'qā' b. Abī Ḥadrad **146**
al-Qa'qā' b. Abī Ḥadrad * 146
Qaraẓah b. Ka'b **300**
Qarībah bt. Umayyah, Qarībah al-Kubrā 76
Qarqisiyā' 138
al-Qāsim, Abū 'Abd al-Raḥmān al-Shāmī * 101
al-Qāsim b. Dīnār al-Qurashī * 246
al-Qāsim b. al-Ḥasan b. Zayd 260
al-Qāsim b. Mukhaymirah * 156, 158
al-Qāsim b. Ṣafwān * 109
al-Qāsim b. al-Walīd * 156
qāṣṣ. See storytellers
Qatādah * 198
Qatādah b. Di'āmah **231–32,** 310, **317**
Qatādah b. Di'āmah * 158, 198
Qatādah b. al-Nu'mān al-Ẓafari 57
Qaṭan **175**
Qaṭan b. Qabīṣah 297 n. 1349
Qaylah bt. Kāhil 130
al-Qayn b. Jasr (tribal group) **6**
Qays 'Aylān (tribal group) **88 n. 424,** 104 n. 495, 228 n. 988, 309 n. 1416, 313 n. 1449
Qays b. Abdallāh b. 'Udas. *See* al-Nābighah al-Ja'dī
Qays b. Abī Ḥāzim **325**
Qays, brother of Ḥārithah 7
Qays b. Makhramah b. 'Abd al-Muṭṭalib **76, 102**
Qays b. al-Makshūḥ **91–92**
Qays b. al-Rabī' * 196
Qays b. Sa'd b. 'Ubādah **296**
Qays b. al-Sā'ib b. 'Uwaymir 116
Qays b. al-Sakan 284 n. 1288
Qays b. Shammās 134
qiblah 247 n. 1090
qiyās 252
Quḍā'ah (tribal group) **6,** 26 n. 115, 214 n. 924, 283, 308 n. 1412, 329 n. 1537
Qudayd 172
Qur'ān 24 n. 108, 46, 54 n. 242, 110 n. 517, 122, 131 n. 605, 135, 157 n. 707, 216, 221 n. 961, 223, 228 n. 988, 231 n. 1005, 237, 238, 247 n. 1091, 248, 254, 265 n. 1184, 268 n. 1197, 280, 284 n. 1287, 293 n. 1329, 294 n. 1335, 304 n. 1383, 305 n. 1394, 307 n. 1403, 309 n. 1417, 312 n. 1434, 323 n. 1497
Qur'ān, collection of **22,** 284, 289 n. 1308, 294 n. 1335

Qur'ānic verses: 2:12 - 213 n. 920; 2:80 - 152 n. 686; 2:138 - 224; 2:184 - 116; 2:205 - 207; 2:238 - 280; 2:285 - 280; 3:104 - 258 n. 1149; 3:114 - 258 n. 1149; 5:59–61 - 178 n. 796; 7:133 - 127 n. 587; 7:157 - 258 n. 1149; 7:200 - 159 n. 720; 8:6 - 200 n. 867; 9:7 - 152 n. 686; 9:33 - 169 n. 803; 9:67 - 258 n. 1149; 9:71 - 258 n. 1149; 9:112 - 258 n. 1149; 16:120 - 37 n. 171; 17:24 - 226; 22:41 - 258 n. 1149; 23:97 - 159 n. 720; 30:3 - 263; 31:17 - 258 n. 1149; 33:5 - 9, 26, 110, 289, 301; 33:28 - 187 n. 823; 33:33 - 155; 33:37 - 181; 33:49 - 9, 197; 33:53 - 184 n. 815, 189; 39:42 - 211; 41:36 - 159 n. 720; 50:18 - 68; 59:23 - 178 n. 801; 61:9 - 179 n. 803; 73:14 - 270 n. 1212; 81:1 - 114; 81:15 - 113; 89:27 - 57; 99:7–8 - 123; 105 - 24 n. 108; 113 - 159 n. 720; 114 - 159 n. 720
Qur'ān reciters, Qur'ān readers 22 n. 93, 32 n. 144, 69, 115 n. 542, 142, 220 n. 957, 222, 237, 239, 241 n. 1060, 242 n. 1065, 244 n. 1075, 248 n. 1096, 254, 269 n. 1203, **276,** 286 n. 1299, 293 n. 1329, 300 n. 1363, 303 n. 1378, 304, 308 n. 1412, 326 n. 1519, 326 n. 1521, 327 n. 1525, 328 n. 1531, 331 n. 1549, 332 n. 1555, 335 n. 1571
Quraysh (tribe of the Prophet) **3 n. 1, 8 n. 27,** 11 n. 41, 14, 15, 21, 37, 41 n. 187, 42, 44, 49, 54, 55 n. 248, 64, 66 n. 303, 68, 73, 78, 90 n. 435, 91, 93 n. 451, 97, 103, 115, 140, 141 n. 647, 143, 144, 166, 167, 171, 174, 180, 197, 201, 212, 213, 232, 235, 236 n. 1033, 254, 261, 276 n. 1248, 301 n. 1365, 305 n. 1391, 311 n. 1426, 314 n. 1545, 318 n. 1472
Quraysh b. Anas * 278
Qurayẓah (Jewish tribe) **130,** 164, 185, 231 n. 1004, 324 n. 1507
Qurrah b. Iyās **292**
Qurrah b. Khālid * 124, 226
qurrā'. *See* Qur'ān readers
al-Qurṭubī, 'Arīb b. Sa'd xv
Qushayr (tribe) **326 n. 1519**
Quss al-Nāṭif **86**
Qutaybah b. Muslim **228**
Qutaylah bt. 'Abd al-'Uzzā 193
Qutham b. al-'Abbās 25, **75,** 95, 201
Qutham b. 'Ubaydalāh b. al-'Abbās 74

R

Rabāb * 125
Rabāb bt. Imri' al-Qays 50
al-Rabadhah **70**
al-Rabī' b. Khuthaym **321**
al-Rabī' b. Ṣubayḥ * 224
al-Rabī' b. Sulaymān * 196, 203, 205, 280
al-Rabī' b. Yaḥyā * 256
Rabī'ah b. Abī 'Abd al-Raḥmān **245,** 250 n. 1107, **335**
Rabī'ah b. al-Ḥārith 19, **61–62, 98,** 198, **288**
Rabī'ah b. al-Ḥārith * 98
Rabī'ah (tribal group) **24 n. 107,** 29 n. 133, 254 n. 1129, 266, 267, 271 n. 1218, 310 n. 1419
Rabī'at al-Ra'y. *See* Rabī'ah b. Abī 'Abd al-Raḥmān
Rāfi' b. 'Amr **122**
Rāfi' b. Khadīj **334 n. 1569**
Rāfiḍah **247**
Rāfid (tribal group) 241
Rajā b. Ḥaywah **321**
raj'ah **218 n. 942,** 238
al-Rajī', battle of 101
Ramlah 19 n. 74
Ramlah bt. Abī Sufyān. *See* Umm Ḥabībah
Ramlah bt. Ḥadath **83**
Ramlah bt. al-Ḥārith. *See* Ramlah bt. Ḥadath
Raqāsh (tribal group) 313 n. 1449
Raqāshiyyūn (tribal group) **266 n. 1190**

al-Raqqah 264, 265
Rāshid b. Ḥubaysh **158**
Rāshid b. Ḥubaysh * 158
Rawḥ * 151, 267
Rawwād b. al-Jarrāḥ * 108
ra'y 265, 335 n. 1571
Rayḥānah bt. al-Hudhayl 166 n. 748
Rayḥānah bt. Zayd **164–65**
Rayṭah * 171
Rayṭah bt. Muḥammad b. 'Alī 235
Rayṭah bt. 'Ubaydallāh b. 'Abdallāh 235
al-Rayy 228 n. 993, 265, 294 n. 1332, 300 n. 1361, 313 n. 1441
religious authority **135 n. 626**
Repenters **53**, 138, 274
Rib'ī * 137
riddah. See Apostasy wars
Rifā'ah b. Rāfi' b. Khadīj **319**
Rifā'ah b. Rāfi' b. Mālik **290**
Ri'l (tribal group) 122
Rishdīn b. Sa'd **329**
riwāyah bi-al-lafẓ **120 n. 554**
riwāyah bi-al-ma'nā **120 n. 554**
Riyāḥ b. 'Uthmān 246
Riyāḥ b. Yarbū' (tribal group) 273 n. 1228
Rubayḥ b. 'Abd al-Raḥmān * 57
Rubayyi' bt. al-Naḍir 222
Rukānah b. 'Abd Yazīd **77, 102**
Ruqayqah bt. Abī Ṣayfiyy 42
Ruqayyah bt. Muḥammad the Prophet **161–62**, 163

S

sa'ādah **62 n. 284**
Saba' 308 n. 1412
al-Ṣa'bah bt. 'Abdallāh 28
al-Sabī' (tribal group) 220, **238 n. 1049**, 268
sābiqah xviii, **16 n. 60**, 43 n. 199
Ṣadaqah b. Khālid * *158*
ṣadaqah, see also legal alms **100 n. 474**, 230 n. 998
ṣadāq. See bridal gift
Sa'd al-'Ashīrah (tribal group) 237 n. 1041
Sa'd b. 'Abdallāh b. al-Ḥakam * 205
Sa'd b. 'Abd al-Ḥamīd * 131
Sa'd b. Abī Waqqāṣ 35, 38, 47, 88, **107, 288**, 299, 314 n. 1450, 337 n. 1585
Sa'd b. Bakr (tribal group) **192**
Sa'd b. al-Ḥārith b. al-Ṣimmah **34–35, 267**
Sa'd b. Hudhaym 130
Sa'd b. Lu'ayy b. Ghālib (clan of Quraysh) **236**
Sa'd b. Mu'ādh **130**
Sa'd al-Qārī' (the Reciter). See Sa'd b. 'Ubayd
Sa'd b. 'Ubādah **290, 296**
Sa'd b. 'Ubayd, Sa'd al-Qārī' **22**, 284 n. 1288
Sa'd b. Zayd Manāh (tribal group) 82, **110**, 248, 311 n. 1427, 316
Sa'd b. Zayd. *See* Sa'īd b. Zayd
Sadūs (tribal group) **231 n. 1005**
Ṣafā **47**
al-Saffāḥ, the caliph **235**, 245, 246, 260, 277 n. 1258, 304
Safīnah, client of Umm Salamah **299**
Ṣafiyy b. al-Ḥārith b. Ḥarb 169, 199
Ṣafiyyah bt. 'Abd al-Muṭṭalib 105, **169, 198–99**
Ṣafiyyah bt. Abī al-'Āṣ 177
Ṣafiyyah bt. al-Ḥārith b. Ṭalḥah 277
Ṣafiyyah bt. Ḥuyayy **184–85**
al-Ṣafrā' **62**
Ṣafwān b. 'Amr * 215
Ṣafwān b. 'Assāl **92**
Ṣafwān b. al-Bayḍā' 301
Ṣafwān b. 'Īsā * 104, 146
Ṣafwān b. Makhramah b. Nawfal, Ṣafwān al-Aṣghar 42
Ṣafwān b. Makhramah b. Nawfal 42, **109**
Ṣafwān b. Mālik b. Jadhīmah 183
Ṣafwān b. al-Mu'aṭṭal **292**
Ṣafwān b. Sulaym **244, 335**
Ṣafwān b. Umayyah 17 n. 65, **81, 118**

Ṣafwān b. Wahb 301 n. 1368
ṣaḥābah. *See* Companions of the Prophet
al-Ṣahbā'. *See* Umm Ḥabīb bt. Bujayr
ṣaḥīfah **255 n. 969,** 222, 322 n. 1493
Sahl b. Ḥunayf **36**
Sahl b. al-Ḥusayn b. Muslim al-Bāhilī * 225
Sahl b. Mu'ādh * 205
Sahl b. Mu'ādh b. Anas * 146
Sahl b. Mūsā al-Rāzī * 154
Sahl b. Sa'd al-Sā'idī **296**
Sahl b. Shu'ayb al-Nihmī * 212
Sahm (tribal group) 84, 284 n. 1289, 291 n. 1316
al-Sā'ib b. Abī al-Sā'ib **115**
al-Sā'ib b. Abī al-Sā'ib * 116
al-Sā'ib b. al-'Awwām 199
al-Sā'ib b. Bishr 247
al-Sā'ib al-Ṭā'ifī * 127
Sa'īd b. 'Abd al-Raḥmān b. Yarbū' * 175
Sa'īd b. Abī 'Arūbah **323**
Sa'īd b. Abī 'Arūbah * 158
Sa'īd b. Abī 'Imrān. *See* Abū al-Bakhtarī al-Ṭā'ī
Sa'īd b. Abī Sa'īd al-Maqbarī 303
Sa'īd b. Abī Sa'īd al-Maqbarī * 174, 211
Sa'īd b. Abī Zayd * 57
Sa'īd b. 'Āmir * 226
Sa'īd b. 'Amr al-Sakūnī * 120
Sa'īd b. al-'Āṣ **193**
Sa'īd b. Bashīr * 157
Sa'īd b. al-Ḥasan al-Baṣrī 225
Sa'īd b. Ḥurayth **114**
Sa'īd b. Ḥurayth * 114
Sa'īd b. 'Imrān. *See* Abū al-Bakhtarī al-Ṭā'ī
Sa'īd b. Jubayr **223,** 314
Sa'īd b. Khālid * 211
Sa'īd b. Manṣūr * 160
Sa'īd b. Muḥammad b. al-Ḥasan * 228
Sa'īd b. Muḥammad b. Jubayr * 79
Sa'īd b. al-Musayyab 216, 240, **316,** 338
Sa'īd b. al-Musayyab * 204
Sa'īd b. Muslim * 243
Sa'īd b. al-Rabī' al-Rāzī * 134
Sa'īd b. al-Sā'ib al-Ṭā'ifī * 127
Sa'īd b. Sa'īd al-Taghlibī, or al-Tha'labī * 136
Sa'īd b. Sallām * 152
Sa'īd b. 'Umayr al-Anṣārī * 136
Sa'īd b. 'Uthmān **75**
Sa'īd b. 'Uthmān al-Tanūkhī * 238, 253
Sa'īd b. Wahb al-Hamdānī **210**
Sa'īd b. al-Walīd * 146
Sa'īd b. Yaḥyā al-Umawī * 279
Sa'īd b. Yarbū' 42
Sa'īd b. Yasār **231, 319**
Sa'īd b. Zayd **37–38, 117, 288**
Sā'idah (a clan of the Khazraj) 188 n. 827, 189, 284 n. 1284
Ṣā'idiyyūn (tribal group) 220
al-Sakāsik (tribal group) 33
al-Sakhāwī xvi, xvii
al-Sakrān b. 'Amr 169, 170
Salām b. Abī al-Ja'd * 135
Salamah b. Abī Salamah 113, 175
Salamah b. al-Akwa' **293,** 319 n. 1476
Salamah b. 'Amr b. al-Akwa'. *See* Salamah b. al-Akwa'
Salamah b. al-Azraq 30
Salamah b. Dīnār 309 n. 1416
Salamah b. al-Faḍl * 5, 13, 14, 146, 160
Salamah b. Hishām **68**
Salamah b. Kuhayl al-Ḥaḍramī **234**
Salamah b. 'Ubaydallāh b. Miḥṣan * 157
Salamah b. Umayyah 105
Salamah b. 'Uthmān * 222
Ṣāliḥ b. Ḥammād * 255
Ṣāliḥ b. Kaysān **336**
Ṣāliḥ b. Kaysān * 23
Ṣāliḥ b. Mismār * 157
Ṣāliḥ b. Muḥammad b. Zā'idah **336**
Ṣāliḥ b. Mūsā al-Ṭalḥī * 279
Ṣāliḥ b. Rustam * 70
Ṣāliḥiyyah 258 n. 1148, 277 n. 1256

Salimah (a clan of the Khazraj) 11, 283 n. 1281
Sālim b. 'Abdallāh b. 'Umar 175
Sālim b. 'Abdallāh b. 'Umar * 174
Sālim b. Abī Ḥafṣah **277–78**
Sālim, client of Abū Ḥudhayfah 300
Sālim, client of Abū Ja'far * 213
Sālim, client of Hishām b. 'Abd al-Malik 233, 234
Sālim b. Ma'qil. See Sālim, client of Abū Ḥudhayfah
Sālim Sabalān * 173
Salīṭ b. Qays 205
Sallām b. Mishkam 185
Salm b. Abī Bilāl * 152
Salmā 87
Salmā, client of the Prophet 66, 99, 194, **199**
Salmā b. Nawfal 73
Salmā bt. Qays. *See* Umm al-Mundhir bt. Qays
Salmā bt. 'Umays, 121, 199, 201, 202
Salmān al-Agharr **319**
Salmān b. 'Āmir al-Ḍabbī **125**
Salmān b. 'Āmir al-Ḍabbī * 125
Salmān al-Fārisī **66, 98**
al-Ṣalt b. Makhramah b. Nawfal, al-Ṣalt al-Akbar 42
al-Ṣalt b. Makhramah b. Nawfal, al-Ṣalt al-Aṣghar 42
al-Ṣalt b. Makhramah b. al-Muṭṭalib **76**
Salūl (tribal group) 84
Sāmah b. Lu'ayy (tribal group) **237, 276,** 312 n. 1437
Samarqand 75, 330 n. 1542
al-Sammāl (tribal group) **166 n. 746**
Samurah b. Jundab 223
Samurah b. 'Umayr. *See* Abū Maḥdhūrah
Sanā bt. al-Ṣalt **166**
Sanā bt. Sufyān. *See* al-Kilābiyyah
Ṣan'ā' 80, 81, 204, 216, 220, 227
Ṣaq'ab b. Sulaym 94
al-Sāqiṭ b. 'Amr al-Anṣārī 191
Sarakhs 326 n. 1519
Sarif **186**
Ṣarrār b. Muḥammad b. Ismā'īl * 216
Ṣa'ṣa'ah b. Mu'āwiyah **123**
Ṣa'ṣa'ah b. Nājiyah **82,** 123 n. 568
Ṣa'ṣa'ah b. Ṣūḥān **275**
Sawdah bt. Zam'ah, wife of the Prophet **169–71,** 172
Sawwār b. 'Abdallāh 259
Saybān (tribal group) **255**
Sayf b. Qays **88–89**
Sayf b. Sulaymān 221
Sayyār b. Abī Sayyār **325**
schools of law 250 n. 1108
scorpions, killing of 279
seal (*khātam*) 317 n. 1469
Shabābah b. Sawwār * 152, 199
Sha'bān (tribal group) 219
Sha'bāniyyūn (tribal group) 220
Shabath b. Rib'ī **273, 321**
al-Sha'bī **218–20,** 278, 304 n. 1383, 314
al-Sha'bī * 83, 92, 182, 268
Sha'biyyūn (tribal group) 220
Shadad, husband of Bilqīs 255
Shaddād b. Aws **295**
Shaddād b. Usāmah b. 'Amr al-Hādi **121,** 202
Shaddād b. Usāmah b. 'Amr al-Hādi * 121
al-Shāfi'ī * **252**
Shāfi'ī school 251 n. 1115
shahīd, **4,** 11, 19, 22, 154, 158, 164, 192, 205, 301
Shahr b. Ḥawshab * 170
Shākir 220
Shamir b. Dhī Jawshan **211**
al-Shammākh b. Ḍirār **72,** 74
al-Shamūs bt. Qays 169
Sharabbah **188**
sharaf al-'aṭā' 274 n. 1239
al-Sharāt **236**
Sharīk * 99, 128, 207, 134, 239
Sharīk b. Salamah al-Murādī 32
Sharqī b. al-Quṭāmī * 166
Shaybah b. Na'āmah * 214
Shaybah b. 'Uthmān b. Abī Ṭalḥah 74, **106**

Shaybān (tribal group of the Bakr b. Wā'il) 231 n. 1005, **239**, 264, 267 n. 1190, 305 n. 1399, 313 n. 1441, 326 n. 1515
Shaybān (tribal group of the Kindah) **89**
al-Shaybānī. *See* Muḥammad b. al-Ḥasan
Shī'ah 25 n. 113, 39 n. 178, 48 n. 218, 54 n. 244, 65 n. 299, 98 n. 468, 231 n. 1002, 236, 237 n. 1041, 245 n. 1084, 246 n. 1087, 247 n. 1090, 249 n. 1104, 256 n. 1141, 257 n. 1143, 258, 268, 271, 275, 276
Shī'ah, Imāmī 229 n. 996, 248 n. 1099, 249 n. 1101
Shī'ah, Ismā'īlī 229 n. 996, 248 nn. 1099, 1100
Shī'ah, Zaydī 233 n. 1012, 234 n. 1016, 258 nn. 1148, 1150, 330 n. 1544
Shī'ī doctrines xix, 50 n. 226, 98 n. 468, 236 n. 1031
Shī'ī propaganda and legitimation 128 nn. 598, 590, 212–213
Shirshīr **250**
shirkat al-'inān. *See* partnership
shirkat al-mufāwaḍah. *See* partnership
Shu'ayb b. Ḥabbān **241**
Shu'bah, client of Ibn 'Abbās **320**
Shu'bah, client of Ibn 'Abbās * 25, 56
Shu'bah b. al-Ḥajjāj **255–56**
Shu'bah b. al-Ḥajjāj * 138, 223, 226, 231, 233, 238, 240, 253, 257, 269
shuhadā'. See *shahīd*
Shuqayr, client of al-'Abbās * 155
shūrā **52**
Shuraḥbīl b. Aws 159 n. 716
Shuraḥbīl b. Ḥasanah **111**
Shurayḥ * 127
Shurayḥ b. Hāni' 298
Shurayḥ b. al-Ḥārith **321**
Shurayḥ, the judge. *See* Shurayḥ b. al-Ḥārith
Shurayḥ b. Salamah * 115
Shurayḥ b. 'Ubayd * 153
Shurayḥ b. Yazīd. *See* Abū Ḥaywah
shurṭah. *See* police guard
Shuways, Abū Raqād * 104
Ṣiffīn, battle of **31**, 32 n. 146, 34, 35, 36, 53, 86, 88 n. 422, 93 n. 453, 117, 138, 151, 207, 208, 233 n. 1011, 247, 266, 267, 269 n. 1205, 270, 274, 275, 282 n. 1278, 295 n. 1340
Sijistān 277 n. 1254, 297 n. 1349
Ṣilah b. Ẓufar al-'Abdī **321**
ṣilat al-raḥim **17 n. 68**
Sinān b. Anas **51**
Sind 228 n. 991
al-Sindī b. Shābak **249**
sīrah 252 n. 1119
Sīrīn, sister of Māriyah 193, 194
Sistān 228 n. 990
Solomon, the king 255
sorcery 134 n. 622
storytellers 227 n. 984, 272 n. 1219, **276 n. 1251**, 298 n. 1351, 317 n. 1468, 319 n. 1479, 328 n. 1533
Successors xv, 20 n. 88, 151 nn. 679, 682, 158 n. 714, 160 n. 721, 205 n. 888, 206, 207 n. 896, 211 n. 912, 223 nn. 970, 971, 271 n. 1217, 303, 308 n. 1408, 309 n. 1413, 313 n. 1445, 314, 315 n. 1455, 319 nn. 1476–77, 325 nn. 1509–10, 326 n. 1518, 327 n. 1523
Su'dā bt. Tha'labah 6
Ṣudayy b. 'Ajlān. *See* Abū Umāmah al-Bāhilī
al-Suddī * 197
Ṣufriyyah **217**
Sufyān * 96, 134, 204, 214, 222, 244, 278
Sufyān b. al-Sā'ib 247
Sufyān b. Sa'īd al-Thawrī 250, 255, 256, **257–58**, 265, 313 n. 1442, 329 n. 1539
Sufyān b. Sa'īd al-Thawrī * 146, 221, 257
Sufyān al-Thawrī. *See* Sufyān b. Sa'īd
Sufyān b. 'Uyaynah 240, **265**, 327 n. 1529, **329**

Sufyān b. 'Uyaynah * 27, 224, 229, 238, 252
Sufyān b. Wakī' * 155
Sufyānids 274 nn. 1234–35
Suhayl b. 'Amr **44**, 170
Suhayl b. al-Bayḍā' **301**
Suhayl b. al-Mughīrah. *See* Abū Umayyah b. al-Mughīrah
suḥuf. See *ṣaḥīfah*
Sukaynah bt. al-Ḥusayn b. 'Alī 50
Sulāfah 49
Sulaym (tribe) 122 n. 559, 242 n. 1065, 269 n. 1203, 285 n. 1295, 292 nn. 1322–23, 301 n. 1366, 312 n. 1436, 313 n. 1444, 323 n. 1500
Sulaym b. al-Aswad, *see also* Abū al-Sha'thā' al-Muḥāribī 314 n. 1451
Sulaym b. Jābir al-Hujaymī, Abū Jurayy **123**
Sulaym b. Jābir al-Hujaymī, Abū Jurayy * 124
Sulaymān * 251
Sulaymān b. 'Abd al-Jabbār * 101, 114
Sulaymān b. Abd al-Malik, the caliph 156 n. 706, 229 n. 993, 316 n. 1462
Sulaymān b. 'Abd al-Raḥmān al-Dimashqī * 150
Sulaymān b. Abī al-Shaykh * 250
Sulaymān b. al-Arqam **324**
Sulaymān b. al-Ḥārith * 190
Sulaymān b. Mihrān al-A'mash **248**, 285, 313, **332**
Sulaymān b. Mihrān al-A'mash * 135, 268, 270, 273
Sulaymān b. al-Mughīrah * 122
Sulaymān b. Qarm 258
Sulaymān b. Qarm * 246
Sulaymān b. Suḥaym * 204
Sulaymān b. Ṣurad **52–53**, **137–138**, **293**
Sulaymān b. Ṣurad * 138
Sulaymān b. Ṭahmān 323 n. 1500
Sulaymān b. Ṭarkhān. *See* Sulaymān al-Taymī
Sulaymān al-Taymī **306**, 323 n. 1500
Sulaymān b. Ukaymah **120**
Sulaymān b. Ukaymah * 120
Sumayyah bt. Khabbāṭ, mother of 'Ammār 29, 30, 117
Sumayyah, mother of Abū Bakrah 29 n. 134
sunnah **157 n. 707**
sunnah, killing of the **225**
Sunnī's 231 n. 1002, 237 n. 1041, 247 n. 1090
the Supplemented, see also *al-Mudhayyal* xx, 81, 209, 233
the Supplement to the Supplemented, see also *Dhayl al-mudhayyal* xv, xvi, xviii, xx
sūrat Āl 'Imrān 84
sūrat al-Baqarah 84, 207
sūrat Maryam 71
Surayj b. al-Nu'mān **331**
Surayj b. Yūnus * 221
Suwā'ah (tribal group) 127 n. 588, 285 n. 1293, 297 n. 1350
Suwayd b. Ghafalah **208**, **320**
Suwayd b. Hubayrah **151**
Suwayd b. Hubayrah * 151
Suwayd b. Sa'īd * 230
Syria 14, 16, 30 n. 136, 32 n. 146, 33 n. 147, 35 n. 159, 53, 62, 63, 70 n. 325, 76, 95, 100, 112, 150 n. 677, 215, 220, 236, 255, 262, 283 n. 1280, 290 nn. 1311, 1312, 291 n. 1316, 292 nn. 1318, 1323, 317 n. 1468, 331 n. 1553, 336 n. 1579
Syrian army 243 n. 1070, 264
Syrian school of law 255 n. 1131

T

Ta'abbaṭa Sharran **73**
Tabālah **19**
al-Ṭabaqāt (by al-Wāqidī) xxiv, xvi
al-Ṭabaqāt (by Ibn Sa'd) xxi, xv–xvi
al-Ṭabaqāt (by Muslim b. al-Ḥajjāj) xvi
ṭabaqāt (categories) xviii, xxv
Ṭabaristān 248, 315 n. 1459
al-Ṭabarī xv, xvi, xvii, xviii, xix,

xx, xxi, xxii, xxiii, xxiv, xxv, xxvi, xxvii, 3, 32, 46, 49, 50, 52, 60, 69, 70, 75, 78, 136, 139, 140, 141, 142, 143, 163, 167, 208 n. 901, 210, 220 n. 956, 223, 250 n. 1107, 253 n. 1121, 256, 258 n. 1148, 281 n. 1272, 295 n. 1338, 301 n. 1366, 310 n. 1424
Tabūk **24,** 34, 105
tadlīs **240**
Taghlib (tribal group) **129,** 271
taḥkīm. See arbitration
taḥnīk **63**
al-Ṭā'if 38 n. 176, 56, 61 n. 277, 103 n. 491, 261 n. 1158, 282 n. 1277, 327 n. 1524
al-Ṭā'if, siege of **11,** 20, 24, 29, 46, 61, 73, 105, 112
ṭalab al-'ilm **218 n. 943**
talbiyah **103,** 128, 277
Ṭalḥah b. 'Abdallāh b. Khalaf **277,** 309 n. 1418
Ṭalḥah b. Kurayz 198
Ṭalḥah b. 'Ubaydallāh 27 n. 126, **28,** 172, 272 n. 1224, 277, **288,** 315 n. 1457
Ṭālibī family 54 n. 246
Tamannī **172**
Tamīm (tribe) **79 n. 377,** 82, 104 n. 498, 112 n. 527, 123, 248 n. 1097, 254 n. 1128, 271 n. 1215, 276, 307 n. 1404, 308 n. 1410, 311 n. 1427, 316, 328 n. 1532, 329 n. 1541
Tamīm b. al-Muntaṣir al-Wāsiṭī * 109
Tamīm al-Dārī 281 n. 1272, **298, 302**
Tammām b. al-'Abbās **75–76,** 96
Tammām b. Rabī'ah 62
al-Ta'rīkh (by Yaḥyā b. Ma'īn) xxvi
tarwiyah 221
Ṭāwūs b. Kaysān **220–21**
tawwābūn. See Repenters
tax collectors 19, 80 n. 380, **83,** 86 n. 410, 91, 135 n. 625, 292 n. 1323, 322 n. 1391
ṭaylasān **229 n. 997**
Taym b. 'Abd Manāh. *See* Taym al-Ribāb
Taym Allāh b. Tha'labah (tribal group) 250, 251 n. 1114, 254
Taym b. Murrah (a clan of the Quraysh) 28 n. 128, 95 n. 461, 111, 240 n. 1057, 245, 261, 333
al-Taymī. *See* Sulaymān al-Taymī
Taym al-Ribāb (tribe) **259**
Ṭayyi' (tribe) 6, 85, 86 n. 411, 209, 239 n. 1055, 305 n. 1392
Thābit al-Buñanī b. Aslam **236, 317**
Thābit b. al-Ḍaḥḥāk **290**
Thābit b. Jidh' **11**
Thābit b. Qays b. Shammās **131,** 183
Thābit b. Tha'labah b. Zayd. *See* Thābit b. Jidh'
Thābit b. Wadī'ah **294**
Thābit b. Yazīd 294 n. 1324
Tha'labah b. Abī Mālik * 39, 164, 187
Tha'labah b. 'Āmir **93**
Tha'labah b. Bakr (tribal group) 166 n. 748
Tha'labah b. Ka'b. *See* Jidh'
Thaqīf (tribe) 11 n. 41, 29 n. 134, **38 n. 176,** 48, 49, 129 n. 596, 244, 257, 299 n. 1360, 310 n. 1420, 327 n. 1525
Thawbān b. Yuḥdad, client of the Prophet **99,** 100
Thawr b. Yazīd **328**
Thawr b. Zayd 328 n. 1535
Thawr 232
Thawr (tribe) **257,** 321 n. 1487
Thu'al (tribe) 86 nn. 410, 414
Thubaytah bt. Ḥanẓalah * 203
Thubaytah bt. Ya'ār 300
Tihāmah 17, **60**
tithe, *see also* 'ushr 221
Tradition of the Covering **155**
treasury 331 n. 1548
tribal nobles, tribal chiefs, tribal leaders 82 nn. 385, 386, 390, 85 n. 404, 86 n. 410, 92 n. 444, 211 n. 912, 228 n. 999, 259 n. 1153, 266 n. 1190, **269,** 270, 275, 277 n. 1254, 297 n. 1349, 298 n. 1352, 298 n. 1355, 316 n. 1466

tribal system, *see also* genealogy 220 n. 953
Tubba' 220
al-Ṭufayl b. al-Ḥārith b. 'Abd al-Muṭṭalib **23–24, 164**
Tujīb (tribal group) **328 n. 1534**
ṭulaqā' **197**
Ṭulayḥah b. Khuwaylid **78 n. 375**
Ṭulayq b. Qays al-Ḥanafī **305**
Twelver Shī'ah. *See* Shī'ah, Imāmī

U

'Ubādah b. al-Ṣāmit **158**
'Ubayd b. Adam * 156
'Ubayd b. Bishr 247
'Ubayd b. Nuḍaylah **328**
'Ubayd b. Rifā'ah al-Zuraqī **134**
'Ubayd b. Rifā'ah al-Zuraqī * 134
'Ubayd b. Zayd 192
'Ubaydah b. al-Aswad * 156
'Ubaydah b. al-Ḥārith 23, 24
'Ubaydah bt. Nābil * 39
'Ubaydallāh * 197, 200
'Ubaydallāh b. al-'Abbās 25, **74–75, 95,** 201, **288**
'Ubaydallāh b. 'Abdallāh b. al-'Abbās 54
'Ubaydallāh b. 'Abdallāh b. al-'Abbās * 55
'Ubaydallāh b. 'Abdallāh b. 'Utbah * 96
'Ubaydallāh b. Abī Rāfi' 66, 99
'Ubaydallāh b. Abī Ziyād * 109
'Ubaydallāh b. Akhnas **325**
'Ubaydallāh b. 'Alī b. Abī Rāfi' * 199
'Ubaydallāh b. 'Alī b. Abī Ṭālib **271**
'Ubaydallāh b. 'Amr * 157
'Ubaydallāh b. al-Arqam 47
'Ubaydallāh b. al-Ḥasan **259–60**
'Ubaydallāh b. Jaḥsh 177, 180
'Ubaydallāh b. Miḥṣan **157**
'Ubaydallāh b. Miḥṣan * 157
'Ubaydallāh b. Muḥammad b. 'Alī 235
'Ubaydallāh b. Mūsā * 119, 122, 145, 204
'Ubaydallāh b. Sa'd al-Zuhrī * 134
'Ubaydallāh b. Sa'īd, Ibn Abī Hind * 187
'Ubaydallāh b. 'Umar * 159
'Ubaydallāh b. Ziyād 211, 274, 315 n. 1459
Ubayy b. Ka'b **289,** 316 n. 1461
'Ūḍah b. Badā 89
'Udhar (tribal group) 220
'Udhrah (tribal group) 71, 165
Uhbān b. Ṣayfī **299**
Uḥud, battle of **10,** 11, 19 n. 79, 22, 24, 26, 30, 36, 38, 40, 47, 57, 58, 66, 67, 69, 71, 73, 74, 118, 133, 155 n. 696, 162 n. 732, 174, 175, 202
'Ujayr b. 'Abd Yazīd **77**
'Ukāshah b. Miḥṣan's mother * 182
'Ukkāẓ **6**
'Ulaybah b. Ḥarmalah * 124
'Ulayy b. Rabāḥ * 156
Umāmah bt. Abī al-'Āṣ 13, 162
Umāmah bt. Ḥamzah **199**
'Umar b. 'Abdallāh b. Abī Rabī'ah. *See* 'Umar b. Abī Rabī'ah
'Umar b. 'Abd al-'Azīz, the caliph 192, 212 n. 916, 309 n. 1416, 310, 318 n. 1473, 319 n. 1475, 322 n. 1491, 326 n. 1522, **332**
'Umar b. 'Abd al-Raḥmān * 157
'Umar b. Abī Rabī'ah **49,** 114
'Umar b. Abī Salamah **113,** 175, **269**
'Umar b. Abī Salamah * 175
'Umar b. Abī Ṭālib, 'Umar al-Akbar **271**
'Umar b. al-Ḥārith al-Khawlānī 32
'Umar b. Hubayrah **228–29,** 242
'Umar b. Ismā'īl al-Hamdānī * 126
'Umar b. al-Khaṭṭāb, the caliph 20, 21, **22–23,** 41, 42, 46, 55, 62, 63, 70 n. 323, 72, 83, 88, 98, 109 n. 512, 110 n. 517, 111 n. 522, 114 n. 538, **117,** 146 n. 657, 147 n. 663, 149 n. 672, 169, 195, 199, 224 n. 976, 231, 252, 277 n. 1254, 279 n. 1265, 285 n. 1295, 290 n. 1311, 294 n. 1336, 307, 314 n. 1450, 321

n. 1486, 325 n. 1509, 335 nn. 1571, 1572
'Umar b. al-Khaṭṭāb, the caliph * 174, 183
'Umar b. Muḥammad b. al-Munkadir 240
'Umar b. Muḥammad b. 'Umar b. 'Alī * 167, 168
'Umar b. Murrah * 100
'Umar b. Sa'd b. Abī Waqqāṣ 211
'Umar b. Sa'īd al-Dimashqī * 149
'Umar b. 'Ubaydallāh b. Ma'mar 309 n. 1418
'Umar b. 'Uqbah * 74
'Umar b. 'Uthmān 309 n. 1418
'Umar b. 'Uthmān * 175
'Umar b. 'Uthmān b. 'Abdallāh al-Jaḥshī * 180, 182
'Umārah b. Khuzaymah b. Thābit * 31, 131, **316**
'Umārah b. al-Muhājir * 185
'Umārah bt. Ḥamzah 202, *see also* Umāmah bt. Ḥamzah
'Umārah b. Zādhān al-Ṣaydalānī * 225
Umaymah bt. 'Abd al-Muṭṭalib 9, 180
Umaymah, client of the Prophet **200**
'Umayr b. 'Abd 'Āmir. *See* Dhū al-Shimālayn
'Umayr b. Sa'd 22 n. 92
'Umayr b. 'Uqbah al-Anṣārī **136**
'Umayr b. Wahb **152**
'Umayr b. Wahb * 152
'Umayr b. Wahb al-Jumaḥī 152 n. 684
Umayyad army, *see also* Syrian army 53 n. 241, 228 n. 990, 229 n. 994
Umayyad period xvi, 82 n. 388, 88 n. 424, 93 n. 453, 168 n. 756, 2212 n. 916
Umayyad propaganda 232 n. 1009
Umayyads, Umayyad dynasty, *see also* Umayyah, family of 31 n. 141, 49, 59 n. 263, 63 n. 286, 178 n. 800, 226 n. 981, 228 nn. 990, 992, 234 n. 1016, 240, 245, 273 n. 1226, 274 n. 1236, 275 n. 1243, 277 n. 1254, 278, 285 n. 1295, 287 n. 1304, 297 nn. 1347–48, 300 n. 1363, 315 n. 1456, 321 n. 1490, 332 n. 1558, 334 nn. 1564–65, 336 nn. 1574, 1576
Umayyah b. 'Abd Shams 9 n. 30, 254 n. 1126
Umayyah, family of **30**, 198 n. 862, 210 n. 907
Umayyah b. Rabī'ah b. al-Ḥārith 198
Umayyah b. Shibl * 218
Umayyah b. Ubayy 105
Umm 'Abdallāh bt. al-Ḥasan b. 'Alī 229
Umm 'Abd bt. 'Abd Wadd **203**
Umm Abīhā, Fāṭimah bt. Muḥammad the Prophet **13**
ummah 37 n. 171
Umm Anmār bt. Sibā' 110
Umm 'Aṭiyyah **12**, 163
Umm Ayman 65, 99, 172, **191–192, 199, 287**
Umm Bakr bt. al-Miswar * 39, 51, 52, 108
Umm Bishr b. al-Barā', Khulaydah bt. Qays **287**
Umm al-Dardā' **205**, 284 n. 1285, **287**
Umm al-Dardā' * 205
Umm Ḍumayrah 100
Umm al-Faḍl. *See* Lubābah bt. al-Ḥārith, Lubābah al- Kubrā
Umm Farwah bt. Ja'far 248
Umm Farwah bt. al-Qāsim 248
Umm Ḥabīb 201
Umm Ḥabīb bt. Bujayr 271
Umm Ḥabībah bt. Abī Sufyān, wife of the Prophet **177–180, 287**
Umm al-Ḥakam bt. 'Abdallāh b. al-Ḥārith 235
Umm al-Ḥakam bt. 'Ammār * 31
Umm al-Ḥakam bt. al-Zubayr **198, 287**
Umm al-Ḥakam bt. al-Zubayr * 198
Umm Ḥakīm bt. 'Abd al-Muṭṭalib **198**, 76
Umm Ḥakīm bt. al-Ḥārith 17
Umm Ḥakīm bt. Zuhayr b. al-Ḥārith 106

Umm Hāni' bt. Abī Ṭālib **196–97, 286–87, 304,** 306 n. 1400
Umm al-Ḥasan bt. al-Zubayr 193
Umm Ḥawshab 87
Umm Ḥumayd bt. 'Abd al-Raḥmān **279–80**
Umm Ibrāhīm. *See* Māriyah
Umm Isḥāq bt. Ṭalḥah 49
Umm Khārijah bt. Sa'd b. al-Rabī' * 205
Umm Kulthūm bt. Asmā bt. Abī Bakr * 279
Umm Kulthūm bt 'Alī b. Abī Ṭālib **279**
Umm Kulthūm bt. al-Ḥasan b. Zayd 260
Umm Kulthūm bt. Muḥammad the Prophet **11–12, 163,** 172
Umm Kulthūm bt. 'Uqbah 198, **287**
Umm Kulthūm bt al-Zubayr b. 'Awwām **279**
Umm Ma'bad al-Khuzā'iyyah 138, 139, 141, 142, **287**
Umm Marthad **205**
Umm Marthad * 205
Umm al-Masākīn. *See* Zaynab bt. Khuzaymah
Umm al-Mundhir bt. Qays **205**
Umm Rūmān bt. 'Umayr 171, 172
Umm Salamah bt. Abī Umayyah, wife of the Prophet 68, 80, 112, 113, **175–76,** 204, 221, **286,** 299, 304, 320
Umm Salamah, wife of al-Saffāḥ 245, 331 n. 1550
Umm Sharīk **204, 287**
Umm Sharīk * 204
Umm Sinān al-Aslamiyyah **203–204**
Umm Sinān al-Aslamiyyah * 203
Umm Ṭalḥah bt. Kurayz 198
'*umrah*. See pilgrimage, lesser
'*umrat al-qaḍiyyah*. See the Pilgrimage of the Consummation
Unays b. Abī Marthad * 102
Unays b. Marthad **101**
Unays b. Mi'yar 48
Unays b. Zurārah 79
'Uqayl (tribe) 125 n. 579
'Uqbah b. 'Abd al-Ghāfir **317**
'Uqbah b. Abī Mu'ayṭ 198
'Uqbah b. 'Āmir al-Juhanī **32, 293**
'Uqbah b. al-Ḥārith b. 'Āmir **103**
'Uqbah b. al-Ḥārith B. 'Āmir * 103
'Uranah **64**
'Urwah b. 'Āmir * 134
'Urwah b. Mas'ūd al-Thaqafī **177 n. 795**
'Urwah b. Zayd al-Khayl **85**
'Urwah b. al-Zubayr 67, 193, **318**
'Urwah b. al-Zubayr * 12, 27, 28, 67, 109, 167, 186, 190
al-'Uryān b. al-Haytham **270**
Usāmah b. Zayd b. Aslam * 174
Usāmah b. Zayd b. Ḥārithah 11, **65, 99,** 172, 192, 194, **289**
Usāmah b. Zayd al-Laythī * 108, 194
Usayd b. Zuhayr **294**
'Uṣayyah (tribal group) **122**
Usayyid (tribal group) **79 n.** 377
'*ushr* 129 n. 599
usury 115 n. 540
'Uṭārid (tribal group) **307 n. 1407**
'Utaybah b. Abī Lahab 163
'Utbah b. Abī Lahab **64,** 161, 163
'Utbah b. Ghazwān **104,** 105
'Utbah b. Ghazwān * 104
'Utbah b. Ḥammād al-Ḥakamī * 150
'Utbah b. Jabīrah * 83
'Utbah b. Rabī'ah **23**
'Uthmān b. 'Abd al-Raḥmān al-Jumaḥī * 118
'Uthmān b. 'Affān, the caliph **22 n. 94, 25, 27, 28 n. 126, 35, 43, 44, 55, 59 n. 263, 63, 66, 70, 76,** 87 n. 418, **92, 95, 99,** 107 n. 505, 109 n. 512, 110 n. 517, 114 n. 538, 116, 162, 163, **191, 192, 198, 206, 207, 222, 227, 239, 269, 270, 272,** 277 n. 1254, **285 n. 1295, 286 n. 1299, 291 n. 1316,** 297 n. 1348, 306, 337 nn. 1581, 1582
'Uthmān b. al-Arqam 47
'Uthmān b. 'Aṭā' al-Khurāsānī * 207
'Uthmān b. Ḥunayf **72, 291**
'Uthmān b. Maẓ'ūn **175**

'Uthmān b. Muḥammad al-Akhnasī * 177
'Uthmān b. Muslim. See al-Battī
'Uthmān b. Sa'īd * 154
'Uthmān b. Ṭalḥah b. Abī Ṭalḥah **107**
'Uthmān b. 'Umar * 209
'Uwaymir b. al-Ashqar **132**
'Uwaymir b. al-Ashqar * 132
Uways b. al-Khulāṣ al-Qaranī **207–208, 266**
'Uyaynah b. Abī 'Imrān, father of Sufyān b. 'Uyaynah 265

V

veil **184 n. 815,** 189, 194
vendetta. *See* blood revenge

W

Wabarah b. Jaḥdar **87**
Wabarah B. Salāmah 87 n. 416
Wādī al-Qurā **65,** 99
Wādī al-Sibā' **28,** 105
Wahb b. Ḥudhayfah **154**
Wahb b. Ḥudhayfah * 154
Wahb b. Kaysān **237, 335**
Wahb b. Munabbih **227, 322**
Wahb b. Rabī'ah b. Hilāl 301
Waḥwaḥ b. Thābit 34
Wā'il b. Ḥujr al-Ḥaḍramī **148**
Wakī' * 135, 136, 226
Wakī' b. al-Jarrāḥ * 113
al-Walīd b. 'Abd al-Malik, the caliph 182, 190, 210 n. 910, 213, 272 n. 1220, 299 n. 1359, 306 n. 1400, 316 n. 1462, 319 n. 1477
al-Walīd al-Bayrūtī * 132
al-Walīd b. al-Mughīrah 202
al-Walīd b. Muslim * 136, 223
al-Walīd b. Muslim, Abū al-'Abbās **326 n. 1518**
al-Walīd b. Muslim, Abū Bishr **326**
al-Walīd b. Rabāḥ * 185
al-Walīd b. Salamah al-Filasṭīnī * 120
al-Walīd b. Shujā' * 250
al-Walīd b. 'Uqbah 198, **297**
al-Walīd b. 'Utbah b. Abī Sufyān 176
al-Walīd b. al-Walīd b. al-Mughīrah **67**
al-Walīd b. Yazīd, al-Walīd II 82 n. 389, 236
waqf **100 n. 474,** 230 n. 998
Wāqid b. Abī Thābit * 78
al-Wāqidī xviii n. 9, xxiv, 253 n. 1119, 330 n. 1543
al-Wāqidī * 4, 5, 10, 12, 17, 23, 25, 26, 30, 31, 32, 33, 34, 36, 38, 39, 41, 42, 43, 45, 46, 47, 49, 50, 51, 52, 56, 57, 58, 59, 62, 63, 65, 66, 67, 69, 70, 71, 73, 74, 78, 79, 80, 81, 83, 90, 91, 92, 106, 115, 116, 161, 162, 164, 165, 166, 167, 168, 169, 170, 171, 173, 175, 176, 177, 180, 183, 184, 185, 186, 187, 188, 190, 192, 193, 195, 203, 208, 209, 213, 214, 217, 221, 227, 229, 230, 232, 233, 234, 239, 241, 244, 245, 249, 253, 255, 257, 260, 262, 265, 283, 289, 293, 298, 299, 319
Warqā' al-Nakha'ī 247 n. 1093
Wāsi' b. Ḥabbān * 154
Wāsiṭ 182 n. 812, 241, 264, 310 n. 1421, 311 n. 1426
waṣiyy 236
Wāthilah b. al-Aṣqa' **291–92**
Wāthilah b. al-Aṣqa' * 101
wine, *see also* alcohol **147,** 178, 200, 297 n. 1348
witr. See prayer, night
Wuhayb * 223

Y

Ya'fur 220
Ya'fur b. 'Abd al-Raḥmān 220 n. 956
Yaf'urid dynasty 220 n. 956
Yaḥmid (tribal group) **210**
Yaḥyā b. 'Abbād * 5, 13
Yaḥyā b. 'Abdallāh b. Abī Qatādah * 162
Yaḥyā b. 'Abd al-Raḥmān * 156

Yaḥyā b. Abī Kathīr **239–40**, 305
Yaḥyā b. Abī Kathīr * 136
Yaḥyā b. Ayyūb * 146
Yaḥyā b. al-Ḍurays * 119, 128
Yaḥyā b. Ḥakīm b. Ḥizām 41, 106
Yaḥyā b. 'Imrān * 47
Yaḥyā b. Ja'far b. Muḥammad 249
Yaḥyā (b. Ma'īn) * 240
Yaḥyā b. Ma'īn; *see also* Ibn Ma'īn xviii n. 9, **52**
Yaḥyā b. Muḥammad b. 'Alī 235
Yaḥyā b. al-Mundhir. *See* Abū Ayyūb al-'Atakī
Yaḥyā b. Sa'īd * 101, 221, 244
Yaḥyā b. Sa'īd al-Anṣārī **336**
Yaḥyā b. Sa'īd al-Anṣārī * 132
Yaḥyā b. Sa'īd b. Dīnār * 192
Yaḥyā b. Sa'īd al-Qaṭṭān 249
Yaḥyā b. Sa'īd al-Qaṭṭān * 207, 221, 223, 240
Yaḥyā b. Ṣāliḥ * 157
Yaḥyā b. Shibl * 167
Yaḥyā b. Sulaymān * 221
Yaḥyā b. 'Urwah b. al-Zubayr **334**
Yaḥyā b. 'Uthmān b. Ṣāliḥ al-Sahmī * 218
Yaḥyā b. Wāḍiḥ * 268
Yaḥyā b. Waththāb 238
Yaḥyā b. Ya'lā al-Aslamī * 101
Yaḥyā b. Ya'lā al-Muḥāribī * 155, 238
Yaḥyā b. Yūsuf al-Zimmī **331–32**
Ya'lā b. al-Ashdaq al-'Uqaylī * 126
Ya'lā b. Munyah. See Ya'lā b. Umayyah
Ya'lā b. Murrah **299, 302**
Ya'lā b. Siyābah. See Ya'lā b. Murrah
Ya'lā b. Umayyah **104, 302**
Yām (tribal group) 220
Yamāmah 239 n. 1055, 240, 305 n. 1392
Yamāmah, battle of 30, 117, 133 n. 616, 208, 286 n. 1301, 300 n. 1363
Yanā'ūn (tribal group) 210
Yanbu' **75**
Ya'qūb b. 'Abdallāh b. al-Ashajj **335**
Ya'qūb b. 'Abdallāh b. Sulaymān * 120
Ya'qūb b. 'Abd al-Raḥmān * 160
Ya'qūb b. Abī Salamah **333**
Ya'qūb b. Abī Ya'qūb * 205
Ya'qūb b. Ibrāhīm * 196
Ya'qūb b. Ibrāhīm b. Jubayr al-Wāsiṭī * 146
Ya'qūb b. Ibrāhīm b. Sa'd * 23
Ya'qūb b. Isḥāq al-Ḥaḍramī * 257
Ya'qūb b. Muḥammad b. Abī Ṣa'ṣa'ah * 193
Ya'qūb b. Muḥammad b. 'Alī 236
Ya'qūb b. Mujammi' * 133
Ya'qūt xix
Yarbū' (tribal group) 83, 307 n. 1404, 308 n. 1410, 330 n. 1542
Yarmūk, battle of **35**
Yasār b. Zayd * 100
Yasār, grandfather of Ibn Isḥāq 253
Yashkur (tribal group) **323 n. 1498**, 325 n. 1514
Yāsir b. 'Āmir 29, 116
Yazīd b. 'Abdallāh b. Qusayṭ * 183
Yazīd b. 'Abdallāh b. al-Shikhkhīr **316**
Yazīd b. 'Abd al-Malik, the caliph 215, 270 n. 1209
Yazīd b. Abī Maryam * 158
Yazīd b. Abī Ziyād **325**
Yazīd b. Abī Ziyād * 12, 97, 168, 207, 216
Yazīd b. Amānāh **89**
Yazīd b. 'Āmir al-Suwā'ī **127**
Yazīd b. 'Āmir al-Suwā'ī * 127
Yazīd b. 'Aṭā * 207
Yazīd al-Faqīr **326**
Yazīd b. al-Hādi * 164, 187
Yazīd b. Hārūn * 109, 123
Yazīd b. Ḥayyān 313 n. 1446
Yazīd b. al-Ḥuṣayn b. Numayr **53**, 138
Yazīd b. 'Iyāḍ, *see also* Ibn Ju'dubah * 212
Yazīd b. Ka'b b. Sharāḥīl 7
Yazīd b. Kaysān **325**
Yazīd b. Mu'āwiyah **40**, 52, 63, 71, 73, 74, 95, 96 n. 466, 186, 215
Yazīd b. al-Muhallab 316 n. 1463
Yazīd b. Rūmān **241**
Yazīd b. Rūmān * 14, 78
Yazīd b. Sinān, Abū Farwah * 200

Yazīd b. Ṭahmān **313**, 323 n. 1500
Yazīd II. *See* Yazīd b. ʿAbd al-Malik
Yemen 17, 29, 74, 94, 114 n. 538, 116, 210, 218, 219, 220, 221 n. 962, 227, 265, 299, 324
Yemen (tribal faction) **88 n. 424**
Yemenī tribes 137
Yuḥābir b. Mālik. *See* Murād
Yūnus * 223, 225
Yūnus b. ʿAbd al-Aʿlā * 100, 108, 132, 133, 147, 204
Yūnus b. Abī Isḥāq * 155
Yūnus b. Bukayr * 200, 218
Yūnus b. Ḥammād al-Maʿnī * 118
Yūnus b. Yazīd al-Aylī * 131
Yūsuf b. Abī Yūsuf. *See* Yūsuf b. Yaʿqūb
Yūsuf b. Muḥammad b. al-Munkadir 240
Yūsuf b. Muḥammad b. Thābit * 133
Yūsuf b. ʿUmar al-Thaqafī **233**, 242, 243, 265
Yūsuf b. Yaʿqūb b. Ibrāhīm **265**
Yūsuf b. Yaʿqūb al-Sadūsī * 124

Z

Zabbān b. Fāʾid * 205
al-Zabīdī * 159
Zād al-Rakb. *See* Abū Umayyah b. al-Mughīrah
Zāhir (tribal group) **91**
Zāʾidah * 238, 242, 268
Zāʾidah b. Qudāmah al-Thaqafī **256–57**
Zakariyāʾ b. ʿAdī * 114
Zakariyāʾ b. Sallām * 226
Zakariyāʾ b. Yaḥyā b. Abān * 101, 155, 268
Zayd Abū Yasār **100**
Zayd Abū Yasār * 100
Zayd al-Ḥibb. *See* Zayd b. Ḥārithah
Zayd b. Abī ʿAttāb * 184
Zayd b. Abī Laylā 312 n. 1438
Zayd b. ʿAlī b. al-Ḥusayn **233**
Zayd b. ʿAmr b. Nufayl **37**
Zayd b. al-Arqam **295**
Zayd b. Aslam * 174
Zayd b. Aslam, client of ʿUmar **335**
Zayd b. Aslam, Companion of the Prophet 335 n. 1571
Zayd b. Būlā. *See* Zayd Abū Yasār
Zayd b. Ḥārithah **6–10**, 14, 65, 162, 172, 180–81, 192, 287 n. 1304, **289**
Zayd b. al-Ḥasan b. Zayd 260
Zayd b. al-Ḥubāb * 152, 221, 205, 258
Zayd b. Jubayr * 200
Zayd b. Khālid al-Juhanī **293**
Zayd b. al-Khaṭṭāb **117**
Zayd b. Muḥammad. *See* Zayd b. Ḥārithah
Zayd b. Rufayʿ * 154
Zayd b. Sahl. *See* Abū Ṭalḥah
Zayd b. Ṣūḥān 330 n. 1545
Zayd b. Thābit **294**, 284 n. 1288
Zaydiyyah. *See* Shīʿah, Zaydī
Zayd al-Khayl **85**
Zaynab bt. Abī Muʿāwiyah **203**
Zaynab bt. Abī Muʿāwiyah * 203
Zaynab bt. Abī Salamah 175
Zaynab bt. Abī Salamah * 184
Zaynab bt. ʿAlī 211
Zaynab bt. al-ʿAwwām 41
Zaynab bt Jaḥsh, wife of the Prophet 9, **180–82**
Zaynab bt. Khuzaymah, wife of the Prophet **163–64**, 177
Zaynab bt. Maẓʿūn 175
Zaynab bt. Muḥammad the Prophet **4**, 13–16, 78, ʻ150, **162–63**, 282
Zaynab bt. Sulaymān b. ʿAlī 263
al-Zibriqān b. Badr **82**
Zimm 331 n. 1554
Zirr b. Ḥubaysh * 51
Zirr b. Ḥubaysh **320–21**
Ziyād b. Abīhi 148 n. 668, 274 n. 1235, 282 n. 1277, 292 n. 1319, 318 n. 1471
Ziyād b. Labīd **135**
Ziyād b. Labīd * 135
Ziyād b. Muṭarrif **155**
Ziyād b. Muṭarrif * 155

Zoroastrians, *see also* Magians, Possessors of the Scriptures 23 n. 99
Zubayd (tribe) 298 n. 1352, 3113 n. 1445
Zubayd, client of al-Ḥusayn b. 'Alī 211
al-Zubayr b. al-'Awwām 16, **27–28,** 41 n. 190, **105,** 169, 172, 199, 272 n. 1224, 279 n. 1267, 281 n. 1272, 287 n. 1304, **288,** 289, 318 n. 1470, 334 n. 1565, 337 n. 1581
al-Zubayr b. al-'Awwām * 78
Zubayrī faction, Zubayrī party 96, 275 n. 1243
Zubayrī family 241, 336 n. 1577
Ẓufar b. al-Hudhayl **251**
Zuhayr * 221
Zuhayr b. Mu'āwiyah al-Ju'fiyy * 190, 191
Zuhayr b. Umayyah 116
Zuhrah (a clan of the Quraysh) **26,** 35, 42, 51 n. 229, 95 n. 461, 107, 110, 111, 152 n. 684, 297 n. 1350, 301 n. 1365
al-Zuhrī, Ibn Shihāb 212, **234–35,** 240, **333,** 335 n. 1572
al-Zuhrī, Ibn Shihāb * 12, 23, 55, 67, 108, 109, 120, 131, 165, 167, 174, 176, 183, 186, 187, 190
Zur'ah bt. Mishraḥ 54, 232
Zurārah b. Awfā al-Ḥarashī **316**
Zurayq (a clan of the Khazraj) 290 n. 1310
Zurayq b. al-Sikht * 152

www.ingramcontent.com/pod-product-compliance
Lightning Source LLC
Chambersburg PA
CBHW020118240426
43673CB00038B/525
9780791428207